CIVIL RIGHTS HISTORY FROM THE GROUND UP

EDITED BY EMILYE CROSBY

# Civil Rights History from the Ground Up

*Local Struggles,*
*a National Movement*

The University of Georgia Press
*Athens and London*

© 2011 by the University of Georgia Press

Athens, Georgia 30602

www.ugapress.org

All rights reserved

Set in Minion by Graphic Composition, Inc.

Printed and bound by Thomson Shore

The paper in this book meets the guidelines for
permanence and durability of the Committee on
Production Guidelines for Book Longevity of the
Council on Library Resources.

Printed in the United States of America

15   14   13   12   11   P   5   4   3   2   1

Library of Congress Cataloging-in-Publication Data

Civil rights history from the ground up : local struggles,
a national movement / edited by Emilye Crosby.

     p. cm.

  Includes bibliographical references and index.

   ISBN-13: 978-0-8203-2963-5 (hardcover : alk. paper)

   ISBN-10: 0-8203-2963-0 (hardcover : alk. paper)

   ISBN-13: 978-0-8203-3865-1 (pbk. : alk. paper)

   ISBN-10: 0-8203-3865-6 (pbk. : alk. paper)

1. African Americans—Civil rights—History.

2. United States—Race relations.

3. United States—History, Local.

I. Crosby, Emilye.

  E185.615.C5844 2011

  323.1196′073—dc22     2010033684

British Library Cataloging-in-Publication Data available

*For Kathy*
*and for "the girls"*

# CONTENTS

List of Illustrations     ix

Acknowledgments     xi

Introduction. The Politics of Writing and Teaching
Movement History    *Emilye Crosby*     1

## Part One. Local Studies as Case Studies

Local People and National Leaders:
The View from Mississippi    *John Dittmer*     43

Challenging the Civil Rights Narrative: Women, Gender,
and the "Politics of Protection"    *Laurie B. Green*     52

Finding Fannie Corbett: Black Women and the Transformation
of Civil Rights Narratives in Wilson, North Carolina
*Charles W. McKinney Jr.*     81

The 1968 Poor People's Campaign, Marks, Mississippi, and
the Mule Train: Fighting Poverty Locally, Representing
Poverty Nationally    *Amy Nathan Wright*     109

## Part Two. From Local Studies to Synthesis

Focusing Our Eyes on the Prize: How Community Studies Are
Reframing and Rewriting the History of the Civil Rights Movement
*J. Todd Moye*     147

Freedom Now: Nonviolence in the Southern Freedom Movement,
1960–1964    *Wesley Hogan*     172

"It wasn't the Wild West": Keeping Local Studies in
Self-Defense Historiography    *Emilye Crosby*     194

Part Three. Creating and Communicating Movement History:
Methodology and Theory

Remaking History: Barack Obama, Political Cartoons, and
the Civil Rights Movement   *Hasan Kwame Jeffries*   259

Making *Eyes on the Prize*: An Interview with Filmmaker and
SNCC Staffer Judy Richardson   *Emilye Crosby, interviewer
and editor*   278

"Sexism is a helluva thing": Rethinking Our Questions
and Assumptions   *Charles M. Payne*   319

Telling Freedom Stories from the Inside Out: Internal Politics
and Movement Cultures in SNCC and the Black Panther Party
*Robyn C. Spencer and Wesley Hogan*   330

That Movement Responsibility: An Interview with
Judy Richardson on Movement Values and Movement History
*Emilye Crosby, interviewer and editor*   366

Accidental Matriarchs and Beautiful Helpmates: Rosa Parks,
Coretta Scott King, and the Memorialization of the
Civil Rights Movement   *Jeanne Theoharis*   385

Why Study the Movement? A Conversation on Movement
Values and Movement History   *Charles M. Payne*   419

Conclusion. "Doesn't everybody want to grow up to be Ella Baker?":
Teaching Movement History   *Emilye Crosby*   448

Contributors   477

Index   481

# ILLUSTRATIONS

1. Mr. Julius Warner, of Deacons for Defense, with the Port Gibson High School Student Council   *2*
2. Fannie Lou Hamer and other protesters during the MFDP challenge   *48*
3. Sanitation strike supporters gathering in front of Clayborn Temple   *53*
4. Fannie Corbett   *82*
5. The children of Bertha Johnson at the Mule Train preparation site   *122*
6. The Mule Train in Batesville, Mississippi   *127*
7. Albany Movement Protestors, Albany, Georgia   *160*
8. Media Focus on Chief of Police Laurie Pritchett and Rev. Martin Luther King Jr. clash   *161*
9. Nonviolent protestors confront lawmen in Albany, Georgia   *177*
10. Lowndes County, Alabama, woman with a typical weapon used for self-defense   *234*
11. R. J. Matson, "The Mountain Top"   *260*
12. Peter Lewis, "American Dream"   *261*
13. David Fitzsimmons, "Obama Wins"   *264*
14. Dwayne Booth, "Water under the Bridge"   *265*
15. J. D. Crowe, "Obama, McCain, and Wallace"   *266*
16. Riber Hansson, "Obama and Resigned KKK Member"   *268*
17. R. J. Matson, "Obama's Cross to Bear"   *270*
18. *New Yorker* cover   *271*
19. Pat Bagley, "Jesse Jackass"   *273*
20. J. D. Crowe, "Obama Race Speech"   *273*
21. Jeff Parker, "Yes We Can"   *274*
22. Judy Richardson with Emilye Crosby   *284*
23. Judy Richardson 1979 memo on naming *Eyes on the Prize*   *289*
24. Citizenship School on Johns Island   *326*

25. Stokely Carmichael canvassing in Lowndes County, Alabama   *327*

26. The Jackson, Mississippi, SNCC "freedom house"   *334*

27. Judy Richardson speaking to students at SUNY Geneseo   *373*

28. Rosa Parks greets children at the Black Panther Party Oakland Community School   *397*

29. Coretta Scott King kicks off the Poor People's Campaign   *404*

30. Geneseo students at Local Studies, a National Movement Conference   *422*

31. Geneseo students at Local Studies, a National Movement Conference   *425*

32. Participants at Local Studies, a National Movement Conference   *429*

33. Partial transcript from a Freedom School class   *434*

34. Ella Baker Reading Group, Geneseo students   *450*

35. Hasan Kwame Jeffries with Geneseo students   *460*

36. Hollis Watkins leading Geneseo students   *467*

37. Rochester teacher Chojy Schroeder and Geneseo student Christopher Basso   *471*

# ACKNOWLEDGMENTS

In many ways my students at SUNY Geneseo are at the heart of this book. Class after class, semester after semester, they remind me of the power and importance of the black freedom struggle, of how distorted or absent it is in their worlds, and of just how much they need to know this history—for themselves and for all of us and our futures. The immediate catalyst for this collection was a March 2006 conference I organized at Geneseo, "Local Studies, a National Movement: Toward a Historiography of the Black Freedom Struggle." An extraordinary gathering, the conference brought together almost two hundred people—students, activists, teachers from K–12 to university professors, scholarly specialists, and other interested folks—for three days of panels, keynotes, and a teaching workshop. The tone was set by panelist Todd Moye, who described the gathering as "the Beloved Community of black freedom struggle scholars," and Geneseo Provost Katherine (Kate) Conway-Turner, who asserted in her welcome that our knowledge of the movement is essential to how we "understand" and "operate in the world." She expressed her desire to see a "deep understanding" of the movement "shape the lives of the young people we all touch" and "those people who make policy and decisions in this country that relate to people in this country and to people outside of this country."* The conference included thought-provoking presentations, dynamic readings of personal accounts, spirited debate, and considerable conversation. It was a wonderful illustration of the potential for rigorous and meaningful academic exchange outside of the Ivory Tower.

I am grateful to the many people who participated in the conference and made it possible. Funding was provided by the Conversations in the Disciplines Program of the State University of New York, Geneseo's Office of the Provost, History Department, Africana/Black Studies Program, Women's

*Todd Moye, "Local Studies: What Do They Tell Us? Why Do They Matter?" panel, March 24, 2006, Conference DVD (in author's possession); Katherine (Kate) Conway-Turner, Welcoming Remarks, March 25, 2006, Conference DVD (in author's possession).

Studies Program, American Studies Program, Sociology Department, School of Education, Xerox Center for Multicultural Teacher Education, Teaching Learning Center, College Auxiliary Services, and the Joseph and Elaine Bucci Endowment Fund for History. A number of people at Geneseo directly contributed to the conference's success. I thank Osman Alawiye, Ed Antkoviak, Susan Bailey, Joseph (Joe) Cope, Joseph (Joe) Dolce, Thomas Greenfield, Jordan Kleiman, Maria Lima, and Rebecca (Becky) Lewis. Sue Ann Brainard went above and beyond, volunteering to actually run the conference, allowing me the luxury of participating fully. Provost Kate Conway-Turner's early endorsement and promise of financial support were critical, as were her insightful suggestions and her willingness to help me think through logistics and framing. Geneseo students helped inspire me to organize the conference and a number of current students and new alumni also helped with the spadework of putting it together. Moreover, Peter Anderson, Sarah Buzanowski, Jackie Chessen, Laura Warren Hill, and Justin Levy enhanced the conference immeasurably by returning to Geneseo and joining the conversations. The students in the Spring 2006 Ella Baker Reading Group were especially enthusiastic and instrumental participants. Christopher Basso, Christopher Bruce, Jared DePass, Gregory Fair, Tiffany Izzo, Tarik Kitson, Christopher Machanoff, Erynne Mancini, Patrick O'Neill, Christina Pinnola, Erin Rightmyer, Claire Ruswick, Kristy Sirianni, and Joseph Zurro prepared intensively (reading, discussing, and writing), and their post-conference reflections are at the heart of my conclusion on teaching movement history. The conference was greatly enhanced by all the Geneseo students who participated; by the students, teachers, and scholars who traveled to out-of-the-way Geneseo; by the Rochester area teachers who struggle day-in-and-day-out to provide their students a quality education and a standard of living necessary for learning; and by my Geneseo colleagues who joined us. The conference presenters were, of course, crucial, and I am grateful to them all—John Dittmer, Wesley Hogan, Hasan Kwame Jeffries, J. Todd Moye, Charles M. Payne, Judy Richardson, Robyn C. Spencer, Jeanne Theoharis, and Komozi Woodard. In the spirit of community and collaboration, everyone pitched in with wonderful presentations and more, ensuring a dynamic conference and spirited exchange.

When Andrew Berzanskis, then an editor at the University of Georgia Press, suggested that we translate the conference ideas into an edited collection, all of the presenters enthusiastically endorsed the idea. The process of putting the book together has become a rewarding way to build on the conversations initiated at the conference—amongst the original participants and those who have joined us along the way. I thank all of the contributors—John Dittmer, Laurie B. Green, Wesley Hogan, Hasan Kwame Jeffries, Charles W. McKinney Jr., J. Todd Moye, Charles M. Payne, Judy Richardson, Robyn C. Spencer, Jeanne Theoharis, and Amy Nathan Wright. This book is a truly collaborative effort. In addition to writing and revising their own pieces, almost everyone pitched in in multiple ways, helping with the conceptualization, offering feedback on my writing, reading each other's work, and more. Todd arranged for Lisa Fox to transcribe Payne's conference presentations and I am indebted to them both. I hope that rather than marking an end, the book's publication will help expand the conversation in new directions and include more people. While I am deeply appreciative and grateful to all of the contributors for all the many ways they made this publication possible, I'd like to especially acknowledge the importance of John Dittmer and Charles Payne in laying the groundwork for the conference, this book, and so much more. I'd venture that it's impossible to overstate the importance of their work on Mississippi for all of us who study and teach the movement. In addition to their groundbreaking scholarship, they have been extraordinary mentors and role models. In his essay, Todd Moye describes carving out space between Dittmer's *Local People* and Payne's *I've Got the Light of Freedom* for his first book. Todd speculated that he probably isn't alone in doing this. I can attest to the accuracy of that; I already have a space waiting for this volume and, like Todd, I hope it belongs there.

The year 2010 was particularly rich in gatherings of movement scholars and activists, all of which reinforced for me the importance of these conversations. I was privileged to participate in the University of Mississippi Porter L. Fortune Jr. Symposium organized by Ted Ownby; the SNCC 50th Anniversary Conference in Raleigh, N.C.; and the Brown University Symposium Celebrating the 50th Anniversary of the Founding of SNCC, organized by Corey D. B. Walker and Charles (Charlie) Cobb Jr. I enjoyed the spirit of camaraderie, lively exchanges, and stimulating conversations and am grateful to all the organizers and participants. The Hamer Institute, which I think of as a contemporary freedom school, has become a second home to me. Led by Dr. Leslie McLemore (now acting president of Jackson State University) and Michelle Deardorff, the institute does wonderful work documenting and teaching movement history. I am delighted to be part of the remarkable and welcoming community of people the institute brings together, including Daphne Chamberlain, David Deardorff, Latosha Garrett, Rickey Hill, Jeffrey Kolnick, Angela Mae Kupenda, Robert Luckett, Keith McMillan, Tiyi Morris, D'Andra Orey, Chauncey Spears, and Hollis Watkins (www.jsums.edu/hamer.institute/). This book and my life have also been enriched by the work and friendship of many other people. I especially want to thank Lori Amy, Curtis Austin, Leslie Brown, Joanna Dipasquale, Nishani Frazier, Deborah Gershenowitz, Françoise Hamlin, Laura Warren Hill, Simona Hill, Ryan Irwin, Patrick Jones, Steven Lawson, Deborah Menkart, Donna Murch, Paul Murphy, Derek Musgrove, Jeffrey O. G. Ogbar, Paul Ortiz, Barbara Ransby, Renee Romano, Christopher Strain, Timothy Tyson, Akinyele Umoja, Anne Valk, Rob Widell, and Yohuru Williams. Renee, Akinyele, and Yohuru read drafts and offered feedback. In addition to wonderful hospitality, Annie and Leslie looked through pictures with me and helped me start thinking about what the cover might look like.

I have had many excellent teachers over the years — in classrooms and out. I'd like to thank my college history professors, especially Emily Rosenberg, Norm Rosenberg, Jim Stewart, and Peter Rachleff. John Dittmer has been reading my work since the earliest drafts of dissertation chapters and is undoubtedly grateful that he didn't have to read (and re-read) all of the pieces in this book. I am constantly reminded of how fortunate I was to have Richard Blackett as my mentor in graduate school. I just wish he didn't live so far away and refuse to visit Rochester in the winter — which he defines with some accuracy as September through June. I particularly want to acknowledge the many outstanding teachers in the Claiborne County Public Schools. In so many ways, they provided the foundation for my interest in this history and my work as a teacher and scholar. I especially thank Gustina Atlas, Harold Liggans, Cynthia Patton, Julius Warner, Pearl Wilson, the late Mason Denham, and the late Percy Thornton. James Miller and Mr. Nate Jones — who might well have been a college professor himself if he had had different opportunities — were important role models and "community" teachers. In a sense, I grew up with Mississippi Cultural Crossroads, a cultural arts organization that Charles Payne once characterized as a freedom school. Cultural Crossroads and the wonderfully talented assortment of folks who helped found the organization and keep it going taught me important lessons about organizing, about history, and about making movement history accessible. Over the years, folks at MCC have gathered and published oral histories, created photographic and multimedia exhibitions, sponsored forums with a wide range of participants, commissioned and performed plays grounded in local history, and so much more. (There's an important book here for someone.) So many people have contributed over the years that naming names will get me in trouble. But I'd like to recognize my mother, Patty, who directed the organization for many years. She and my father, Dave, along with James Miller, Worth Long, Roland Freeman, Ms. G. (Gustina Atlas), Geraldine Nash, and others accomplished a tremendous amount. I am grateful to them for all that I had a chance to participate in and for Tara Wren-Douglas, who is leading the organization into the future (www.msculturalcrossroads.org).

At Geneseo, many people have contributed to this book directly and indirectly. My ideas about teaching movement history and its contemporary importance have been influenced and shaped by my work with Geneseo students. The interactions between campus visitors, students, formal coursework, and a variety of projects has been particularly rewarding and formative. Unita Blackwell, Julian Bond, Charlie Cobb, David Dennis, Worth Long, Charles (Chuck) McDew, Judy Richardson, Maria Varela, Hollis Watkins, and Robert Zellner were all inspiring and generous in their campus visits, giving talks, speaking to classes, and talking informally with students. They shared stories of their 1960s movement activism and gave us a sense of what it means to have a lifelong commitment to racial equality and social justice. Photographer and cultural documentarian Roland Freeman has presented his work several times. Most recently he exhibited and talked about "Some Things of Value: African American Expressive Culture" and "The Mule Train: A Journey of Hope Remembered." Three groups of Geneseo students have read and discussed drafts of Hasan Kwame Jeffries's work on Lowndes County with him. This tradition started when he spent lunch during the Conversations in the Disciplines conference talking with a dozen students who had just read his dissertation. Dr. Ysaye M. Barnwell, who was one of a handful of African Americans on campus when she earned her BS and MS degrees from Geneseo in 1967 and 1968, gave many of us a boost when she returned to campus in 2007 to support students organizing around racial justice on campus. Closer to home, we have been fortunate to meet with William Bradbury, Iris Banister, Walter Cooper, Jean Howard, and J. Bediaku Afoh-Manin. All of these visitors—and more—have been generous and inspiring, greatly enriching our community.

Since my earliest days at Geneseo, there have always been students who want to do in-depth study of the movement, beyond a course or two, and who want to make connections between the history and their contemporary world. In many ways, these students have been the driving force behind our invitations to these movement activists and scholars. They have also worked with me in creating directed study and "co-curricular spaces" for study, research, and conversation, including the Local Studies, a National Movement Conference, the Ella Baker Reading Group, the Race and Social Justice Learning Community, the Dramatic Readings from the Civil Rights Movement performances, and the Geneseo History Project. Many were also involved in teach-ins on Hurricane Katrina and "Race and Campus Culture," and helped create "Conflicted Histories: Geneseo and the Struggle for Justice," the keynote for the latter. I would like to thank all of those at Geneseo who share my interest in the movement and who have participated in these projects, especially students Lauren Akin, Peter Anderson, Christopher Basso, Christopher Bruce, Sarah Buzanowski, Jackie Chessen, Anna Delaney, Alexandria Coubertier, Jared DePass, Joseph Easton, Alexis Everson, Daniel Gaffney, Sara Germain, Janine Giordano, Brian Hartle, Tiffany Izzo, Cortez Jones, Matthew Kellogg, Tarik Kitson, Ryne Kitzrow, Justin Levy, Erynne Mancini, Jasmine Montgomery, Christopher Neels, Christopher Machanoff, Hannah Prescott-Eberle, Erin Rightmyer, Shanna Reulbach, Claire Ruswick, Mark Schuber, Scott Snowden, Alex Waldauer, Candace Walton, and Joseph Zurro. I would also like to recognize and thank others who have supported these projects. Joe Dolce has helped us document events and work with video. Ed Rivenburgh and the entire Milne Library staff are all extraordinarily helpful and supportive all the time. Steve Dresbach and Corey Ha are patient and generous as we come back with more and more questions and more and more requests for help. To say Sue Ann Brainard has supported this work is to do her a disservice. She has been absolutely integral to all of it. And while the students may be most appreciative of her generous contributions of home cooking to our various communities, I am particularly moved by her embrace of learning. During her years as Geneseo's provost, Kate Conway-Turner encouraged and facilitated many of these projects, and made it clear that she valued this work.

I am also grateful to others at Geneseo for their friendship, interest, and collaboration on campus projects, especially Catherine Adams, Anne Baldwin, Rose-Marie Chierici, Betsy Colón, Archie Cureton, Betty Fearn, Cynthia Hawkins, Paula Henry, Enrico Johnson, Fatima Rodriguez Johnson,

Jennifer Katz, Becky Lewis, Margaret Matlin, Susan Preston Norman, Alice Rutkowski, Linda Shepard, and Ren Vasiliev. President Christopher C. Dahl was an enthusiastic participant at the conference and has consistently followed the book's progress in the intervening years. Provost Carol Long joined Geneseo as I was entering the homestretch and I appreciate her interest and encouragement. The Geneseo Foundation provided several small grants and funded several student research assistants. Claire Ruswick, Christopher Basso, and Anna Delaney worked directly on this book, transcribing interviews, looking up footnotes, and helping in a range of important ways. Joel Dodge and David O'Donnell, whose research assistant work has focused on other projects, also helped out with last minute details. Ed Rivenburgh has been unfailingly supportive and encouraging. Brian Bennett helped tremendously with photographs and permissions and has done much over the years to document campus events related to the black freedom struggle. Steve Dresbach spent many hours helping me navigate digital images and the pitfalls of putting the final manuscript together using Microsoft Word. At the very end, Sue Ann Brainard took on the tedious work of proofreading and cleaning up endnotes, a contribution matched by her excitement and enthusiasm for the book and the history. Colleagues Justin Behrend, Joe Cope, and Carol Faulkner (who abandoned us for Syracuse) read portions of the manuscript, offering invaluable feedback and support. Joe attended the entire conference, and our conversations about the ideas at the core of the project and the issues involved in moving from conference to book were particularly helpful. Celia Easton was one of the first people I met at Geneseo and remains one of the most important. Susan Bailey is another good friend and I look forward to many more shared projects, events, meals, and conversations.

Many people helped with the photographs, granting permission to use their work, sharing their personal collections, and finding, creating, and editing the necessary files. I thank Gabrielle Begue, Brian Bennett, Barbara Blackston, Richard Campbell, Sarah C. Campbell, Matt Herron, Adrian Jenkins, Ericka Huggins, and Susan Williams. I especially thank Roland Freeman, who is always extremely generous with his photographs. Since Andrew Berzanskis suggested this collection, I've enjoyed working with the skilled and helpful folks at the University of Georgia Press, including Anne Boston, Jon Davies, John McLeod, and Beth Snead. The anonymous readers offered constructive and quite helpful critiques. Rachel Cabaniss improved the manuscript with her careful copyedit. I am particularly grateful to my editor, Derek Krissoff, who has been patient, encouraging, and helpful at every turn.

I can't really imagine doing this book or much of anything else without the friendship of Wes, Hasan, and Judy. Individually and collectively they brighten my world and I just about can't write anything without running it by each of them. I'm always looking forward to our next conversation, conference, and collaboration. Worth Long was my first SNCC teacher. For almost as long as I can remember he and Roland Freeman have helped shape my world. I hope they can recognize their influence in this book and know how much I appreciate their work and their friendship. My friendship with Michele Mitchell goes back to the Woodson Institute and I am always grateful when we have a chance to fall into the kind of long, easy conversation that marked those days. Janis Forbes continues to encourage me to vacation, something I clearly need to do more of and get better at.

I'd also like to thank my parents, Patty and Dave, and sisters, Sarah and Jessica. I suspect I'm a historian because my parents moved to Mississippi and enrolled their children in the local public schools. I hope they know how much I appreciate both of those decisions. Sarah and my mother read and commented on parts of this book. For a couple weeks in July, Sarah's feedback and help with printing (not to mention the endless supply of paper and clips) were absolutely essential as I juggled work on the manuscript and full days with the Hamer Institute. I am especially grateful to my brother-in-law Richard, who used his artistry and skill to rescue several photos and to create a readable copy of a SNCC document. Graeme, Nathan, Douglas, Tanner, and Griz were all good for distraction. My sister Jess is a teacher herself and I'm waiting to see what she thinks of this.

Kathy Connelly has lived with this book, as she lives with all my projects (and my dogs!). Over the years, she has taught me much of what I know about writing and I hope this work lives up to her insistence that history doesn't have to be deadly dull. Mostly, though, I thank her and the girls for their support and distraction and their considerable patience with my stories and my struggles to make sense of them.

CIVIL RIGHTS HISTORY FROM THE GROUND UP

EMILYE CROSBY

# Introduction

## *The Politics of Writing and Teaching Movement History*

**M**y earliest exposure to civil rights movement history came informally, through community programs and my teachers' stories. Those early accounts provided a crucial introduction and alternative framework that helped offset the very different, sanitized narrative that has come to dominate textbooks, the popular culture, and too many accounts by historians. For example, I first learned about self-defense, a topic that has become particularly significant to my own scholarly work, from stories about the "Black Hats" or "Deacons for Defense" from my tenth-grade social studies teacher, Mr. Julius Warner. He taught world history, and a group of us would hang out in his classroom during his "free" period. He would question us about current events and we would pester him for his opinion and for stories about the local movement in our hometown of Port Gibson, Mississippi. In the mid-1960s, before he completed his college degree and began teaching, Mr. Warner was a factory worker and movement activist, canvassing for voter registration, supporting a boycott of white merchants, and sending his children to the formerly whites-only public school (where, because of white flight, we now studied in a virtually all-black environment). He was also president of the local self-defense group, known as the Black Hats, or the Deacons.

I was lucky to have this introduction—to the civil rights movement generally and self-defense specifically. Although I knew these stories when I first proposed a study of my hometown community for my dissertation, I argued

I thank Sarah Campbell, Joseph Cope, Patricia Crosby, Michelle Deardorff, John Dittmer, Carol Faulkner, Laurie Green, Hasan Kwame Jeffries, Todd Moye, Judy Richardson, Renee Romano, and Kathleen Connelly for their comments and insights. Wesley Hogan put her own work aside to read and offer extensive comments on several drafts, for which I am greatly appreciative.

Figure 1  Mr. Julius Warner (*far right*), former head of the Port Gibson "Black Hats" or "Deacons," pictured here as advisor to the Port Gibson High School Student Council on Crazy Sock/Faded Blue Jeans Day, 1983 (the year after Emilye Crosby graduated from high school). Coach Percy Thorton (*far left*), the Student Council's other advisor, taught Crosby her first Afro-American history class. From the collection of Sarah C. Campbell.

its significance primarily in terms of the Port Gibson Boycott and *Claiborne Hardware, et al. v.* NAACP, *et al.*, the Supreme Court case that emerged out of it. The U.S. Supreme Court ruled unanimously in 1982, the summer before my senior year in high school, that protesters could use economic boycotts for political goals. This was big news. After years of litigation, many local defendants (including some of my teachers, a former bus driver, and Mr. Warner's father) were exonerated from the charges that they had been part of an illegal boycott conspiracy. Moreover, national leaders from the NAACP (National Association for the Advancement of Colored People) came to town to celebrate and the case was covered by the news media around the country.[1] National media, national leaders of a major civil rights organization, and a Supreme Court victory—these made the Port Gibson movement significant . . . right?

Years later when I began doing research for my dissertation, a few oral history collections and first-hand accounts remained virtually the only published and easily accessible sources that addressed self-defense in the movement.[2] And yet, when I interviewed local residents (whether active in the movement or not) and scoured the archival records, including reports from the Mississippi Highway Patrol, the Mississippi State Sovereignty Commission, and the Lawyers' Committee for Civil Rights Under Law, it was clear that armed self-defense and its more morally ambiguous sibling, boycott enforcement, were central to the local movement. I came to believe that understanding the role of self-defense and what it meant to African Americans and whites was just as important as the distant Supreme Court decision. And, in many ways, the local issues that had precipitated the litigation had been outpaced by events on the ground as blacks and whites negotiated new ways of interacting.[3] The successful national movement and new federal laws were an essential backdrop, but meaningful local change came through daily interactions that included confrontational rhetoric and individual and collective self-defense.

Though Mr. Warner only reluctantly agreed to a formal interview and never conceded to a follow-up, his stories got me started on the right path, long before I had any idea I would be writing this history. When I was distracted by the existing framework and traditional notions of what makes something historically significant (that is, the emphasis on the legal and political milestones of a "nonviolent" movement), he and others kept me on track with their accounts of both dramatic events and daily life. From them, I learned that self-defense was widely accepted and integral to the local movement. For example, when Marjorie Brandon was threatened because all six of her children were desegregating the white school, she put a gun in her purse and continued to attend mass meetings. She took the older children along, while her husband stayed home with the younger ones. Brandon also let the sheriff know that she intended to protect her family and property. When the children involved in school desegregation (including those of Mr. Warner and Mrs. Brandon) were having trouble with fights and threats at school, NAACP president Rev. James Dorsey met with school leaders and explained that if school personnel could not protect the children, the black community would be forced to do it themselves. School officials immediately took steps to limit white harassment, making black intervention unnecessary. In other incidents, Leesco Guster stood guard all night after a Klansman threatened her over the phone and organizer Rudy Shields returned fire when whites tried to drive him out of town by shooting at his temporary home. When white lawmen walked up to First Baptist Church during the regular Tuesday night mass meeting on a hot August evening in 1966, a group of armed black men stepped out of the bushes and confronted them.[4]

Mr. Warner also taught me that sometimes repression backfires. He went from being a relatively passive bystander to a movement stalwart when white lawmen attacked a crowd of peaceful demonstrators, including his father (who had to be hospitalized for a week). Warner's experience also demonstrated that if blacks threatened retaliation, whites sometimes backed off. When the mayor tried to intimidate the movement with the Klan shortly after Warner became president of the self-defense group, he and others let the mayor know that "if you get one of us, we gon' get one of you all."[5] Because blacks had already made clear their commitment to self-defense, the threat carried some weight and helped keep the Klan from establishing a toehold. The Black Hats, organized by Rudy Shields and led by Mr. Warner, were all male, but as these stories suggest, women were quite active in protecting their homes and families.

Though many see self-defense and nonviolent protest as antithetical, in Claiborne County (and elsewhere throughout the South), most blacks saw no contradiction. Marjorie Brandon was probably typical, explaining that although she carried a gun, she did not want to "do anybody any harm." At the same time, she believed both that the movement "needed" protectors to keep whites from "doing us harm in the church" and that the movement "was nonviolent." Rev. Eddie Walls, who became NAACP president in 1969, asserted, "I always preached nonviolence. . . . [T]he NAACP stood for that nonviolence, like Dr. King always said, nonviolence. . . . But yet and still people always went prepared to take care of themselves."[6]

The Claiborne County movement also included psychological warfare. Playing on white fears, in June 1966 the local self-defense group took the name Deacons (borrowed from the Louisiana group then guarding the Meredith March from Memphis to Jackson) and created a fake minutes book that inflated membership numbers, referenced imaginary weapons caches, and detailed nonexistent plans for acquiring guns from Chicago. In another instance, when a few blacks spread a false rumor that they were going to burn the downtown, highway patrolmen flooded the community and a number of white merchants stayed up all night, armed to the teeth, waiting for "something akin to the Watts Riot." A local leader told an informant, "One thing about these people down here, we can put out anything, and with all that is going on all over the state, they will believe it." Real or implied threats, especially when accompanied by action like shooting back or openly drilling and carrying weapons, could sometimes translate into changes in policy or practice. In this instance, the town aldermen passed an ordinance banning guns in public and the Claiborne County sheriff implored movement leaders to de-escalate, pledging to enforce the law equitably.[7]

I learned all of these stories and more as I was doing the research for my dissertation. None of them fit easily into the narrative of "*the movement*" as it was presented in the existing top-down literature that focused so heavily on Martin Luther King Jr., nonviolence, national organizations, and the legal and legislative victories that served as movement milestones—the story of the movement that my students still learn, in its most simplistic and, in their words, "sugarcoated" form.[8] In most of that literature, black self-defense was invisible. If it did appear, it was typically portrayed as a momentary aberration or, even more commonly, as part of a declension model that emphasized the "breakdown" of the "nonviolent" movement as it moved North and/or "deteriorated" into Black Power. I say that I *learned* all this about self-defense, but it is probably more accurate to say that I was gathering the evidence and developing the analytical tools that would help me make sense of it. I got quite a bit of help when, as I was writing my dissertation in 1994 and 1995, John Dittmer and Charles Payne published their accounts of the movement in Mississippi. Together with Adam Fairclough's 1995 monograph on Louisiana, their books helped make self-defense visible and demonstrate how integral it was to the story.[9]

Local studies, then (by Dittmer, Payne, Fairclough, and many who have followed their lead), have made it clear that if we look at the movement through the experiences of local people throughout the South, we have to acknowledge and understand the role of self-defense. And, like self-defense, we must also confront and reexamine many other aspects of the movement, including those that are dominant and those that remain invisible as long as we are overwhelmed by King's compelling presence or our attention is focused primarily on Washington. In this way, self-defense is a helpful illustration of the potential and significance of local studies both in providing details *and* in forcing us to rethink assumptions and frameworks.

Although William Chafe's groundbreaking 1980 community study of Greensboro, North Carolina, came a decade and a half earlier, the almost simultaneous publication of the local and state studies by Dittmer, Payne, and Fairclough in the mid-1990s marked a major shift in the field.[10] Collectively, these books called into question many of the top-down generalizations introduced and reinforced by studies of national leaders, major events, and pivotal legal and political milestones. In contrast, they highlighted how acknowledging and studying the importance of the movement's local, indigenous base fundamentally alters our picture of the movement and its significance. The subsequent decade and a half has seen a proliferation of local studies that range widely in terms of their emphases, approaches, time frames, conclusions, and location (including those focused on counties, states, and portions of states, as well as communities that are urban and rural and situated throughout the country, from the Deep South, to the Northeast, to the West Coast and in between). Collectively this work has laid a foundation for reshaping movement history, for changing our understanding of many things, including chronology, the role of women, the significance of self-defense, the nature and persistence of white resistance, the failures of the federal government, the differences between long-term organizing and short-term mobilizing, the development of Black Power, the importance of economics and human rights issues, and the possibilities and limitations of nonviolent tactics and ideology.

The past thirty years of southern movement-based local studies has clearly had a meaningful impact on the field. Despite this, the insights of the field remain too peripheral to historiographical debates and essentially invisible or nonexistent in popular versions. The pieces in this book literally refocus our attention. The local studies and bottom-up history here, including overviews, syntheses, and case studies, demand a rethinking of *what* and *who* we think is important. The transcripts and pedagogical essays in the final part of the book explore crucial questions of both interpretation and communication. How can we make sure that our history is as accurate as possible *and* that we are able to share it effectively with our students and the larger society?

Since the mid-1980s, historians have fairly consistently acknowledged the pivotal contributions of local studies (and pointed to the importance of more work in this vein). Local studies have also been crucial in raising many issues that are central to today's most visible historiographical discussions. These incorporate debate over chronology (including movement origins and end point), southern distinctiveness (or the relationship between northern and southern movements), definitions (including what we mean by "movement" and how we understand terms like civil rights, black freedom struggle, and Black Power), and the role partisanship or politics should play in historians' work.[11] Ironically, even though local studies have been recognized in virtually all of the significant recent historiographical essays and this approach has been embraced, even by those scholars whose own work fits more readily into the top-down category, the insights of local studies scholarship have been strangely sidelined and are virtually invisible in the specifics of the current arguments and conclusions.[12] For example, although both Charles Eagles and Jacqueline Dowd Hall give a nod to local studies in their influential historiographical overviews, in different ways they each push local studies (and the closely related bottom-up approach) to the side, reinforcing a somewhat top-down angle.[13]

In his 2000 *Journal of Southern History* essay, Eagles argued that historians should pay more attention to white opponents of the movement and extend the chronology backward and forward (beyond the *Brown* to Memphis framework), but he may be best-known for calling out movement historians for, in his words, sharing "a sympathetic attitude toward the quest for civil rights" and, consequently, for "telling the story . . . essentially from the perspective of the movement."[14] He insists that movement historians are not sufficiently "detached," and the result is an "imbalance" that, he suggests, grows out of historians' failure to be "critical of the civil rights movement" or to produce "sympathetic" accounts of segregationists. What is particularly important here is that in pushing this critique Eagles argues that this partisanship has resulted in an "immature" field without enough divisions or debate. He asserts that "the writing on the movement has yet to produce a range of strikingly different interpretive schools or consistently clashing interpretations."[15]

In making this argument, Eagles either does not see or does not acknowledge the extent to which movement historians were (and are) actually offering up competing interpretations, especially related to top-down and bottom-up approaches to the history.[16] Perhaps this has something to do with how he understands the movement and concepts of difference. For example, in praising Charles Marsh's *God's Long Summer* for including "activists on both sides of the freedom struggle," Eagles portrays divisions in fairly superficial ways— white against black, segregationist against movement. This seems to suggest that he sees the movement and its participants as largely monolithic, not acknowledging that there were considerable differences *within* the movement, not just between the movement and its opponents.[17] Perhaps this comes in part from not sufficiently recognizing or engaging in the complexity highlighted in local studies. It is almost as if he is looking for historians to restage something akin to the battles between the Citizens' Council and the NAACP. Short of that, he appears to miss or not take seriously either the differences within the movement or the well-developed debates among movement historians.

Moreover, at least some of what he calls for in 2000 was already present in local studies (and other movement scholarship). Sympathetic to movement goals or not, most of the published work evaluated and critiqued aspects of the movement, often from different angles and leading to different conclusions. In addition, local studies were consistently putting the 1950s and 1960s mass movement in a context that extended well beyond the *Brown* to Memphis time frame, often starting with World War II (or earlier) and extending into the 1970s or 1980s. For most, this chronology was not used to argue for a long continuous movement (something that Eagles appears to be simultaneously seeking and critiquing) but instead provided essential context for exploring precise questions of movement origins and evolution and for examining and understanding the period of the mass movement against the backdrop of long-term struggle and daily life.[18]

Similarly, though I certainly agree with Eagles's call for expanding the research agenda "within the 1954–68 model," his framework for arguing this need is so thoroughly top-down, it is hard to see how it can coexist in an essay that acknowledges Dittmer's and Payne's work on Mississippi and praises Chafe's *Civilities* and Fairclough's *Race & Democracy* as crucial models worthy of emulation. Eagles writes, "Currently scholars typically stress the importance of the NAACP only up through the *Brown* verdict and then shift the focus to Martin Luther King and the development of nonviolent passive resistance; beginning with Freedom Summer in the mid-1960s, SNCC [the Student Nonviolent Coordinating Committee] and more radical activists gain nearly equal billing with King." This summary could come right out of a textbook and ignores virtually all of the complexity of the movement found in the scholarship he surveys, even though it comes several pages after his observation that "diverse later works further expanded coverage and broadened understanding of the black freedom movement beyond the traditional major events, individuals, and institutions."[19] In this regard, Eagles appears to establish a pattern that too many follow. He points to the value and important innovations of local studies work but then proceeds to marginalize them in assessing and synthesizing the field.

Perhaps some of the emerging debate around the long civil rights movement, most explicitly articulated by Jacquelyn Dowd Hall in her 2005 *Journal of American History* essay, is more what Eagles has in mind when he calls for scholarly differences. Hall, despite agreeing with Eagles on the need to extend the chronology and giving considerable attention herself to white resistance (especially in the years before and after the "classical phase" of the movement), would undoubtedly draw his ire for her forthright calls to wrest the movement narrative from political conservatives. In Hall's view, the key to reestablishing the movement's radical vision (and its related contemporary potential) is tied to what she sees as the centrality of "civil rights unionism," a coalition of "laborites, civil rights activists, progressive New Dealers, and black and white radicals, some of whom were associated with the Communist Party." She insists that "civil rights unionism was not just a precursor of the modern civil rights movement. It was its decisive first phase." Moreover, Hall sees the movement fundamentally in terms of "the link between race and class," which, for her, is an explicitly interracial vision rooted in "a national movement with a vital southern wing."[20] In highlighting civil rights unionism, the national nature of racism and civil rights struggle, the links between race and class, and the long-term persistence and effectiveness of white resistance, Hall addresses important points but simultaneously downplays what she refers to as the "classical" phase of the movement, the southern struggle from the *Brown* decision to the Voting Rights Act. In the process, she implies that the corrective to the conservative master narrative and to, in her words, the important work of making "civil rights harder" lie outside this aspect of the history.[21]

The implications of Hall's emphasis are reinforced by her contested claim that the southern movement of the 1950s and 1960s emerged "largely from the prophetic tradition within the black church," her assertion that the Cold War "diverted the civil rights movement into new channels," and her persistent focus on, it seems, *everything but the movement*. (She spends approximately three pages of thirty-one on the classical southern movement.) Whether intentional or not, together these contentions and emphases seem to imply that the southern movement of the 1950s and 1960s, not just the normative portrayal of it, was fairly narrow and conservative, focused primarily on pursuing the "civil rights" of political access and desegregation, not human rights or economic issues. Aside from a few passing references, Hall generally does not engage with community studies (or much of the literature of the 1950s and 1960s movement). As a result, she essentially fails to explore the ways that community studies and bottom-up history themselves offer significant critiques of the normative history and illuminate a messier, more complex, and more radical movement *centered within* the timeline of the southern classical phase.[22]

While local studies are obviously not Hall's particular interest or focus, they do provide a critical lens for evaluating various ways of framing and understanding the movement. It is important, for example, to consider how the six points Hall identifies as central to the long civil rights movement framing look when we turn our attention to the Mississippi movement, as portrayed by Dittmer, Payne, Todd Moye, Chana Kai Lee, Kay Mills, and others. How does the long civil rights conceptualization fit with our picture of the Alabama movement—in cities and in the rural—developed by Hasan Kwame Jeffries, Cynthia Griggs Fleming, Glen Eskew, Robert Norrell, and J. Mills Thornton? Or the movements in Georgia, Louisiana, Memphis, North Carolina, Maryland, Florida, and Kentucky chronicled by Stephen Tuck, Winston Grady-Willis, Adam Fairclough, Greta de Jong, Laurie Green, William Chafe, Christina Greene, Timothy Tyson, Charles McKinney, Peter Levy, Glenda Rabby, and Tracy K'Meyer?[23]

One of Hall's points is that a number of factors have, in her words, whitened "the memory and historiography of the Left." And yet, her own prioritizing of civil rights unionism itself leads to a whiter, more interracial history than you will find in virtually any southern-based local studies of the freedom movement.[24] Moreover, as any number of people have observed, one of the important contributions local studies have made to the historiography is to highlight some of the problems with a rigid adherence to a *Brown* to Selma (or Memphis) framework that obscures earlier roots and continuing struggle—the ways that the movement connects to what came before and after.

Consider Todd Moye's *Let the People Decide* on Sunflower County, Mississippi. Moye begins his account in the early twentieth century and extends it into the 1980s.[25] In this instance, his chronology is useful for challenging the master narrative and for adding to our understanding of how black organizing *before Brown* (both the year before and the decades before) helped inspire white organizing *after Brown*, while also highlighting the distinctions between the 1960s and 1980s movements in the community. Though his work is not confined to either a *Brown* to Selma timeline or a narrow definition of "civil rights," neither Moye's longer chronology nor his conclusions about Sunflower County fit easily with Hall's framework. For example, as Moye points out, the Sunflower movement was more about "human rights than civil rights" and this "radicalism" emerged from the lived experience of southern African Americans, including Fannie Lou Hamer. Moye writes that

Hamer's "first priority as a public figure was to make sure that her neighbors, many of them desperately poor and ill-educated, had clothes to wear, access to decent health care, and enough food to eat. As she understood it, having the bare material essentials of life was a human right that could be guaranteed only through political organizing in the political economy she inhabited." Similarly, Hasan Kwame Jeffries's work on Lowndes County, Alabama, makes it clear that we must take seriously rural southern African Americans' own traditions and conceptions of freedom as we define and analyze the origins and trajectory of movement radicalism. Though blacks in Lowndes were exposed to the New Deal coalition of civil rights unionists through the Sharecroppers' Union and the community's strong ties to Detroit, the local movement's radicalism was deeply rooted in what Jeffries identifies as "'freedom rights'—the assortment of civil and human rights that emancipated African Americans identified as the crux of freedom."[26]

Although they approach it from a somewhat different perspective than Hall, Jeanne Theoharis and Komozi Woodward have also pushed to extend our sense of the boundaries and contours of the movement. In *Freedom North* and *Groundwork*, they highlight local studies and emphasize movements outside the South. Theoharis, in particular, has urged scholars to reconsider the declension model and take the nonsouthern struggle seriously. In work published before and after Hall's call for a long civil rights approach, Theoharis has drawn attention to the pervasiveness of racism, the overlapping range of tactics and ideologies that populated black activism in the South and North over extended periods of time, and the potential downfalls of ignoring the state's role in perpetuating "de facto" segregation.[27]

Sundiata Cha-Jua and Clarence Lang took up a number of the threads in this debate in a 2007 *Journal of African American History* essay. Responding primarily to Hall, Theoharis, Woodard, and Peniel Joseph (who has coined the term "Black Power studies" and, mirroring Hall, is putting forth a vision of a long Black Power movement), they made a compelling argument for more careful attention to context and for the importance of time and place. They assert that there is, in fact, something distinctive about the southern movement during the classical phase and that historians would do well to distinguish between the civil rights movement (with its mass activism) and its antecedents and legacies.[28]

I agree with much of Hall's compelling critique of the normative narrative, share her urgency about the need to replace it with a more accurate "harder civil rights," and greatly appreciate the way she and others (especially Theoharis and Woodard) insist that we expand and refine our understanding of broad spacial and chronological context. It is indisputable that the problems of white supremacy were (and remain) national. This is well-documented in our nation's history, in the specifics of the burgeoning scholarship on the North, West, and Midwest, *and* in what southern-based histories reveal about the vast limitations to the national commitment to racial equality and economic justice.[29] But does this mean that what the public and scholars initially saw as a southern-based mass movement is better understood as one national in scope? Is there really a compelling argument for situating the mass movement's "first phase" in the 1930s, as opposed to the 1950s, or World War II or the moment of emancipation? Is it appropriate to locate movement radicalism in interracial "civil rights unionism" rather than in ideologies developed within black southern communities? Have we addressed sufficiently the key issues raised by considering top-down and bottom-up interpretations, or sufficiently incorporated local studies into our assessments and considerations?[30]

In fact, it seems clear that we have hardly begun to incorporate the insights of local studies into the movement's "big picture" at the popular *or* scholarly level. And while the local studies angle is insufficient on its own, it is crucial to any complex and realistic portrayal of what Clayborne Carson described as the "black freedom struggle."[31] I think the starting place for tackling problems with the master narrative and the (mis)use of that history actually comes from *within* the scholarship on the "classical phase," especially local studies that are grounded in the particulars of time and place, but also those works that explore the full range of movement topics from the vantage point of the bottom up. Part of the answer to Hall's call to make "civil rights harder[,] harder to cast as a satisfying morality tale[, and] most of all, harder to simplify, appropriate, and contain," must come, not primarily from privileging "civil rights unionism" or the Communist Party-influenced left labor coalition that she highlights, but from greater engagement with community studies, with works that are centered on (without being confined to) the classical phase.[32] As we consider various theories and possible frameworks, I think we need to hold them up to the light of local studies (individually and collectively) and, with local studies at the center, add up similarities, make sense of differences and change over time, evaluate the distinctions of time and place, and test out theories.

Perhaps now, with thirty years of local studies scholarship to draw on, we might consider revisiting and updating Steven Lawson's call for interactive movement history. Since we now know quite a bit more about the intersections between local and national in particular places, we should do more to develop an interactive synthesis, one that seriously engages the collective insights of local studies, while simultaneously considering the full range of movement-related scholarship—from top-down studies of leaders, organizations, and federal (in)action to those works addressing previously neglected or distorted topics, including analyses of women/gender, religion, segregationists, the role and impact of class, northern bases of structural inequality, community-based Black Power, civil rights unionists, and much more. As we work on creating a meaningful synthesis, we might also do well to consider the implications of Clayborne Carson's argument, made more than twenty years ago, that the phrase "black freedom struggle" was more appropriate than "civil rights movement" for accurately representing the full range of tactics, ideologies, visions, and radicalism of that intense period of southern mass movement activism *within* the 1954 to 1965 or 1968 period. While we certainly should not confine ourselves to a narrow look at the South in this period, neither should we ignore the centrality of the southern movement in the "classical" period. It must be at the heart of an accurate and usable movement history.[33]

Even a very brief look at William Chafe's seminal work on Greensboro, published in 1980, and Hasan Kwame Jeffries's July 2009 monograph on Lowndes County, Alabama, illustrate the need and potential of this type of narrative. Both books offer compelling models for looking at events of major national significance in the context of particular communities over an extended period of time. In the national story, Greensboro features polite, well-dressed college students who, on the surface, were seeking integration and the right to buy a Coke and a hamburger. On the other hand, you have Lowndes County, home to the snarling black panther and base for launching Stokely Carmichael's and SNCC's call for Black Power. In these superficial characterizations, Greensboro and Lowndes represent very different aspects of the normative national narrative.

Although these two communities *are* different in significant ways and point to the critical role of context, both places and both stories share a good bit. Both highlight the importance of communities and generations of resistance, the persistence and adaptability of white supremacy, and the ways

African Americans shaped and revised tactics in response to particular con-
texts/situations. In both places, the movement was based on a foundation of
struggle that emerged in brief periods of mass movement, during and after
the typical chronology. In both instances, the local movement worked for
civil and human rights, what Jeffries calls "freedom rights." (Lowndes County
tax assessor candidate Alice Moore campaigned on a platform of "tax the rich
to feed the poor," while Greensboro African Americans highlighted the centrality of economic issues decade after decade after decade.)[34] And in both
cases blacks insisted on self-determination and refused to accept white supremacy, whether it came cloaked in the civility of Greensboro or the violence of Bloody Lowndes. Moreover, both books add to our understanding of Black Power. Chafe provides not only one of the earliest, but one of
the best explorations of community-based Black Power, taking us from the
iconic sit-in moment into the mass demonstrations of 1963 and the late 1960s
community organizing around housing, economics, and cultural autonomy.
For Jeffries, Black Power is what draws the national attention. Putting SNCC's
often-mentioned but little understood June 1966 call for Black Power in the
context of the group's organizing work in Lowndes County, he illustrates how
SNCC's Black Power program drew on the organization's strong ties to indigenous black communities and strategic efforts to translate the Voting Rights
Act into meaningful political power in Lowndes County.[35] We need a synthesis that can convey all of what is important about the movements in Greensboro and Lowndes, not just what we get in narrow and typically distorted
snapshots. The movements in Greensboro and Lowndes were national and
local, unique and typical, and (as portrayed by Chafe and Jeffries), they represent well the potential of a synthesis that seriously engages with the insights
of local studies scholarship and why it is so essential.

In fact, as Hall notes, these issues have considerable significance beyond
historical debate. While we scholars might have differences over the centrality of the Communist Party-inspired Left, the extent to which the struggle
in the South and North are similar and different, whether the World War II
era is a precursor or part of the movement proper, and exactly how something we call the "civil rights movement" relates to something we call the
"Black Freedom Struggle," our students and the larger public are largely di-
vorced from any meaningful awareness of either the "classic" or the "long"
civil rights movement. In the fifteen or so years I have been teaching at SUNY
Geneseo, there has been a disturbing consistency and persistence in what my

students believe they know about the civil rights movement. In fact, today, in 2010, despite the explosion of scholarship that has added more and more complexity to our understanding of the movement, my students' perceptions seem more, not less, wedded to a very superficial, very normative view, one that helps set up and reinforces contemporary talk of a "post-racial America."

Like most undergraduates, my students arrive in class with a simplistic mythology that a former student captured perfectly with this short synopsis. "One day a nice old lady, Rosa Parks, sat down on a bus and got arrested. The next day, Martin Luther King Jr. stood up and the Montgomery Bus Boycott followed. And sometime later King delivered his famous 'I Have a Dream' speech and segregation was over. This is how the story was taught to me."[36] Another student extends the common story into the Black Power era: "Martin Luther King was a wonderful leader who single-handedly changed the course of history. Malcolm X was another leader, but a different kind of leader who hated white citizens and whose militant perspectives were dangerous."[37] When my students and I analyze survey texts and movement overviews, we see very little evidence that they are influenced by local studies and bottom-up history.[38] Moreover, as Jeanne Theoharis's essay on the memorializations of Rosa Parks and Coretta Scott King makes clear, our students' high school history is amply reinforced by the popular culture (see chapter 13). Not just students, but journalists and politicians, including U.S. presidents, Cabinet members, and members of Congress, share (and help perpetuate) a distorted, mythological version of the movement untouched by local studies (or much other) scholarship.

Many of the most powerful members of our society, including policymakers and Supreme Court justices, act on these distortions in ways that reinforce and extend centuries-old inequalities. For example, a majority on the Supreme Court seems unable to distinguish between legally-required segregation in the service of white supremacy and race-conscious policies designed to offset the pernicious legacies of state-sponsored inequality.[39] Moreover, for many, Barack Obama's election serves as conclusive evidence that America has become a post-racial society, the fitting end to the triumphant story of a heroic, interracial America responding to the moral imperative of a King-led nonviolent movement to eliminate all vestiges of racial discrimination.[40] This distorted history lives side-by-side with a distorted present, allowing far too many people to ignore the extent to which statistics (and qualitative evidence) on race, income, wealth, education, health, health care, and housing point to the persistence of white advantage. Moreover, Justice Sonia Sotomayor's nomination illustrates that, for many, white and male is still normative. Her perspective, as a Latina, is both visible and suspect in a way that Justice John Robert's white, male perspective is not. That is, the ways her experiences have shaped her perspective are perceived by many as being inherently political, while the experiences that have shaped her white, male counterparts are perceived as neutral, invisible, and not so much irrelevant as appropriate.

A recent incident at SUNY Geneseo (which has been replicated with variation at institutions across the country), offers one small example of how these historical and contemporary omissions and inaccuracies intersect and impact individual and institutional actions. When black students protested white students' use of blackface caricatures for Halloween (in the context of other racist incidents and pervasive "ghetto theme" parties"), many white students responded with surprise and, in some cases, anger. Many in our community, including some faculty, defended the white students, suggesting that they were not responsible, as their actions came from ignorance, not malice. While it is true that many of our students, whether white, black, Asian, Asian American, Latino/a, or multiracial, are poorly educated, even miseducated, about race, it is also true that many white students (and the adults in their lives) are deeply vested in maintaining their ignorance and preserving the myths that smooth the way for their sense that it is not whites, but African Americans and other racial minorities who experience racial privilege today. And for many, that certainty is grounded in and reinforced by the mythologies of the civil rights movement. As one student explained, "[W]e truly were raised in what we were taught was a post-racial world" where "racism is a quenched evil."[41]

While many college faculty, administrators, and students deplore explicitly racist name-calling, blackface, and offensive imagery in student parties, far fewer understand or are willing to examine how these outward manifestations are deeply connected to long-standing policies and practices, many of which continue to privilege curriculum, admissions, and hiring priorities that reinforce white access and a white-dominated worldview. Too many faculty, staff, and administrators, even those who are politically liberal or were young people during the movement years, readily accept and act on versions of the mythologies that so inform our students.[42]

As scholars and teachers, it is our job to give our students the best critical thinking tools we can fashion as all of us confront an increasingly complex, multiracial society and world, with challenging problems grounded in differences in religion, race, worldview, and resources. Too often, young (white) people are taught that they have no responsibility for the white supremacy in our country's past, while being encouraged to believe that our society has fully addressed any problems associated with slavery or Jim Crow. This reinforces white students' sense of privilege and leaves all students ill-equipped to understand, much less work to address, the persistent inequalities that make a truly "post-racial" society impossible. For many students, learning a more accurate and complex history, especially one that looks at the civil rights movement from a bottom-up perspective, is an essential starting point for a more realistic approach. This history can provide the background that is crucial for understanding contemporary issues, while exposing students to a world beyond their immediate experience, and with it, the opportunity to understand more fully the power of perspective. (See the conclusion for more on teaching movement history.)

It seems imperative, then, that we take seriously the problem of conveying more of what historians know about the movement to young people and a general audience. To do this well, I think we must put local studies at the center of our historiographical analysis and begin developing a movement synthesis that truly engages with this scholarship. But, I believe we must also expand the conversation beyond the confines of the Ivory Tower. It is too important, too essential to our country's "racial literacy" and future, to be limited to academic conferences and esoteric scholarly debates. If we develop the history (and the strategies for sharing it widely) in conversation with movement activists, as well as teachers and students (from the earliest grades through graduate school, including those connected to formal educational institutions and those grounded more in community organizations and cultural arts centers), we will have a better chance of getting the history right and of making it relevant and accessible to many more people.

Of course, not everyone agrees that we should listen closely to the insights and perspectives of movement activists. In the midst of his overall criticism of movement scholars for being too sympathetic to the movement, Charles Eagles singled out Charles Payne. After observing that Payne reached "out to include the otherwise ignored and forgotten," Eagles asserted that Payne relied too uncritically on oral history, concluding, "Just repeating such stories, however compelling they may be, makes for incomplete history."[43] Alan

Draper, in a joint review of Payne's *I've Got the Light of Freedom* and Dittmer's *Local People*, makes an almost identical argument, asserting, "[B]oth Dittmer and Payne are uncritical of their sources and, consequently, of their subject. They both use oral histories and published reminiscences by civil rights activists extensively, so that civil rights activists effectively shape the history of the movement they made."[44] Draper concludes that Dittmer's is "a partisan account," while Payne "is so eager to offer a history that instructs, he is sometimes guilty of ignoring inconvenient facts that get in the way of the lesson he wants to impart."[45]

Few would argue with Draper's assertion that "[h]istorians need to examine the testimony of Movement activists skeptically, test whether activists interpreted their experience accurately, . . . and not prejudge the evidence."[46] Yet there are several somewhat interrelated issues that neither Draper nor Eagles (or others) acknowledge. First, they see some perspectives and voices, typically those that are at odds with the normative view (which tend to be the SNCC and local voices), as more suspect than others. Like those who identify Justice Sotomayor's Latina perspective as problematic while not even noticing Justice Robert's white male perspective, the critiques offered by Draper and Eagles, though framed as objective or neutral, emerge from a normative orientation. They fit easily with the larger political trends where top-down or white or male (or whatever the elite perspective is) is considered objective. It is essential that we recognize that *all* history, not just bottom-up movement history, is political. It is political in what we center and consider important, in the sources we use and prioritize, in the questions we ask and try to answer. What these critics ignore, then, is that the decision to rely primarily or exclusively on the traditional, written sources produced by elites is just as political as drawing heavily on and taking seriously oral history. Disregarding or downplaying the accounts of SNCC workers and their local allies is as political as the decision to listen to them. To take seriously the stories of movement participants, to engage in thoughtful discussion and exchange, does not require suspending the standards of scholarship.[47] Moreover, you can believe in racial justice, that our history matters to contemporary issues, and still produce rigorous and sound scholarship about the movement.

Second, it is not just that historical actors have important stories and details to share about their experiences, but they can often make insightful analytical contributions to framing the history they participated in. For example, in a 1978 interview, Bernice Johnson Reagon, who joined the Albany, Georgia, movement as a college student and went on to work with SNCC and earn a PhD in history (among many other things), offered an early and still relevant critique of the scholarship on the Albany Movement. She explains, "When I read about the Albany Movement, as people have written about it, I don't recognize it. They add up stuff that was not central to what happened." For her, the common emphasis on the local movement's meaning for Martin Luther King Jr., the tactics of white police chief Laurie Pritchett, and a short-term assessment of "specific achievements" was "not central." Instead, what mattered to her was that the Albany Movement gave "[me] the power to challenge *any* line that limits me. . . . And that is what it meant to me, just really gave me a real chance to fight and to struggle and not respect boundaries that put me down."[48] Here, in the late 1970s, before Chafe's pioneering community study, before Dittmer's and Payne's work on Mississippi, and when the field of civil rights movement history was in its infancy, Reagon (speaking from the vantage point of a participant—albeit one who had a PhD in history), identified many of the crucial differences in framing and emphasis that have come to reflect top-down versus bottom-up debates among movement scholars.

As Todd Moye's essay on local studies (see chapter 5) points out, these divergent perspectives on Albany persist and Reagon probably still does not recognize or agree with most of what has been put forward by scholars. But let's be clear: this is not simply a case of one (or many) activist/participant(s) disagreeing with an "objective" historical assessment. The dominant scholarly interpretation that emphasizes Albany as a failure (and learning experience) for King is one that closely follows the perspective held by King and others in the Southern Christian Leadership Conference (SCLC). And this, of course, is the version that makes it into movement syntheses and textbooks. But what makes that framework, that perspective, the correct one? Can we say, without question, that what makes Albany most significant is Chief Pritchett's nonbrutality, the federal government's inaction, and the lack of immediate, tangible victories? Is it accurate or objective to decenter and even disregard Reagon's view of the Albany Movement, one that focuses on its meaning for the many hundreds of local people who stepped up and provided the impetus for King to come in the first place?[49]

And if historians prioritize the movement's meaning for local participants, like those hundreds of African Americans in Albany who decided to directly challenge institutional white supremacy (even when it almost certainly meant going to jail), are they to be dismissed for simply accepting or following an activists' perspective? The fact that the dominant, visible portrait of Albany is so consistent with King's and SCLC's view (one set of historical actors) reinforces just how much diversity there was *within* the movement. It also suggests that the issue for those critics is the bottom-up framing itself, not that scholars' interpretations are sometimes similar to those of activists. The problem for these critics, then, comes when scholars' interpretations too closely match those of a *particular subset* of activists, the ones who themselves have a bottom-up perspective. So it is historians who ask the questions and seek out the evidence that puts local people (along with their on-the-ground organizers) at the center of the story who are perceived as political and as too uncritically accepting of the accounts of activists.

In addition to pointing out that we need to be clear about what the objection really is, I think this example also illustrates that, more often than not, the problem is not that historians' scholarly standards are undermined by taking the views of activists/participants seriously, but that in our failure to hear the contributions activists have to make, our histories contribute to distorting the movement they helped create. It is not just arbitrary, but actually counterproductive to advocate for an immutable divide between historians and activists in constructing accurate movement history. In fact, I would contend that in some instances the vision and framing of activists/historical participants can help identify and counter historians' own unacknowledged or unseen biases, offering analytical insights that can help us more effectively make sense of all of the available evidence. My argument is not that either activists or scholars are always right or always wrong or that oral history is always the best source or the bottom-up perspective is always superior. As Charles Payne writes in the preface to the 2007 edition of *I've Got the Light of Freedom*, "[E]very way of seeing is a way of not seeing."[50] What I believe is that in working together, effectively using the fullest range of sources available, and being very aware of the consequences of our choices around framing and emphasis, we have the potential for a richer, more meaningful history that is both accurate and usable.[51]

Self-defense offers a good illustration of the importance of taking seriously activist voices and the evolving intersection between scholarship, firsthand perspectives, and popular culture. Even as the first generation of movement scholars were typically ignoring, overlooking, downplaying, or misinterpreting self-defense, activists were including it in their stories, their memoirs, and their oral history accounts. Then, and even today, these activist discussions of self-defense remain among the most nuanced and accurate available. I think my own experience in learning about self-defense is useful. It is not just that I was exposed to self-defense through personal stories when it was largely invisible in the scholarship, it is that what I learned from the stories of people I knew, the formal oral history interviews I conducted, and reading published oral histories and memoirs was as complex, nuanced, and accurate as anything I have read since from scholars.

This is not to say that scholars, led by John Dittmer, Charles Payne, Adam Fairclough, and Timothy Tyson, have not made important contributions in analyzing self-defense in terms of the broad patterns and important variations, all while grounding it in local, national, and international contexts. But it is to say that both the *details and the analysis* in the firsthand accounts hold up and are entirely consistent with the very best of the existing scholarship. Moreover, though we now have good work on self-defense, especially in biographies and community studies, the story is not simply one of ever-improving scholarship. Perhaps in their zeal to correct egregious earlier omissions, some of the more recent scholars who have focused explicitly on self-defense have gone too far in overemphasizing the centrality of a certain kind of visible and confrontational self-defense. Some of this work tends to valorize "armed resistance" and denigrate nonviolence.[52] (See my essay on the historiography of self-defense, chapter 7.)

And yet, as angry as many movement participants were with the ways that self-defense was obscured (in favor of a moralistic nonviolence) in both the early scholarship and the popular culture, they have largely failed to embrace this new wave of scholarship, which has its own distortions. The accounts of activist/participants remain consistent *and* point the way toward a more perceptive and nuanced framing for addressing the full range of movement tactics and philosophies. For example, Charles (Charlie) Cobb Jr., a SNCC field-worker who spent several years in Sunflower County, Mississippi, in the early 1960s, explains that self-defense was just a given. It was ubiquitous and local blacks felt no need to even discuss it. They had guns and they were going to use them to protect themselves. Period. But he also insists that "it wasn't the wild west." Self-defense was about "defense" and about providing the protection and space people needed to do the political work of voter registration and building up black institutions.[53] While his insights are reflected in local studies, they are lost in top-down works that generally see the movement either in terms of nonviolence alone or nonviolence versus self-defense, a framework that is misleading and inadequate, obscuring quite a bit of movement work that does not easily fit in either category.

In my view, the best analytical framework for addressing the problems that emerge from this dichotomy comes, not from any of the many scholars who have studied and written about the topic, but from SNCC staffer Worth Long. He asserts that the movement was more "un-violent" than nonviolent. Robert (Bob) Moses, another SNCC organizer, makes a related point in insisting that the voter registration work that dominated the Mississippi movement did not require nonviolence and did not employ nonviolent tactics. At the same time, he and others sought to limit any kind of direct conflict or confrontation that would undermine their ability to function. This is essentially what Long was describing, a movement that was more un-violent than nonviolent. And even though self-defense was pervasive, it was practical rather than provocative.[54] These activists have provided scholars, if we are willing to listen, a useful blueprint and way of rethinking the intersections between various movement approaches and philosophies (and the ways that people understood them on the ground). These insights, this nuance, belong at the heart of our scholarship (not because it comes from activists, but because it is effective) and must be part of any attempt at synthesis.

Meanwhile, as we work on that synthesis, how can we communicate this complexity to our students and a popular audience? When I began teaching, the popular 1988 film *Mississippi Burning* was one of my students' most important touchstones for the movement. I initially struggled to effectively combat this egregiously normative and racist depiction of the movement, including its caricatures of white violence and complete obliteration of black agency. The only black character who picked up a gun was hanged for his efforts. At the same time, I found that my students were really wedded to the movement as nonviolent and many unquestioningly bought into a racist double standard that essentially expected African Americans to "earn" their (Constitutional) rights by remaining nonviolent (in word, thought, and deed). My students clung to this viewpoint no matter how much they learned about the violence movement activists faced from the Klan, the police, and their neighbors, and no matter how much they learned about the failure of the local, state, and federal law(men) to provide protection or prosecute perpetrators. I had little success making a dent in the views they had so thoroughly absorbed from the media, their social studies textbooks, and the New York State Regents curriculum *until* I put together a set of oral history interviews, primarily from rural Mississippians. These firsthand accounts, far more than my explanations or the scholarly passages I had assigned, got my students' attention and convinced them to use their own analytical skills to think critically about both the movie and the racist, "sugar-coated" history they had been exposed to. Through reading these firsthand accounts, my students were able to begin using the specific details and stories to grapple effectively with the larger concepts that were at odds with so much that they believed.

I still remember quite clearly, though, the many students who insisted that we had no business holding *Mississippi Burning* up to the light of historical analysis and, furthermore, that there was no other way to make a dramatic, compelling movie about the movement. Imagine how much easier my teaching became when the TNT (SNCC) movie, *Freedom Song*, became available in 2000. Made at least partially in response to *Mississippi Burning*, *Freedom Song* draws extensively on first-hand accounts, existing and new oral history interviews, and even community-based discussions about the history portrayed in the film. Former SNCC staff were crucial in choosing and framing the story and in connecting the writer/director with many of the local people who are portrayed in the film.[55] The result is both excellent history and a compelling story. Through focusing on SNCC's early organizing efforts in southwest Mississippi, *Freedom Song* brings to life many aspects of the movement, including—to mention just two relevant and interrelated examples—the realities of white violence and black self-defense. While *Mississippi Burning* assaults the viewer with scene after scene of hooded Klansmen beating and burning African Americans who cringe and run, *Freedom Song* shows that blacks were organizing and acting publicly, while armed and prepared to defend themselves at home. And, following the historical truth, it also illustrates the institutional nature of white violence. The deadliest attack in southwest Mississippi did not come from the Klan under the cloak of darkness, but from state legislator E. H. Hurst, who murdered Herbert Lee, an NAACP activist and farmer, in broad daylight. *Freedom Song*, then, shows the reality of white violence and black self-defense, without making a caricature of the one or glamorizing the other. *Freedom Song* also makes it clear that the costs of fighting for freedom were high, and in southwest Mississippi in the early 1960s the victory came through individual and community transformation, not a shoot-out at the O.K. Corral.

Created through a collaboration between movement activists, scholars, and Hollywood stars, *Freedom Song* offers one model for how to present good scholarship and a compelling story in an accessible medium. My students love *Freedom Song* <u>and</u> they learn as much or more from it as they do from the more traditional primary and secondary sources I assign. (They learn best when they watch the film in conjunction with some reading.) While I would like to see everyone in our country read a couple dozen of my favorite movement books, I think a good start would be to use *Freedom Song* as the basis for what middle and high school students learn about the movement.

Through a variety of emphases and formats, the contributors to this book join the ongoing historiographical discussions about how best to *interpret* the significance of the movement and offer possibilities for how best to effectively *communicate* it beyond a small group of specialist scholars. This book illustrates that we have much more to learn about movement history and that local studies remain central to our still growing field. Scholarship that draws on oral history and activist insights (along with traditional sources) and that brings the specificity of time and place into dialogue with broad themes and a national context is crucial as we continue to engage in scholarly debates, evaluate newer conceptual frameworks, and do the related work of figuring out how to replace the superficial, sugar-coated narrative that persists in the popular imagination.

The ongoing significance of the movement and movement history may have been more immediately obvious twenty-five years ago in Mississippi than it is today in upstate New York. But as Barack Obama's election reinforces and intensifies talk about a "post-racial America," I think my students (and others) need this history every bit as much as my classmates and I did. And, based on their comments and reflections, many of them agree. This book will help ensure that scholars' history of the movement is as accurate and complex as possible and that more of what scholars know reaches students and the rest of our society. In bringing together syntheses and case studies, as well as interviews and pieces that address theoretical and practical issues, the contributors to this book illustrate the continuing importance of bottom-up, local studies and of expanding the conversation to include scholars, teachers, and activists.

Part 1 brings together case studies by John Dittmer, Amy Nathan Wright, Charles W. McKinney Jr., and Laurie Green, illustrating some of the crucial lessons of local studies and offering a glimpse of how much more we have to learn. John Dittmer's discussion of what the federal government did and did not do in relation to the Mississippi movement offers a forceful rebuttal to the celebratory story that is so central to my students' mythology. Amy Nathan Wright uses a case study of the Mule Train from Marks, Mississippi, to the nation's capitol (part of the Poor People's Campaign that King was working on at his death) to explore a movement that was simultaneously local and national. Drawing on the Wilson, North Carolina, movement, Charles McKinney makes an argument about the connections between gender and what is defined as "the movement." He finds that in Wilson, a traditional narrative centered around male leadership and narrowly defined civil rights—voting and desegregation—obscures the late 1960s community organizing that relied on the leadership and activism of women and that focused on decent housing and other issues more explicitly connected to quality of life. Laurie Green draws both on her work on Memphis and that of other scholars to expose the ways that gender has shaped the civil rights narrative. In addition to revisiting leadership and the complex interactions between local and national, she offers new insight into the "politics of protection" through an examination of the intersections between gender and racial violence, health, hunger, and poverty. At the heart of Green's argument is the importance of grappling with the complexity of gender and shifting the frame so that women become more central to our analysis, not just fuzzy objects on the periphery.

Part 2 brings together a series of essays that draw collectively on local studies to offer overviews and critiques of significant topics. Todd Moye combines a personal account of how he came to write a book on the civil rights and white resistance movements in Sunflower County, Mississippi, with an overview of some of the most significant themes to come out of local studies scholarship. Among other things, he suggests that we need to acknowledge that the movement was probably "less incrementalist, more revolutionary" and "less successful than we like to tell ourselves."[56] Wesley Hogan's essay "Freedom Now: Nonviolence in the Southern Freedom Movement, 1960–64" and mine on self-defense provide complementary reevaluations of these important aspects of the movement, how they are interrelated, and the ways historians have addressed them.

Part 3 addresses methodology and theory, focusing on the ways we interpret and communicate movement history. Hasan Kwame Jeffries offers a compelling analysis of the ways that political cartoons addressing Barack Obama's presidential campaign reflect common distortions of movement history. He gives us a glimpse of what is obscured and why it matters. Among other things, he touches briefly on the ways popular (and some historical) portrayals of white resistance too often frame it as isolated, individual, and distinct from larger white communities and those whites in power. The same is typically true of Black Power, which is too often marginalized and caricatured as angry and counterproductive, with no attention to its strong grounding in African American history and communities. There are two edited interviews with SNCC staffer Judy Richardson who, in addition to her movement activism, has done extensive work documenting and teaching movement history. The first interview highlights her involvement with the making of *Eyes on the Prize*. The second interview explores her approach and priorities in sharing movement history with teachers and popular audiences. Jeanne Theoharis's analysis of the popular response to the deaths of Rosa Parks and Coretta Scott King provides a clear illustration of the mythology that passes for movement history. She also discusses some of what that myth obscures, about Parks and King and the movement more broadly. In "Telling Freedom Stories from the Inside Out: Internal Politics and Movement Cultures in SNCC and the Black Panther Party," Wesley Hogan and Robyn C. Spencer write in conversation with each other about the intersections between the personal and political and about the challenges and importance of unearthing movement culture. Charles M. Payne has contributed edited transcripts of two presentations from a Local Studies Conference at Geneseo in March 2006. In "Sexism is a helluva thing," he offers some cautions about the questions we ask, the sources we use, and the assumptions we make, especially as they relate to gender and radicalism. "Why Study the Movement?" is drawn from his closing keynote, a wide-ranging discussion that focused on teaching and learning movement history, movement values, and the movement's relevance to contemporary issues. It includes reflections from many of the conference participants. The book closes with my essay, "Doesn't everybody want to grow up to be Ella Baker?" I draw on students' reactions to the March 2006 Local Studies conference at Geneseo to reflect on some of the possibilities of teaching bottom-up history and the importance of not just what, but how we teach. Taken together, these pieces force a rethinking from scholars and teachers alike. What does the scholarship tell us about the history? What is most important for us to convey in our teaching? How does our understanding of the movement impact our actions today?

## NOTES

1. Emilye Crosby, *A Little Taste of Freedom: The Black Freedom Struggle in Claiborne County, Mississippi* (Chapel Hill: University of North Carolina Press, 2005), 127, 130, 138, 183, 187, 235–7, 240, 255.

2. Some of the early published primary sources that discuss self-defense in the movement include: James Forman, *The Making of Black Revolutionaries* (Seattle: Open Hand, 1972, 1985); Howell Raines, *My Soul Is Rested: The Story of the Civil Rights Movement in the Deep South* (New York: Penguin, 1977, 1983); Rural Organizing and Cultural Center, *Minds Stayed on Freedom: The Civil Rights Struggle in the Rural South: An Oral History* (Boulder: Westview Press, 1991); John R. Salter Jr., *Jackson, Mississippi: An American Chronicle of Struggle and Schism* (Hicksville, N.Y.: Exposition Press, 1979); James Farmer, *Lay Bare the Heart: An Autobiography of the Civil Rights Movement* (Westminster, Md.: Arbor House, 1985; New York: Penguin, 1986); Tracy Sugarman, *Stranger at the Gates: A Summer in Mississippi* (New York: Hill and Wang, 1966); Cleveland Sellers, *The River of No Return: The Autobiography of a Black Militant and the Life and Death of* sncc (Jackson: University Press of Mississippi, 1990; reprint of 1973 edition); Clayborne Carson, David J. Garrow, Gerald Gill, Vincent Harding, and Darlene Clark Hine, *The Eyes on the Prize Civil Rights Reader: Documents, Speeches, and Firsthand Accounts from the Black Freedom Struggle, 1954–1990* (New York: Penguin, 1991). Some of the early secondary works that contained brief references to self-defense include: David R. Colburn, *Racial Change & Community Crisis, St. Augustine, Florida, 1877–1980* (Gainesville: University Press of Florida, 1985, 1991); Clayborne Carson, *In Struggle:* sncc *and the Black Awakening of the 1960s* (Cambridge, Mass.: Harvard University Press, 1981); George Lipsitz, *A Life in the Struggle: Ivory Perry and the Culture of Opposition* (Philadelphia: Temple University Press, 1988); Taylor Branch, *Parting the Waters: America in the King Years, 1954–1963* (New York: Simon and Schuster, 1988); Doug McAdam, *Freedom Summer* (New York: Oxford University Press, 1988).

3. Two of the most important boycott demands were for "courtesy titles" and better jobs. By the time the Supreme Court ruled in *Claiborne Hardware v.* naacp, many African Americans held jobs as cashiers, while merchants and other whites were typically careful to use courtesy titles in addressing blacks. See Crosby, *A Little Taste of Freedom.*

4. Crosby, *A Little Taste of Freedom*, 162, 163, 180; Emilye Crosby, "Common Courtesy: The Civil Rights Movement in Claiborne County, Mississippi" (PhD diss., Indiana University, Bloomington, 1995), 301.

5. Crosby, *A Little Taste of Freedom*, 127, 167, esp. 168.

6. Ibid., 169–70.

7. Ibid., 179, 183–6, esp. 184, 185.

8. Kristen Geroult reflection, Hist266, Spring 2009 (this and other student reflections in author's possession).

9. John Dittmer, *Local People: The Struggle for Civil Rights in Mississippi* (Urbana: University of Illinois Press, 1994); Charles M. Payne, *I've Got the Light of Freedom: The Organizing Tradition and the Mississippi Freedom Struggle* (Berkeley: University of California Press, 1995); Adam Fairclough, *Race & Democracy: The Civil Rights Struggle in Louisiana, 1915–1972* (Athens: University of Georgia Press, 1995).

10. William Chafe, *Civilities and Civil Rights: Greensboro, North Carolina and the Black Struggle for Freedom* (Oxford: Oxford University Press, 1980).

11. Clayborne Carson and Steven Lawson were among the first to highlight local studies in historiographical reviews. See Clayborne Carson, "Civil Rights Reform and the Black Freedom Struggle," in *The Civil Rights Movement in America*, ed. Charles W. Eagles (Jackson: University Press of Mississippi, 1986), 19–32; Steven F. Lawson, "Comment," in *The Civil Rights Movement in America*, 32–37; Steven F. Lawson, "Freedom Then, Freedom Now: The Historiography of the Civil Rights Movement," *American Historical Review* 96 (April 1991): 456–71; Steven F. Lawson, "Freedom Down to Now" (addition to "Freedom Then, Freedom Now") in Steven F. Lawson, *Civil Rights Crossroads: Nation, Community, and the Black Freedom Struggle* (Lexington: University of Kentucky Press, 2005), 19–28.

For the most influential and visible historiographical essays in the past decade, see Charles W. Eagles, "Toward New Histories of the Civil Rights Movement," *Journal of Southern History* 66 (Nov. 2000): 815–48; Jacquelyn Dowd Hall, "The Long Civil Rights Movement and the Political Uses of the Past," *Journal of American History* 91 (March 2005): 1233–63; Jeanne Theoharis, "Black Freedom Studies: Re-imagining and Redefining the Fundamentals," *History Compass* 4, no. 2 (2006): 348–67; Sundiata Keita Cha-Jua and Clarence Lang, "The 'Long Movement' as Vampire: Temporal and Spatial Fallacies in Recent Black Freedom Struggles," *Journal of African American History* 92, no. 2 (2007): 265–88. More recently, Eric Arnesen and David Chappell have responded to Jacqueline Hall's call for a long civil rights movement. See Eric Arnesen, "Civil Rights Historiography: Two Perspectives," *Historically Speaking* 10 (April 2009): 31–34; David Chapell, "The Lost Decade of Civil Rights," *Historically Speaking* 10 (April 2009): 37–41.

See also David Chappell, "Civil Rights: Grassroots, High Politics, or Both?," *Reviews in American History* 32 (Dec. 2004): 565–72; Peniel Joseph, "Introduction: Toward a Historiography of the Black Power Movement," in *The Black Power Movement: Rethinking the Civil Rights-Black Power Era*, ed. Peniel Joseph (New York: Routledge, 2006), 1–25; Peniel Joseph, "The Black Power Movement: A State of the Field," *Journal of American History* 96 (Dec. 2009): 751–76; Kevin Gaines, "The Historiography of the Struggle for Black Equality Since 1945," in *A Companion to Post-1945 America*, ed. Jean-Chrisophe Agnew and Roy Rosenzweig (Malden, Mass.: Blackwell, 2002); Stephen Tuck, "'We Are Taking Up Where the Movement of the 1960s Left Off': The Proliferation and Power of African American Protest during the 1970s," *Journal of Contemporary History* 43, no. 4

(2008): 637–54; William Chafe, "The Gods Bring Threads to Webs Begun," *Journal of American History* 86 (March 2000): 1531–51; Adam Fairclough, "State of the Art: Historians and the Civil Rights Movement," *Journal of American Studies* 24, no. 3 (1990): 387–98.

12. For example, Clayborne Carson, David Garrow, and Steven Lawson all point to the importance of local studies, although none have emphasized that perspective as part of their own primary work. Carson, "Civil Rights Reform and the Black Freedom Struggle," in *The Civil Rights Movement in America*, 19–32; Lawson, "Comment," in *The Civil Rights Movement in America*, 32–37; Lawson, "Freedom Then, Freedom Now," 456–71, esp. 456–59, 471; Lawson, "Freedom Down to Now," in Lawson, *Civil Rights Crossroads*, 19–28.

Jeanne Theoharis and Komozi Woodard have been particularly important in highlighting local studies scholarship in their two influential edited collections, *Freedom North* and *Groundwork*. The latter was conceived as a tribute to John Dittmer, acknowledging the importance of Dittmer's 1994 *Local People* in legitimizing local studies scholarship on the civil rights movement. Jeanne F. Theoharis and Komozi Woodard, eds., *Freedom North: Black Freedom Struggles Outside the South* (New York: Palgrave, 2003); Jeanne Theoharis and Komozi Woodard, eds., *Groundwork: Local Black Freedom Movements in America* (New York: New York University Press, 2005). See especially, Theoharis, Introduction, *Freedom North*, 1–16; Payne, Foreword, *Groundwork*, ix–xv; Theoharis and Woodward, Introduction, *Groundwork*, 1–16. Charles Payne, in the preface to the 2007 edition of *I've Got the Light of Freedom*, comments on the significant expansion of movement scholarship since 1995, especially local, bottom-up studies that challenge normative work. He observes, "The last decade has witnessed a remarkable flowering of movement scholarship, much of it trying to dismantle the mainstream narrative, assertion by assertion. . . . [T]he scholarly literature has expanded and changed in ways that could not have been foreseen just a decade ago. Ideas which were oppositional then have a hint of a new orthodoxy about them now." Payne, Preface, *I've Got the Light of Freedom*, 2007, xiv.

David Chappell would undoubtedly agree, but from a somewhat more critical angle. In a December 2004 review of Steven Lawson's *Civil Rights Crossroads*, he suggests that local studies have supplanted top-down scholarship, writing, "While other historians of his generation made a great show of discovering and celebrating the once unsung folk heroes of the rural southern movement, Lawson ground on with unfashionable, often unappreciated, but vital work on national legislation, lobbying, and litigation. . . . Though Lawson resisted the fashion of grassroots historiography—the main trend in civil rights studies for the last 25 years—he did not object to it on philosophical or methodological grounds." He goes on to criticize Lawson for not being more vigorous (in this book and other work) in challenging bottom-up scholarship. For example, Chappell asserts, "It does not seem to have occurred to him that he could do the grassroots historians a greater service by establishing a real debate with them than by echoing their principles, which after all requires no special talent or perspective." Chapell, "Civil Rights: Grassroots, High Politics, or Both?," 565–72. Despite this attention to local studies and Chappell's assertion that local studies work has "supplanted" other approaches, local studies still remain fairly marginalized when it comes to the framing and details that dominate recent historiographical debates and attempts at synthesis.

13. Eagles observed that the earliest community-based histories "marked a significant departure" and observed that more community studies would be "of even greater interest," including those on communities that were home to well-known events and "otherwise unknown centers of activities." Even as he notes the persistence of a *Brown* to Memphis time frame, Eagles appears to give community studies credit for complicating this chronology, noting their longer view, but concluding that "[t]he examination of events in individual communities and among ordinary people has failed to inaugurate a different chronological conception of the movement." Eagles, "Toward New Histories," 827, 836–37. Hall observes that "[e]arly studies of the black freedom movement often hewed closely to the journalistic 'rough draft of history,' replicating its judgements and trajectory. More recent histories, memoirs, and documentaries have struggled to loosen its hold." She adds in a footnote that "community studies tend to blur the boundaries of the dominant narrative." Hall, "The Long Civil Rights Movement," 1236, 1236n8.

14. Eagles, "Toward New Histories," 816.

15. Ibid., 840–41.

16. Eagles ignores this debate, despite Charles Payne's quite explicit bibliographic essay on the shortcomings of top-down, normative history, published in 1994, as well as his subsequent debate with Steven Lawson, first published in 1998. Payne, "Bibliographic Essay: The Social Construction of History," in *I've Got the Light of Freedom*, 413–42; Steven F. Lawson and Charles Payne, with introduction by James Patterson, *Debating the Civil Rights Movement, 1945–68* (Lanham, Md.: Rowman & Littlefield, 1998, 2006). Even earlier, Steven Lawson's essay, "Freedom Then, Freedom Now," includes extensive discussion of historiographical debates. He notes in conclusion that "[d]ifferences of interpretations are as evident among civil rights scholars as they were among civil rights activists." Lawson, "Freedom Then, Freedom Now," 456–71, esp. 456–9, 471, quote on 471. See also, Carson, "Civil Rights Reform and the Black Freedom Struggle," in *The Civil Rights Movement in America*, 19–32; Lawson, "Comment," in *The Civil Rights Movement in America*, 32–37, esp. 32; Steven F. Lawson, "Freedom Down to Now," in Lawson, *Civil Rights Crossroads*, 19–28; Cha-Jua and Lang, "The 'Long Movement' as Vampire," 265–88, esp. 267.

17. Eagles, "Toward New Histories," 830–31. Scholars are also giving attention to the diversity among those whites committed to resistance. David Cunningham's work on the Klan in Mississippi offers one example. David Cunningham, presentation at the Porter

Fortune Symposium at the University of Mississippi, February 2010. Even before Eagles's essay, other scholars had begun to sketch out some of the differences and debates within the white community. See, for example, Dittmer, *Local People*; Payne, *I've Got the Light of Freedom*; and Neil R. McMillen, *The Citizens' Council; Organized Resistance to the Second Reconstruction, 1954–64* (Urbana: University of Illinois Press, 1971).

18. Eagles writes, "Most works, however, have presented only positive interpretations of the movement that shy away from searching criticism of its leaders, tactics, and strategies, as well as its larger failure to achieve the goal of racial justice. Again, the writing on the movement has yet to produce a range of strikingly different interpretive schools or consistently clashing interpretations." He goes on to use Martin Luther King Jr. as an example. Eagles, "Toward New Histories," 837–41, quote on 841. Steven Lawson disagrees with Eagles's assertion that scholars have not been critical of the movement and directly counters Eagles's assessment of King scholarship. Lawson, "Freedom Down to Now," 27. From a different political perspective, Alan Draper gives considerable attention to what he considers the unfair critiques by Charles Payne and John Dittmer of "middle-class" movement activists. Alan Draper, "The Mississippi Movement: A Review Essay," *Journal of Mississippi History* 60, no. 4 (1998): 355–66, esp. 360–3.

In terms of chronology, Eagles appears to acknowledge the significance of local studies work for evaluating chronology, noting that "the examination of events in individual communities and among ordinary people has failed to inaugurate a different chronological conception of the freedom struggle." He then asserts, however, that "while considerable variety exists among the publications on the civil rights struggle, most conform to a similar chronological outline. . . . [M]ost historians have apparently accepted a periodization that proceeds essentially from *Brown* to Memphis." He then notes that "[a]s a number of works have already indicated, students should at the very least be increasingly dissatisfied with the standard 1954–1968 scenario. . . . Too often, however, earlier people and events are viewed as precursors rather than parts of the actual civil rights movement; the relationship between the 1930s and 1940s and the more conventional 1954–1968 period needs to be clarified." He continues, "To balance the growing interest in the pre-1954 history, however, more attention needs to be paid to the period after 1968 and the legacies or ramifications of the movement." See Eagles, "Toward New Histories," 837–38. Thus Eagles acknowledges and overlooks the complexity of local studies' timelines. Moreover, Eagles's push to have historians extend the time frame for the movement beyond the typical end point is particularly ironic since he also argues that historians are too sympathetic *because* they have not yet "acknowledge[d] the end of the movement." Eagles, "Toward New Histories," 848.

19. Eagles, "Toward New Histories," 838–39, 831.

20. Hall, "The Long Civil Rights Movement," 1245.

21. Ibid., 1235.

22. Ibid., 1251. Hall observes that "[e]arly studies of the black freedom movement often hewed closely to the journalistic 'rough draft of history,' replicating its judgements and trajectory. More recent histories, memoirs, and documentaries have struggled to loosen its hold." This work she references is absolutely crucial, yet she cites only three community studies, along with several top-down overviews, and a range of work outside the classic movement. In a footnote she also notes that "[c]ommunity studies tend to blur the boundaries of the dominant narrative" and acknowledges that the normative narrative persists *despite* the efforts of recent scholarship. Hall, "The Long Civil Rights Movement," 1236, 1236n8. For the three pages of text on the classical period, she references only two works that are grounded in local communities: Charles Payne's, *I've Got the Light of Freedom* and an essay by Laurie Green, based on her study of Memphis, Tennessee. Other references that might fall into the bottom-up category are Barbara Ransby's biography of Ella Baker and Aldon Morris's classic, *The Origins of the Civil Rights Movement.* Hall, "The Long Civil Rights Movement," 1251–54, see esp. 1251n48, 1253n453, 1253n54.

Hall makes a number of important observations that could point in a different direction. She notes, for example, that "black southerners were schooled in a quest *both* for access and for self determination that dated back to emancipation," that they utilized a wide range of tactics (including intraracial and interracial), and that the movement's success "depended not just on idealism and courage, but on a keen sense of understanding and ready use of the fulcrums of power." (Emphasis in original.) She cites Charles Payne's, *I've Got the Light of Freedom* several times, referring to a number of his critical insights on the movement and the historiography, including some that highlight different ways of seeing the movement than the one she is advocating. However, there is little evidence that Payne's insights influence her framing and her footnote referencing the diversity of the southern black struggle cites scholarship that focuses only on the era before the New Deal. Hall, "The Long Civil Rights Movement," 1251, 1251n49.

The Long Civil Rights Movement Conference, organized by Hall and hosted by the University of North Carolina in April 2009, had the same general emphasis. "The Long Civil Rights Movement: History, Politics, Memories," a conference hosted by the Southern Oral History Program in the Center for the Study of the American South, University of North Carolina at Chapel Hill, April 2–4, 2009 (program in my possession and available online at https://lcrm.lib.unc.edu/blog/wp-content/uploads/2009/04/lcrm -program.pdf, accessed February 27, 2010).

23. Hall, "The Long Civil Rights Movement," 1239. Dittmer, *Local People*; Payne, *I've Got the Light of Freedom*; J. Todd Moye, *Let the People Decide: Black Freedom and White Resistance Movements in Sunflower County, Mississippi, 1945–1986* (Chapel Hill: University of North Carolina Press, 2004); Chana Kai Lee, *For Freedom's Sake: The Life of Fannie Lou Hamer* (Urbana: University of Illinois Press, 1999); Kay Mills, *This Little Light of*

*Mine: The Life of Fannie Lou Hamer* (New York: Penguin, 1993); Hasan Kwame Jeffries, *Bloody Lowndes: Civil Rights and Black Power in the Alabama Black Belt* (New York: New York University Press, 2009); Cynthia Griggs Fleming, *In the Shadow of Selma: The Continuing Struggle for Civil Rights in the Rural South* (New York: Rowman & Littlefield, 2004); Glen T. Eskew, *But for Birmingham: The Local and National Movements in the Civil Rights Struggle* (Chapel Hill: University of North Carolina Press, 1999); Robert J. Norrell, *Reaping the Whirlwind: The Civil Rights Movement in Tuskegee* (New York: Knopf, 1985); J. Mills Thornton, *Dividing Lines: Municipal Politics and the Struggle for Civil Rights in Montgomery, Birmingham, and Selma* (Tuscaloosa: University of Alabama Press, 2006); Stephen G. N. Tuck, *Beyond Atlanta: The Struggle for Racial Equality in Georgia, 1940–1980* (Athens: University of Georgia Press, 2003); Fairclough, *Race & Democracy*; Greta de Jong, *A Different Day: African American Struggles for Justice in Rural Louisiana, 1900–1970* (Chapel Hill: University of North Carolina Press, 2002); Laurie B. Green, *Battling the Plantation Mentality: Memphis and the Black Freedom Struggle* (Chapel Hill: University of North Carolina Press, 2007); Winston Grady-Willis, *Challenging U.S. Apartheid: Atlanta and the Black Struggles for Human Rights, 1960–77* (Durham: Duke University Press, 2006); Chafe, *Civilities and Civil Rights*; Christina Greene, *Our Separate Ways: Women and the Black Freedom Movement in Durham, North Carolina* (Chapel Hill: University of North Carolina Press, 2005); Timothy B. Tyson, *Radio Free Dixie: Robert F. Williams & the Roots of Black Power* (Chapel Hill: University of North Carolina Press, 1999); Charles McKinney, *Greater Freedom: The Evolution of the Civil Rights Struggle in Wilson, North Carolina* (Lanham, Md.: University Press of America, 2010); Peter B. Levy, *Civil War on Race Street: The Civil Rights Movement in Cambridge, Maryland* (Gainesville: University of Florida Press, 2003); and Glenda Alice Rabby, *The Pain and the Promise: The Struggle for Civil Rights in Tallahassee, Florida* (Athens: University of Georgia Press, 1999); Tracy E. K'Meyer, *Civil Rights in the Gateway to the South: Louisville, Kentucky, 1945–1980* (Lexington: University of Kentucky Press, 2009).

24. Hall, "The Long Civil Rights Movement," 1253.

25. Moye, *Let the People Decide*; Moye, "Focusing Our Eyes on the Prize: How Community Studies Are Reframing and Rewriting the History of the Civil Rights Movement," chapter 5, this volume.

26. Moye, "Focusing Our Eyes on the Prize: How Community Studies are Reframing and Rewriting the History of the Civil Rights Movement," chapter 5, this volume; Jeffries, *Bloody Lowndes*, 26–27, 29–31, quote on 4. In this instance, even the Communist Party-affiliated Sharecroppers' Union was indigenous to Alabama.

27. With these points in mind, Theoharis insists that local studies help us rethink and reframe the dichotomies that grow out of the normative version of the history. Too often we see, in her words, "a nonviolent movement born in the South during the 1950s that

emerged triumphant in the early 1960s but then was derailed by the twin forces of Black Power and white backlash when it sought to move North after 1965." Theoharis, Introduction, *Freedom North*, 2; Theoharis, "Black Freedom Studies: Re-imagining and Redefining the Fundamentals," 348–67; Theoharis and Woodward, Introduction, *Groundwork*, 1–16. Unlike Hall, Theoharis explicitly draws on and emphasizes the importance of local studies.

28. Cha-Jua and Lang explicitly point to the significance of local studies, especially in highlighting the agency of southern African Americans. Moreover, their critique, with its emphasis on context and precision, implicitly reinforces the importance of local studies. At the same time, their framing of a fourth wave of scholarship as part of the "long movement" appears to obscure or subsume quite a bit of important work that does not appear to easily fit that category. They note, for example, that scholars are particularly attracted to the "Long Movement's focus on local movements, especially in the urban North." While I agree with this and with their follow-up, that some of the long civil rights movement work can go too far in "de-centering the southern-focused narrative," it is not clear how they would categorize the extensive outpouring of southern-based local studies (and other) work that counters that emphasis. For example, Cha-Jua and Lang argue that "[p]erhaps the most important contribution of fourth-wave scholarship has been its re-centering of African American women and gender into Civil Rights and Black Power narratives." Again, I agree with their assessment of the importance of the work that has given serious attention to women and gender, but it is not at all clear to me why Barbara Ransby's biography of Ella Baker, to give one example, would be categorized as part of the "long movement" scholarship. By framing recent scholarship, their "fourth wave," primarily or exclusively in terms of the "long movement," they appear to disregard much of the southern-based, bottom-up, local studies work that continues to strengthen our understanding of the southern freedom movement. Cha-Jua and Lang, "The 'Long Movement' as Vampire," 265–88, esp. 266–69.

29. For just a few examples, see Yohuru Williams, *Black Politics/ White Power: Civil Rights, Black Power, and the Black Panthers in New Haven* (St. James, N.Y.: Brandywine Press, 2000); Robert Self, *American Babylon: Race and the Struggle for Postwar Oakland* (Princeton, N.J.: Princeton University Press, 2003); Thomas J. Sugrue, *Sweet Land of Liberty: The Forgotten Struggle for Civil Rights in the North* (New York: Random House, 2008); Thomas J. Sugrue, *The Origins of the Urban Crisis: Race and Inequality in Postwar Detroit* (Princeton, N.J.: Princeton University Press, 1996); Matthew Countryman, *Up South: Civil Rights and Black Power in Philadelphia* (Philadelphia: University of Pennsylvania Press, 2006); Yohuru R. Williams and Jama Lazerow, *Liberated Territory: Untold Local Perspectives on the Black Panther Party* (Durham: Duke University Press, 2008); and Patrick D. Jones, *The Selma of the North: Civil Rights Insurgency in Milwaukee* (Cambridge, Mass.: Harvard University Press, 2009).

30. Eagles, as noted before, ignores the bottom-up versus top-down debate and bottom-up critique, while Hall, though she does not take it up explicitly, emphasizes the primacy of national institutions and the centrality of the government (whether for good or ill). Eagles, "Toward New Histories," 815–48; Hall, "The Long Civil Rights Movement," 1233–63.

31. Carson, "Civil Rights Reform and the Black Freedom Struggle," in *The Civil Rights Movement in America*, 27–28.

32. Hall, "The Long Civil Rights Movement," 1233–35, esp. 1235.

33. Carson, "Civil Rights Reform and the Black Freedom Struggle," in *The Civil Rights Movement in America*, 19–32, esp. 27–28; Lawson, "Freedom Then, Freedom Now," 456–71, esp. 457, 471.

34. Jeffries, *Bloody Lowndes*, 197.

35. Chafe, *Civilities and Civil Rights*; Jeffries, *Bloody Lowndes*.

36. Alex Waldauer, quoted in *A Little Taste of Freedom*, xiii.

37. Samantha Maurer reflection, Hist266, Spring 2009.

38. For just one example, see John Mack Faragher, Mari Jo Buhle, Daniel Czitrom, and Susan H. Armitage, *Out of Many: A History of the American People*, Combined Volume (Englewood Cliffs, N.J.: Prentice Hall, 2009). See also, John Mack Faragher, Mari Jo Buhle, Daniel Czitrom, Susan H. Armitage, *Out of Many: A History of the American People*, Vol. II (Englewood Cliffs, N.J.: Prentice Hall, 1994). A comparison of these two editions makes it painfully obvious how little impact the local studies scholarship of the past fifteen years has had on the textbook authors' approach to the civil rights narrative.

39. In a plurality opinion, the Supreme Court severely limited race-conscious school assignment policies, with some Justices equating them with the legally-mandated segregation overturned by *Brown*. Opinions of Justice Roberts, Justice Thomas, Justice Kennedy, Justice Breyer, Justice Stevens, *Parents Involved in Community Schools v. Seattle School District No. 1, et al.* and *Crystal D. Meredith v. Jefferson County Board of Education, et al.*, June 2007.

40. The following song lyrics, versions of which became popular among progressives during and after Barack Obama's election, provide a telling example of this tendency. "Rosa sat so Martin could walk. Martin walked so Obama could run. Obama runs so our children can fly." There are many variations on this. For this version, see http://www .democraticunderground.com/discuss/duboard.php?az=view_all&address+132x7641350 (accessed March 1, 2010).

41. As I write this, the University of California, San Diego, is trying to deal with a number of similar and highly visible racist incidents, including the so-called "Compton Cookout," an off-campus party mocking black history month, and the presence of a noose hanging from a campus library. In response to these incidents or, perhaps, the unwelcome publicity surrounding them, UCSD reported that it is accepting recommendations

from the Black Student Union that it take steps to address recruitment of faculty of color, examine declining black student enrollment, and look for space for a Black Resource Center. "UCSD Frat Denies Involvement in 'Ghetto-Themed' Party: UCSD Officials Condemn 'Compton Cookout' Held Last Weekend," February 17, 2010, http://www.10news .com/news/22588063/details.html (accessed February 28, 2010); "Student Admits Hanging Noose in Library," February 26, 2010, CNN, http://www.cnn.com/2010/us/02/26/ california.noose/index.html?iref=allsearch (accessed February 28, 2010). Kevin Muller, Honr203 journal, November 25, 2008 (in author's possession).

42. "Conflicted Histories: Geneseo and the Struggle for Justice," keynote presentation for Race and Campus Culture Teach-In, Spring 2008 (in author's possession); Daniel Bailey, final reflection, Hist220, Fall 2009; Kevin Muller journal, Honr203, November 25, 2008; Joseph Cope, teach-in reflection, Spring 2008; Ronald Herzman, teach-in reflection, Spring 2008; Jasmine Montgomery, teach-in reflection, Spring 2008. These teach-in reflections (and others), along with general readings and information, can be found at http://eres.geneseo.edu/library/cdc/race.shtml (accessed February 28, 2010). News coverage, editorials, and letters to the editor can be found in the student newspaper, *The Lamron*, online at http://www.thelamron.com. There is considerable coverage of blackface, race, the Race and Campus Culture Teach-In, and related issues throughout the 2007–2008 academic year, especially following a Halloween 2007 blackface incident.

43. Eagles, "Toward New Histories," 836. In offering this critique, Eagles offers no examples or evidence to support his conclusions.

44. Draper, "The Mississippi Movement: A Review Essay," 355–66, esp. 356; Charles Payne, responding to such critiques, argues, "Giving young people a history they can use doesn't require any bending of the record. Quite the contrary. The more precisely and completely we can render the history, the longer it will be useful." Payne, *I've Got the Light of Freedom* (2007), xxi. Suggesting the ways that oral histories were considered suspect, William Chafe explained and justified his use of oral histories in the introduction to his 1980 community study on Greensboro, writing, "[T]his book is based up on a combination of oral and written sources. Only through extensive use of oral interviewing, grounded in written sources, has it been possible to gain even a glimpse of the rich multiracial fabric that is Greensboro's civil rights history. Oral sources are used here not as a substitute for other historical research techniques—rather as a supplement. But without a combination of the two there would be no possibility of discovering what happened in Greensboro." Chafe, *Civilities and Civil Rights*, 10.

45. Draper, "The Mississippi Movement: A Review Essay," 363–64.

46. Ibid., 366.

47. Howard Zinn addresses this in his essay, "Knowledge is a Form of Power." He writes, "Our values should determine the questions we ask in scholarly inquiry, but not the answers." Howard Zinn, *The Politics of History* (Boston: Beacon, 1970), 10. There are,

of course, challenges in developing effective collaborations between scholars and activists. At least some activists are intensely critical of historians. For an example of both the anger and some of the reasons for it, see the comments by historians and activists at a 1988 SNCC reunion at Trinity College. "SNCC and the Practice of History," in *Circle of Trust: Remembering* SNCC, ed. Cheryl Lynn Greenberg (New Brunswick: Rutgers University Press, 1998), 177–99. Although some movement people are very conversant with the current scholarship and how it has evolved over the years, many judge the history based either on the first generation of scholarship published in the 1970s and 1980s or through the lens of popular culture, assuming that since the normative story is so unchanging, historians must be reinforcing, not challenging, it. Anger over this popular version and the sense that historians are both distorting and controlling movement history has been expressed publicly on a SNCC listserv several times in recent years (copies in author's possession). Reflecting on the gap between the popular portrayals of the movement and the reality, one of my students wrote, "I wonder what it means to some of these people who risked their lives in towns all across the country, to have their histories simplified and glossed over and their heroism become part of someone else's myth" (Joseph Zurro reflection, Spring 2006). In response to a discussion that emerged around the Long Civil Rights Movement Conference in Chapel Hill, N.C., in April 2009, Patrick Jones offered a thoughtful discussion of the existing divisions between scholars and activists and the ways we could each benefit from closer collaboration. Patrick Jones to SNCC-List, February 24, 2009 (in author's possession).

48. Bernice Johnson Reagon and Dick Cluster, "The Borning Struggle: The Civil Rights Movement: An Interview with Bernice Johnson Reagon by Dick Cluster," *Radical History* 12, no. 6 (1978): 9–25, esp. 21.

49. During a question and answer session following a presentation in March 2009, Reagon was asked if she ever marched with Dr. King. She responded that she had not and then explained that in December 1961, King came to Albany, Georgia, *because* she was in jail (along with hundreds of other black residents), and that by the time she came out of jail, he had left town. In other words, King responded to the collective action of people struggling before he arrived and those same people continued to struggle after he left. Bernice Johnson Reagon, "She Said: Women's Words Featuring Bernice Johnson Reagon," March 15, 2009, Pittsburgh Cultural Trust, Bynam Theater, Pittsburgh, Pennsylvania. For a few sources by activists that reflect or include a King/SCLC-centered perspective, see Ralph Abernathy, "Albany," in *The Walls Came Tumbling Down* (New York: Harper & Row, 1989), 201–29; Henry Hampton and Steve Fayer, eds., "Albany, Georgia, 1961–62," in *Voices of Freedom: An Oral History of the Civil Rights Movement from the 1950s through the 1980s* (New York: Bantam Books, 1990), 97–114, esp. 104–6, 111–13; and Coretta Scott King, *My Life with Martin Luther King, Jr.* (New York: Holt, Rinehart, and Winston, 1969), 187–92.

50. Payne, *I've Got the Light of Freedom* (2007), xx.

51. Charles Payne, in his talk "Sexism is a helluva thing," reflects on the issue of framing, while giving an example that illustrates the diverse views of movement participants and how important it can be to hear and take seriously as many of those perspectives as possible. He explains how his use of the SNCC papers and interviews with SNCC staff contributed to his conclusion that Freedom School work was "devalued" in the 1964 Mississippi Summer Project. Years after he published that assessment, a Freedom School teacher called his conclusion into question by directing attention away from SNCC staff and toward the local African Americans whose children attended Freedom Schools. As Payne explains, her critique resonated, leading him to rethink the framework he employed and sending him back to look again at the evidence (see chapter 10, this volume).

Among those who critique oral history, there tends to be an assumption that scholars simply accept what they are told at face value. These critics also tend to ignore the fact that all sources require critical analysis and corroboration. Any serious oral historian evaluates and verifies interviews as rigorously as any other source. There are, of course, problems that can be more pronounced with oral history, including the potential for failed or distorted memories. For example, Judy Richardson realized, after years of thinking (and telling oral historians) that male SNCC workers (including Stokely Carmichael) rescued her and others from a white mob outside a hospital in Greenwood, Mississippi, in summer 1964, that in fact, it was actually the local white police who eventually came to escort them home. She "discovered" this when I shared an archived copy of an affidavit describing the incident. In this instance, Richardson's memory is not accurate, something that was possible to check. At the same time, the fact of her altered memory is interesting in its own right, for what it says about how she has made sense of the history for herself.

52. The best example is Lance Hill, *The Deacons for Defense: Armed Resistance and the Civil Rights Movement* (Chapel Hill: University of North Carolina Press, 2004). See also, Emilye Crosby, "'It wasn't the Wild West': Keeping Local Studies in Self-Defense Historiography," (chapter 7, this volume).

53. Charles (Charlie) Cobb Jr., July 2009, speaking at "Landmarks of American Democracy: From Freedom Summer to the Memphis Sanitation Workers' Strike," NEH (National Endowment for the Humanities) Institute for Community College Teachers, Hamer Institute, Jackson State University; Charles Cobb Jr., e-mail to author, June 17, 2010.

54. In a tribute to Worth Long, Charlie Cobb writes that one of his "favorites" of Long's words "is 'unviolent' rather than 'nonviolent' to describe the tactics of the 1960s Southern Civil Rights Movement." Charlie Cobb (Charles Cobb Jr.) in *A Tribute to Worth Long: Still on the Case: A Pioneer's Continuing Commitment*, by Roland L. Freeman (Washington, DC: Smithsonian Center for Folklife and Cultural Heritage, 2006), 43. See also, Worth Long, quoted in Moye, *Let the People Decide*, 102, 233n35; Molly

McGehee, "'You Do Not Own What You Cannot Control': An Interview with Activist and Folklorist Worth Long," *Mississippi Folklife*, 31 (Fall 1998), 15; Robert Parris Moses, interview by Joseph Sinsheimer, November 19, 1983, Joseph Sinsheimer papers, Duke University, transcript, 19, 20; Charles Cobb Jr., quoted in Joanne Grant, *Fundi: The Story of Ella Baker* (Brooklyn: First Run/Icarus Films, 2005); Cobb, July 2009, "Landmarks of American Democracy," Hamer Institute.

55. The egregiously racist and historical inaccuracies of *Mississippi Burning* were at least part of the impetus for the making of *Freedom Song*. *Mississippi Burning* brought together Mississippi movement activists who had not seen each other in decades. Moreover, Charles (Chuck) McDew describes calling the producer of *Mississippi Burning*, asking that a disclaimer be added to the end of the film. Flatly rejecting the request, the producer showed no awareness of who McDew was and, among other things, suggested that if SNCC workers did not like the movie, they should make their own. So, in conjunction with some allies in the film business, they did. As they began working on the project, SNCC workers insisted that the movie focus on the years *before* Freedom Summer, in an attempt to counter the persistent Big Event/white focus that tends to dominate popular understanding of the Mississippi movement. Charles McDew, presentation, SUNY Geneseo, Spring 2003 (video in author's possession); Charles McDew, presentation at NEH Institute "Civil Rights Movement: History and Consequences," Harvard University, Summer 2000; David Dennis, Forward, *Radical Equations: Math Literacy and Civil Rights*, by Charles E. Cobb Jr. and Robert P. Moses (Boston: Beacon, 2001), vii–viii. Jefferson Graham, "'Freedom Song' fulfills a dream," February 23, 2000, *USA Today*. TNT (Turner Network Television), which produced the film, has some information on its website, including some support for teachers. See http://alt.tnt.tv/movies/tntoriginals/freedomsong.

56. Moye, "Focusing Our Eyes on the Prize," chapter 5, this volume.

# PART ONE

# Local Studies as Case Studies

JOHN DITTMER

# Local People and National Leaders

## *The View from Mississippi*

**T**his chapter explores the relationship between civil rights activists in Mississippi and national political leaders and institutions over a twelve-year period, beginning in the aftermath of the *Brown* decision and ending with the Meredith March in June of 1966. Blacks and their white allies made extraordinary progress during this brief span of time, sweeping aside Jim Crow laws and guaranteeing African Americans the vote, while setting an example of courage and determination that continues to inspire us today. Given the white supremacist mentality that governed all aspects of Mississippi life, however, local people needed allies in Washington if they were to succeed in cracking open the Closed Society. That help was slow to arrive, as an examination of the racial policies of presidents Eisenhower, Kennedy, and Johnson will reveal.

The white reaction to *Brown v. Board of Education* in Mississippi was predictable. Senator James Eastland breathed defiance: "The South will not abide by nor obey this legislative decision of a political court. We will take whatever steps are necessary to retain segregation in education." Shortly thereafter, the white Citizens' Council was formed in the Delta for the express purpose of thwarting the Court's decision. When the NAACP filed school desegregation petitions in five Mississippi cities the Citizens' Council used publicity and economic retaliation to stop the desegregation effort in its tracks.[1]

Faced with this bald-faced challenge to the law of the land, the administration of Dwight Eisenhower looked the other way while Mississippi whites made a mockery of *Brown*, responding indifferently to repeated pleas for help by local and national NAACP officials. Privately, the president had opposed the school decision, and regretted nominating Earl Warren as chief justice. The Supreme Court itself also must bear responsibility for the failure to desegregate any Mississippi schools, for its implementation decree had in fact placed the burden of compliance on black parents rather than the school districts, with disastrous results. Black Mississippians had welcomed the *Brown* decision as a sign that the federal government was now on their side. But for the rest of the decade segregationists took whatever steps necessary to maintain their supremacy, including the murder of black leaders, while the federal government watched from the sidelines. As one white Mississippian observed: "It's open season on Negroes now. They've got no protection, and any peckerwood who wants to can go out and shoot himself one and we'll free him. Our situation will get worse and worse."[2]

Black leaders greeted the election of John F. Kennedy in 1960 with mixed emotions. He had made the famous telephone call to Coretta King after her husband had been jailed in Georgia, but Kennedy was also known in Mississippi as a friend of James Eastland, who along with other southern senators had supported Kennedy in his unsuccessful bid for the Democratic Party's vice presidential nomination in 1956. Kennedy's first big test in the area of civil rights came early in the spring of 1961 with the Freedom Rides. Foreign policy, not civil rights, was the priority for the president, who in early 1961 was preparing for his summit meeting with the Soviet leader Nikita Khrushchev in Vienna. When he first learned that the Congress of Racial Equality (CORE) leaders were planning to test the *Boynton* decision outlawing separate terminal facilities serving interstate passengers, an angry John Kennedy demanded that White House assistant Harris Wofford "tell them to call it off. Stop them!" As the riders headed south he adopted a wait-and-see attitude, but when a bus carrying the riders was burned outside Anniston, Alabama, Attorney General Robert Kennedy became directly involved.[3]

Avoiding violence would be the Kennedy administration's major goal during the Freedom Rides. When the riders insisted on pressing on into Mississippi the Kennedys feared a bloodbath, and with Eastland as their intermediary they cut a deal with Governor Ross Barnett: if the state promised to protect the riders, the White House would not interfere when local police officers arrested them as they entered the "white" waiting room at the Jackson terminal. The Kennedys could have provided protection. The Supreme Court had outlawed segregated waiting rooms. Assistant Attorney General Burke Marshall later wrote that "to enforce segregation in a place that was prohibited by federal law from being segregated [is] unconstitutional in my opinion without any question." But Robert Kennedy told interviewer Anthony Lewis that he believed "our authority was limited" in Jackson, adding that "it's better not to impose things from above just because people resent it." Burke Marshall attempted to justify this policy on constitutional grounds, invoking the doctrine of Federalism: "[T]he responsibility for the preservation of law and order, and the protection of citizens against unlawful conduct on the part of others is the responsibility of local authorities." Scores of attorneys and law school professors disagreed, citing legal precedents including *In Re Debs*, where the Supreme Court had ruled that "[t]he entire strength of the nation may be used to enforce in any part of the land . . . the security of all rights entrusted by the Constitution to its care." The administration stood its ground: there would be no federal protection for civil rights workers. "We didn't have the power," Burke Marshall later told an interviewer. "And," he added candidly, "we didn't want it."[4]

Avoiding violence became the keystone of the Kennedys' Mississippi policy, as they preferred to remain in the background and avoid crises. When conditions demanded White House action, such as James Meredith's integration of Ole Miss a year later, they were more comfortable working behind the scenes with Mississippi segregationists than with movement activists, a preference that, according to Martin Luther King, "made Negroes feel like pawns in a white man's political game." Leslie Dunbar, then head of the Southern Regional Council, has perceptively observed that in the Kennedy administration there was "a great reluctance to accept the fact that you had to be on somebody's side in the South."[5]

Not until the Birmingham crisis in the spring of 1963 did John Kennedy weigh in strongly on the side of the movement. His speech of June 11, the strongest ever by a president, formally endorsed the passage of a civil rights law. "We are confronted primarily with a moral issue," he said. "The heart of the question is whether all Americans are to be afforded equal rights and opportunities, whether we are going to treat our fellow Americans as we want to be treated." Still, the president's actions did not match his rhetoric. Only hours after his speech, a Citizens' Council member named Byron de la Beckwith gunned down Medgar Evers, who had been leading a movement in Jackson to end segregation and discrimination in downtown businesses. The city had refused to negotiate. When black outrage after Evers's death increased racial tensions to the breaking point, John Kennedy personally persuaded black leaders to accept a compromise that was in fact a sellout. They won none of their demands. Jackson remained a segregated city.[6]

So it went down during the last months of the president's life. As early as the fall of 1962 the Civil Rights Commission had planned to hold hearings in Mississippi to dramatize conditions facing African Americans in the Closed Society. The administration used various subterfuges to persuade the Commission to put off the hearings, for in requesting that human rights abuses in Mississippi be publicized nationally and declaring (as it did) that the administration had the obligation to protect civil rights workers, the commission was challenging the Kennedys' southern strategy. By March of 1963 four members of the commission were threatening to resign over this issue. In a scribbled note to Burke Marshall, Robert Kennedy asked, "Isn't there something that would be worthwhile for the Civil Rts. Commission to do? There must be something useful. I don't want them to resign." Nine days before his brother's assassination the attorney general recommended that the chairman of the Civil Rights Commission, John Hannah, be relieved of his duties.[7]

The news of John Kennedy's death saddened movement activists in Mississippi, just as it was cause for celebration among many segregationists. In Washington, SNCC opened its fourth leadership conference with a moment of silence for the slain president. But author James Baldwin no doubt voiced the sentiments of many in the audience when he said, "Let us not be so pious as now to say that President Kennedy was a great civil-rights fighter."[8]

The new president, Lyndon Johnson, had pledged to continue the Kennedy program, including passage of the civil rights bill, which was then bogged down in Congress. Johnson also adopted the Kennedys' "hands off" policy toward Mississippi, and as a result by early 1964 the Klan was running wild in the Magnolia State.[9] SNCC leader Bob Moses recalled that "we were just defenseless. There was no way to bring national attention. People were just going to be wiped out." Faced with a reign of terror at home and apparent indifference in Washington, the Council of Federated Organizations (COFO) leaders made plans for a "Summer Project" in 1964, a massive program that would bring upwards of a thousand volunteers to the state, most of them white college students. In addition to working on voter registration, opening community centers, and teaching in the freedom schools, the volunteers worked with the new Mississippi Freedom Democratic Party (FDP), which was to challenge the seating of the state's all-white, segregationist delegation at the Democratic Party's national convention in Atlantic City.[10]

Lyndon Johnson knew that his opponent in November would be the nation's leading conservative, Senator Barry Goldwater. Their differences on civil rights for black Americans could not have been more clear cut: LBJ had just pushed the Civil Rights Act of 1964 through Congress; Senator Goldwater had voted against it. Johnson took justifiable pride in his civil rights record—indeed, no president in our history can match it—but he opposed the FDP challenge, fearing that if the delegation were seated the other southern states would walk out of the convention and Goldwater would win the election. In a recorded telephone conversation with Senator Hubert Humphrey, Johnson exploded: "There's no justification for messing with the Freedom Party at all. . . . If we mess with the group of Negroes that were elected to nothing, and throw out the governor and elected officials of the state, we will lose fifteen states without even campaigning." To which Humphrey, who had been given the task of resolving this problem, said of the Mississippi activists: "We're just not dealing with emotionally stable people on this, Mr. President."[11] Johnson became obsessed by the FDP challenge, employing thirty undercover FBI agents at the convention, who wiretapped Martin Luther King's hotel telephone and installed microphone surveillance at SNCC's headquarters, passing intelligence on FDP strategy to presidential aide Bill Moyers at the White House. Unaware of these measures, the Freedom Democrats worked tirelessly to gain delegate support. The high point was the appearance before the Credentials Committee of Fannie Lou Hamer, the former sharecropper who had come to symbolize the grass-roots struggle in Mississippi. So compelling was Mrs. Hamer's testimony that the president called a press conference just to get her off the air.[12]

Ultimately the president resorted to arm-twisting to get his way with the credentials committee, and proposed a compromise in which two FDP delegates chosen by the White House would be given seats at large on the convention floor, along with a pledge that the Democratic Party would eliminate racial discrimination at all future conventions. The compromise was rammed through the Credentials Committee by Humphrey protégé Walter Mondale before the FDP had a chance to consider it—or lobby against it. At a meeting the following day, Fannie Lou Hamer expressed the anger of the challengers when she said, "We didn't come all this way for no two seats, 'cause all of us is tired." White liberals could not understand why the FDP rejected the compromise. The journalist Theodore White summed up this feeling of disappointment bordering on anger when he wrote that the Freedom Democratic Party "had stained the honor that so much courage and suffering had won it." The British journalist Godfrey Hodgson, on the other hand, believed that "in a longer perspective, the episode of the Mississippi Freedom Democratic Party

Figure 2 Fannie Lou Hamer and other protesters during the MFDP challenge to the all-white delegation at the Democratic National Convention in Atlantic City (Aug. 10, 1964). *Foreground, left to right*: Emory Harris, Stokely Carmichael, Sam Block, Fannie Lou Hamer, Eleanor Holmes Norton, Ella Baker. © 1978 George Ballis/Take Stock.

was perhaps even more ominous. That was the moment when the more radical black leaders finally lost faith in the presidency, in the Democratic Party, and the coalition between the liberal intellectuals and the labor unions."[13]

Mississippi activists were hurt by their rejection at the convention, but they came back home and endorsed the Johnson-Humphrey ticket, ran candidates of their own, and intensified the effort to be recognized as the state's official Democratic Party. This task proved especially difficult because the FDP insisted on preserving its independence rather than submitting to the dictates of the Democratic National Committee. Only five months after Atlantic City the Freedom Democrats crossed the Johnson administration again by unsuccessfully challenging the seating of Mississippi's congressional delegation. They invited Malcolm X to speak at their convention, and came out against the war in Vietnam before Martin Luther King made his opposition public. The FDP would never win recognition from the national party. (At the 1968 national convention in Chicago, a "Loyalist" delegation was seated. This was an integrated delegation more willing to follow the dictates of the Democratic National Committee.)[14]

Although the more militant black activists were not welcome at the White House, the Johnson administration, through its antipoverty programs, did improve the quality of life for thousands of poor Mississippi blacks. Head Start provided jobs for local people as well as early childhood education, and the Voting Rights Act added hundreds of thousands of black names to the registration books. Shortly after the passage of that law, in a speech at Howard University, President Johnson told the black students and faculty in his audience that the need was not mere equality of opportunity but rather equality of condition: "not equality as a right and a theory, but equality as a fact and a result."[15] This speech was the high-water mark of the liberal commitment to the goal of racial equality.

Over the next twelve months events conspired to undermine this commitment. Race riots in northern cities led to a white backlash. Activists in SNCC and CORE began talking about black nationalism. Their hero was Malcolm X, not Martin Luther King. And looming over all of this was the escalating war in Vietnam, with all its attendant consequences.

Things came to a head, once again, in Mississippi. In the spring of 1966 James Meredith set out on a 220-mile walk from Memphis to Jackson. His purpose was "to challenge the all-pervasive and overriding fear" still dominant among most black Mississippians, and to convince them it was now safe to register to vote. On the second day of his journey, Meredith was shot by a white man, and civil rights leaders from across the country came to Mississippi to continue Meredith's march. As Martin Luther King, Stokely Carmichael, and hundreds of others wound their way through the Delta, it was clear that fundamental changes were occurring, that the shaky alliances between black activists and northern white liberals was coming apart. Two events during the latter stages of the march drove this point home. The first was Carmichael's raising the cry of "Black Power" at a rally in Greenwood, a slogan that many whites saw as a threatening example of "racism in reverse." And then several days later in Canton, marchers attempted to pitch their tents on the campus of a black public school after they had been denied permission to do so by city officials. Sixty-one state troopers in full battle gear ordered the crowd of some 2,500 people to disperse, and two minutes later began firing tear gas across the field. Then they waded in with their guns and nightsticks. Paul Good, a journalist on the scene, wrote that the troopers "came stomping in behind the gas, gun-butting and kicking the men, women, and children. They were not arresting. They were punishing."[16]

The police riot in Canton was as brutal as the assault on the marchers at the Selma bridge a year earlier. Then the president had federalized the National Guard to protect the marchers, but in Canton the Johnson administration's response was strikingly different. The next day Attorney General Nicholas Katzenbach merely said that he "regretted" the use of tear gas against the marchers because "it always makes the situation more difficult." Katzenbach refused to condemn the police attack, commenting that the whole matter was under investigation. More revealing, the White House press secretary told reporters that the president had "no specific reaction" to the gassing of the demonstrators. Back in Canton, Martin Luther King told Paul Good that he had "heard the terrible statement of Katzenbach's. I've heard nothing from President Johnson. I don't know what I'm going to do," King confessed. "The Government has got to give me some victories if I'm gonna keep people nonviolent. . . . But a lot of people are getting hurt and bitter, and they can't see it that way anymore."[17] The national civil rights coalition and the ideology that united it were among the casualties on that battlefield in Canton.

Looking back on the twelve years between *Brown* and the last great march of the civil rights years, a couple of conclusions are in order. First, it took a grass-roots insurgency in the South to persuade a reluctant federal government to act. Neither Dwight Eisenhower nor John F. Kennedy regarded righting racial wrongs as their priority. Lyndon Johnson, in my opinion, did have a strong commitment to racial equality, but he wanted to lead the civil rights crusade, and did not take kindly to those like King and Carmichael and the Mississippi Freedom Democrats who had their own black agendas.

Second, strong federal support for the civil rights movement's program began with Kennedy's "Birmingham" speech and ended with Johnson's inspiring address at Howard. During this brief three-year span the Civil Rights and Voting Rights acts passed Congress, and the Office of Economic Opportunity attempted to come to grips with the problems of poverty. This period of promise ended abruptly in the summer of 1966. Black Power and Vietnam were of course in part responsible. But by then Martin Luther King and other established leaders were becoming convinced that equality of opportunity did not lead to equality of condition on a playing field that was not level, and when they began to demand that white people make sacrifices to achieve the greater good they lost the support of the White House and Congress.

We can now see that the civil rights movement had pretty much run its course long before King's assassination in Memphis. Nationally, there began a period of benign neglect in matters of race—by both major political parties. But for a brief moment in the mid-1960s the nation got a glimpse of the possibilities of democracy, when ordinary people accomplished extraordinary things in the bastions of white supremacy. Looking back on the freedom struggle in the Magnolia State, Bob Moses observed that the movement "brought Mississippi, for better or worse, up to the level of the rest of the country."[18] That was no small achievement. It also reminds us of the distance still to be traveled.

## NOTES

1. John Dittmer, *Local People* (Urbana: University of Illinois Press, 1994), 37, 45, 46–47.

2. Ibid., 52, 58.

3. Ibid., 92–93.

4. Ibid., 93–94.

5. Ibid., 94.

6. Ibid., 166, 168.

7. Ibid., 195–98.

8. Ibid., 211.

9. Ibid., 37; John Dittmer, "Fighting for the Soul of the Democratic Party," *YES! Magazine,* Fall 2003.

10. Dittmer, *Local People,* 219, 244, 237, 273.

11. Ibid., 286, 290–91; Michael R. Beschloss, ed., *Taking Charge: The Johnson White House Tapes, 1963–1964* (Simon & Schuster, 1997), 515–16.

12. Dittmer, *Local People,* 292, 288.

13. Ibid., 297, 302; Godfrey Hodgson, *America In Our Time: From World War II to Nixon—What Happened and Why* (New York: Vintage Books, 1976), 216–17.

14. Dittmer, "Fighting for the Soul of the Democratic Party."

15. Dittmer, *Local People,* 363; Hodgson, *America In Our Time,* 216–17.

16. Dittmer, *Local People,* 389, 392, 396, 397, 399.

17. Ibid., 400–1.

18. Ibid., 430.

LAURIE B. GREEN

# Challenging the Civil Rights Narrative

## Women, Gender, and the "Politics of Protection"

### WHO'S IN THIS PICTURE?

In the upper right-hand corner of the frame, striking Memphis sanitation workers sporting recently printed placards that read, "I AM A MAN," mill around in front of Clayborn Temple in anticipation of a mass strike support march to be led by Dr. Martin Luther King Jr. later that Thursday morning of March 28, 1968. Paradoxically, perhaps, dozens of black women of various ages—many talking and laughing, others more serious, some holding signs with messages such as "Workers Walk for Wages," and all poised to move out—fill most of the rest of the image. As photographer Ernest C. Withers snapped the picture, women at the center of the frame proudly lifted up their signs. At the time, then, both men and women, the preprinted "I AM A MAN" signs and these handmade ones, all proved newsworthy.[1]

This photograph, however, has not become an iconic image. It is symbolic of neither the 1968 strike nor the black freedom movement in general. The strike pictures that instead come to mind focus on the male workers bearing the "I AM A MAN" placards. So emblematic has the sign become of the crucial year 1968, and indeed a whole era of struggle, that one preserved sign recently sold at auction for $34,000.[2] The repeated reproduction of these images, especially over the last decade, frames a historical narrative in which the

I warmly thank Nancy Bercaw, Martin Summers, Denise Spellberg, Linda Ferreira-Buckley, Elizabeth Englehart, and especially Emilye Crosby, for their careful reading, thoughtful insights, and helpful suggestions.

Figure 3 A crowd of sanitation strike supporters gathering in front of Clayborn Temple, March 28, 1968. © Ernest C. Withers Collection, courtesy of Decaneas Archive.

struggle for dignity by otherwise subordinated black men stands in for the larger African American quest for freedom. Ironically, even as local scholarly studies now regularly make visible the extent of women's activism, the repetition of these representations suggests otherwise. What brought these women out to the streets that Thursday morning, on a workday? Even the question begs explanation.

As seen in this volume and in other recent studies, the shift over the last two decades from national to local civil rights studies, from stories about political leaders to those centered on the grass roots, has revealed the scope of women's activism. Viewing the movement through these new lenses is uncovering dimensions of struggle eviscerated in historical accounts based on national narratives, including those most frequently cited in popular and educational accounts of civil rights. These local grass-roots studies demonstrate the extent, the determination, and the creativity of women's participation in the civil rights movement. In addition, they expose the pernicious consequences of failing to grapple with the scope of women's activism. So why does black women's activism remain invisible to many and undigested to most? Why has the overall historical narrative of the movement proved so resistant to change?

Building on previous efforts to answer these questions, this chapter takes a step back to further assess underlying ways in which gendered understandings of racial inequality, oppression, and citizenship, and the means of achieving them, have structured the civil rights narrative. Analyzing how gender has influenced historical narrativity itself can become a prism that illuminates how freedom and rights were articulated and pursued in various contexts. By gender, I do not refer only to men and women's different roles as activists, about which we now know a good bit. In this essay, I am equally concerned with assumptions about manhood and womanhood built into struggles against racial injustice during the civil rights era—which for the purposes of this chapter I take to mean the period from World War II through at least the sixties—and into subsequent historical writing.

As indicated by the example of "I AM A MAN" and the sanitation strike, what may have been more flexible and expansive meanings of freedom and rights during the actual strike have nevertheless been discussed in much historical literature such that freedom equals manhood equals dignity and authority denied to black men in racist U.S. society. In addition to precluding an analysis of women's activism and aspirations, this approach takes the perquisites of white manhood as the measure of black freedom. By boxing rights into those typically associated with manhood in that era (individualism, particularly in labor and politics, authority as head of household), it thwarts consideration of concerns such as raising one's children in a racist society, or rescuing oneself from charges of promiscuity, both of which women made pivotal to the idea of freedom.

The chapter as a whole critically explores areas that have become focal points for studying women, gender, and race in civil rights history. Each section uses examples from the research of other historians, as well as my own research on the black freedom movement in Memphis, as points of departure for considering how civil rights historians have scrutinized the impact of gender in mainstream narratives and, in some cases, how we might push this analysis further. The first two sections, for instance, address how and why historians of women in the movement have confronted gendered assumptions about leadership and about local versus national campaigns. A third section examines issues of labor and household that have captured attention in recent historical literature, and borrows from historians of Reconstruction to speculate about further work.

The final sections—one on racial violence and another on health, hunger, and poverty—juxtapose two sides of what I refer to as the "politics of protection," which I argue is as cogent to the problem of gender and historical narrativity as are leadership and local dynamics. Historians have convincingly argued that when the sanitation strikers and myriad other male activists staked their claim to freedom in terms of manhood, they rejected the racist degradation and demonization of black men that obstructed their efforts to economically support and physically protect mothers, sisters, wives, and daughters from sexual assaults by white men. And yet this very insight can obscure other aspects of the politics of protection equation: struggles *among* African Americans about who bore the responsibility for safeguarding black women and communities; women's investments in their own roles as protectors, not just as dependent recipients of protection, against racial violence and other hardships; and the impact of conflicting beliefs about race, gender, and protection on the civil rights movement.

Scholars of women and gender have illuminated how traditional concepts of leadership and politics have rendered women's activism invisible. In countering these standpoints, we have made more visible their extensive mobilization, most often at the grass roots in local movements, but also in national settings. Given this greater visibility, we can now delve more deeply into women's motivations, aspirations, and ideas about freedom while asking why they frequently get subsumed in ideas about manhood.[3] Again, what impelled black Memphis women to support the sanitation strike, even if that meant skipping work and other obligations to march downtown? By posing "politics of protection" as a category of analysis, this chapter explores one pathway for further analyzing how gender has impacted the historical narrative of the civil rights movement.

## WOMEN, GENDER, AND LEADERSHIP
## IN CIVIL RIGHTS SCHOLARSHIP

Historians concerned with women and gender in the history and memory of the civil rights movement have extensively documented women's activism and critiqued silences in the mainstream literature. As far back as 1988, a group of civil rights scholars and activists convened in Atlanta to address the persistent obscuring of the scope and significance of women's participation in what had become the accepted narrative of the movement, based on charismatic leadership and national organizations. Georgia State University and the Martin Luther King Jr. Center for Nonviolent Change cosponsored "Women in the Civil Rights Movement. Trailblazers and Torchbearers: 1941–1965," a conference organized by Marymal Dryden and Judith Allen Ingram. Participants referenced historian William Chafe's 1980 statement, based on his research on Greensboro, North Carolina, that women formed "the backbone" of the freedom movement. They demonstrated that women had comprised a majority of local activists and contributed ideas rooted in their own experiences that became crucial to organizing.[4]

The 1988 Atlanta conference thus created a space for a set of scholars to collectively confront women's invisibility in mainstream civil rights literature and the misconceptions that resulted when they dropped out of the historical narrative. Charles Payne titled his paper, "Men Led, but Women Organized," and cited SNCC member Lawrence Guyot's assertion, "It's no secret that young people and women led organizationally." Other papers explored women's theological and organizational groundings in the black church; their understandings and pursuit of "empowerment, citizenship, and community building"; and the intersections of race, class, and gender that shaped women's activism. Speakers addressed the historical legacies of Ella Baker, Septima Clark, Fannie Lou Hamer, Gloria Richardson, and Modjeska Simkins. They discussed local movements ranging from Mississippi to Boston and institutions as diverse as the radically oriented Highlander Folk School and the Methodist Church. These papers appeared in an anthology by the same title as the conference edited by Vicki Crawford, Jacqueline Rouse, and Barbara Woods, still in print.[5] Together, this conference and volume set the stage for an extensive body of work that has expanded upon these early studies and taken them in important new directions.

Nevertheless, authors of such works continue to question why women activists commonly appear in the sidebars of social studies and history textbooks, while the overall narrative in textbooks and in many widely acclaimed studies remains the same. Christina Greene eloquently declares in her 2005 book on women in the Durham freedom movement that "analysis of women's activism suggests new ways of understanding protest, leadership, and racial politics. The inclusion of women, especially African American women, in this history demands an entire rethinking of a movement that changed forever a region and a nation." The problem may begin with a lack of inclusion, she argues, but it ends with distorted interpretations of the movement.[6]

Along similar lines, authors of recent studies of the welfare and tenant rights movements argue emphatically that absenting poor black women from chronicles of the civil rights movement reinforces truncated perceptions of rights and freedom and struggles to achieve them. From the perspective of these historians, one cannot imagine the civil rights movement concluding in the mid-sixties, rather than finding new life through the antipoverty movement, which was just then gaining steam. Nor can one identify "Black Power" solely with young, urban, single men and their claims to manhood when one analyzes the language of self-respect and community solidarity used by welfare rights and other antipoverty activists. When we acknowledge that women headed the national welfare rights movement and personally confronted a gamut of local, state, and federal officials, leadership also takes on different parameters.[7]

Historian Kathy Nasstrom in a 1999 publication interrogates the construction of historical memory of the civil rights movement, after wondering why black women's extensive roles in postwar voter registration campaigns in Atlanta seem to have been forgotten by all but the aging participants. She constructs a "genealogy" of historical memory in which she explores how and why the accepted narrative of these voter registration movements shifted at different junctures. Ultimately, grass-roots participation by women, not to mention youth, took a backseat to black candidates' success in garnering the votes to win public office. This gendered dynamic of historical memory, Nasstrom asserts, nearly erased the legacy of black Atlanta women—not to mention youth and some working-class men in these communities—who collectively defied the political disempowerment of black Atlanta residents.[8]

Scholars of women in social movements have increasingly rejected conceptions of leadership that focus exclusively on formal authority figures. Anthropologist Karen Sacks assigns the term "centerwomen" to women who were highly respected in their communities and took on informal authority roles in movement activism. Sociologist Belinda Robnett casts such women as "bridge leaders," in recognition of their crucial roles in negotiating the spaces between grass-roots communities on the one hand, and official, frequently national, leaders on the other. Together, Sacks, Robnett, and others show that the movements they study would have disintegrated without the intervention of "centerwomen" and "bridge leaders." This gendered concept of leadership has opened new avenues for evaluating women's activism.[9]

Life stories of women who younger movement activists did hail as leaders—if not heads of organizations—suggest that some earned respect precisely because they challenged traditional leadership hierarchies inherited from black churches, businesses, and older civil rights organizations. Biographies of Septima Clark and Ella Baker, for instance, highlight their articulation of a radical vision of democracy and citizenship. Both women perceived the domination of male charismatic leaders as injurious to the freedom movement, and instead promoted a kind of democracy in which the voices of even the most oppressed became important to the direction of the movement. Charles Payne argues in his study of Mississippi that what was distinctive about the two women was their support for—as Ms. Clark put it—"broadening the scope of democracy to include everyone and deepening the concept to include every relationship." Barbara Ransby expands on this view, asserting that "[Ella] Baker's message was that oppressed people, whatever their level of formal education, had the ability to understand and interpret the world around them, to see that world for what it was and to move to transform it." Both Clark and Baker closely associated the top-down leadership structure with male charismatic leadership, especially that of the ministers affiliated with King's Southern Christian Leadership Conference.[10]

Historians of local movements, however, have also had to confront more contradictory approaches to gender and leadership in the freedom movement that involve households as well as organizations. Christina Greene writing on Durham, North Carolina, and Emilye Crosby analyzing the movement in Claiborne County, Mississippi, found that women who took on formidable, sometimes dangerous work in the freedom movement frequently considered it a given that men would lead both their organizations and their households. Crosby asserts, "In Claiborne County, [Leesco] Guster and other women stepped up to do the work that needed doing—whether it was canvassing, challenging whites through public marching, or defending their homes with weapons—and simultaneously accepted prevailing gender hierarchies."[11] And yet, understandings of manhood and womanhood did not necessarily remain static in such circumstances. Women "defending their homes with guns" hardly fit bourgeois assumptions about gendered power relations, an issue to which I return later in this chapter.

To further complicate matters, many women identified with the language of manhood that had for generations been used by some church and community leaders to exhort their constituents to shed fears of white reprisals and adopt a bolder standpoint. In Memphis, Hazel McGhee, wife of a sanitation worker, mother, and worker at an industrial steam laundry plant, recalls pushing her husband to "be a man" by living up to *her* example as a tenacious participant in a lengthy strike with the laundry workers union that directly preceded the sanitation strike. "I would not have liked it," she asserts, "after I done been out seven months and two weeks, and he done went out and stayed two days. That would make me feel like that he wasn't like the slogan, a man." McGhee rejected neither her sense of herself as a woman nor her husband's position as head of household, but in her memory the boundaries between manhood and womanhood blurred.[12]

At one level, then, some of the most articulate and respected women, like Ella Baker and Septima Clark, openly espoused conceptions of leadership and participation that countered precisely the national political formations that many civil rights historians have reified. At another level, many women activists in local, grass-roots movements pushed the cultural boundaries of manhood and womanhood just shy of the breaking point, even as they continued their investments in existing gendered ideas of authority.

## RETHINKING THE OPPOSITION BETWEEN NATIONAL AND LOCAL

Turning away from national studies and toward analyses of local grass-roots black freedom struggles opens both opportunities and hazards for historians concerned with women and the gendering of the civil rights movement narrative. Although there is no doubt that analyses of the local and the "grass roots" have illuminated gendered racial and class dynamics of black freedom struggles—indeed, assessing the extent and significance of women's activism proved impossible until a critical mass of historians and social scientists departed from national studies and embarked on local ones—terms like "local" and "grass roots" can convey unintended gendered meanings. We run the risk of consigning women and, for that matter, working-class people, to the local, and counterposing them to the national. Similarly, identifying women with the grass roots hazards obscuring their significance to the larger movement.

In their introduction to *Groundwork: Local Black Freedom Movements in America*, Jeanne Theoharis and Komozi Woodard address such concerns when they warn against efforts to "reaffirm a binary opposition between the local and the national," and insist upon a more nuanced understanding of the relationship between the two. They argue that local activists, through exposure to movement ideas, frequently began to ascribe greater meaning to what they had previously perceived as merely personal or individual problems. Concomitantly, they assert, local struggles in many cases spurred national initiatives and inspired national leaders. "The local," Theoharis and Woodard argue, "is where the national and international are located."[13] No doubt this last point holds true for Memphis in 1968. Only the unity, determination, and deep-reaching ideas of justice among both sanitation workers and their communities convinced King to interrupt planning for the national Poor People's Campaign and come to Memphis—not just once, but three times in as many weeks. Addressing a crowd of over fifteen thousand, March 18, he announced that the Poor People's Campaign would start in Memphis, because this kind of freedom movement exemplified what the campaign was about.[14]

Theoharis and Woodard do not directly address gender here, but the binary opposition between local and national they contest usually assigns women to the local. In some cases, this move inadvertently neglects the far-reaching consequences of women's activism. Acknowledging women as the backbone of local campaigns as organizers, networkers, and supporters does not necessarily lead to assessing their impact on national politics and leaders. If the national is construed as the place from which initiative and leadership emanate, then the local can mistakenly be relegated to a dependent or satellite status—a source of energy and momentum, but not direction.

The outpouring of new scholarship on antipoverty activism challenges this gendered duality of local/national. It shifts attention from the Johnson administration's federal War on Poverty to community-based organizing without ignoring the national political scene. Several scholars reconfigure the opposition between local and national, for example, detailing cross-country trips made by community-based women activists to attend national conferences, testify at congressional hearings, and support other local battles. Out of this local activism and national networking emerged a set of formidable and talented leaders, most black, many young, all poor mothers who had a seat at the table in larger discussions of civil rights, poverty, politics, and policy.

These historians also illuminate how poor black activists involved in antipoverty struggles deliberately politicized issues of household, parenting, health care, nutrition, and intimacy, and forced them onto the agenda of the larger black freedom movement. Their successful efforts to push these issues onto national agendas emanated from their determination to protect and advance their children. Although this activism did not exclusively involve women, it rested on a gendered understanding of rights that bridged the gap between domestic and political by acknowledging political ideas of freedom forged in neighborhood, household, and even intimate spaces.

## RACE, WORK, AND THE HOUSEHOLD

The civil rights narrative shifts if we consider how ideals of freedom itself may have been gendered. Civil rights scholars might look to historians who have analyzed how gender infused political meanings of freedom during the American Revolution and Reconstruction. Writing about these contested ideas of freedom during Reconstruction, Nancy Bercaw contends that the destruction of the antebellum plantation household during the Civil War made the very concept of household, along with attendant issues of mastery, autonomy, dependency, and intimacy, central to the politics of Reconstruction. In contrasting ways, planters and freed people strived to reimagine and reconfigure the household, perceiving this process as key to their claims to freedom and citizenship.[15] Hannah Rosen moves this discussion in a different direction by analyzing racialized sexual violence wreaked upon black women. Women's testimony revealed that these assaults usually began with invasions of freed people's homes by disguised white male "night riders." Ku Klux Klansmen and others who resorted to violence as part of the "redemption" of the South staged belligerent disruptions of the domestic arrangements established by ex-slave men and women, culminating with the rape of women.[16] Bercaw and Rosen both build on Elsa Barkley Brown's insights into freed women's claims to citizenship, which she argues were grounded more in ideas about the rights of families and communities than on liberal ideas of individualism. Brown illustrates how women ensured that the ballot itself belonged not only to their husbands but themselves, despite the fact that the Fifteenth Amendment had extended suffrage only to black men.[17] By looking outside more familiar sites of political conflict and rethinking categories of political analysis, these historians and others provide deeper understandings of the contested meanings of freedom during Reconstruction.

Our scholarship on the civil rights movement might examine similar sites. Deeply rooted problems of race and gender imbedded in household forms persisted in the twentieth century and spurred responses ranging from migration to participation in the black freedom movement. In complicated ways, urban migrants who left plantation regions during and after

World War II, especially young adults, seized upon opportunities to disrupt tenant farmer household arrangements that emerged during Reconstruction. These included power dynamics that prevailed both *within* these households—particularly the imposition of adult male authority as both father and foreman—and *between* these households and white landowners or managers. That rural black women increasingly took jobs as domestic servants or in cafés during and after the Great Depression further complicated this scenario. Yet the fact that most women migrants to the city and a significant number of men continued to labor as domestic servants in private households or in cafeterias, hospitals, and laundries underscored their inabilities to fully uproot the gendered equation of dependency and authority they associated with the old plantation form.

Although rural and urban contexts differed from each other, rhetorically migrants and others compared their city workplaces, including factories, to plantations, and brought historical memory to bear on the present. As I have discussed elsewhere, they rejected a set of power relations and mental attitudes associated with both labor and domesticity. Hazel McGhee, the laundry worker and sanitation striker's wife quoted earlier—a migrant from Tallahatchie County, Mississippi, where she had been raised in a tenant farm family—illuminated these connections when she condemned supervisors in the urban sweatshop because they "wanted to . . . drive you, that you hadn't worked enough," and that they "talked to you . . . like you was their child. . . . You don't talk to adults like you're talking to a child," she declared. "And you ask them to do things, don't tell them you got to do nothing."[18] Her choice of the adult/child metaphor is significant in that it articulated a deeply rooted critique of a set of historical social relations that encompassed both production and the household in the plantation and the city.

Indeed, the sanitation workers, all of them African Americans, performed labor that identified them as both public employees and mobile domestic servants. Despite being organized in crews, they trudged as solitary individuals through the yards of families not their own bearing leaking tubs on their shoulders, in an act repeated hundreds of times a week. Although the view of black men stepping onto the terrain of white households might otherwise have sounded alarms, the familiar image of the black domestic servant shaded them into a part of the scenery. Frequently they wore outsized garments cast off and donated by homemakers, making it appear as if they were dependents incapable of choosing and purchasing clothes. In their own homes these men represented heads of household, and yet low wages and nonexistent benefits forced many to depend on earnings of wives and older children or on government assistance. Workers and strike supporters alike recognized that manhood struck a deep chord precisely because it staked black men's rights to authority and respect as heads of households to their demands for recognition in the workplace.

Working-class women strike supporters identified with these sentiments, albeit from different positions. They toiled outside their homes to support their families yet racist labor practices kept most in servant jobs. Or, if they secured manufacturing work—which women increasingly did in the 1960s, especially after passage of the 1964 Civil Rights Act—employers paid them wages low enough for them to qualify for food stamps. This situation also impacted women, who as sole supporters of their children, had become heads of household but had been forced by circumstances to leave jobs and depend fully on government income.

*Both* black men and women articulated gendered understandings of freedom and racial justice that counterpoised these ideals to their actual consignment by white racist practices and attitudes to economic dependency, vulnerability, and disrespect. Their critiques acknowledged historic links between labor and household that had obviously changed since Reconstruction yet continued to serve as reference points in the postwar politics of race, gender, and freedom.

## RACIAL VIOLENCE AND THE "POLITICS OF PROTECTION"

The sanitation strike turned on the dime of racial violence, however. A week and a half into the strike policemen attacked a march of strikers and supporters by opening fire with their new riot control weapon, mace, spraying it directly into the marchers' faces. The provocation came with a rapid-fire series of occurrences: a police car edging marchers to the curb, a prominent female supporter screaming when the car rolled over her foot, and angry men rocking the police car in protest of this injury to black women. The macing of the marchers (soon to be known as the macing of the ministers who, to their shock, became police targets) united black Memphians as never before, transforming the strike into a mass community movement that drew in King and captured national attention. Police assaults on sanitation workers, professionals, and ministers convinced the latter that regardless of their station, race marked them as objects of derision, dehumanization, and violence.[19]

Looking backward on the black freedom movement from the vantage point of 1968, racial violence stands out as the issue that fueled both the most heated reactions against white domination and the most fraught controversies within black communities over how to respond. One has only to consider the impact that news of the 1955 Mississippi lynching of Emmett Till had on young African Americans who later joined the civil rights movement to grasp the intense—and gendered—symbolic significance of this violence. The point here is not only to trace struggles over racial violence during the civil rights era but to show how they fueled and complicated the movement for racial justice.

Fully comprehending the fierce responses evoked by certain kinds of violence—for instance, against veterans and young women—involves grappling with a highly charged, gendered "politics of protection" that surrounded them. Although this politics of protection involved more than racial violence, it sharply emerged in that context. Within black communities racially inflected ideas of manhood and womanhood, which frequently intersected with class, ascribed powerful meanings to police brutality and influenced debates about how to respond. Although masculinity and femininity were hardly the sum of what was at stake, these gender issues riddled nearly every aspect of postwar racist police violence. Together they became a lightning rod for fighting over what was at stake, who mattered in U.S. society, who had the right to power over whom, who were the aggressors, and who were considered the potential victims. In essence, the question of who had responsibility for protecting and defending the vulnerable galvanized and complicated postwar conflict over racist police violence, both between black activists and white officials and among them.

Until recently the scholarship around gender and racial violence has largely addressed earlier time periods: the slavery era, when there was no legal category addressing the rape of slave women because they were deemed property; and the post-emancipation period, when lynching and "night riding" skyrocketed amidst contests over equal citizenship rights, segregation, and economic autonomy. Several historians writing about post-emancipation lynching, mob violence, sexual assault, and other forms of vigilantism see gender as crucial to their historical analysis. Most take off from black journalist and antilynching crusader Ida B. Wells's incisive observation in the

1890s that lynching was really about white men destroying black men's economic and political advances, not protecting defenseless white women from bestial black rapists.[20]

Nearly a century later, in 1983, historian Jacquelyn Hall extended Wells's analysis of the vicious cycle that tied together lynching and rape. Lynching, she agreed, constituted an act of terror against the authority and bodies of black men under the guise of protecting white women from rape. Hall added that interracial rape in fact usually comprised acts of white male brutality against black women that violated their bodies and flouted their marital and maternal status. Hall's work challenged analyses of rape that dealt with gender by reducing rape to a struggle among men, as articulated in structuralist anthropologist Claude Lévi-Strauss's oft-noted theory of kinship and communication in which women symbolize the "verbs" in men's transactions over power and property. Hall recognized the partial truth in Lévi-Strauss's analysis; the rape of black women threatened black men's power and property. However, she underscored the racial misogyny of sexual violence and its impact on black women. She also analyzed the antilynching activism of some white southern women, asserting that it represented a rejection of sexist stereotypes of them as passive victims.[21]

Several recent studies develop Hall's argument by further exploring the extent and historical significance of sexual violence and lynching. Hannah Rosen argues that sexual assaults associated with mob violence and "night riding," and protests against them, reveal what was at stake in the postemancipation struggle. She analyzes women's official reports of rape, arguing that they illuminate the meanings of freedom for newly emancipated ex-slaves. Women insisted that citizenship made rapes of black women illegal. Moreover, their narratives framed the sexual violence of "night riders" as contraventions of marital, maternal, and political rights they linked to citizenship. Crystal Feimster extensively documents the previously forgotten murders and rapes of women at the height of racial terrorism (1880–1930), and analyzes black and white women's political activism in this same period. Numerous scholars have studied women's club and suffrage campaigns, but Feimster uses the lens of lynching to confront parallels and sharp racial tensions that surfaced as black and white women both sought to use the vote to address lynching and rape, but from opposing racial standpoints.[22]

Studies of racial violence in the mid-twentieth century must address its continuities and discontinuities in the changing historical context. In rural areas, historian Hasan Jeffries argues, police violence rose in importance during the postwar era as lynching became less frequent, a result of both federal intervention against mob violence and advances such as road paving and use of automobiles that afforded more mobility to police officers.[23] Police brutality was no newcomer to southern cities, but it became more prevalent in the postwar era as migration brought millions of rural black and white southerners into high-density northern and southern cities from World War II through the 1960s.[24] Migrants from farms and small towns in agricultural regions transformed by mechanization moved into crowded, segregated neighborhoods patrolled by white policemen (at least in the South for most of this period). Within these neighborhoods black youth walked to school and congregated. Both youth and adults rode segregated city buses, bringing them into close, tense contact with whites. Active-duty and demobilized servicemen became far more visible in the downtown—and heavily policed—sectors of cities near military bases.

Policemen may have winked at or supported lynching—and sheeted individual officers may have participated—but they increasingly *were* the face of racial violence during the civil rights era, whether their assaults were conducted as part or outside of official police business. Protest against police brutality thus pitted black families and communities against city and county police departments and governing public officials, politicizing racial violence even more than had been the case in the intervening years since Reconstruction. Deeper into the civil rights era, large contingents of Ku Klux Klan members and white mobs revitalized earlier modes of extralegal racial violence through murders of activists and threats of mob retaliation. Even then, however, civil rights groups strived to secure police protection, pressuring the federal government when local and state assistance was denied or, even worse, turned against the movement.

And yet, there is no necessary reason that the narratives about racial violence would continue to be gendered ones. Even so, gender did persist as a central component of postwar police violence that affected who police targeted and how communities reacted. Police officers stirred up by public outcry against supposed outbreaks of crime beat, shot, and killed young black men identified as perpetrators, and harassed neighborhood youth as both potential criminals and violators of their authority. With some notable exceptions, the victims of these attacks failed to win universal community support because they were deemed outside the bounds of respectability. However, the cases that provoked the most outrage usually revolved around assaults of servicemen and veterans, labor and civil rights activists, and sexual abuse of young women. Reactions to these incidents of racial violence were fraught with imagery about violations of manhood and womanhood.

African American men's ability to protect and defend African American women figured as a primary axis of black community politics in the post–World War II period. Two scholars of women and gender in urban racial politics identify historical changes in ideologies framing such politics. In her study of African American women in Detroit, Victoria Wolcott marks a shift during the Great Depression from female "bourgeois respectability" as the driving force behind racial advancement to a masculinist discourse of black self-defense and self-determination, to which the protection of women, children, and families was key. As the latter ideology became predominant, it partially eclipsed women's activism by depicting them as the objects, not subjects, of self-defense. Marilynn Johnson demonstrates that gendered rumors served as triggers for wartime race riots. She too identifies an ideological shift from the earlier period among black Detroiters. Instead of focusing on sexual violations of black women and men's abilities to protect them, the rumors that sparked the 1943 race riots involved either police brutality against servicemen, or rumored incidents of white violence aimed at women and children. The family, she argues, became the primary object of black protection.[25]

As Wolcott and Johnson demonstrate, grasping the continuities and discontinuities in postwar black urban movements is crucial. Urban migration to southern cities did not simply wipe out plantation-based narratives of racial violence in part because neither black nor white migrants had purged themselves of recent memories and narratives of violence. Additionally, the gendered narrative of black male defense of black women from sexual abuse may not have receded as quickly as Johnson's analysis of the wartime riots suggests. Tragically, in the postwar era actual sexual assaults of black women, not rumored ones, were what spurred outpourings of rage and militant assertions of black male defense. And yet the complicated politicization of racial violence did mark important discontinuities.

That tension between continuities and discontinuities sets the stage for analyzing the gendered narratives of black protest as a "politics of protection." This term builds on Wolcott and Johnson's work by marking a further dynamic in the postwar era within this pursuit of racial justice.

"Politics of protection" refers to a complex set of struggles, both between blacks and whites, and within black communities. Competing claims to manhood were central to this dynamic, but so were bold assertions of responsibility by women. Gendered conflicts among various organizations, leaders, and individuals, including women, about black self-defense and protection of families and communities significantly impacted the course of the civil rights movement.

Local communities, sometimes aided by the NAACP, protested a slew of police assaults and shooting deaths of servicemen and veterans in the immediate aftermath of World War II. They denounced white officers' demands for servility from black men who had served the nation at war and their assaults when the men failed to comply. In Columbia, Tennessee, in February 1946, an altercation between a white veteran and a black veteran culminated in the armed defense of the black community against a police rampage. Rage over the racial emasculation of these servicemen nourished a politics of black manhood based on the power to not only serve the nation but defend and protect their own communities.[26]

Collective responses to police sexual assaults of black women concentrated on women's vulnerability to rape by white men in positions of authority and black men's responsibility to protect and defend them. In Memphis in 1945 and Montgomery in 1949, white patrolmen forced women into squad cars by claiming they were streetwalkers or drunk, then sexually molested them. The outrage that followed translated into political mobilization against police officials and city administrators. As stories of police sexual assaults and the brutalizing of veterans entered into political parlance, they energized black voter registration, community meetings, and election day turnout. In Memphis, these responses impacted the outcome of key elections in 1948, while in Montgomery uproar over the 1949 assault spurred the community organizing that culminated in the Montgomery Bus Boycott. Important developments in the civil rights narrative, in other words, cannot be fully understood without analyzing the gender dynamics of these protests against police brutality and their implications for the freedom movement.[27]

Historian Timothy Tyson, writing about Black Panther forbearer and World War II veteran Robert Williams in North Carolina, for example, stresses that Williams's notorious enjoinder to "fight violence with violence," as opposed to King's advocacy of a philosophy of nonviolence, followed several assaults of black women by white men. Williams declared that they represented "a challenge to our manhood, especially to veterans, who had been trained to fight. . . . We as men should stand up as men and protect our women and children." He also declared, "I am a man and I will walk upright as a man should. I WILL NOT CRAWL." This encounter with racist sexual violence came on the heels of Williams's and other Monroe NAACP members' confrontation with threats of race war from the Ku Klux Klan. The militant stance Williams and his comrades adopted in the face of sexual assault and the threat of mob violence impacted the course of both the Monroe movement and the black freedom movement more generally. Williams's defiant public support of armed resistance led to the Monroe group's expulsion from the NAACP, and he became a role model of sorts for the founders of the Black Panther Party several years later. [28]

This gendered "politics of protection" in some cases also helped incite the 1960 sit-in movement for Freedom Now. Typically, civil rights histories view the movement as the outcome of young people's growing impatience with the slow legal process pursued by the NAACP to force the implementation of *Brown v. Board of Education* (1954), combined with extended rage at the lynching of fourteen-year-old Emmett Till (1955). Certain evidence suggests that in some locales fury over racial and sexual violence at the end of the 1950s persisted beyond the Till slaying and helped tip the balance toward direct action (e.g., sit-ins). Danielle McGuire demonstrates that in Tallahassee, the spring 1959 Mississippi lynching of Mack Charles Parker after he was accused of raping a white woman, followed immediately by the gang rape of a Florida A&M student by four white men, ignited mass protest among college students in Tallahassee. To a crowd of 1,500 A&M students, female and male, the student government president declared they "would not sit idly by and see our sisters, wives, and mothers desecrated." Some speakers criticized the young woman's date for not confronting the armed attackers, while a speaker at another rally exhorted college men to protect their women: "You must remember it wasn't just one Negro girl that was raped—it was all of Negro womanhood in the South."[29] These fiery gendered declarations helped catapult the Tallahassee students into the sit-in movement that swept across the South less than a year later.[30] This 1959 context differed significantly from the 1945 situation in Memphis, yet in both cases standing up to racist and sexual violence and legal injustice became central to an ascendant militancy by a new generation that rejected passivity, fear, and dependency.

The politics of protection that infused postwar responses to racial violence

sometimes erupted into public denunciations of black leaders, who were accused of being spineless in the face of such attacks. In 1945, such statements
in the local black newspaper pressured some black elites to speak out against
the police rapes of two young women, and to push city officials—part of the
Boss Crump political machine—to prosecute the policemen. Similarly, a 1952
editorial in the Durham *Carolina Times*, also a black paper, railed against established leaders for their "lethargy" and silence following the rape of Mrs.
Ersalene Williams by Thomas Clark, after he had engaged her supposedly
to clean his house. As in Memphis, this public criticism made their lack of
"manhood" symbolic of a broader political anemia. Christina Greene shows
that the *Carolina Times* underscored this point through a gender reversal that
contrasted male leaders' quiescence to the support offered to Mrs. Williams
by the female Sojourners for Truth and Justice.[31]

As Greene shows in further comments on activism by the Sojourners for
Truth, this internal politics of protection involved more than exhorting black
men to defend their communities against white men's racial and sexual domination. Historical analysis that begins and ends there eclipses women's protest against racial and sexual violence and their participation in this politics of protection. Mothers of the young Memphis women, both heads of
household, contacted civil rights leaders, pressed charges, and submitted testimony. Their daughters withstood a court trial, the first in Memphis to try
white men on charges of sexually assaulting black women. White attorneys
attempted to taint their characters by portraying them as promiscuous and
dishonest. McGuire shows that substantial numbers of female students participated in the Tallahassee rallies despite the rhetoric of masculinity. To reduce this complex politics of protection to declarations of manhood misses
the complexity of political dynamics *within* black communities, and the
gendered activist identities that adhered in protest against racial and sexual
violence.

In addition to recouping women's historical agency, we need to puzzle
through what it meant for women to embrace and rally behind a politics of
protection that was articulated in terms of manhood. Both women and men
pushed back against the dehumanization at the core of racial violence including rape, but they used gendered terms to stake out their right to protect
themselves and their families and communities. The language of manhood
heard at the Tallahassee rallies had become a familiar, universal mode of political expression, yet it was also quite literally about men protecting women.

Not surprisingly, women strongly supported men's determination to stand up for them, but that support could shade into emasculating criticisms when they felt men weren't living up to the ideal of manhood. Following the Tallahassee trial, a female reader of the New York *Amsterdam News* accused black men of being "mice" because they failed to protect their women. In North Carolina, Robert Williams faced condemnation by angry black women who blamed him for the lack of justice accorded by the courts in two 1959 assault cases, after Williams resisted their demands for armed responses to the attackers.[32]

Beyond their support for and/or criticism of men as protectors, there is further significance in black women's participation in protests such as the Tallahassee student rallies. Besides identifying with manhood as a universal, women's claim to their own agency articulated a kind of split or dual female subjectivity, in which they represented both dependents and activists, both object and subject of protection. Moreover, confronting racial violence, dehumanization, and injustice cultivated collective identities that encompassed more than those of individuals, of daughters, wives, or mothers. In the context of the postwar black freedom movement, in other words, protection was not just a feature of manhood (in either its universal or gender-specific meanings), but was central to a politicized understanding of womanhood that broke down divisions between individuals, households, and communities. Yet the prevailing emphasis on men's claims to manhood in historical accounts of the civil rights movement instead of the full complexity of this politics of protection partially obscures the dynamics and goals of the movement.

## EXPANDING THE MEANING OF RIGHTS:
## HEALTH, HUNGER, AND POVERTY

This politics of protection also shaped conflicts over health and poverty that were integral to the black freedom movement. This section builds on work by historians of welfare rights and other antipoverty campaigns by examining how a dynamic of protection, to which gender, race, and class were central, influenced these struggles around health and poverty.[33] It is not insignificant that the Memphis sanitation strike erupted in the midst of the antipoverty movement of the mid-1960s to mid-1970s. Indeed, strike supporters including welfare rights activists emphasized that the sanitation workers and many other black city service employees earned such low wages that they qualified for food stamps. These concerns underscored that problems of labor were also problems of the household. As we have seen, this was true decades before poverty and labor entered the spotlight in new ways in the 1960s.

The sanitation strike highlighted indignities faced by male service workers whose wages were insufficient to support their families. However, it also reflected efforts by black women in low-income communities to address health and hunger crises, in another manifestation of the politics of protection. Poor women in Memphis, Mississippi, and elsewhere helped redefine the black freedom movement in spring 1968 when they publicly articulated these concerns during U.S. Senate hearings conducted at the same time when they and thousands of others were encamped in the nation's capitol for the Poor People's Campaign. In their roles as witnesses, they presented gripping testimonials that helped shift hunger, malnutrition, and poverty to center stage.

Although much popular discourse at the time portrayed women receiving public assistance as lazy, licentious dependents on tax monies, welfare rights activists focused on their need to support and protect their children. Only when health crises prevented them from working, they insisted, had they sought government support. These requests for public assistance placed them in dependent positions but did so because of their determination to care for their children. While the sanitation workers' positions as heads of household rested on childcare by wives and older children, these women became heads of household following the deaths or departures of their husbands. Several heroines of Annelise Orleck's *Storming Caesars Palace* applied for welfare only after illness or injury made it impossible for them to hold down jobs. Ruby Duncan, a leader of the Las Vegas welfare rights movement and Operation Life, a community development corporation that eventually hosted a full-fledged medical clinic, sought public assistance after an accident at work injured her spine in 1967. Until then, she had eked out a living for herself and seven children by laboring as a hotel cook. Mary Wesley, Orleck writes, supported eight children by working two waitress jobs until her health failed. Losing these jobs in 1965 forced her to place her children temporarily in a home for destitute children and apply for public assistance. Ongoing medical problems and inadequate health insurance meant she had to rely on welfare and Medicaid periodically for years. And Rosie Seals suffered a stroke while trying to support her children by working two jobs, one as a domestic worker, the other in a laundry.[34]

Yet the materiality of indigence and poor health did not alone transform these women into activists. Indignation at humiliating treatment by social workers, combined with the larger social climate engendered by the black freedom movement, motivated them to collectively pursue policy changes they believed would win them both adequate income and respect. In Las Vegas, Memphis, and other cities, young women in the welfare rights movement participated in multiple aspects of civil rights, antipoverty, and Black Power movements. They seized on the language and symbols of the movement to reject prevailing racist images of black womanhood that dominated discourse around welfare, and claimed different ones based on dignity and respect. In doing so they, like the Las Vegas women, expanded "civil rights" to include their right as mothers to provide for and protect their children.[35]

Civil rights investigations in the 1960s, meanwhile, documented egregious racial discrimination in the medical system that exacerbated poor women's efforts to ensure the health of their children as well as their own health. During U.S. Civil Rights Commission hearings held in Memphis in 1962, commissioners made racism in the health care system one of their priorities. Statements by public health officials, hospital administrators, and black medical professionals convinced them that racist practices had impacted the provision of health care for African Americans. Their hearings revealed that major private hospitals, most of them church-run, all excluded black patients and doctors, and that the one public hospital that admitted blacks as patients excluded black doctors from its active medical staff. Commissioners found this situation so troubling that a 1963 report on nationwide racial discrimination in hospitals relied on evidence from Memphis.[36] A half decade after the Civil Rights Commission issued this report, a nonprofit black community organization in south Memphis reported that formidable barriers—inconvenient locations, lengthy bus rides, lack of nighttime hours, and packed waiting rooms—made it difficult for poor African Americans to secure medical care for themselves and their children at public health clinics.[37]

The 1962 Civil Rights Commission hearings also revealed that city health officials made decisions about health care based on racist beliefs about poor black women, which limited their efforts to tackle the high black infant mortality rate. A city/county health department official attributed this differential not to factors such as sparse prenatal care, poor nutrition, and unsanitary conditions, but to a high rate of "illegitimacy" among black mothers.[38] The health department report concluded that quelling immoral behavior was the antidote to black infant mortality. Such reports may not have been as dramatic as acts of racial violence, yet they ultimately had equally severe consequences.

Poor women's welfare rights activism directly countered this ideology with one of their own. It made problems of black womanhood as significant as those of black manhood when it came to protecting black families and showed that women held positions of responsibility that equaled those of men. Few women would have disrespected black men's claims to manhood, but in this complicated politics of protection they combated stereotypes of immoral and lazy black women, established new health programs, and demonstrated that poor women's rights were as important to the movement for racial justice as those of men. By claiming identities as caring and protective mothers who were the experts in determining their children's needs, poor women activists fused these qualities to their identities as activists. Conversely, they posited the state's denial of economic and medical assistance as racial injustice that thwarted their efforts to protect and provide for their children. Based on this alternative narrative, welfare rights activists shifted the discussion from laziness, immorality, and dependency to prenatal care, pediatric medical screening, adequate nutrition, and income. In the same period the Black Panther Party expanded self-defense from police brutality to the self-determination of poor black communities and created free medical clinics and breakfast programs—run largely by women—independent of government assistance.

## GENDER AND THE BLACK FREEDOM MOVEMENT, FROM FORTY YEARS LATER

If we flash back to the scene captured by camera in late March 1968 in light of this "politics of protection," it becomes more complicated to answer the question posed at the beginning of this chapter about what brought all these men and women to Clayborn Temple that weekday morning to rally around the sanitation workers' declaration, "I AM A MAN!" The presence of both civil rights leaders, including King, and union officials from AFSCME (American Federation of State, County, and Municipal Employees) and elsewhere underscores that the strike united the labor and civil rights movements. Yet the strike also reflected struggles over poverty, welfare, health, and hunger—all issues that were starkly highlighted later that spring when a "mule train" surrounded by freedom movement activists departed from the Lorraine Motel, where King had been shot on April 4, to mark the beginning of the Poor People's March.[39] (For more on the Mule Train, see Amy Nathan Wright, "The 1968 Poor People's Campaign, Marks, Mississippi, and the Mule Train: Fighting Poverty Locally, Representing Poverty Nationally," chapter 4, this volume.) Similarly, support for the strike invoked decades of protest against police brutality in its numerous forms. Rather than focusing on pictures that show only the pending arrival of King, or the strikers with their "I AM A MAN!" signs, we need to expand narratives of this pivotal moment in the civil rights movement to explore the multiple strands of activism that co-alesced in this same movement, to which the gendered politics of protection was central.

A majority of histories of the movement concentrate on attempts to break down de jure and de facto racial segregation in all facilities open to the public, whether they were under the aegis of local and state government, such as schools and libraries, or privately owned and operated, such as res-taurants and movie theaters. Or, they trace voting rights campaigns, includ-ing efforts to register, educate, and rally potential voters despite legal and extralegal barriers. Despite significant local distinctions, African Ameri-cans across the South assailed their exclusion from the mainstream political process and fought for political expression and clout. These two avenues of struggle shaped and energized postwar civil rights movements, and they at-tracted massive attention and support from outside of the South.

Together, however, they comprise a gendered narrative of civil rights that revolves around public facilities and public policies. As a number of scholars point out, particularly those writing about antipoverty struggles, this narra-tive obscures equally hard-fought struggles centered on home, work, fam-ily, and community—areas of daily life commonly perceived as outside the realm of political conflict. These struggles became absolutely germane to the freedom movement. They represented key concerns in and of themselves and also redefined the larger civil rights movement by shaping activists' beliefs about meanings of rights and justice. Deepening understanding of the free-dom movement demands a regendering of the narrative, not just by mapping out women's contributions, but by rethinking what constitutes the political and which domains of struggle matter in the claiming of freedom.

Just as importantly, we need to assess, not reproduce the ways in which manhood and womanhood became pivotal to understandings of freedom.

Manhood became the medium through which many activists conceived of freedom. However, as seen in the cases of Durham, Memphis, and Monroe, North Carolina, that language also animated contention among different voices within black communities, as certain parties with conflicting ideas about manhood vied with each other over the direction of local movements. That power struggle pressured some African American leaders to take positions from which they might otherwise have shirked, resulting in changes of course that influenced the larger direction of local and national movements.

These power struggles based on conflicting claims to manhood, however, can still keep the civil rights narrative trained on black male leadership. Women, too, appropriated a masculinist language of self-defense to goad male activists into adopting more militant positions. As we have seen, during the Tallahassee demonstrations a woman observer demanded that men be more than "mice"; female activists in Monroe pressured Williams to punish the white rapists of black women by taking up arms; and some working-class women supporters of the sanitation strike like Hazel McGhee insisted that the workers live up to the claims to manhood exhibited on their signs—"I AM A MAN!" Such exhortations may or may not have influenced the men at which they were aimed, but they certainly allowed women to carve out unique spaces for themselves in which they kept pressure on male activists in the limelight of these movements. In addition, their critical mobilization in supporting roles also energized their pursuit of other struggles, from welfare rights to labor battles.

Finally, we need to take stock of activism by poor black women who served as heads of households in lieu of male breadwinners. In this case, women did not deploy a language of manhood, but made the provision for and protection of their children the basis for their identities. In doing so, they articulated an idea of womanhood that was shorn of the racist images of black women as pariahs that adhered to them in white public discourse. Such parlance, unlike bourgeois ideals of womanhood, rejected dependency while claiming authority as protectors of their households. By firing up women's convictions in their own value, these assertions spurred women to pursue struggles that might otherwise have appeared too daunting.

All movement activists could unite behind the idea of protecting black communities from racist violence. However, there was not necessarily unanimity about what that entailed (prayer and patience? armed self-defense?). Black masculinity, defined in terms of self-defense and protection, offered a language through which to mobilize activists but it also provided a means by which both male and female activists challenged authority figures and their agendas within black communities. Concomitantly, both men and women fought against demeaning racist labels of dependency that depicted men as boys and women as lazy during and even after the Jim Crow era, and that produced material consequences exemplified by the sanitation workers' plights. For women, doing so involved a significant contradiction; particularly in the context of 1960s antipoverty struggles they insisted upon the respect and security accorded to white women yet rejected racist images of dependency assigned specifically to black women. Moreover, they demanded the right to protect their own dependent children and households. During the postwar civil rights era, these questions of who would or could protect African American women, men, children, and families from white racist violence and other forms of injustice alternately defined, motivated, and complicated the movement for freedom.

## NOTES

1. Ernest C. Withers, Sanitation strike supporters gathering outside Clayborn Temple, March 28, 1968, Panopticon Gallery. Some signs read, "Dignity and Respect for the Sanitation Workers," and "Keep Your Money in Your Pocket"—a reference to a downtown boycott.

2. Michael Lollar, "'I Am A Man' poster from Memphis strike draws $34K bid at auction," *Commercial Appeal*, posted February 25, 2010, http//www.commercialappeal .com/news/2010/feb/25/i-am-man-poster-memphis-strike draws-five-figures-/, accessed June 13, 2010.

3. Biographies of leading women activists explore their motivations particularly well. See, for example, Chana Kai Lee, *For Freedom's Sake: The Life of Fannie Lou Hamer* (Bloomington: University of Illinois Press, 2000); Barbara Ransby, *Ella Baker and the Black Freedom Movement: A Radical Democratic Vision* (Chapel Hill: University of North Carolina Press, 2002).

4. William Chafe, *Civilities and Civil Rights: Greensboro, North Carolina, and the Black Struggle for Freedom* (New York: Oxford University Press, 1980), 125.

5. Vicki L. Crawford, Jacqueline Anne Rouse, and Barbara Woods, eds., *Women in the Civil Rights Movement: Trailblazers and Torchbearers, 1941–1965* (1990; Bloomington: Indiana University Press, 1993), Payne quote on p. 1. See also Bettye Collier-Thomas and V. P. Franklin, eds., *Sisters in the Struggle: African American Women in the Civil Rights– Black Power Movement* (New York: New York University Press, 2001).

6. Christina Greene, *Our Separate Ways: Women and the Black Freedom Movement in Durham, North Carolina* (Chapel Hill: University of North Carolina Press, 2005).

7. See Premilla Nadasen, *Welfare Warriors: The Welfare Rights Movement in the United States* (New York: Routledge, 2004); Annelise Orleck, *Storming Caesars Palace: How Black Women Fought Their Own War on Poverty* (Boston: Beacon, 2005); Rhonda Y. Williams, *The Politics of Public Housing: Black Women's Struggles Against Urban Inequality* (New York: Oxford University Press, 2005); and Greene, *Our Separate Ways*.

8. Kathryn L. Nasstrom, "Down to Now: Memory, Narrative, and Women's Leadership in the Civil Rights Movement in Atlanta, Georgia," *Gender & History* 11, no. 1 (April 1999): 113–44.

9. Karen Brodkin Sacks, "Gender and Grassroots Leadership," in *Women and the Politics of Empowerment*, ed. Ann Bookman and Sandra Morgan (Philadelphia: Temple University Press, 1986), 77–94; Belinda Robnett, *How Long? How Long? African-American Women in the Struggle for Civil Rights* (New York: Oxford University Press, 1997).

10. Charles M. Payne, *I've Got the Light of Freedom: The Organizing Tradition and the Mississippi Freedom Struggle* (Berkeley: University of California Press, 1995), 68; and Ransby, *Ella Baker*, 7.

11. Emilye Crosby, *A Little Taste of Freedom: The Black Freedom Struggle in Claiborne County, Mississippi* (Chapel Hill: University of North Carolina Press, 2005), 137–38. Greene notes, "Even when they were in the majority, women sometimes relinquished public roles to males" (Greene, *Our Separate Ways*, 97).

12. Hazel McGhee, interview by author, Memphis, August 11, 1995, transcript in "Behind the Veil: Documenting African American Life in the Jim Crow South," Special Collections, Duke University, Durham, cited in Laurie B. Green, *Battling the Plantation Mentality: Memphis and the Black Freedom Struggle* (Chapel Hill: University of North Carolina Press, 2007), 261 (hereafter cited as *Battling*).

13. Jeanne Theoharis and Komozi Woodard, Introduction, *Groundwork: Local Black Freedom Movements in America* (New York: New York University Press, 2005), 7.

14. Green, *Battling*, 251–52.

15. Nancy Bercaw, *Gendered Freedoms: Race, Rights, and the Politics of Household in the Delta, 1861–1875* (Gainesville: University Press of Florida, 2003).

16. Hannah Rosen, *Terror in the Heart of Freedom: Citizenship, Sexual Violence, and the Meaning of Race in the Postemancipation South* (Chapel Hill: University of North Carolina Press, 2008), esp. 202–20.

17. Elsa Barkley Brown, "To Catch the Vision of Freedom: Reconstructing Southern Black Women's Political History, 1865–1880," in *African American Women and the Vote, 1837–1965*, ed. Ann D. Gordon, with Bettye Collier-Thomas, John H. Bracey, Arlene V. Avakian, and Joyce A. Berkman, (Amherst: University of Massachusetts Press, 1997), 66–99.

18. McGhee interview, quoted in Green, *Battling*, 260–61.

19. Details of this incident are in Joan Turner Beifuss, *At the River I Stand: Memphis, the 1968 Strike, and Martin Luther King* (Brooklyn: Carlson Publishing Inc., 1985), 109–21; and Michael K. Honey, *Going Down Jericho Road: The Memphis Strike, Martin Luther King's Last Campaign* (New York: W.W. Norton & Co., 2007), 200–10.

20. Ida B. Wells-Barnett, *On Lynchings*, Introduction by Patricia Hill Collins (Amherst, N.Y.: Humanity Books, 2002).

21. Jacquelyn Dowd Hall, "'The Mind That Burns in Each Body': Women, Rape, and Racial Violence," in *Powers of Desire: The Politics of Sexuality*, ed. Ann Snitow, Christine Stansell, and Sharon Thompson (New York: Monthly Review Press, 1983), 328–49; Hall, *Revolt Against Chivalry: Jessie Daniel Ames and the Women's Campaign against Lynching* (New York: Columbia University Press, 1993, rev. ed.); Claude Lévi-Strauss, *The Elementary Structures of Kinship* (Boston: Beacon Press, 1969), 52–68.

22. Rosen, *Terror in the Heart*; Crystal Nicole Feimster, *Southern Horrors: Women and the Politics of Rape and Lynching* (Cambridge, Mass.: Harvard University Press, 2009).

23. Hasan Kwame Jeffries, *Bloody Lowndes: Civil Rights and Black Power in Alabama's Black Belt* (New York: New York University Press, 2009), 34–35.

24. The following analysis draws on the work of several historians but where not noted otherwise it is based on my research for *Battling the Plantation Mentality*.

25. Victoria W. Wolcott, "Gendered Perspectives on Detroit History," *American Historical Review* 27, no. 1 (Spring 2001): 75–91; and Victoria W. Wolcott, *Remaking Respectability: African American Women in Interwar Detroit* (Chapel Hill: University of North Carolina Press, 2001); and Marilynn S. Johnson, "Gender, Race, and Rumours: Re-examining the 1943 Race Riots," *Gender & History* 10, no. 2 (August 1998): 252–77.

26. Gail Williams O'Brien, *The Color of the Law: Race, Violence, and Justice in the Post–World War II South* (Chapel Hill: University of North Carolina Press, 1999). On police brutality over a longer period, see Leonard Moore, *Black Rage: Police Brutality and African American Activism from World War II to Hurricane Katrina* (Baton Rouge: Louisiana University Press, 2010).

27. Green, *Battling*, 81–111, 136–40; J. Mills Thornton, *Dividing Lines: Municipal Politics and the Struggle for Civil Rights in Montgomery, Birmingham, and Selma* (Tuscaloosa: University of Alabama Press, 2002), 34–35; Stewart Burns, ed., *Daybreak of Freedom: The Montgomery Bus Boycott* (Chapel Hill: University of North Carolina Press, 1997), 8; and Danielle L. McGuire, "'It Was Like All of Us Had Been Raped': Sexual Violence, Community Mobilization, and the African American Freedom Struggle," *Journal of American History* 91, no. 3 (December 2004): 910–13 (hereafter cited as "'All of Us Had Been Raped'").

28. Timothy B. Tyson, *Radio Free Dixie: Robert F. Williams & the Roots of Black Power*

(Chapel Hill: University of North Carolina Press, 1999), quotes from 141, 158, discussion of Klan 86–89.

29. McGuire, "'All of Us Had Been Raped,'" quotes from 916, 917, aftermath of trial, 930. Tyson, *Radio Free Dixie*, 143–49.

30. McGuire, "'All of Us Had Been Raped,'" 930; Tyson, *Radio Free Dixie*, 144.

31. Green, *Battling*, quote on 96; Greene, *Our Separate Ways*, 7–8.

32. McGuire, "'All of Us Had Been Raped,'" 928; Tyson, *Radio Free Dixie*, 146–49.

33. Orleck, *Storming Caesars Palace*; John Dittmer, *The Good Doctors: The Medical Committee for Human Rights and the Struggle for Social Justice in Health Care* (New York: Bloomsbury Press, 2009), 229–50; Jennifer Nelson, "'Hold Your Head Up and Stick Out Your Chin': Community Health and Women's Health in Mound Bayou, Mississippi," *National Women's Studies Association Journal* 17, no. 1 (Spring 2005); Bonnie Lefkowitz, *Community Health Centers: A Movement and the People Who Made It Happen* (New Brunswick, NJ: Rutgers University Press, 2007), 29–49; and Greta de Jong, "Staying in Place; Black Migration, the Civil Rights Movement, and the War on Poverty in the Rural South," *Journal of African American History* 90, no. 4 (2005), esp. 400–2. Alice Sardell, *The U.S. Experiment in Social Medicine: The Community Health Center Program, 1965–1986* (Pittsburgh: University of Pittsburgh Press, 1988).

34. Orleck, *Storming Caesars Palace*, 73–74, 79–82, 94.

35. Willie Pearl Butler, interview by author, Memphis, August 19, 1995, transcript in "Behind the Veil: Documenting African American Life in the Jim Crow South," Special Collections, Duke University; and Juanita Miller Thornton, interview by author, Memphis, June 6, 2001, tape in possession of author.

36. *Hearings before the United States Commission on Civil Rights: Hearings Held in Memphis, Tennessee, June 25–26, 1962* (U.S. Commission on Civil Rights, 1962); U.S. Commission on Civil Rights, ed., *Equal Opportunity in Hospitals and Health Facilities: Civil Rights Policies under the Hill–Burton Program* (Washington, D.C.: U.S. Commission on Civil Rights, 1965).

37. Autry Parker, "Memphis Area Project—South Annual Report for 1967," unpublished report, 1968; and Autry Parker, "Politics of Community Organization: Map South, Inc.," unpublished paper for Administrative Theory class, Memphis State University, 1975. Memphis Area Project-South Offices, Memphis.

38. *Hearings in Memphis, Tennessee, June 25–26, 1962.*

39. "Poor People Remain in Citadel of Poverty: Poor People's Campaign More Than A March," and accompanying photograph, "On To Washington," by Ernest Withers, *Tri-State Defender*, May 11, 1968; and Thornton interview.

CHARLES W. MCKINNEY JR.

# Finding Fannie Corbett

## Black Women and the Transformation of Civil Rights Narratives in Wilson, North Carolina

In 2000, Fannie Corbett retired from the Wilson Community Improvement Association (WCIA) after thirty-two years of service to the community of Wilson, a midsize town in eastern North Carolina. As one of the principal founders of the organization in 1968, Corbett oversaw the evolution of the WCIA from a loose consortium of programs—such as a daycare, peer counseling, and job training—into an organization that through the years developed over three hundred units of affordable housing for low-income residents. An effusive article in the *Wilson Daily Times* praised Corbett's three-decade effort to provide housing for the less fortunate, particularly for elderly citizens. The article congratulated Corbett on the good works she performed in the region; state representatives praised her for her hard work and determination and several city officials lauded her efforts to improve the lives of the less fortunate. Fellow Wilsonian, civil rights activist (and future U.S. congressman) G. K. Butterfield Jr. proclaimed that, when it came to being an advocate for the dispossessed, Corbett "[had] done just as much if not more than any citizen in this community." He went on to praise her as a "positive force in the lives of countless people."[1]

This essay is adapted from a larger project, *Greater Freedom: The Evolution of the Civil Rights Movement in Wilson, North Carolina* (University Press of America 2010). I would like to thank Dee Garceau-Hagen for her many helpful suggestions when this project was in its early stages, and Emilye Crosby for her generosity of spirit and thoughtful insights. I would like to thank Barbara Blackston for providing the image of her mother at work at Wilson Community Improvement Association, Inc.

Figure 4 Fannie Corbett, community activist and one of the principal founders of the Wilson Community Improvement Association, helped transform the movement in Wilson by expanding the traditional boundaries of protest and participation. Photograph courtesy of Barbara Blackston.

However, while these newspaper accounts extol Corbett and her community work, they also commit a substantial sin of omission by decoupling Corbett's decades-long efforts to "build a better Wilson" from the city's civil rights movement and the central role she played in giving voice to working-class black communities in that struggle. In fact, in the dozen articles written about Corbett that appeared in both the Raleigh *News and Observer* and the *Wilson Daily Times* prior to her retirement, none of them mentioned her training as a community organizer by one of the most progressive civil rights organizations in the state, her essential role in organizing Wilson's poor and working-class African American communities in the late 1960s and early 1970s, or her efforts to increase black electoral participation. Indeed, in all of the articles on her life and work, there is not one explicit reference to her work in the civil rights movement that served as a training ground for all of her subsequent accomplishments. The failure to explicitly connect Corbett's community work with the civil rights movement is all the more troubling when compared to articles produced about Butterfield Jr. during the same time period. Stories about him are replete with references to his civil rights activities in the 1960s. In the feature article on his promotion from the State Superior Court to the State Supreme Court, the Raleigh *News and Observer* referred to Butterfield Jr. as a "well-connected Democratic politician and heir to a civil-rights legacy." The label was not without merit: Butterfield's father, G. K. Butterfield Sr., worked for years as a tireless advocate for black equality, helped create Wilson's branch of the NAACP, and won election to Wilson's City Commission in the early 1950s, an achievement that consolidated his place in the city's civil rights lore.[2]

Like countless other women who worked and struggled to attain black equality during the middle decades of the twentieth century, Corbett has fallen victim to an interpretation of the black freedom struggle characterized by activist and scholar Julian Bond as the "master narrative." In this rendering of the story, black male middle-class reformers and activists are almost solely responsible for the conception, execution, and—with the assistance of the federal government—eventual completion of the civil rights movement. In this middle class, masculinist version of the civil rights story, black women—particularly working-class women—are relegated to the margins of the action, where they eagerly await direction and inspiration from bold, dynamic, visionary male leadership. Or, as in Corbett's case, their activities are redirected and repackaged as important "community work" that is separate and distinct from issues deemed central to Wilson's movement—desegregation, voter registration, and an end to legal segregation. Although scholars continue to challenge the master narrative and its narrowly defined version of the civil rights story, there is much work to be done. The narrative—by now a fully grown commodity employed by corporate interests seeking to "celebrate diversity"—continues to wield significant sway over yearly celebrations of the King holiday or Black History Month that take place in local communities across the country.[3]

To place gender at the center of a civil rights story is to launch a frontal assault on the master narrative and many of its essential tenets. In Wilson, working-class women frequently thought differently about the tension between community organizing and mobilizing, the socioeconomic implications of the movement, and the very definition of "civil rights" than did their middle-class counterparts in the movement. Corbett, like other working-class women across the country who became politicized in the late 1960s, understood the unsung work of community organizing as the lifeblood of their movement—the single most important element in a movement (supposedly) dedicated to the expansion of democracy and the procurement of equality, dignity, and self-determination. She drew direct lines between the lack of available drinking water, unpaved streets, and substandard housing in East Wilson to the reality of continued racial discrimination that dogged the lives of all black residents. Given this outlook, it comes as no surprise that Corbett came to view civil rights as a subset of a larger struggle for economic and human rights. This perspective confounded traditional leaders of the movement, highlighted growing differences between middle- and working-class activists over goals and tactics, and threw open the question of how movement participants would define leadership. Centering gender in our analysis allows the multiple layers of tension and opportunity within the movement to be more fully explored. It can get messy, but the results are infinitely more satisfying—and accurate.[4]

The dogged adherence to the master narrative necessarily obscures these tensions. The contemporary story of the Wilson civil rights movement, the one that excludes Fannie Corbett, focuses on familiar tactics and goals, including large-scale protests and electoral victory. It highlights the election of the elder Butterfield to the City Commission, mass marches and demonstrations in the 1960s, and the election of African Americans in larger numbers to political office in the 1970s—venues of the movement traditionally dominated by men. Regrettably, in the frequently zero sum game of civil rights history, the process that historian Charles Payne refers to as the "slow respectful work" of community organizing seldom finds a place in the narrative. As a result, the most compelling and enduring contributions of the WCIA— its deep involvement with and commitment to the development of change agents in working-class communities—get relegated to something akin to pleasant background music, happily (and quietly) supporting the main overtures of the movement. The relegation of this deep work—frequently led by women—to the margins of the civil rights story perpetuates the invisibility of women and leads to a reemphasis of the "big ticket" events of the movement that are already deified.[5]

Throughout East Wilson, the life and work of several civil rights era luminaries are memorialized with streets and structures named in their honor. Butterfield Lane and Fitch Drive (named for Milton Fitch Sr., a long-time civil rights activist and onetime state coordinator for the Southern Christian Leadership Conference) both empty out onto Martin Luther King Jr. Parkway in Southeast Wilson, literally connecting the two men and their accomplishments with the movement's most popular icon. In September of 2001, the board of the WCIA voted to name a resource center at one of its housing sites after Charles Branford, a long-time educator at Darden High School who mentored generations of students and actively participated in the movement throughout the late sixties and seventies as a WCIA board member. At the unveiling ceremony, held as part of the organization's King Day celebrations in 2002, the executive director of the WCIA likened Branford to Dr. King, calling him a man who "dreamed of freedom through education and business development." Ironically, none of the participants at the ceremony made mention of the fact that Branford emerged as one of the earliest and most vocal middle-class supporters of the WCIA, a position he assumed at great cost to himself and his own economic self-interest. Additionally, the successful political careers of Milton Fitch Jr. (a long-time member of the state legislature and the first black Majority Leader) and Butterfield Jr. combine with the physical monuments to reinforce the narrative's central indicator of black achievement—political inclusion and participation.[6]

Markers like roads, buildings, and successful political campaigns invoke familiar, commonly referenced stories by bringing the viewer back to the master narrative.[7] To be sure, this is not the sole function of these sites; the streets, resource center, and other public markers also serve as potential areas of reinterpretation and debate about the past. However, in the absence of critical inquiry and vigorous engagement of the dominant narrative, these sites marginalize the activities of the movement's nonelite participants and the bread and butter issues they prioritized. This narrow version excludes women, blocks realistic assessment of how change occurred, and obscures the centrality of economic/human rights issues for many African Americans, particularly in a context where the dominant stories and themes go unchallenged.[8]

This chapter points the way toward a more complete understanding of the movement in Wilson by giving particular attention to black working-class women and their efforts to garner what I refer to as greater freedom. In the process, it reflects on a number of crucial questions: How does the story change with the creation of a civil rights narrative that centers and frames the work of black women like Corbett? That recognizes organizations like the WCIA? What constitutes leadership, and why are some leaders valued more than others? How do we define and understand the goals and tactics of the civil rights movement? How should the movement be periodized? What do we know about who acted and why? What are the implications of these framings?

Fannie Corbett was born into a sharecropping family in 1932. Along with her mother, stepfather, and four siblings, she worked in the tobacco fields of Stantonsburg, a small town in Wilson County, planting, cultivating, and harvesting the golden leaf that dominated both the countryside and the region's economy. To supplement their income, the family raised and sold cotton on their small farm and engaged in the vigorous informal economy of the area. Endowed with her mother's passion for education and civic involvement, Corbett participated in 4-H, sang in the church choir, and performed in plays put on by her elementary school. She thought nothing of the daily three-mile walk to school, and frequently snuck out of the house during winter—against her mother's wishes—to get there. An avid reader, Corbett skipped several grades and advanced rapidly at the segregated, two-teacher, two-room school she attended.[9]

It was during these early years that Corbett caught a glimpse of life beyond the tobacco and cotton fields. Income from tobacco cultivation and cotton picking in the fall and winter enabled the family to make occasional weekend trips into the city of Wilson to purchase clothes and other supplies for the upcoming year. The few extra dollars in the family budget also enabled Corbett's parents to take her and her siblings to Barnes Street in East Wilson, the town's black business and entertainment center. The Corbetts treated their children to soda, popcorn, and—if the budget permitted—an opportunity to "see the cowboys" at the Negro movie theater. Corbett, like many other young people of her generation, became enamored of the city and all of the possibilities it represented. Specifically, city life held with it the potential to earn a better living, or at least a better living than sharecropping had to offer. During the tobacco curing process, the most lucrative stage of cultivation, the family earned just over two dollars a day. In 1949, the last year she worked in a cotton field, Corbett earned $1.25 for every one hundred pounds of cotton she picked. She set her sights on completing her education and moving to Wilson. However, marriage and motherhood forced her to drop out of school. After the breakup of her marriage, Corbett finally moved to Wilson in 1956 and found work as a cafeteria cook at Hearne Elementary School, a school for white students. Although she made it to the city, she did so under very different circumstances than the ones she'd envisioned.[10]

Not long after starting her new job, Corbett confronted the type of economic pressure that largely defined life for working-class people in Wilson. When the principal of the school announced that all food and cafeteria workers would work for the annual fundraiser without compensation, Corbett uttered a lonely dissent in the presence of the stunned principal and a room full of black women—all of whom were painfully aware of the workers' tenuous economic position. After identifying one other worker who felt as strongly as she did, the two of them went to the Employment Security Commission to file a grievance.

Even though their meeting with the ESC did not produce the desired administrative reaction (an agent informed them that they would have to go to the Raleigh office—sixty miles away—in order to find a suitable venue for their grievance) their visit did have the effect of convincing the principal to amend her previous comments. Claiming that her statements were misinterpreted, the principal clarified any potential misunderstanding by stating that the event merely offered school workers an opportunity to "volunteer" at the upcoming function. Although reluctant to do so, Corbett ultimately worked on the evening in question. Fearful of being fired, the welfare of her children far outweighed any stand that placed her economic well-being at risk. Yet, in a substantial way, Corbett's actions constituted a serious statement. She became one of the first African Americans in Wilson to lodge a formal employment complaint in recent memory, and modeled the behavior of a woman whose simmering discontent with the economic status quo was only beginning to manifest itself.[11]

Corbett's solitary stand for self-respect did not take place in a vacuum. By the mid-1950s, a growing number of black individuals and groups in East Wilson engaged employers and city officials in contentious dialogues about the nature (and future) of segregation. Black locals of the Tobacco Worker's International Union (TWIU) flourished in all of the city's major tobacco processing factories, and drew members because of their increasing willingness to confront white supremacy. Organized for over a decade, union members had seen their minimum wage almost double since the late 1940s. In addition to wage increases, the collective strength of the locals enabled them to obtain washing facilities for African Americans, lunchrooms, and prior notice of overtime shifts. Black workers also utilized their union to defend access to unemployment compensation, Social Security, and vacation time. While Corbett sought to form a collective response to the unfair working conditions she experienced, TWIU locals thrived in the city, securing benefits for their members and playing a prominent role in the political life of East Wilson.[12]

The Men's Civic Club (MCC) represented another center of black civic and political influence in the city. From its inception, the club worked diligently and behind the scenes to secure improvements in the quality of black life. Founded in the 1930s, this elite, all-male organization comprised of middle-class professionals worked to, in the words of its founders, "press with greater boldness for an opportunity to practice the duties of good citizenship." Dedicated to the politics of respectability and accommodation, the group used racial diplomacy to create and maintain relationships with white elites and then used those relationships to gain concessions for East Wilson. By the end of the 1950s, the MCC won the successful integration of the municipal stadium and persuaded the city (with the threat of litigation) to fund major improvements for black educational institutions in town. The club also engaged in frequent voter registration efforts, which culminated in the election of G. K. Butterfield to the Board of Aldermen in 1953. Butterfield became the first black elected official in eastern North Carolina in the twentieth century.[13]

Throughout the early sixties, East Wilson's political leadership continued to work behind the scenes to win concessions from the city's elected officials and businessmen. Then, in the spring of 1963, students at East Wilson's Charles Darden High School began a series of marches to protest segregation, a display that reflected their growing impatience with the slow nature of racial change in Wilson. After receiving an abbreviated training in nonviolent protest from a local minister, a small contingent of students targeted three downtown movie theaters and several restaurants that did not cater to blacks. For the better part of August, students made their way downtown, attempted to eat in white-only establishments and gain seating in white sections of the theaters. Within several months of the marches, numerous downtown stores and all three theaters quietly desegregated. The MCC complemented student efforts by creating a local branch of the Good Neighbor Council, a statewide interracial initiative created by Governor Terry Sanford designed to encourage private employers to voluntarily hire black workers. Several restaurants, department stores, and a local bottling company hired black workers for nonblack positions. After meeting with the Council, city leaders removed all signs pertaining to race from the city's drinking fountains, restrooms, and courtrooms. Segregated tax listings, a practice most blacks found particularly insulting, were also abolished.[14]

To be sure, the civil rights apparatus of East Wilson made notable strides toward greater freedom in the late 1950s and early 1960s. Yet these achievements did little to alter many of the fundamental challenges that Corbett faced as a poor woman of color in the city. As an elementary school cafeteria worker, she confronted unfair labor practices without the benefit of union membership. When she attempted to file a complaint against her employer, she did so knowing full well that she alone would have to face the consequences. As an emerging activist, Corbett fell through the organizational cracks in the late 1950s and early 1960s.[15]

In addition to her sense of organizational alienation, the freedom agenda constructed by black elites in Wilson failed to consistently confront one of the most central challenges facing the black community—deplorable housing conditions. In 1960, officials with the Department of Conservation and Development classified 11 percent of the homes in West Wilson (the white side of town) as substandard. In East Wilson, the Department classified 87 percent of the homes as either dilapidated or unfit for occupation. In a report submitted to the city, officials with the Department declared that nothing short of the "total clearance" of a majority of the dwellings would "return [East Wilson] to an environment fit for human habitation." The collective reluctance by the city's political elites on both sides of the train tracks to confront the housing issue consigned Corbett and thousands of others to the inhumane conditions in which they lived.[16]

The city's vigorous commitment to segregation stifled any systematic attempt to confront its housing problems. In October of 1965, the Board endorsed an urban renewal proposal that reflected its continued dedication to racial inequality. The plan called for the condemnation and destruction of substandard properties in and around Warren Street, the only enclave in West Wilson that housed black residents. The city's plan offered no solutions for housing the residents who would lose their home if the plan were approved; there were no vacant rental properties or homes for residents to move into once the clearance started. Even after the City Board gave the initial go-ahead on the project, the majority of the commissioners remained extremely wary of the federal government's reach and influence into the city's local affairs. Several commissioners, led by Edgar Norris, remained adamant in their opposition. "I don't think the government needs to tell us what to do," stated Norris prior to voting against the city's redevelopment plan. The plan passed with a final vote of four to three, with the mayor voting in the affirmative to break the tie.[17]

The plan drew the immediate ire of newly energized housing activists throughout East Wilson. Indeed, the frustration of living in communities that suffered from years of municipal neglect easily bubbled to the surface whenever the subject of housing dominated city meetings. Frequently, the staid nature of traditional political communication structured by Robert's Rules of Order gave way to a new type of civic dialogue that quickly stripped away pretense and exposed the city's culpability. "The blight on Warren Street developed because the city didn't enforce the codes!" exclaimed one exasperated (and unidentified) resident in an October 1965 City Board meeting. According to another citizen, the city's failure to collect the garbage on a regular basis on Warren Street "contributed to making it a slum area!" In his view, garbage collection represented one of the more rudimentary elements of the city's obligation to its citizens. It made little sense to act as if this failure did not play a central role in the street's deterioration.[18]

In the wake of the October meeting, residents contacted Floyd McKissick, a prominent civil rights attorney from Durham, and asked him to intervene on behalf of an East Wilson resident. McKissick, who would become the National Executive Director for the Congress of Racial Equality within months, began to attend City Board meetings in October of 1965. When McKissick queried the Board about the adequacy of rental facilities and the city's statutory requirements to house dislocated residents, Board members replied that the city would have additional public housing "at some point in the future." When asked specifically about the relocation of property owners who would lose their homes, city manager Jack Maynard replied that the families could always attempt to buy the refurbished properties with long-term low interest rates provided by the government. This was highly unlikely, McKissick replied, as the vast majority of the ninety-four black families scheduled for removal were working class and elderly. Under the city's plan, those who could not qualify for loans would then become renters. To this observation, Maynard replied that the city was building twenty-eight more units of public housing. Those who did not find a place to live in Wilson were free to go elsewhere with the money they would receive from the city.[19]

In early 1966, the Department of Housing and Urban Development (HUD) responded to the concerns raised by McKissick and local residents. In a letter to Wilson mayor E. B. Pittman, Bruce Wedge, regional director of HUD in Atlanta, suggested a number of changes that would make the city's proposal more viable. To address the issue of dislocation, the city might use a portion of the grant money to provide a staff person to assist people with obtaining better housing. Also, the city could give relocated families priority in public housing. Finally, Wedge suggested that if the urban renewal lots remained unsold after a period of time, the city could amend the selling method to create terms more amenable to displaced residents. If the city would adopt one or all of these measures, the problem could be considered solved. In March, Pittman answered Wedge by saying that, after polling the Board, it was clear that they would not adopt any part of Wedge's statement. The Board, he informed Wedge, was "adamant about altering their original conception," and remained determined to use federal money to reinforce residential segregation.[20]

The city's actions aggravated an already deplorable scenario. A housing survey conducted in 1965 found thirteen hundred substandard houses in East Wilson. Of these, a majority were considered beyond repair to meet even the minimum standards of Wilson's housing code. Tentative efforts to implement the code enforcement program were slowed "due to the inability to find standard housing to accommodate the people who would be displaced by code enforcement."[21] Although the city had recently completed four hundred new units of public housing, they filled up quickly with sixteen hundred people. An additional three hundred applications for housing sat in the Housing Authority office. In a context of increased distrust and growing animosity, city leadership and an increasingly impatient group of black residents continued to struggle over the ultimate direction of the city's housing policy.

Local anxiety about housing overlapped with the advent of antipoverty programs supported by both legislation and funding from Washington and within the state. Federal programs—and their statewide counterparts—provided resources for local organizations willing to address an array of issues, such as underemployment, health disparities, and housing. In North Carolina these efforts resulted in the creation of the Foundation for Community Development (FCD) in 1967. This new, statewide organization had two objectives—to stimulate economic development and facilitate community organization of the poor into autonomous, politically active groups. In May of 1968, FCD created a summer internship program that trained three-dozen college students as community organizers. While the program taught students the basics of organizing, staff members identified "target areas" throughout the state, locations regarded as having strong local movements. In August of 1968, FCD staffers Minnie Fuller and Sondra Philpot accompanied five graduates of the

internship program to Wilson, one of the six "target areas" in the state identified by FCD.[22]

FCD officials chose wisely in identifying Wilson as an area ready for
grass-roots mobilization. The student-led marches of 1963 and increased desegregation in 1964 placed Wilson firmly on the state's activist radar. By 1965,
black youth in Wilson had created one of the largest student branches of the
NAACP in the state. Floyd McKissick, a major national figure in the civil rights
arena, spent time in the city working to improve housing policy and in doing
so connected the city's activists with the larger, statewide civil rights community. Almost immediately after their arrival and initial canvassing efforts,
FCD's organizers encountered a coterie of black women who stood ready to
do *something* about the conditions they, their families, and other residents
lived in. After their arrival, Fuller and Philpot—the two lead organizers—led
small teams into East Wilson to gather as many residents as possible to discuss their lives, assess their challenges, and begin to visualize a course of action. The two began hosting a series of meetings across East Wilson designed
to engage community members about the myriad challenges that faced their
communities.[23]

When FCD organizers first met Fannie Corbett in the summer of 1968,
they found the single mother enrolled in a job training program at Wilson's Industrial Education Center. Although she still made roughly twenty
five dollars a month, the same amount she made working at the elementary
school, the training component of the program held with it the promise of
better employment in the near future, a point in time that, for Corbett, could
not come fast enough. Her monthly income from the Center, coupled with
welfare benefits, enabled the family to maintain their meager standard of living. When FCD organizers approached Corbett that summer about the state
of housing in her neighborhood she remembers being receptive to their comments: "They went around telling people that you didn't have to live like you
were living, there are better ways for black people now, and that things have
changed for black people, but black people had to come together in order to
get the things they really needed. One Sunday—they were sent from God!—
Sondra came to my home and we just connected. They had afros and things
and we just didn't know what they were. So when she came there and was telling me about the opportunities that were here, I bit like the biggest fish you
ever seen in your life. Whew I bit that!" Corbett attended the first neighborhood gathering the young organizers hosted.[24]

Lillian Weaver recalled a similar story about her initial involvement with FCD organizers. Prior to her first interaction with FCD workers, she cast a skeptical eye on the efforts of civil rights activists. Throughout the 1960's, whenever Martin Luther King Jr. appeared on her television screen, she turned the channel. Convinced that the marches and protests that King led were primarily designed to "stir up trouble," Weaver refused to listen to anything King had to say. The confrontations that met King wherever he marched spoke volumes to Weaver. Though he championed nonviolence, his actions usually led to the dissemination of large helpings of violence, with blacks most often as the unhappy recipients. Weaver concluded that King's decision to postpone a scheduled march and rally in Wilson on April 4, 1968 would be in the city's best interest. After all, she concluded, white reactions to his presence were bound to be aggressive.[25]

Her attitude toward King changed radically with the crack of a rifle shot in Memphis. "After he got shot," she recalls, "I said 'why would they kill him? What was he doing?' And so then I started listening and paying attention."[26] Once Weaver began "paying attention," she quickly discovered that she had a lot to be discontented about. Like most blacks in East Wilson, she lived in a home that bore little resemblance to the domiciles on Wilson's tourism brochures. Weaver paid six dollars a week for a rundown apartment that had no hot water. Fearful of summary eviction, she refrained from complaining to her landlord about the conditions in which she lived. Nor did she tell anybody of the epiphanies she experienced in the wake of King's death. But after a few months, she felt confident of the fact that the key to making improvements in the city lay in some sort of collective action. One Sunday during the summer, there was a knock on the door. After a pleasant introduction, Sondra Philpot informed Weaver that the FCD was hosting a meeting at the Reid Street Community Center to discuss the poor housing that afflicted East Wilson. Weaver remembers clearly her response to Philpot's invitation: "I'm going to that meeting."[27]

Initially, FCD organizers worked in five different neighborhoods and encouraged local residents to create neighborhood associations. Fuller and Philpot encouraged the nascent groups to identify the major problems that faced their community. At first, people were reluctant to attend these weekly gatherings held in various churches and homes across East Wilson. Local residents confronted the young activists with high levels of disengagement from the political process, and a profound skepticism about their capacity to make any substantive changes in the city. Residents also feared reprisals from vindictive landlords. Wealthy landowners were known to drastically increase the rent of tenants who complained about the conditions in which they lived. However, the persistence of FCD organizers was matched by the insistence of a small—but growing—number of residents eager to engage the city with both dialogue and, if need be, other forms of interaction. Corbett, Weaver, and other local conveners worked tirelessly with residents in all of the areas, convincing them that these initial meetings, designed to let residents speak their minds about the challenges facing their community, represented the beginning of a larger, more inclusive process for change.[28]

The concerns that individuals in their respective neighborhoods identified read like a litany of substandard housing woes. Residents in the Washington Carver Heights area—an unincorporated section of town—wanted clean water, paved streets, and the other benefits of annexation. Residents in the Elvie Street area wanted school signs, streetlights, and a park in the area so children wouldn't have to leave the neighborhood to play. The communities around Suggs Street and Mercy Hospital wanted the city to address the stark deficiencies in housing that plagued residents. The basic community needs that residents identified became a "wish list" that would be presented to the appropriate governmental body. While residents continued creating their list of grievances, FCD organizers also began to discuss with them the mechanics of social change; they let it be known that their objective was to create autonomous community organizations that would address the issues that residents articulated. Initially, the process did not go smoothly. Accustomed to generations of neglect and disrepair, scores of people doubted the efficacy of forming a grass-roots organization that could successfully lobby the City Board for improvements in housing.[29]

Corbett played a key role in the process of building the community groups across East Wilson and quickly earned a reputation as someone who could serve as the connective tissue between local residents and unfamiliar activists. Corbett joined with Fuller, Philpot, and the rest of the FCD staff to canvas neighborhoods, and introduced them to key individuals throughout East Wilson. During these initial meetings, she used her existing relationships to challenge residents to not only confront city officials about their needs, but to take an active role in creating programs in their communities. "After all," she reminded them, "we're taxpayers." As citizens of Wilson, she reasoned, each resident had an obligation to engage in the effort to build a better community. Residents could not chastise the city for its lack of engagement and responsibility while remaining inactive themselves. Besides, it was time for black folks to start making major changes in the way they interacted with the city, and those changes started with the perception that blacks should be content with second-class citizenship. In order to make improvements in their communities, blacks had to reject the notion that, by virtue of their being black, they were in Corbett's words, "supposed to have less than the white man." Throughout the summer, Corbett worked with other volunteers to craft a variety of programs for residents, all designed with the implicit assumption of full citizenship and inclusion into Wilson's mainstream. She helped coordinate voter registration drives in East Wilson, and worked with fellow volunteers Velma Farmer and Wallace Bailey to set up recreational programs for children.[30]

As part of FCD's aim to fund and train autonomous groups across the state that would then pursue community improvement and increased inclusion in the mainstream of American life, the organization gave the Wilson groups a start-up grant of $5,300, helped them to find an office, and provided them with technical assistance. FCD members taught volunteers about the basic functions of city government and the role that the City Board played in running the city. FCD staff helped residents interpret the housing code so they could gain a clear understanding of the city's legal obligations and their individual rights. When the state legislature passed laws that impacted Wilson's low-income residents, organizers helped residents to understand their meaning and impact and then typed up and distributed handouts that used accessible language to explain the legislation. Minnie Fuller, FCD's chief organizer in Wilson, became legendary for her ability to type up flyers, leaflets, and fact sheets and get them quickly distributed throughout East Wilson.[31]

Volunteers learned the fundamentals of parliamentary procedure, such as how to run a meeting and recognize speakers on the floor. Fuller encouraged residents to start taking photographs of houses, unpaved streets, and unrepaired sewage lines in their communities—evidence that would eventually be used in meetings with city officials. Howard Fuller, FCD's director of Community Organization, conducted training designed to teach effective methods of mobilization and the successful retention of volunteers. Minnie Fuller and her team expected the volunteers to "start small" in their efforts before the Board, by asking for items that would not impose too much of a burden on the city. However, this tactic merely represented the beginning of a sustained interaction with city officials.[32]

Staff members also encouraged Wilson residents to view their impending struggle as a long-term endeavor; if they remained dedicated to affecting change, they had to understand that the process would take time. City streets would not get paved, nor would streetlights be put up if residents simply conducted a series of marches or sit-ins. Although these tactics had their place in the struggle, they didn't comprise the central elements of social change. Nothing short of a sustained, consistent presence represented the best way to get recognized by city officials. They would have to break the cycle of municipal neglect that had built up over the decades, and a sustained interaction with city officials represented a key element in the process. In several meetings before their first scheduled interaction with the City Board, Minnie Fuller continually repeated an admonition: "[D]on't be intimidated by their red faces."[33]

Minnie Fuller assisted the groups in forming a cooperative structure that enabled them to act in a more unified manner. The individual groups now pledged themselves to collective action in areas such as fundraising or going before the City Board. Meeting participants voted to officially name their consortium the Wilson Community Improvement Association (WCIA). Each community group selected a representative to serve on the WCIA board of directors. The group hired Fannie Corbett as its first full-time organizer and board chair.[34] Corbett's hiring as the WCIA's first paid organizer merely formalized an unofficial reality. Throughout the early tenure of what would eventually become WCIA, she embodied the group's ethos—she possessed a willingness to build relationships while at the same time building a sense of commitment to both those relationships and a larger purpose. While still working and attending classes, Corbett knocked on doors throughout East and West Wilson, urging people to join in their efforts to improve Wilson as a whole. Her dedication to WCIA was intense from the start. When the fledgling organization couldn't pay its rent, Corbett organized teams of people to make and sell peanut butter and jelly sandwiches.[35]

Corbett stood out because she understood the value of nurturing indigenous leadership. In workshops hosted by FCD, organizers continually stressed the importance of allowing people to "come into their own sense of direction" when it came to recruiting and interacting with neighborhood residents. Corbett took this lesson to heart with great effect. She played a key role in identifying men and women who soon became chief lieutenants in the WCIA. These people in turn were able to identify others whose passion for community improvement and political assertion matched their own. The dedication and camaraderie generated by WCIA was palpable, particularly in its early days, when funding from groups other than FCD was at its most precarious. "The leaner we got," recalls Corbett, "the closer we came together."[36]

On August 15, 1968, members of the Wilson Community Improvement Association arrived en masse at their first monthly City Board meeting. Dwight Bailey (another FCD recruit) and Nathaniel Tucker spoke on behalf of the seventy-five members present. Residents stood in the back of the auditorium with picket signs expressing their discontent with the city. When recognized to speak, Bailey produced a copy of the city's housing code, inspection reports, and copies of photographs of houses in substandard condition. Bailey and Tucker, using pictures provided to the board, highlighted the myriad violations seen in the pictures and corresponded each section of the housing code to a particular violation. After a lengthy presentation, the two men closed their remarks with a question: why didn't the city enforce the housing code? A board member reminded the audience that vigorous enforcement of the code would result in the displacement of hundreds of people. Bailey responded by urging the city to find a middle way, navigating between outright condemnation and continued neglect. Bailey and Tucker exchanged ideas and suggestions with the Board in a vigorous debate punctuated by the shouts of affirmation from WCIA members in the back of the room. Mayor John Wilson, who chaired the meeting, became impatient with the increasingly heated debate. Though he'd remained silent throughout the session, he suddenly made a motion to move to the next agenda item. After the motion passed and the Board began to discuss another issue, he informed WCIA members that it was unnecessary for them to go over the ordinances "section by section, criticizing [them]."[37]

City officials in Wilson were ill prepared for the arrival of such a radically different political entity. To be sure, black groups had used the public space of City Board meetings in the past to varying degrees of effectiveness. But WCIA's approach represented something altogether unconventional. Like previous community groups before it, WCIA leaders understood the importance of popular support and sizable presentations. However, the presence and influence of FCD transformed WCIA into a well-trained, independently funded organization—a group anchored by the principle of community organizing. With roots planted throughout working-class enclaves in East Wilson and a political agenda that resonated with almost every black person in town, WCIA had all the elements in place to become the city's first mass-based civil rights organization. Additionally, WCIA leaders were becoming versed in the city's own language of codes and ordinances; this enabled them to make specific legislative recommendations regarding housing concerns. It soon became apparent to literally every elected and appointed body in Wilson that WCIA did not intend to be a flash in the city's political pan.

If city officials found WCIA's conduct to be disconcerting, their demands proved to be wholly exasperating. In addition to the standard requests that black neighborhoods all over the city made (streetlights, paved roads, street signs in school areas, housing code enforcement) officials in the group demanded representation on all of the city's appointed councils. As fixtures at meetings of the Wilson Housing Authority, Corbett and others insisted on the equal representation of blacks and whites on the body. When informed that changing the Authority's composition would require a change in the city's charter, spokeswoman Leslie Farmer immediately inquired about the intricacies of the procedure and demanded that the city begin the process.[38] As city officials soon discovered, WCIA's leadership style articulated a radically different perspective on the relationship between citizens and elected officials. In years past, black leaders appeared before the City Board to make requests; now the racial diplomacy of the MCC gave way to a cadre of activists who viewed themselves as vocal shareholders in municipal government. More importantly, FCD activists trained WCIA members to view *themselves* as a group who both wielded and sought to gain political power for the purposes of improving their section of the city. This new orientation, coupled with the various programs that WCIA began sponsoring in the city, heightened the group's expectation that city officials would view them as partners in municipal administration.

These tentative efforts to alleviate the more extreme cases of housing inequality coincided with increased opportunities to receive federal funding for urban renewal projects. Yet, the possibility of matching federal funds did little to decrease the city's determination to avoid integrated housing. In January 1969, the Department of Housing and Urban Development summarily rejected Wilson's request for public housing funds because the city sought to place the proposed project in East Wilson for the sole purpose of housing dislocated families from the same side of town. In the letter, HUD officials reminded the City Board that any attempts to place housing only in areas of "racial concentration" would be considered "*prima facie* unacceptable." HUD officials also expressed concern over the fact that the city knew this to be the case and proceeded to request funds for segregated housing anyway. In the wake of this setback, and in the midst of constant lobbying by the WCIA, city manager Bruce Boyette encouraged the City Board to begin talking with HUD officials in Atlanta about the feasibility of securing funds for the annexation of the Washington-Carver Heights community, another course of action that could lead to improved housing.[39]

From August of 1968 through 1969, WCIA members continued to pack into City Board meetings to demand housing reform. Their efforts did not go un-rewarded; under increasing pressure from federal housing authorities, the city began to take substantive steps. The city applied for and received a code enforcement grant from HUD, enabling it to hire additional housing inspec-tors. In August, the city applied for a grant to build three hundred additional public housing units. The WCIA responded with a two-pronged approach. First, WCIA leaders asked the City Board why it didn't apply for grants to annex Washington-Carver Heights, clearly the most deficient area in town. Second, they asked the city to forgo building more public housing in order to build houses for low-income residents. The federal government's new low income housing program, called Turnkey 3, could provide the city with the resources it needed to expand the tax base in East Wilson. Surely, Corbett surmised during a City Board meeting, Wilson should move in a direction where "black people can become taxpayers."[40]

Throughout the early months of 1970, the WCIA—which now claimed over a thousand active members—maintained its presence in City Board and Housing Authority meetings in order to request construction of the addi-tional homes. City manager Bruce Boyette countered by offering to build two hundred units of public housing and one hundred low-income homes. Cor-bett, Weaver, and other leaders of the WCIA emphasized to the City Board the importance of giving as many people as possible the chance to own a home. In March, several dozen public housing residents attended the City Board's monthly meeting to voice their support of the Turnkey 3 initiative. WCIA rep-resentatives informed the Board that, if the city made housing available to them, the spaces they occupied in public housing could be used for elderly residents on the city's waiting list. In May, over one hundred people packed the City Board meeting room to voice their support of WCIA's proposal. Finally, in July of 1970, under significant pressure from both the WCIA and Boyette, the City Board relented. Boyette drafted and the Board approved a resolution of intent to submit an application for three hundred low income homes in East Wilson.[41]

More than any other factor, the constant political pressure and presence of the WCIA lay at the heart of the city's political evolution. Throughout its first years of existence, the WCIA imbued in its rapidly increasing membership a sense of civic engagement unique in Wilson's black freedom struggle. Corbett, her lieutenants, and the hundreds of members who participated in the WCIA's numerous programs took active roles in the democratic dialogue they worked to construct with the city. WCIA members who asked the city for improvements in East Wilson were also likely to present the city with options for implementing those improvements. From the perspective of the WCIA, to do any less would be unproductive.

Moreover, this new relationship with the city's elected officials—coupled with external political pressure to modernize East Wilson—provided cover for many of Wilson's black civic groups who were still heavily invested in the politics of racial diplomacy. Largely as a result of the groundswell caused by the emergence of the WCIA, the Men's Civic Club, the East Wilson Ministerial Association, and the Good Neighbor Council began petitioning the Board about the problems associated with inadequate housing and sewage in the black sections of town. In the case of the MCC, actions by the WCIA lent credence to their tentative foray into the city's housing issue. In January of 1968—two years after initial protests and seven months before the emergence of the WCIA—MCC president John Wesley Jones wrote a letter to the City Board endorsing the need for an increase in low income housing and calling the housing issue "one of the most urgent problems confronting our segment of the population." Within months, working-class activists confirmed this assessment by making housing the central issue on Wilson's political agenda. By the turn of the decade, black civic groups were increasingly speaking with one voice in regards to housing policy. However, in a significant departure from the recent past, the leading voices in the chorus for change now belonged to some of the most marginalized members of the black community—working-class men and women.[42]

Throughout the late 1960s and into the early years of the new decade, the impact and full potential of community action dramatically energized the city's black freedom struggle and created several tangible results. In 1970, the City Board responded to years of intransigence on the part of landlords by passing an ordinance that allowed the city to pave streets without the permission of the landowners who lived in the vicinity. The new law—pushed by the WCIA—overrode the prerogatives of landlords who routinely refused to petition for paving because they would be partially responsible for the financing. Absentee owners who failed to assist with paving costs faced having a lien placed on their property. This ordinance removed one of the most enduring obstacles to the construction of sidewalks throughout Wilson.[43]

The efforts and activities of the WCIA placed the organization in the vanguard of Wilson's civil rights movement in the late sixties and early seventies, and established the group as a permanent fixture in Wilson's social and political life for the next three decades. With financial and organizational support from the FCD, the WCIA extended the tenets of participatory democracy well into Wilson's working-class enclaves, transforming the political terrain of the city. Within the first two years of its existence, the group developed a cadre of activists who—supported by a burgeoning, insurgent organization—directly confronted city officials about pervasive disparities in black communities and actively worked with them to address those issues. Throughout the WCIA's early tenure, Fannie Corbett embodied both the process of political evolution and the possibility of sustained community action. However, in the organization's early years, both Corbett and the WCIA—despite their early successes—faced a number of obstacles to their inclusion into the mainstream of Wilson's political culture. Accordingly, these obstacles are also intimately tied to the continuing challenges surrounding Corbett and the WCIA's place in Wilson's civil rights narrative.

Wilson's popular civil rights story—which mirrors the structure of the overall master narrative of the black freedom struggle—remains deeply rooted in conventional notions regarding social change and leadership. As such, it is ill prepared to account for the complex processes that comprise a social movement, or what an analysis of these processes can tell us about alternative forms of leadership. For most people in Wilson—on both sides of the train tracks—"civil rights" largely boils down to political engagement between white and black elites, a formulation that invariably conflates the concepts of "male" and "leader." This self-fulfilling view (men lead, therefore men are leaders) continues to choke off the possibility of alternative realities regarding civil rights leadership, and remains a presumption hard-wired in the minds of Wilson's residents.[44]

As a working-class woman of color recruited and trained by activists focused on long-term organizing, Fannie Corbett employed a different style of leadership, recruiting other community members into WCIA and becoming one of the main liaisons between community members, a rapidly evolving organization, and the city's elected officials. These activities embody the type of principal participant that Belinda Robnett defines as a *community bridge leader*—an individual who connects the divide between grass-roots constituencies and civil rights organizations. Several of the black women (and more than a few men) who worked with WCIA did this type of work (defined by Robnett as community bridge leadership). They laid the groundwork for a viable community organization by recruiting members into WCIA and encouraging those members to take an active role in the life of the city, whether by attending a protest, volunteering at a community program, or helping the WCIA in some other way. They built relationships between working-class neighborhoods and the WCIA and, perhaps most importantly, remained deeply committed to the needs and demands of their constituents.

Another barrier to the WCIA's inclusion in the civil rights narrative lay in the fact that, for many middle-class activists and residents, the frequently confrontational efforts of the WCIA represented an ill-advised attempt to disrupt the well-established machinery of social change. From the perspective of East Wilson's elites, poor and working-class blacks were ill prepared when it came to creating and sustaining autonomous protest organizations. Fanny Corbett remembers being reminded of this fact frequently when WCIA first started operation: "We had people like [the funeral home director]. One of the men that ran it said 'they'll never make it. She don't know how to carry out no organization.' . . . They wanted the little poor folks to go and tell them what the problem was, then they'd take what they want up there to the Man, and the Man would tell him, '[W]ell, wait a minute . . . we can do this but we can't do that.' Put 'em out and they accepted it. That's what had been going on." For the middle-class critics of the WCIA, the pursuit of greater freedom represented an endeavor best left to the professional classes. In their minds, working class inroads into these unfamiliar waters would come to nothing in the end, and would most certainly strain the relationships between black and white elites—a relationship that took decades to build. However, social change by way of intermediary possessed clear downsides, particularly for working-class people whose agenda for greater freedom often diverged from that of their middle-class counterparts. Unfortunately, with a continued narrative emphasis on electoral politics and desegregation, these notable divisions within the movement are frequently papered over in the retelling of the story.[45]

Fannie Corbett's work with the WCIA increased the capacity of working-class community action in Wilson, and laid the groundwork upon which three decades of the black freedom movement rested. Assisted by the FCD, organizers of what would eventually become the WCIA started identifying and working with groups of high school age youth, single mothers, retired individuals, and everyone in between to train a cadre of activists and organizers. This small band then went out and worked intensely with citizens in East Wilson, familiarized them with the inner workings of city and municipal politics, gave them the tools to improve their neighborhoods, and enabled them to assume the mantle of engaged citizenship. Within two years of its founding, the WCIA helped secure affordable housing for thousands of low income residents, supported marginalized black high school students, registered hundreds to vote, and became a force in local politics. More than any other civil rights organization in town, the WCIA fostered the growth of participatory democracy in Wilson's African American community. The group—urged by Corbett and others—laid claim to their ability to shape the political terrain of the city, and moved quickly to use that power, frequently in ways that expanded the notion of "civil rights" work. Before the arrival of the WCIA, no major black organization in East Wilson engaged in a sustained conversation with city officials that framed housing and other municipal issues as a matter of civil rights. The rise of the WCIA forcefully expanded the definition of civil rights to include issues such as housing, garbage removal, annexation, and a host of related subjects. For Corbett and her compatriots, the achievement of "greater freedom" meant a radical expansion of the list of items that people saw as essential to their actual liberation; it also meant the inclusion of the voices of the most marginalized members of Wilson's black community.

Fannie Corbett embodied the intimate relationship between the WCIA and Wilson's working-class African American population. Her status as a poor, working-class single mother of color served as a key ingredient in her ability to effectively organize and mobilize a critical constituency in the city. For much of her life, she'd lived in substandard housing in Wilson, and confronted the daily quandary presented by low wages, unsanitary neighborhoods, and substandard housing—all reinforced by persistent discrimination. These realities, combined with a determination to change her community and the training she received from FCD enabled her to play a central role in creating one of the most influential black social/political organizations in the city, an organization primarily dedicated to addressing the concerns of the city's most marginalized segment of the population.

Finally, Corbett's detachment from the larger record of civil rights activism blinds us to a central implication of her legacy. Placing Corbett and the WCIA firmly within Wilson's civil rights story enables us to understand the implications of the intensely local nature of civil rights activity. The procurement of paved streets, recreational programs, the enforcement of the housing code, and availability of affordable housing formed a central component of the movement in Wilson in the late 1960s. Moreover, these issues provided fertile ground for community organizers who adhered to a grass-roots perspective that respected the importance of "home grown" obstacles, and used them to craft long-term participants in the movement. Corbett's effort in these areas helped mobilize hundreds of black citizens who demanded and then fashioned a radically different relationship with city officials than the one previously endured by blacks. In East Wilson, it was only after this process began in earnest across working-class enclaves that residents turned their attention to issues such as school desegregation and the election of black candidates. In this instance, then, a focus on economic issues (typically understood as following an initial focus on civil rights) paved the way for additional struggle—around issues typically thought to be the starting point and more central to the struggle.

In Wilson, as in other cities across the South, the sum of the black freedom struggle always consisted of more than a national agenda hammered out in faraway places and acted upon by local black leaders. For Corbett and the WCIA, local concerns formed the centerpiece of the movement and helped shape the political perspective and subsequent course of action for movement participants. Corbett's work with the WCIA embodies the concentric nature of the movement in Wilson, and represents perhaps the most essential starting point in an effort to reconstruct a fuller, more inclusive civil rights narrative for the city.

## NOTES

1. *Wilson Daily Times*, June 22, 2000 (hereafter cited as *WDT*).

2. *Raleigh News and Observer*, February 6, 2001.

3. Emilye Crosby provides a compelling snapshot of the challenges facing local historians and activists who seek to create a narrative that more accurately reflects the history and legacy of the movement in Claiborne County, Mississippi. See Emilye Crosby, *A Little Taste of Freedom: The Black Freedom Struggle in Claiborne County, Mississippi* (Chapel Hill: University of North Carolina Press, 2005), 255–282. For an excellent example of corporate efforts to appropriate the legacy of the movement, see McDonald's Web site "365 Black" at http://www.365black.com/365black/whatis.jsp.

4. There are a number of recent works that effectively center gender and class in an effort to accurately gauge women's activism in local movements. Among them are Laurie B. Green, *Battling the Plantation Mentality: Memphis and the Black Freedom Struggle* (Chapel Hill: University of North Carolina Press, 2007); Christina Greene, *Our Separate Ways: Women and the Black Freedom Movement in Durham, North Carolina* (Chapel Hill: University of North Carolina Press, 2005); Rhonda Williams, *The Politics of Public Housing: Black Women's Struggles Against Urban Inequality* (New York: Oxford University Press, 2005); Annelise Orleck, *Storming Caesar's Palace: How Black Women Fought Their Own War on Poverty* (New York: Beacon Press, 2005); Winston A. Grady-Willis, *Challenging U.S. Apartheid: Atlanta and Black Struggles for Human Rights, 1960–1977* (Durham: Duke University Press, 2006).

5. Kathryn Nasstrom's groundbreaking article remains a definitive work on this phenomenon. See Kathryn Nasstrom, "Down to Now: Memory, Narrative, and Women's Leadership in the Civil Rights Movement in Atlanta, Georgia," *Gender and History* 11 (April 1999): 113–44. See also Green, *Battling the Plantation Mentality*, chapter 3.

6. *WDT*, January 22, 2002.

7. Renee Romano and Leigh Raiford, eds., *The Civil Rights Movement in American Memory* (Athens: University of Georgia Press, 2006), xiv.

8. Joseph Tilden Rhea, *Race Pride and the American Identity* (Cambridge, Mass.: Harvard University Press, 1997), 113; Derek Alderman, "Street Names as Memorial Arenas: The Reputational Politics of Commemorating Martin Luther King, Jr. in a Georgia County," in *The Civil Rights Movement in American Memory*, 67–95.

9. During the first half of the century, Wilson County produced more bright leaf tobacco than any other location in the world. On Wilson's dominance in the tobacco industry, see Patrick Valentine, *The Rise of a Southern Town: Wilson, North Carolina, 1849–1920* (Baltimore: Gateway Press, 2002); Nannie May Tilley, *The Bright-Tobacco Industry, 1860–1929* (Chapel Hill: University of North Carolina Press, 1948); Scott Matthews, "Farm Tenancy and Race in the Tobacco Culture of Wilson County, North

Carolina, 1866–1992" (senior honor's thesis, Guilford College, 1995); Roger Biles, "Tobacco Towns: Urban Growth and Economic Development in Eastern North Carolina," *The North Carolina Historical Review* 84 (2007): 156–90; Fannie Corbett, interview by the author, August 22, 2001. On the informal economy in eastern North Carolina, see Lu Ann Jones, *Mama Learned Us to Work: Farm Women in the New South* (Chapel Hill: University of North Carolina Press, 2002).

10. Corbett interview.

11. Ibid.

12. On union activity in Wilson, see contracts and wage agreements between TWIU and the R. P. Watson Tobacco Company, James I Miller Tobacco Company, and Export Leaf Tobacco Company from 1947 to 1959. See also Nettie Speight to R. J. Petree, January 29, 1958. Tobacco Workers International Union Papers, Special Collections, University of Maryland Libraries; Janet Irons and Steve Unruhe, "Black Wilson: The Second City, 1930–1980" (paper written for NAACP Legal, Educational and Defense Fund, in author's possession), 9.

13. G. K. Butterfield, interview by the author, August 23, 2001; Men's Civic Club, "A History of the Men's Civic Club" (privately printed, in author's possession); William Chafe, Raymond Gavins, and Robert Korstad, eds., *Remembering Jim Crow: African Americans Tell About Life in the Segregated South* (New York: The New Press, 2001), 281–85. G. K. Butterfield to Wiley Branton, Voter Education Project, May 27, 1964, reel 182, Papers of the Southern Regional Council.

14. Grover Bridgers, interview by the author, November 9, 2001; Joanne Woodard, interview by the author, February 1, 2003; Charles Davis interview, February 2, 2003; *WDT*, August 19, 1963; *WDT*, September 2, 1963; Wilson Good Neighbor Council, "Good Neighbor Council Update" (report submitted to Wilson City Board of Commissioners, 1963), 3.

15. Corbett interview.

16. The U.S. Census Bureau defined the term "dilapidated" in 1960 as housing that "does not provide safe and adequate shelter and in its present condition endangers the health, safety, or well-being of the occupants." For the definition, see Hasan Kwame Jeffries, "Organizing for More Than the Vote: The Political Radicalization of Local People in Lowndes County, Alabama, 1965–1966," in *Groundwork: Local Black Freedom Movements in America*, ed. Jeanne Theoharis and Komozi Woodard (New York: New York University Press, 2005), 1960. See also Division of Community Planning, Department of Conservation and Development, *A Preliminary Land Development Plan for Wilson, North Carolina* (Raleigh: State Printing Office, 1960), 8.

17. Minutes, City Board of Commissioners, October 1965. Throughout the decade, city officials constantly refused federal aid unless it was for agricultural or infrastructure projects. Bruce Boyette, interview by the author, August 21, 2002; Irons and Unruhe, "Black Wilson," 32.

18. See minutes, City Board of Commissioners, monthly meetings from June 1965 throughout the rest of the decade. See especially October 7, October 14, 1965.

19. Minutes, City Board of Commissioners, October 14, 1965.

20. E. Bruce Wedge to E. B. Pittman, February 12, 1966, in minutes, City Board of Commissioners, February 23, 1966. E. B. Pittman to E. Bruce Wedge, March 1, 1966, in minutes, City Board of Commissioners, March 11, 1966; Irons and Unruhe, "Black Wilson," 32, 77.

21. E. B. Pittman to E. Bruce Wedge, March 1, 1966, in minutes, City Board of Commissioners, March 11, 1966.

22. Dwight Womble, "History of the Foundation for Community Development" (master's thesis, North Carolina Central University, 1980), 32.

23. Corbett interview; "Corporate Data and Early History of FCD" (report prepared for the Ford Foundation, in author's possession). Howard Fuller, interview by the author, June 1, 2002.

24. Corbett interview.

25. Lillian Weaver, interview by the author, February 11, 2003.

26. In Wilson, over a thousand people attended a memorial service in King's honor on April 7. That night, widespread looting occurred throughout the city. Looters shattered thirty windows and local authorities arrested thirty-three people. City manager Jack Maynard called a meeting of the City Board, who promptly declared a state of emergency in the city. See *WDT*, April 1, April 8, 1968; February 17, 1996; Minutes, City Board of Commissioners, April 7, 1968; Darlene Johnson, "The Civil Rights Movement in Wilson, North Carolina, 1968–1971" (unpublished master's thesis, North Carolina Central University, 1998), chapter two; Boyette interview.

27. Weaver interview.

28. Corbett interview; Weaver interview.

29. Corbett interview; Farmer interview.

30. Corbett interview; Wallace Bailey, interview by the author, 2003.

31. Corbett interview; Foundation for Community Development Papers, Folder 891, in the North Carolina Fund Records no. 4710, Southern Historical Collection, the Wilson Library, University of North Carolina at Chapel Hill (hereafter cited as FCD Papers); Nathan Garrett to Fannie Corbett, December 12, 1968, folder 891, FCD Papers.

32. Corbett interview; Fuller interview.

33. Weaver interview; Corbett interview; Bailey interview. In her work on Durham, N.C., Christina Greene illuminates the crucial nature of providing residents with the skills to organize their community and how these efforts were essential in providing the movement its forward momentum in the late 1960s. See Greene, *Our Separate Ways*, chapter 4. On the recruitment of black women into the freedom movement, see Jenny Irons, "The Shaping of Activist Recruitment and Participation: A Study of Women in the

Civil Rights Movement," *Gender and Society* 12 (December 1998): 692–709; Charles M. Payne, *I've Got the Light of Freedom: The Organizing Tradition and the Mississippi Freedom Struggle* (Berkeley: University of California Press, 1995); Chana Kai Lee, *For Freedom's Sake: The Life of Fannie Lou Hamer* (Urbana: University of Illinois Press, 1999).

34. Bailey interview; Thomas Stott, interview by the author, January 29, 2001; Corbett interview.

35. Farmer interview.

36. Corbett interview. Anthropologist Karen Sacks defines the type of role Corbett played in Wilson as that of a "centerwoman," a person capable of utilizing strong informal relationships within neighborhoods to facilitate community organizing efforts. See Karen Sacks, "Gender and Grassroots Leadership," in *Women and the Politics of Empowerment*, ed. Ann Bookman and Sandra Morgen (Philadelphia: Temple University Press, 1986); and Karen Sacks, *Caring by the Hour: Women, Work and Organizing at Duke Medical Center* (Urbana: University of Illinois Press, 1988).

37. Minutes, City Board of Commissioners, August 15, 1968. Bailey interview; Corbett interview.

38. City Board Minutes, August 15, 1968.

39. Minutes, City Board of Commissioners, January 16, 1969; Irons and Unruhe, "Black Wilson," 38. After serving as long-time assistant city manager, Bruce Boyette was promoted to city manager after Jack Maynard became seriously ill. Boyette functioned with a relatively moderate style of leadership that sought to directly address issues of long-term discrimination. See minutes, City Board of Commissioners, February 6, 1969. Boyette interview; Irons and Unruhe, "Black Wilson," 45.

40. City Board Minutes, August 25, October 7, 1969; March 12, 1970.

41. City Board Minutes, March 12, May 14, July 16, 1970. Boyette interview; Irons and Unruhe, "Black Wilson," 49.

42. Corbett interview; Branford interview; Bailey interview; Irons and Unruhe, "Black Wilson," 48; *WDT*, March 13, March 15, 1968. John Wesley Jones to City Board of Commissioners, January 9, 1968, letter in Board minutes for January 11, 1968.

43. Irons and Unruhe, "Black Wilson," 49; *WDT*, December 8, 1972.

44. There are a number of notable efforts in this regard. See Belinda Robnett, *How Long? How Long? African American Women in the Struggle for Civil Rights* (New York: Oxford University Press, 1997), 165; Greene, *Our Separate Ways*; Lee, *For Freedom's Sake*; Green, *Battling the Plantation Mentality*. In her work on SNCC, Wesley Hogan also pays particular attention to these issues. See Wesley C. Hogan, *Many Minds, One Heart: SNCC's Dream for a New America* (Chapel Hill: University of North Carolina Press, 2007).

45. Corbett interview. In MCC's organizational history, there are few references to any other civil rights organizations in the work.

AMY NATHAN WRIGHT

# The 1968 Poor People's Campaign, Marks, Mississippi, and the Mule Train

## Fighting Poverty Locally, Representing Poverty Nationally

> Why don't you see it? Why don't you feel it? I don't know! I don't know!
> You don't have to live next to me. Just give me my equality.
> Everybody knows about Mississippi. Everybody knows about Alabama.
> Everybody knows about Mississippi Goddamn!
> —Nina Simone

> I was in Marks, Mississippi the other day and I found myself weeping
> before I knew it. I met boys and girls by the hundreds who didn't have
> any shoes to wear, who didn't have any food to eat in terms of three
> square meals a day, and I met their parents, many of whom don't even
> have jobs. But not only do they not have jobs, they are not even getting
> an income. Some of them aren't on any kind of welfare, and I literally
> cried when I heard men and women saying that they were unable to
> get any food to feed their children.
> —Martin Luther King Jr.

During the mid-to-late 1960s, Martin Luther King Jr. was moved to tears on two occasions when visiting the small Delta town of Marks, Mississippi. The poverty he witnessed prompted King to focus his attention and

Epigraphs: Nina Simone, "Mississippi Goddamn!," Sam Fox Publishing/ASCAP, 1963; Martin Luther King Jr., "Conversation with Martin Luther King," *Conservative Judaism* 22, no. 3 (Spring 1968): 17.

the Southern Christian Leadership Conference's (SCLC) resources on fighting poverty. King made his first trip to Marks in 1966 to attend the funeral of activist Armstead Phipps, who died of a heart attack along the "Meredith March Against Fear" from Memphis, Tennessee, to Jackson, Mississippi.[1] Ralph Abernathy, King's closest friend and successor as head of SCLC, recounts that while in Marks the two civil rights leaders visited a Head Start day care center where they watched as four hungry students eagerly awaited their lunch—an apple their teacher had quartered. King uncharacteristically broke into tears and said to Abernathy, "I can't get those children out of my mind. . . . We've got to do something for them. . . . We can't let that kind of poverty exist in this country. I don't think people really know that little school children are slowly starving in the United States of America. I didn't know it."[2] After a largely unsuccessful effort to tackle housing issues and other poverty-related problems in Chicago, King and his staff began planning a national poverty campaign during the summer and fall of 1967.

King knew he wanted to take action and began researching his possibilities and the amount of potential support for a national poverty campaign, especially since both funding and support for LBJ's War on Poverty were waning. After traveling through Mississippi's most impoverished areas at the behest of Marian Wright Edelman, Senator Bobby Kennedy pleaded with King to "bring the poor people to Washington." Kennedy's appeal prompted King to quickly formulate a plan and take action while the mood was right. He and Andrew Young visited with editors from some of the nation's top publications and received even more enthusiasm for their campaign. King proposed that a racially, geographically, and politically diverse coalition of poor people join forces under the leadership of SCLC and caravan to Washington, D.C., where they would enact civil disobedience to protest the unseen poverty they suffered from on a daily basis. Journalists, politicians, and even his own staff urged King to abandon his plans of having thousands of poor people protest in the nation's capital, but he insisted that poor people caravan to the capital where they could meet with their political representatives face-to-face and where the public could see the otherwise invisible poor. Most thought the campaign was ill-timed and destined to fail, but King declared that if the Poor People's Campaign (PPC) failed, it would be America's fault, not his or the activists who joined him in protest.[3]

According to SCLC's plan, a coalition of thousands of African American, American Indian, Puerto Rican, Mexican American, and white Appalachian poor people would caravan to Washington, D.C., where they would build a temporary shantytown in an attempt to bring poverty into the national spotlight and expose the bleak conditions impoverished people experienced on a daily basis. The city, which would be named Resurrection City after King's assassination, would also provide participants with social services and basic necessities they lacked at home, as well as direct access to government institutions where they could protest for their basic needs of adequate jobs, housing, and food.

On March 19, 1968, King returned to Marks as part of his people-to-people tour of the nation to rally support for the 1968 Poor People's Campaign. He had recently become involved in the Memphis Sanitation Workers' Strike, which he argued was a local example of the national antipoverty movement, but which the majority of his staff insisted was an unnecessary distraction from the PPC. While in the area, King also toured the nearby Mississippi Delta, one of the epicenters of U.S. poverty. After witnessing the dire circumstances Marks residents were suffering, he used their stories to rally the nation for the national poverty campaign. On March 31, 1968, just days before his assassination, King delivered a stirring sermon, "Remaining Awake through a Great Revolution," at the National Cathedral in Washington in which he testified to the conditions Marks residents and impoverished people throughout the Delta were experiencing. One young girl explained: "We go around to the neighbors and ask them for a little something. When the berry season comes, we pick berries. When the rabbit season comes, we hunt and catch a few rabbits. And that's about it." After providing evidence of hunger and starvation in one of the wealthiest nations, King told the story of how he wept after entering a dilapidated shack on Cotton Street in Marks and then encouraged others to follow him in his quest to combat this kind of poverty.[4] Yet King understood that in order to convince the people and the government to enact a radical redistribution of wealth, while already strapped with a costly war, they would need more than tales of hard times in one black community. King, SCLC, and the countless activists and participants who joined the PPC had to use examples of the *local experience* of poverty to mobilize grass-roots support for the national campaign, while emphasizing the *national scope* of the problem to justify the prolonged protest and need for national action.

My work draws and builds on recent local studies and work that explicitly connects antipoverty campaigns, labor union actions, and welfare rights movements to the broader civil rights struggles of the post–World War II era. The Mule Train from Marks—the most dramatic of the nine regional PPC caravans to the capital—was an important component of the national movement while being grounded in a local movement. In addition, the Mule Train and the other caravans created a movement, literally in motion, that fostered grass-roots organizing simultaneously at the local, regional, and national scales. As communities across the nation organized local people to join the PPC's caravans, they bolstered existing organizations or built new ones to provide the resources participants needed for their journeys and to meet the needs of those at home. All along the caravans' journeys, participants encountered local people and organizations that sought to help them meet their immediate goal of reaching the nation's capital for the national stage of the PPC. Some developed relationships that extended beyond the actual campaign.

The Mule Train, with its cavalcade of approximately fifteen mule-drawn covered wagons, served as a moving political theater, displaying southern poverty for all in its path. Many participants were still day laborers on the same plantations that generations of blacks before them had worked, and the Mule Train served as a visual reminder that some poor black southerners were still trapped in a system of racial and economic domination similar to the one that their predecessors had endured. Through their performance of poverty, participants challenged images of the poor as shiftless and employed an outdated form of transportation as an innovative and dramatic, yet challenging, display of resistance. Participants enjoyed the opportunity and excitement of the trip but also sacrificed and struggled to reach Washington in the mule-drawn wagons, which were symbolic of their lack of economic mobility.

The PPC and its caravans also helped local people recognize that their individual and local problems were symptomatic of much larger, systemic issues rooted in the nation's economic system and racial order.[5] And while the Mule Train displayed rural southern poverty both for those along its path and to the nation through nightly news reports, SCLC's organizing in Marks on behalf of the Mule Train sparked events that generated local support for the PPC and created opportunities for black residents to more effectively organize around local issues. Tracing the Mule Train's journey reveals the ways in which a local community responded to the opportunity to dramatically display poverty and take action. Journalists and some civil rights scholars have dismissively characterized the PPC as the last gasp of the civil rights movement—a failed campaign with no substantial lasting consequences.[6] Yet if the movement's effects at the local level are taken into consideration, it becomes clear that the PPC had a profound effect both on individuals and local communities. The PPC put the small Delta town of Marks, Mississippi, on the map. The national media's spotlight on Marks, which helped generate important change, was the result of the combined efforts of SCLC activists and local people's determination to challenge the town's power structure.

## MARKS, QUITMAN COUNTY, MISSISSIPPI: "THE POOREST COUNTY IN THE NATION"

Marks became a focal point of the PPC not only due to King's connection to the town, but also because it was the hub of Quitman County, which had the notorious title of being the poorest county in the nation. Marks native Hilliard Lackey describes the town in 1968, with its almost 2,500 residents, as "the queen city in a county of 21,000 that boasts of towns and villages such as Sledge, Darling, Lambert, Crenshaw, Falcon, and Vance, with populations of less than 500 each."[7] Yet, in a letter from SCLC activist R. B. Cottonreader to Hosea Williams on February 12, 1968, Cottonreader detailed the numerous problems people throughout the county were facing: "Quitman County's black people are among the poorest if not the poorest in Mississippi, and said that they would support the Poor People's Campaign to Washington in any way that they can, but they further stated that they felt that financial support within the county would be very limited, as lots of the black people in Quitman County are near starvation and out of work and the ones working are underpaid. Mr. Franklin told me of four families that had been recently put off the white man's plantation."[8] In fact, Cottonreader explained that the only space available for meetings and organizing was an office and a hall where a family recently thrown off a plantation was living.

The data SCLC gathered revealed that Marks residents and their neighbors throughout the Delta suffered a gamut of problems that reflected failures at all levels of government. Limited, substandard, and overcrowded housing conditions, as well as frequent evictions from plantations, were some of Marks residents' central concerns. Leon Hall, an SCLC staff member, reported that "rents are often absurdly high in contrast to the usually shabby condition of the property. This is especially true when the ability of poor people to pay (based upon their income) is considered." Other problems included unemployment and underemployment, what residents identified as "rigid segregation in hiring policies" and the "lack of training programs for the skilled labor market, segregation in the trade unions." SCLC's leaders connected these local concerns to the PPC's central demands—a guaranteed job or annual income. Education was also a major issue since the schools remained segregated, and the schools black children attended were overcrowded. The local black schools reportedly lacked new and up-to-date textbooks and athletic and recreation facilities and even "basic essentials such as proper sewage, ventilation, lighting conditions, etc., to the point of being unhealthy conditions for children to learn in."[9] SCLC's organizing efforts in Marks enabled black parents to publicly vent their frustrations with the school's inadequacies and its white administrative staff as local protests emerged alongside preparation for the Mule Train.

Along with local systemic problems, residents complained about federal programs. Local blacks reported that those most in need were not receiving sufficient welfare, with families receiving as little as fifty dollars a month and individuals relying on nine or ten dollars of support each month. Irene Collins, a Marks resident, describes how the shift from free commodities programs to food stamps exacerbated an already grim situation: "During that time you had to buy your food stamps. . . . You paid so much for your food stamp and got so many, but they wasn't free then like they is now. . . . They provide for some, but if you look at, there is some they are providing for that don't really need it, and the needy is going without."[10] With the passage of the Food Stamp Act of 1964, the government began to replace the monthly dispersal of free commodities, which included staples such as powdered milk, eggs, and flour, with food stamps that could be used for a wider range of food items. The problem with the program was that it required a minimum of two dollars to purchase the stamps, which many Mississippians lacked. John Dittmer reports that in 1967 the shift in fifty Mississippi counties "left an estimated 64,000 people who had received free food unable to buy food stamps."[11] While many called for making food stamps available at no cost, those who touted the "culture of poverty" perspective, like Mississippi Congressman Jamie Whitten, argued that giving poor people free food would "destroy character more than you might improve nutrition."[12] This attitude was widespread, and contributed to the problem many Delta families faced with malnutrition and even starvation.

Communicating the extent of poverty throughout the nation was a vital component of the ppc since many middle-class Americans incorrectly assumed that if poor people were unable to provide for themselves, they were receiving what they needed from New Deal–inspired government programs, such as welfare and Social Security. The predominant attitude in the United States, both then and now, was best reflected by the culture of poverty theory and Horatio Alger-type myths that if poor people were suffering, it was due to their own behaviors or lack of effort rather than structural inequalities and racism that prevented them from accessing resources. ppc participants' registration forms and questionnaires reveal that the vast majority of poor people were not receiving social services or federal aid and had no steady income. When asked to fill in their annual income, the overwhelming majority of participants listed none, while a few listed incomes that ranged from a few hundred dollars a year to a high of about $2,000, all of which were well below the national poverty line, which was approximately $3,000 for a family of four in 1968. The participants' responses to questions regarding their access to Social Security benefits, welfare checks, or food stamps were staggering. Only twenty participants of 140 reported that they were receiving any form of Social Security; twenty-five of the 104 respondents received welfare, with six receiving ADC benefits. With no income and very little relief available, only forty-two of 128 participants reported that they could afford the two dollars required to purchase food stamps; the rest had to rely on the insufficient surplus commodities program, which was not even available in some places.[13]

In addition to the registration forms, some participants filled out more extensive questionnaires, painting an extremely stark picture of their lives in the Mississippi Delta in 1968. Out of the approximately 140 questionnaires archived, only forty-three people reported having owned their own home—the key to financial stability in the United States—while eighty-two said they rented; of these, only fifty reported having indoor fixtures and both hot and cold water. Eighty-three respondents indicated that they had at some point been sharecroppers, while forty-two currently lived on white-owned land. The overwhelming majority had never seen a doctor or dentist.[14] Both registration forms and questionnaires indicated that most participants had few if any resources to help them get by.

While many Americans subscribed to "culture of poverty" arguments that suggested that poor people were lazy, apathetic, and thus responsible for remaining stuck in a cycle of poverty, testimony from participants clearly reveals that the white power structure—at the local, state, and federal levels—played an active role in keeping minorities poor. The experience of poor southern blacks was not unique. Government policies at all levels across the nation perpetuated systemic economic and racial inequalities, which is clearly demonstrated by the participation of different ethnoracial groups from across the nation in the PPC. Although different groups had specific needs and complaints that they wanted addressed, all of the participants struggled to receive adequate government assistance, decent housing, consistent food supplies, and other basic needs.[15] Virginia Robinson, a seventy-four-year-old experienced activist from Hattiesburg, who had no income and no hot water or indoor bath fixtures and who received no welfare or Social Security except food stamps, explained how whites had destroyed all that she had worked for: "Once I own my own home in the 40's. I own a farm, stocks, and plenty of land. But the white people taken it away. They killed my cattles, horses, and chickens. And next they said if I didn't move away I would be next. So I was forced to leave everything I owned."[16] Robinson does not provide further explanation of why she lost her property, but local residents report similar occurrences of being thrown off of white-owned land in both the question-naires SCLC collected and in personal testimony.[17]

While much of the data SCLC gathered from local blacks indicated dire need for economic opportunity and improved access and quality of social services, SCLC staff member Leon Hall explained that in addition to improved services, black residents felt that local black control over the administration of federal social programs was essential to combat racially-based inequities in distribution of federal resources: "One of the main questions was how to insure that these jobs and money are given in proportion to the Black population. In regard to this, most Black people want a voice in running these programs at the 'grass roots' level, i.e., they want to have sincere, qualified people from their own ranks who understand their problems, to participate in the administration of the programs, and the decision-making."[18] Some voiced more radical aims, calling for "the possibility of making a demand for reparations as a part of the program" and "the possibility of having petitions for land grants to establish economic bases for Black people to work from." Farm cooperatives were proposed as another way to gain self-determination and economic independence from whites.[19] Many blacks saw economic independence as key to making the other goals of the movement, such as desegregation and voting rights, a reality. Yet, there was little interest among Marks residents in joining the PPC's journey to Washington until local authorities challenged their right to protest.

## THE HIGH SCHOOL PROTEST: LOCAL EVENTS, NATIONAL NEWS

In late April after King's assassination, SCLC organizers Willie Bolden, Jimmie L. Wells, Andrew Marisette, and Margie Hyatt—all in their twenties—arrived in Marks to rally local support for the PPC.[20] Bolden and his staff went to the Quitman County Industrial High School on the morning of May 1 and quickly garnered a crowd of several hundred students eager to participate. Shortly after the crowd gathered, the principal alerted the sheriff, who promptly arrested and charged Bolden with trespassing on school property and disturbing the peace. One of the students present, Samuel McCray, explains the students' response to their principal's overreaction to Bolden's presence: "We felt the high school was our turf. And under normal circumstances, he would have been able to speak."[21] Within minutes of discovering Bolden's arrest, the senior class, which was practicing for graduation ceremonies, created a spontaneous protest with approximately three hundred students and several teachers marching to the county jail to protest.

One of the students observes that while he and others were prepared to go to jail for protesting, they did not expect the physical confrontation with police that ensued outside the jail. McCray recounts: "They waited till they were right up on us. . . . We were crunched over laying down waiting for some tear gas and ready to ride that out. So we really weren't prepared for the Billy clubs; I certainly wasn't. They came over, and literally started beating people, literally just walking right through. And I think that was the only time they stepped out of formation, they just kind of . . . beating everybody that would get in the way."[22] Black residents were stunned after witnessing the unprovoked violent attack on nonviolent demonstrators, which left many protesters injured. Lydia McKinnon, one of the teachers who participated, suffered severe blows. In a later interview, she describes her reasons for protesting and how she was injured: "White folks had the best of everything, and what we blacks were getting was worse than second best, and we were expected to do a good job with hardly anything. So, for that one crazy moment, I stood up for what I knew to be right, and with the butts of their guns and the heels of their boots, they knocked me unconscious for it."[23] Like many other Marks natives, the melee at the courthouse emboldened McKinnon, transforming her from a shy and timid schoolteacher into a courageous civil rights activist.

SCLC leaders quickly responded to the violence and sought to transform frustration and outrage into productive antipoverty activism. That night Ralph Abernathy led a mass meeting at the Eudora AME Zion Church and a lengthy prayer service and singing session at the jail. While law enforcement officials peacefully stood guard and the protest appeared to be nonviolent, a local man, Ned Gathwright, remembers that several marchers were "armed to the teeth," hiding weapons beneath their coats in case another unprovoked attack occurred.[24]

The following day, May 2, between 1,000 and 3,000 marchers, including some from nearby Memphis, joined SCLC and local residents in a third march to the courthouse. With a stronger coalition of activists locked in arms and singing triumphantly and the national media present, law enforcement remained peaceful. The greater numbers and more experienced and well-known protesters, as well as the media's presence, enabled this group to safely inhabit the space of the courthouse lawn with an authority that the smaller group of teachers and students lacked. But the violence at the courthouse also sparked local resistance that only Marks residents could enact. Black families led a boycott of the schools, keeping their children out of school for days, both out of fear and to protest the violent and unprovoked attack against their children and their teachers.[25] The spontaneous walkout, the melee at the courthouse, and the peaceful demonstrations that followed ignited Marks and transformed SCLC's organizing efforts into both a local and national movement.

Many Marks residents agree that the protests at the courthouse and the unprovoked police violence sparked increased interest and participation in the PPC and the Mule Train. According to Marks native and Mule Train leader Bertha Burres Johnson, Bolden's arrest and the violence against non-violent protesters is what sparked interest in the Mule Train: "They were upset then, so you got a lot more people to go then."[26] Samuel McCray concurs: "The incident at the high school probably inspired more folks to get involved than anything else. You had people here that were working here all the time, people engaged in the whole civil rights movement and all that. But the galvanizing force was the fact that you had people who would invade a school and attack children for no other reason than that people don't want to live in poverty anymore, and I think that was at the core."[27] The series of events, originally prompted by the local officials' overreaction to an "outside agitator," led Marks residents not only to join the PPC but also to more vocally protest conditions at home. Bolden's arrest and the violence enacted against peaceful demonstrators at the courthouse highlighted the lack of power poor blacks had in Marks. Doris Shaw Baker declares that the overreaction to SCLC's presence and the violence at the courthouse invigorated the community because it "exposed the poverty, racism, [and] hidden injustices" that plagued Marks.[28] Despite the efforts of longtime local activists, Marks remained highly segregated and a small number of white families dominated both the economic and political systems in the area. The violent reaction to this small act of protest was a breaking point for many Marks residents who had suffered for decades from stark physical segregation and economic exploitation. As one Marks native declared: "Those people there across them tracks—they use a Negro for what they want, but they don't respect him, and here on this side, the Negroes done decided that they ain't gonna take it no more."[29] The combined outrage and sense of possibility for change expressed at the courthouse demonstrations spread quickly and convinced some skeptics to register to participate in the PPC and go to Washington.

The incident at the high school and the local police's response to the courthouse demonstrations enraged many local blacks. Together with the enhanced sense of efficacy that came from the presence of SCLC organizers and the national media, these incidents helped energize local residents and convince them that joining the Poor People's Campaign and working for change at home were worthwhile. A *Washington Post* article titled "The 20th Century Tests Marks, Mississippi," declared that the small Delta town had already experienced a "minor revolution affecting the Negro community to its very core."[30] The *New York Times* and other media outlets covered every detail of the SCLC's stay in Marks. The national media coverage persuaded local people that participating in the PPC might provide the exposure and assistance needed to force local officials to provide better social services.

## TENT CITY

Plantation owners retaliated against workers for any involvement in civil rights activity. According to Roland Freeman, who photographed the Mule Train and Resurrection City for SCLC, after one planter found out SCLC staff had visited a female worker, he returned to her house the following day and, with "shotgun in his hand, kicked open her door, and scared her kids half to death. By the time the SCLC field-workers got there, he had thrown out all this woman's belongings—which consisted of a couple of spreads tied with rags."[31] According to questionnaires, 15 percent of those signed up to participate in the PPC were evicted from their homes on white-owned land.[32] Thus, one of the most immediate needs of the campaign was locating a place to house both local activists, who had been evicted from plantations, and out-of-town activists and media. Like Resurrection City in the nation's capital, the tent city provided safety, lodging, and other necessities for those willing to participate. The tent city would also serve as the site of mass meetings and freedom rallies.[33] A *Newsweek* article insisted that the media coverage had persuaded city officials to accommodate both the press and the activists, at least temporarily. In addition to allowing the PPC to use a forty-four acre industrial park for a tent city, the local white-power elite (horrified at their negative portrayal in the media) offered electricity, water, and chemical toilets for the marchers' campsite and an office with free Cokes for the press—a show of hospitality aimed mainly at speeding the pilgrims on their way.[34] Mayor Howard C. Langford's accommodations, along with his public endorsement of the PPC's "goals but not the methods," infuriated many other local whites who had already called for a curfew for the black activists.[35]

## WHY THEY WENT

The Mule Train, the most theatrical of the PPC's nine regional caravans, not only dramatized the rural poverty that southern blacks experienced, it also displayed the determination and courage of poor people to protest their poverty, challenging culture of poverty depictions of a lazy and apathetic underclass. When photographer Roland Freeman asked a white, middle-class volunteer from Huntsville, Myrna Copeland, whether participants fully comprehended the PPC's goals and purpose, she insisted that they did: "When it comes down to the nitty-gritty of what this campaign is all about, they know more than we do because they've lived through the destitution and the poverty that has caused a movement like this, and when they're put up against the wall, they can tell you why they are going to Washington and can tell it in a much more sorrowful way than we could."[36] Fifty-five-year-old Ms. S. C. Rose Kendrick explained her understanding in an SCLC questionnaire: "Washington is the center of government power and the national government have the money and we are ask for our support we want it right now. Poor People do not get decent job and decent school. They do not get decent health care, do not get decent government and decent police. Poor People do not even get respect as human being. . . . Congressmen, you have the job and you have the money. I want some of it so I can live too."[37] She and others consistently articulated the specific patterns of oppression that had contributed to the cycle of poverty many faced in the region. The questionnaires illustrate the participants' understanding of the issues.

While racism severely limited job opportunities for both sexes, single mothers—the majority of those who joined the Mule Train—faced a unique set of challenges. Bertha Burres Johnson, a twenty-eight-year-old single mother of six and Mule Train leader, explained that she joined the movement to protest for a job and to end racial discrimination in the workplace: "I would like to be able to get a good paying job, so I can take care of my family. The factories won't hire too many black people. We can't get a chance to show our talent."[38] In an SCLC brochure for the PPC, another single mother from Marks described the experience many young mothers shared: "Quitman County is on starvation. I have five children. Don't have a job. Don't have a husband. I get sixty dollars out of the month from welfare and I have to pay my rent, buy food, buy clothes and buy fuel and I am just starving to death. And it's not me by myself. There is a lot of us like this. We have to pay rent for houses with no bath and put on our boots to wade out in back. We done worked all our lives and we are just starving to death. No home fit to live in. I stay up all night. The roaches all night. My children have to stay out half of the night. I'm holding the light over them to help them sleep. Now you know something needs to be done now—not a while—now."[39] While many feared the month-long journey and indefinite stay in unpredictable conditions in Washington, these young mothers recognized the PPC as a unique opportunity to transform their situation and help their local community meet its basic needs.

While some joined the movement to save their families, other young, single women like twenty-one-year-old Genevista Williams saw participating in the PPC as a once in a lifetime opportunity for a free trip full of adventure and excitement. Williams explains, "My reason for going is I might can learn something I don't know and see something I haven't seen before and I think it would be fun to go. . . . I haven't been there before. . . . I hope as many of my friends can go as possible."[40] Most of the people on board the Mule Train

Figure 5 The children of Bertha Johnson at the Mule Train preparation site (*back row*) Brian, Terence, and Nelson; (*front row*) Trudy, Charles Jr., and Brenda Marie. Bertha Johnson emerged as a leader during the Mule Train and rode with her children from Marks, Mississippi, to Resurrection City on the National Mall, Washington, D.C. Photograph © 2010 Roland L. Freeman.

had never traveled beyond their home state, and for the children in particular, the trip was more like a joyride than a social movement.[41] The Mule Train became an exciting journey for the young and old alike, but its fundamental purpose was to improve the participants' economic status.

Many were uncertain about whether the PPC was likely to transform participants' lives. When Roland Freeman asked Myrna Copeland what she expected the participants to gain from the PPC, she responded: "I don't know. I think it's probably a bad year to ask Congress to respond favorably to a movement like this. There are a number of congressmen, particularly liberals and moderates who are up for reelection this November, and putting them on the spot like this is going to be very difficult."[42] Copeland focused on the broader political landscape rather than the potential effects for local communities and argued that the reelection of left-leaning politicians was more important than risking the fallout that might come from trying to enact more fundamental economic changes. Responding to Copeland's skepticism about the potential for the PPC, Freeman questioned why she would participate and what she hoped to gain, to which she responded: "I wish you hadn't asked me that! I think this is something that has to be done. Perhaps this can be looked on as an education for the people of America. I think a lot of Americans just don't realize, are ignorant of how many poor people live in the U.S. . . . . [T]here are a lot of people in the U.S. that are in that same situation, and until we can actually show them the poor, the great numbers of poor people we have in America, they won't be motivated to do something to back Congress to do something in Washington."[43] Although some of the people involved with the PPC were skeptical about its potential for enacting a major redistribution of wealth, the Mule Train served as a powerful tool to communicate to the nation that poverty existed and to expose the conditions the rural poor experienced on a daily basis. It also enabled the poor to articulate their understandings of citizenship.

## CHRONICLING THE CARAVAN

On May 13, as the PPC launched the national campaign by breaking ground to build Resurrection City on the National Mall, approximately one hundred poor people and fifteen SCLC staff set off in seventeen mule-drawn covered wagons. Due to multiple rain delays and inexperience assembling covered wagons and harnessing and shoeing mules, the Mule Train was almost ten days behind schedule.[44] The two lead mules, Bullet and Ada, steered the Mule Train along the first day of its journey as it headed from Marks to nearby Batesville. The following day, the caravan continued south on to Courtland, five miles south of Batesville, and on May 16 reached Grenada, where SCLC had been active. After spending a few days in Grenada, the Mule Train picked up additional Mississippi participants as it headed through Duck Hill, Winona, Kilmichael, Europa, Starkville, and Columbus between May 20 and May 25. The Mule Train stopped for two days in Reform, Alabama, before heading into its first city, Tuscaloosa, on May 28, where the caravan remained for a couple of days. The caravan traveled on through Cottondale and Bessemer in the last days of May and headed into Birmingham on June 2. The group left Birmingham on June 5 and traveled on to Anniston, another city known for violent reactions to civil rights activism, such as the 1961 fire-bombing of one of the Freedom Riders' buses. After spending four days in Anniston, the Mule Train left for Georgia.

The group included more than forty women and twenty children, whose ages ranged from eight months to over seventy years old; most participants' were between seventeen and thirty. Each family had a wagon, and some large families received two wagons. Two cars and a truck provided portable toilets, food, and the participants' belongings. Dealing with the forces of nature made Wagon Master Willie Bolden and other participants compare their experience to that of pioneers: "We used to just sit down late in the evening and talk about what life must have been like for the pioneers going out West and how they traveled in mule trains and similar situations. I mean, I know that for us it was raining and cold, and in almost every town that we went into, we didn't sleep in hotels."[45] Photographer Roland Freeman recounts that after traveling all day, there was still much to do each evening: "Food would be inventoried, distributed, and prepared; mules would be watered and fed; wagons and equipment would be inspected and repaired; passengers would access their personal belongings; children would play; and staff would organize rallies, prayer meetings, and community support. All in all, it was an awesome amount of daily logistics to attend to more than a hundred people and their travel across the South."[46] Much of this daily work fell on the shoulders of the women on board the Mule Train.

Despite the fact that their names rarely appeared in the press, several women were responsible for making the Mule Train function on a daily basis. For instance, Margorie Hyatt kept records of supplies, Faye Porche,

SCLC's financial administrator, managed the caravan's expenses, while Marks native Bertha Burres Johnson—with her six children in tow—kept track of the ever-fluctuating number of participants.[47] Having worked as a secretary for local civil rights groups, Burres Johnson had some experience with organizing activists, so SCLC leaders placed her in charge of tracking and making sure participants had something to eat, somewhere to sleep, and medical care if needed.

For some, traveling in mule-drawn wagons was too much to handle, so SCLC paid for bus tickets for any participants who wanted to return home or go somewhere else, but the majority of participants withstood the harsh conditions and made the entire journey.[48] Almost thirty years later, Willie Bolden explained how the community that formed among Mule Train participants and the spirit of unity they found with the local people they encountered propelled them along the long and arduous trip: "I think that it was because of unity and commitment, and that we got folks to understand that this was not going to be an easy journey. It had never been done before. We didn't know of anyone in our time that had undertaken such a task. We were going to have to stick together. . . . I would solicit help from the local communities at these meetings. We were received well in almost every community we stopped in. They were poor folks just like us."[49] Some aboard the Mule Train slept in their wagons or under the stars, but many stayed in the churches or homes of local people along their path. SCLC staff encouraged each local community they worked in to rally support and to ensure food and lodging for the poverty pilgrims whenever and wherever possible. Some of these accommodations were better than what many of the participants had back home.

Several Marks residents recounted the generosity of people along their travels. Bertha Burres Johnson remembers: "The first family gave us a mattress to go on the bottom of the wagon. . . . [W]e got radios, TVs, cameras, any of those little appliances they didn't want, they gave us food, they gave us toys for the children."[50] Many acquired not only food and lodging, but also books, clothes, and even money. The PPC organizers hired a truck to transport the collected goods from the local communities the Mule Train encountered to Quitman County. Hosea Williams also sent a Western Union telegram to the Fifteenth Annual Conference on Marketing and Public Relations in the Negro Market asking for their help developing a "Poor People's Store" in Marks, Mississippi, based on the donations of furniture, farming equipment, school supplies, medical supplies, clothing, shoes, and nonperishable foods acquired along the Mule Train's journey.[51]

Many people were interested in witnessing the spectacle of the Mule Train and experiencing the carnivalesque atmosphere it sparked. Hundreds of rural blacks, and at times a smaller contingent of whites, were scattered along the highways to show their support for the campaign or simply witness the most exciting thing in town. Most were spectators in awe at the sight of the mule-drawn covered wagons moving along a busy highway, but others were galvanized to form "emergency groups" to feed, clothe, and house the poverty pilgrims. Some formed support organizations that became local, grass-roots organizations.[52]

The participants used the canvasses covering the wagons to communicate their message to the local people hovering along the highway and to the nation through nightly television coverage. One asked, "Which is Better? Send a Man to Moon or Feed Him on Earth?," while another proudly declared, "Everybody's Got a Right To Work, Eat, Live."[53] Others invoked common movement slogans like "I Have a Dream," "We Shall Overcome," and "Freedom." One slogan reminded southerners that their protest was grounded in their faith and exhibited the true teachings of Christianity; it read, "Don't Laugh, Folks: Jesus was a Poor Man."[54] Alabama activist John Cashin, who located and paid for the mules and covered wagons, was also responsible for many of the Mule Train's messages, such as "Stop the War, Feed the Poor" and "Jesus Was a Marcher Too." The Mule Train enabled the participants to interact with local people across their path and persuade them to help fight poverty. As John Cashin explains, the Mule Train not only served as a traveling billboard for the PPC across the South but also as a national advertisement since members of the national media followed the caravan along its journey and televised images of the Mule Train to the nation five or six times a day.[55]

The Mule Train served as a dramatic symbol of the limits on poor people's physical and economic mobility, while demonstrating the strength and determination of the participants to endure unpredictable and arduous circumstances due to such outdated transportation. Each night as the major network news televised images of the Mule Train, viewers witnessed the dramatic contrast between the modern day transportation systems and the mule-drawn covered wagons, as well as the will of the protesters to travel in this manner. Bertha Burres Johnson recounts that the Mule Train was both exciting and dangerous: "We were going down this slope, this hill. I guess it was a

Figure 6  The Mule Train in Batesville, Mississippi, on a rest stop the second day.
Photograph © 2010 Roland L. Freeman.

downgrade about two to three miles. Behind us was this eighteen-wheeler; he had to breakdown. It was exciting to see this eighteen-wheeler behind a mule train."[56] The image of an eighteen-wheeler stuck behind a train of mule-drawn wagons dramatized the sharp contradiction of rural poverty in a wealthy, modern, industrialized nation. This image also indicated the bravery required of the participants to travel in rickety covered wagons across the Deep South and leave the familiarity of home, despite its conditions, in order to improve their lives.

While there were some risks involved and sacrifices to be made, many participants embraced the journey. Most of the participants had never traveled beyond their home state, so the Mule Train provided local poor people both with an opportunity to protest their condition, as well as a chance to travel and temporarily escape their daily lives. And despite the difficulties of traveling in covered wagons, the Mule Train participants developed a strong camaraderie along their journey, received a free trip to Washington, D.C., courtesy of sclc, enjoyed three square meals a day, and experienced little trouble from local white authorities and almost no violence.

Unlike some other civil rights actions where state troopers prevented marchers from proceeding, the troopers escorted the Mule Train through both Mississippi and Alabama to prevent any problems that might garner media attention and federal intervention, perhaps as part of the new "southern strategy." Moreover, in the wake of riots that had swept the nation's cities after King's assassination, local authorities were more interested in getting the Mule Train along its journey and out of their state than obstructing the caravan's trip. In addition to the local police escorts, extensive surveillance of the Mule Train occurred at the local, state, and federal levels. In Mississippi alone twenty-six uniformed officers and three plainclothes investigators from the state police, fourteen FBI agents, and one supervisor along with the network of informants kept the Mule Train under around-the-clock surveillance.[57] The caravan did face some resistance along its journey, particularly at its starting and ending points. Wagon master Willie Bolden recalls how local whites in Marks "would drive by blowing their horns, purposely trying to spook the mules and us," causing the mules to run off the road, which resulted in some minor injuries.[58] Along with harassment from white civilians, there were several encounters with local law enforcement. On the first day of the Mule Train's journey, SCLC staff member Andrew W. Marrisett was arrested for "obstructing a highway when he refused to move a car," but after Bolden threatened to protest at the local jail, officials quickly released Marrisett, who had indicated that his arrest was not about the car but resulted from an altercation with an officer who called him "boy."[59]

While the Mule Train traveled relatively incident-free throughout Mississippi and Alabama, when it reached Georgia on June 13, the caravan confronted greater opposition. Georgia's Governor Lester Maddox commanded state troopers to block the entrance to Interstate 20 and arrested sixty-seven participants when the caravan arrived outside Bremen, Georgia, on June 13. Though Mule Train leaders refused Maddox's offer to transport the group on flatbed trucks or provide an escort along an alternate path, after ninety minutes of debate Sheriff Caude Abercrombie and Wagon Master Willie Bolden reached a compromise that allowed the Mule Train to use the emergency lane of Interstate 20 between 7:00 AM and 7:00 PM.[60]

When they finally arrived in Atlanta on June 15, participants had traveled approximately five hundred miles aboard mule-drawn covered wagons, averaging about twenty-five miles per day. The participants spent several days visiting civil rights landmarks in Atlanta and then boarded trains for Alexandria, Virginia. After experiencing several delays for their initial departure and further weather delays, SCLC leaders decided that the Mule Train participants needed to take trains to Washington so that they could be in the nation's capital for the PPC's highlight, Solidarity Day, which was scheduled for June 19, 1968.

Once they arrived in the D.C. area on June 18 some Mule Train participants joined friends and family who were already living in Resurrection City. However, Resurrection City was overcrowded at the time with swelled numbers for the upcoming Solidarity Day, so most Mule Train participants stayed at a nearby Methodist church center. Each day SCLC coordinated buses to pick up Mule Train participants so that they could be involved in the day's events.[61]

While the Mule Train was just arriving in the nation's capital, the other eight caravans—the Freedom Train (a caravan of buses from the South that carried predominantly young black men who were responsible for helping construct the temporary city), the Southern Caravan (which included blacks from across the South), the Northeastern Caravan, the Midwestern Caravan, the Indian Trail, and three Western Caravans—had arrived weeks before and were already settled into their shanties in Resurrection City or in their bunks at the nearby Hawthorne School. After constructing the city, participants engaged in a range of activities that included daily protests at a variety of government buildings, as well as enjoying all that Resurrection City had to offer—food, clothing, health care, education, childcare, and entertainment.

On June 19, SCLC reassembled the wagons and harnessed the mules with the hopes of having the Mule Train enter the city to join with the some 50,000 people who traveled to Washington, D.C., for the PPC's showcase march, Solidarity Day. Intended to replicate the diverse participation and peaceful protest of the 1963 March on Washington, it ultimately had only a quarter of the participation of the earlier march. Although the Mule Train was supposed to have been one of the highlights of the Solidarity Day celebration, at the last minute SCLC leader Andrew Young informed the press that the Mule Train "would have caused too much 'confusion' in the march."[62] While the Mule Train did not end up being a central focus of the Solidarity Day celebration as the organizers had intended, even its short journey from Alexandria into the nation's capital made big news. *Washington Post* reporter Paul W. Valentine described the tension between the protesters and D.C. residents sitting in traffic, and law enforcement trying to manage the scene: "Traffic was tied up behind the mule train as Alexandria, Arlington County, and Park

Police shepherded the group along in the curb lane on the northbound side of the Parkway. The train moved at a steady gait except at two points—once when a wheel rim broke off a wagon and had to be fixed and later when an auto driver behind the last wagon began shouting angrily and found himself surrounded by about 35 youths from the train. The youths dared him to get out of his car. A Park Police sergeant moved in, dispersed the youths and directed the driver into the open lane around the mule train."[63] Roland Freeman's photographs of the Mule Train blocking traffic in the nation's capital reveal the sharp contrast of the mule-drawn covered wagons alongside the sleek 1960s cars on a busy modern highway. The image exemplifies the contradiction of poverty in a nation of plenty, while illustrating the effect the Mule Train had on the nation's capital—it literally stopped people in their tracks! While many D.C. residents might have seen both the Mule Train and Resurrection City as nuisances, both elements of the PPC were successful in terms of making both local people and the nation pay attention to the protest and see the nation's poverty.

When the Mule Train participants finally settled in at Resurrection City after the Solidarity Day events on June 19, most of the participants agree that some of their unity and commitment deteriorated. After weeks of rain, the temporary shantytown had been transformed into a muddy pit and most of the late-arriving Mule Train participants were dispersed, making the unity experienced on the caravan difficult to sustain. Bertha Burres Johnson recounts: "Everybody on the Mule Train was more together, much more together than in Resurrection City. . . . There was all kind of trouble there. As soon as we got there, we got put out."[64] Wagon master Willie Bolden agreed: "Well, as I recall, I don't think they lost hope. . . . The truth of the matter was that we really hadn't gotten a lot of direction from senior SCLC staff. People just kind of got scattered, where before we had been together for some forty to fifty days, traveling down the highway through Mississippi, Alabama, and Georgia. Then, all of a sudden, when we got our destination, people just got scattered."[65] Congress rejected the PPC's appeal for an extension for their permit to use the National Mall shortly after the Mule Train arrived, so these participants had a very short stay in Resurrection City. Though most returned to their hometowns, some used their free one-way bus ticket to move somewhere new. Several of those who returned home feared the consequences of having participated in the movement. One young woman from Marks, Minnie Lee Hills, exclaimed "I'm afraid to go back there to live; they might be mad at me for coming here."[66] Other participants were willing to face these risks, and, for many, the journey resulted in positive changes.

## REFLECTING ON THE JOURNEY

While the thousands of activists who participated in the PPC failed to sway the nation to provide the poor with a guaranteed job or income or meet a myriad of the movement's other demands, many individuals' lives changed as a result of their participation in the PPC and the Mule Train. Marks residents recount how the local participation in this national movement led to increased access to social services and more job opportunities. Some emphasized practical goods they obtained as a result of participating, while others commented on how participating in the campaign fostered lasting and empowering psychological transformation. Participants' interactions with other poor people of color transformed their views of the world and inspired some to become lifelong activists.

Perhaps one of the most significant and dramatic changes that occurred as a result of mass local participation in the PPC and media coverage of the movement in Marks was a shift in the dynamic between the white power structure and local blacks. In 2006, Burres Johnson recounted how the explosion of local activism and participation in this national antipoverty movement threatened the local white power structure, prompting them to make improvements in local services: "For me, it was quite an experience. And when I got back here, I didn't have any problem with anyone. I went to see the health people about a health problem that I needed assistance and they was very nice to me because I guess they were afraid not to be because they thought I would call the SCLC staff if they weren't."[67] Her role as a leader on the Mule Train and as a staff member for SCLC might account for the reaction to her as an individual, but Burres Johnson explains that the changes that occurred affected local blacks countywide regardless of whether or not they actually participated in the PPC. These transformations resulted from a combination of local people's activism and participation in the Mule Train and PPC, the media's coverage of events in Marks, and the black population's ties to SCLC and the national campaign.

The collective activism displayed along the Mule Train and during the PPC's national stage inspired the small Delta community and its welfare services to help participants once they returned from Washington. A local church raised money for Augusta Denson, so she and her family, who had been kicked off a plantation for her participation in the PPC, received a new house shortly after returning to Marks.[68] But she agrees that the PPC contributed not only to individual lives, but also made substantial changes throughout Quitman County. Denson explains that the local movement and Marks residents' participation in the national stage of the PPC improved both job opportunities and welfare administration in the area: "It was a good thing they did. At that time in Mississippi there wasn't no good jobs, and they started bringing the good jobs. We got one factory, the other's closed now, but one's still open. Before that, we didn't have no jobs except for working in private homes as domestics. . . . [P]eople on welfare, they wasn't giving you more than ten or fifteen dollars, that's all you'd get. But when we went up there and explained it to them, it did go up. It went up to forty, and then it started going up and up. . . . I didn't get no welfare until I come back. . . . I really think it had something to do with it. They would turn you down; they would treat us so bad at the welfare office."[69] Before joining the PPC, Denson was not receiving any Social Security for her children after their father's death. Using information she gained from participating in the movement and with assistance from local activists, she learned how to navigate the system and access available resources. Bertha Burres Johnson attributes the increase in access to social services to the mass participation of Marks residents in the PPC and the information they gained while in Washington: "Because then people began to learn about social security and food stamps because everybody didn't know about that, just a few them knew that they could apply for food stamps, apply for social security, that they could get dental care. It was just that way. People were here, and they were just ignorant to everything that they had a right to. And by me going up there, it opened up my life to where I could share with them."[70]

The psychological transformation that occurred for many PPC participants has been lasting. In 1997, Bertha Burres Johnson recounted how joining the movement not only changed her economic situation, but also transformed her ability to stand up for herself in all of her relationships with men: "I gained the courage to speak up for myself. I got married young, you see, and the first time I spoke up to my husband I almost had a nervous breakdown. He was not very secure and had trouble coping with life, so he sort of dominated me—you understand what I mean? SCLC taught me that there is no harm in speaking up. That's the only way you can let people know what you think and feel."[71] Dora Lee Collins from Clarksdale, Mississippi, expressed a similar change in how she related to her employer after going to Washington: "I really enjoyed the whole experience and I learned what we could do if we stuck together. I never marched like that before. I saw my government turn us down. But the experience lifted my spirits and changed the way I think forever. I got back here and I didn't say 'yes sa boss' anymore."[72] Doris Shaw Baker, another female leader, remembers the Mule Train as "the most soulful experience I've ever encountered. The old folks had so much soul." Baker attributes her decision to become a lifelong activist not only to the mentorship she received from other activists and the skills she acquired as a protestor by participating in the PPC, but also to the courage the Mule Train inspired in her during protests and confrontations with police.[73]

Along with abandoning any form of deference to their partners or to southern whites, many women experienced a new sense of universal humanism. Augusta Denson insists that her participation in the movement made "life better in a lot of ways." She recounts that she not only received a new home from sympathetic neighbors after returning home with no place to go, she also learned "how to treat people, too." She declared, "I ain't got no hatred in my heart. We came together as a big family, white, black, Mexican, Puerto Rican. All of us marched together, hand in hand."[74] For the first time, Denson and many other southern blacks recognized that other minority groups also suffered the effects of poverty. While blacks, Chicanos, Appalachian whites, and American Indians all had particular needs rooted in their unique historical experiences in the United States, all of these groups shared the experience of economic exploitation, sometimes exacerbated by racial discrimination. The PPC enabled participants to recognize their shared oppression and propose national solutions that would help all of the nation's poor.

This generation of female activists, who are now in their sixties and seventies, agree that the PPC and the Mule Train transformed their lives and contributed to significant improvements in Quitman County. The U.S. Census for 1959 and for 1969 support the testimony of Marks's residents, demonstrating that the black population in Quitman County experienced a measure of improvement in their economic status within this decade. In 1959, 76 percent of families in Quitman County were living under the poverty line, which at that time was $3,000 for a family of four. While only 42 percent of white families were living in poverty, a staggering 94 percent of black families in Quitman County had fallen below the poverty level. By 1969, the total number of families living below the poverty line fell to 64 percent, with 71 percent of black families and 52 percent of white families falling below the poverty level.[75] While the PPC is not wholly responsible for these improvements, the combination of PPC-related activism and the efforts of other antipoverty campaigns, in particular the government's War on Poverty, contributed to blacks' economic gains.[76] Many participants have touted the positive effects the PPC and the Mule Train had on Quitman County, but they all bemoan the persistent racism and economic inequality in the area.

## MARKS TODAY AND MEMORIALIZING THE MULE TRAIN

Despite its status as one of the poorest towns in the poorest county in the nation in 1968, Marks was once the cultural and economic hub of the county. Today, the small Delta town remains an economic disaster. In fact, the population of Quitman County has shrunk by over half, from 21,019 in 1960 to just 8,724 in 2008, with the county experiencing a 13.8 percent decline since 2000.[77] While it is no longer the poorest county in the nation, the people of Quitman County are still suffering.[78] The rise of a post-industrial, post-agricultural service economy has continued to disproportionately affect Marks's black population. While the percentage of people living below the poverty line has dropped to approximately 30 percent overall, with the black poverty rate at approximately 40 percent, the county still falls behind both the state and the national averages. The median income in Quitman County is $24,144, which is over 50 percent lower than the state of Mississippi's median of $36,656 and over 100 percent lower than the national median income of $49,133.[79] The shift to a service economy has led to a dearth of both jobs and capital in this community.

While a system of complete domination has crumbled, racism persists. Samuel McCray explains, "There's a real resistance. It's not hostile in terms of people calling people names anymore. We've gotten sophisticated, so now people are real nice about it."[80] According to McCray, some churches have voluntarily integrated, but desegregating the schools is an ongoing struggle. By 1975, although the vast majority of black students in Quitman County were attending public schools, most white students had fled to private academies (where they remain into the twenty-first century). McCray explains that this unwillingness to desegregate has left both blacks and whites with economic problems and inadequate educations: "You've got white people in this county probably at the numbers of black that live in poverty. It's high. Some are probably more so, but they will struggle to keep their kids in private schools that academically are not performing any better and in many cases worse."[81] A lack of jobs and local businesses in Marks and the persistence of racism have left both blacks and whites with little economic opportunity.[82]

Some of Marks's black residents have sought to revitalize the local economy by promoting tourism based on the town's participation in the Mule Train and Poor People's Campaign, but others question whether Marks has an economic future in a post-industrial, post-agricultural service economy. The irony of promoting the town's involvement in an anti-poverty movement to promote economic viability is hard to escape. Samuel McCray explains that garnering support from Marks's white residents to memorialize the Mule Train has been a struggle; local whites have even protested the small billboard posted at the town's entrance that designates it as the home of the Mule Train. While using Marks's participation in this antipoverty campaign to promote tourism remains contentious, many black residents insist on preserving the past for younger generations. In October of 1997 during the planning stages for the thirtieth anniversary of the PPC, Bertha Burres Johnson explained: "Most young people around here today don't think that something like the Mule Train leaving here really happened. But I am really excited about folks knowing our history and that we did something that a lot of people thought couldn't be done."[83] As the fortieth anniversary of the PPC and the Mule Train has come in conjunction with the worst economic recession in recent history, the Mississippi Delta has again become a focus for antipoverty activism.

More recently, the Southern Christian Leadership Conference joined forces with Antoinette Harrell and Ines Soto Palmarin, leaders of an antipoverty organization based out of Louisiana and Mississippi called the Gathering of Hearts, to relaunch the Poor People's Campaign. Harrell and Soto Palamarin led poverty tours in Quitman County throughout the spring and summer of 2009 to bring attention to the problems Mississippi Deltans continue to face. They convinced SCLC to join in their efforts, and in addition to the poverty tours, held public hearings at which both adults and children from Lambert, Mississippi, and the surrounding area testified to the conditions they were living in and detailing their basic needs.[84] The poverty hearings on June 19, 2009, the forty-first anniversary of the PPC's Solidarity March, were followed by a march to the state capitol in Jackson, Mississippi, which approximately 1,000 people attended, including two notable civil rights activists who integrated two of the South's largest universities, James Meredith and Amelia Boynton Robinson. SCLC interim president Rev. Byron Clay announced plans to take a group of poor people to Washington, D.C., in October of 2009 to confront Congress with the issue of poverty, but the trip never occurred after the minimal turnout for the protest in Mississippi and increasing conflict within SCLC.[85] While the 1968 Poor People's Campaign took place in a relatively positive economic environment, this latest effort has occurred during the nation's worst economic period since the Great Depression, signaling the fact that even in a harsh economic climate, the poor remain invisible. Therefore, it seems apparent that connecting the local conditions and protests with a larger national movement is necessary in order for a renewed Poor People's Campaign to gain sufficient attention from the government to take action. While the original PPC was highly critiqued for taking the poor to the nation's capital rather than letting legislators visit the pockets of poverty, the challenge of making poverty visible and of generating a social movement strong enough to prompt systemic change still remains.

Typically, historians have dismissed the 1968 Poor People's Campaign because it failed to enact the proposed economic bill of rights, the centerpiece of which was national legislation that guaranteed citizens a job or minimum income. While the movement did not achieve these ambitious legislative goals, it was a success for many of the individuals who took part in the campaign and prompted more national organizing for many of the groups involved, signaling the emergence of the Chicano and American Indian movements. Resurrection City and the caravans, particularly the Mule Train, did display American poverty for the nation, and the world, to see. The campaign exposed the hypocrisy of a wealthy nation that boasts a classless society while its poor are typically hidden from sight. In the short-term, the PPC also provided poor people with a gamut of services normally unavailable—three square meals a day, shelter, clothing, childcare, health care, education, and information about access to services back home. They also received a free trip to the nation's capital, the opportunity to see some of the most popular performing acts of the era, and the chance to confront their government and demand they receive help. In addition, participants gained a number of intangible goods from their involvement in the movement, such as the pride and confidence that comes from protesting for your rights, the camaraderie that both activism and travel engender, and the gratification that they did something to try to improve their condition. Marks residents speak to both the initial concrete reforms they saw as a result of their participation in the PPC and the Mule Train and the limitations of this success in the years since. Here, the local and national remain intertwined; the failure to achieve the national antipoverty agenda has made lasting change at the local level difficult if not impossible.

While scholars have typically ignored or dismissed the national Poor People's Campaign, those that have studied the local movement in Marks have used different criteria for assessing the value of the campaign and have, overall, produced much more positive discussions of its effects and its overall significance. Despite his initial skepticism about the goals and tactics of the movement, photographer Roland Freeman's overall assessment of the movement changed after conducting interviews with participants. Rather than being the last gasp of the civil rights movement, Freeman declares: "It irreversibly changed the terms of reference and the agenda for change in the United States by incorporating, and then making inseparable, the economic and political dimensions of poverty in America. It also manifested the requirement that the ongoing struggle reach across racial and ethnic lines, and provided an arena to accelerate the process of coalition building." But Freeman also recognized how fragile and temporary these alliances could be and, like others involved in the PPC and in the Mule Train, continues to have mixed feelings about the movement. In his own tribute to the Mule Train and PPC, he asks, "Why then does the Poor People's Campaign still seem so amorphous, and why do I—and seemingly many others with whom I spoke—feel so ambivalent about the experience?" He answers, "Perhaps it is because the work that began then is still unfinished thirty years later."[86]

If we include in the civil rights historiography those movements that exposed how racism, sexism, and regional exploitation have led to the cyclical poverty that people of color continue to face in disproportionate numbers, then we must acknowledge that the struggle for economic and racial equality is unfinished. While there were many civil rights campaigns that preceded the PPC that demanded both economic and racial equality, as Freeman suggests, the PPC solidified the connection between the two, in part due to the fact that a multiracial alliance united to demonstrate their shared suffering from poverty. The PPC complicates our understanding of SCLC by demonstrating that the organization was committed to combating not only racial inequality, but also the economic injustice to which it is connected. The movement also challenges "culture of poverty" arguments about the apathy and disorganization of the poor by demonstrating the willingness of thousands of poor people from a wide range of ethnoracial and geographic backgrounds to leave their homes and travel to the nation's capital for weeks at a time to protest for better living conditions.

Despite its status as the first multiracial, national, antipoverty campaign of the era, the PPC and its Mule Train have largely been ignored. While recent civil rights scholarship has included intensely local studies, we need to do more to connect the history of individual local movements with the national civil rights movement. The Mule Train—a social movement literally on the move—allows us to study activism simultaneously on the local, regional, and national scales and demonstrates the interconnectedness between these different levels of activism. The national stage of the PPC would not have been possible had hundreds of local organizations not mobilized their communities and had thousands of poor people not decided to make the trip to D.C. to protest. Yet the local changes experienced in Marks and in other places around the nation would likely not have occurred without the national exposure the PPC gave to the local economic and racial injustice people suffered in poverty pockets throughout the nation. The effects of the Mule Train and the PPC on local people demonstrate the importance of linking local grass-roots campaigns with the broader national movements when assessing the effectiveness and significance of activism at all levels.

## NOTES

1. Lawrence Lackey, *Marks, Martin, and the Mule Train* (Jackson, Miss.: Town Square Books, Inc., 1998), 17.

2. Ralph David Abernathy, *And the Walls Came Tumbling Down: An Autobiography* (New York: Harper & Row Publishers, 1989), 413.

3. See Abernathy, *And the Walls Came Tumbling Down*, 415. For LBJ's response to the PPC, see David Garrow, *Bearing the Cross: Martin Luther King, Jr. and the Southern Christian Leadership Conference* (New York: Vintage Books, 1958), 595. For the responses from several senators reported on by the press, see "A Threat of Anarchy in Nation's Capital," *U.S. News and World Report*, May 20, 1968, 47–49; and Milton Viorst, "Martin Luther King Intends to Tie the City in Knots this Spring," *Washingtonian* (February 1968), Martin Luther King, Jr. Center for Nonviolent Social Change, King Library and Archives, Files of the Southern Christian Leadership Conference, Box 178, Folder 9 (hereafter cited as F9, B178, SCLC Papers, KL). For resistance from King's staff, see Henry

Hampton and Steve Fayer, eds., *Voices of Freedom: An Oral History of the Civil Rights Movement from the 1950s to the 1980s* (New York: Bantam Books, 1991), 455.

4. Martin Luther King Jr., "Remaining Awake Through a Great Revolution" (Delivered at the National Cathedral, Washington, D.C., on March 31, 1968). *Congressional Record*, April 9, 1968.

5. For more on the politicization process see Jeanne Theoharis and Komozi Woodard, eds., *Groundwork: Local Black Freedom Movements in America* (New York: New York University Press), 7.

6. See Charles Fager, *Uncertain Resurrection: The Poor People's Washington Campaign* (Michigan: William B. Eerdmans Publishing Company, 1969); Robert T. Chase, "Class Resurrection: The Poor People's Campaign of 1968 and Resurrection City," *Essays in History* 40 (1998). The following are just a small spattering of the numerous responses from the press condemning the campaign: "'Poor March' on Washington: A City Braced for Trouble," *U.S. News and World Report* (May 20, 1968): 11, 47–49; "Insurrection City," *Time*, June 14, 1968; Tom Kahn, "Why the Poor People's Campaign Failed," *Commentary* (September 1968): 50–55.

7. Lackey, *Marks, Martin, and the Mule Train*, 1.

8. Letter from Cottonreader to Williams, February 12, 1968; F9, B178, SCLC Papers, KL. It is unclear whether these individuals lost their jobs and were therefore put off the plantation, or whether they were thrown off the property as a result of political action.

9. Leon Hall, SCLC project director, Grenada, Mississippi, letter to Hosea Williams, SCLC field director, February 21, 1968; F9, B178, SCLC Papers, KL.

10. Irene Collins, interview by the author, Marks, Mississippi, September 1, 2006.

11. John Dittmer, *Local People: The Struggle for Civil Rights in Mississippi* (Urbana: University of Illinois Press, 1994), 386.

12. Quoted in Dittmer, *Local People*, 386.

13. While there are some registration forms from participants from other areas of the nation, the vast majority of those archived are participants from the Mississippi Delta, and primarily from Marks. See F4, F5, B181, SCLC Papers, KL.

14. Like the registration forms, the questionnaires archived primarily depict the social status of black Mississippians who lived in the Delta; F4, F5, F6, F7, B181, SCLC Papers, KL.

15. For more on the government policies that perpetuated inequality for all of these groups, see Ira Katznelson, *When Affirmative Action Was White: An Untold History of Racial Inequality in Twentieth-Century America* (New York: W. W. Norton, 2005); Thomas J. Sugrue, *The Origins of the Urban Crisis: Race and Inequality in Postwar Detroit* (Princeton, N.J.: Princeton University Press, 1996); and Thomas J. Sugrue, *Sweet Land of Liberty: The Forgotten Struggle for Civil Rights in the North* (New York: Random House, 2008).

16. F6, B181, SCLC Papers, KL.

17. Of the 131 who responded to the question asking if they had been "put off white people's land" only twenty-one answered that they had. F4, F5, F6, F7, B181, SCLC Papers, KL.

18. Leon Hall, SCLC project director, Grenada, Mississippi, to Hosea Williams, field director, February 21, 1968; F9, B178, SCLC Papers, KL.

19. Ibid.

20. Lackey, *Marks, Martin, and the Mule Train,* 21–22.

21. Samuel McCray, interview by the author, Marks, Mississippi, September 1, 2006.

22. Ibid.

23. Roland L. Freeman, *The Mule Train: A Journey of Hope Remembered* (Nashville: Rutledge Hill Press, 1998), 100.

24. Lackey, *Marks, Martin, and the Mule Train,* 41.

25. Ibid., 49, 53.

26. Bertha Burres Johnson, interview by Roland Freeman, May 14, 1968. See Freeman, *The Mule Train,* 114.

27. Samuel McCray, interview by the author.

28. Doris Shaw Baker, interview by the author, Marks, Mississippi, September 2, 2006.

29. Robert Maynard, "The 20th Century Tests Marks, Mississippi," *Washington Post,* Sunday, May 5, 1968.

30. Ibid.

31. Freeman, *The Mule Train,* 122.

32. F4, F5, F6, F7, B181, SCLC Papers, KL.

33. Freeman, *The Mule Train,* 96.

34. "We're on Our Way," *Newsweek,* May 6, 1968, 30–32. The campsite the article refers to is the site for Tent City.

35. Walter Rugaber, "Mississippi Mayor Backs Goals of March of Poor," *New York Times,* May 4, 1968.

36. Myrna Copeland, interview by Roland Freeman. See Freeman, *The Mule Train,* 123.

37. F20, B180, SCLC Papers, KL.

38. Ibid.

39. F19, B179, SCLC Papers, KL.

40. F20, B180, SCLC Papers, KL.

41. See Bertha Burres Johnson, interview by the author, Marks, Mississippi, September 2, 2006; and Augusta Denson, interview by the author, Marks, Mississippi, September 2, 2006. These women provide details on their children's experiences on the Mule Train and in D.C.

42. Myrna Copeland, interview by Roland Freeman. See Freeman, *The Mule Train,* 122.

43. Ibid.

44. Most of the delays were due to a lack of preparation or inclement weather, but

Bolden charged a Marks police officer with cutting the corral fence shortly before dawn on May 12, enabling approximately thirty mules to wander off, further postponing the mission. See "30 Mules in March Back After Fleeing Through Cut Fence," *New York Times*, May 13, 1968.

45. Freeman, *The Mule Train*, 126.

46. Ibid., 38–39, 57.

47. Freeman, *The Mule Train*, 126.

48. Bertha Burres Johnson, interview by the author.

49. Willie Bolden, interview by Roland Freeman. See Freeman, *The Mule Train*, 127.

50. Bertha Burres Johnson, interview by the author.

51. F2, B177, SCLC Papers, KL.

52. Bertha Burres Johnson, interview by the author.

53. Freeman, *The Mule Train*, 41.

54. Ibid., 34, 42, 45, 49.

55. John Cashin's prepared comments, February 9, 1998, Freeman, *The Mule Train*, 124.

56. Bertha Burres Johnson, interview by the author; see also Freeman, *The Mule Train*, 112.

57. Gerald D. McKnight, *The Last Crusade: Martin Luther King, Jr., the F.B.I. and the 1968 Poor People's Campaign* (Boulder: Westview Press, 1998), 97. McKnight makes an important contribution by outlining how the government, the FBI in particular, surveyed, infiltrated, and disrupted the Poor People's Campaign, as well as the Memphis Sanitation Workers' Strike. He provides significant details about the PPC's inner workings in the process, but his focus remains on explaining why the movement failed.

58. Freeman, *The Mule Train*, 127–28.

59. Ibid., 104.

60. "Georgia Yields on March Mule Train," *Washington Post*, June 15, 1968.

61. Freeman, *The Mule Train*, 68.

62. "After an 1,100-Mile Trip, Mule Train Misses Rally," *New York Times*, June 20, 1968.

63. "Rickety Mule Train Plods in to Wait for March," *Washington Post*, June 19, 1968.

64. Bertha Burres Johnson, interview by the author.

65. Freeman, *The Mule Train*, 128.

66. Quoted in Lackey, *Marks, Martin, and the Mule Train*, 120.

67. Bertha Burres Johnson, interview by the author.

68. Augusta Denson, interview by the author. Denson did not indicate the racial makeup of the church, but I assume that it was a local black church considering the local white reaction to the movement.

69. Augusta Denson, interview by the author.

70. Bertha Burres Johnson, interview by the author.

71. Bertha Burres Johnson, interview by Roland Freeman, Marks, Mississippi, October 1997, Freeman, *The Mule Train*, 114.

72. Roland L. Freeman, "Mule Train: A Thirty-Year Perspective on the Southern Christian Leadership Conference's Poor People's Campaign of 1968," *Southern Cultures* 4, no. 1 (Spring 1998): 91–119.

73. Doris Shaw Baker, interview by the author, Marks, Mississippi, September 2, 2006.

74. Augusta Denson, interview by the author.

75. See U.S. Department of Commerce, *U.S. Census Population: 1960, Mississippi* (Washington, D.C.: Bureau of the Census, 1960); and U.S. Department of Commerce, *1970 Census of Population*, Volume 1, Characteristics of the Population, Part 26, Mississippi (Washington, D.C.: Bureau of the Census, 1973). It is interesting to note that the percentage of white families living in poverty actually increased by 10 percent, whereas the number of black families living in poverty fell by over 20 percent. Black participation in the PPC and in War on Poverty programs may account for this disparity.

76. The interviews I conducted with Marks residents demonstrate the improvements that occurred on the local level. For a more thorough discussion on what the PPC accomplished in terms of federal legislation, see chapter seven in Amy Nathan Wright, "Civil Rights' 'Unfinished Business': Poverty, Race, and the 1968 Poor People's Campaign" (PhD diss., University of Texas, 2007).

77. See http://www.fedstats.gov/qf/states/28/28119.html (accessed July 15, 2009).

78. U.S. Census Bureau, Population Division, reported at http://www.google.com/publicdata?ds=uspopulation&met=population&idim=county:28119&q=Quitman+County+population (accessed July 15, 2009).

79. See http://www.ecanned.com/MS/2007/01/income-and-poverty-in-quitman-county.shtml (accessed July 28, 2007).

80. Samuel McCray, interview by the author.

81. Ibid. The continued segregation or resegregation of public schools is not exclusive to Marks or the South in general. For example, see John Charles Boger and Gary Orfield, eds., *School Resegregation: Must the South Turn Back?* (Chapel Hill: University of North Carolina Press, 2005); and Beverly Daniel Tatum, *Can We Talk About Race? And Other Conversations in an Era of School Resegregation* (Boston: Beacon Press, 2007).

82. Obviously, the economic struggles and racial inequality that Marks residents experience are also not unique to the Mississippi Delta. For a recent study that documents the extent to which blacks and Latinos are facing economic inequality, see Ammad Rivera, Jeannete Huezo, Christina Kasica, and Dedrick Muhammad, *The Silent Depression: State of the Dream 2009* (United for a Fair Economy), 2009: 4–6, http://www.faireconomy.org/dream.

83. See Bertha Burres Johnson, interview by Freeman, *The Mule Train*, 115.

84. For more on the poverty tours and hearings the Gathering of Hearts has led,

see the videos Antoinette Harrell has provided on youtube: http://www.youtube.com/watch?v=YiMscjAoE8Q (accessed July 15, 2009).

85. Timothy R. Brown, "SCLC Renews Poverty Campaign Before Small Crowd," www.WTOP.com, June 20, 2009, http://www.wtop.com/?nid=104&sid=1701128 (accessed July 15, 2009). For other press accounts on these recent events, see Lawayne Chidrey, "Poor People's Campaign Comes to Jackson," Mississippi Public Broadcasting, June 20, 2009, http://www.mpbonline.org/content/poor-people's-campaign-comes-jackson; Daniela Carieda, "Local Charity, SCLC to Lead Poor People's March," *The Bay State Banner* 44, no. 36 (April 30, 2009), http://www.baystatebanner.com/local13-2009-04-30; Desiree Evans, "Shining a Light on Poverty: SCLC Renews King's Campaign," *Facing South: The Online Magazine of the Institute for Southern Studies* (June 25, 2009), http://www.southernstudies.org/2009/06/post-29.html; Shelia Byrd, "Group Relaunches Poor People's Campaign," *Commercial Appeal Online* (June 19, 2009), http://www.commercialappeal.com/news/2009/jun/19/group-relaunches-poor-peoples-campaign/.

86. Freeman, *The Mule Train*, 132.

# PART TWO

# From Local Studies
# to Synthesis

J. TODD MOYE

# Focusing Our Eyes on the Prize

## How Community Studies Are Reframing and Rewriting the History of the Civil Rights Movement

I n 1980 Randall Kennedy had this to say about William Chafe's *Civilities and Civil Rights: Greensboro, North Carolina, and the Black Struggle for Freedom*: "Thoughtful, well written and thoroughly researched, it is a work of disciplined, committed scholarship that is likely to inspire imitation." Neil McMillen wrote, "Viewing Greensboro as a microcosm of the nation, Chafe has boldly suggested an interpretive framework in which to examine the larger struggle for Afro-American rights." These would prove to be two of the most prescient sentences in the annals of book-review prophecy. The flood of community studies that followed the publication of *Civilities and Civil Rights* has reshaped the historiography of the civil rights movement in the span of a quarter-century, leaving a vastly changed (and ever-changing) field in its wake.[1]

The community studies that followed Chafe's lead made the body of literature on the civil rights movement one of the most vibrant in the field of United States history. They have also revolutionized both historians' periodization of the movement and our understanding of what the movement really looked like and meant to the people who conceived, organized, staffed, and led it. In this chapter I examine what community studies have done and are doing to reframe and reconceptualize the larger historiography of the modern American black freedom struggle.[2]

In the spirit of the inspiring conference Emilye Crosby organized at SUNY

The author thanks Joe Crespino, Emilye Crosby, Steve Estes, and Kathryn Nasstrom for the helpful suggestions that have improved this chapter immeasurably.

Geneseo in March 2006, "Local Studies, a National Movement: Toward a Historiography of the Black Freedom Movement," I have written this chapter in a more conversational and less academic style than I might have otherwise, and with the goal of raising more questions than I answer. I also include some informal intellectual autobiography. I do so, at least in part, in the hope that my discussion of the historiographical questions that most interested me when I embarked on my own community study of Sunflower County, Mississippi, more than a decade ago will encourage others to wrestle with similar issues.

Community and statewide studies have done much more than add new layers of detail to our understanding of this chapter in the black freedom struggle. By reframing the questions that historians ask about civil rights movements (the concept must be understood in the plural; there was no monolithic civil rights movement), they have reconceptualized the struggle itself. In fact, they question whether the term "civil rights movement" fits at all; many of the local movements they bring to our attention defined *themselves* as movements for human rights, for freedom and self-determination, more so than as movements for constitutional protections and civic rights. As Clayborne Carson has argued, local black movements whose preeminent goal was the creation of enduring local institutions, not protest marches or lobbying campaigns, can more properly be called parts of the "black freedom struggle"—even if what happened during the decades of the 1950s and 1960s was categorically different from earlier (and later) chapters in that struggle's history. (Nonetheless, in the interest of clarity I will use the term "civil rights movement" throughout this essay.)[3]

When Chafe published *Civilities and Civil Rights* there was already a large and growing body of literature on civil rights organizing—this just two decades after the assassination of Martin Luther King Jr., the point at which most scholars then agreed that the movement had ended. David Levering Lewis's King biography was already a decade old; Taylor Branch and David Garrow were well into the research that would result in their own King biographies, *Parting the Waters* (the first of a three-volume set) and *Bearing the Cross*, respectively. August Meier and Elliott Rudwick had published their study of the Congress of Racial Equality (CORE), and Clayborne Carson was nearing completion of his institutional history of the Student Nonviolent Coordinating Committee (SNCC). Steven Lawson had published his first work on black voting power in the South since World War II (two additional volumes would follow), and Harvard Sitkoff published his survey of the movement the following year. There were already enough journalistic treatments and movement memoirs to strain a bookshelf. In rereading the bibliographic essay that accompanies Sitkoff's *The Struggle for Black Equality, 1954–1980*, I am struck by the amount of work, some of which has stood the test of time quite well, that had already been published by the early 1980s.[4]

In the years since, historians have written important biographies of movement participants, from "national leaders" like King to grass-roots activists and foot soldiers like Fannie Lou Hamer and Ruby Doris Smith Robinson, and they have turned their attention to more thematic studies exploring such topics as religion in the movement, southern whites' responses to the movement, the role of mass media, and gender and masculinity concerns within the movement. Each of these approaches yields important new insights into the history of the civil rights movement, but I will focus my attention here on the community studies that followed Chafe's trail and will confine myself to those that have studied southern communities.[5]

Chafe's deeply researched monograph distinguished itself from the dozens of other civil rights histories then in existence by shifting attention away from national leaders and national lobbying campaigns toward local people and their local struggles to define problems, conceive of solutions, and manage complex movements themselves, over a long period of time. Two other first-rate community studies followed close behind *Civilities*: Robert J. Norrell's examination of the voting-rights movement in Tuskegee, Alabama, and David Colburn's study of St. Augustine, Florida. Colburn challenged orthodoxy when he concluded that Martin Luther King Jr. and his Southern Christian Leadership Conference (SCLC) did more harm than good by involving themselves in St. Augustine blacks' fight against segregated bus lines, because they did nothing to develop indigenous institutions that could carry on the fight after they left.[6]

The community studies that followed these three seminal works have done more than just pile on detail to an unchallenged and unchanging narrative of the movement. To make that case, I will revisit some of the questions that most interested me as I embarked on the research project that led to my dissertation and first book, a community study of the civil rights and white resistance movements that emerged from an economically poor, rural, majority-black county in the Mississippi Delta. The questions that interested me in that project may not interest other civil rights historians, and vice versa, and that is for the best. I have argued that the Mississippi Delta's experience is central to the American experience, and I get frustrated when others try to pretend that Mississippi is somehow outside of the United States. But I stop short of arguing that the experience of people in Sunflower County, Mississippi, was somehow normative for the South or the nation as a whole. My goal was to write a book that accurately placed one community's history of race relations within the context of that community's particular history, which took place in the context of a unique state and regional political culture, and which impacted and was impacted by so-called "national" events in the civil rights timeline. I hope I accomplished that.

I knew long before I had even heard of Sunflower County, Mississippi, that I wanted to use the community-study approach to study the history of American civil rights movements. As a freshman in an introductory U.S. history survey course at the University of North Carolina I read *Civilities and Civil Rights*, the history of a local movement in Greensboro, N.C., that coalesced in the 1940s and 1950s, nurtured the college students who engaged in the first sit-ins in the early 1960s, and continued in various iterations through the next two decades. One of Chafe's arguments, that the Greensboro movement exposed the myth of North Carolina's racial progressivism as a powerfully self-satisfied justification for white supremacy, almost literally struck me.

I can grandly characterize my life as a historian in the terms of BC and AC: "Before *Civilities*" and "After *Civilities*." For me the book was history about incredibly engaging people, but not larger-than-life heroes—it described real people I could recognize. As I first read the book, my maternal grandparents lived in Greensboro, an hour's drive from where I was in Chapel Hill; my family had lived in the Atlanta area nearly all my life, but I had been to Greensboro dozens of times as a child and young adult to visit them. My mother had been a student at the Woman's College of the University of North Carolina, now UNC–Greensboro, when the North Carolina A&T students staged a sit-in at the Woolworth's lunch counter in 1960. I heard firsthand from my mother and her friends about how young whites in Greensboro, who would have self-identified as liberal, reacted to the sit-ins: that is, with fear.

I knew many, many North Carolinians of my grandparents' and parents' generations, some of them family members, who proved Chafe's civility thesis for him. It wasn't uncommon to hear my father's relatives speak, unbidden, about how well they all got along with "the coloreds" in Greenville, N.C., over on the eastern side of the state. For instance, the Greenville city council considered in the late 1980s a proposal to rename Fifth Street to Martin Luther King Jr. Boulevard. Fifth Street was where my grandparents lived throughout my father's childhood and my own, and where my grandfather's straight-out-of-Flannery O'Connor sisters still lived in my great-grandparents' Victorian home. My great-aunt Jesse despaired. "Why can't they just change the name of Fifth Street where it goes through Colored Town and leave us alone?" she keened—and that's more or less what the town council eventually did.

Seeing this mind-set chronicled and analyzed in Chafe's book, having it placed in a richly detailed context, seeing its three-dimensional characters portrayed as historical actors, was powerful for me. It made me want to be a historian, too. Luckily, I got that chance. When Bill Clinton was elected to the White House in 1992, the very same great-aunt Jesse somehow got the idea that Clinton was going to tax all the money she had inherited from her parents decades ago, so she gave much of it away in chunks to her great-nephews. Mine paid for my first year of graduate school.

When I began my graduate studies at the University of Texas and started hunting for a research topic, I had a general idea that I wanted to do something in line with Chafe's methodology. But the community studies on the civil rights movement that were published by this point (the early 1990s) tended to be about communities with long-established black middle classes. (Chafe's Greensboro and Norrell's Tuskegee are the two classic examples.) The way civil rights historians tended to frame their narratives placed well-educated African Americans with good, stable jobs at the center of the stories, and I thought that the very fact that they wrote about middle-class blacks might mean that the movements were defined too narrowly. The movements covered by the existing literature tended to push for equal access to public spaces, better (racially integrated) public schools, and the ballot. I wanted to explore the history of a place without much of a black middle class to see whether the movements that emerged from that locale looked any different from the movements in communities we already knew about.

In my view at the time, scholarship on the civil rights movement, on both the local and national levels, was also taking too much for granted about the goals that movement participants created for themselves. I wanted to ask more basic questions about *how* people became civil rights activists. Decades after the fact, it seems so natural that a father whose children are being educated at a substandard school would start advocating for better educational opportunities for his children. It seems self-evident that a woman born in the United States who was denied the ballot would of course march around the courthouse until she was afforded her due. But we know that most of the people in these circumstances did not and do not become activists. Life tends to get in the way of social protest organizing: among a million other things there are kids to take care of and employers to satisfy, and to become a civil rights activist in most parts of the South during this period was, by definition, to put your family and your livelihood at risk.

So why did some people "get organized," as the saying goes? Once they did get organized, how did they come up with the vocabulary they needed to define the problems that faced them? Did they wait to hear what Martin Luther King had to say about it on the television news? Once they defined the problems, how did they imagine the solutions to address them? From what sources did they draw their ideas? How did they decide who to try to convince to join them, and who to leave out? These are all basic questions about the development of social movements; I wanted to jump in and wrestle with them, and the community studies model seemed the ideal way to do it.

(An aside: as I began to ponder these issues and dig around in the archives, John Dittmer published *Local People* and Charles Payne published *I've Got the Light of Freedom* within a year of each other. What timing! I know that every one of the authors in this collection has been profoundly influenced by these books, and even more so by the examples that John and Charles set for us as scholars and colleagues. I have heard Komozi Woodard describe the books as "force fields" that made the study of poor people's movements legitimate in the academy and protected people like us from the charge that our work was marginal. I think he's right about that. In any case, these books were so influential on me as a graduate student that I literally had to put them away and force myself not to look at them while I wrote my dissertation. It was too tempting to just pick a page in one of their books and run with whatever idea was there. When my book on Sunflower County was finally published and I received my first hardback copy, the first thing I did was wedge out a space for it on the bookshelf between *Local People* and *I've Got the Light of Freedom*, hoping that it might actually belong there. I may be crazy, but I doubt I'm the first or last author to do that.[7])

One of the first big historiographical issues I wanted to take on in my project was white resistance to the movement. At the time, historians tended to describe organized white resistance to the civil rights movement in terms of a backlash that began in response to *Brown* and really coalesced only after the movement succeeded in forcing Congress to pass the important pieces of reform legislation in the mid-1960s. There was, of course, white violence at every stop along the way in the common civil rights timeline, from Montgomery to Greensboro to Birmingham to Memphis, but there was little attention paid to white organizing. Much of the attention that *was* paid to white organizing tended to frame it in terms of the political organizing and reorganizing that swept the Solid South away from the Democrats and into the Republican party. This narrative picked up with Nixon's southern strategy in the 1968 election and culminated with the snowballing Republican majorities in the South in the 1980s and 1990s, a process that resulted in retreat on the part of the federal government in its commitment to upholding minority rights.[8]

Again, I suspected there was more to this. I was interested in how whites organized proactively to preserve Jim Crow segregation, and I was interested in how this kind of organizing did or did not affect the goals and tactics of those in black freedom struggles. Because I wanted to write about a community without a black middle class and because of my interest in interaction between white segregationists and the black freedom struggle on the local level, I settled on the community of Sunflower County for my study.

Sunflower was the home of Fannie Lou Hamer, a sharecropper with almost no formal education who became the embodiment of SNCC's organizing ethic, "Let the People Decide." It was also the home of James Eastland, the reactionary planter and U.S. senator who was almost single-handedly responsible for delaying federal civil rights legislation for as long as possible in the halls of Congress. Those two celebrities drew me to Sunflower, but what hooked me were the people's movements that the county produced. On the one hand, Sunflower generated a homegrown black freedom struggle that ended up looking as much like a human rights movement as a civil rights movement, and on the other hand it brought into being the self-named Citizens' Councils, the preeminent pro-segregation organization that ended up sweeping through the South.

A fair amount had been written about the Citizens' Councils by that point, including a terrific monograph from Neil McMillen that examined the Councils' founding and spread, and Numan V. Bartley's examination of white pro-segregation organizing throughout the South. So I knew that the Councils had formed because white men in Indianola, the Sunflower County seat, were worried about the implications of the *Brown* decision. I wanted to see if maybe there were local events that encouraged them to organize where and when they did—again, not everyone becomes an activist. Why did these particular men in this particular place choose to organize?[9]

I kept coming back to something the president of the town's bank was reported to have said at the first meeting of the Indianola Citizens' Council. "This meeting should have been held 30 years ago . . . when it was very noticeable that the Negro was organizing," Herman Moore announced. "Then there was a light in every Negro church, every night, regardless of the time you passed. . . . The Negro continued to meet and organize and through their concerted efforts, with the help of what I believe to be subversive groups and others, have made them a force to be reckoned with." That jumped off the page at me the first time I read it. Moore and his compatriots perceived that black freedom organizing had been proceeding for too long, and that they— the good white male citizens of Indianola, Mississippi—needed to do something to stop it. The organization they created defined racial segregation as a positive good, created and maintained a genteel image in the press (the Citizens' Councils were popularly known as "the white-collar Klan"), and set out to terrorize blacks who asserted their rights as American citizens—not so much through physical violence (though they used plenty of that, too), as through economic intimidation. The effect was just as pernicious either way.[10]

Indeed, after a little digging I found that the Mississippi NAACP State Conference of Branches held its state convention in Indianola just a few months before Moore spoke in 1954. As the justices of the U.S. Supreme Court debated the merits of the *Brown* case—this predated the announcement of their decision—state NAACP officials gathered in Indianola to offer optimistic predictions of a favorable outcome and relatively strident rhetoric about what the decision would mean for Mississippi. They came to Indianola because a charismatic young medical doctor moved back to his hometown in 1951, reinvigorated the local NAACP chapter, and began organizing a voter registration drive that threatened to upset the community's balance of power. I argued in my book that the Citizens' Councils movement could have emerged from any one of literally hundreds of communities in the southern states, but it emerged from Indianola specifically because local whites found that kind of activism so threatening.

The modus operandi of the Citizens' Councils was to create something close to a pro-segregation monolith among whites in their communities, and then to use that unanimity to threaten African Americans who dared assert their citizenship rights. In Indianola, that meant terrorizing Clifton Battle, the young medical doctor who had returned to Indianola and led a voter registration drive in 1953–1954. Interestingly, the county registrar had allowed Battle, his wife, and around fifty other well-to-do black farm owners and small business owners to register, but that door slammed shut when the *Brown* decision came down. Herman Moore's bank and others called in loans from local blacks who joined the NAACP, and they knew exactly who was joining because someone at the Indianola post office intercepted and read black people's mail.

Ironically, by punishing these African Americans and driving them away—they literally drove Battle out of town—they ensured that whatever civil rights organizing occurred in the future would have to concentrate on poor people. Indeed, the civil rights movement that Fannie Lou Hamer led in Sunflower County beginning in 1962 was a poor people's movement. Over the long haul it had as much in common with a human rights movement, as we understand that term in an international context, as it did with a civil rights movement, as we understand that term in the context of American history. Two biographies of Hamer make it clear that her first priority as a public figure was to make sure that her neighbors, many of them desperately poor and ill-educated, had clothes to wear, access to decent health care, and enough food to eat. As she understood it, having the bare material essentials of life was a human right that could be guaranteed only through political organizing in the political economy she inhabited.[11]

Hamer and her comrades formed the Mississippi Freedom Democratic Party to provide themselves access to the electoral process that had been systematically denied them as blacks. But when the Sunflower County Freedom Democrats gathered to discuss political strategies, they discussed how they could win a minimal standard of living for their neighbors through the electoral process. They also debated their party's stance on U.S. policies toward Cuba and the apartheid regime in South Africa. Hamer and the Freedom Democrats understood their mission as a civil rights struggle to change the political economy of Mississippi and the United States, but they also saw themselves as actors on the world stage.

What I found as I dug deeper into the history of the Citizens' Council and the history of black organizing in Sunflower is something that other authors of community studies have discovered: the more you learn, the more convinced you become that the chronology of the civil rights movement as it is popularly understood is just plain wrong. The creation of the Citizens' Council is commonly understood as a knee-jerk reaction to the *Brown* decision. Well, it was that, at least in part. But the organization emerged *when* it did and *where* it did because black Sunflower Countians began organizing, began pushing, began refusing to be constrained by white expectations of their behavior under the sharecropping system, long before the Supreme Court announced its *Brown* decision. And local movements did not respond to "national" events per se. Indianola whites formed their Citizens' Council in response to *Brown*, but they would not have organized in the first place had it not been for Battle's activism on the local and state level. As Herman Moore's telling admission makes clear, African Americans in Sunflower County did not wait for the justices of the United States Supreme Court to tell them the coast was clear to begin organizing in their own interest. And Sunflower County whites certainly did not wait for a "national" organization to tell them what to do. They organized themselves.

I also found that the chronology for the movement in Sunflower County had to stretch forward in time to include a school boycott and a strike among unionized catfish processors that both occurred in 1986. My study essentially tested the SNCC method of organizing for social change over a long period of time, and I considered questions about how that method succeeded or failed in Sunflower County. SNCC field-workers who moved into communities like Sunflower came with the goal of training local people to be leaders who could create their own free-standing, community-sustaining institutions. By 1986 Fannie Lou Hamer had been dead for nine years; no figure as charismatic as she led either of the 1986 movements. The school boycott was organized by a group of middle-class blacks. This by itself made the movement new and different in the county's history; there had been no black middle class to speak of in Sunflower before then. The middle-class blacks of the 1986 movement called themselves Concerned Citizens, and they had wide, cross-class support from the entire African American community. The school boycott succeeded, and white leaders were forced to accede to Concerned Citizens' demands. In contrast, the black middle class failed to support the striking catfish workers later that year, and their strike failed. The creation of intraracial, cross-class coalitions, I concluded, was the key to success for social protest movements in communities like Sunflower.

In pushing the chronology forward in my study I concluded that the 1986 movements responded to many of the same conditions, defined their goals similarly, and used many of the same tools that earlier movements had used, though the demographics of the movements were different. I also tried to demonstrate how terribly difficult it is to build and sustain a mass social protest movement. Any signs of progress to be found in Sunflower County over the span of the four decades my study covered were the results of painstaking, two-steps-forward-and-one-step-back community organizing and indigenous institutions, not charismatic personalities or outside organizations.

Others have learned that defining success and failure in social protest movements is a tricky business, and so much depends on how historians frame and reframe these questions. The best example of the ways in which framing determines conclusions about movement success or failure can be found in historians' writings on the movement that developed in Albany, Georgia. David Levering Lewis, David Garrow, and Taylor Branch, the authors of major first-generation King biographies who to varying degrees attempted to tell the whole story of the civil rights movement through King's involvement in it, all devoted considerable attention to the black freedom struggle in Albany and King's role there. Adam Fairclough did as well, in an organizational history of SCLC and in a short King biography.[12]

The self-named Albany Movement was formed in the autumn of 1961 when Charles Sherrod and Cordell Reagon, field workers for SNCC, moved into Albany to begin a voter-registration campaign, and formed a coalition with a local NAACP chapter and other indigenous organizations. The Albany Movement demanded an end to Jim Crow segregation in public and municipal facilities, progress toward the fair employment of blacks in the community, and the elimination of police brutality. Less than a month after the coalition's initial founding, a faction invited King and SCLC into Albany, prompting a bitter power struggle among SNCC, SCLC, and the NAACP for control of the Albany Movement.

King's methods of creative antagonism produced headlines throughout the country but they failed to advance the Albany Movement's program, due in large part to Albany police chief Laurie Pritchett's nonviolent jujitsu. Pritchett read King's book on the Montgomery Bus Boycott, *Stride Toward Freedom*, and studied his methods. Pritchett directed his police force not to use violence against the Albany protesters (at least in front of the news cameras) and arranged for additional space in neighboring counties' jails so that the mass arrests of protesters would not cripple the city. He succeeded in blunting the campaign's impact. Lewis, Garrow, Branch, and Fairclough agreed that King and SCLC learned important lessons from the Albany campaign, and for all intents and purposes each ended the history of the movement in Albany in August 1962, when King and SCLC pulled up stakes in southwest Georgia, taking with them all national media attention. The Albany Movement continued, however, and SNCC redoubled its commitment to the area with the creation of its Southwest Georgia Project the following year.[13]

Vincent Harding, a somewhat more imaginative King biographer and movement historian, explored what the Albany experience meant for King as an activist and an organizational leader. In a 1979 essay he emphasized the creative tensions between SNCC field-workers and King, whom the representatives of the antihierarchical SNCC had by then begun to refer to derisively as "De Lawd." Others had criticized King and SCLC for asking for too much in Albany—complete desegregation of public facilities and practical steps toward economic justice—but Harding argued that the strategy conceived by King and other leaders was "one forced upon them by the powerful thrust of the freedom movement," an illustration of the way that the people often led the leaders in this social movement. "The internal force of the people's rush toward justice, their sense that the new time was indeed upon them, the growing understanding of the wider significance of their movement . . . all these pushed the black freedom fighters out of the churches, out of the train and bus stations, out of the dime stores, out into the streets," Harding wrote. Although short-lived, King's involvement in the Albany Movement was essentially positive as Harding defined it, if for no reason other than the important and practical lessons on organizing King and SCLC learned from it, and then applied to the Birmingham campaign.[14]

Howard Zinn, a participant-observer of the Albany Movement and the author of the first tentative history of SNCC, wrote in his own memoir, "It has often been said, by journalists, by scholars, that Albany, Georgia, was a defeat for the movement, because there was no immediate victory over racial segregation in the city. That always seemed to me a superficial assessment." Zinn concluded, "Social movements may have many 'defeats'—failing to achieve objectives in the short run—but in the course of the struggle the strength of the old order begins to erode, the minds of the people begin to change; the protesters are momentarily defeated but not crushed, and have been lifted, heartened, by their ability to fight back." His last point is, I think, especially salient. True *movements* occurred when the people of a given community found in themselves—both as individuals and as members of a group— the courage and strength to define the obstacles they faced in an inherently unequal society and began to propose solutions that would allow them to overcome. It is exactly this understanding of the development of civil rights movements, I think, that best characterizes the new generation of community studies. (Those of us who plow this ground owe a great debt to Lawrence Goodwyn, who first identified how important it was for local people to create "a movement culture . . . a new way of looking at things" that helped them develop "a new democratic language" in his history of the Populists.)[15]

John A. Kirk, a British historian, stepped into this debate in 2005 when he published yet another King biography. Kirk's treatment of the Albany Movement, a freedom struggle that preceded King's 1961–1962 involvement and continued long after King and sclc left, drew the ire of movement veterans. Because his narrative focused on the charismatic figure of King, Kirk was able to call what happened in Albany a "defeat" because the Albany Movement failed to tear down every vestige of Jim Crow within a matter of months. After all, King's retreat from southwest Georgia left local blacks "disillusioned, frightened and bitter," according to a contemporaneous report from a leader in the Albany Movement, and Pritchett was able to brag that his town was "as segregated as ever" in 1963. Kirk's narrative left Albany with sclc's retreat, never to return.[16]

Joan Browning, a white Georgia native who spent time in an Albany jail as a member of the first group of Freedom Riders into the town, publicly challenged Kirk's framing of the story. "Albany was not 'King's' campaign—he was an ineffective interloper in Albany," she wrote in an e-mail to the publicly accessible H-South e-mail listserv in response to a review of Kirk's biography. "That was an Albany Movement and a sncc campaign and when one looks at the Albany Movement's goals for the campaign, then it is a success." When King left Albany in 1962, she pointed out, the Confederate battle flag flew over city hall. By the time Kirk's tale of "defeat" was printed in 2005, Albany police cars sported a city crest that included the image of a black hand clasping a white hand in cooperation, an appropriation of the classic sncc symbol. Had Kirk bothered to look at the goals local people defined for their own movement, and not the goals King and sclc publicized, Browning charged, he would have understood that the Albany Movement succeeded.[17]

Figures 7 and 8  The Albany Movement was a mass movement—including a coalition
of organizations that attracted individuals from many walks of life—and was active
for many years (*above*). But journalists and a first generation of historians reduced the
movement to a dramatic clash of personalities between Chief of Police Laurie Pritchett
and Rev. Martin Luther King Jr. (*facing page, Pritchett and King at center*). Photographs
courtesy of AE Jenkins Photography/Cochran Studio..

The Albany argument owes much to conflicting perspectives and differing understandings of movement periodization and chronology. From the
perspective of a King biographer, the Albany Movement existed for a few
months before King entered the picture in 1961, and it ended when he left
in 1962. In contrast, Stephen G. N. Tuck utilized the community-study approach, took the ideas and goals of local people seriously, and traced the history of the Albany Movement over several decades in his study of black freedom movements in Georgia. The opening pages of Tuck's *Beyond Atlanta:
The Struggle for Racial Equality in Georgia, 1940–1980* include a telling 1962
quote from Charles Sherrod: "[O]ur criterion for success is not how many
people we register, but how many people we can get to begin initiating decisions solely on the basis of their personal opinion." "For Sherrod," Tuck

writes, "civil rights activism was 'a psychological battle for the minds of the enslaved.'"[18]

Almost by definition such a program would require decades to bear fruit. Indeed, Sherrod remained and worked for racial justice in Albany for years after the civil rights movement purportedly ended there. Sherrod directed the Southwest Georgia Project for Community Education until 1987 and New Communities, Inc., a cooperative farming project, from 1969 to 1985. He served on the Albany City Commission from 1976 to 1990, where he forced the city to make many of the changes Joan Browning mentioned as signs of progress for which the Albany Movement was directly responsible. Kirk was not the first to step into this minefield; he is hardly alone among King biographers and movement historians in ignoring what happened in Albany after

King retreated. (For instance, in an influential survey of the civil rights literature Charles Eagles touched on the Albany Movement just long enough to refer to it as "one of King's major setbacks" and "the debacle.") But as the author of a very perceptive community study of the Little Rock movement, Kirk might have been more attuned to the issues Browning and others have raised.[19]

The example of the Albany Movement also illustrates what community studies have done and are doing to shift historians' understanding of movement chronology and periodization. Today a King-centric book that purported to tell the whole story of the civil rights movement but only spanned the years between the Montgomery Bus Boycott and King's assassination would be laughed out of the Ivory Tower. (If you don't believe me, read Charles Payne's blistering bibliographic essay, "The Social Construction of History.") I hasten to add, however, that, as Steven Lawson pointed out way back in 1986, from the beginning most efforts to topple a Montgomery-to-Memphis chronology have involved a certain amount of setting up and knocking down straw men.[20]

Community studies have proven beyond all doubt that local civil rights movements drew inspiration, learned tactics from, and in many cases included the same cast of characters of resistance movements from previous eras. They also lasted long past the lifetime of Dr. King. Adam Fairclough argued that activism before the *Brown* decision "constituted more than a prelude to the drama proper; it was the first act of a two-act play." Tuck does him one better: "[I]f there was a first act of protest before the King years, there was also a third act afterward. . . . The removal of legal segregation raised new questions about the meaning of racial equality at the local level. In many smaller communities, organized challenges to white supremacy occurred only after Lyndon Johnson had signed the [1964] Civil Rights Bill."[21]

The periodization argument is a good one for civil rights scholars to have, but its value goes far beyond academic debate. If the civil rights movement started not with Rosa Parks's seemingly impromptu decision to defy Jim Crow segregation on a Montgomery bus or with the U.S. Supreme Court's decision in the *Brown* case, if it instead began years earlier in the black church organizing tradition and NAACP activism and continued with the political organizing of radicals and liberals in the New Deal era, gained momentum during World War II, and continued to inspire citizens to change their communities through the 1970s and 1980s and longer, then the civil rights movement wasn't what the American public thinks it was. It was less incrementalist, more revolutionary than the general public thinks. It was energized not by black preachers but by black Christians. The movement, in fact, involved something more than courageous individuals bearing witness to injustice so that good white Americans could recognize the error of their ways and change. It involved the creation of an alternative culture, a new way of looking at the world, which included economic objectives in addition to the goals of equal citizenship rights and the deracialization of public spaces. If that is what it really involved, then I believe we have to conclude that it was less successful than we like to tell ourselves it was.

If the community studies have shifted historians' understanding of the nature of the civil rights movement and its chronology, they have also overturned our understanding of its geography. (The concept of a "long civil rights movement" has captured scholars' attention. It may be possible now to identify a "wide civil rights movement," too.) I will not go into great detail here, but I do want to acknowledge the watershed importance of Jeanne Theoharis's and Komozi Woodard's coedited 2005 volume, *Groundwork: Local Black Freedom Movements in America*. The authors of essays in this collection consider historical figures, communities, and issues outside of the "normal" civil rights narrative—Father James Groppi of Milwaukee; the Des Moines, Iowa, Black Panther Party—and familiar figures and organizations—the Lowndes County Freedom Organization, the Oakland Black Panther Party—with fresh eyes. Their contributions moved the historiography well past familiar and superficial dichotomies (good early 1960s/bad late 1960s, nonviolent southern movements/violent northern rebellions) and offered original interpretations. Most importantly, they proved that urban and nonsouthern freedom movements developed from similar concerns and similar organizing traditions as their southern counterparts. As Tim Tyson put it, "'[T]he civil rights movement' and 'the Black Power movement' emerged from the same soil, confronted the same predicaments, and reflected the same quest for African American freedom." I believe this is true, at least generally. But we should be careful not to conflate the northern and southern freedom movements.[22]

The post-*Civilities* generation of community studies has added detail and nuance, introduced complicated personalities beyond the movement's "heroes," reframed and reconceptualized the movement, and reshaped academic debates. However, this generation of scholarship has not yet produced a synthesis to replace the grand narrative of the movement—although Raymond Arsenault's *Freedom Riders: 1961 and the Struggle for Racial Justice* offers clues as to how that synthesis may come about. Arsenault provides something of a travelogue of grass-roots civil rights movements in his wonderful history of the 1961 Freedom Rides and makes great use of the community studies available to him. More than any other civil rights historian before him, Arsenault combines a grand-narrative writing style with attention to local detail that captures the dramatic tensions among local and national movements, leaders, and agents of change. If interpretation of the Albany Movement can be used as a litmus test, Arsenault's treatment is among the very best histories of the civil rights movement available.[23]

Even so, much work remains to be done. Writing in the *Journal of Southern History* in 2000, Charles Eagles argued that taken as a whole, historians of the movement lacked critical perspective and scholarly detachment from the figures and events they chronicled, and questioned whether civil rights historians of an older generation could ever compose objective treatments of the movement. Given their "profound and justifiable moral commitment to the aims of the civil rights movement," Eagles wrote, scholars of the black freedom struggle had produced no better than asymmetrical treatments of the civil rights era, the time of what he called "the most profound change in southern history." He charged that historians had uncritically taken the side of movement participants without making significant attempts to understand the movement's opposition—white segregationists—but he also offered hope. Eagles suggested that a new generation of movement historians would move in to write more nuanced, balanced, and comprehensive chronicles of the revolution as movement participants, the journalists who covered them, and the first generation of fellow-traveling civil rights historians exited the stage. He called for more "imaginative monographic work, new syntheses, and . . . new bold reconceptualizations of the movement's history."[24]

I concur with a large part of Eagles's critique of civil rights historiography—the part that says civil rights historians must do a better job of placing the movement within the context of biracial southern communities. (This critique has been important for my own work, but not necessarily for the work of others.) I agree, too, that we need to better understand the motivations of white supremacists over a long period of time and am always in favor of imaginative monographs and new syntheses. But I find it difficult to accept Eagles's point about generational scholarship and take it to its logical conclusions.

Eagles also criticized scholars who "rely on oral histories but too often accept the voices as telling true stories without verifying the material either with corroborating testimonies from others or with more traditional sources. Just repeating such stories, however compelling they may be, makes for incomplete history." His point is well-taken. Any historian worth her salt will apply the same rigorous, critical analysis of oral histories that she applies to written sources. But I would also argue that we run a far greater risk of writing incomplete history if we ignore these sources. Oral histories, if rigorously collected and analyzed, offer a rich vein of information and analysis for civil rights historians. Those who are interested not only in collecting oral histories but in reading them critically and comparing them against written sources over a span of time should be familiar with Steve Estes's essay, "Engendering Movement Memories: Remembering Race and Gender in the Mississippi Movement." Estes provides a case study for how we can explore the "dialogue between historians and historical actors, between scholarship and activism, between the past and the present[.]"[25]

The very act of recording oral history has played a significant role, I believe, in historians' reconceptualization and reperiodization of the civil rights movement. The vast majority of the scholars whose work I mention in this chapter recorded oral histories with movement participants in researching their studies. Of these, the majority undoubtedly used "life history" approaches, in which narrators conceptualized the turning points in their own life stories. Kathryn Nasstrom, for example, based her biography of the white Georgia activist Frances Freeborn Pauley on a series of oral history interviews between the two of them. Nasstrom concluded from this experience, "The storytelling that emerges from oral history practice is a narrative act in which experience is ordered and interpreted, and the life history approach, which aims at a full narration of personal history, leads naturally to a consideration of beginnings and endings. Implicitly, each life story opens onto the question of periodization." To put it another way, it is possible that historians would have arrived at a new understanding of movement periodization anyway, but the fact is that the accumulation of thousands of these life stories accounts for this particular revolution in civil rights scholarship. Perhaps it should come as no surprise that Chafe was among the first civil rights historians to engage in systematic oral history interviewing; the research behind *Civilities* combined the written record with more than seventy oral histories that he recorded and that he considered "[t]he indispensable core of this book."[26]

The beat goes on. Graduate students and assistant professors throughout the land are toiling in the vineyards of community studies even as you read this—I hope that at least one of them is in Albany—and important new works continue to appear at the rate or two or three per year. In 2006 Winston A. Grady-Willis accomplished what I had until then thought was impossible, publishing a community study of Atlanta that made sense of the interplay among the "national" civil rights organizations that were headquartered there, neighborhood campaigns, and actors in the city's byzantine system of racial politics. He did so within a framework of human-rights challenges to "apartheid," a concept that will not sit well with everyone but which I (a white who grew up in the Atlanta suburbs) found convincing. Hasan Kwame Jeffries's 2009 book, *Bloody Lowndes: Civil Rights and Black Power in Alabama's Black Belt*, proves beyond all doubt that Stokely Carmichael's call for "Black Power" was not just sloganeering but was instead firmly rooted in Carmichael's practical organizing experience on behalf of SNCC in Lowndes County, Alabama. Jeffries introduces the concept of "freedom politics," an ultra-democratic, transparent form of movement organizing for "freedom rights" that disintegrates the artificial divide between civil rights and Black Power. I look forward to the challenges that the next round of community studies will offer to my own evolving understanding of the movement.[27]

On the evidence already provided by community studies, scholars now understand the civil rights movement to have been more female, more grass roots, less philosophically nonviolent, and less pulpit-directed than they understood it to be thirty years ago, and where they see successful changes having taken place they are more likely to find decades worth of organizing and struggle behind them. If I can offer a tremendous generalization, scholars now see the civil rights movement preeminently as a movement for self-determination rather than a movement for integration of the races or even for equal civil rights. They see Black Power not in the terms of an earlier generation's declension model, whereby Black Power rushed in to fill the vacuum that the decline of the civil rights movement created, but as an ideology (amorphous though it may have been) that invigorated local movements long before Stokely Carmichael issued his famous call in 1966. When the next major synthesis of civil rights history is written, its author will have to contend with all of the nuances and details that community studies have added to the history of the movement. She or he will also have to wrestle with these and other examples of the reframing and reconceptualization that the community studies have brought about for this, the most consequential—and endlessly fascinating—social movement in America's history.

## NOTES

1. Randall Kennedy, "Review of *Civilities and Civil Rights: Greensboro, North Carolina, and the Black Struggle for Freedom*," *The New Republic* (February 16, 1980): 39–40; Ncil McMillen, "Review of *Civilities and Civil Rights: Greensboro, North Carolina, and the Black Struggle for Freedom*," *American Historical Review* 87, no. 2 (April 1982): 565–66.

2. To take just a few recent examples, the focused and solidly researched community studies of Memphis, Tennessee, Durham, North Carolina, and Atlanta, Georgia, recently provided by Laurie B. Green, Christina Greene, and Winston A. Grady-Willis, respectively, have taught us a great deal about the dynamics of the disparate movements that developed in these very different southern cities. Each of these works examined a local movement (or series of movements) through the lenses of gender and class, in addition to race. In their own way, each made an important contribution to the intellectual history of the civil rights movement. Laurie B. Green, *Battling the Plantation Mentality: Memphis and the Black Freedom Struggle* (Chapel Hill: University of North Carolina Press, 2007). Christina Greene, *Our Separate Ways: Women and the Black Freedom Movement in Durham, North Carolina* (Chapel Hill: University of North Carolina Press, 2005). Winston A. Grady-Willis, *Challenging U.S. Apartheid: Atlanta and Black Struggles for Human Rights, 1960–1977* (Durham: Duke University Press, 2006). See also J. Mills Thornton, *Dividing Lines: Municipal Politics and the Struggle for Civil Rights in Montgomery, Birmingham, and Selma* (Tuscaloosa: University of Alabama Press, 2002), a massive and finely detailed examination of movement dynamics in three Alabama communities; and Glenn T. Eskew, *But for Birmingham: The Local and National Movements in the Civil Rights Struggle* (Chapel Hill: University of North Carolina Press, 1997), a study of the interplay among a national civil rights advocacy organization, a local movement in Birmingham, and separate economic classes within the city's black community. This approach has yielded key insights into how social movements developed and operated in other communities. Statewide studies from the likes of Adam Fairclough, John Dittmer, Charles Payne, and Stephen G. N. Tuck have helped civil rights historians develop the deep and nuanced understanding we now have of issues as diverse and as crucial to movement dynamics as the role of violent self-defense, relations between local people and national organizations and "leaders," and the organiz-

ing networks created by women in every aspect of local civil rights movements. These scholars legitimized the study of "local people," bringing new depth and energy to the literature. Adam Fairclough, *Race & Democracy: The Civil Rights Struggle in Louisiana, 1915–1972* (Athens: University of Georgia Press, 1995); John Dittmer, *Local People: The Struggle for Civil Rights in Mississippi* (Urbana: University of Illinois Press, 1994); Charles Payne, *I've Got the Light of Freedom: The Organizing Tradition and the Mississippi Freedom Struggle* (Berkeley: University of California Press, 1995); Stephen G. N. Tuck, *Beyond Atlanta: The Struggle for Racial Equality in Georgia, 1940–1980* (Athens: University of Georgia Press, 2001).

3. Clayborne Carson, "Civil Rights Reform and the Black Freedom Struggle," in *The Civil Rights Movement in America*, ed. Charles W. Eagles (Jackson: University Press of Mississippi, 1986), 19–32.

4. David Levering Lewis, *King: A Critical Biography* (New York: Praeger, 1970); Taylor Branch, *Parting the Waters: America in the King Years, 1954–1963* (New York: Touchstone, 1988 ); David Garrow, *Bearing the Cross: Martin Luther King, Jr., and the Southern Christian Leadership Conference, 1955–1968* (New York: William Morrow, 1986); August Meier and Elliott Rudwick, CORE: *A Study in the Civil Rights Movement, 1942–1968* (New York: Oxford University Press, 1973); Clayborne Carson, *In Struggle:* SNCC *and the Black Awakening of the 1960s* (Cambridge, Mass.: Harvard University Press, 1981); Steven F. Lawson, *Black Ballots: Voting Rights in the South, 1944–1969* (New York: Columbia University Press, 1976); Harvard Sitkoff, *The Struggle for Black Equality, 1954–1980* (New York: Hill and Wang, 1981).

5. Fairclough, Tuck, Eskew, Greene, and other authors of community studies have illuminated class divisions within black movements. Emilye Crosby has done much by herself to move our understanding of the movement past the "heroic southern blacks/ evil southern whites" dynamic portrayed by Hollywood's version of the civil rights movement, the film "Mississippi Burning." Emilye Crosby, *A Little Taste of Freedom: The Black Freedom Struggle in Claiborne County, Mississippi* (Chapel Hill: University of North Carolina Press, 2005). See also Kay Mills, *This Little Light of Mine: The Life of Fannie Lou Hamer* (New York: Plume, 1993); Chana Kai Lee, *For Freedom's Sake: The Life of Fannie Lou Hamer* (Urbana: University of Illinois Press, 1999); Cynthia Griggs Fleming, *Soon We Will Not Cry: The Liberation of Ruby Doris Smith Robinson* (Lanham, Md.: Rowman & Littlefield, 1998); Charles Marsh, *God's Long Summer: Stories of Faith and Civil Rights* (Princeton, N.J.: Princeton University Press, 1997); David Chappell, *A Stone of Hope: Prophetic Religion and the Death of Jim Crow* (Chapel Hill: University of North Carolina Press, 2004); Jason Sokol, *There Goes My Everything: White Southerners in the Age of Civil Rights, 1945–1975* (New York: Alfred A. Knopf, 2006); Joseph Crespino, *In Search of Another Country: Mississippi and the Conservative Counterrevolution* (Princeton, N.J.: Princeton University Press, 2007); and Steve Estes, *I Am a Man!: Race, Man-*

*hood, and the Civil Rights Movement* (Chapel Hill: University of North Carolina Press, 2005).

6. Robert J. Norrell, *Reaping the Whirlwind: The Civil Rights Movement in Tuskegee* (New York: Random House, 1985); David R. Colburn, *Racial Change and Community Crisis: St. Augustine, Florida, 1877–1980* (New York: Columbia University Press, 1985).

7. J. Todd Moye, *Let the People Decide: Black Freedom and White Resistance Movements in Sunflower County, Mississippi, 1945–1986* (Chapel Hill: University of North Carolina Press, 2004).

8. The legal scholar Michael J. Klarman contributed to this debate with his influential article, "How *Brown* Changed Race Relations: The Backlash Thesis," the *Journal of American History* 81, no. 1 (June 1994): 81–118. For new examinations that tell considerably more complicated stories of how this process developed, see Crespino, *In Search of Another Country*; Matthew D. Lassiter, *The Silent Majority: Suburban Politics in the Sunbelt South* (Princeton, N.J.: Princeton University Press, 2005); and Kevin Kruse, *White Flight: Atlanta and the Making of Modern Conservatism* (Princeton, N.J.: Princeton University Press, 2005).

9. Neil McMillen, *The Citizens' Council: Organized Resistance to the Second Reconstruction, 1954–1964* (Urbana: University of Illinois Press, 1971); Numan V. Bartley, *The Rise of Massive Resistance: Race and Politics in the South During the 1950's* (Baton Rouge: Louisana State University Press, 1969).

10. Moore's quote appeared in Stan Opotowsky, "Dixie Dynamite: The Inside Story of the White Citizens Councils," an investigative series that ran in the *New York Post*, January 7–20, 1957. See Moye, 65, 227n1.

11. See Lee, *For Freedom's Sake*; and Mills, *This Little Light of Mine*.

12. Adam Fairclough, *To Redeem the Soul of America: The Southern Christian Leadership Conference and Martin Luther King, Jr.* (Athens: University of Georgia Press, 1987); and Adam Fairclough, *Martin Luther King, Jr.* (Athens: University of Georgia Press, 1990). See also Clayborne Carson, "SNCC and the Albany Movement," *Journal of Southwest Georgia History* 2 (1984): 15–25. Though none of them consider Albany directly, several of the authors in the collection *The Civil Rights Movement in American Memory*, ed. Renee Romano and Leigh Raiford (Athens: University of Georgia Press, 2006) tackle the questions of who gets to write movement history and how.

13. Martin Luther King Jr., *Stride Toward Freedom* (San Francisco: Harper, 1958).

14. Vincent Harding, "So Much History, So Much Future: Martin Luther King, Jr., and the Second Coming of America," in *Have We Overcome? Race Relations Since Brown*, ed. Michael V. Namorato (Jackson: University Press of Mississippi, 1979), 51.

15. Howard Zinn, *You Can't Be Neutral on a Moving Train* (Boston: Beacon Press, 1994), 54. See also Howard Zinn, SNCC: *The New Abolitionists* (Boston: Beacon Press,

1965). Lawrence Goodwyn, *Democratic Promise: The Populist Movement in America* (New York: Oxford University Press, 1976), xi.

16. John A. Kirk, *Martin Luther King, Jr.* (Harlow, UK: Pearson Longman, 2005), 77–78.

17. Joan C. Browning, "Re: H-South Review: Hustwit on Kirk, Martin Luther King, Jr.," e-mail to the H-South Listserv, March 29, 2006, and "Re: Albany failure," e-mail to the H-South listserv, April 12, 2006. See also Joan C. Browning, "Shiloh Witness," in *Deep in Our Hearts: Nine White Women in the Freedom Movement* (Athens: University of Georgia Press, 2000), 37–83.

18. Sherrod quoted by Tuck, 3.

19. For Sherrod's biography see http://www.reportingcivilrights.org/authors/bio.jsp ?authorId=147; Charles W. Eagles, "Toward New Histories of the Civil Rights Era," the *Journal of Southern History* 66, no. 4 (November 2000): 842; John A. Kirk, *Redefining the Color Line: Black Activism in Little Rock, Arkansas, 1940–1970* (Gainesville: University Press of Florida, 2002).

20. Payne, *I've Got the Light of Freedom*, 413–41. Steven F. Lawson, "Response to Clayborne Carson," in *The Civil Rights Movement in America*, 33.

21. Fairclough, *Race & Democracy,* xii; Tuck, 2.

22. See Jacquelyn Dowd Hall, "The Long Civil Rights Movement and the Political Uses of the Past," the *Journal of American History* 91, no. 4 (March 2005): 1233–63; and, for a dissenting view, Sundiata Keita Cha-Jua and Clarence Lang, "The 'Long Movement' as Vampire: Temporal and Spatial Fallacies in Recent Black Freedom Studies," *Journal of African American History* 92, no. 2 (Spring 2007): 265–88. Jeanne Theoharis and Komozi Woodard, *Groundwork: Local Black Freedom Movements in America* (New York: New York University Press, 2005); see especially Theoharis and Woodard's introductory essay. Timothy B. Tyson, *Radio Free Dixie: Robert F. Williams & the Roots of Black Power* (Chapel Hill: University of North Carolina Press, 1999), 3.

23. Raymond Arsenault, *Freedom Riders: 1961 and the Struggle for Racial Justice* (New York: Oxford University Press, 2006).

24. Eagles, "Toward New Histories," 815–6, 844.

25. Ibid., 836. Steve Estes, "Engendering Movement Memories: Remembering Race and Gender in the Mississippi Movement," in *The Civil Rights Movement in American Memory*, ed. Renee C. Romano and Leigh Raiford (Athens: University of Georgia Press, 2006), 290–312.

26. Kathryn Nasstrom, "Beginnings and Endings: Life Stories and the Periodization of the Civil Rights Movement," the *Journal of American History* 86, no. 2 (September 1999): 700–11. See also William H. Chafe, "The Gods Bring Threads to Webs Begun," the *Journal of American History* 86, no. 4 (March 2000): 1531–51. Chafe, *Civilities and Civil Rights*, 421.

27. Grady-Willis, *Challenging U.S. Apartheid*; Hasan Kwame Jeffries, *Bloody Lowndes: Civil Rights and Black Power in Alabama's Black Belt* (New York: New York University Press, 2009). See also Jeffries, "Organizing for More Than the Vote: The Political Radicalization of Local People in Lowndes County, Alabama, 1965–1966," in *Groundwork: Local Black Freedom Movements in America*, 140–63, and Cynthia Griggs Fleming, *In the Shadow of Selma: The Continuing Struggle for Civil Rights in the Rural South* (Lanham, Md.: Rowman & Littlefield, 2004).

WESLEY HOGAN

# Freedom Now

## Nonviolence in the Southern Freedom Movement, 1960–1964

### NONVIOLENCE IN ACTION

Nashville, Tennessee: Everything in 1959 was segregated—the movie theaters, city parks, drinking fountains, prison cells. Black women couldn't try on hats or dresses, nor were their children allowed to play on the carousel in the tearoom at Harvey's Department Store. Jobs as bank cashiers, police officers, city council members, and store clerks were all reserved for whites only. When Diane Nash, John Lewis, and James Bevel arrived in Nashville to pursue college degrees, all felt stifled by the lockdown of Jim Crow. "I came to college to grow and expand, and here I am shut in," Nash recalled. They turned eagerly to divinity doctoral candidate James Lawson, just back from three years in Nagpur, India, where he studied Gandhi's nonviolent assault on the British. Lawson hoped to make Nashville a "nonviolent laboratory," a place to try out on American soil the ideas he learned in India, a place to wield what he called the "nonviolent anvil."[1]

A group of twenty or so young people went through Lawson's first nonviolent workshop in 1959, learning the "nonviolent method" and considering ways to act. First they gathered information: they asked, "What would happen if Negroes stopped shopping downtown?" Fisk economist Vivian Henderson explained that blacks in Nashville spent $8 million a year downtown;

The author expresses gratitude to the following people, without whom this essay would have remained mere speculative musing: Emilye Crosby, Dirk Philipsen, Sara Leland, Nishani Frazier, Hasan Jeffries, and Tim Tyson. Any errors of fact or interpretation remain mine.

if one looked at metropolitan Nashville, a ninety-mile radius, blacks brought in $100 million a year. Armed with this information, the students decided to target the big department stores with a boycott and the direct action that became known as sit-ins.[2]

Lawson, their leader, did not advocate immediate action. To make Nashville's movement long term, he knew the students needed time to experience and internalize the ideas and possibilities of nonviolent direct action. So five months before the Greensboro, North Carolina, sit-ins began in February 1960, he set out to show the members of the group how nonviolence as an idea could be traced from the early Christians and the New Testament's concept of *agape* love, through William Penn's experiment in Pennsylvania to peacefully coexist with native people, through the abolitionist movement, and on to nonviolent resistance against the Nazis and Gandhi's campaigns against British colonialism in South Africa and India.[3]

Others had brought these ideas forward in the United States before. What made Lawson different? Simply put, he taught the ideas not to people sitting in a church basement or to college students in a lecture hall trying to expand their minds. He taught these ideas to people who were desperately trying to find a way to act. The students were astounded by his examples. To think that their situation could be compared to those of people in biblical times, or colonial India, or France under Nazi occupation gave them an entirely new sense of their struggle. "To learn that the tension between what was right and what was wrong that had torn at me since I was old enough to think," recalled John Lewis, to learn "that people of all cultures and all ages had struggled with the same issues" and realities, "it was mind-blowing."[4]

Lawson's broad historical context gave the students a new perspective, and they began to discuss, week after week, the way segregation made them feel, how it worked, how it diminished a person's sense of self. As they described their individual experiences, they realized a menacing, existential fear held them back. The system of segregation made "thousands of Negroes feel that they are 'nobodies' and they have no right to aspire to nobler things," as they would write later in a newsletter.[5] But together, sharing common experiences, they realized it was segregation, not individual weakness, that needed to change. If they all refused to participate in the segregated system, they came to see, it could not be maintained. Lawson told them the best way to undermine segregation would be to develop compassion for the insecurities that drove their oppressors. He demonstrated that approach. When a man spat in his face, he responded with dignity, asking him for a handkerchief. The spitter handed one over, suggesting the possibility for different future behavior. Compassion, within Lawson's nonviolent tradition, was practical. He set up role-plays of confrontations and they tried to figure out potential scenarios: How would I respond if someone hits me? Calls me a black bitch? Calls me "boy"? Punches my sister? And then Lawson would tell them to freeze, and he'd have others in the group walk around the outside of the role-play, commenting, analyzing what worked and what didn't. People figured out how they personally could handle these situations, learned from others' ideas, and gained confidence.[6]

Now they initiated the nonviolent process. In December 1959, right before leaving for winter break, they tried to negotiate with managers to desegregate at Harvey's and Cain-Sloan. No response. They tried the second step: to sit-in at the department stores, a few people at a time. No one was arrested, no one seemed to notice. Two months passed. On February 1, 1960, students in Greensboro, North Carolina, conducted sit-ins at lunch counters in that city, and called the Nashville students to see if they'd join them by sitting-in at lunch counters in Nashville. On February 13, five hundred students turned out. They wore their Sunday best, brought their schoolbooks, purchased something from the store, and then sat down at the lunch counter and ordered. When refused service, they continued to sit. When they were arrested, others moved in to take their place. They adhered to a strict code of conduct: "under no conditions were they to strike back, either physically or verbally." "Do not block entrances to stores outside nor the aisles inside. Do show yourself friendly and courteous at all times."[7]

The arrests prompted a wider black boycott of downtown stores, so much so that white merchants began to pressure Mayor Ben West to negotiate. Tensions mounted downtown, and unknown assailants firebombed the house of NAACP leader Z. Alexander Looby. Outraged, the students organized a march to city hall. They walked silently, two abreast and unarmed, to confront the mayor. Upon arrival, the Reverend C. T. Vivian condemned Mayor West for his inaction. They traded angry insults. Diane Nash, twenty years old, then stepped forward. She engaged the mayor in a different manner, asking quiet, determined questions, such as "Do you feel it's wrong to discriminate against a person solely on the basis of his race or color?" The mayor responded honestly, won over by her earnestness, and her interest in addressing him as a person, "not as mayor." He said it was morally wrong to sell someone merchandise and refuse them service. Within three weeks, Nashville's lunch counters were desegregated.[8]

The students in Nashville had mobilized nonviolence in three obvious ways. First, it was a tactic safe enough to try in Nashville, where the white power structure considered itself moderate; indeed, they referred to their city as the "Athens of the South." Furthermore, the presence of three black colleges gave the students a large pool of potential recruits, supported by a well-organized adult church community. Indeed, over five hundred students participated in the first February sit-in. In a city where no large groups had formed to protest Jim Crow since Reconstruction, this can't be overestimated. Second, tactically speaking, it worked: the lunch counters were desegregated because the cash-starved merchants pushed the mayor to negotiate a settlement. Third, in this particular situation, Diane Nash was able to reach out to Ben West on a human level. He responded to her approach of treating him as a man, not the mayor, and admitted that the law was immoral. This undermined the police force's ability to enforce segregation. In a setting where people had for decades lamented that nothing seemed to ever change, Nashville student activists created their own victory in the space of six months and in the process witnessed the opening up of new possibilities for a transformed world, one where people would be judged by character, not color.

Many variations on the lunch counter sit-ins followed. All over the South, groups of black students (sometimes with white student allies) sat-in together at amusement parks, movie theaters, concert halls, and restaurants; swam-in at county pools and beaches; kneeled-in at all-white churches. Entering courthouses to support fellow activists who had been arrested, they refused to abide the instructions of the court marshal to sit whites on one side, blacks on the other. They insisted on their own dignity, as well as that of the people who denied them equal treatment.[9] In 1961, over six hundred people rode interstate buses from Washington, D.C., and other points north toward Jackson, Mississippi, integrating the "whites only" and "colored" sections of both the buses and the bus stations. They were called "Freedom Riders," and the term stuck: after 1961, all civil rights workers throughout the South were thusly called. And so a basic pattern continued between 1961 and 1964: when arrested for "breach of peace" or breaking segregation laws, Freedom Riders used jail to recruit others. They inspired those on the outside to march for their release. When marchers were subsequently arrested, this often resulted in the recruitment of more movement people.[10]

These early nonviolent activists insisted on living as if the South were not segregated, armed only with their dream and their willingness to die for the cause. Theirs was a daily challenge to Jim Crow, day in and day out. Whether beaten, jailed, or spat upon, they refused to back down, and refused to quit. In many locales, they wore out the ability of local law enforcement to enforce segregation. Sometimes this was just a short-term victory, such as nonviolent campaigns in Jackson's department stores, St. Augustine's lunch counters and beaches, or Maryland's eastern shore restaurants. In other cases, in Atlanta, Georgia, or in Petersburg, Virginia, and on interstate buses, the changes lasted through the passage of the 1964 Civil Rights Act. In some cases, like McComb, Mississippi, or Albany, Georgia, in 1961, it did not lead to desegregation, but it did lead to movement: sit-ins recruited young people and forced older people to consider how far they were willing to go to support "freedom now." In several explosive situations like the Freedom Rides, activists forced a recalcitrant federal government, embarrassed by their international claim as the world's most finely tuned democracy, to protect activists and enforce federal law.[11]

## KINDS OF NONVIOLENCE

People understood nonviolence and believed in nonviolence in different ways. The most widespread understanding in the freedom movement was pragmatic. For Stokely Carmichael (Kwame Ture), a Howard University student who later became chair of the Student Nonviolent Coordinating Committee (SNCC), it was simply a pragmatic way to draw attention to southern injustice and American hypocrisy. Charles (Chuck) McDew, also a SNCC chair, saw the philosophy of SNCC as taking on segregation wherever it existed and using nonviolence "as a tactical method to do so. It was a way to break down the traditions and laws separating the races."[12] Between 1960 and 1964, it was this unbelievable ability of SNCC to act "as if" segregation didn't exist that truly opened up new views of what a nonsegregated country would look like. This ability to act "as if," and to organize others to do the same, led a fiery Mississippian named Charles McLaurin to call SNCC's voter registration projects "revolutionary": "People going to the courthouse, for the first time. Then telling their friends to go down."[13]

What is not captured in McLaurin's shorthand is the colossal battles black

Figure 9 The nonviolent anvil: members of the Albany, Georgia, movement stand their ground in the face of local law enforcement's violation of the 14th Amendment. Photograph courtesy of AE Jenkins Photography/Cochran Studio.

Mississippians experienced in their own minds about whether to go to the courthouse. It could mean loss of a job, a house, or even one's life. Yet, when over one hundred people stood with McLaurin in front of Bryant's Chapel in Indianola during July 1964, despite thunder and lightning, "They felt the meaning of ONE MAN ONE VOTE," reported Eddie Johnson. "To vote out police brutality; to vote out officials that keep the Negro down. To vote in people that care about people—black and white. They saw a policeman ask to talk to McLaurin. And they saw McLaurin say, 'Wait till I'm finished talking.' And McLaurin went on and talked. And they sang 'Ain't gonna let no policeman turn us around.' Brave people ready to join you in the fight for freedom."[14] Such activity was not only groundbreaking, it won the revolution against the caste system of white supremacy. People witnessed McLaurin acting "as if," and joined him, because they could do so and still live. When

McLaurin had this many people behind him, it gave pause to police officers who might otherwise arrest him for "talking fresh" to a white officer. Nonviolent direct action might be "sitting-in" at a lunch counter, but it also was embodied in McLaurin's refusal to obey Jim Crow customs preventing blacks' right to assemble. When he drew people together and told the police officer to wait, people could suddenly see a new way to act.

Many of those within Dr. King's organization, the Southern Christian Leadership Conference (SCLC), and some within SNCC—people like Charles Sherrod and Prathia Hall and many who first practiced it in Nashville with Jim Lawson—did not see nonviolence merely as a useful coercive tactic. Instead, they came to nonviolence from a philosophical and spiritual place. Sometimes people referred to this as "strict nonviolence," and three basic strands of thinking emerged within this tradition of philosophical nonviolence.

First, activists like Diane Nash, James Lawson, and Texan SNCC activist Casey Hayden learned that nonviolent direct action allowed them total self-control. One did not have to wait for anyone or any law to be free. To act "as if" black and white could sit together in a park or at the movies was freedom one could experience here, now, regardless of how opponents responded. The experience of acting on their deepest values permanently changed how they saw themselves, their own ability to impact events around them, and their sense of what was politically possible. "Nonviolence is not docility," James Lawson stated. "Nonviolence is the courage to be—in very personal terms. It is the tenacity in insisting upon one's own life." Diane Nash, through the 1959–1960 school year, and into 1961, learned to her great surprise that by withdrawing support from a system—not a person—that oppressed them, nonviolent activists no longer saw themselves as victims. When a person was able to identify his or her responsibility in the maintenance of systems of oppression, "it puts you in a position of power," Diane Nash would later explain, "because then you are able to withdraw your participation and therefore end the system."[15] It was a central experiential reality for people adhering to nonviolence as a way of life: simply by refusing to participate in segregation, Nash was contributing to its dissolution.

A second, and sometimes overlapping, strand of nonviolent philosophy was the Christian idea of redemptive suffering. In the context of the Cold War, southern black church-based communities acted from a position of moral authority that allowed students to see protest as honest and dignified rather than subversive and unpatriotic. Further, part of the thread of egalitarianism that infused the movement was rooted in certain religious themes. Throughout the life of the movement, these themes became encased in the cultural and spiritual rhythms of the black freedom church. The church provided both a direct link to the heritage of black struggle and the space and opportunities for people to develop their own sense of self. African American leaders drew on religious traditions, forms, and experiences to move members of their congregations, their communities. Mississippi activist Fannie Lou Hamer stated that the police beating of voter registration worker Annell Ponder in the Winona jail in 1963 could only be understood in a political *and* religious context: "That was somethin'. . . . She kept screaming, and they kept beatin' on her, and finally she started prayin' for 'em, and she asked God to have mercy on 'em, because they didn't know what they was doin'." Ponder herself felt that the people who beat her were not evil themselves but that they needed "training and rehabilitation." Her actions echoed those of SNCC's Charles Sherrod, who stated that the movement's capacity for suffering was going to overcome their opponents' ability to inflict harm.[16]

This is frankly counterintuitive to many inside and outside of Christian traditions. Yet people like Ponder, Sherrod, and Diane Nash who remained unbowed in these situations often credited their Christianity as essential to their ability to endure. Their collective backbone was strengthened by their basic understanding of Christianity's teaching that all people are equal in the eyes of God. As James Bevel reported, "[A]ccording to the Bible and the Constitution, no one has the power to oppress you if you don't cooperate. If you say you are oppressed, then you are also acknowledging that you are in league with the oppressor; now it's your responsibility to break the league with him." In jail in Selma and sick, Bevel was taunted by an officer. The man warned that Bevel wouldn't make it out of jail alive. Bevel responded that his stomach might be aching, and the officer might beat him, but he was going to shake the man's hand and walk out of jail in the morning. Bevel and the officer talked most of the night, and indeed, rather than beat him, the officer talked with Bevel about the nature of man and society, justice and God, and they shook hands when Bevel departed the next day. Bevel's willingness to endure suffering, to open himself to someone who wished him dead, had, at least momentarily, changed the behavior of his enemy.[17]

The third strand of nonviolence as a philosophy, or basic approach to life, centered on the idea of creating a "beloved community." The central idea, as articulated by SNCC chair John Lewis, was that throughout human existence, people "from ancient Eastern and Western societies up through the present day have strived toward community, toward coming together." The community might be delayed by hatred, greed, or ambition, but believers in the beloved community "insist that it is the moral responsibility of men and women with soul force, people of goodwill to respond and struggle nonviolently against the forces that stand between a society and the harmony it naturally seeks." Lewis learned this lesson firsthand from James Lawson. When a white biker spat on Lawson as he sat in the front seat of a Nashville bus, Lawson calmly turned and asked the man for a handkerchief. Stunned, the tough guy pulled one out of his pocket and handed it to Lawson, who then asked the spitter about his motorcycle. Engaging in this kind of open conversation, Lawson compelled the other man to "do some searching" and to see Lawson as a fellow human being.[18] It was a response that required courage as much as poise, and there was no guarantee that it would work. For Lawson, however, it was clear that in order to bring down customary barriers between people that had been followed for generations, one had to act simply as if there were no barriers. Instead, one had to act from the premise that all humans are entitled to equal dignity and respect.

For some in SNCC, part of creating the beloved community was acting on the motto "black and white together." For a time, they took it literally. In counties where police routinely pulled over blacks and whites who were driving together, SNCC's black and white organizers drove together, walked together, flew together, ate together, lived together, and of course, acted together against segregation. For three hundred years, both custom and law forbade this kind of activity. Indeed, when they were trying to avoid police attention in practical day-to-day situations, SNCC often hid people under blankets in backseats, or instructed black men and white women workers to keep their distance from one another in public. However, more often than not, SNCC people routinely began to act "as if" Jim Crow's custom and laws did not exist.[19] Their courage both inspired and recruited others.

Thus, when people took this insight, that all humans are entitled to dignity and respect—beyond a basic one-on-one human interaction—nonviolence as a way of life pulled people into the larger movement involving political activism. This is not to say nonviolence was easy, or that large numbers accepted nonviolence as a way of life. More often, people entered the movement because watching others (on television, or seeing a picture in the paper) act with full dignity appealed to them, made people outside the movement recognize that there was, in fact, another way to be. One could live publicly as a full human being and live to see another day. Consequently, many in SNCC, as well as in the Congress of Racial Equality (CORE) and SCLC, went beyond nonviolent action. They worked to register people to vote, but also ran citizenship training schools, freedom schools, and cooperatives. They believed citizens needed to act as if their voices could make an impact on policy and government in order to bring about the "beloved community" in reality.

Finally, pursuit of the beloved community meant people had to work out their conflicts in ways that enhanced, rather than diminished, the whole community. Inside SNCC, for example, people tried to work out conflict face-to-face. They came together at the end of sometimes fiercely contentious, even belligerent, meetings to sing, dance, and laugh together. Every act of every person either reinforced the drive toward "beloved community" or delayed it. Thus each person could choose to contribute to the solution. Those who believed in nonviolence not simply as a coercive tactic that worked but in nonviolence as a way of life, organized their day-to-day existence around the idea of living "as if" humans had already created the beloved community.[20]

Within the movement, there were others whose belief in the beloved community and the common humanity of people worked well with philosophical nonviolence, even though they were not philosophically nonviolent. Ella J. Baker's life best exemplifies this and some in SNCC followed her lead. Many movement people and scholars acknowledge Baker as the "mother of SNCC." And she was. She provided so many of the key ingredients the young group needed to strike out on its own: infrastructure support, contact lists, a calming presence, a person who stiffened others' backbones by seeing their best selves within. Yet she was not nonviolent. While she supported nonviolence as a tactic, she had been raised by self-reliant farmers who had always carried guns for self-defense. She insisted numerous times she would not let anyone "step on my neck." Still, several aspects of philosophical nonviolence intersected with Baker's philosophical beliefs about how to treat people: her insistence on horizontal democracy, nonhierarchical organization, and the belief that everyone's voice was important. Baker, because of her instrumental role spanning over fifty years in the freedom movement, is a helpful exemplar of the nuance required to see the role of nonviolence within that movement. She didn't practice nonviolence as a way of life, but she didn't see it only as a tactic, either. She noticed how nonviolence provided support to the insides of the movement, promoting a way of being with one another that sustained people.[21]

For example, in the Albany SNCC project, those who believed in nonviolence as a way of life strengthened the rural voter registration projects by giving ongoing attention to two principles. First, everyone was valuable and potentially a leader, and a humane relationship had to be established with every single person, adversary or friend. Such relationships created the opportunity to break through stereotypes, allowing people to see the multifaceted person at the core. While Charles Sherrod, James Bevel, and others spoke about seeing adversaries as complex and reachable human beings, scholar Charles Payne noted, Ella Baker saw this having an impact on relationships within the movement as well: people "were so keen about the concept of nonviolence that they were trying to exercise a degree of consciousness and care about not being violent in their judgment of others." Payne later noted this as one of the "moral anchors" that helped regulate relationships within the movement, enabling people to keep working together. In Albany, at least, and perhaps in SNCC in general, nonviolence strengthened long-term community organizing. To be clear, the pursuit of the beloved community was not confined to those who believed in pure nonviolence as a spiritual discipline. Things like face-to-face conflict resolution, being good to each other, and acting in egalitarian ways also happened in political activity that did not center on nonviolence. The point is simply that people committed to nonviolence as a way of life did often privilege these egalitarian modes of interaction because of their belief in nonviolence.[22]

## ASSESSING WHERE NONVIOLENCE
## WORKED AND WHERE IT DIDN'T

Forty-plus years after the height of the movement, activists, scholars, and those interested in the freedom movement have to carefully sort out, with the benefit of hindsight, where nonviolence worked, where it did not, and how it intersected with other tactics. And when nonviolence did not work, what then? As historian John Dittmer has fruitfully asked, what do you do after nonviolent direct action fails to bring results?[23] No campaign lasts very long without tangible victories.

Nonviolence was tactically practical in the 1960 sit-ins and on the Freedom Rides of 1961. Courageous to the point of disbelief, perhaps, but practical: it worked, it bent the arm of the moral universe toward the protestors, and it forced a day-to-day change in that lunch counters, interstate buses, and bus stations were no longer segregated throughout the urban South. Nonviolent direct action drew recruits in Albany, Georgia—including a SNCC staff culled from local high schools and Albany State—even though nonviolent direct action did not break down Albany's segregation in 1961. Once SNCC had this staff, they used them to spread to Albany's four surrounding counties between 1961 and 1963. Using ideas emerging from nonviolence as a way of life, Charles Sherrod built the Albany project into another "laboratory of nonviolence," where these ideas informed the large-scale voter registration efforts of SNCC and SCLC over the coming four years, as well as ongoing attempts at desegregation, and campaigns to hire black workers in Albany.[24]

The Mississippi movement, according to the literature SNCC sent to media outlets and liberal contributors in the North and West, was nonviolent. However, its central focus was not on nonviolent direct action but on voter registration and community organizing. Approaching the registrar before the Voting Rights Act went into effect in 1965 was, to many, a form of nonviolent direct action, tactically speaking. Trying to engage the U.S. Justice Department on the moral high ground by embarrassing them into enforcing the Fifteenth Amendment was a use of nonviolence as a moral suasion technique. But in reality, while sometimes going to the registrar looked like nonviolent direct action (as in McComb, Mississippi, in the fall of 1961), at other times it just looked like nonretaliation, not nonviolent direct action.[25] In other words, we need to sort out what campaigns used nonretaliation in order to get the federal government to do its job of enforcing law and what campaigns were more broadly informed by nonviolence as a way of life, trying to create a better world.

Local histories have helped raise the question of how much that has been commonly considered "nonviolence" can actually fit the definition. They have also begun to show us the detail we need to more precisely understand the range of approaches people used and how they worked together. Emilye Crosby's study of Claiborne County finds very little activism classifiable as nonviolent. Black citizens used a massive boycott of white merchants, but while this tactic is often a part of nonviolent struggle, it involved *not* doing something, namely shopping. It was not nonviolent direct action. Further, some of the boycott enforcement clearly involved physical coercion. Hasan

Kwame Jeffries shows that the Lowndes County, Alabama, movement involved school boycotts, voter registration and political party formation, and a major attempt to bring federal programs to area blacks. Which of these activities might be considered nonviolent? In Sunflower County, Mississippi, Todd Moye demonstrates that local people and SNCC people learned a great deal from one another but that many on both sides saw the limited nature of nonviolent direct action or voter registration when police auxiliaries in the county "cooperated with Sunflower County's suppression of civil rights" to the extent that "at a moment's notice, any white man in the county can be deputized."[26] So who in the local movements, at any given time, understood their actions to be nonviolent? How did they challenge or support leaders who insisted on nonviolence? Was a boycott itself nonviolent? Could boycott enforcement (verbal berating, pulling groceries out of someone's arms) be characterized as nonviolent? The work of Crosby, Moye, and Jeffries, as well as Adam Fairclough in Louisiana, indicate we have much to learn about how nonviolence and voter registration tactics and campaigns related to each other.

Timothy Tyson's account of the movement in Oxford, North Carolina, indicates that even when nonviolent marches took place, some participants refused to rely on the state police patrol for protection. "Ben [Chavis] and them said it had to be nonviolent," Eddie McCoy stated. "But we all had our shit with us. That wagon with the mule had more guns on it than a damn army tank."[27] We see self-defense, often in conjunction with nonviolence, throughout the movement. Joseph Mallisham of Tuscaloosa, Alabama, accepted nonviolence as "the only possible strategy in the freedom struggle," while simultaneously forming a black defense agency to protect nonviolent activists. He "sought to defuse rather than aggravate volatile situations." His reasoning was that if activists were committed to nonviolence, police lost any pretext for arrest, and this was good for the movement. However, Mallisham wanted to make sure his (armed) people were in the background, guaranteeing the nonviolent activists' survival to fight another day. Similarly, Fannie Lou Hamer believed in the transformative power of nonviolent practitioners like Annell Ponder. Yet just as her mother before her, who took a gun in her lunch pail to keep the white overseers off of female family members in the fields, Hamer insisted on her right to self-defense.[28] Movement leaders like Ella Baker, Mallisham, and Hamer, with their flexible approach to nonviolence and their support of self-defense, are critical to understanding the full role of nonviolence in the freedom movement. They prevent us from simply seeing nonviolence and self-defense as either/or propositions for the movement as a whole. But they also allow scholars, citizens, and particularly young people to see that we can't write off the actions of individuals who weren't "purely" nonviolent, or only committed to self-defense. Activists "had to make a movement out of human beings," after all, Tyson noted, "and we're all complicated."[29]

There are also places where nonviolence did not achieve long-term success: It did not work in Cambridge, Maryland, in 1963 because when local people fought back, the governor used that as cover to call in the National Guard. Nor did it work for more than a few weeks at a time in St. Augustine, Florida, in 1963–64 because Klan terror effectively ended movement activity. While some groups like SCLC remained committed to the ideals and practices of nonviolence, SNCC and field-workers in CORE showed a great deal more ambivalence. Yes, the Nashville cohort in SNCC was able to persuade most of their peers in 1960 that nonviolence was the way to go. By June 1964, however, many in SNCC felt nonviolence could no longer be the primary tool in the toolbox.

When a young boy was shot in Albany, Georgia, in May 1964 by a police officer, 1,200 people showed up at a mass meeting, SNCC worker Don Harris reported. "They were mad. Young people and people on the fringes of the movement were expressing themselves. That night they could have had as big a demonstration as ever," Harris continued, but when SNCC people began to talk about nonviolence, it had a chilling effect on many in attendance. Harris asked what right did SNCC have to stop people from using self-defense? Sam Block explained the escalating tension in Greenwood, Mississippi: "Mrs. McGhee has guns and has been able to stop some violence. What are we to say to her?"[30] As these questions show, it was hard to sort out what exactly nonviolence meant or how it could be used in all situations. In Albany, Harris knew that SNCC as an organization was committed to nonviolence. But he needed guidance: How could he have organized people to shut down the police station nonviolently, to let police know that people would not accept the abuse? And in Mississippi, if people were using guns to protect their homes at night, wasn't it still possible to use nonviolent tactics during the day to desegregate downtown stores?

When SNCC people were housed with Mississippi activists, some felt caught between their preference for nonviolence and the very real need for self-defense. Longtime Quaker activist and Spelman historian Staughton

Lynd had traveled west to Mississippi to serve as the 1964 Freedom School coordinator. In Carthage, when SNCC volunteers tried to set up a Freedom School, the whites said the deed to the land was invalid and "were talking about getting their guns and setting fire to the schoolhouse." A volunteer reported Lynd's dilemma: "In a situation like this, what do we do? It's necessary to ask other people to protect you, and this is something we are trying to avoid." Lynd said he had "an uneasy feeling about getting someone else to do my dirty work for me. It seems to me that some time we are going to have to go one way or the other—either asking all the people in the movement to drop their guns, or picking them up ourselves."[31]

After 1964, events in the wider movement, especially in the North, also began to ripple throughout the southern freedom struggle. Local and state governments pursued a military response to uprisings in Harlem, and later in Watts, Detroit, Newark, and other urban areas. This had a profound impact on the way activists thought about nonviolence. In such cities, black people were killed by police for walking in the street: how, then, could anyone be expected to train residents within a few days to respond nonviolently? Between 1965 and 1967, increasing knowledge of U.S. military policy and its impact on Vietnamese civilians prompted some movement workers to focus greater attention on how they might—"by any means necessary"—prevent the U.S. government from pursuing the war. Even people utterly committed to nonviolence as a way of life, such as Diane Nash, gave up on nonviolence as "probably an ineffective way to struggle for liberation." For a few years, Nash, perhaps the most innovative nonviolent strategist of her generation, could not imagine a way for the tactic to work against economic inequality, northern racism, or the Vietnam War.[32]

As the 1960s wore on and more and more civil rights workers were brutalized, raped, beaten, and even killed for acting as if they were free, those activists most dedicated to nonviolence found themselves questioning it. Nonviolence did not work for many individual activists after people had experienced too many emotionally wrenching deaths to allow these murders to go unanswered in kind. As I have written elsewhere, piled-up memories of white brutality became unbearable: when white prison guards stripped seventeen-year-old Ruby Doris Smith naked, then scrubbed her with a wire brush in Parchman; or when Camilla, Georgia, police officers beat Marion King so badly she miscarried at the seventh month of pregnancy; when a group of whites in Selma beat Bernard Lafayette until pieces of his skull hung open; when white police in Rolling Fork, Mississippi, put a gun to Ivanhoe Donaldson's temple, raised the hammer and screamed, "You ain't gonna get nothin' but a bullet in the head!"; when the whites who beat James Chaney left evidence for the forensics team at Ole Miss that was so grotesque, so unprecedented, that it produced near incoherence in the doctor charged with the responsibility for writing the autopsy report; when a white officer murdered Jimmy Lee Jackson as he tried to protect his mother in Alabama . . . then what? Fay Bellamy, a black SNCC staff member, tried to write about the anguish of living through these events: "Can one write about pain? What I'm also attempting to ask is how does one get used to it? How many people will have to die before we can make it a two-way street?" She was afraid of war but "would much rather us die fighting to defend ourselves, since we die all of the time anyway."[33] In the face of what seemed in 1964 or 1965 like very limited gains for the movement, living life as if one was a part of the beloved community did not seem worth this devastatingly high cost. As a tactic, then, as well as a philosophy, nonviolence appeared to have lost its widespread efficacy in the southern freedom struggle beginning in 1964.

Many nonviolent practitioners were questioning nonviolence as a tactic by mid-decade: Could it still work in any situation? If so, which ones? Was it worth the cost? Could they live with themselves given that they had felt the costs so personally? But these questions were largely shoved under the rug for one fundamental reason: white supporters in the North and West only donated funds to southern freedom organizations who remained formally committed to nonviolence. Thus, many in SNCC were unable to be clear or honest with themselves about nonviolence, unable to speak frankly in an environment where they were still dependent on these liberal monies. In addition to their questions about whether nonviolence was working, SNCC people had been socialized within American culture and, like any other Americans, needed a way to cope with or understand the emotional tendency to settle the score by inflicting retaliatory damage on the oppressor. But how did the public relations arm of SNCC or CORE explain their field staff's disillusionment to its funders, as those funders sat in the suburbs of St. Louis, San Francisco, and Boston? Warning a SNCC worker against telling northerners about how carrying guns stopped racist assaults, longtime civil rights activist Anne Braden noted, "Don't get me wrong. I don't think anybody sitting in a safe comfortable apartment in New York has any right to tell you not to arm yourself . . . but frankly some people react this way." Still, the promotional and fund-raising literature from SNCC and CORE continued to portray the groups as uniformly committed to nonviolence as a way of life, despite the momentous disagreements within the organizations on this central issue.[34]

The challenges to understanding the role of nonviolence in the freedom struggle are not just a result of the conflict between daily practice in the southern movement and the very different experiential reality of northern liberals who funded it. Many top-down and popular culture accounts of the civil rights movement privilege nonviolence in ways that obscure the movement's flexibility. Nonviolence has also been critiqued and ridiculed by activists and bystanders. In his 1962 book *Negroes with Guns*, Robert F. Williams, ignoring his own use of tactical nonviolence, went as far as asserting that only elite blacks practiced nonviolence: "Nor should we forget that [these] same deceiving pacifist-preaching well-to-do southern blacks profit from the struggle, living lives of luxury while most Afro-Americans continue to suffer."[35] From outside the movement, Malcolm X cut down nonviolent activists for being naïve.[36]

Recently, Ward Churchill published a book read widely in young activist circles, *Pacifism as Pathology*. Without any evidence from the southern freedom struggle, he argues that the only people who have the luxury to practice nonviolence are those in the middle and elite classes who have the choice of many tools for struggle. For Churchill, nonviolence is a hoax, a pathology, another way to rob those in the freedom struggle of their right to resist the dominant culture.[37] Such portraits of nonviolence as an elite tactic, rather than a "weapon of the weak," combined with the fact that nonviolent practitioners did not always feel able to tell the rest of the country the truth about their experiences, has led to a huge amount of cultural confusion as to what nonviolence is, what ideas and values informed it, and in what circumstances it worked.

And yet, despite these critiques and some of its own inherent limitations, nonviolence did provide people a concrete way to act, a way forward. And when it did work, it broke open huge new vistas of freedom. Those who used it tore down the southern caste system—permanently. Perhaps once we are able to see more clearly where nonviolence worked, and where it did not, we will be able to acknowledge an elemental fact: people understood nonviolence in multiple ways. They used it in varying situations. It worked often enough that others stood witness and used it in their own struggles: at the Pentagon in 1967, in Prague in 1968, at Tiananmen Square in 1989, and in the Middle East's West Bank in 2003. One thing seems obvious: those who merely speechify about nonviolence, either as the "be-all-and-end-all" of the freedom struggle or by condemning it as "elitist," can make their cases only by ignoring a vast amount of evidence and experience. We still await a clear-eyed assessment of the complex ways that activists mobilized nonviolence in the southern movement and the ways that it intersected with other tactics.

## NOTES

1. See Wesley C. Hogan, *Many Minds, One Heart: SNCC's Dream for a New America* (Chapel Hill: University of North Carolina Press, 2007), ch. 1. Benjamin Houston's dissertation *The Nashville Way: A Southern City and Racial Change, 1945–1975* (University of Florida, 2006) is an important source on Nashville's movement, as is David Halberstam's *The Children* (New York: Ballantine, 1999).

2. Hogan, *Many Minds, One Heart*, 17–26.

3. Ibid., 20.

4. John Lewis, *Walking with the Wind: A Memoir of the Movement* (New York: Simon and Schuster, 1998), 87.

5. Hogan, *Many Minds, One Heart*, 301.

6. "Attention all Students: Why We Must Fight Segregation," October 11, 1960, folder 12, Box 74, Kelly Miller Smith Papers, Vanderbilt University, Nashville, Tenn.; Lewis, *Walking with the Wind*, 87; James Lawson, interview by the author, August 14, 2001; Bevel quoted in Henry Hampton and Steven Fayer, eds., *Voices of Freedom: An Oral History of the Civil Rights Movement from the 1950s Through the 1980s* (New York: Bantam Books, 1990), 226.

7. Hogan, *Many Minds, One Heart*, 28, 303.

8. Ibid., 33–34.

9. Harvard Sitkoff, *The Struggle for Black Equality, 1954–1980* (New York: Hill and Wang, 1981), 72.

10. Several helpful examples of movement-supporting activities are documented by Tiyi Morris, "Local Women and the Civil Rights Movement in Mississippi: Revisioning Womanpower Unlimited," in *Groundwork: Local Black Freedom Movements in America*, ed. Jeanne Theoharis and Komozi Woodard (New York: New York University Press, 2005), 193–214; Aldon Morris, *Origins of the Civil Rights Movement* (New York: Free Press, 1984); and Adam Fairclough, *Race & Democracy: The Civil Rights Struggle in Louisiana, 1915–1972* (Athens: University of Georgia Press, 1999). On how going to jail recruited people, see Hogan, *Many Minds, One Heart*, ch. 2.

11. On the Freedom Rides, see Ray Arsenault, *Freedom Riders: 1961 and the Struggle*

*for Social Justice* (New York: Oxford University Press, 2006). On St. Augustine, see Lawrence Goodwyn, "Anarchy in St. Augustine," *Harpers*, July 1965, 78–81; Taylor Branch, *Parting the Waters: America in the King Years 1954–63* (New York: Simon and Schuster, 1989); Taylor Branch, *Pillar of Fire: America in the King Years 1963–1965* (New York: Simon and Schuster, 1999); and oral histories available online at http://www .crmvet.org/nars/staugbar.htm; http://www.crmvet.org/nars/conway.htm; and http:// www.crmvet.org/nars/staugwhi.htm. On the Atlanta movement, see Branch, *Pillar of Fire;* Ronald Bayor, *Race and the Shaping of Twentieth-Century Atlanta* (Chapel Hill: University of North Carolina Press, 1996); Julian Bond, *A Time to Speak, A Time to Act* (New York: Harper and Row, 1972); David Garrow, *Atlanta, Georgia 1960–1961: Sit-ins and Student Activism* (New York: Carlson, 1989); Harry Lefever, *Undaunted by the Fight: Spelman College and the Civil Rights Movement, 1957–1967* (Macon, Ga.: Mercer University Press, 2005); and Aldon D. Morris, *The Origins of the Civil Rights Movement: Black Communities Organizing for Change* (N.Y.: Free Press, 1984). On Maryland's eastern shore, see Hogan, *Many Minds One Heart*, 125–28; and Peter B. Levy, *Civil War on Race Street: the Civil Rights Movement in Cambridge, Maryland* (Gainesville: University of Florida Press, 2004).

12. Stokely Carmichael, with Ekwueme Michael Thelwell, *Ready for Revolution: The Life and Struggles of Stokely Carmichael (Kwame Ture)* (New York: Scribner, 2003), 172; Chuck McDew, quoted in interview for *Freedom Song*. Available online at http://turner learning.com/tntlearning/freedomsong/home.html (accessed July 23, 2009).

13. Hogan, *Many Minds, One Heart*, 91.

14. Ibid., 91–92.

15. Nash, quoted in *Circle of Trust: Remembering* SNCC, ed. Cheryl Lynn Greenberg (New Brunswick, N.J.: Rutgers University Press, 1998), 21; Lawson and Hayden quoted in Hogan, *Many Minds, One Heart*, 23, 36, 84.

16. Fannie Lou Hamer, quoted in Howell Raines, *My Soul is Rested: Movement Days in the Deep South Remembered* (New York: Putnam, 1977), 253; Annell Ponder, quoted in Charles M. Payne, *I've Got the Light of Freedom: The Organizing Tradition and the Mississippi Freedom Struggle* (Berkeley: University of California Press, 1995), 309.

17. Bevel quoted in *Voices of Freedom*, 132.

18. Lawson, interview by author, March 23 and 27, 2000.

19. Hogan, *Many Minds, One Heart*.

20. Ibid.,104, 110, 162, 171, 197–218, 235–36, 253–55.

21. Barbara Ransby, *Ella Baker and the Black Freedom Movement* (Chapel Hill: University of North Carolina Press, 2003), 193–94, 211–12, 323; Payne, *I've Got the Light of Freedom*, 372.

22. Ransby, *Ella Baker*, 193–94, 211–12, 323; Payne, *I've Got the Light of Freedom*, 372.

23. John Dittmer, March 25, 2006, comments at conference, "Moving Beyond Dichotomies," SUNY Geneseo, Geneseo, New York, notes in author's possession.

24. See Hogan, *Many Minds, One Heart*, ch. 3.

25. Robert Moses and others in SNCC stayed committed to nonretaliation. But, as Moses would later assert, "[T]here's nothing in terms of going down to register which required that they take the nonviolent stance." Courtland Cox asserted a different point, one that echoed the Nashville workshops with Lawson in 1959. Namely, that armed self-defense was a step back, a retreat, not a step forward. "To the extent that we think of our own lives, we are politically immobilized," he suggested. "We volunteer for this situation knowing what's happening and we must accept the implications. Self-defense can only maintain the status quo, it can't change the existing situation." During the 1964 Summer Project, staff and volunteers would be living with rural people—nearly all of whom were armed, Cobb noted. What would happen if someone attacked a local person's homestead—someone who was housing SNCC people? Would SNCC stand by their workers who were there, "even though SNCC advocates nonviolence"? Moses quote from Robert Moses, interviewed by Joseph Sinsheimer, November 19, 1983, Cambridge, Mass., Box 3, Joseph Andrew Sinsheimer Papers, Duke University, Durham, N.C.; Harris, Cobb, Cox, Block, McLaurin quoted in staff meeting minutes, June 10, 1964, 14–15, Frames 982–83, Reel 3, SNCC Papers. See also Ransby, *Ella Baker*, 322–24.

26. Emilye Crosby, *A Little Taste of Freedom: The Black Freedom Struggle in Claiborne County, Mississippi* (Chapel Hill: University of North Carolina Press, 2005), 74–75, 138–47, 168, 178–83, 240, 263; J. Todd Moye, *Let the People Decide: Black Freedom and White Resistance Movements in Sunflower County, Mississippi, 1945–1986* (Chapel Hill: University of North Carolina Press, 2004), 143, chs. 4, 5; Fairclough, *Race & Democracy*; Hasan Kwame Jeffries, "Organizing for More than the Vote: The Political Radicalization of Local People in Lowndes County, Alabama, 1965–1966," in *Groundwork*, ed. Theoharis and Woodard, 140–63.

27. Timothy B. Tyson, *Blood Done Sign My Name* (New York: Random House, 2004), 213.

28. Ransby, *Ella Baker*, 193–94, 211–12, 323; Payne, *I've Got the Light of Freedom*, 372; Simon Wendt, *The Spirit and the Shotgun: Armed Resistance and the Struggle for Civil Rights* (Gainesville: University of Florida Press, 2007), 60–61.

29. Quoted here is the incomparable Tim Tyson, who is right of course, but only this one time. Correspondence with author, January 6, 2009.

30. Harris, Cobb, Cox, Block, McLaurin quoted in staff meeting minutes, June 10, 1964, 14–15.

31. Staughton Lynd, quoted in Sally Belfrage, *Freedom Summer* (New York: Viking Press, 1965), 176.

32. Nash quoted in *Circle of Trust*, ed. Greenberg, 19.

33. Hogan, *Many Minds, One Heart*, 246.

34. Anne Braden quoted in Wendt, *Spirit and Shotgun*, 106. Wendt's book raises the

issue of fund-raising on SNCC and CORE's nonviolent stance repeatedly in his fascinating study. See pp. 68, 71, 106, 110, 130, 142, 145, 148. However, we still need to integrate this more forcefully into our understanding of how SNCC and CORE functioned.

35. Robert F. Williams, *Negroes with Guns* (New York: Marzani and Munsell, 1962), 114.

36. Malcolm X, "Message to the Grassroots," November 10, 1963. Available online at http://www.americanrhetoric.com/speeches/malcolmxgrassroots.htm. Malcolm X's critique is worth quoting at length, as most people still aren't as familiar with his rhetorical brilliance as they are with his iconic image.

> You don't have a peaceful revolution. You don't have a turn-the-other-cheek revolution. There's no such thing as a nonviolent revolution. [The] only kind of revolution that's nonviolent is the Negro revolution. The only revolution based on loving your enemy is the Negro revolution. The only revolution in which the goal is a desegregated lunch counter, a desegregated theater, a desegregated park, and a desegregated public toilet; you can sit down next to white folks on the toilet. That's no revolution. Revolution is based on land. Land is the basis of all independence. Land is the basis of freedom, justice, and equality. The white man knows what a revolution is. He knows that the black revolution is world-wide in scope and in nature. The black revolution is sweeping Asia, sweeping Africa, is rearing its head in Latin America. The Cuban Revolution—that's a revolution. They overturned the system. Revolution is in Asia. Revolution is in Africa. And the white man is screaming because he sees revolution in Latin America. How do you think he'll react to you when you learn what a real revolution is? You don't know what a revolution is. If you did, you wouldn't use that word. A revolution is bloody. Revolution is hostile. Revolution knows no compromise. Revolution overturns and destroys everything that gets in its way. And you, sitting around here like a knot on the wall, saying, 'I'm going to love these folks no matter how much they hate me.' No, you need a revolution. Whoever heard of a revolution where they lock arms, as Reverend Cleage was pointing out beautifully, singing 'We Shall Overcome'? Just tell me. You don't do that in a revolution. You don't do any singing; you're too busy swinging [from a tree].

Nonviolence has at times been very effectively satirized by activists as the last refuge of elite scoundrels. See Williams, *Negroes with Guns*; Ward Churchill, *Pacifism as Pathology: Reflections on the Role of Armed Struggle in North America* (Edinburgh: AK Press, 2007).

37. Williams, *Negroes with Guns*, 114; Ward Churchill, *Pacifism as Pathology*. Lance Hill's *The Deacons for Defense: Armed Resistance and the Civil Rights Movement* (Chapel Hill: University of North Carolina Press, 2004), equates nonviolence with passivity and the middle class/elite sections of communities, and posits that self-defense was workers' and local people's most effective method of struggle. This inversion of the

dominant mythology ("nonviolence is good, self-defense is bad") prevents illumination of the multilayered realities in much the same way that Churchill's study does. Hill notes, "Freedom was to be won through fear and respect, rather than guilt and pity" (9), and so promotes the very same misunderstanding of nonviolent direct action that runs throughout Churchill's work. Christopher Strain began to break down this misleading dichotomy in his *Pure Fire: Self Defense as Activism in the Civil Rights Era* (Athens: University of Georgia Press, 2005), but clearly we need new models for understanding the ways nonviolence and self-defense worked in concert, in opposition, or parallel to one another. Local studies are still not numerous enough on this front to do more than point us in new directions and to ask new questions.

EMILYE CROSBY

# "It wasn't the Wild West"

## *Keeping Local Studies in Self-Defense Historiography*

The earliest scholarship on the movement—with its focus on Martin Luther King Jr., major media events, and legislative victories—tended to foreground and overemphasize nonviolence, highlighting it as the driving force behind the movement. It is this version—which typically ignores self-defense and downplays the role of force or coercion—that continues to dominate the "movement narrative" in the popular culture (in its most oversimplified form) and even much of the scholarship (in its more sophisticated forms). To some extent this is related to the top-down lens: nonviolence is more prominent if the focus is on King and dramatic demonstrations. It is probably also connected to the ways some people find an emphasis on nonviolence appealing and reassuring, as a story of the triumph of morality and high ideals, along with individual and national redemption.[1]

In shifting the lens, local studies unearthed self-defense and called into question the extent to which philosophical nonviolence dominated the movement. Away from the media spotlight in the rural communities of the Deep South, activists tended to emphasize voter registration more than direct action protest. Though attempting to register to vote (alone, in small groups, or as part of an organized Freedom Day) always held the potential for confrontation, direct challenge wasn't necessary or even desirable. Much of the work of voter registration—canvassing, Citizenship School classes, and mass meetings—took place within the black community. Here, open conflict with

The title quote comes from Charlie Cobb. Charles (Charlie) Cobb Jr., July 2009, speaking at "Landmarks of American Democracy: From Freedom Summer to the Memphis Sanitation Workers' Strike," NEH Institute for Community College Teachers, Hamer Institute, Jackson State University; Charles (Charlie) Cobb Jr., e-mail to author, June 17, 2010.

segregationists was less likely than during direct action protests, both because organizers tried to move quietly and because blacks routinely protected themselves, something whites were well aware of.[2]

The most important early scholarship on self-defense came in the local and state studies of Mississippi and Louisiana published by John Dittmer, Charles Payne, and Adam Fairclough in 1994 and 1995.[3] Although Dittmer, Payne, and Fairclough did not focus on self-defense as much as some subsequent authors, their groundbreaking monographs, together with Timothy Tyson's biography of Robert Williams published a few years later, make it crystal clear that during the movement self-defense was pervasive, essential, and closely tied to other kinds of activism.[4] Dittmer's and Payne's books are filled with details about individual and collective self-defense. We learn that during the 1950s and 1960s, every NAACP leader in Mississippi was armed at some point, including presidents Emmett Stringer and Aaron Henry, well-known Delta activist Amzie Moore, and state field secretaries Medgar and Charles Evers. Most of these men periodically relied on armed guards. Others, including C. C. Bryant and his sister-in-law Ora Bryant, Laura McGhee (and her sons), Hartman Turnbow, and Vernon Dahmer fired back at attackers. Dahmer's stand enabled his family to escape their burning home, although he died the next day of burns and smoke inhalation. In contrast, many Holmes County blacks believe Turnbow killed one of his attackers and "whites covered it up by saying the man had a heart attack." Turnbow's wife, Mrs. "Sweets" Turnbow, carried her gun along in a paper bag when she went to the 1964 national Democratic Convention in Atlantic City and had it with her as she lobbied the Oregon delegation to support the Freedom Democrats.[5]

All of these people, and many more, were prepared to defend themselves. In fact, Dittmer's and Payne's accounts make it clear that you would be hard pressed to find a native Mississippi movement activist who did not, at some point, carry a weapon or stand guard. For all of these people and many others, self-defense came *after* and *because* they joined the movement and were involved in other kinds of activism. That is, they turned to self-defense not as a primary means of organizing or challenging white supremacy but because they were under attack for using other tactics. Many tried to register to vote and engaged in canvassing, encouraging others to make the registration attempt. A few enrolled children in the formerly whites-only schools. Some initiated sit-ins or went on marches. Others joined and organized the Mississippi Freedom Democratic Party, taught Citizenship School classes, housed and fed civil rights workers, and attended mass meetings.

For the most part, John Dittmer lets self-defense speak for itself. His text incorporates extensive examples in a matter-of-fact way that reinforces how absolutely ordinary and commonplace it was. He does explain, however, that in Holmes County, white vigilante "violence was not as severe . . . in part because black residents set up nightly patrols, letting it be known that they had weapons and were prepared to use them." Self-defense is part of the fabric of Charles Payne's text as well, though he offers more speculation about the positive roles it played. He suggests, for example, that "the success of the movement in the rural South" might owe "something to the attitude of local people toward self-defense." Observing that vigilante violence became more clandestine and less deadly, Payne credited self-defense, noting that "the old tradition of racist violence was coming to mean that you really could lose your life or your liberty." Adam Fairclough found a similar pattern in Louisiana, observing, for instance, that "many ordinary blacks regarded strict nonviolence as nonsensical. In rural Louisiana the ownership of guns was commonplace, and here, where blacks were isolated and most vulnerable, guns were often seen as the *only* deterrent to white violence." Fairclough also profiles the well-organized and highly visible Deacons for Defense. Founded in Jonesboro in late 1964, the best-known chapter emerged in Bogalusa in 1965 where their insistence on protecting the movement and refusal to back down from the Klan helped convince the federal government to aggressively intervene.[6]

In 1998, Timothy Tyson first published his influential work on Robert Williams, one of the best-known advocates of what he called "armed self-reliance." Situating Williams within the local Monroe, North Carolina, movement and the broader national and international context, Tyson's work straddles the forms of community studies and a subsequent generation of self-defense scholarship. He argues that Williams's commitment to self-defense was "more ordinary than idiosyncratic" and demonstrates that in some cases self-defense could do more than keep people alive. In 1957, when "a large, heavily armed Klan motorcade attacked" the home of a prominent NAACP leader, "Black veterans greeted the night riders with sandbag fortifications and a hail of disciplined gunfire. The Monroe Board of Alderman immediately passed an ordinance banning Klan motorcades, a measure they had refused to consider before the gun battle." Drawing on Robert Williams's life and beliefs, Tyson used the topic of self-defense to explicitly challenge the "cinematic civil rights movement" that focused exclusively on "nonviolent civil rights protest," insisting that during World War II and after, there was a "current of militancy" among African Americans "that included the willingness to defend home and community by force. This facet of African American life," he argued, "lived in tension and in tandem with the compelling moral example of nonviolent direct action."[7]

Collectively, Dittmer, Payne, Fairclough, and Tyson laid out the basic contours and identified most of what is significant about self-defense in the movement. They demonstrated that self-defense was widespread and commonplace; it was closely tied to and complemented the "nonviolent" movement. Women, men, and sometimes children regularly used self-defense to protect their families and property. In some instances, self-defense was more organized and formal. Here men dominated and typically worked together to patrol black communities, monitor lawmen, guard mass meetings, and protect the most visible leaders. More rarely, self-defense extended to public spaces and demonstrations. All of these aspects of self-defense were necessary because of widespread white vigilante violence and because there was essentially no viable law enforcement for African Americans. Local, state, and federal governments openly conspired with or utterly failed to control white terror. Occasionally, as with the incident in Monroe, self-defense itself led to changes in policy or practice. Moreover, as Adam Fairclough noted, few blacks had any problems with the practice of self-defense. Charles Payne found that "[i]n rural areas particularly, self-defense was just not an issue among Blacks. If attacked, people were going to shoot back."[8]

Despite this pervasive acceptance among rural activists, these books also point to some internal movement conflicts over self-defense. Adam Fairclough explains that at times some of the national staff of the Congress of Racial Equality (CORE), with their commitment to philosophical nonviolence, were at odds with local activists in Louisiana. National leaders tended to be particularly uneasy when support for self-defense was visible and forceful. Tyson chronicles one of the best-known examples when, in 1959, Robert Williams angrily asserted that blacks should "meet violence with violence" and "lynching with lynching." NAACP head Roy Wilkins immediately suspended him and was unmoved when, the next morning, Williams clarified his views, explaining that he was simply insisting on the Constitutionally-protected right to self-defense. A few months later, Martin Luther King Jr. debated the relative merits of nonviolence and self-defense with Williams in the pages of *Liberation* magazine. King's task was challenging since the sit-ins had not yet turned nonviolent direct action into a viable tactic and he, too, accepted self-defense. Tyson explains that "the philosophical position from which King centered his argument—preferring nonviolence but endorsing the principle of self-defense, even involving weapons and bloodshed—was in fact, the same position that Williams had taken."[9]

A second generation of scholarship that is more explicitly focused on self-defense has sought to reinforce and build on these insights to further challenge the pervasive stereotype of a nonviolent movement.[10] In 1996, two years before Tyson previewed his biography of Robert Williams with an article in the *Journal of American History*, Akinyele Umoja completed his dissertation, "Eye for an Eye: The Role of Armed Resistance in the Mississippi Freedom Movement." A year later, Lance Hill finished a dissertation on the Deacons for Defense. Christopher Strain added an insightful article, also on the Deacons, that was based on the research for his dissertation, "Civil Rights and Self-Defense: The Fiction of Nonviolence, 1955–1968," defended in 2000. Umoja's dissertation produced several important articles on armed resistance, published in 1999, 2003, and 2004, and is the basis for a forthcoming book. Hill and Strain published their dissertation-based books, *The Deacons for Defense: Armed Resistance and the Civil Rights Movement* and *Pure Fire: Self-Defense as Activism in the Civil Rights Era* in 2004 and 2005, while Simon Wendt weighed in with his 2004 dissertation (completed in Germany) and his 2007 book, *The Spirit and the Shotgun*.[11] A number of newer local studies also make important contributions to the ongoing conversation about self-defense. These include Greta de Jong's *A Different Day: African American Struggles for Justice in Rural Louisiana, 1900–1970*; Peter Levy's *Civil War on Race Street: The Civil Rights Movement in Cambridge, Maryland*; Todd Moye's *Let the People Decide: Black Freedom and White Resistance Movements in Sunflower County, Mississippi, 1945–1986*; and Hasan Kwame Jeffries's *Bloody Lowndes: Civil Rights and Black Power in Alabama's Black Belt*.[12]

Akinyele Umoja and Lance Hill both focus on relatively narrow geographical areas. Starting with a nuanced overview of self-defense in the Mississippi movement, Umoja argues that events in 1964, including the Freedom Summer project, were pivotal in marking the "beginning of the end of nonviolence as the Southern freedom movement's philosophy and method." Moreover, based on a close study of Natchez and other southwest Mississippi communities in the post-1964 era, he insists that "the capacity of the movement to protect itself and the Black community and to retaliate against White supremacist terrorists gave … Black leaders more leverage in negotiating with local White power structures." Lance Hill adds an organizational history of the Deacons for Defense, focusing primarily on Jonesboro and Bogalusa, Louisiana, where the Deacons were founded and had their biggest impact. Concluding his book with a chapter each on the Deacons in other parts of Louisiana, in Mississippi, in the North (meaning not South), and during the emergence of Black Power, especially the 1966 Meredith March, Hill goes further than any other scholar in framing nonviolence and self-defense as opposing tactics. He argues that the Deacons represented a working-class rejection of nonviolence, asserting, for example, that "the Deacons reflected a growing disillusionment of working class blacks with the pacifistic, legalistic, and legislative strategies proffered up by national civil rights organizations. Many African Americans, men in particular, refused to participate in nonviolent protests because they believed that passive resistance to white violence simply reproduced the same degrading rituals of domination and submission that suffused the master/slave relationship."[13]

Christopher Strain and Simon Wendt both contribute broad overviews, situating self-defense in the larger context of the movement by addressing key people and events, including Robert Williams and the Deacons for Defense. Both authors also distinguish between philosophical and tactical nonviolence and highlight the ways self-defense supplemented the nonviolent movement. Strain's is an intellectual history, and he emphasizes that throughout African American history, blacks' use of self-defense was "an essential part of the struggle for citizenship." He insists that in the context of white supremacy, even "individual acts of defiance" had "important political and constitutional roles in black empowerment." Wendt's most original contribution is attention to the connection between civil rights organizations' fund-raising and their public projections of nonviolence. Like Umoja, he highlights the relationship between nonviolence and self-defense in the Mississippi organizing of the Student Nonviolent Coordinating Committee (SNCC). He also adds a case study of Tuscaloosa, Alabama, that reinforces much that we learned about self-defense from earlier local studies.[14]

Umoja, Hill, Strain, and Wendt all stress a number of important aspects of self-defense, most of which were at least implicit in earlier studies. However, in these studies, their forcefulness and centrality give them greater visibility and demand engagement by other historians. Collectively, they argue that historians must more fully acknowledge the crucial role of "armed resistance" and what they tend to characterize as "militancy." In his 1999 article "The Ballot and the Bullet," Umoja asserts that we "must revise the definition of the civil rights movement to include the role of armed militancy as a complement and alternative to nonviolent direct action." Wendt and Strain would likely agree. According to Wendt, "[A]rmed resistance served as a significant auxiliary to nonviolent protest," while Strain notes that "the traditions of armed self-defense and nonviolence co-existed."[15]

These authors also highlight the importance of rejecting a racial double standard related to violence, whether perpetuated by those present during the movement or by subsequent commentators. Strain, for example, takes issue with journalists and early movement histories that portrayed a pre- and post-1965 dichotomy framed as a negative shift from nonviolence to violence, insisting that they "have perpetuated a historical double standard regarding the use of violence by black and white Americans (i.e., whites can, blacks cannot)." (Activist Robert Williams made this same argument in his 1962 *Negroes with Guns*.) Though Hill, in particular, frames nonviolence and self-defense in fairly oppositional ways, he also emphasizes the importance of challenging the double standard, pointing out that "[t]he Deacons boldly flouted the age-old southern code that denied blacks the right of open and collective self-defense, and by doing so they made an implicit claim to social and civil equality."[16]

This recent generation of self-defense scholarship has done invaluable service by drawing attention to the basic outline of self-defense, especially as it relates to the national story, and by insisting that historians confront its significance and role. At the same time, there are ways that some of this scholarship has, in moving away from the complexity of community studies, gone too far in overemphasizing the centrality of self-defense, in and of itself, without enough attention to the ways it was always part of a larger movement that utilized a range of tactics (not all of which fit either nonviolence or self-defense). One result is that the self-defense focused books have, in some ways, created a new top-down, media-driven narrative that, even as it replaces or stands alongside the King-centric one, still largely follows visible people, organizations, and events. It typically includes King and Montgomery as a way to explore the contested nature of early nonviolence, turns to Robert Williams to illustrate the competing or alternative ideology of assertive armed resistance, and chronicles SNCC's encounter with black Mississippians, like Hartman Turnbow, as context for the organization's internal debates about self-defense during the Mississippi Summer Project in 1964. The Deacons represent the high point or epitome of southern self-defense and then the story shifts North, including some or all of the following: Malcolm X and the Nation of Islam, urban rebellions (or riots/conflagrations, depending on the author), and the Oakland-based, southern movement-inspired Black Panther Party for Self-Defense. Although there are variations, most of the new self-defense scholarship fits within and contributes to this framework.

Moreover, in their efforts to correct the blindspots and perversions of the traditional narrative, these works can sometimes slip into caricaturing nonviolence while glorifying guns and violence. This has a number of implications. It can overstate the effectiveness and primacy of self-defense in generating change, while obscuring the dynamic interactions of multiple tactics. It can also translate into a disproportionate focus on men and manhood that obscures quite a bit about men and women. Similarly, while most of these scholars highlight the limitations of the strict nonviolence versus self-defense dichotomy, stressing that these were more complementary than contradictory, it is a difficult dichotomy to leave behind. At times, they still have a tendency to perpetuate this analytical framework. And yet, to some extent, the categories of nonviolence and self-defense, whether set up as contradictory or complementary, are too limited and imprecise to fully capture the flexibility and complexity of the freedom struggle.[17] In addition, while all of these works point to changes over time (especially around 1964) and the distinctiveness of the Deacons, many questions about the nature of and reasons for these changes remain unanswered, especially as they relate to the specifics of chronology and location. Finally, we need more precision around the definition of "armed resistance" and more clarity about the role of violence (broadly defined) within the movement, including those aspects that are not so easily categorized as self-defense.

Thus, while these books have collectively helped reinforce the significance of self-defense and begun the work of creating a synthesis of key events, people, and topics, much work remains. In particular, we need to reconsider and reframe our understanding of movement tactics so that we can move beyond the persistent nonviolence/self-defense framework; revisit gender and militancy; examine the role of "other" forms of violence or resistance, not easily categorized as self-defense; and analyze the nature and extent to which self-defense changed in 1964 (in general and in relation to the Deacons for Defense).

Self-defense is an important topic in its own right, one that is crucial to a complete and accurate picture of the civil rights movement. By revisiting local studies and developing new conceptual frameworks—ones that avoid the either/or traps and overstatements of both the nonviolence- and self-defense-oriented frameworks—we can more precisely bring self-defense into the narrative of movement history. As this suggests, self-defense also offers a useful case study for illustrating both the challenges and importance of revising and reorienting "the movement narrative" to reflect what we know from local studies and bottom-up history.

## NONVIOLENCE AND SELF-DEFENSE, MOVING BEYOND THE DICHOTOMY

Part of the conceptual problem is that too often "nonviolence" has been used as a catchall for every strategy that did not involve self-defense or violence. That simply does not work. In his study of Sunflower County, Mississippi, Todd Moye notes that "[f]ew local people made the commitment to nonviolence as a way of life." Drawing on a framework articulated by SNCC worker Worth Long, Moye argues "the term 'un-violent,' as opposed to 'nonviolent,' may best describe the movement." In a 1983 interview, SNCC activist Robert (Bob) Moses, who worked in Mississippi from late 1961 through the end of the 1964 Summer Project, described the Mississippi movement in similar terms, telling the interviewer, "I don't think violence versus nonviolence is such a good dichotomy." He added that during the movement, the discussion about nonviolence, self-defense, and guns "had a lot of negative qualities because the emotional pitch was so high," making it difficult to address the "practical issues." In his view, openly carrying weapons could be counterproductive, making it more difficult to "move as quietly as possible among people so that you could work. Because the strategy was not to pick a fight and just throw yourself into the wave of mechanisms." At the same time, he asserted that none of the local Mississippians "were practicing nonviolence . . . and while they sometimes acknowledged that we ourselves were practicing nonviolence . . . they would not buy it. And we weren't selling it." In fact, he explains that the attempt to initiate a nonviolent movement in Mississippi failed in the aftermath of the 1961 Freedom Rides and, instead, the movement organized around the "more practical program of voter registration . . . which didn't require either on the part of the staff or the people a commitment to nonviolence." He elaborates, "There is nothing in the federal government that says you have to be nonviolent to go register."[18] Because the Mississippi movement was organized around voter registration with few public demonstrations, for the most part tactical nonviolence was neither necessary nor appropriate.

Most authors who focus on self-defense miss this nuance. Even those who argue that nonviolence and self-defense were complementary, not antagonistic, still tend to reinforce a dichotomy and overlook or mischaracterize "un-violent" tactics.[19] Although a number of authors contribute to sustaining this dichotomy, Lance Hill is distinct in arguing forcefully that there was an explicit conflict between nonviolence and self-defense that went well beyond public relations. In this regard, Hill's influential work on the Deacons reflects some general shortcomings, while also being somewhat at odds with other scholarship. Because of this, his arguments are worth exploring in some detail. In his determination to argue for the significance and primacy of self-defense, Hill caricatures much of the movement, ignores considerable scholarship (especially local studies), and makes huge generalizations about national organizations.

For example, he insists that national organizations tried to impose nonviolence, which he characterizes as passive and emasculating, on local activists. He asserts that "[f]rom the beginning of the modern civil rights movement, opposition to black armed self-defense was an article of faith for national organizations." He includes the NAACP, SNCC, CORE, and the Southern Christian Leadership Conference (SCLC) in this group, though he does note that "SNCC and CORE moderated their official positions near the end of the movement." Contending that "the national organizations took a stand against self-defense that placed them at odds with local movements besieged by police and Klan violence and hobbled by passive stereotypes," Hill asserts that the Deacons became a "symbol of the revolt against nonviolence." He also argues that the Bogalusa movement proved the effectiveness of self-defense, especially in contrast to what he terms "nonviolence."[20] In making these claims, Hill disregards variations among the national civil rights organizations, their internal conflicts, the reality of local movements, and shifts over time. For example, while the national NAACP *did* suspend Robert Williams for assertively insisting that blacks had the right to self-defense, at the same convention, the membership passed a resolution reaffirming the right to self-defense. Moreover, as Dittmer, Payne, and others have illustrated, at the local level NAACP activists across the South routinely armed themselves, something national staff must have known. And the same Roy Wilkins, who earlier suspended Robert Williams, authorized a fund to pay bodyguards for Charles Evers (who also troubled Wilkins with his periodic public statements threatening black retaliation).[21]

Whatever the NAACP's positions were on self-defense, the national staff was never particularly excited about philosophical or tactical nonviolence. Both were more important in the creation and early histories of SNCC and CORE. Yet by the time the Deacons were founded in the fall of 1964 and emerged on the national scene in Bogalusa in 1965, SNCC and CORE, both in terms of the beliefs and practices of individual organizers and broader organizational debates and policies, had long since abandoned any single-minded devotion to nonviolence. In fact, nonviolence was always contested within SNCC, and by 1962 field staff were living and organizing in local Mississippi communities where, as Dittmer and Payne illustrate, white terror and black self-defense were givens. Payne claims that "[w]hatever they felt about nonviolence personally, SNCC workers seem to have almost never tried to talk local people into putting down their guns" and concludes that black "farmers may have done more to change the behavior of SNCC workers in this respect than vice versa." Bob Moses explained to Akinyele Umoja, "Local people carried the day. They defined how they and the culture was going to relate to the issue of using guns."[22]

CORE's approach to self-defense is particularly relevant because it was the primary national civil rights organization in the Louisiana communities that Lance Hill studies. Compared with SNCC, CORE had a longer, more explicitly nonviolent history. It was also more hierarchical and included a number of national staff who more insistently promoted nonviolence. And yet, Adam Fairclough and Greta de Jong illustrate that by 1963 CORE field staff in Louisiana (including some who remained personally committed to nonviolence) had come to accept and appreciate self-defense. Many CORE workers welcomed the presence of armed men at meetings, some staff carried guns, and there was even discussion of possible retaliatory violence. In 1963, white CORE worker Miriam Feingold captured both the pull of violence and the conflict between the national staff and CORE workers on the ground, writing in her diary, "[CORE leader] Jim McCain says CORE can't afford to advocate retaliation. But [field staff] Dave Dennis, [and] Jerome Smith say to hell with CORE, we're with the people."[23]

Greta de Jong, especially, details how CORE's national staff and some volunteers attempted to influence local people to accept nonviolence, though she notes that they had very limited success. Fairclough explains that in 1964, the "director of CORE's southern regional office, sent staff members a memo directing them to cease carrying weapons or resign." When they failed to comply, however, "he turned a blind eye to the practice." As this suggests, local realities and preferences typically trumped the official line coming from the national office. In Louisiana, as in Mississippi, local people did more to influence CORE workers than the other way around. In 1963, Feingold wrote her family, "Most everyone, especially the kids who have been most active, are disillusioned with non-violence, & see the situation very much turning toward violence. They think that we must do as the masses feel—& if it means violence, then that's what we do." Akinyele Umoja and Simon Wendt also detail how black southerners' insistence on their right to self-defense had an increasing impact on CORE at the national and policy level. At the 1963 national convention, field staff warned about the possibility of a "violent racial explosion." Though the group reaffirmed its commitment to nonviolence, it did so in more practical and less idealistic terms. The debate continued in subsequent conventions until, in 1966, CORE publicly asserted what had long been practiced in the field, that self-defense was a "natural, constitutional, and inalienable right" and that "nonviolence and self-defense are not contradictory."[24]

Hill's narrative fails to acknowledge that national organizations did not always speak with one voice and the national view did not always prevail. Local studies make it clear that black southerners *always* brought their realities and priorities to the table. In varying degrees, they shaped not only their own local movements but the experiences and attitudes of those civil rights organizers they worked with most closely *and* broader national trends and priorities. Interestingly, the specifics of the Deacons' own history, including much of Hill's account, point to the ways that local communities influenced the national organizations. They also suggest that Hill overstates the conflicts between the Deacons (self-defense) and CORE/national organizations (nonviolence). In both Jonesboro and Bogalusa, the men who founded and belonged to the Deacons worked closely with CORE, participated in a wide range of movement activities (including nonviolent demonstrations), and in some instances, publicly articulated their support for nonviolence. Here, as in other communities, self-defense supplemented and supported other, nonviolent *and* unviolent, forms of protest, including direct action, voter registration, boycotts, litigation, and negotiations. Ironically, according to Hill and Fairclough, two white, philosophically nonviolent CORE workers actually facilitated the establishment of the Deacons, originally in Jonesboro and then in Bogalusa. Moreover, at the 1965 CORE convention, Deacon Earnest Thomas urged CORE delegates to continue their support for tactical nonviolence.[25]

In attempting to stake out a place for the Deacons and what he considers black militancy, Hill also overstates the Deacons' singular role in the Bogalusa "victory." The victory that Hill attributes almost solely to the Deacons was also based on the work of CORE, the Bogalusa Voters League, and other activists, as well as assertive federal intervention (in response to open racial conflict). Without CORE workers (and others, including some Deacons), demonstrating and insisting on their right to congregate, picket, enter restaurants, and use parks, there would have been no one for the Deacons to protect. Self-defense was just that, *defensive*, and while in many cases it was *essential*, it was never the primary organizing tactic in Bogalusa or the movement as a whole. Moreover, even in Bogalusa where the Deacons escorted activists, guarded the black community, and exchanged gunfire with the Klan, they were unable to effectively protect public demonstrations. With inadequate protection from local lawmen and extensive Klan violence and intimidation (even with the Deacons' determined stand), the significant break in Bogalusa came when a federal judge, with Justice Department urging, took steps to dismantle the Klan and ordered local officials to protect demonstrators. Thus, Hill's effort to stress the Deacons' significance and place self-defense front and center comes at the expense of other aspects of the movement and a nuanced understanding of the interplay of numerous factors.[26]

Although Hill uses most of his book to emphasize the Deacons' rejection of nonviolence and their centrality in challenging the existing civil rights movement leadership, in his conclusion, he backtracks a little and puts forward an interpretation that is much more in line with the general consensus on self-defense. He writes,

> The Deacons did not see their self-defense activities as mutually exclusive of nonviolent tactics and voter registration. Viewing themselves as part of the broader civil rights movement, they did not oppose nonviolent direct action — indeed, they supported it, employed it as a tactic, and expended most of their

energy defending its practitioners. What the Deacons opposed was the dog-
matic idea that nonviolent direct action precluded self-defense. . . . The choice
confronting the black movement was not, as Martin Luther King and his disciplines maintained, strictly a choice between nonviolence and violence.[27]

Hill is right. The choice was not strictly "between nonviolence and violence." Moreover, few people really saw it that way. His decision to employ
this dichotomy ignores and dismisses the realities of Jonesboro and Bogalusa, along with quite a bit of movement history. It obscures the pervasiveness of self-defense, its essentially complementary nature, its acceptance by
many CORE activists and others within national organizations, and the wide
range of movement tactics that are not easily categorized as either nonviolence or self-defense. Though direct action was important to Bogalusa, so
were many other tactics that were *unviolent*, like voter registration, boycotts,
and litigation. In perpetuating this dichotomy, Hill loses an opportunity to
explore more precisely the tensions that did exist over nonviolence, the ways
that self-defense in Bogalusa was distinct, how the local/national interactions
evolved over time, and how the organized, assertive, and visible nature of
self-defense in Bogalusa actually did impact the movement more broadly.
Moreover, by constructing a framework that equates the Bogalusa Deacons'
form of self-defense with an evolution toward militancy and manhood for
black men, Hill implies that it was somehow a natural development, rather
than a response to a particular set of circumstances.

## GENDER AND MILITANCY

The nonviolence/self-defense framing also has implications for understanding the topics of gender and militancy. During the movement and since, many
activists, bystanders, commentators, and historians have perpetuated and reinforced stereotypes whereby militancy is defined primarily in terms of guns
and violence (or the potential for violence) and nonviolence is denigrated
as passive and humiliating, especially for men. While this does reflect a particular view, as a framework for understanding the movement it has severe
limitations. It overlooks the coercive and positive elements of nonviolence,
obscures activism that was essentially "unviolent," and largely ignores wom-
en's experiences, while distorting those of many men. In the end, although
a few self-defense scholars give some attention to gender and occasional lip

service to women, for the most part they keep the lens on men. With this approach, both women and men appear somewhat one-dimensional and much of the scholarship accepts too much at face value—be it the gendered language, assumptions, and claims of the 1960s or the unsupported speculations of participants and scholars. In part this reflects the reality that within the movement, men *were* typically more vocal about self-defense and clearly dominated self-defense efforts as they became more organized and formal. Ultimately, though, it seems more connected to stereotypes and an unquestioning acceptance of the idea that self-defense is a "male prerogative."[28]

In 1959, before the sit-ins and Freedom Rides illustrated the potential effectiveness of nonviolent action, Robert Williams "denounced the 'emasculated men' who preached nonviolence while white mobs beat their wives and daughters." Many other black men shared these attitudes (including many who remained outside the southern movement), but the Deacons were among the most assertive proponents of self-defense in terms of masculinity. Christopher Strain titled his 1997 article on the Deacons "We Walked Like Men" and argues that the organization became "an expression of manhood." Simon Wendt insists, "The Deacons' armed militancy also reflected southern black men's determination to assert their manhood." Hill claims that the Deacons offered "black men a way to participate in the movement while maintaining their concept of male honor and dignity" and that in Jonesboro, Deacons' meetings "became a pulpit for the new creed of manhood." According to Hill, for the Deacons, "[f]reedom for black men depended on manhood, and manhood meant the willingness to use force to defend one's family and community. Black men could not attain manhood through the strategy of nonviolence, since nonviolence prohibited the use of force. And without manhood status, rights were meaningless. For black men to be free, whites had to fear as well as respect them." Wendt, too, asserts that for Deacons "there was no freedom without dignity, and sometimes, dignity could only come from the barrel of a gun."[29]

Following this line of thinking, some authors insist that the "nonviolence" supposedly required by the movement was a major factor in limiting male participation and that the supposed "passivity" of nonviolence was somehow more problematic for men than women. (The unspoken corollary is that it was somehow problematic that more women than men joined the movement.)[30] For example, Simon Wendt observes that "[t]o the primarily working-class men who joined the Deacons, Martin Luther King's idea of nonviolence was degrading to their notion of male identity." Even as he observes that women regularly used self-defense, he expresses surprise that "women practiced what most men considered a male prerogative" and speculates that "[o]ne explanation could be that white supremacy had traditionally impeded the ability of black men to defend themselves and their community."[31] Lance Hill offers a blanket description of nonviolence as a "pacifistic" attempt at moral suasion that required blacks to cater to whites' fears and preferences. He also contends it was "emasculating," leading black men to "boycott" the movement rather than "passively endure humiliation and physical abuse."[32] Hill asserts that "the physical and emotional risks that black men assumed when they joined a nonviolent protest far outweighed what black women and children suffered." Moreover, he continues, "Bound by notions of masculine honor, black men had much more to lose than women and children: what was at stake was their pride, their manhood, and, very likely, their life." Wendt adds, "Men were generally more reluctant to become involved in civil rights activism. Many were afraid of losing their job or of white retaliation. Others refused to participate because of their opposition to nonviolence."[33] Though Wendt acknowledges that a range of factors influenced black men's participation or lack thereof, neither he nor Hill offer much evidence to support their broad claim that antipathy to nonviolence, more than other factors, kept black men (and men more than women) out of the movement. Instead, they speculate about the psychological impact of white supremacy on black men and rely heavily on the rhetoric of a few men, most of them Deacons, to make the connection to manhood.[34] Unfortunately, they and others too often fail to go beyond such relatively superficial characterizations.

Here again, some of the earlier local studies offer useful insight and point to the possibilities for a more nuanced, complex assessment. Through an accumulation of details, it is clear that black women in the Mississippi movement were actively involved in defending themselves and their families. In Dittmer's and Payne's accounts, the ways women and men used and understood self-defense do not appear so starkly different and do not easily fit with the gendered stereotypes that populate some of the self-defense oriented books. Moreover, in an entire chapter devoted to considering women's disproportionate movement participation, Payne's focus is ultimately on efficacy: what does it take for women and men to have the courage and faith to act in the face of seemingly insurmountable odds? Neither he nor any of those he quotes so much as speculate that nonviolence was a factor in the participation rates of women or men. Payne analyzes and discounts the somewhat-related "differential-reprisal theory" offered by some, that women joined the movement because they were somehow less vulnerable to violence or economic retaliation. Furthermore, in his counter-example of Holmes County—where men joined the movement early and in large numbers, bucking the pattern of neighboring Delta counties—Payne points to the significance of high rates of contiguous black landownership, along with a history of working in cooperatives. Thus, he speculates that it was these positive experiences that led to increased efficacy, and increased movement participation, among Holmes County men. Nonviolence—its presence or absence—appears irrelevant.[35]

Even more than Dittmer and Payne, Timothy Tyson gives particular attention to the intersection of gender and self-defense in the Monroe movement where women and men used and advocated armed self-defense. Tyson argues that black women "both deployed" and "defied" gender stereotypes. For example, women urged Robert Williams and other men to stand up and protect them, while simultaneously insisting on weapons training and agitating to participate in the self-defense network. In one instance, a crowd of armed women crowded into the police station and demanded the release of Dr. Albert Perry, a jailed movement leader. In another, Mabel Williams, Robert's wife, used a .12-gauge shotgun to keep police at bay when they came to arrest her husband. And yet, women and men both had gendered expectations related to self-defense. Robert Williams recalled that although women "wanted to fight[,] . . . we kept them out of most of it." For their part, black women "turned on Robert Williams" when two white men were acquitted of crimes against black women and "bitterly shamed him for failing to provide for their protection." Earlier, Williams had discouraged them in their calls for extralegal revenge. Grounding his analysis in the context of race and gender in the 1950s, Tyson explains that black men considered it their duty and right to protect black women "not as an abstract rhetorical commitment to black patriarchy but as a deep and daily personal responsibility." At the same time, Tyson argues that "[t]he rhetoric of protecting women was an integral part of the politics of controlling women" and that protecting "'their' women" was also as much about black men's identities as it was about "the security" of women.[36] Taken together, Tyson's examples and analysis offer a complex picture of self-defense and gender that extends to the attitudes and actions of men and women.[37]

More recently, historian Steve Estes challenges the stereotype that nonviolence was inherently unmanly, claiming that the "young men in the movement created militant new models of black manhood." In fact, he argues that despite its passive connotations, nonviolence "could be courageous and even manly." Stokely Carmichael (Kwame Ture), who introduced the "Black Power" slogan to the nation during the 1966 Meredith March, takes up the nonviolent stereotype in his posthumously published memoir, *Ready for Revolution.* He carefully explains the differences between tactical and philosophical nonviolence and asserts that both required considerable discipline and were anything but "passive." Moreover, according to Carmichael, rather than limiting participation, strategic nonviolence "gave our generation—particularly in the South—the means by which to confront an entrenched and violent racism. It offered a way for *large* numbers of [African Americans] to join the struggle. Nothing passive in that." He also explains that he "gloried" in "*direct action*" because although it was nonviolent, it was also "directly confrontational, even aggressively so." He reiterates that one of the important aspects of nonviolent action was that it allowed "the entire community, everyone who would, [to] be a part and hope to survive."

In talking about the Albany, Georgia, movement, Bernice Johnson Reagon describes the "sense of power" that she and others got from "confronting things that terrified you, like jail, police, walking in the street—you know, a whole lot of Black folks couldn't even walk in the street in those places in the South." Though she does not define her experience in terms of nonviolence, direct action was a key component of the Albany Movement and was one way that African Americans actively resisted segregation and challenged white authority. Reagon explains that, for her, the central aspect of the Albany Movement was that it gave her a "real chance to struggle" and "the power to challenge *any* line that limits me."[38]

At times, it seems that scholars accept (or project) facile characterizations of nonviolence as a way to excuse or justify women's more widespread participation in the movement, while failing to offer a compelling argument for why men might have found "nonviolence" more problematic than women. Thus, the idea that nonviolence was both passive and emasculating, along with the corollary that self-defense was a crucial antidote, particularly essential to black "manhood," remains a powerful theme in the work of self-defense scholars. However, in many ways this issue of "nonviolence" is a red herring since many men and women used it assertively in ways that enhanced their feeling of dignity, while others joined the movement without submitting to the discipline of nonviolence or giving up their right to armed self-defense. It is hard to seriously consider the Mississippi movement, just to take an example, and conclude that it was based on a cringing form of nonviolence that was emasculating and geared toward appeasing whites. And certainly, as Dittmer and Payne make clear, the *men and women* who tried to register to vote or participated in the Mississippi movement in any way, were prepared to and did defend themselves with guns. I cannot think of one single cringing emasculated man who *joined* the movement. A facile glorification of guns and disparagement of nonviolence becomes a substitute for careful analysis of gendered differences in movement participation. Thus, these scholars miss the opportunity to contribute to a fuller understanding of the reasons both men and women chose to join or not join.

In fact, anyone joining the movement had to consider the likelihood of job loss, violence, and other forms of repression. This certainly extended to men as well as women. Hill himself notes that there was actually widespread fear among black men, fear and passivity (unrelated to nonviolence) that the Deacons tried to combat. He explains, for example, that the Jonesboro Deacons sought to "shock black men out of the lethargy of fear." Umoja, who avoids these gendered stereotypes, notes that actively engaging in armed resistance helped many men overcome fear. In 1964, when SNCC's Charles McLaurin was leading a demonstration composed of "kids and women," he urged the black men watching from the sidelines to join and accused them of being "afraid." A number of movement activists (including those who believed in self-defense) suggest, in fact, that men (and women?) sometimes tried to cover up their fear and inaction through disparaging nonviolence. Stokely Carmichael recalls listening to Malcolm X assail "the 'unmanliness' of leaders who would watch white men brutalize their women and children while professing 'nonviolence.'" This gave Carmichael pause, but he also observed that "all the brothers in the room who'd never been on our picket lines suddenly found justification for their absence." Similarly, SNCC organizer Worth Long explains that "people who were afraid would say 'I would go out with you and march with you . . . except that I'm violent. I might hit somebody.' Basically they're saying they're afraid. So I would say things like, 'Well, I'm scared too.' Get to the heart of the matter."[39]

Most of the assessments of men and masculinity are too superficial, but the attention to women is even more cursory, with little or no analysis of how they understood their use of self-defense, what they thought of nonviolence, what they wanted from the men they lived and worked with, or any other of the many questions we might ask. The self-defense scholarship also tends to ignore the possibility that the explanation for women's more frequent movement participation might lie in something positive related to women, rather than something negative related to men.[40] Hill does note that women joined the Jonesboro Deacons and that women in both Deacon strongholds, Jonesboro and Bogalusa, held target practice and contemplated a women's auxiliary. Moreover, in all these communities, even after self-defense became organized, women continued to wield and use weapons. In Bogalusa, Jackie Hicks pulled a pistol out of her purse to "fend off" a mob during an attempt to desegregate a public park. Despite these important snippets, Hill fails to offer much detail or any analysis, simply observing in one endnote that "[t]here are no studies of the role of women in the self-defense movement, though it would be a fascinating and useful subject." Similarly, Hill gives a nod to the fact that some women, like some men, had problems with nonviolence, writing, "[L]arge numbers of women refused to participate in nonviolent activities for some of the same reasons as men."[41] Although this is an important point, it remains buried, included as an aside. There is no systematic analysis of the responses, attitudes, and actions of men and women in relation to nonviolence, self-defense, and a wide range of movement tactics—an approach that might offer some insight and one that is certainly relevant to Hill's gendered conclusions.

Wendt also focuses on the meaning of self-defense for men and defines men's use of self-defense in terms of masculinity, even when their explanations appear gender neutral. In one instance, Wendt argues that "[i]n assuming the protection of women and children, [Medgar] Evers, [Hartman] Turnbow, and other black Mississippians regained part of their manhood that whites had long denied them." While there is undoubtedly some truth to the idea that black men believed that they should protect black women and children, this assertion includes a number of blindspots. One, it assumes that, separate from self-defense, these men felt unmanly. Two, it ignores the longstanding history of self-defense among African Americans. As Payne and others have pointed out, self-defense did change and was different when it was connected to an organized political movement, but there were *always*

African Americans who used weapons to protect themselves and their families.[42] In addition, given the number of women among the black Mississippians who used self-defense, it is problematic to imply, as this does, that self-defense was the province of men. Did women's use of self-defense help them regain their manhood? Their womanhood? Though Wendt follows up with quotes by a number of male activists, their explanations for self-defense appear fairly universal and it is not clear why they would not apply just as well to women. Comparisons are difficult, however, since Wendt did not include the voices of any women on their use of self-defense. The logic seems to go like this: self-defense is somehow inherently masculine; therefore, no matter the explanation, men who use it do so in order to assert their manhood.

Self-defense was undoubtedly gendered. For some, it was almost certainly related to ideas of manhood, masculinity, and the male "prerogative" of protecting one's family and community. Yet it is important not to read "manhood" into every instance of self-defense or every explanation of it. Did women and men understand self-defense differently? Why did self-defense become more male as it became more organized? Does it follow the typical pattern in the movement, where women are most visible and apparent at the grass-roots level, while men tend to dominate more formal and visible leadership positions? Or is there something different at work here? Were there men who participated in the movement only through organized self-defense efforts? If so, who were they? How did they differ from men who also (or only) participated in other movement activities?

Women are a significant part of this story, too, and we need to acknowledge that and bring them into the narrative in meaningful, not superficial, ways. How did Laura McGhee understand her use of self-defense? (Not only did she and her sons shoot back at violent night riders, she punched a police officer in the Greenwood jail.)[43] Did protecting her family mean something different to McGhee than it did to Hartman Turnbow? Did Turnbow feel more manly after shooting back at the men who firebombed his house? Or was it security in his manhood that brought him into the movement and made him a target in the first place? Did joining the Deacons mean something different to women than men in Jonesboro? Why do we know so little about these women? And what about Jackie Hicks in Bogalusa? She consistently defended her home and pulled a gun on lawmen in a public park. According to Hill, she organized target practice for women and tried to form a Deacons' auxiliary. How did she feel about being excluded from the group?

Did it matter to her? Did she feel discriminated against? Proud of the men who stepped forward? Disgusted at the chauvinism that limited the pool of participants? And what of her Deacon husband? How did he feel about her active self-defense? He is unarmed at the park, while she has a gun. Does he feel unmanly? Or proud? Would he feel safer if she was in the Deacons? Or is he emasculated by her assertiveness?

## FIGHTING BACK IN THE "NONVIOLENT" MOVEMENT

One of the problems with this kind of superficial and flawed gender analysis, especially when combined with the persistence of the nonviolence and self-defense dichotomy, is that it actually makes it more difficult to acknowledge and fully grapple with the experiences, perspectives, and impact (on the movement) of the people, *men and women,* who chose not to join the movement or who limited their participation because they were unable or unwilling to submit to nonviolent discipline.[44] Timothy Tyson gives a glimpse of this complexity through his profile of Mae Mallory, who became an avid supporter of Robert Williams after hearing his outspoken insistence on armed defense. Though Mallory was "among those who would never enlist in the armies of nonviolence," she was a movement activist in Harlem and as a supporter of Williams and the Monroe movement. In 1961, when a group of freedom riders went to Monroe and escalated demonstrations, Mallory came immediately to help Mabel Williams with "household chores." Once in Monroe, she stayed away from demonstrations because of her unwillingness to "submit to nonviolent discipline." In fact, Robert Williams recalled that several times he had to discourage her interest in initiating violence.[45]

This is just the tip of the iceberg and another problem with the nonviolence/self-defense framework. Just as many tactics did not require nonviolence, many people broke nonviolent discipline and/or used, considered, reacted with, or threatened violence in ways that stretched the boundaries of self-defense. The example of Judy Richardson, a nineteen-year-old SNCC activist who had spent a year at Swarthmore, is probably somewhat typical. During an arrest at a January 1964 demonstration in Atlanta, she reacted angrily to the rough handling of another demonstrator by police. Struggling to get away and help, she unintentionally kicked an officer in the groin. According to the *New York Times,* several others "sought to tear off a policeman's jacket." Many of the personal accounts in *Hands on the Freedom Plow,* a collection of autobiographical narratives by SNCC women, feature self-defense, while a few describe similar incidents of breaking discipline during ostensibly nonviolent protests. For example, Mildred Forman, wife of SNCC's executive secretary James Forman, fought with a police officer in Atlanta who was determined to drag her on the ground during an arrest. She reflected later that "nonviolence was only a tactic, not my Chicago way of life." She also remembered Martin Luther King Jr. teasing her husband about seeing the incident on the news and suggesting to Forman that he "keep [his] wife in the office" so she would not "ruin our nonviolent concept!" In another instance, a "group of black youngsters . . . brandishing sticks and . . . shouting 'Freedom! Freedom!'" saved her and other picketers from a Klan attack in front of the Atlanta restaurant owned by Lester Maddox, later an aggressively segregationist governor. Fay Bellamy recalls being shocked to find herself "locked in mortal combat" with a state trooper who knocked her down the Capitol steps during another Atlanta demonstration. When a police officer refused to stop pinching her arm after a later arrest, she hit "him with all the power I could muster." After the second incident, she decided that "being nonviolent" during demonstrations was not one of her "strengths" and she would have to focus on other ways to be part of the "nonviolent struggle."[46]

Nashville is often held up as an ideal for nonviolence, in part because it was home to James Lawson's nonviolent workshops. These fostered disciplined and effective sit-ins, while producing a committed group of philosophically nonviolent practitioners. These influential activists insisted the Freedom Rides continue, even in the face of extreme violence and federal demands for a cooling off period, and many became leaders in SNCC and SCLC. Despite this, SNCC activists James Forman and Stokely Carmichael both recall that in the summer of 1961, there were heated debates in Nashville over the appropriate role of nonviolence in the movement and considerable resistance to strict nonviolence from some segments of the black community. Neither Forman nor Carmichael embraced philosophical nonviolence, though both saw it as an important tactic. For example, Forman writes that he viewed nonviolence "as a means to build a mass movement and to build the self-confidence of our people as a whole." Despite reservations about his ability to maintain nonviolence, Forman joined a picket line (part of an ongoing protest) and recalls that when he "faced" the "hecklers" he "had to steel" himself, noting that "I didn't want to break the discipline of the group by striking back." Though he found this a "terrible test of my nerves," Forman's

belief in "collective discipline" kept him in "the nonviolent group." He recalls, however, that Bill Hargrove, a freedom rider who had abandoned nonviolence, was among a group of "young blacks" who stood watch across the
street, prepared to battle whites if they attacked the nonviolent demonstrators. Writing in 1972, Forman characterized this group as "forerunners of the
Deacons" who themselves, he argues, were "an inevitable parallel to the development of nonviolence."[47]

Carmichael, probably describing the same protest (that extended over several weeks), recounts a conversation with "a group of brothers off the corner" who expressed support for the movement, but said, "We don't go for
none a' that nonviolence stuff." Carmichael responded that "nonviolence is
hard, it ain't for everybody." With fellow SNCC activist Dion Diamond, he asserted that they did not have to be nonviolent, but urged them to "find a way
to struggle." According to Carmichael, they did. A few nights later when a
white heckler knocked him into a plate glass window and the police moved
in to arrest him, "the young brothers on the corner" responded by "throwing
bricks and bottles and whatever else they had stockpiled." Carmichael found
that not everyone was happy with his ecumenical organizing and at a "heavy,
heavy meeting," leaders of the Nashville movement accused him of "causing the violence at the demonstration" and threatened to expel him from the
"nonviolent movement."[48] As these examples suggest, there were people who
supported the movement, but had trouble with the idea or practice of nonviolence. At least some of them still found ways to act.

Moreover, as these examples illustrate, violence or its potential was always
present in the movement. In a 2001 essay, Jenny Walker argues that the media
(followed by many historians) "often seemed inclined to ignore, downplay or
de-politicize incidents of black violence and inflammatory rhetoric in civil
rights protests." Revisiting the well-known bombing of King's home during
the Montgomery Bus Boycott when "an angry and armed crowd . . . gathered
outside intent on revenge," she notes that many "journalists and historians in
telling this story have focused on the fact that King persuaded the seething
mob to return home peacefully. Thus, the departure from nonviolent discipline is reduced to a parable" about King's commitment to nonviolence and
his ability to "revitalize the black community's own momentarily wavering
passion for nonviolence." More recently, those focusing on self-defense have
shifted the focus a bit, often analyzing the Montgomery Bus Boycott to illustrate King's own wavering and slow conversion to nonviolence as well as

the fluidity of nonviolence and self-defense. Christopher Strain, for example, notes that "while King defused the volatile situation with a message of peace, he prepared for war." He concludes that although King came to embrace nonviolence in a way that "made self-defense obsolete," other African Americans "needed more convincing." In fact, Strain insists, King's "faith in nonviolence ran counter to the pervasive, if sometimes unspoken sentiment among black Americans that freedom should come 'by any means necessary.'"[49]

Walker makes a similar argument, though she turns her lens even more purposefully away from King and toward the angry crowd and their counterparts in black Montgomery. In her view, the incident is less a parable about the triumph of nonviolence than a warning about the potential for violence. She argues that the crowd reflects "a willingness to take up arms to resist white aggression, sometimes spilling over into a desire for vengeance . . . [that] lurked permanently beneath the respectable surface of the nonviolent boycott." She then devotes several paragraphs to effectively illustrating this point, including examples of black women threatening retaliation if King should come to harm. In her 1992 memoir for young adults, Rosa Parks, often used as a symbol of respectable nonviolence, reinforces Walker's conclusions. She explains that for most blacks in Montgomery, "On an individual level, nonviolence could be mistaken for cowardice. The concept of mass nonviolent action was something new and very controversial. Some people thought it was risky and would invite more violence." Though she and others came to see "that the tactic could be successful," Parks concluded that she was never "an absolute supporter of nonviolence in all situations."[50]

As with self-defense, the local studies by Dittmer and Payne provide considerable detail and context for the ways that black violence was woven into the fabric of the ostensibly nonviolent movement. For example, in late 1954, after an inaccurate rumor that black leader T. R. M. Howard's wife had been assaulted, fifteen carloads of armed blacks offered their assistance. Also in the 1950s, Medgar Evers followed news of the Kenyan liberation movement and seriously considered the possibility of guerilla warfare. Laura McGhee, like Evers, was assertive and open to options. After one attack on her farm, she called the sheriff to warn him that next time she called, he would be "picking up bodies." In another incident, she punched a police officer who was harassing her as she tried to bail out one of her sons. John Dittmer observes that in the months before the 1964 Summer Project, Justice Department head Burke Marshall was concerned that blacks and whites were arming themselves and

"preparing for confrontation." In Natchez in late 1965, NAACP state field secretary Charles Evers explicitly threatened retaliation in response to white violence. He also encouraged the harassment of African Americans who violated an NAACP-sponsored boycott in Natchez (and elsewhere). In a more
recent local study of Cambridge, Maryland, Peter Levy makes it clear that
self-defense was widely accepted and practiced among local blacks. Black
men kept regular watch, firing back at white vigilantes who rode through
the black community shooting at African American homes and residents.
He also observes that, anticipating violence, black protesters sometimes carried weapons on demonstrations. In June 1963, in the midst of considerable
tension, several white-owned businesses were burned in the black neighborhood, blacks and whites exchanged gunfire, and when the police entered the
black community, they "were met with a barrage of bricks and bottles."[51]

John Dittmer details a number of instances in which black Mississippians
engaged in or considered collective retaliation. When police stopped Medgar Evers's funeral procession in 1963, "angry blacks fought back, shower-
ing the police with bricks, bottles, and other available missiles." In February 1964, after a black woman was hit by a car, more than seven hundred
students at Jackson State "went on a rampage, throwing rocks, bricks, and
bottles at cars driven by whites." A few months later, when Greenwood activist Silas McGhee was shot in his car, a crowd of armed black men converged
on the movement office. Dittmer describes McComb, Mississippi, after a series of bombings in fall 1964, as an "armed camp." The late September bombing of movement activist Aylene Quin's home was, apparently, one bombing
too many. "Several hundred angry blacks stormed into the streets. . . . Some
were carrying guns, while others made molotov cocktails by pouring gasoline
into empty beer bottles."[52]

In describing the Greenwood incident, Dittmer notes that these were
"new faces." These were "black men in their late twenties and thirties who
had not previously been involved in the movement." CORE worker Dave Dennis makes much the same point about many of those who reacted violently in
response to the repression at Medgar Evers's funeral. He explains, "There was
a different element of people who had never participated in the movement
before. They didn't want to have anything to do with us, because they felt that
they could not cope with the nonviolence. It's not that they disagreed with the
movement, but with the tactics that we used. These guys off the street were
just angry, you know, and that day they decided to speak up." During Evers's

funeral march, Dennis was among those trying to calm the angry crowd. SNCC workers did the same in Greenwood and McComb. In each of these cases and others, activists tried to limit violence and control crowds, not because they had any inherent objection to violence or desire to cater to whites, but for fear that black attackers would bear the brunt of the violence. Dittmer notes, for example, that after McGhee was shot SNCC workers convinced the armed newcomers, along with "several hundred other angry local people," to engage in "peaceful protest and thus avoid a bloodbath."[53]

In this respect, Mississippi was typical. Movement history is full of examples of spontaneous collective retaliation (or potential retaliation) that highlight the point that should be clear—nonviolence was never universal or inevitable. Many blacks were prepared and willing to fight back. Some incidents are fairly well-known. In July 1962 in Albany, Georgia, for example, African Americans threw bricks and bottles at white police officers and passing motorists. In May 1963 in Birmingham, bystanders did the same after police attacked nonviolent protesters with fire hoses and police dogs. The violence in Birmingham was even more extensive a few weeks later when an angry crowd poured into the streets after the bombing of the Gaston Motel, where King and other SCLC leaders had been staying. Outraged African Americans attacked police cars and fire trucks, looted and burned businesses, and assaulted passing motorists.[54]

Black citizens and movement activists did have disagreements over the role and appropriateness of both nonviolence and violence. In some instances, black retaliation or advocacy of violence explicitly reflected or caused friction within the movement and the larger community. At times these tensions were related to pragmatic concerns about fund-raising and public relations. For example, James Forman, who had his own difficulties with nonviolence, chastised Judy Richardson for kicking the police officer (at least partially because she did it in front of a *New York Times* reporter). Simon Wendt contends that civil rights organizations purposefully misrepresented their work, projecting "King's philosophy" as "the movement's official creed" and promoting "a false polarity between nonviolence and armed resistance as a tactical ploy to nurture and sustain white support." He insists that even as SNCC and CORE became less and less committed to philosophical nonviolence, they continued to highlight it to the media and in their promotional and fund-raising materials.[55]

Some of the internal conflicts were more serious and reflected strongly divergent philosophical beliefs. Carmichael's experience in Nashville, for example, exemplified disagreement both within the movement and between some activists and the larger black community. In fall 1961, some of the Freedom Riders who went to Monroe, North Carolina, to support the local movement there "considered themselves philosophical if not personal adversaries" of Robert Williams and came "to prove that Williams was wrong about [the limitations of] nonviolence." One explained to reporters that what happened in Monroe was crucial to the future of "nonviolence" and "will determine the course taken in many other communities throughout the South." In July 1962 when blacks in Albany, Georgia, threw "rocks and bottles" at police officers, Martin Luther King was "deeply upset." At a news conference, he emphasized that those who were involved in the disorder were "onlookers" and not "part of our movement." He also announced a "twenty-four-hour moratorium on all demonstrations" and a "day of penance" to serve "as a symbolic apology." Historian Wesley Hogan describes a different incident in Albany, Georgia, in 1964 after a white policeman shot a young black child. She writes, "1200 people showed up to a mass meeting." However, "when SNCC people began to talk about nonviolence, it had a chilling effect on many in attendance."[56]

SNCC activist Prathia Hall witnessed another conflict between SCLC leaders and angry local residents. At a meeting in the wake of the January 1965 Bloody Sunday violence in Selma, Alabama, she recalled that because SCLC staff "were afraid that the anger would turn to violence," they were emphasizing love and nonviolence, even to the extent of trying to manipulate the religious faith and singing of those present. Although Hall came into the Movement embracing nonviolence as a way of life, she was upset in this context by what she felt amounted to "spiritual extortion," explaining, "If a person has spent all of his or her life living and suffering in the expectation of seeing Jesus at the end, it is troubling to be told if you cannot sing this song right now, you will not be saved. . . . Folks were not feeling very loving and they were not singing. This was a theological crisis for me."[57]

Who were the people who threw rocks and bottles or showed up armed, ready to retaliate for white violence? They appear in the fringes of movement histories, sometimes as foils or threats to King's nonviolence, sometimes as evidence of the limits of nonviolence, and sometimes as the sources of an implicit (or explicit threat) that forced white concessions. But we know very little about who they were, how they related to the movement, or how their actions impacted the movement as a whole. There is evidence to suggest that some may have rejected "nonviolence," but this tells us little. If we move beyond the framework of nonviolence versus self-defense/violence dichotomy, we have the potential to see a much more complex picture. In Albany, for example, we might shift our focus from King's response and the media's coverage and turn toward those who threw the rocks. Though one historian notes that SNCC workers considered the "day of penance" humiliating, we know little about how local blacks (the "bystanders" and those in the movement) felt about the retaliation or King's response to it. And why did blacks in Albany choose that day, after months of demonstrations, to fight back? Was it triggered by the beating hours earlier of Marion King, the pregnant movement supporter whose husband was a prominent leader? And how did the retaliation and King's response impact the local movement? Several historians note that SCLC subsequently had difficulty recruiting local blacks to go to jail.[58] Was there a connection? In Albany and later in Selma, how did SCLC's insistence on "nonviolence" impact those struggling to come to grips with the violence against themselves, their families, and their community? And similarly, what did SNCC's calls for "nonviolence" mean to the angry crowd after the 1964 police shooting in Albany? Did it prevent retaliation and more violence? Or did it undermine the possibility for other types of protest or action? And how did movement tactics and the projection of nonviolence impact those who joined the movement and those who did not? This is particularly important to understand when it is clear that only a small fraction of movement participants believed in philosophical nonviolence and many people found ways to participate, with or without engaging in tactical nonviolence. Thus, attitudes toward nonviolence seem far too simplistic as a singular explanation for whether one chose to participate or not.

## HOW DOES SELF-DEFENSE CHANGE IN 1964?
## WHAT DO WE MEAN BY ARMED RESISTANCE?

One of the key historiographical issues that needs more attention and clarity is the precise nature of the ways self-defense changed (and didn't) in the mid-1960s. Through local studies, especially, we have a good sense of how self-defense worked at the level of individuals acting alone or with close friends and family. We also know that by 1964 armed self-defense was more visible, more organized, and there was a general shift toward more open and collective efforts to protect demonstrations and public space, not just private homes, leaders, and meeting spaces. Though the Deacons are the most visible manifestation of this trend, it was well under way when they burst onto the national scene in Bogalusa in the summer of 1965. Before the 1964 Mississippi Summer Project, many individuals in SNCC and CORE accepted self-defense and both organizations were debating their official policies. By July 1964 there was an armed self-defense group in Tuscaloosa committed to protecting the movement, including nonviolent demonstrators who were testing enforcement of the newly passed Civil Rights Act. Throughout that summer, a number of collective, though still somewhat informal, groups protected well-known activists and the rural Mississippi communities of Harmony and Mileston. That fall, the Deacons organized in Jonesboro, expanding to Bogalusa in February 1965. With the Deacons, movement-related self-defense gained more national attention, offered a more explicit public challenge to double standards (surrounding race, violence, and law enforcement), frightened some whites, and helped inspire many African Americans.

Beyond these basics, historians disagree on the extent to which the Deacons precipitated (or reflected) a major shift in self-defense and overall movement tactics; the nature of (and reasons for) their success in Bogalusa; and the degree to which they expanded beyond Jonesboro, Bogalusa, and the 1966 Meredith March. There are also major differences in how historians assess the impact of self-defense and the ways scholars use the phrase "armed resistance."

For Wendt and Fairclough, the Deacons' most important contribution came in Bogalusa, as part of that particular movement. They both emphasize the positive interplay between the Deacons' self-defense and nonviolent tactics (especially in prompting federal intervention), stress the similarities in the self-defense of the Deacons and others in the movement, and reject claims (by the Deacons and other scholars) that the group experienced any significant expansion beyond Louisiana. Fairclough concludes, for example, that "the emergence of the gun-toting Deacons for Defense and Justice, regarded by many at the time as a harbinger of deadly armed conflict throughout the South, turned out to be less important than it first seemed. Contrary to exaggerated press reports, the Deacons never grew into a statewide, let alone a southwide, organization, and by 1967 it was defunct."[59]

In different ways, Christopher Strain, Akinyele Umoja, and Lance Hill see the Deacons as representing significant shifts in the movement and tend to emphasize the organization's expansion and relevance beyond Bogalusa.[60]

Strain evaluates the Deacons in the context of broad national developments, rather than primarily within a southern movement context. He argues that the Deacons "combined Robert Williams's pragmatic real-world approach to self-defense with Malcolm's insistence on" its "constitutional significance." He sees the Deacons, then, as representing a stage in the "politicization of self-defense" and part of a "trend [that] would reach its zenith with the actions of another group, the Black Panther Party for Self-Defense." For his part, Umoja emphasizes the ways the Deacons served as an important model within a larger shift from nonviolence to armed resistance, specifically within the context of the southern movement. He asserts that, given the massive failure of federal, state, and local law enforcement officials to protect African Americans, "the paramilitary organization of the Deacons seemed to be the natural progression."[61]

In assessing the Deacons' overall impact, Hill's claims are, again, somewhat atypical. For one, he appears to overemphasize the role of the Deacons in almost single-handedly achieving an unambiguous victory in Bogalusa. (Ironically, given his seeming disdain for those activists who he characterizes as appealing to the federal government for change, he concludes that the victory came through forcing the "Yankee government to invade the South once again.") For Hill, however, the Deacons' real significance is that they precipitated a sharp break *in the movement* and, building on that, they successfully expanded throughout Louisiana, Mississippi, and beyond. In highlighting the Deacons' distinctiveness, Hill hammers a number of interrelated, recurring themes: that the Deacons' version of self-defense was unique; that only the Deacons' public, organized, and visible version of self-defense had political meaning; and that the Deacons represented an explicit challenge to (and victory over) the existing "nonviolent" movement. Like Umoja, he appears to see a shift toward "armed resistance" as a natural progression, but unlike Umoja, he sees it as an entirely new development that included an explicit rejection of previous approaches. For example, Hill asserts that the Deacons "transformed self-defense from a clandestine and locally restricted activity into a public and wide-ranging organization capable of challenging the entrenched movement leadership and its creed of nonviolence."[62] (Here and elsewhere, Hill's emphasis implies that the Deacons' primary concern was contesting movement tactics and ideology—presumably nonviolence—not defying white supremacy and protecting movement activists under attack for challenging the status quo.)

These divergent assessments of the Deacons reflect considerable difference in the ways scholars frame and evaluate self-defense. Wendt and Strain are somewhat restrained and ambivalent in their conclusions about the extent to which self-defense and other forms of violence and coercion were productive and contributed to the movement's success. After chronicling the emergence of the Deacons, Strain focuses largely on events outside the South. To some extent he emphasizes continuity, arguing that Malcolm X's rhetoric, the Watts "conflagration," and the early work of the Oakland Black Panther Party could all be considered self-defense, but he also sees these as stages through which self-defense develops and evolves. Though he insists that African Americans' use of self-defense "represented a watershed in race relations" and was a "form of empowerment," he also concludes that "armed self-defense offered few easy solutions" and may have helped undermine the movement. He concludes, "If self-defense proved effective in the struggle and complementary to nonviolence, then it did so at no small cost, and one must be careful not to romanticize the practice of self-defense. . . . Armed self-defense provided no panacea capable of curing four hundred years of racial transgressions."[63]

Wendt devotes most of his book to the South and more explicitly contrasts southern self-defense, which he sees as largely effective, with northern self-defense (based largely on a study of the Black Panther Party), which he argues was primarily symbolic and ultimately self-defeating. In contrast to Umoja and, especially, Hill, he argues that self-defense did not replace nonviolence but that in fact, self-defense disappeared along with nonviolence. "Given the symbiotic relationship between protest and protection in the southern civil rights struggle, the demise of nonviolent demonstrations also led to the end of the region's era of armed black resistance." Though he largely accepts self-defense as a necessary and useful corollary to the southern "nonviolent" movement, especially in providing protection, reducing white violence, boosting morale, and adding a coercive element to black efforts to negotiate, Wendt does express caution in his assessment, arguing that self-defense sometimes led to increased white repression and that it could undermine the movement's "moral power in the eyes of white moderates."[64]

Although Umoja and Hill differ in their interpretations of how nonviolence and self-defense evolved, they both insist that after 1964 and the Deacons there was a dramatic change toward more "militant" action by African Americans. Umoja argues that after 1964, "armed resistance would take on a more institutionalized and paramilitary character." Dismissing pre-

Deacons self-defense efforts, Hill asserts that "[a]rmed self-defense had no political significance until it became collective and public and openly challenged authority and white terror." Moreover, for Hill this shift was singularly responsible for the movement's victories. He concludes, "Only after the threat of black violence emerged did civil rights legislation move to the forefront of the national agenda. Only after the Deacons appeared were the civil rights laws effectively enforced and the obstructions of terrorists and complicit law enforcement agencies neutralized."[65]

To bolster their arguments, both Hill and Umoja turn to events in southwest Mississippi where, starting in Natchez in late 1965 and extending throughout southwest Mississippi over the next few years, NAACP state field secretary Charles Evers used a combination of economic boycotts, self-defense groups, boycott enforcement, and confrontational rhetoric to mobilize black communities and force concessions from the local white power structure. Hill uses this as evidence that the Louisiana Deacons were effective in using "the gun" as their "principal organizing tool" to successfully expand beyond Jonesboro and Bogalusa. He further argues that Evers "employed the strategic model for community organizing that the Louisiana Deacons perfected before the Natchez campaign. It was a strategy that eschewed appeals to northern conscience and instead forced local concessions through a combination of legal protest, economic coercion, and most importantly, militant force—in the form of armed self-defense and community discipline."[66] For Umoja, who emphasizes that these southwest Mississippi self-defense groups had no formal affiliation with the Louisiana Deacons, the "Natchez model" (his name for what Hill attributes to the Deacons) is also important, but as evidence of the emergence of armed resistance (which he defines as including but going beyond self-defense) as a primary strategy in Mississippi. He highlights the new prominence of "confrontational and inflammatory rhetoric," along with "the open threat of violent response." He asserts, moreover, that paramilitary groups in these communities were responsible for protection and boycott enforcement, while representing the possibility of retaliation against whites. Thus, in his view, the Natchez model was significant for "using the threat of coercive response to defeat external and internal enemies of the Mississippi freedom movement."[67]

The Port Gibson/Claiborne County self-defense group is crucial to both Hill's and Umoja's arguments. They describe the Port Gibson "Black Hats" (the most common local name) as one of the "strongest Deacons chapters in

Mississippi" and as being "among the best organized and most effective para-military organizations in the state."[68] For both, then, the Port Gibson/Claiborne County Black Hats (and the overall local movement) represent a new brand of organized, paramilitary black militancy that differed significantly from the earlier movement. In drawing their conclusions about Claiborne County, they both tend to focus on a few visible, dramatic events and emphasize the movement's use of boycott enforcement (a form of internal policing against African Americans), which they see as evidence of coercive force and increased militancy. (According to Umoja, boycott enforcement should be considered "armed resistance" because it helps "undermine the authority of white supremacy and establish the power of movement forces.")[69]

There *are* ways that the Claiborne County movement differed from earlier movements in Mississippi, but these variations had little direct connection to the Deacons or an explicit move toward "armed resistance." Instead, they were primarily related to its timing—after the Civil Rights and Voting Rights Acts of 1964 and 1965—and its connection to Charles Evers, rather than SNCC (or its local organizational affiliates, COFO and the MFDP). Moreover, if we acknowledge the extent to which self-defense was ubiquitous in the southern movement and the extent to which the movement was unviolent as well as nonviolent, then the shifts in 1964 and with the Deacons are not nearly as stark as they have been portrayed. In Claiborne County, as in most places, self-defense was supplemental, augmenting other, more proactive tactics and activities, like voter registration, mass meetings, marches, and boycott picketing. In fact, outside of the spotlight and away from the insistent arguments about armed resistance, self-defense in Claiborne County looks much like the self-defense practiced throughout the movement, *but* with a few twists that were almost certainly inspired by the Deacons and facilitated by broad shifts in context.[70]

Throughout the Claiborne County black community, most people greatly admired Martin Luther King Jr., strongly identified with the NAACP, perceived the movement as essentially nonviolent, and saw no contradiction in the simultaneous use of weapons and threats. Here, as elsewhere, activists typically made strategic decisions based on practical, common-sense considerations. Self-defense was widely, maybe even universally, accepted. It was most often used by individuals defending their homes and families. A relatively informal group did take on the responsibility of protecting mass meetings and movement leaders and, for several months starting in June 1966, this group employed psychological warfare (through adopting the name Deacons, wearing uniforms, drilling in public, threatening retaliation, and creating a fake minutes book that included inflated numbers and references to imaginary weapons caches). For most, utilizing armed self-defense and trying to scare whites into backing off made good tactical sense. They did not, however, see these actions as first steps in an armed revolution or even as distinguishing them in any significant ways from the larger movement (that most associated with King). Therefore, when the Sheriff answered their escalation with a plea to disarm, they responded positively, believing it was worth a try.[71]

Moreover, the Claiborne County movement was very much shaped by the intersection between the broader movement's accomplishments and the specific local context. For example, by the time the Claiborne County movement began, the Mississippi movement had, as John Dittmer and Charles Payne illustrate, "won the right to organize." The Claiborne County movement itself was actually precipitated by the 1965 Voting Rights Act and organized around voter registration, not by the Deacons or around guns/self-defense/armed resistance. Similarly, while the Deacons were significant to Claiborne Countians as a source of inspiration and a useful threat, the most important local influences were Charles Evers and Rudy Shields, his close ally and key organizer. Shields and Evers, not the Deacons, spearheaded the voter registration campaign. Shields and Evers, not the Deacons, introduced and encouraged boycott enforcement against African Americans. (The use of boycott enforcement was typically one of the things that distinguished movements led by Evers and appears in Jackson as early as fall 1963, after Medgar Evers was murdered.)[72] Shields and Evers, not the Deacons, were behind the local effort to heighten white fears by making the existing self-defense efforts more visible and explicitly threatening. Instead of joining or being organized by the paramilitary Deacons, local activists, influenced by Shields and Evers, recognized and used white fears of those Deacons for their own ends.[73]

Self-defense, public confrontations, and assertive language were all very important to the Claiborne County movement. High school student activists, in particular, reflected on how proud the "Black Hats" (Deacons) made them feel, and how safe. The students and others recall gaining courage from Rudy Shields when he would stand up to whites, refusing to be intimidated, talking back, and staring down guns. They laughed and stood tall as Charles Evers insulted and challenged white officials and merchants. Clearly, African American assertiveness and willingness to fight back were fundamental to the movement and its success.[74] This is important history and a compelling story. But it does not easily fit either the traditional saccharine account of nonviolent love and moral transformation *or* the narrative of a movement defined by militant gun-toting paramilitaries. Umoja's and Hill's assertions that the Claiborne County self-defense group was an especially well-organized paramilitary organization fighting internal and external enemies as part of a larger shift toward "armed resistance" (with the implication that this was a distinct break from the earlier movement) simply does not fit.

The Port Gibson, Claiborne County movement does, however, offer some insight into the Deacons' broad significance beyond Bogalusa. The Deacons' vocal, aggressive insistence on the right to self-defense, their willingness to exchange gunfire with Klansmen, and their highly visible, well-organized, and collective move into public spaces frightened whites and served as an inspiration for blacks. Virtually everyone who studies the Deacons highlights their psychological impact. In a 1988 account, George Lipsitz wrote that the Deacons' "discipline and dedication inspired the community, their very existence made black people in Bogalusa think more of themselves as people who could not be pushed around." Christopher Strain asserts that "[t]he Deacons became . . . a mindset, a broad concept of empowerment and protection." This idea was put forward earlier by Deacon Charles Sims, who insisted that whenever "the Negro decide he going to fight . . . back, he's a Deacon." The importance of the Deacons in generating black pride and white fears is reflected in the ways that other, unrelated self-defense groups, like the Port Gibson Black Hats, adopted their name. Wendt, who argues that the Deacons were unsuccessful in their efforts to expand, suggests that this failure was at least partially related to the pervasiveness of self-defense. Downplaying the Deacons' distinctiveness, he asserts that "expansion proved unnecessary since the gospel that [Deacon Earnest] Thomas and others preached was already widely practiced across the region."[75]

More than reflecting a sharp break with the previous "nonviolent" movement, it seems that the Deacons took the already existing tradition of self-defense, combined it with an assertive, confrontational attitude, and brought both into the public eye. They contributed to making black assertiveness and armed self-defense more visible—to whites and blacks. With regional and national visibility came a more explicit challenge to the double standard that whites somehow had more right to use violence than blacks. The Deacons, then, may have contributed broadly to breaking down black fears (of white violence), while increasing white fears (of race war) and giving law enforcement officers more incentive to protect African Americans. Strain sums this up, writing that the Deacons "punctured the double standard of self-defense in America. They honed in on the lesser amounts of protection offered blacks by southern polity and made a conscious effort to change the discrepancy."[76]

The Deacons' visibility was a significant development in self-defense, but it seems clear that there was a broader related shift in 1964 as organized self-defense moved into public spaces. The Deacons were part of this trend, though they did not initiate it. We know that for most people, whether or not to defend oneself at home was never an issue. The question, really, was whether to defend oneself in public or on a demonstration. Why did people begin to answer this question differently in 1964? Why did some local movements utilize organized, public self-defense while others did not? Akinyele Umoja offers a partial answer to the first question by focusing on internal movement dynamics and arguing that because of their experiences with segregationist terrorism and federal inaction, many activists were moving away from nonviolence. It may also be that late 1964 and into 1965 provided an unusual opportunity for the freedom struggle because of the national movement's accomplishments. Although many activists were disgusted with the federal government's many failures, this period saw the most significant legislation (the Civil Rights and Voting Rights Acts), unprecedented national awareness and sympathy, and an increase in federal intervention. Given this, the movement of self-defense into public space and the Deacons' ability to survive and support the movement may have actually been an illustration of the larger, ostensibly nonviolent movement's achievements, not, as Hill argues, a rejection of nonviolence and "passivity."[77]

From this perspective, the Deacons' ability to organize openly could be understood as evidence of the movement's success in creating more legitimacy and protection for open resistance. Adam Fairclough, for example, believes the Bogalusa movement signaled "a transition," but not "between a mild movement and a militant one, or between nonviolence and Black Power." Instead, he speculates that "it was a transition . . . between a movement that had been struggling for recognition and one that had just achieved a political breakthrough."[78] Robert Williams's experiences offer a useful counterexample. In many ways, he and others in Monroe, North Carolina, foreshadowed the Deacons, vocally articulating their right to self-defense, while aggressively organizing and utilizing defense at home and in public. Unlike the Deacons, however, Williams and the local movement were unable to withstand the combined repression of white vigilante violence and the white-controlled legal apparatus. In 1961, Williams fled the country and the local movement was destroyed.

The timing of collective, organized self-defense in public spaces, coming almost exclusively *after* the 1964 Civil Rights Act, points to a number of significant factors. The Civil Rights Act, by putting the force of law behind demands for desegregation, helped stimulate a new wave of direct action protests as African Americans used the law as an additional tool. And as activists moved into public spaces, self-defense groups sometimes organized to protect them.[79] In fact, most public self-defense was closely connected to nonviolent protest. One result is that organized self-defense groups were typically associated with local movements that utilized direct action (as opposed to those that focused more exclusively on things like voter registration). Part of the explanation, then, for the 1964 and 1965 emergence of armed self-defense in public space, may be related to African American assertiveness in demanding that the Civil Rights Act be implemented. In fact, one might even see the Deacons and others utilizing self-defense in public as extending, not rejecting, tactical nonviolence. Their insistence on their right to public space and on their right to protection in public spaces, from the formal law or from themselves, could easily be understood as a form of direct action, a way of claiming rights that, while different, is very much in the tradition of the early direct action movement to desegregate public space. The Civil Rights Act also gave the federal government more explicit tools for intervening on behalf of the movement. Activists were quite willing to use this to their advantage. Rather than back down in the face of white threats and violence, they often pushed harder, insisting the government intervene or deal with the possible consequences of open racial violence (by blacks as well as whites).

Furthermore, by 1964, the movement was moving increasingly in the direction of parallel institutions, including the Freedom Schools and the Mississippi Freedom Democratic Party, organized as part of the Summer Project. African Americans who used self-defense always claimed it as a human and Constitutional right. They also acted on their own, rather than depend on white lawmen. It may be, then, that organized self-defense is yet another example of African Americans stepping up to develop creative alternatives to mainstream institutions. In this case, they responded to the flagrant absence of meaningful protection by acting as a parallel law enforcement group that, in Umoja's words, "represented the forces of the Movement." At least some activists understood their actions in this light. For example, several Claiborne County "Black Hats" compared themselves to a "police department" or "state troopers." In fact, it appears that the concessions won through collective, visible self-defense or retaliation were most often connected to law enforcement or protection. By fighting back, African Americans *persuaded* white officials to take steps to provide at least a modicum of protection and consideration for black citizens. Moreover, in Claiborne County (and perhaps elsewhere) a significant number of the men involved in self-defense eventually held jobs in law enforcement. By organizing around self-defense, African Americans won some measure of protection and took steps toward claiming larger movement goals of jobs and full participation in government.[80]

There are also other general patterns that offer partial explanations for the ways self-defense varied from place to place. Self-defense appears to have been most organized in relatively compact or cohesive spatial communities, mostly urban but also rural areas where black landowning farmers were clustered together or living on contiguous land, places that Akinyele Umoja characterizes as "haven communities."[81] Organized self-defense also seems to have been more prevalent when white violence was perpetrated by an organized, active Klan, rather than by individuals acting alone or in loosely organized groups. In part then, black organization matched white organization.

It appears that the movement's political successes, its access to additional tools, and its increased attention to parallel institutions, along with the federal government's increased authority for intervening (supplemented by its old fears of race war), may have contributed to the development of the more public and collective version of self-defense that emerged in 1964. Thus, the Deacons' founding in Jonesboro, and especially Bogalusa, may be due less to the working-class revolt against nonviolence that Hill sees than to the particulars of time and place, which include the juxtaposition of movement successes with a relatively compact black community using direct action protest and facing extensive Klan repression. This combination of factors may have contributed to the need for the Deacons, the space that made them possible, and the context for their successful contribution to the local and national movements.

Hasan Kwame Jeffries's local study of the Lowndes County, Alabama, movement, organized by SNCC following the 1965 Selma-to-Montgomery march, also helps illustrate the freedom struggle's wide-ranging, flexible use of self-defense. Building on their Mississippi experiences and trying to make the Voting Rights Act meaningful, SNCC organizer Stokely Carmichael and others set out to develop an all-black independent political party in the rural, majority-black county. In addition to their usual canvassing, SNCC organizers developed extensive political education workshops and used comic books to explain voting and politics. Because of its black panther emblem, its association with Stokely Carmichael, and its refusal to participate in the (white supremacist) Democratic Party, many in the press and around the country connected the Lowndes County Freedom Organization (LCFO) to Black Power and vilified the group as violent.[82]

In Lowndes, where the movement was built around voter registration and political organizing, tactical nonviolence was nonexistent and self-defense was commonplace. Activists defended their homes and mass meetings. They traveled in armed convoys and provided weapons to SNCC organizers. After a white volunteer was murdered, black leaders "sent word to whites that they were prepared to meet violence with violence." When the local sheriff and a Justice Department lawyer discouraged the LCFO from using the courthouse lawn for its nominating convention, insisting it was too dangerous, local leader John Hulett assured both that the Freedom Organization would meet. If necessary, they would provide their own protection. They might not be able to stop white violence, but they were ready to answer it. Talking to the Justice Department attorney, Hulett added, "If shooting takes place . . . we are going to stay out here and everybody die together. . . . There's no place to hide, so whatever happens, you can be a part of it." Afraid of a race war, the Justice Department lawyer quickly negotiated with Alabama state officials to allow the LCFO to hold its nominating convention at a nearby church instead of at an official polling place (as required by Alabama law).[83]

Despite the pervasiveness of self-defense and Hulett's threat to engage in a shoot-out, Jeffries observes that in Lowndes, African Americans "did not use guns as organizing tools" and had "no need for suicidal displays of bravado." He explains, "Everyone in the black community knew of their commitment to armed self-defense, and each time they repulsed an attack they made whites aware of their pledge to meet violence with violence." In fact, because white violence was decentralized and typically executed by neighbors, rather than the Klan, blacks in Lowndes made a "conscious decision to decentralize armed resistance" instead of organizing a "paramilitary group."

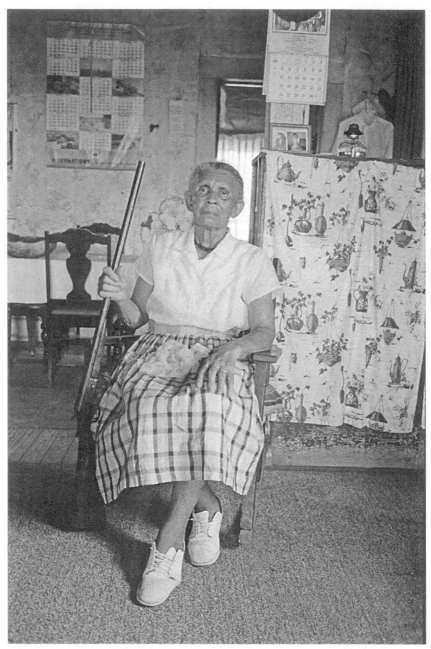

Figure 10  Lowndes County, Alabama, woman with a typical weapon used for
self-defense (1965). Photograph courtesy of the Library of Congress, Prints and
Photographs Division, *Look* magazine, Photograph Collection, LC Look-Job 65-2434.

Lowndes activists had no hesitation in standing up to violent whites *and* no interest in escalating tension or precipitating a confrontation. Furthermore, Jeffries argues, because Lowndes African Americans had no interest in nonviolence, there was no need to protect nonviolent protests and no need for a division of labor between those who demonstrated and those who defended them.[84]

The Lowndes example suggests the need for different ways to categorize and evaluate the role of self-defense locally and nationally. By Hill's definitions, for example, because self-defense in Lowndes was not handled by a paramilitary organization, it should be considered apolitical.[85] Because it was not accompanied by assertive public rhetoric, it could be dismissed as being intentionally obscured or, perhaps, accommodating. And yet, you would be hard pressed to find a local movement that was more explicitly political or more widely considered militant. The local movement spent no time on moral appeals and was always focused on securing power, something many whites, including the national media, found quite threatening. In fact, the LCFO and the promise of independent political organizing became the basis for SNCC's policy shift to Black Power and led to a widespread critique and backlash from white liberals. In terms of self-defense specifically, African Americans in Lowndes were comfortable using it to protect their homes and families *and* to demand access to formerly white-only public space as part of an explicit effort to secure political rights.[86]

The idea that there was a natural progression whereby self-defense became more militant and political as it was organized and visible falls apart when we examine it through the lens of local studies. While there are some identifiable trends and patterns, it is also evident that to a considerable extent African American activists made choices based on their priorities, the tools available to them, and the specific contexts of their local circumstances. They took advantage of opportunities and drew inspiration from others as they crafted approaches that made sense in their communities. The Lowndes example, for instance, suggests that it might make sense to evaluate the extent to which self-defense was political, not based on a level of formal organization, but on whether it was part of a broader political movement. There are similar issues with visibility. Hill refers to self-defense before the emergence of the Deacons as the "movement's family secret" and implies that to some extent the secrecy was about appeasing whites.[87] Among other things, it is important to distinguish between national visibility and local visibility.

When activists used self-defense, local whites and blacks almost invariably knew about it. White editor Hazel Brannon Smith warned her newspaper readers in Holmes County, Mississippi, to avoid Hartman Turnbow's farm at night if they did not want to be shot.[88] In Leflore County in 1962 and in Claiborne County in 1966 African Americans publicly articulated their plans to shoot back, hoping that by making their intentions clear, whites would have sense enough to back off. In Lowndes and other places, it is also evident that the Justice Department and other federal officials knew about black threats.

The question of visibility then, must be addressed and analyzed more specifically and in terms of the particular audiences involved. As discussed earlier, Simon Wendt suggests that, for some, downplaying self-defense was a strategic decision related to fund-raising among northern liberals. This seems to be another important arena for additional research. To what extent did civil rights organizations and local activists consider the ways their actions in the rural South would play in the liberal North? What impact did that have on tactical decisions? Charles Payne, for example, observes that in planning "Freedom Summer," SNCC consciously used the nation's racism to try to expose and protect themselves from Mississippi's racism.[89] How did the white supremacist context impact movement decision making? Can we distinguish between pragmatic considerations and appeasement? For historians, rather than trying to rank levels of militancy, it might be more useful to analyze the nature and uses of self-defense in particular communities at particular times. Was self-defense limited to protecting individuals and their property? Did it extend to meeting places or into public space? Was self-defense handled by family and friends or was it collective and part of a division of labor? Was the right to self-defense (at home or in public) simply claimed by action or was it articulated? Did the local movement include breaks in nonviolent discipline? Confrontational rhetoric? Threats of retaliation? Aggressive violence?

There are other questions related to the effectiveness and impact of self-defense, including its limitations. The Deacons, for example, found it difficult or impossible to protect picketers during demonstrations in Bogalusa and, in at least one instance, decided to "temporarily withdraw the pickets and file a complaint with city officials." During the 1966 Meredith March from Memphis to Jackson the Deacons' self-defense was a point of contention within the movement, and journalists consistently contrasted their use of weapons with King's nonviolence (though some journalists and historians have also emphasized that, despite King's opposition to violence, he accepted and was grateful for the Deacons' protection as he and others walked along highway 51 through the Mississippi Delta). Yet it is not clear where the Deacons were or what role they played when white lawmen launched a vicious attack on marchers setting up tents in Canton, Mississippi. Hill ignores this attack, asserting in a somewhat misleading manner that "[t]he Meredith March ended without incident."[90] The point here is not to criticize these self-defense efforts or discount the crucial role they played in countering white violence, but simply to suggest that we need to examine the role, effectiveness, and limitations of self-defense, as carefully as we do nonviolence and other freedom movement tactics. There was no single approach that guaranteed success, something that the best-known advocates of self-defense, including Robert Williams and the Deacons, knew well. There is quite a bit of evidence to suggest that activists made sensible decisions based on circumstances and goals, rather than simply adopting an ideological position and pursuing it at all costs.

We also need to know more about the broad impact of collective retaliation and visible self-defense. We have some evidence to suggest, for example, that actual or threatened public self-defense and retaliation *could*, in particular situations, influence white officials to make some concessions to movement activists.[91] It is not clear, however, that coercion alone was ever responsible for these shifts. Simon Wendt, in particular, argues that "the legitimacy of the nonviolent movement remained a vital counterbalance to perceived threats of violence."[92] It is also important to consider whether there were contexts in which black threats and self-protection translated not into some measure of relief but into escalating tensions. The example of Robert Williams and Monroe is interesting. Though Tyson makes a compelling argument that Williams was typical in his use of self-defense, Williams's very visible and assertive public claim to self-defense was unusual in the late 1950s and early 1960s. As noted, Tyson points to several instances in which self-defense won victories and created some breathing space for African Americans. And yet, by the end of August 1961 Williams had fled the country, while a number of his key supporters were eventually convicted of trumped up kidnapping charges. With Williams in exile and others in jail, what about the Monroe movement itself? How did the community that came to symbolize armed self-defense fare in terms of movement goals?[93]

Finally, it is important that we more precisely define terms like "armed resistance" and "paramilitary." Christopher Strain and Simon Wendt focus exclusively on self-defense and appear to use "armed resistance" interchangeably with self-defense. Lance Hill employs similar usage, though at times he appears to include boycott enforcement in his discussion of the Deacons' "armed resistance." Akinyele Umoja's focus and his definition of "armed resistance" are the most expansive, including and extending beyond self-defense. The lack of consistency in the use of these terms complicates our efforts to assess the various arguments, especially in terms of those who look beyond narrowly defined self-defense.

For example, at times, both Hill and Umoja imply that the "Natchez model," which they attribute variously to the Deacons or Charles Evers, shifted the movement in a more militant direction, one that included a willingness to use force or violence. With a close read, it is evident that this violence was essentially limited to assertive rhetoric and boycott enforcement against African Americans. Despite this, both authors still appear to imply that this "armed resistance" was something more encompassing, maybe a step away from revolution, but, at the very least, a distinct shift from what went before and a move toward something more radical.

In reality, however, the Port Gibson self-defense group had more in common with the earlier, semi-organized, informal self-defense groups than with a paramilitary organization. Aside from boycott enforcement, black violence in the movement appears almost entirely limited to self-defense, threats, spontaneous retaliation, and breaking nonviolent discipline on demonstrations. Most of the few concrete examples we have of planned, aggressive violence are from Timothy Tyson's work. In *Blood Done Sign My Name*, he describes the military-like precision that Vietnam vets used to carry out firebomb attacks on white property in Oxford, North Carolina, in 1970. He also mentions a number of suspicious fires in his biography of Robert Williams.[94] Tyson's work raises a number of questions for consideration. How widespread were such attacks on property? What do we know about African American considerations of guerilla war or retaliatory violence in the late 1960s and 1970s? Many scholars have noted the significance of World War II veterans to the emergence of the modern civil rights movement. What role did returning Vietnam veterans play in the southern struggle in the late 1960s and early 1970s?

Self-defense, threats, and spontaneous retaliation were present in varying degrees throughout the movement. But they were always, from beginning to end, connected to a larger movement employing a wide range of available tactics. As Tyson observed in his biography of Robert Williams, "[F]or most black southerners nonviolence was a tactical opportunity rather than a philosophical imperative." One could undoubtedly make a similar point about self-defense and other forms of violence. Many activists probably fit Tyson's description of Williams as "practical, eclectic, and improvisional." Charles Payne captures something similar in a 2006 essay, insisting that "[t]he masses were committed to change, not to particular methods. If nonviolence worked, fine; but if not, they were willing to use other methods." Moreover, Bob Moses recalls that rather than violence or nonviolence, SNCC workers and community members were considering more nuanced and practical questions about "what you do, what the limits are, what means you take toward defending yourself." For him, one of the important considerations was avoiding anything that would disrupt his ability to work effectively. In pointing out that Medgar Evers could simultaneously contemplate "guerilla warfare against whites in the Delta" and believe that if he spent enough time talking to "hate callers" he "might be able to change them," Payne argues that rather than simple inconsistency, this diversity reflects the "breadth of social vision some southern blacks developed."[95]

While we *must* have self-defense in our picture of the movement, along with threats, retaliation, and other forms of violence, it is absolutely crucial that we not substitute a narrow glamorization of or overemphasis on self-defense or violence. We gain little if we lose sight of the full range of tactics and ideologies that comprised the freedom struggle. Moreover, it is important to understand these choices not simply as being about what is or was "moral" or appealing to whites, but in terms of pragmatic choices based on an evaluation of success, failure, or even survival. Local studies are crucial in helping us understand more about the intersections of "unviolent" political organizing and activism, a broad national projection of nonviolence, black willingness to take up arms in defense, and both actual and threatened black retaliation. Understanding and evaluating the role of self-defense within the movement should be connected to a broader reorientation that reassesses nonviolence and offers a more precise evaluation of tactics, how they ranged and varied and were connected to particular circumstances and contexts. This changed understanding should also give more nuanced attention to gender, examine the range of black militancy, engage with the extent to which white lawlessness and whites' unchecked, apparently exclusive "right" to use violence against blacks impacted the movement, acknowledge federal neglect, explore the interplay between morality and coercion, and place all of these pieces within the larger black tradition of struggle.

Worth Long, the SNCC activist who contended that most of the movement was "unviolent," not nonviolent, and who suggested that often people hid their fear behind claims of opposing nonviolence, insists that "if you let someone negate your human rights . . . then you are always in danger, it seems to me. Now you can pray with them or pray for 'em, but if they kill you in the meantime you are not going to be an effective organizer."[96] In the freedom struggle, self-defense could be a tactic and a demand. It was pragmatic and ideological, a civil and a human right. It helped people survive and continue the struggle *and* it offered up a fundamental challenge to white supremacy and the enduring double standards related to violence and race. Our histories must be thoughtful and nuanced enough to engage with each of these pieces in all of their complexity as we craft an accurate and precise picture of the freedom movement.

## NOTES

I would like to thank the many people who have shared this essay with me—reading, questioning, discussing, and encouraging. Geneseo students, along with the presenters and other participants in the "Local Studies, a National Movement" Conference at Geneseo in March 2006, helped me begin to think through these questions. I am grateful to friends and colleagues who discussed these ideas and read drafts of this essay, including Justin Behrend, Joseph Cope, John Dittmer, Laurie Green, Wesley Hogan, Hasan Kwame Jeffries, Steven Lawson, Timothy Tyson, Akinyele Umoja, Yohuru Williams, and especially Kathleen Connelly. Among other things, Justin saved me from a title that didn't work. Wesley and Hasan have been particularly generous in reading multiple drafts and especially helpful in pushing me to clarify these ideas. During a leisurely breakfast in Birmingham that was as productive as it was enjoyable, Hasan and I made an important start on tackling the significance of 1964. Although Akinyele Umoja and I have some differences in interpretation when it comes to this history, I remain grateful for the spirit of collaboration that has characterized our overlapping work on southwest Mississippi and for our many conversations—starting back in the early 1990s when we were both working on our dissertations. In particular, our June and July 2010 "e-mail conversation" has been extremely helpful as I have worked to clarify some of these ideas.

1. For an overview of the top-down scholarship and its orientation toward nonviolence and normative, see Charles M. Payne, *I've Got the Light of Freedom: The Organizing Tradition and the Mississippi Freedom Struggle* (Berkeley: University of California Press, 1995), 413–41; Charles Payne, "Debating the Civil Rights Movement: The View from the Trenches," in *Debating the Civil Rights Movement, 1945–1968*, Steven F. Lawson and Charles Payne, with introduction by James T. Patterson (Lanham, Md.: Rowman & Littlefield, 2006), 115–55. The emphasis on nonviolence persists. In a published interview following the SNCC fiftieth anniversary conference, Branch argued that the "overwhelming lesson [from SNCC's success eliminating segregation] is that they grounded themselves in nonviolence and in the notion that people will respond to the moral values of equal citizenship and democracy and basic religious morality, if it's dramatized sufficiently. And they discovered a kind of nuclear energy in nonviolent witness from the sit-ins to the voting rights era." Taylor Branch, interviewed by Susan Lehman, Brennan Center for Justice, New York University School of Law, http://www.brennancenter.org/blog/just_books/categorytaylor_branch/ (accessed April 29, 2010).

2. Robert Parris Moses, interview by Joseph Sinsheimer, November 19, 1983, Joseph Sinsheimer papers, Duke University, transcript.

3. John Dittmer, *Local People: The Struggle for Civil Rights in Mississippi* (Urbana: University of Illinois Press, 1994); Payne, *I've Got the Light of Freedom*; Adam Fairclough, *Race & Democracy: The Civil Rights Struggle in Louisiana, 1915–1972* (Athens: University of Georgia Press, 1995).

4. Timothy Tyson, *Radio Free Dixie: Robert F. Williams & the Roots of Black Power* (Chapel Hill: University of North Carolina Press, 1999.

5. Payne, *I've Got the Light of Freedom*, 44, 51, 59, 114, 138–39, 205, 209, 211, 213–14, 279, 287, 398, esp. 205; Dittmer, *Local People*, 47, 49–50, 106, 191–92, 267–68, 278–79, 285–86, 391.

6. Dittmer, *Local People*, 253–54; Payne, *I've Got the Light of Freedom*, 202–6, esp. 206; Adam Fairclough, *Race & Democracy*, 341, 371.

7. Timothy Tyson, "Robert F. Williams, 'Black Power,' and the Roots of the African American Freedom Struggle," *Journal of American History* 85 (Sept. 1998): 551, 570.

8. Payne, *I've Got the Light of Freedom*, 205.

9. Tyson, *Radio Free Dixie*, 214–16, esp. 216.

10. In 1997, Tyson asserted that an exclusive emphasis on "nonviolent civil rights protest obscures the full complexity of racial politics. It idealizes black history, downplays the oppression of Jim Crow society, and even understates the achievements of African American resistance." Tyson, "Robert F. Williams, 'Black Power,' and the Roots of the African American Freedom Struggle," 570. Seven years later, Lance Hill offered a similar argument, critiquing narratives that feature "nonviolence as the motive force

for change," insisting this is "a reassuring myth of American redemption—a myth that assuaged white guilt by suggesting that racism was not intractable and deeply embedded in American life, that . . . the system had worked and the nation was redeemed. It was a comforting but vacant fiction. In the end, segregation yielded to force as much as it did to moral suasion." Lance Hill, *The Deacons for Defense: Armed Resistance and the Civil Rights Movement* (Chapel Hill: University of North Carolina Press, 2004), 258–59.

11. Akinyele O. Umoja, "Eye for an Eye: The Role of Armed Resistance in the Mississippi Freedom Movement" (PhD diss., Emory, 1996); Lance E. Hill, "The Deacons for Defense and Justice: Armed Self-Defense and the Civil Rights Movement" (PhD diss., Tulane, 1997); Christopher B. Strain, "'We Walked Like Men': The Deacons for Defense and Justice," *Louisiana History* 38, no. 1 (1997): 43–62; Christopher Barry Strain, "Civil Rights and Self Defense: The Fiction of Nonviolence, 1955–1968" (PhD diss., University of California, Berkeley, 2000); Akinyele O. Umoja, "The Ballot and the Bullet: A Comparative Analysis of Armed Resistance in the Civil Rights Movement." *Journal of Black Studies* 29, no. 4 (1999): 558–78; Akinyele Omowale Umoja, "'We Will Shoot Back': The Natchez Model and Paramilitary Organization in the Mississippi Freedom Movement." *Journal of Black Studies* 32, no. 3 (2002): 271–94; Akinyele O. Umoja, "1964: The Beginning of the End of Nonviolence in the Mississippi Freedom Movement." *Radical History Review* 85 (2003): 201–26; Hill, *The Deacons for Defense*; Christopher B. Strain, *Pure Fire: Self-Defense as Activism in the Civil Rights Era* (Athens: University of Georgia Press, 2005); Simon Wendt, "The Spirit and the Shotgun: Armed Resistance and the Radicalization of the African American Freedom Movement" (PhD diss., Freie University, Berlin, 2004); Simon Wendt, *The Spirit and the Shotgun: Armed Resistance and the Struggle for Civil Rights* (Gainesville: University Press of Florida, 2007); Akinyele O. Umoja, "Eye for an Eye: The Role of Armed Resistance in the Mississippi Freedom Movement," book manuscript. A 2006 article by Ohio State graduate student Annelieke Dirks illustrates that the topic continues to attract attention. Annelieke Dirk, "Between Threat and Reality: The National Association for the Advancement of Colored People and the Emergence of Armed Self-Defense in Clarksdale and Natchez, Mississippi, 1960–1965," *Journal for the Study of Radicalism* 1, no. 1 (2006): 71–98. See also, Emilye Crosby, "'This nonviolent stuff ain't no good. It'll get ya killed.': Teaching about Self-Defense in the African-American Freedom Struggle," in *Teaching the Civil Rights Movement*, ed. Julie Buckner, Houston Roberson, Rhonda Y. Williams, and Susan Holt (New York: Routledge, 2002), 159–73; Emilye Crosby, "'You Got a Right To Defend Yourself': Self-Defense and the Claiborne County, Mississippi Movement," *International Journal of Africana Studies* 9, no. 1 (Spring 2004): 133–63; Simon Wendt, "God, Gandhi, and Guns: The African American Freedom Struggle in Tuscaloosa, Alabama, 1964–65," *Journal of African American History* 89 (Winter 2004): 36–56; Simon Wendt, "The Roots of Black

Power? Armed Resistance and the Radicalization of the Civil Rights Movement," in *The Black Power Movement: Rethinking the Civil Rights-Black Power Era*, ed. Peniel E. Joseph (New York: Routledge, 2006), 145–65; Simon Wendt, "Protection or Path Toward Revolution? Black Power and Self-Defense," *Souls* 4, no. 4 (2007): 320–32. See also, Craig S. Pascoe, "The Monroe Rifle Club: Finding Justice in an 'Ungodly and Social Jungle Called Dixie,'" in *Lethal Imagination: Violence and Brutality in American History*, ed. Michael A. Bellesiles (New York: New York University Press, 1997), 393–423; Harold A. Nelson, "The Defenders," in *Black Power in the Belly of the Beast*, ed. Judson L. Jeffries (Urbana: University of Illinois Press, 2006), 163–84.

12. Greta de Jong, *A Different Day: African American Struggles for Justice in Rural Louisiana, 1900–1970* (Chapel Hill: University of North Carolina Press, 2002); Peter B. Levy, *Civil War on Race Street: The Civil Rights Movement in Cambridge, Maryland* (Gainesville: University Press of Florida, 2003); J. Todd Moye, *Let the People Decide: Black Freedom and White Resistance Movements in Sunflower County, Mississippi, 1945–1986* (Chapel Hill: University of North Carolina Press, 2004); and Hasan Kwame Jeffries, *Bloody Lowndes: Civil Rights and Black Power in Alabama's Black Belt* (New York: New York University Press, 2009). See also, Cynthia Griggs Fleming, *In the Shadow of Selma: The Continuing Struggle for Civil Rights in the Rural South* (Lanham, Md.: Rowman & Littlefield, 2004); and Emilye Crosby, *A Little Taste of Freedom: The Black Freedom Struggle in Claiborne County, Mississippi* (Chapel Hill: North Carolina, 2005).

13. Umoja, "1964," 202; Umoja, "'We Will Shoot Back,'" 291; Hill, *The Deacons for Defense*, 3.

14. Strain, *Pure Fire*, 3, 7; Wendt, *The Spirit and the Shotgun*, 99, 102, 110–11, 123, 124, 130, 42–65, 100–30.

15. Umoja, "The Ballot and the Bullet," 577; Wendt, *The Spirit and the Shotgun*, 1; Strain, *Pure Fire*, 4.

16. Strain, *Pure Fire*, 4; Hill, *The Deacons for Defense*, 3; Robert Franklin Williams, *Negroes with Guns* (New York: Marzani & Munsell, 1962). Both Umoja and Hill argue that there was a transition from nonviolence to violence/armed resistance, but unlike most of the early commentators, they see this as a positive development. Hill, *The Deacons for Defense*, 108–19; Umoja, "The Beginning of the End of Nonviolence in the Mississippi Freedom Movement."

17. Charles Payne makes essentially this point in a short essay analyzing John Dittmer's *Local People*. Charles Payne, Foreword, in *Groundwork: The Local Black Freedom Movement in America*, ed. Komozi Woodard and Jeanne Theoharis (New York: New York University Press, 2005), ix–xv, esp. x–xii.

18. Moye, *Let the People Decide*, 102, 233n35. In a tribute to Worth Long, Charlie Cobb writes that one of his "favorites" of Long's words "is 'unviolent' rather than 'nonviolent' to describe the tactics of the 1960s Southern Civil Rights Movement." Charlie

Cobb (Charles Cobb Jr.) in *A Tribute to Worth Long: Still on the Case: A Pioneer's Continuing Commitment*, by Roland L. Freeman (Washington, D.C.: Smithsonian Center for Folklife and Cultural Heritage, 2006), 43. Bob Moses observes that most people did not want to say they were "violent" or "nonviolent." Robert Parris Moses, interview by Joseph Sinsheimer, November 19, 1983, Joseph Sinsheimer papers, Duke University, transcript, 19–21.

19. Strain and Wendt explicitly argue that self-defense and nonviolence were mutually reinforcing, not antagonistic. This is, in fact, one of their key contributions. Yet they often reference these as if they are opposing categories and as if they encompass all movement tactics. In one typical instance, Strain notes that Gloria Richardson "acknowledged armed self-defense as an alternative to nonviolent direct action." In another, he explains that "there was a misunderstanding on both sides" of the nonviolence versus self-defense debate. Strain, *Pure Fire*, 80, 176. Wendt observes that "nonviolence remained the driving force behind social change in the Deep South, but armed resistance complemented civil rights protest and frequently enhanced its effectiveness at the local level." In another instance he concludes that "although violence and fear of violence might have enhanced the bargaining position of civil rights leaders, tactical nonviolence remained the driving force behind social change." Wendt, *The Spirit and the Shotgun*, 2, 197. In contrast, however, Hill argues that the Deacons' use of self-defense was an explicit rejection of nonviolence and that the "two strategies invariably competed." Hill, *The Deacons for Defense*, 44–45. Despite his argument, many of Hill's examples actually show the complementary nature of self-defense and other movement tactics. For example, Hill notes that the Deacons worked closely with the Bogalusa Voters League. Hill, *The Deacons for Defense*, 108–10.

20. Hill, *The Deacons for Defense*, 6, 8, 147. Other scholars who study the Deacons tend to emphasize their cooperation with and support for nonviolence. For example, Strain writes, "Given their menacing public image, it might have surprised the public to learn that the Deacons reaffirmed the principle of nonviolent direct action." Strain, *Pure Fire*, 106. Fairclough writes that the Jonesboro "Deacons insisted that they shared the same aims as CORE, differing from other civil rights groups only in their readiness to use weapons to protect the black community from attack." Fairclough, *Race & Democracy*, 342; Hill, *The Deacons for Defense*, 150–64.

21. John Morsell to Henry E. Briggs, March 16, 1966, Charles Evers, 1966–68 folder, Box 58, Series C, Group 4, NAACP papers, Library of Congress; Crosby, *A Little Taste of Freedom*, 86–90, 189–99.

22. Umoja points out that the NAACP "never took an overt stance on armed resistance or self-defense." Umoja, "Eye for an Eye," 86; Payne, *I've Got the Light of Freedom*, 203–5; Moses quoted in Umoja, "1964," 221.

23. Fairclough, *Race & Democracy*, 341–43, 193–94; de Jong, *A Different Day*, 193–94.

24. de Jong, *A Different Day*, 175–76, 193; Fairclough, *Race & Democracy*, 342; Wendt, *The Spirit and the Shotgun*, 69–70; Umoja, "The Ballot and the Bullet," 563.

25. For examples of the Deacons' involvement in other forms of activism, see Hill, *The Deacons for Defense*, 108–10, 113, 138. For the Deacons' articulating support for or willingness to participate in nonviolent protest, see Hill, *The Deacons for Defense*, 132. Hill writes that CORE workers helped form a Deacons group in Ferriday, Louisiana, in the summer of 1965. Hill, *The Deacons for Defense*, 175. For the role of the white CORE worker in the formation of the Bogalusa Deacons, see Fairclough, *Race & Democracy*, 357; Hill, *The Deacons for Defense*, 44–45; Wendt, *The Spirit and the Shotgun*, 97.

26. Hill, *The Deacons for Defense*, 114, 123, 130–31, 156–57. My intent here is not to downplay the significance of the Deacons in prompting this federal action. Clearly the presence of armed black men willing to publicly engage with violent racists "encouraged" the government to step in. It is important to acknowledge, however, that the Deacons alone did not trigger this intervention. Strain, Fairclough, and Wendt tend to more explicitly emphasize the Deacons' collaboration with CORE and nonviolent protest. They also offer different interpretations of the Deacons' impact. For example, while Fairclough acknowledges the Deacons' role in pressuring the state and local governments to get involved in Bogalusa, he also argues that the recently passed Civil Rights Act and the public violence in Selma gave the federal government more ammunition and more incentive to intervene. The Civil Rights Act, for example, provided the legal basis for several notable lawsuits. Fairclough, *Race & Democracy*, 377–80. Wendt stresses the importance of both nonviolent direct action and "armed resistance" in prompting federal intervention and local success. Wendt, *The Spirit and the Shotgun*, 92–93. See also, Strain, *Pure Fire*, 106.

27. Hill, *The Deacons for Defense*, 268. This conclusion seems at odds with the argument Hill makes throughout his book. For example, Hill notes that by 1966 the Deacons "were resolute opponents of nonviolence and, compared to the national civil rights organizations, had a radically different approach to winning equality." In another instance, Hill asserts that the Deacons "transformed self-defense from a clandestine and locally restricted activity into a public and wide-ranging organization capable of challenging the entrenched movement leadership and its creed of nonviolence." Hill, *The Deacons for Defense*, 166, 217; see also 11, 44, 58, 147, 217, 268.

28. Umoja and Tyson were the first historians to draw attention to a pattern that others confirm—that women actively participated in self-defense, especially of their homes and families. But, as Umoja observes, the connection between manhood and "defending the community . . . became more entrenched as the work of armed defense became more formally institutionalized." Akinyele Umoja, "Eye for an Eye," 189; Tyson, *Radio Free Dixie*, 141. Strain adds, "It would seem that self-defense as a personal right was recognized regardless of gender, but that it became the domain of men once it be-

came more organized and more politicized." Strain, *Pure Fire*, 74. See also, Strain, *Pure Fire*, 111–12; Wendt, *The Spirit and the Shotgun*, 83, 120, 121; Hill, *The Deacons for Defense*, 45, 46.

29. Tyson, *Radio Free Dixie*, 141; Strain, "'We Walked Like Men,'" 54; Wendt, *The Spirit and the Shotgun*, 87, 88; Hill, *The Deacons for Defense*, 261–62, 51, 226.

30. For example, Lance Hill writes, "Ultimately nonviolence discouraged black men from participating in civil rights protests in the South and turned the movement into a campaign of women and children." Hill, *The Deacons for Defense*, 28. Writing about white CORE organizer Charlie Fenton in Jonesboro, Hill asserts, "The men were not going to subject themselves to humiliation and physical abuse simply to conform to his philosophy. Without the men, Fenton's frontline protest troops would be women and children." Hill continues that Fenton was "unwilling to use children as shock troops against the police and Klan," implying that Fenton, the white CORE organizer, was making the decisions. Hill, *The Deacons for Defense*, 44.

31. Wendt, *The Spirit and the Shotgun*, 87, 121; Hill, *The Deacons for Defense*, 2, 8, 44, 236–37, 268.

32. Hill, *The Deacons for Defense*, 2, 8, 44, 236–37, 268, 27. Hill makes similar assertions throughout his book. He argues, for example, "Throughout the South, most black men boycotted the civil rights movement; the campaigns in Birmingham, New Orleans, Bogalusa, and Jonesboro became movements of women and children. Many civil rights leaders explained the absence of men as some character failing—apathy, alienation, or fear. Yet black men did participate in the black freedom movement in the Deep South— but not under the discipline of nonviolent organizations." Hill, *The Deacons for Defense*, 260–61; see also 28, 107.

33. Hill, *The Deacons for Defense*, 28; Wendt, *The Spirit and the Shotgun*, 87.

34. See for example, Wendt, *The Spirit and the Shotgun*, 2–3, 54, 87, 88, 101–2, 108, 115–16, 120–21; Hill, *The Deacons for Defense*, 3, 28, 38, 46, 51, 95, 161, 260–61, 308–9n34. Christopher Strain mentions a psychiatry resident who spent time in Jonesboro, La., and speculated that the Deacons' guns were a "phallic symbol." Strain observes, "This psychological evaluation of the Deacons might be highly questionable; however, the Deacons' assertion of their masculinity was not." Strain, *Pure Fire*, 112. In assessing self-defense, Strain also speculates on the important psychological role it played for African Americans, writing, "[T]his sense of subordination may have been particularly acute in black men, who shouldered the burden of defending not only themselves but also the women and children in their lives. Self-defense represented a man's prerogative and a man's duty: it was a manly response to white transgressions. Consistently, male activists expressed the impulse to defend themselves in terms of gender roles and sexual divisions of labor. Most black men felt it was their responsibility to protect the women in their lives; in fact, they guardedly viewed self-defense as their domain, and theirs alone. . . .

[W]omen often subverted these traditional gender roles and implemented defensive measures themselves to protect their homes, bodies, and families." Strain, *Pure Fire*, 180.

35. Dittmer, *Local People*, 268, 276–79, 285–86, 306–7; Payne, *I've Got the Light of Freedom*, 203–6, 209, 213–14, 265–83.

36. One of Robert Williams's most important influences was his grandmother, who left him his politically active grandfather's rifle as a final gift. Tyson, *Radio Free Dixie*, 25, 141, 259–60, 183, 141, 148–49, 142, 141–42.

37. Other historians capture bits of this. Akinyele Umoja observed that in Mississippi women were extensively involved in informal self-defense efforts, but, as in Monroe, men dominated as this work became more organized and public. Umoja, "Eye for an Eye," 189; Tyson, *Radio Free Dixie,* 141. Strain, *Pure Fire*, 74. See also, Strain, *Pure Fire*, 112; Wendt, *The Spirit and the Shotgun*, 83, 120; Hill, *The Deacons for Defense*, 45, 46. Strain reiterates a number of Tyson's observations, especially related to Robert Williams. He also suggests that sexism played a role in explaining the exclusively male nature of organized self-defense, while choosing to highlight the experiences of Rebecca Wilson, a twenty-two-year-old black woman who acted alone (and outside of a movement context) to defend her home and family from a white attack in 1962. Strain, *Pure Fire*, 73–77. For the most part, though, the details offered by Payne and Dittmer and Tyson's model of complex analysis are too often overlooked.

38. Steve Estes, *I Am a Man! Race, Manhood, and the Civil Rights Movement* (Chapel Hill: University of North Carolina Press, 2005), 62–63, 66, 67, 71, esp. 62, 63; Stokely Carmichael, with Ekwueme Michael Thelwell, *Ready for Revolution: The Life and Struggles of Stokely Carmichael (Kwame Ture)* (New York: Scribner, 2003), 165–66, 176; Bernice Johnson Reagon and Dick Cluster, "Borning Struggle: The Civil Rights Movement: An Interview with Bernice Johnson Reagon," *Radical America* 12, no. 6 (1978): 20–21. There are many possible examples to illustrate the practical possibilities of nonviolent action and the ways that it appealed to African Americans. In many cases, these activists never identified with philosophical nonviolence and were quite willing to explore a wide range of tactical possibilities. For example, Cleveland Sellers, another SNCC activist closely associated with the organization's shift toward Black Power, recalls that the early sit-in participants "looked so magnificent, the men and the women." Connie Field, Marilyn Mulford, Michael Chandler, and Rhonnie Lynn Washington, *Freedom on My Mind* (San Francisco: California Newsreel, 1994). A high school student at the time, he immediately helped organize sit-ins in his Denmark, South Carolina, community. Cleveland Sellers, *The River of No Return: The Autobiography of a Black Militant and the Life and Death of SNCC* (Jackson: University Press of Mississippi, 1990; reprint of 1973 edition), 20–25. As Carmichael suggests, for Sellers and many others, direct action was empowering and offered a way to act. Historian Steven Lawson, in a published review, contends that Hill "fails to understand that the kind of disciplined nonviolence that King preached and

practiced also bolstered feelings of self-confidence and self-worth in those who practiced it." Steven F. Lawson, review of *Deacons for Defense*, in *The Historian* 67, no. 3
(2005): 523–24, quote on 524.

39. Hill, *The Deacons for Defense*, 104; see also 51, 105; Umoja, "Eye for an Eye," 241;
McLaurin quoted in Dittmer, *Local People*, 254; see also Estes, *I Am a Man!*, 74; Carmichael, with Thelwell, *Ready for Revolution*, 260; Molly McGehee, "'You Do Not Own
What You Cannot Control': An Interview with Activist and Folklorist Worth Long," *Mississippi Folklife* 31 (Fall 1998): 15.

40. For the most part, these authors tend not to engage with Charles Payne's thoughtful analysis of those differences in the Mississippi Delta. He finds that in the early 1960s,
women may have been more likely than men to join the movement because of the ways
they were tied into networks of family and friends. Payne also points to the significance
of efficacy, for women and men, suggesting that faith and social networks may have
been most important for women and landownership most important for men. Payne,
*I've Got the Light of Freedom*, 265–83. See, for example, Hill, *The Deacons for Defense*,
260–61, 330n8.

41. Hill, *The Deacons for Defense*, 127, 290n43, 45, 46, 118, 127, 161, 290, 308–9. In one
example, Hill describes a woman, who he refers to not by name, but as "Jackson's wife,"
and notes that she "unloaded her gun" at the Klan. In addition to not naming Mrs. Jackson, Hill implies that the home is her husband's, rather than hers or theirs. "The Klan
attempted to light a cross at the home of the Reverend Y. D. Jackson." Hill, *The Deacons
for Defense*, 40.

42. Wendt, *The Spirit and the Shotgun*, 108. In her history of the Louisiana movement, Greta de Jong does a good job of illustrating how self-defense ranged from individual protection to playing a role in political movements. de Jong, *A Different Day*,
16–17, 58–61, 111, 139, 140, 170–71, 192, 193, 195. Charles Payne points out that Fannie Lou
Hamer's mother carried a gun to the fields when she expected trouble and that Medgar
Evers's "standard of manhood was set by his father's refusal to kowtow to whites." Evers's
great-grandfather killed two whites and escaped the community. His father fought
whites in front of his sons on at least one occasion. Payne, *I've Got the Light of Freedom*,
233, 47–48.

43. Payne, *I've Got the Light of Freedom*, 213–14.

44. Though I believe many of the gendered conclusions about male and female
movement participation as it relates to nonviolence are seriously flawed, there is evidence to suggest that some African Americans did object to the movement's nonviolence
or nonviolent image and that they were among those who periodically reacted to white
violence with collective retaliation. There is also some evidence to suggest that during
the movement black men were more likely than black women to engage in spontaneous (and planned) retaliatory violence, but there has been no systematic study of this—

either for movement participants or bystanders. For example, David (Dave) Dennis, talking about those who reacted violently in response to the repression at Medgar Evers's funeral, explains, "There was a different element of people who had never participated in the movement before. They didn't want to have anything to do with us, because they felt that they could not cope with the nonviolence. It's not that they disagreed with the movement, but with the tactics that we used. These guys off the street were just angry, you know, and that day they decided to speak up." Henry Hampton and Steve Fayer, eds., *Voices of Freedom: An Oral History of the Civil Rights Movement from the 1950s through the 1980s* (New York: Bantam, 1990), 156. John Dittmer observes that after the shooting of a local movement activist in Greenwood, Mississippi, in 1964, young black men who had previously not been involved in the movement showed up with weapons, prepared to retaliate. Dittmer, *Local People*, 279. Before we can draw conclusions, we need to know quite a bit more about those who engaged in retaliation. How many were men? Women? What were their ages? What was their economic status? Did they interact with the movement in any way before or after their participation in violent retaliation? If they were nonparticipants, was that primarily about the movement's nonviolence or was it related to other factors?

45. Tyson, *Radio Free Dixie*, 268, 275, 278–80.

46. Claude Sitton, "Negroes to Step Up Pressure in Atlanta," *New York Times*, January 18, 1964; Judy Richardson, "sNCC: My Enduring 'Circle of Trust,'" in *Hands on the Freedom Plow: Personal Accounts by Women in sNCC*, ed. Faith Holsaert, Martha Prescod Norman Noonan, Judy Richardson, Betty Garman Robinson, Jean Wheeler Smith Young, and Dottie Zellner (Urbana: University of Illinois Press, 2010), 354; Mildred Forman Page, "Two Variations on Nonviolence," in *Hands on the Freedom Plow*, 54; Fay Bellamy, "Playtime is Over," in *Hands on the Freedom Plow*, 479–81.

47. James Forman, *The Making of Black Revolutionaries* (Seattle: Open Hand, 1972, 1985), 148–49.

48. Carmichael, with Thelwell, *Ready for Revolution*, 236–40.

49. Walker argues that the media downplayed violence in the early sixties and emphasized it in the latter sixties, which helped obscure significant "continuity in the character and extent of black violence between the two eras." Jenny Walker, "A Media-Made Movement? Black Violence and Nonviolence in the Historiography of the Civil Rights Movement," in *Media, Culture, and the Modern African American Freedom Struggle*, ed. Brian Ward (Gainesville: University Press of Florida, 2001), 47, 48–49, 44.

50. Walker, "A Media-Made Movement?," 49–50, esp. 49; Rosa Parks with Jim Haskins, *Rosa Parks: My Story* (New York: Dial Books, 1992), 195–96.

51. Dittmer, *Local People*, 47, 278, 279, 238; Payne, *I've Got the Light of Freedom*, 213–14; Levy, *Civil War on Race Street*, 81–83, 85–86, 92, 99.

52. Dittmer, *Local People*, 167, 238, 279, 306, esp. 307.

53. Ibid., 279; Dave Dennis, interview in Hampton and Fayer, *Voices of Freedom*, 156.

54. Glen Eskew, *But for Birmingham: The Local and National Movements in the Civil Rights Struggle* (Chapel Hill: University of North Carolina Press, 1997), 280–83, 300–1.

55. Richardson recalls that Forman "scolded me, reminding me that we were supposed to be nonviolent and that this kind of negative publicity could hurt our fundraising efforts. I left his office feeling very hurt by his anger and guilty that I had in some way jeopardized the organization." Judy Richardson, "SNCC: My Enduring 'Circle of Trust,'" in *Hands on the Freedom Plow*, 354; Claude Sitton, "Negroes to Step Up Pressure in Atlanta," *New York Times*, January 18, 1964; Wendt, *The Spirit and the Shotgun*, 4, 99, 102, 110–11, 123, 124, 130.

56. Tyson, *Radio Free Dixie*, 265; David Garrow, *Bearing the Cross: Martin Luther King, Jr., and the Southern Christian Leadership Conference* (New York: Vintage, 1986, 1988), 208–9; Taylor Branch, *Parting the Waters: America in the King Years, 1954–63* (New York: Simon & Schuster, 1988), 618–19; Clayborne Carson, *In Struggle: SNCC and the Black Awakening of the 1960s* (Cambridge, Mass.: Harvard University Press, 1981), 61; Stephen G. N. Tuck, *Beyond Atlanta: The Struggle for Racial Equality in Georgia, 1940–1980* (Athens: University of Georgia Press, 2003), 149. Hogan is quoting SNCC worker Don Harris, speaking at a SNCC meeting. Wesley Hogan, "Freedom Now: Nonviolence in the Southern Freedom Movement, 1960–1964," chapter 6, this volume.

57. Prathia Hall, "Bloody Selma," in *Hands on the Freedom Plow*, 497.

58. Garrow, *Bearing the Cross*, 208–9; Branch, *Parting the Waters*, 618–19.

59. Wendt argues that the Deacons were significant within Louisiana because of their "ability to thwart the worst forms of white terror and their inspiring effect on local African Americans." He also stresses the importance of both nonviolent direct action and "armed resistance" in prompting federal intervention and local success. Wendt, *The Spirit and the Shotgun*, 92–93. Fairclough focuses primarily on the Deacons' local impact, asserting that although the Deacons were heavily outnumbered, they "enabled the Bogalusa movement to hang on" and, together with CORE, "clashed with the Klan head-on," creating a "crisis of such magnitude that neither the state nor the federal government could afford to look the other way." Fairclough, *Race & Democracy*, 359, 342, 345.

60. Hill claims that the "Deacons became organizational expansionists" and developed seventeen southern affiliates. Hill, *The Deacons for Defense*, 167. Hill and Umoja both point to southwest Mississippi as an important site of the Deacons' expansion. Hill, *The Deacons for Defense*, 184–215; Umoja, "'We Will Shoot Back.'" Strain's interpretation falls somewhat in between. He appears to largely accept the Deacons' claims of rapid expansion throughout the South and beyond (with approximately fifty chapters by June 1965 and more shortly thereafter), although he does suggest that the claims of a membership between 5,000 and 15,000 were probably inflated. Strain, *Pure Fire*, 104, 111, 115, 120, 122. He also notes that the organization had faded from view by 1967 and, through

his emphasis on Jonesboro, Bogalusa, and the 1966 Meredith March, reinforces these as the crucial sites for the Deacons. Strain, *Pure Fire*, 97–126, esp. 120.

61. Strain, *Pure Fire*, 97, 125–26; Umoja, "Eye for an Eye," 194–95.

62. Hill asserts that "[t]he source of SNCC's difficulties was its emphasis on federal intervention." Hill, *The Deacons for Defense*, 197. Hill argues that the Deacons "crystallized around a challenge to the doctrine of nonviolence, which, as a matter of principle, deprived African Americans of an indispensable means of countering white terror." Hill, *The Deacons for Defense*, 11, 44, 58, 147, 217, esp. 166.

63. Strain, *Pure Fire*, 179, 176, 172, 182. In the end, Strain emphasizes the psychological issues of "respect" more than practical or tangible benefits of self-defense. Strain, *Pure Fire*, 176–83, esp. 179–80.

64. Wendt, *The Spirit and the Shotgun*, 152, 189–99, esp. 193–94.

65. Umoja, "1964," 222; Hill also asserts that "individual acts of self-defense did not in themselves constitute a sign of militancy or a leap of consciousness. Physically defending oneself can be motivated by nothing more than common sense and the instinct to survive." Hill, *The Deacons for Defense*, 276n4, 258–59.

66. Hill, *The Deacons for Defense*, 206. Hill writes that the Natchez "Deacons" were responsible for organizing the Claiborne County "Deacons." Ignoring Evers's primacy in southwest Mississippi and his antipathy to other civil rights groups, Hill further ties the Deacons to Evers, writing, "Between 1965 and 1968 Charles Evers' extensive local campaigns provided the main framework for Deacons organizing in Mississippi. The Natchez Deacons went on to organize several Deacons chapters and informal groups in Port Gibson. . . ." Moreover, although Hill acknowledges that the Natchez Deacons and most of the other active groups in Mississippi had no formal affiliation with the Louisiana Deacons, he still appears to use these groups as evidence that "the Deacons" became a "southernwide organization." Hill, *The Deacons for Defense*, 206, 207, 182, 212, 214, 265, 268, and vii (Contents). He writes that the Port Gibson group was "officially a Deacons' chapter" without explaining what that means. Furthermore, if the Deacons were a southernwide organization, they had to have a presence outside of Louisiana. However, the only southern, non-Louisiana "Deacons" that Hill gives any significant attention to are in Mississippi, especially the Natchez "Deacons" and the Port Gibson "Deacons." The overall implication appears to be that these groups are evidence of the Louisiana Deacons' expansion. My research suggests that, in the case of Port Gibson at least, the connections are more of inspiration than anything tangible or formal. The Port Gibson self-defense group was organized by Rudy Shields and later began using the name "Deacons" in the context of the Meredith March. For more on self-defense in Claiborne County, see Crosby, *A Little Taste of Freedom*, 168–88, esp. 178–80. Hill also argues that Evers secured a major victory in Natchez and takes issue with John Dittmer for discounting it. Ironically, he praises Evers for eschewing federal intervention in

Natchez (while noting the Deacons' ability to force federal intervention in Bogalusa as key to their victory). Moreover, in comparing Natchez with the McComb movement which, he notes, registered only six voters in six months, Hill ignores the huge changes that had occurred in Mississippi and throughout the country between the 1961 McComb movement and the late 1965 Natchez movement. Among other things, activists had considerably more resources to draw on through the earlier movement's successes, including the Civil Rights Act of 1964 and Voting Rights Act of 1965. Hill, *The Deacons for Defense*, 205.

67. Akinyele Umoja defines "armed resistance" as "insurgent individual and collective use of force for protection, protest, or other goals of political action." Akinyele Umoja, e-mail to author, June 24, 2010. See also, Umoja, "Eye for an Eye: The Role of Armed Resistance in the Mississippi Freedom Movement," Book Prospectus, summer 2010, in author's possession. Umoja notes that the Claiborne County self-defense group was "autonomous from the Natchez group." He also observes that the Natchez group did not affiliate with Louisiana Deacons and points out that Evers's advocacy for armed resistance predates the founding of the Deacons. Umoja, "'We Will Shoot Back,'" 275, 272, 287. Umoja also insists that "[t]he capacity of the movement to protect itself and the Black community and to retaliate against White supremacist terrorists gave Evers and other Black leaders more leverage in negotiating with local White power structures." Umoja, "'We Will Shoot Back,'" 291. See also Umoja, "1964," 211.

68. Hill implies that the Port Gibson, Claiborne County group was connected to the Louisiana Deacons. Umoja, more accurately, observes that they drew inspiration from the Deacons and borrowed their name, but were ultimately an independent organization. Hill, *The Deacons for Defense*, 207; Umoja, "'We Will Shoot Back,'" 287–88; Crosby, *A Little Taste of Freedom*, 178–80. Umoja, "Eye for an Eye," 216, 217. For more on the way Hill characterizes the relationships between various Deacons' groups, see note 66.

69. Hill notes that in engaging in boycott enforcement, the Deacons were "clearly crossing the line between defensive and offensive force." Hill, *The Deacons for Defense*, 208. Umoja argues that "[t]he formula developed in Natchez to combat the local White power structure and win concessions toward human and civil rights was used throughout the state, particularly in southwest Mississippi communities. . . . The Natchez model had proven the necessity of using the threat of coercive response to defeat external and internal enemies of the Mississippi freedom movement." He also writes, "The Natchez model, combining economic boycotts with paramilitary defense and the potential for retaliation, proved more effective in winning concessions and social and cultural change on the local level than nonviolent direct action or voter registration campaigns depending on federal protection." Umoja, "'We Will Shoot Back,'" 287, 272, 291. See also, Umoja, "An Eye for an Eye," 186–87. The quote is from Akinyele Umoja, e-mail to author, June 23, 2010.

70. In addition to Hill and Umoja, Wendt also writes about the Claiborne County Deacons, or Black Hats. Wendt, *The Spirit and the Shotgun*, 148–49. Of the self-defense scholars, only Strain, who turns his attention to the West Coast after the emergence of the Deacons, fails to address Claiborne County.

71. Crosby, *A Little Taste of Freedom*, 178–86.

72. Ibid., 139–40; Payne, *I've Got the Light of Freedom*, 360–61.

73. Crosby, *A Little Taste of Freedom*, 89, 101–17, 178–86; Hill, *The Deacons for Defense*, 201.

74. Crosby, *A Little Taste of Freedom*, 169–88. Evers and Shields do appear to have used a more aggressive and threatening tone than many earlier activists. However, there was a long history of African Americans standing up to and challenging whites. Charles Payne writes, "Public defiance of the 'laws' was an important element in the style of many of the [SNCC] workers in the Delta, and it was certainly a part of [Sam] Block's style." Payne, *I've Got the Light of Freedom*, 147. During the Hamer Institute NEH Landmarks Workshops for Community College Teachers, the oral history panels are filled with accounts of confrontational activities during the pre-1964, ostensibly "nonviolent" phase of the movement. This is particularly true of the comments by Charles (Charlie) Cobb, Judge Mamie Chinn, Hollis Watkins, and Charles McLaurin. The oral history panels and tours were recorded by the Hamer Institute. "Landmarks of American Democracy: From Freedom Summer to the Memphis Sanitation Workers' Strike," NEH Institute for Community College Teachers, Hamer Institute, Jackson State University, July 2009, July 2010.

75. George Lipsitz, *A Life in the Struggle: Ivory Perry and the Culture of Opposition* (Philadelphia: Temple University Press, 1988), 96; Strain, *Pure Fire*, 123, 178–80. Charles Sims, in *Black Protest: History, Documents, and Analyses, 1619 to the Present*, ed. Joanne Grant (New York: Ballantine Books, 1983), 342; Wendt, *The Spirit and the Shotgun*, 93.

76. Umoja, "Eye for an Eye," 241; Strain, *Pure Fire*, 123.

77. The group in Tuscaloosa that defended nonviolent demonstrators in the summer of 1964, for example, preceded the Deacons. Wendt, *The Spirit and the Shotgun*, 54. Umoja, "1964," 201–26. Hill, *The Deacons for Defense*, 27, 44, 261–62, 268.

78. Fairclough, *Race & Democracy*, 380.

79. Others have noted the importance of the Civil Rights Act of 1964 in providing African Americans with another tool. See Payne, *I've Got the Light of Freedom*, 320; Sundiata Keita Cha-Jua and Clarence Lang, "The 'Long Movement' as Vampire: Temporal and Spatial Fallacies in Recent Black Freedom Struggles," *Journal of African-American History* 92, no. 2 (2007): 278; Nelson, "The Defenders," 163–84, esp. 163–67.

80. Umoja, "Eye for an Eye," 189; Crosby, *A Little Taste of Freedom*, 185–88; Nelson, "The Defenders," 163–84, esp. 163–67.

81. Umoja, "1964," 210.

82. In fact, state investigators spying on the Claiborne County movement imagined Panther logos, presumably from Lowndes County, on the shirts of local men active in self-defense and expressed panic that they were forming a chapter of the "panthers." Crosby, *A Little Taste of Freedom*, 182. For a discussion of the media's response to the Lowndes County Freedom Organization and their distinct preference for Charles Evers, see Emilye Crosby, "'God's Appointed Savior': Charles Evers's Use of Local Movements for National Prestige," in *Groundwork*, ed. Woodard and Theoharis, 165–92.

83. Jeffries, *Bloody Lowndes*, 83, 102–4, 116, 143–44, 171–73, esp. 83. John Hulett, "How the Black Panther Party Was Organized," in *The Eyes on the Prize Civil Rights Reader*, ed. Clayborne Carson, David J. Garrow, Gerald Gill, Vincent Harding, and Darlene Clark Hine (New York: Penguin, 1991), 275.

84. Jeffries, *Bloody Lowndes*, 103–4, 116, esp. 103.

85. Strain, by contrast, considers all self-defense political. See, for example, Strain, *Pure Fire*, 7.

86. Hasan Kwame Jeffries, "SNCC, Black Power, and Independent Political Party Organizing in Alabama, 1964–66," *Journal of African American History* 91, no. 2 (2006): 171–93; Jeffries, *Bloody Lowndes*, 103–4, 116.

87. Hill, *The Deacons for Defense*, 58.

88. Payne, *I've Got the Light of Freedom*, 279.

89. Lawson and Payne, *Debating the Civil Rights Movement, 1945–1968*, 142.

90. Hill, *The Deacons for Defense*, 122–23, 246–250, esp. 249. According to Hollis Watkins, who was present, the Deacons did not try to protect the group from the attack by the highway patrol. He believes this was because they were so out-gunned that to attempt self-defense in that context would have led to more violence. Hollis Watkins, conversation with Emilye Crosby, March 5, 2010.

91. Tyson, *Radio Free Dixie*, 88; Strain, *Pure Fire*, 106; Wendt, *The Spirit and the Shotgun*, 92–93; Fairclough, *Race & Democracy*, 342–45, 359.

92. Dittmer, *Local People*, 310, 398; Wendt, *The Spirit and the Shotgun*, 198.

93. Wendt quotes an observer that the Monroe movement was "completely shattered" after Williams left the community. Wendt, *The Spirit and the Shotgun*, 191. In contrast, Stokely Carmichael observes that he and others in the movement were inspired by Williams. Carmichael, with Thelwell, *Ready for Revolution*, 225–28. James Forman, who traveled to Monroe and devotes several chapters to Williams and the Monroe movement in his memoir, makes a similar point. Forman, *The Making of Black Revolutionaries*, ch. 19–28; Wendt offers some brief comments on negative responses to black retaliation, focusing in particular on northern liberal responses and repression by southern law enforcement. Wendt, *The Spirit and the Shotgun*, 191–92, 196–98.

94. Timothy B. Tyson, *Blood Done Sign My Name: A True Story* (New York: Three Rivers Press, 2004), ch. 7, 9, 10, esp. 220–24; Tyson, *Radio Free Dixie*, 263.

95. Tyson, *Radio Free Dixie*, 192; Lawson and Payne, *Debating the Civil Rights Movement, 1945–1968*, 132; Moses, interview by Sinsheimer, transcript, 19–20; Payne, *I've Got the Light of Freedom*, 314.

96. McGehee, "'You Do Not Own What You Cannot Control': An Interview with Activist and Folklorist Worth Long," 18.

# PART THREE

# Creating and Communicating Movement History: Methodology and Theory

HASAN KWAME JEFFRIES

# Remaking History

## *Barack Obama, Political Cartoons, and the Civil Rights Movement*

On the forty-fifth anniversary of Dr. Martin Luther King Jr.'s "I Have a Dream" speech, which he delivered on August 28, 1963, during the March on Washington, Barack Obama accepted the Democratic Party's nomination for president of the United States. In doing so, he became the first African American to earn the top spot on a major political party's presidential ticket. This historical twist of fate was not lost on Obama, but in keeping with his campaign strategy, which called for him to avoid discussing race, he downplayed the happenstance, alluding to it only with a passing reference to "a young preacher from Georgia."[1] The media, however, did not hesitate to point out the coincidence, freely invoking the spirit of King and the March on Washington. Political cartoonists reflected this tendency in their work. While covering Obama's nomination, they made frequent reference to that historic day nearly half a century earlier. Cartoonist R. J. Matson, for example, published a piece the day before Obama's acceptance speech that featured King, standing on steps not unlike those of the Lincoln Memorial (from which King delivered his most famous speech), holding an oversized replica of Obama's campaign emblem high above his head.[2]

Allusions to King and the March on Washington made by those covering Obama's campaign neither began nor ended with the Democratic National Convention. Instead, they spanned the full length of Obama's run for the White House, starting in earnest the day he announced his candidacy in February 2007 and continuing through his electoral victory in November 2008.

The author would like to thank the College of Arts and Humanities at The Ohio State University for generous financial assistance that made it possible to include the images that appear in this chapter.

Figure 11  R. J. Matson, "The Mountain Top," *Roll Call* (Aug. 27, 2008).

This affinity for the past was a part of a larger trend of remembering the civil rights movement and reflecting on its legacy that was sparked by Obama's emergence as a viable African American presidential candidate. Looking back at the movement in this way was unprecedented. At no other time had so many people tried so publicly for such a sustained period of time to draw meaning from the African American freedom struggle. Unfortunately, much of what they derived was incorrect, owing to the innumerable myths about the movement that abound.

In this chapter, I explore the ways in which popular misconceptions about the civil rights movement have served to remake history, altering everything from the freedom struggle's leadership, goals, strategies, tactics, and guiding philosophies, to the depth and breadth of the white opposition, including the form and function of racial terror. I use political cartoons, composed by award-winning artists from across the political spectrum and published during Obama's campaign, to identify leading movement myths. The cartoons also serve as a starting point for discussing the origin of key myths, for clarifying the truths that these fabrications conceal, and for illuminating the ways these stories shape contemporary discourse on racial inequality and African American activism.

The dominant view of the civil rights movement holds that Martin Luther King Jr., who was thrust into the nation's consciousness in 1955 during the Montgomery Bus Boycott, was the movement's singular voice, chief strategist, and principal decision maker. The *Britannica Concise Encyclopedia*, for instance, describes King as the person who "led the civil rights movement in the United States."[3] It is hardly surprising, then, that throughout Obama's run for the White House, cartoonists used images of King to invoke the civil rights movement. Cartoonist Peter Lewis, for example, conjured the movement in a sketch published the day after Obama won the presidency by depicting a young Obama watching a televised broadcast of King's "I Have a Dream" speech.[4]

Figure 12  Peter Lewis, "American Dream," *The Herald* (Australia) (Nov. 5, 2008).

This King-centric view of the movement, however, obscures far more than it reveals. Among other things, it marginalizes the movement activists with whom King worked, frequently overlooking leaders of national organizations such as John Lewis, the chairperson of the Student Nonviolent Coordinating Committee (SNCC), and his successor Stokely Carmichael, except on those occasions when they said or did something that challenged King. In a similar way, it ignores local leaders such as John Hulett, the chairperson of the Lowndes County (Alabama) Freedom Organization (LCFO), apart from when they crossed paths with King or were affiliated with his Southern Christian Leadership Conference (SCLC). In a like manner, it pushes aside women such as Ella Baker, who helped bring both SCLC and SNCC into being. The King-centric perspective also overemphasizes mass mobilizing events such as marches and demonstrations, and deemphasizes the importance of grass-roots organizing, the slow and hard work of getting ordinary people to act on their deeply held desire to change the status quo. The sustained canvassing activities of SNCC organizers in Mississippi, for example, is given short shrift compared to marches led by King in Alabama, regardless of outcome.[5]

The King-centric view of the movement also misrepresents the movement's goals. The infatuation with King inevitably leads to a fixation on color blindness—the absence of racial acknowledgment in any way.[6] Cartoonists, for example, frequently point to color blindness as the movement's main objective, and like Peter Lewis, typically use King to buttress their point. King famously gave voice to color blindness as a movement aim during the March on Washington when he spoke eloquently about his desire—his "Dream"— that his children would "one day live in a nation where they will not be judged by the color of their skin but by the content of their character."[7] King's version of color blindness, however, differed substantially from present-day notions. Above all else, he believed that it was necessary to consider race when devising solutions to racial inequality. "A society that has done something special against the Negro for hundreds of years," wrote King in 1967, "must now do something special for him, in order to equip him to compete on a just and equal basis."[8]

Lost in the contemporary discourse surrounding color blindness is the movement's diverse array of goals. Among other things, civil rights activists fought relentlessly for fair employment practices. In New York City during the 1940s, they organized for the creation of city and state committees, modeled after the federal Fair Employment Practices Committee (FEPC), to enforce nondiscrimination in hiring, promotions, and wages. They also fought for decent housing. In Milwaukee, Wisconsin, during the late 1960s, they secured open housing legislation to help end housing discrimination. They agitated for quality education. In Jackson, Mississippi, in the 1950s, some lobbied for improving segregated black schools; in the 1960s, others petitioned for desegregating white schools; and in the 1970s, still others worked for community control of neighborhood schools. Civil rights activists also organized to participate fully in the political process. In Lowndes County, Alabama, in the mid-1960s, African Americans formed their own political party—the first Black Panther party—in order to gain control of the county government. These activities reflected the movement's broadly configured agenda, which sought to bring about an equal society with equal opportunities and equal outcomes regardless of race. Movement activists had little interest in a society that purported to ignore race yet maintained the systems and structures that created and reproduced racial inequality.[9]

While King tends to dominate popular understandings of the civil rights movement, President Abraham Lincoln looms large in the conventional narrative of the broader African American freedom struggle. Cartoonists, drawn to the notion that Lincoln's vision of a nation without slavery embodied America's democratic promise, used images of the former president to connect Obama to the African American past almost as often as they used images of King. David Fitzsimmons, for example, in a cartoon published just ahead of Election Day, portrays the statue of Lincoln at the Lincoln Memorial with its arms raised in celebration of Obama's victory while a park ranger explains to a tour group that "[h]e's been like that ever since Election Day 2008."[10] The insinuation, of course, is that Lincoln, the Great Emancipator, would have been overjoyed to witness an African American elected president. Lincoln, however, was not a racial egalitarian. A product of his times, he believed unfailingly in white supremacy, a position that was compatible with abolition. In fact, Lincoln was slow to embrace abolition, and when he finally came around to the idea, he did so out of military necessity and political expediency rather than moral obligation. He worked to save the Union, not to make it "more perfect" through racial equality. The thought of an African American occupying the Oval Office would have caused him distress and dismay, not delight.

Emancipated African Americans, however, would have been ecstatic

Figure 13  David Fitzsimmons, "Obama Wins," *The Arizona Star* (Nov. 2, 2008).

about Obama's election. Unlike Lincoln, their vision of post-emancipation America was truly democratic. They imagined a nation incorporating them into the body politic, allowing them equal and unfettered access to the ballot box so that they could participate in political decision making and hold public office. In Richmond, Virginia, for example, following the enfranchisement of African American men pursuant to the Fifteenth Amendment, freed people mobilized to register black men to vote and to elect black candidates to office.[11] Obama's election, therefore, exemplified their political beliefs. Cartoons depicting freed people, or their enslaved predecessors, however, were practically nonexistent.

By overlooking freed people, the origins of the freedom struggle's objectives, along with the depth and breadth of civil rights era aims, are lost. When freedom dawned, African Americans immediately began to organize for freedom rights, the combination of basic civil rights and fundamental human rights that they had been denied during slavery. In Lowndes County, Alabama, for instance, freed people worked tirelessly not only for the ballot, but also for economic independence by acquiring their own land, for cultural integrity by establishing their own churches, and for social autonomy by securing legal recognition of their marriage and kinship bonds. Their determined efforts created a blueprint for future agitation and laid the groundwork for civil rights era victories.[12]

Misinterpretations of what African Americans were fighting for stem from misunderstandings about what African Americans were fighting against. In the minds of many, the principal, if not the sole obstacle to racial equality before the civil rights era was Jim Crow, the system of de jure segregation that touched every aspect of southern life. Jim Crow, however, is often misconstrued as a benign form of racial discrimination, a kind of bigotry that inconvenienced black people by prohibiting them from enjoying life's simple amenities, from eating at restaurants to sitting in the front of buses. Cartoonist Dwayne Booth captures this sentiment in "Water under the Bridge," which appeared shortly after Obama's election. Booth tweaks a familiar image of Jim Crow—a black man drinking from a public water fountain designated for African Americans while standing next to a fountain reserved for whites—by replacing the "Colored" label above the fountain the man is drinking from with "House," so that the combined Jim Crow signage reads "White House."[13] Jim Crow, however, was much more than the denial of public conveniences. It was an institutionalized system of racial discrimination—designed to control black labor by regulating black behavior—that was sanctioned by the federal government and enforced locally through vicious forms of racial

Figure 14 Dwayne Booth, "Water under the Bridge," *Mr. Fish* (Nov. 6, 2008).

terrorism. No election, presidential or otherwise, can wipe away the vestiges of Jim Crow.

Alongside the idea that the chief impediment to racial equality was the inconvenient nature of Jim Crow is the mistaken notion that white supremacy was essentially a matter of personal prejudice, a product of anachronistic attitudes that led to atypical individual behavior. It is also widely held that white supremacy was embraced by only a handful of racial demagogues who spoke mainly for themselves. Late in the presidential campaign season, during the dustup surrounding Congressman John Lewis's likening of Republican campaign events (at which racist catcalls could be heard) to the campaign rallies of arch segregationist George Wallace, J. D. Crowe drew a cartoon featuring Wallace seated between Obama and John McCain. Wallace, appearing old and decrepit, asks, "How the [expletive] did I get dragged into this?"[14] Crowe's depiction of Wallace as aged and infirm captures Wallace's physical essence late in life, but not during his heyday. When Wallace was winning gubernatorial races in Alabama and presidential primaries nationwide, he was not a geriatric jester—some southern hayseed embraced only by a racist fringe—but a multiterm governor whose rhetoric and policies, including his "Stand in the Schoolhouse Door" at the University of Alabama in 1963, were in keep-

Figure 15 J. D. Crowe, "Obama, McCain, and Wallace," *Mobile Register* (Oct. 15, 2008).

ing with the beliefs of white conservatives throughout the South and beyond Dixie's borders.

Reducing the causes of racial inequality to the deviant behavior of a couple of supposedly "out-of-control crackers" ignores how deeply embedded white supremacy was in the framework of American society. It also obscures the fact that movement activists, with the important exception of the minority who embraced nonviolence as a way of life, worried less about personal prejudice—changing white hearts and minds—and more about the ways systems and institutions perpetuated the status quo. SNCC organizer Stokely Carmichael, who viewed the movement as a political struggle rather than a moral crusade explained, "I never saw my responsibility to be the moral and spiritual reclamation of some racist thug. I would settle for changing his behavior, period. Moral suasion, legal proscription, or even force of arms, whatever ultimately it took, that's what I'd be for."[15] In addition, the focus on personal prejudice treats white supremacy strictly as a southern issue, confined to the states of the former Confederacy, rather than as a national problem that touched every corner of the country.[16]

In keeping with the notion that white supremacy was the province of a small number of "out-of-control crackers," it is commonly asserted that racial violence, which undergirded Jim Crow, was the exclusive domain of terror groups, specifically the Ku Klux Klan. Riber Hansson, a Swedish cartoonist, uses Klan imagery to explain the transformative implications of Obama's victory. In a cartoon published immediately after the election, Hansson shows a victorious Obama walking past a dejected Klansman dressed in full Klan regalia, complete with a cross ready for burning and a container of kerosene, as the president-elect makes his way to the White House.[17] The inference about the future is clear—Klansmen have little choice but to accept the new racial order, one based on racial equality rather than racial hierarchy. The suggestion about the civil rights past is equally apparent—Klansmen, the archetypal "out-of-control crackers," were the principal practitioners of racial intimidation, as symbolized by the fictional Klansman's cross and the kerosene.

Blaming Klansmen for America's long and brutal history of racial terror, however, conceals much more than it brings to light. It hides the array of perpetrators of racial violence who were bound neither by class nor gender. On August 7, 1930, white men and women, of great and limited means, assembled in the streets of Marion, Indiana, and lynched African Americans Thomas Shipp and Abram Smith.[18] Blaming Klansmen blurs the causes of racial

Figure 16  Riber Hansson, "Obama and Resigned KKK Member," *Svenska Dagbladet* (Nov. 6, 2008).

violence, which transcended racial hatred and included a range of economic and political factors. On December 4, 1947, in Lowndesboro, Alabama, local white resident Clarke Luckie murdered African American entrepreneur Elmore Bolling. According to an NAACP investigative report, Bolling's body was "riddled with shotgun and pistol shots" simply because he was "too prosperous as a Negro farmer."[19] Holding Klansmen solely responsible for racial terror also glosses over the widespread social acceptability of racial violence, as well as the complicity of the state. In October 1919, in Elaine, Arkansas, nearly six hundred federal troops, along with one thousand area whites, terrorized local African Americans, killing several hundred, in an effort to prevent black sharecroppers from organizing a union. Following the massacre, county sheriffs, judges, and justices of the peace, together with the governor of Arkansas, conspired to prevent the victims of the violence from receiving justice.[20] Racial terror was not an American anomaly; it was an American tradition.

Unlike contemporary political commentators, movement activists were fully aware of the nature of racial violence. They were also cognizant of the extent to which American society accepted white supremacy, and of the ways in which white supremacy operated systemically and institutionally. These understandings framed their critique of the nation, which for increasing numbers of civil rights activists revolved around structural analyses that refuted personal prejudice as the chief obstacle to racial equality.

Liberal white friends of the movement, however, tended to hold on to the idea that personal prejudice was the problem, flatly rejecting structural critiques. What's more, they often argued their point by disparaging those who advocated the contrasting position. During the late 1960s, as structural analyses gained popularity under the rubric of Black Power, critics of the structural point of view became more vociferous in their denunciations. Editors and journalists at the *Chicago Tribune*, for example, variously referred to proponents of structural analyses as "rabid spokesmen," "civil rioters," "wild men," "fanatics," "angry young men," "Negro extremists," and "hotheads."[21] And they singled out for special ridicule Stokely Carmichael, who introduced the nation to the Black Power slogan in 1966, mocking him as a "rabid evangelist" and as the chief "apostle of Black Power."[22]

Critics of structural analyses intentionally chose demeaning language to describe radical black activists in order to depict them as senseless and impractical. From the perspective of those who were convinced that personal prejudice was the issue, it was insane to suggest that the nation's most basic systems and institutions were fundamentally flawed and should be completely overhauled in order to create a just, humane, and equitable society. It was equally insane to suggest that well-meaning whites were somehow complicit in the perpetuation of racial inequality. Falling back on a default analysis of black radicalism that had been used over the centuries to dismiss black freedom fighters from Nat Turner to Marcus Garvey, they wrote off proponents of structural analyses as unstable. By portraying black radicals as "crazy Negroes," they were able to reject without consideration or deliberation everything they said and did, from the pragmatic solutions they offered to the organizing projects and community programs they developed.

The "crazy Negro" mischaracterization of radical black activists has endured. Its persistence became abundantly clear during the presidential campaign when media outlets broadcast snippets of sermons by black theologian Rev. Jeremiah Wright in which he criticized American foreign policy lead-

"AND FURTHERMORE, BARACK, WHO GAVE YOU THE CRAZY IDEA THAT PEOPLE WHO ARE BITTER CLING TO THEIR RELIGION ?!?"

Figure 17  R. J. Matson, "Obama's Cross to Bear," *St. Louis Post Dispatch* (April 29, 2008).

ing up to 9/11. The endlessly looping sound bites of his passionate homilies prompted widespread condemnation of his remarks and denunciations of him as traitorous, nonsensical, and even fanatical. Cartoonist R. J. Matson captured these sentiments in "Obama's Cross to Bear," in which he depicts Wright as a Bible thumping, pulpit banging, bug-eyed rabble-rouser who is as bitter about his place in America, and is clinging as tightly to his black liberation Christianity, as the white conservative evangelicals whom Obama accused of doing the same.[23]

The persistence of the "crazy Negro" mischaracterization also shapes the ways in which black radicalism during the civil rights era is typically understood. Few cartoons illustrate this better than the one of Barack and Michelle Obama that appeared on the cover of *The New Yorker* during the height of the campaign. Satirizing conservative portrayals of Barack as a closeted Muslim and Michelle as unpatriotic, the cartoon depicts him in traditional Islamic garb and her in the imaginary fashion of a 1960s black radical, complete with fatigues, Afro, automatic weapon, and bandolier.[24] Michelle's appearance is meant to bring to mind the urban riots and "crazy Negro" politics of the late sixties, from the Watts and Newark uprisings to the revolution-

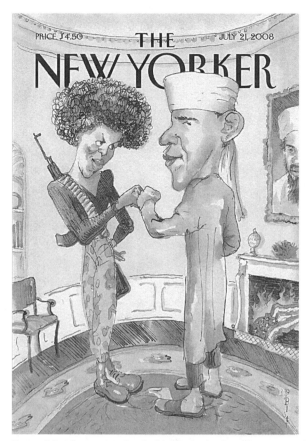

Figure 18 *The New Yorker* (July 21, 2008). Blitt/The New Yorker/Condé Nast Archive, copyright © Condé Nast.

ary black nationalism of Huey Newton and the cultural black nationalism of Amiri Baraka.

Lingering stereotypes of black radicals perpetuate many of the misconceptions about the black freedom struggle in general, and about the Black Power movement in particular. They harden the fictitious line separating civil rights protest and Black Power politics, which at best minimizes and at worst overlooks important linkages between the two, making it nearly impossible to see the ways in which civil rights breathed life into Black Power. They reinforce the false notion that Black Power activism was responsible for waning interest in grass-roots organizing and for alienating whites, the combination of which is blamed for movement ineffectiveness near the end of the 1960s.

They strip Black Power ideologies of real meaning, reducing them to violent, anti-white philosophies. And they misconstrue black radicals' understanding of racial inequality, which revolved around structural analyses, robbing the black radical critique of real meaning and lasting value.

The failure to take black radicals and their structural analyses seriously has made it more difficult to make sense of racial inequality in the post–civil rights era. It has prompted many people to fall back on personal prejudice as the major cause of race-based disparities, and in the wake of the declining social acceptability of public displays of racism, to suggest increasingly that African Americans bear primary responsibility for their inability to get ahead in life. Following Rev. Jesse Jackson's crass, off camera criticism of Obama for repeatedly calling on African Americans to assume more responsibility for their families and communities, the *Salt Lake Tribune* published a Pat Bagley cartoon featuring Jackson with his arms wrapped around Obama's ankle saying, "We're always bein' held back by 'The Man'. . . ."[25] For Bagley, Jackson's tactless censure of Obama underscored that racial discrimination today is a figment of African Americans' imagination, the product of race-card profiteers, the heirs to the "crazy Negroes" of the sixties.

Bagley's take on Jackson's remarks hints at the dominant way of interpreting racial divisions, which holds that racialized views of the present are shaped wholly by emotional baggage from the past. For African Americans, it is rage held over from the distant Jim Crow era, the apex of de jure segregation. For whites, it is animosity born during the immediate post-civil rights era, the period of affirmative action, which many whites point to as the start of reverse racism. Cartoonist J. D. Crowe's interpretation of Obama's Philadelphia race speech speaks directly to this point of view. Crowe depicts Obama as a Moses-like figure with the power to heal the racial divide, the parameters of which he suggests are defined by black anger and white resentment.[26] Framing the present as an emotional conflict, however, ignores the historic and persistent causes of racial inequality and disregards the social value and economic legacy of white privilege.

Viewing racial divisions as a simple misunderstanding born of oversensitivity about the past has led to premature declarations of the triumph of racial equality. Across the political spectrum, Obama's victory has been heralded as the dawn of a post-racial age, one in which all things are possible for people of color, particularly children of color, who unlike their parents, are

Figure 19  Pat Bagley, "Jesse Jackass," *Salt Lake Tribune* (July 10, 2008).

Figure 20  J. D. Crowe, "Obama Race Speech," *Mobile Register* (March 19, 2008).

Figure 21  Jeff Parker, "Yes We Can," *Florida Today* (Nov. 11, 2008).

unburdened by memories of bygone eras. Cartoonist Jeff Parker depicts this point of view in his cartoon "Yes We Can," which appeared the day after the general election, and features children of Latino, Asian, and African American descent watching Obama celebrate his victory while thinking, "Yes, we can," or that they too can now achieve their dreams.[27] The willingness of whites to vote for an African American presidential candidate is taken as prima facia evidence that racial egalitarianism has supplanted personal prejudice as the dominant mode of thinking, eliminating racism as a barrier to success, and making simple positive thinking the key to achieving one's goals.

Obama's historic run for the White House created a unique opportunity for public reflection on the civil rights movement. Political cartoonists were among the many who looked back at the past and found meaning in the movement. Unfortunately, their understanding of the movement as expressed in their illustrations reveals the persistence of innumerable myths about the struggle, from the alleged predominance of King's leadership to the supposed aberrant behavior of "out-of-control crackers." These myths have remade history, altering everything from the movement's internal dynamics to the nature of the opposition. As a result, critical aspects of the movement are consistently overlooked, including its freedom rights goals, and important lessons are routinely disregarded, including insights pertaining to the structural causes of racial inequality. These myths also continue to shape the public discourse on race, limiting the usefulness of these conversations. Although deeply ingrained in the public consciousness, these myths are not indelible. Dispelling them, however, requires recentering those aspects of the movement that have been pushed to the margins of history.

## NOTES

1. For details of Barack Obama's race-avoidance campaign strategy see Adam Nagourney, Jim Rutenberg, and Jeff Zeleny, "Near-flawless run is credited in victory," *New York Times*, November 5, 2008. For the complete text of Barack Obama's presidential nomination acceptance speech go to http://www.nytimes.com/2008/08/28/us/politics/28text-obama.html?pagewanted=1&_r=1.

2. R. J. Matson, "The Mountain Top," *Roll Call*, August 27, 2008.

3. "Martin Luther King, Jr.," *Encyclopedia Britannica* (Encyclopedia Britannica Online, 2010). Available at http://www.britannica.com/EBchecked/topic/318311/Martin-Luther-King-Jr.

4. Peter Lewis, "American Dream," *The Herald (Australia)*, November 5, 2008.

5. For an example of how the King-centric view obscures more than it reveals about the civil rights movement, see Robert Weisbrot, *Freedom Bound: A History of America's Civil Rights Movement* (New York: W. W. Norton & Co., 1989).

6. For examples of works that reduce the aim of the movement to color blindness see Tamar Jacoby, *Someone Else's House: America's Unfinished Struggle for Integration* (New York: Basic Books, 2000), and Paul M. Sniderman and Edward G. Carmines, *Reaching Beyond Race* (Cambridge, Mass.: Harvard University Press, 1999).

7. For the full text of King's "I Have a Dream" speech see Clayborne Carson and Kris Shepard, *A Call to Conscience: The Landmark Speeches of Dr. Martin Luther King, Jr.* (New York: Warner Books, 2002), 75–88.

8. Martin Luther King Jr., Coretta Scott King, and Vincent Harding, *Where Do We Go From Here: Chaos or Community?* (Boston: Beacon Press, 1968), 95. For an excellent essay on how King's view of color blindness has been misinterpreted see Tim Wise, "Misreading the Dream: The Truth about Martin Luther King, Jr. and Affirmative Action," *LiPmagazine.org* (2003). Available at http://www.lipmagazine.org/articles/featwise_mlk.shtml.

9. For more on the diverse array of movement goals see Martha Biondi, *To Stand and Fight: The Struggle for Civil Rights in Postwar New York City* (Cambridge, Mass.: Harvard University Press, 2003); Patrick D. Jones, *The Selma of the North: Civil Rights Insurgency in Milwaukee* (Cambridge, Mass.: Harvard University Press, 2009); Charles Bolton, *The Hardest Deal of All: The Battle over School Integration in Mississippi, 1870–1980* (Jackson: University Press of Mississippi, 2005); Hasan Kwame Jeffries, *Bloody Lowndes: Civil Rights and Black Power in Alabama's Black Belt* (New York: New York University Press, 2009).

10. David Fitzsimmons, "Obama Wins," *The Arizona Star*, November 2, 2008.

11. For an example of African American political mobilization after emancipation see Elsa Barkley Brown, "Negotiating and Transforming the Public Sphere: African American Political Life in the Transition from Slavery to Freedom," in *The Black Public Sphere: A Public Culture Book*, ed. Black Public Sphere Collective (Chicago: University of Chicago Press, 1995), 111–50.

12. For a detailed explanation of freedom rights and for a close look at the fight for freedom rights in Lowndes County, Alabama, during the post-emancipation and Reconstruction eras, see Jeffries, *Bloody Lowndes*, 7–38.

13. Dwayne Booth, "Water under the Bridge," *Mr. Fish*, November 6, 2008.

14. J. D. Crowe, "Obama, McCain, and Wallace," *Mobile Register*, October 15, 2008.

15. Stokely Carmichael with Ekwueme Michael Thelwell, *Ready for Revolution: The Life and Struggles of Stokely Carmichael (Kwame Ture)* (New York: Scribner, 2003), 172.

16. In recent years, scholars have increasingly turned their attention to the African American freedom struggle outside the South. For overviews of black activism and white supremacy in regions other than the South see Jeanne F. Theoharis and Komozi Woodard, *Freedom North: Black Freedom Struggles Outside the South, 1940–1980* (New York: Palgrave Macmillan, 2003); Thomas J. Sugrue, *Sweet Land of Liberty: The Forgotten Struggle for Civil Rights in the North* (New York: Random House, 2008).

17. Riber Hansson, "Obama and Resigned KKK Member," *Svenska Dagbladet* (Swedish newspaper), November 6, 2008.

18. For details of the lynching of Thomas Shipp and Abram Smith see James H. Madison, *A Lynching in the Heartland: Race and Memory in America* (New York: Palgrave Macmillan, 2003).

19. Jeffries, *Bloody Lowndes*, 32.

20. For the full story of the Elaine massacre see Nan Elizabeth Woodruff, *American Congo: The African American Freedom Struggle in the Delta* (Cambridge, Mass.: Harvard University Press, 2003).

21. "Who Stands to Profit from Riots?" *Chicago Tribune*, August 3, 1967; "Backing Away from the Consequences," *Chicago Tribune*, October 7, 1966; "A Few 'Theories' about Revolution," *Chicago Tribune*, September 3, 1967; "Photog, Delegate Beaten dur-

ing New Pol Parley," *Chicago Tribune*, September 4, 1967; "Riots Are Subsidized as Well as Organized," *Chicago Tribune*, August 6, 1967; "Plain Talk about Hatred and Violence," *Chicago Tribune*, May 28, 1968; "Ominous Talk from the Hotheads," *Chicago Tribune*, July 6, 1966.

22. "'Black Power' Again," *Chicago Tribune*, October 30, 1966.

23. R. J. Matson, "Obama's Cross to Bear," *St. Louis Post Dispatch*, April 29, 2008.

24. *The New Yorker*, July 21, 2008.

25. Pat Bagley, "Jesse Jackass," *Salt Lake Tribune*, July 10, 2008.

26. J. D. Crowe, "Obama Race Speech," *Mobile Register*, March 19, 2008.

27. Jeff Parker, "Yes We Can," *Florida Today*, November 11, 2008.

EDITED BY EMILYE CROSBY

# Making *Eyes on the Prize*

## *An Interview with Filmmaker and* SNCC *Staffer Judy Richardson*

**N**ote: This interview text is drawn from several in-depth interviews with Richardson, conducted by Emilye Crosby, between July 2005 and July 2007. The interviews have been consolidated, organized, and edited for clarity and readability. A brief introduction precedes the interview.

### INTRODUCTION

*Eyes on the Prize* first aired in 1987 when I was a senior in college. I know this because it literally stopped me in my tracks one day as I was walking past the communal television where it was showing. I have no idea which episode I saw. I remember only that I was absolutely transfixed and unable to continue on my way until it was over. Nearly twenty-five years later, I still use portions of *Eyes* in my courses and it continues to grab my students' attention and draw them into the history.

In this interview with Judy Richardson, we get a glimpse of *Eyes* as a work-in-progress, *before* it became a cultural touchstone powerful enough to generate the recent national campaign to renew the rights and keep the series available.[1] What we all know as *Eyes on the Prize*, the two-part series totalling fourteen one-hour episodes, was initiated in 1978 by Blackside founder, Henry Hampton. At the time, he envisioned it as a two-hour documentary titled, "America, We Loved You Madly." Richardson was one of a handful of people who began working on the documentary in this pre-*Eyes* period. In fact, it might be appropriate to thank her for the 1979 memo she wrote pleading for a title change and offering up more than twenty freedom song alternatives, including "Keep your Eyes on the Prize." (See figure 23 in this chapter for a copy of the memo.)

This interview with Richardson is not an official history of *Eyes on the Prize*. Rather, it focuses on Judy's perspective and personal experiences. I was curious, for example, about what it felt like for her to interview others and do research on the movement she had been part of. I was interested in her sense of the scholarship at the time and what it was like to engage scholars (and others) around the issues of interpretation. I wondered how the production team developed their stories and figured out the framework. I had other questions, too: what was it like to see the documentary take shape? What did she think of the way it portrayed the movement? Did it capture what she experienced? What did she see as its strengths? Weaknesses?

As Judy reflects, we get a glimpse of her excitement at uncovering pieces of the history and her joy in reliving aspects of the movement, of having her own sense of the movement reinforced and validated through the stories and memories of those she interviewed. Through Judy's memories, we get a sense of how uncertain and tenuous the project was at times, of the luck and perseverance involved, of the challenges, and of the contested nature of the interpretations. We get a sense of the many, many people who made contributions to the series. In fact, one of the strongest themes that comes through in Richardson's interview is how absolutely crucial collaboration was to the project and how much making *Eyes* was a learning experience for all involved. For example, filmmakers who had little background in the civil rights movement became, in essence, historians, doing research, interviewing participants, and attending Scholar Schools. I can only imagine that the Scholar Schools—which brought the production team together with a wide range of movement scholars, journalists, government officials, and activists—must have made for a lively and contentious classroom, one I'd love to join. (Too bad the Blackside filmmakers didn't record those sessions!)

When Richardson began working on *Eyes on the Prize*, she had no background in film. Instead, she brought with her the contacts and skills that she had developed in the movement. She joined SNCC in fall 1963 after a year at Swarthmore, working briefly in Cambridge, Maryland, before relocating to the national office in Atlanta. Over the next three years she went with the national office to Greenwood during the 1964 Mississippi Summer Project, and then worked in southwest Georgia, Lowndes County, Alabama, and on Julian Bond's first campaign for the Georgia House of Representatives. She left SNCC in 1966 and two years later joined several of her former SNCC colleagues to organize Drum and Spear Bookstore in Washington, D.C. After quickly becoming the largest African American bookstore in the country, Drum and Spear added a publishing house with offices in Washington and Tanzania and Richardson spent a few years as the children's book editor.

In the early 1980s when Henry Hampton rejuvenated his documentary project on the civil rights movement, now named *Eyes on the Prize*, Richardson was working in New York as Director of Information for the United Church of Christ (UCC) Commission for Racial Justice. In that capacity, she wrote the Commission's weekly commentary and coordinated public information campaigns and research. While continuing her work with the Commission on Racial Justice, she rejoined *Eyes* as a research consultant. As she explains in the interview, there was considerable overlap as she moved back-and-forth between her work on movement history with *Eyes* and the UCC's ongoing projects, including anti-police brutality campaigns in New York City and two Freedom Rides from New York to the Alabama Black Belt to counter Reagan administration intimidation of black voters.

It is interesting to revisit *Eyes on the Prize* in the context of current historiographical debates and the larger challenge we face of replacing the popular "master narrative" of the movement with a more nuanced story that incorporates bottom-up history and reflects the movement's complexity. There are ways that, collectively, the six episodes of the first series reinforce the tendency to see the movement as a story of national success, moving from the 1954 Supreme Court decision in *Brown* through the Voting Rights Act of 1965. Going from this triumphant story of victory to the emergence of Black Power with the opening of the second series feeds the stereotypical dichotomy between what is portrayed as the good southern nonviolent movement of the early 1960s versus the bad, violent Black Power movement of the late 1960s. Moreover, the *Eyes* framework recreates some of the limitations of top-down movement history. Because Blackside chose to develop the stories in *Eyes* around archival footage, producers were tied to those stories that the media considered newsworthy at the time. *Eyes*, then, shares some of the blindspots of the media's coverage of the movement, with an overemphasis on "big events," on white participants, and on public, confrontational violence.[2] For example, the episode on Mississippi is framed almost exclusively around the assassination of Medgar Evers and the 1964 Summer Project, known popularly as Freedom Summer. Although both are important, and the attention to Evers at least hints at the existence of local black organizing, generally this kind of focus on high profile violence, interracial activism, and big events tends to obscure the longer term, less visible, less dramatic organizing of southern African Americans.[3]

And yet even within this episode centered on the Mississippi events that were considered most media-worthy, the *Eyes* producers go beyond the surface story that drew the cameras. In particular, they introduce us to local activists, the people who provided the base for the movement and did much to sustain it. For example, we meet and hear from Unita Blackwell, Victoria Gray Adams, and Fannie Lou Hamer, a few of the African American women who embraced SNCC organizers and helped transform the state. Through archival footage and interviews, we get a sense of their work, their motivation, and their understanding of the issues. And in *Eyes on the Prize* it is they, not white liberals, who offer a final assessment of the Mississippi Freedom Democratic Party's decision to reject the token compromise offered by the national Democratic Party in 1964. These leaders, black women from Mississippi, make it clear that they were not, as some of the media at the time portrayed them, politically unsophisticated people unable to comprehend the realities of a national convention. Rather, they were people who, after risking their lives in the movement, had no interest in settling for a mess of pottage.[4]

In addition to outpacing much of the existing scholarship in its attention to local people and grass-roots activism, *Eyes* anticipates a number of more recent historiographical developments and debates. For example, *Eyes* includes both movement-era footage and extensive contemporary interviews with white supremacists years before Charles Payne critiqued historians for too often depicting white racists as "stupid, vulgar, and one-dimensional" and Charles Eagles made his own appeal for more serious scholarship on whites, including movement opponents.[5]

Similarly—though the absence of self-defense in the first series and the way *Eyes* I and *Eyes* II are divided contribute to the stereotypical good sixties/bad sixties—if we take the first and second series together and examine the specifics that emerge in the eight episodes that make up *Eyes* II, the picture is more complex. The second series gives the Black Power movement serious scholarly attention, carries the story into the early 1980s, and features many events centered outside the South.[6] Here *Eyes* predates the recent scholarly interest in extending the chronology beyond the 1965 or 1968 framework, exploring black activism in the North and West, and developing more nuanced histories of Black Power. It challenges, rather than reinforces, the triumphant popular framing that obscures both the continuing problems of economic and racial inequality and the national nature of white supremacy.[7]

In her interview, Richardson highlights another important *Eyes* II contribution and one that historians might consider building on. When the *Eyes* staff was considering which campus protest story to include, she believed they should feature the Howard University students' campus takeover, as opposed to Cornell student protests for Black Studies, because "[i]t's not always black folks trying to get white folks to do right. Sometimes it's black folks trying to get *black* folks to do right. And sometimes we're only talking to ourselves, we're talking internally. So that's why, for me, the Howard story was important." Charles Payne made a similar point in one of his "Local Studies" Conference talks at Geneseo in 2006, observing that "[o]ur literature on how blacks relate to other black folk is thin. It's thin over a 150 year period." In fact, he argues that race relations and even black militancy are typically understood in terms of how "black people relate to white people." Like Richardson discussing the importance of telling the Howard story, Payne argues that scholars need to explore how African Americans "relate to one another— on a day-to-day, ordinary way."[8] (For more of Payne's discussion, see chapter 10, this volume.) As the recent nature of Payne's comments suggest, internal black community conversations, relationships, and organizing is still an underdeveloped area of scholarship and another in which scholars might want to follow the lead of *Eyes on the Prize*.

So, while the first series of *Eyes* did important work in highlighting some of the many "ordinary" African Americans who created and sustained the civil rights movement, the second series made it clear that the struggle for racial justice continued long after the passage of the Civil Rights and Voting Rights Acts. Portraying this post-1965 period was a challenging and contested task, however, and Richardson's interview gives us a glimpse of the internal debates and tensions that emerged around choosing and interpreting this history. As *Eyes* II tackled stories featuring not just electoral politics and school integration, but also ones focusing on black nationalism and community control, Richardson often found herself at odds with Hampton and others. While she saw the key role that black self-determination and institution-building played in the larger freedom struggle, she notes that Hampton opposed all-black anything. Moreover, she laughingly explains, he was very conscious of PBS's white viewers and his sense that they needed to "see themselves." Richardson's memories of these conflicts and differences reinforce my sense of the rich, collaborative environment in which *Eyes* was created. Hampton insisted on integrated production teams (with black and white coproducers on every episode) and struggled with Richardson's assertion—based on personal experience—that the Lowndes County Freedom Party was organized as an all-black political party. At the same time, he created space for multiple perspectives and gave the producers room to use their research to develop and argue for stories and to push for the framing that emerged from that research.

Looking back at the largely top-down, King-centric scholarship that existed when *Eyes* was created and reflecting on the popular version of the movement that persists today, the fact that *Eyes* has weaknesses related to a top-down, media-driven orientation is probably less surprising than the series' many strengths. As Judy notes in her interview, not only did *Eyes* producers and staff read widely and attend rigorous Scholar Schools, they also did extensive primary research and in-depth audiotaped pre-interviews (partly to assess potential for on-camera interviews, but also for research). It seems clear that these "oral histories" helped offer a counterpoint to the limitations of the existing framework generated by the media and by early top-down studies. So, although *Eyes* chronicles a recognizable national story, it attempts to ground that story in local communities, while highlighting the agency of "ordinary" African Americans. It is both a testament to *Eyes* and a troubling commentary on the shortcomings of popular culture and contemporary textbooks that, despite its limitations, the history *Eyes* conveys is far more accurate and complex than the one my students learn today. Sadly, even the most up-to-date textbooks, ones written by professional historians with access to the full range of scholarship that has proliferated in the two decades since the second series aired, fall far short of *Eyes*, not only in communicating the drama and power of the movement, but also its conflicts and complexity and its grounding in the struggle of ordinary African Americans.[9]

In the following interview, Judy Richardson shares her memories of working on and helping to create *Eyes*, including her perspective on the challenges and the joys and her assessment of its strengths and weaknesses. Richardson came into *Eyes* as a movement person, utilizing the contacts and skills that she developed in SNCC. Through her work on *Eyes* and other Blackside projects she developed new skills and became a filmmaker in her own right. *Eyes*—her work on the project and its public reception—also pushed her into a role of public speaker and workshop leader. Although Judy recalls that for

Figure 22 Judy Richardson (*left*) with Emilye Crosby, April 2010. Photograph by Wesley Hogan, courtesy of Wesley Hogan.

most of her life "speaking to a room with more than 3 people scared the hell out of me," she was propelled forward by her passion for movement history and desire to share it with others.[10] In this first interview, she focuses on *Eyes* and in "That Movement Responsibility" (see chapter 12, this volume), she talks more generally about her work interpreting movement history, especially through lectures and teacher workshops.

## INTERVIEW

EMILYE CROSBY (EC): Can you tell me how you got started working with *Eyes on the Prize*?

JUDY RICHARDSON (JR): Before *Eyes*, Henry Hampton and Blackside had mainly been doing industrial, nonbroadcast stuff, but wanted to do what he thought would be a two-hour documentary on the civil rights movement. I had done a movement chronology for Henry and when he finds out I'm moving up to Boston, he says, "That's great. Why don't you come on as an AP?," an associate producer. He was about to get the grant from Cap Cities for this documentary, so he asked me to be the office manager until the money comes in and I can be the AP. I said "fine," because I had no money. But of course, that didn't work out so well because I was supposed to open the office, and I can't be anywhere at 9:00 a.m. consistently. So that was a problem, but that's a whole other thing.*

I think the reason he hired me, and I'm not even sure if he ever stated it, but the assumption was nobody knows Blackside. The people in the movement don't know Henry, they don't know Blackside, they don't know anything Blackside's done before. And I think what he hoped is that I'd be an entrée to some of the movement people. So I mainly come because I have what Henry believes are connections to the movement. I had no—absolutely no—experience in film when he hired me.

It took six months before we got a producer, Henry Johnson, who had just come from WGBH, the PBS station in Boston. And, it wasn't really clear which stories we were doing. So Henry Johnson and I went out and started doing pre-interviews, "pre" meaning it was not being filmed, just audio-taped. We started on the phone and then I did my first-ever in-person pre-interview with Myrlie Evers in L.A. at ARCO, where she worked in the Corporate Giving office. By the time the work on *Eyes on the Prize*, the real one, begins in '84, it was clear to me that she had already told the story of Medgar's death many times. But when I'm talking to her in '78, it seemed so fresh to me. It seemed like not many people had asked her, it was different, it was a little rawer. And not so much rawer, more from the heart. You know? And I remember what really grabbed me was when she talked about the kids, that when they heard the shots the kids got to the floor and then to the bathtub as they had been taught to do. And that just took me out, it was just amazing to me.

And then I asked her, "Look, if we had no footage, how would you describe a mass meeting to people so even if they aren't looking at anything, they will see that mass meeting, and they will feel that mass meeting?" And she just did it. She just recreated the sense of exhilaration and energy and the emotion of it, and just being carried away by it all. And I started to tear up. She just had done it again for me. And it was like, *okay*. It made me feel I had not made this up. That's what it was. I have not made up this movement. I have not romanticized it through these years. And the other part of

---

* Capital Cities Communication later bought the whole ABC–TV network, then sold it to Disney. But at that point they were just distributors of independent programming.

it was, this could really be an amazing film. That was the other thing that came at me from her.

And then on that same trip, I went next to Dave Dennis. And he was in New Orleans at that point. And we just hit every club, because he did not want to talk about Chaney, Goodman, and Schwerner,* and I told him, "That's what I'm coming to talk about." He delayed and delayed it as much as he possibly could. And then we went back to the hotel, I set up the tape recorder and it would not operate. He was so happy [*laughter*] because he really did not want to talk about it. So then I of course felt pissed because I really wanted to get his thoughts down on what happened. He was will- ing to talk about it a little bit when we were walking and going through the clubs and stuff, but to actually focus on it, he didn't want to do that.

When I did that first interview with Myrlie and then the attempted one with Dave, I was very aware that I was calling on skills developed in the movement. That I knew, because people had taught me how to do this, how to get information out of people and how to do it in a way that could be fairly concise. Because I was used to getting information from people call- ing from the field about church bombings or freedom house burnings and all that kind of stuff. And also because, even though much of my SNCC life had been working in an office, some of the organizing stuff rubbed off on me. And so I actually kind of knew how you deal with people. I knew how to talk to people so that they would want to give me their story, that's really what it was. Now, that really helped me when I was doing that first piece, that first two hours of what became *Eyes*.

EC: Do you remember having conversations in that pre-*Eyes* stage with Henry Hampton and whoever else was involved on what the film should focus on, and what stories it should tell?

JR: Yeah. As a matter of fact Henry let us go off, Henry Johnson, Blackside writer Steve Fayer, and I, and Audrey Barnes, a black female editor who also was part of that. She was doing research. And we were trying to figure out what the stories are going to be. And Henry Hampton was part of that to-

---

* James Chaney, a native Mississippian working with CORE, Michael Schwerner, a New Yorker on CORE's staff, and Andrew Goodman, a summer volunteer, were all killed at the beginning of the 1964 Summer Project sponsored by SNCC and COFO. Dave Dennis was CORE's top staff person in Mississippi and the assistant director for the Summer Project.

wards the end. But it was very clear it was going to be . . . well, there was no term at that point for local movement history, but it was very clear it was going to be local movement based. One of the things I try and remind folks of, is that the kind of local movement scholarship that you have now, that just wasn't available to me then. I'm sure people were working on their books and working on their theses, but they were not published at that point. And so everything was *Bearing the Cross,* and King and wherever King went. And the interpretation of those events was always through the lens of Dr. King. So I just wasn't seeing any of the people that I knew were amazing and incredible to the movement. And what was lucky for me was that Henry understood that. But we were really trying to figure out: is it going to be the Freedom Rides and the sit-ins? is it going to be—I don't even think Albany was part of it at that point. But it was trying to figure out: What is the through-line? What are the stories and stuff? We knew we had to do Montgomery.

Montgomery was the one where I'm looking through *Stride Towards Freedom.* And I hadn't been finding any women. I hadn't been finding anybody but King most of the time, and anybody who worked with King. I'm not finding any stuff on Fannie Lou Hamer, and Ms. Ella Baker and Mrs. Victoria Gray, and you know, anybody. So when I'm going through *Stride Towards Freedom,* and I find Jo Ann Robinson's name, that's when I start to look for her. And I'm trying to think because Dave Garrow had this humongous rolodex, but he wasn't the one who actually gave me the number for her. I called Gerald Fraser, from the *New York Times,* and he's the one who says, "You need to look at the phone book." And she was listed and I called her. She was so excited that I was calling to ask about this, so there was that whole thing about how people get validated through their oral histories. She started telling me part of the story, and I stopped her because I was afraid she was going to tell all this stuff and then be wiped dry by the time the camera got there. I can't remember who filmed that, but it's one of the few exterior interviews we do. Those earlier interviews are the only ones done outside, before it is decided that everything will be a sit-down standard interview format. We also filmed one of the Montgomery Bus Boycott walkers outside. And it's the only time where you hear an off-camera question too.

That was the times of figuring it out. We had used Julian Bond in that earlier version as an on-camera narrator. And Julian's very gifted at that, as well as a number of other things. He's gifted at being able to do narration, either stand-up or voice-over. In the Montgomery section, initially in that first version, he was going to show what it was like to be on a bus. So we had gotten one of those old buses, and he talks about going to the back of the bus on the outside and then boarding at the side door. That's when we didn't know what the format was going to be. We didn't know—okay, is it all going to be voice-over? Or are we going to have recreations?

In that first two-hour version, the thing that gets done is I get the title changed. It had been "America We Loved You Madly." That's Henry's title. I wrote this memo and it's 1979 October. I talk about how— "Y'all know about how much I dislike the current working title. I have therefore perused freedom song titles for alternatives. Herein is the list. I am not wedded to any of these titles although there are a couple I kinda like. I am circulating this mainly to get us thinking about other possibilities. Also, since they are all related to actual freedom songs there is a tie in musically. . . . There is no, underlined, no order of preference on this listing." Number six is "Their *Eyes on the Prize*," or "Keep Your *Eyes on the Prize*." And then I go through all these other freedom song titles and then number twenty-two has an as- terisk, and the asterisk says . . . the title of twenty-two is "We Placed our Trust in the Lord . . . and they beat the shit out of us anyway." And then on the bottom it says "my favorite." And then I have a P.S., "I know many of these are tacky but while you're laughing at the yucky ones (and you should have seen what the first list looked like . . .) keep the better ones in mind."

So what's good about Henry is that he picks number six. When the first two hours goes down for lack of funding, it lays fallow from about '80 to about, maybe '82 or so when he starts fund-raising again. So when it comes back up again he has now called it "Eyes on the Prize." And our writer, Steve Fayer, who had been working with Blackside long before I came on in '78, said that he thought that Henry had chosen the wrong title. And Steve says, Steve's a white guy, and Steve said, "I was telling them they're going to mis- pronounce it. They're going to say 'Eyes on de Prize.' They're going to make fun of it." And he said that almost up until broadcast. So what was great is when you saw people starting to use the phrase, unrelated to the series, and it became part of the culture.

The work on the two hour version for Cap Cities goes for two years, from about '78 to '79, I would say the end of '79. And then Cap Cities pulls the plug. They pulled the plug both because, I think, we really did not know what we were doing. But more than that, it was that they wanted some- thing much more King-centered than either Henry or I wanted to do. And

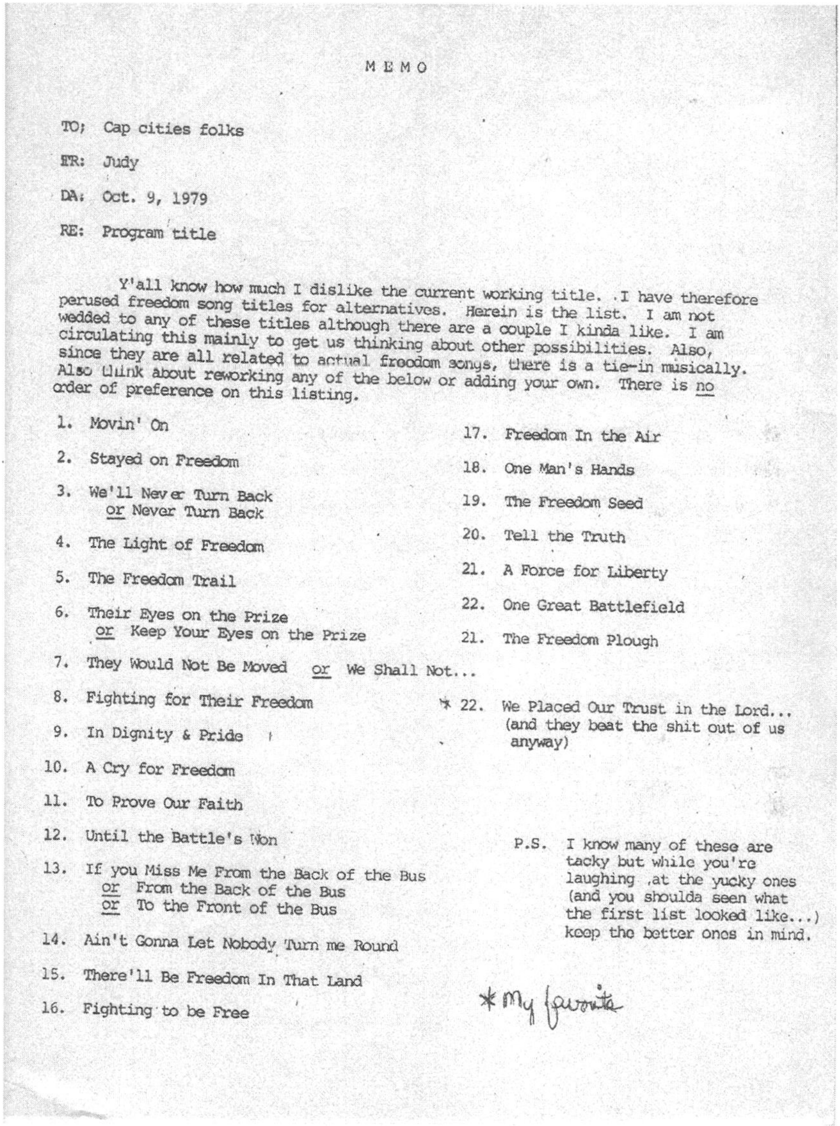

MEMO

TO: Cap cities folks

FR: Judy

DA: Oct. 9, 1979

RE: Program title

Y'all know how much I dislike the current working title. .I have therefore perused freedom song titles for alternatives. Herein is the list. I am not wedded to any of these titles although there are a couple I kinda like. I am circulating this mainly to get us thinking about other possibilities. Also, since they are all related to actual freedom songs, there is a tie-in musically. Also think about reworking any of the below or adding your own. There is no order of preference on this listing.

1. Movin' On

2. Stayed on Freedom

3. We'll Never Turn Back
   or Never Turn Back

4. The Light of Freedom

5. The Freedom Trail

6. Their Eyes on the Prize
   or Keep Your Eyes on the Prize

7. They Would Not Be Moved   or   We Shall Not...

8. Fighting for Their Freedom

9. In Dignity & Pride

10. A Cry for Freedom

11. To Prove Our Faith

12. Until the Battle's Won

13. If you Miss Me From the Back of the Bus
    or   From the Back of the Bus
    or   To the Front of the Bus

14. Ain't Gonna Let Nobody Turn me Round

15. There'll Be Freedom In That Land

16. Fighting to be Free

17. Freedom In the Air

18. One Man's Hands

19. The Freedom Seed

20. Tell the Truth

21. A Force for Liberty

22. One Great Battlefield

21. The Freedom Plough

* 22. We Placed Our Trust in the Lord...
      (and they beat the shit out of us
      anyway)

P.S.   I know many of these are
       tacky but while you're
       laughing .at the yucky ones
       (and you shoulda seen what
       the first list looked like...)
       keep the better ones in mind.

* my favorite

Figure 23  Judy Richardson 1979 memo on naming *Eyes on the Prize*. Courtesy of Judy Richardson.

it wasn't so much what I wanted to do. I was only a little AP at that point. It was clear that Henry did not want to do the film that Cap Cities wanted.

I stay with Blackside for another six, seven months, and then I go to L.A. with my boyfriend and Henry goes back to doing industrials and government spots and stuff like that. Then a friend of Henry's, Ruth Batson, says "Henry you can't let this go. You have got to continue fund-raising."

Batson was part of the Boston NAACP and was one of the main people pushing school desegregation in the 1960s. It's funny because she was basically a nationalist. In her heart, that's who she really was. But her feeling was her daughters were not getting what they needed from the local schools, and she couldn't force the school board to put the money into the black schools. So they started doing a survey to find out were there empty classrooms, not up to capacity, in the white schools. And yes, there were. And so she comes back, and they get this court order and all that stuff.

So, after Batson pushes Henry, he goes to some of his friends in the Unitarians. He goes to Marian Wright Edelman and her husband, who really reached out to a number of folks. And also, what was great was that there were a number of black women whom he always credited, who were in key positions at Ford and the Corporation for Public Broadcasting, who really helped boost some of this through and get some funding for it. So he gets the funding in '84.

During the work on *Eyes* I, I would come up for six weeks at a time and then go back to my job as Director of Information at the United Church of Christ Commission for Racial Justice. But people who were working full-time on the production remember, in a way that I don't, that folks never really knew from day to day whether this was really going to pan out, whether there was going to be enough funding to complete it, whether they would have enough money to keep the salaries going. It was all of that.

They bring in Judith Vecchione, who had been a series producer, I think, on the Vietnam series for PBS. Now, when Vecchione comes, she brings the kind of rigor of doing a multi-part series for PBS. Henry, however, had already come out of a journalistic thing. He had been the publicist for the Unitarian Universalist Association, so he absolutely understood the importance of the journalistic grounding, the scholarly grounding, and keeping a fact book. So, for example, there was always a fact book for every show. The final fact book has every page of script with citations from the scholarship validating anything that could be questioned either in the narration or in one of the interviewee's comments. And so that went through all of Blackside's series. We carried that through for everything else.

EC: How did you deal with interviews? They're presumably fact-based, but they're also people's perspective and interpretation.

JR: Yeah, well then you get into that thing about whether you let somebody say something that you know is wrong. For example, John Dittmer had a problem with the way the Till piece was framed by one of the interviewees, and still does. To John, it makes it seem that Till called it upon himself by showing the picture of the white girl that was in his class. And that story is told by William Bradford Huie, the *Life* reporter. And that's what he says the murderers told him. So then the question becomes, do you say that's not what happened? That certainly is what they told Huie. Now, whether in fact Till did that is another question. I don't know, but that's one of those times where it did stay in.

EC: Can you tell me about the Scholar Schools for *Eyes*?

JR: At Blackside we had to be grounded in the scholarship, so the schools were to ground the producers, the associate producers, and researchers, to give them common ground, in terms of the research of this period. We did a humongous amount of reading and we did ten days of school for *Eyes* I. That was at the Kennedy Library. We had activists who were there. Fred Shuttlesworth came up. And scholars like John Dittmer, Clay Carson, and David Garrow. And you had media people who were active. I don't think we were able to get Claude Sitton, of the *New York Times*, but we had some other people who represented the media. Then you had Burke Marshall and John Doar from the Justice Department. Julian Bond came up and did a piece. Oh, it was amazing!

EC: What was it like for you to be part of those schools?

JR: It was actually fascinating because when you're in a movement, there are lots of pieces that you don't know are going on at the same time. So for me, hearing some of those other pieces was very interesting. And part of it for me was renewing my sense that it *had happened*. So that's what was important to me. Even in school, particularly when you heard the activists, there was a sense that it was real, that this was important to a lot of other people in the same way that it was important—well, mmmm . . . in much the same way as it was important to me. Not for everybody. But there were enough people that it validated my feelings about it. *Yeah*.

EC: Did you have any issues with any of the scholars about what they thought was important versus what you thought was important?

JR: I don't remember so much the scholars, as I do some of the government people. Burke Marshall really was an apologist, to me, for the inaction of the government. And so, when he talks about Lyndon Johnson doing all this wonderful work and stuff, it was like "*please*." But, as a member of the production staff, you were not to get into any arguments with them. Now, you could ask them questions, but you couldn't argue. And besides which, my feeling was, I could talk at staff meetings. And also in some ways this was really new to me, as it was to all the producers, I think. And so although there were things that made me mad, I guess we didn't know what *Eyes* was gonna become and how important it was gonna be and we were really kind of feeling our way in a lot of ways.

EC: Was it difficult to frame *Eyes on the Prize* in ways that didn't just reflect the existing King-centric scholarship that you described earlier?

JR: Not once people started calling folks. People did a lot of phone interviews for the two-hour version. When you ask about how do they compensate for there not being this scholarship? It really does come through the local, the movement people who they're talking to. I think, for example, on the Albany section, most of the scholarship, and I suspect, even Henry's sense of this, was that it was a failure, because it was a failure for King. So, in my mind, and I hope I'm correct about this—What I remember is certainly Callie Crossley (who goes on to ABC-TV) and possibly her coproducer, Jim DeVinney, change that ending. So you now have this ending with SNCC's Charles Sherrod saying, "We didn't stop a beat," you know. "We kept moving. King might have left, but we kept moving." Now that's a different ending than would have been done if they had depended only on the scholarship. And I'm thinking that Callie did tell me that in fact they had to struggle over that. But that it was clear from talking with Sherrod and the local people, and Bernice Reagon, and everybody else that that was not seen as a failure by them. So that is one case where that happens, yeah.[11] And producers are constantly shaping their shows, based on their interviews and the other research they and their teams are doing.

EC: So it sounds like in terms of making *Eyes*, that the interviews were important not just so you got footage of people telling the stories, but that they're also part of the research process.

JR: Absolutely.

EC: And was that always clear that that was part of the interviews?

JR: Yes, we always knew that you're also doing that for research. You're calling them up certainly to find out whether they'd be good as an on-camera interview. But you're also calling up because you really do need this research. And so you're talking to people you'd never want to interview, or who might not even agree to an interview, so that you have this base of knowledge.

I remember talking to Mrs. Annie Devine from the Canton movement in Mississippi. That was the fourth Congressional District, so that was CORE, and I didn't have that contact with her in the movement. But I remember saying, we're doing this two-hour documentary—again, that was before it became the real *Eyes*—and she says she wouldn't be interviewed for it because, she says, "We're going to do" ("we" meaning the local people here), "are going to do our own film." Of course that never happened, which is what always—People don't know what it takes, the amount of money to get the skills base that you need to do something like that. But they understand also that if they don't tell the story themselves, it could be really perverted, as it had been so often before. So I understood all that she was dealing with. It's just that I felt so sorry we didn't have her voice in there, except in the archival footage.

In terms of research, you tend to get more from the newspapers than you do from the footage, just because you get more analysis pieces. And you have longer television pieces in that first six hours because TV is covering the movement differently, they're giving more time to it, they're sending people down, people spending three, four, five weeks in a city. By the second series of *Eyes on the Prize*, that's no longer happening. And also they're not keeping the footage in the same way because they're now on videotape, and so they're taping over stuff, they're getting rid of it. So the archives you have access to are different. But yeah, we always knew that the research was part of the interviews.

I remember when I was working at the United Church of Christ Commission for Racial Justice that Orlando Bagwell, an *Eyes* I producer, called and asked if I could meet the person from the Mississippi state archives.

And this is the change that comes between when we're first doing it in '78 and then by now in '84, because they're now willing to share some of these archives. And our footage is from, I think, WLBT [TV station in Jackson, Miss.], which had been the really horrible—They lose their license and stuff because it was so overtly racist during the movement. So now the Mississippi state archivist has that footage and what the archivist had said was that he would not even trust to ship it. So he was going to take the train from Jackson, Mississippi, all the way up to Boston. But he wanted someone to meet him at Penn Station. And then he could walk around, get some lunch and stuff, and come back and continue on up to Boston. And the person I sent then sat there, guarding the footage. Once the archivist gets to Blackside and reviews the footage with the team, Orlando—with all kinds of pleas and assurances—was allowed to keep some of the footage. They duplicated it and sent all the originals back down. But they found footage. It was amazing the level of research that went on for those stories.

EC: How did the "larger you" decide who to talk to?

JR: The producers do. Like, for example, when Orlando Bagwell goes down to do interviews on sit-ins and Freedom Rides, he had already talked to Leo Lillard about the local Nashville movement during the sit-ins. And so he gets down there, and his whole crew's there, and he's talking to Leo, not on camera, and just says, "Do you know anybody whom I should talk to?" So Leo says, "Well, my friend Freddie Leonard could do this." And so he calls, and they go over, and Freddie's looking at some ball game, and so they don't disturb him. They look at it with him and when it's over Orlando says, "So I understand you were part of the Nashville movement," and Freddie says, "No." And so they're talking and at first Orlando's a little crestfallen because it's like: "I've wasted this time. I have the crew and we have to do interviews tomorrow." But then Freddie happens to mention: "But I was on the Freedom Rides." So Orlando says, "Oh! Okay." And Freddie starts to tell him the story and Orlando says, "Hold it, I want to get you on film tomorrow." And Freddie says, "I'm too nervous. I'll only do it if my friend Leo comes with you tomorrow." And so they agree. Orlando shows up with the film crew. No Leo. So Orlando ends up giving him a couple shots of liquor, and they do that interview in one take. It was one take. And, it's just, it's one of those seminal interviews. It's like I show it at teacher workshops. *Everybody* remembers that Freddie Leonard interview, and him talking about the mattress. "I just kept holding my mattress." [*laughter*] And the trustee, Peewee, who was one of the inmates. "I mean, *in*mates," he says. "Then," Freddie says, "Peewee came down on my head, womph, womph." And the thing about the tears, that Peewee was crying. "You know how your mother says that this is going to hurt me more than it hurts you. It hurt Peewee more than it hurt me." Now, everybody remembers it. It's amazing. But that was, you know, that was happenstance. Who knew.*

EC: That is a really incredible interview and I know it's one that my students always respond to. And you're saying that happened almost randomly, by following the story and asking activists who else to talk to?

JR: That's right.

EC: What was it like to see *Eyes* take shape?

JR: I guess for me it was amazing because a lot of stuff I'd forgotten. Oh, and of course they were also doing stuff that I didn't know about. I didn't know the Albany Movement. I didn't know Birmingham. I will say that it was a little irritating to me for the Mississippi segment to focus so much on Mississippi Freedom Summer and the white volunteers, because that wasn't the story that I lived in Mississippi in '64. I was glad that they started with Medgar Evers, because it gave a sense that the local movement was doing stuff— even before SNCC or CORE ever gets there. And PBS may be a notch above CBS or NBC, but it is still a white viewer's network, and mostly white people look at it. Henry said to me once, "White people got to see themselves." And he almost [*laughter*], I think, almost had it down to a science. "Maybe they should see themselves"—he never said this, but I always got in my mind this thing—"and they need to see themselves every three-and-a-half min-

---

* Freddie Leonard and other Freedom Riders were transferred to Mississippi's notorious Parchman Penitentiary. In the interview Richardson is discussing, Leonard recounts the back-and-forth as prison officials use various threats and coercive tactics to try to stop Freedom Riders from singing. Leonard describes how, after spending a night without a mattress as punishment for singing, he defies the order to again give up his mattress. In response, prison officials order a black trustee to beat Leonard. The excerpts Richardson describes are in Henry Hampton, et al., *Eyes on the Prize (Ain't Scared of Your Jail)* (Alexandria, Va.: PBS Video, 2006). A transcript is available at the PBS *Eyes on the Prize* website (http://www.pbs.org/wgbh/amex/eyesontheprize/about/pt_103.html). The quotes in the text reflect Richardson's account, not the actual transcript.

utes or. . . ." But you couldn't have too many all-black things with Henry. Part of that was him, but part of it was what he thought was going to fly on PBS with the viewership. And he wanted people to see it and tune in. And, I gotta say, now that I've been in the business longer, I gotta agree with him.

EC: When you did interviews for *Eyes* or anything else, is it different to interview people who you knew or worked with, or were interviewing about something you knew versus people—

JR: Well, for example, when I did Stokely for the second series, I had to remind him, well, a couple of things. One is, I said, "Act as if you're not talking to someone who knows this history. So, you really do have to explain things, and you can't say, 'Well, you know.' You're doing this for the viewer." And I also took him out for breakfast before. Now this is when he's on the run and the government's after him, so we had to go out somewhere near LaGuardia Airport, so if he had to go run to the airport, he could do it quickly. Stokely at that point is not saying "black folks" or "African Americans." He's just saying "Africans." And that's because he's a pan-Africanist and he has lived in Ghana and Guinea, and for him it is, "We're all Africans, we're all part of the Diaspora." So I said, "Stokely, they won't know what the fuck you're talking about." He laughed, and he said, "Well, you know, I can't say it any other way." And I said, "But they won't understand. The point is to make yourself understood, to tell the story that you want told." He said, "Okay." So we get to the shoot, and he does figure out how to do it. And then, at some point he uses "Africans," and it's so funny because the crew breaks up. It's an all-black crew. And Stokely continues with the thought, because I'm not going to interrupt him anyways, until he finishes. And he has, it's like this little smile. It's like, "Yeah, I'm gonna do it, one of these times I gonna, yeah." [*laughter*] Just playing with it.

EC: Could somebody else have gotten an interview from Carmichael?

JR: They wouldn't have gotten the same interview, no. They would have gotten an interview. But that's the reason why we did—when I realized Stokely really was sick, I mentioned it to Henry. And I think Henry was the one who suggested that I just do another interview with him, for the archives. This is after *Eyes* II. It wasn't, "Oh, we're going to need him for this film, or this film." It was just so that he would be recorded. And so it was true that because Stokely knew me he did a fuller, day-long interview. And I went back for a second day. He couldn't do the full second day. That's what was amazing to me. He had the cancer, it was getting worse, and yet when I left him that first day at five, he was going to a rally in Brooklyn right after that.

I do think that Stokely was less formal than he can be sometimes on interviews. Less guarded. Which can be good, can sometimes not be good, particularly if this is an interview for the record. Because, his seeing me, in some ways there's no reminder that this is an interview for public consumption. This is not just you and I talking. So at the beginning, for example, he starts—You know, because this is Stokely, so he starts doing this little kinda come-on, "come hither" look and does it in the camera. [*laughter*] And of course the crew, which is, again, all-black, is just having a ball with this. And I said to the folks at Washington University, which has the Blackside archives, "Please be careful, because I don't want—particularly given the way Stokely's statement about 'prone' is misused—I don't want the clip to feed into that." So I don't know what they're doing about it, but I have cautioned them about this.[12] That's a disadvantage of having somebody whom the interviewee knows, particularly in the position that Stokely was in, Kwame was in. The other thing is, like I said, to remind him that he has to explain for people who don't know the story and not just use short-hand because of our shared experiences.

EC: I know when you first started working on *Eyes*, you thought it was gonna be a two hour segment and then that fell through and you ended up with the six hour first series. At what point does the second series become part of the mix?

JR: Because people told Henry he had to do it. This was not his favorite period of the movement. He did not want to do it. He felt just that it was incumbent upon him because people were saying, "Well you know you've got to do the second part now." And, even with that, he is fund-raising for a second series that he doesn't really want to do, I think.

EC: So, he starts dealing with the second series—

JR: Almost immediately after the first series airs. And he gets all this wonderful publicity for the first series. To get an Academy Award nomination, to get glowing reviews in the *New York Times* and *Washington Post* and *TV Guide*, etc. And the problem was, Henry thought that he was going to be able to just sit there and people would just offer him money, which would normally happen for this kind of successful series. Didn't happen. So he is beating the bushes.

And Henry also can't decide on whether we're gonna move into the five stories old place on the South End to do the production. That's before it becomes this chi-chi place to live, as it is now in Boston. Back then it was on the edge of Roxbury and hadn't been gentrified. But people were trying to get him to make a decision. Are you going to house the production of the second series of *Eyes* in this place that you own, in this building, or where he had put us at the last minute, which was on Mass Ave, Massachusetts Avenue in a building that was very central, but was horrible for production? Had no lights. Sound bounced off all the walls. It was an open space. We ended up putting black foam on the walls that cut the light even more. You could barely see. It was the most horrible place. So, some of us started working at home and then Henry decides, because people were grousing about it, he has them come over with this big-assed conference table that he used to use for table tennis, ping pong, because he thinks that'll kind of help ease our piss-ed-ness. And it only increased it, of course. It was like, you can't get us a decent working environment and you're gonna send us a ping pong table?!

EC: You mentioned that Hampton didn't really want to do *Eyes* II, but that after *Eyes* I comes out, people tell him he needs to do the follow-up. Who's telling him this? And how are they framing what he needs to do?

JR: That I don't know. Truthfully, I don't know. I once heard him say publicly that people said there's another part of the movement that you've not told. And basically, you have a responsibility to tell the second part. It doesn't end with that and you need to show the extension of what happened. And that's why he thought there would just be money hand over foot, and then it wasn't. As a matter of fact, the reason we got some funding was because there was an article in both the *Wall Street Journal* and the *New York Times* about the fact that Henry was having to beat the bushes for *Eyes* II and wasn't that a shame. And Charlayne Hunter Gault called Bill Cosby and said, "You know, this doesn't make any sense, would you do a fund-raiser?" Bill Cosby says he will do a fund-raiser at his apartment on the East side of New York City. So, I went down for it. Henry went down. Dave Lacy was a producer on *Eyes* II and he was there. So we were the three production people. And it was all black, which is interesting. They were all black funders. It was the grant officer from the Rockefeller Foundation. I'm sure Andrea Taylor was there from Ford. There were probably about fifteen people there who could write checks. And, at some point, Cosby hands me this check for $42,000 and says, "This was Las Vegas," meaning, this was the take from Las Vegas. So, I say, "Well, thank you Las Vegas." And we laughed and we went off and I had this check for $42,000. Then Henry says that he had just gotten a commitment for either ten or twelve thousand dollars from Concord Baptist Church in Brooklyn. It was a commitment, a pledge. And he says, "Do you think they'll be good for it?" And I say, "I don't know," not knowing this is probably the biggest black church in Brooklyn, and yes, they were *definitely* good for it. And sure enough, they came forward with this—I think it was $12,000. And we had one of the first premiers of the second series at the church.

EC: It sounds like black individuals working for these foundations—

JR: Were very helpful. I would say, though, that Janet Axelrod, who is white and was very active in South African anti-apartheid stuff and all that, was also very helpful. She worked for Lotus, and she hooks Henry up with Jim Manzi, the head of the firm, and he becomes a major funder of the second series.

EC: Okay, so there's some white funding, there's some white support. But, it sounds like there is a real strong black push that makes these possible.

JR: Yes. I would agree with that. And also at PBS and Corporation for Public Broadcasting, there are black people now, finally in place, to help move this through the system.

EC: Do you think these people are in these positions because of the movement?

JR: Correct.

EC: Do they see that connection?

JR: I think most of them do, most of the ones that are involved in our funding. Now whether other people do or not. . . . But, yes, this particular group of black folks does.

EC: On *Eyes* I you are listed as the research consultant and on *Eyes* II you are listed as the series associate producer. How did your role differ in the two series?

JR: On *Eyes* I, I was finding and contacting some interviewees for the teams, looking over scripts, helping a bit on rewrites on the book Juan Williams was doing with other Blackside staff—basically being a resource in terms of movement stuff. And I was going back and forth between my job as information director at the United Church of Christ Commission for Racial Justice in New York and the *Eyes* production in Boston. And what was so funny was that there was no disconnect for me.

At the UCC we were in the midst of protesting, with other groups in the city, the mushrooming of police brutality. Ed Koch was mayor and he wasn't doing diddly except supporting the police. Five transit police officers beat Michael Stewart to death when they found him drawing graffiti in the subway—and there'd been a bunch of other incidents. There were also all these incidents of racially motivated violence, like Howard Beach. And I remember one where three black guys were leaving work—around 2–3 o'clock in the morning. They had gone into a donut shop in Graves End—way out on the other end of Brooklyn—and they'd been chased and beaten by a white mob. So we were having rallies and demonstrations and stuff. And, what was amazing was that I'd leave that and come up to *Eyes* and I felt like *Eyes* was just part of that continuum.

On *Eyes* II, I came on as series associate producer as well as associate producer to one of the four teams. Henry was right. He said I'd learn more about production if I was based in a team. And as series AP, I did some of the interviews that might be used series-wide. And I was in all the so-called "lock" sessions—the last session with Henry, the two show producers, and Steve Fayer, the writer—before the film was finalized. And for *Eyes* II I was full-time, no going back and forth to the UCC. And I did that because one of the producers from *Eyes* I, Callie Crossley, said to me, said, "Look, you could go back and forth on *Eyes* I." But, she said, "*Eyes* II you need to be present." So I took a leave from the UCC even though I didn't know what she was talking about until I got here. And then I realized, "Oh, I see. She's right."

EC: What did she mean?

JR: Oh, well she knew Henry's politics. And he was a liberal Democrat, and very much an integrationist in the truest sense of that word. And the series was focusing on a period of Black Power, and nationalism, and people doing "black stuff." I had more of a nationalist orientation and had been involved in building black institutions. And even though Callie wasn't on the production,

I think she felt that someone on staff needed to be able to represent that point of view, at least include it in the discussion. And she was right. [*laughter*] She was absolutely right. There were times when Henry and I were barely talking to each other. You know, just coming from such opposite poles.

I remember, early on, before he brought the teams on, Henry and I had gone to dinner with Steve Fayer and his lady friend Charlotte, and I realized after that conversation at Steve's house that we really were different. Our point of view was different, Henry's and mine. I remember sitting in that car driving back to Boston and he realized it too. And yet, when we brought the full staff together and we had our first production staff retreat, that first day he actually asked me to comment. And it was just open-ended. He said, "And I want to call on Judy." Had not told me he was gonna do this. Which was the good part about Henry. He would allow people like me who had totally opposing—not totally—had opposing points of view, to be heard. And because he said, "I would like Judy to now say something, too," it had the authority of his asking me to do that.

EC: Can you explain what the political differences are between you and Henry and why they're more apparent in *Eyes* II than *Eyes* I?

JR: Mmmm. Because Henry really doesn't, didn't believe in self-defense. And he didn't believe in all-black organizations. So he had difficulty with the direction, certainly, that SNCC was taking at that point. He was much more in favor of the "John Lewis, Nashville" SNCC, than he was the "Black Power, Stokely" SNCC. He certainly had a good sense of the economic stuff. And he definitely wanted to tell regular people's stories. But he was very much—as a matter-of-fact, a white mutual friend of ours said, "You know, Henry's very much a liberal Democrat." And I said, "Yeah, I guess that's true, isn't it?" Which I'm not. [*laughter*] And that's not what the second series was.

EC: What political perspective did you contribute to *Eyes* II?

JR: To say blacker is not, is too easy, too facile. I just had a sense of the nationalism that was not, as they say, narrow. A sense of why black folks thought that they had to go out on their own in some ways. That yeah, you could do coalitions, but some of the stuff we have to do on our own and not always in integrated groups. And that was part of it. Also the idea of self-defense, I think. I had a certain political frame, and I remember sitting in a production meeting with Steve Fayer, and Steve turning to me, saying something about,

"You have a certain, you come with politics," as if to dismiss whatever point I'd just made. Now Steve is someone I respect and stay in touch with, but that day I looked at him and I said, "Steve, everybody around this table has politics, I'm just much more open about mine." And he didn't say anything else.

I remember Toni Cade Bambara being at one of the Scholar Schools. She was a little too strong for Henry. It was so funny. She really was talking about black militancy in a way that was, [*laughter*] was not something Henry really wanted to deal with. And I can't remember the specifics of it. But he really did not like her point of view. And the thing is, she was very strong. Yeah, she was really strong. For me, not so much with the first series, but with the second series there were points where I wondered if it was going to be possible to say it the way it really happened and get it through lots of different, I don't want to say, "filters." I don't know. Whether it, internally and externally, was going to be able to come across the way it should.

I had been on Henry kind of consistently, talking about the fact that we have to have Malcolm in this second series, that you could not do *Eyes* II without explaining, without understanding the importance of Malcolm. And he had been resisting that except in a cursory way. So, we're at the Scholar School for *Eyes* II, and at the end, Henry would always give the lineup of what the shows were gonna be. First of all, what the team composition was gonna be and then what shows that team was gonna be responsible for. And the idea was always to make sure that all the producers were listening to all the information because if you told them at the beginning what shows they were gonna do, they would only listen to the information that would pertain to their show. So, it was that. And he does the lineup and Malcolm's nowhere in there. So I raise my hand from the audience and I said, "But, Henry, how are we gonna deal with Malcolm?" And he said, "Oh, well, he'll, you know, he'll be a presence in there." And so I say, "Yeah, but it seems to me that he has to be, he's the through line. He has to be based in a story." And he gave some perfunctory response that made me know this was not the place to argue this point. So, it's only when we lose a producer on that team and Dave Lacy comes up and is working with Jim DeVinney and they figure out a way to frame it, not so much as a biography of Malcolm, but really as Malcolm in his time and Henry buys it. But, he would have been perfectly happy not having Malcolm in there. He didn't like Malcolm. [*laughter*]

EC: So, does Henry object to him because of—

JR: He's a nationalist. He's perceived as anti-white. And I don't think Henry understood the man's amazing intelligence. I think he saw him as just, as somebody who's just spouting off at the mouth.

Terry Rockefeller was a white producer, white female producer, along with Louis Massiah. They were two equal coproducers on two shows. And I should parenthetically mention that Henry's thing was always to integrate the production teams, keeps them honest, he said. He didn't say it that way. That's just what he believed. It was funny—in *Eyes* II, we actually had a party for just the black production staff, unbeknownst to Henry. And we did it because there's a point where you get tired of always explaining your position to white people. And that was happening on those production teams, because of this forced black-white configuration on the teams. I don't think any of them were nationalists. I absolutely don't believe—I might have been, but they weren't. But they just needed a break, and so we did a Fourth of July party. It was great. Because we left behind all that other stuff.

EC: Was it your idea?

JR: No, it wasn't actually. Isn't that funny? It wasn't. It was one of the other producers who said "We need a break." [*laughter*]

Anyway, when we were proposing the Attica prison rebellion as one of these stories, Henry was resisting it up and down. Henry didn't see Attica as a civil rights story. And Henry already didn't want to put Angela Davis in. Louis Massiah and Terry Rockefeller, both of them, were just *so* clear that they wanted Angela Davis to be one of those stories in that series. And Terry did a lot of research on that, too. Never happened. Henry didn't want mention of the Communist Party in anything he touched. He finally did say, "No, she will not be the focus of a story." I think it's because she's CP. He never said that. He never framed it that way. His thing was, "I don't want this to be a profile of somebody." And a lot of folks. . . . I will say that the majority of the production staff felt that Angela should be there and also that Attica should be there. And again, we're trying to figure out what stories are going together. And we're still struggling over Attica, and Henry's still not getting it. And then he comes in one morning during a production meeting and says, yeah, he gets it. And it's some white guy who was a friend of his who told Henry, "Yeah, when Attica happened, I absolutely saw how linked it was to the traditional civil rights movement." And so we were fine after that about Attica.

Now, I will say, Henry was right about Muhammad Ali. I was not. Henry wanted Muhammad Ali. I thought it was just gonna be a sports story and I said, "You're just trying to popularize and soften the series." But, he was absolutely right. Because, of course, that story was so much more than that. It was a very important story and it became really a wonderful story. And it was perfect once they found the footage that put Muhammad Ali talking about, "Everything's white," you know, "snow white," and so and so. And because you're at Howard University, it's the link, he's now the segue into the Howard student takeover story, and it's so perfect.

With *Eyes* II, it was also which school rebellion you do? And I proposed the Howard takeover because I said, "Okay, Cornell is black folks trying to get Black Studies in there. But with Howard, you get black folks talking to the black community. It's not always black folks trying to get white folks to do right. Sometimes it's black folks trying to get *black* folks to do right. And sometimes we're only talking to ourselves, we're talking internally. So that's why, for me, the Howard story was important. That was important to me. On the Howard story, Henry was actually willing to allow it. It was still always in the background that we might have to shift to the Cornell takeover or one of the others. And there was a problem because we couldn't find any footage. And then this one black male production assistant, who was at one of the local network affiliates, he went over to the storeroom and came back and said, "I found a couple of cans of film." And he said, "I want to tell you the state of that storeroom." He said, "rats, rat droppings, everything, all over the place."

And I was glad, also, that I had fought for Howard because I wanted people to see: yeah, Stokely Carmichael came out of there, Michael Thelwell, all these people, Cleve Sellers. And yeah, you had the poet Sterling Brown, who's transmitting all this black culture. But, you also couldn't play jazz in the music room because it was seen as low class. You're supposed to only play classical music. So, there was also the other side of that . . . the contradictions.

Now, what we didn't get into in that story was that, what a lot of the young folk who were part of the leadership of the movement there told us. It wasn't just the anti-war stuff. It wasn't just trying to reclaim and get Black Studies and stuff. It was also that they were pissed at the way they were treated, by faculty, and particularly by the administration, that the administration would disrespect them and would mess over their scholarship money. They said the telephone operators would be nasty and discourteous to you. Paula Giddings mentioned that. I had called her for a recommendation for the Howard story, to find out who could tell me about what happens when they crown Robin Gregory, who is the first homecoming queen with an Afro. So, I'm calling her at 10 o'clock at night. And I'm calling her to find out whom can she recommend. And she starts to tell me this story. She was in the audience and she starts to talk about it. And I say, "Oh my God, wait a minute, don't tell me. We got to get this on camera. Can we film you?" So, we filmed her. And it was funny because when she was first being interviewed, Sam Pollard is doing the interview, because he's the producer for that. But she's doing it at a historian's distance. So I go up to her and I said, "Paula we need to have you in the room, have your experience." And then she says, "And I was there, too." So it's this cute little thing. But, when we were talking about it on the phone, she also mentioned, "When we took over the switchboard, that was the nicest. Students would call and they would talk about how like a breath of fresh air it was to be treated courteously by the operator of the switchboard." But we never got into that part on *Eyes*.

EC: For you, was it different to work on things that you knew about from firsthand experience versus things that you knew about from the research?

JR: Yes. Yeah, I could speak with more assurance and clarity about stuff I knew. With the things that I did not know, it was harder. There was one point where I went downstairs to the edit room, where they were doing the Lowndes County story in "The Time Has Come." And so I happened to look through, and I mentioned to Henry—I don't know if I'd seen some footage or not on the monitor in the edit room. But in any event, I said something to Henry about the fact that, "You know the Lowndes Country Freedom Organization was organized as an all-black party." And he said, "No it wasn't." And I said, "Yeah it was, Henry. It really was." I said, "I was there." And he got stone-faced, he was so angry! Because, number one, I'd stepped across the line from production person to participant in the event. The other thing is, I was presenting a view that he really did not want to put in here. So I immediately said, "No, no, ask Mants, ask Bob Mants, ask any of the people, they'll tell you." He said, "Alright, alright," still gruff.

EC: It's interesting, though, because part of why he wants you on production staff is because of your movement connections. So, is it that you're an activist or is it that you're drawing on your activist background to assert an authority to disagree with him?

JR: Yes, it is the latter because if I had used that authority to agree with him, he would not have had that problem. Yeah. And yet, again, as mad as it made him, he always left room for it.

EC: You talk about that one example with Lowndes where you sort of used your being there as your authority to challenge Hampton on some stuff he didn't want to be challenged on. Was it always one way or the other, where being a participant gave you more legitimacy or—

JR: It did with the producers, definitely with the producers. Although I was more left of center than some of the producers, too, so it was easy for them to say, "Oh, that's just Judy." Now they wouldn't do that to my face, but I think there were people, black and white, who would say, "Well that's just— she's bringing that other stuff in there."

EC: I wondered about that because being a participant doesn't always bring legitimacy when you're working on historical work. And so that's part of what I'm curious about.

JR: No, I think it did. I think the producers did respect the fact that I had actually experienced this stuff. Most of the production team had not had any contact with the movement one way or the other. So everything is new for them, both on *Eyes* I and *Eyes* II. Orlando had had some contact with CORE, but he was younger, and it was mainly through his parents.

Now, I will say, in *Eyes* II I tried to get something in about Drum and Spear Bookstore and black institution building, because that was important to me. I thought it was important that in D.C. you had a black bookstore that becomes the largest in the country, and a black publishing house, and the Center for Black Education that's teaching diasporic history. And then, down the street you have a third world cultural center, where you'd have poetry readings and Don Lee, who is now Haki Madhubuti, he would do readings at the bookstore. Shirley Du Bois would have a reading at the bookstore. And there was this ferment, there was an intellectual ferment. It was great, and that was important in terms of understanding, first of all the nationalist aspect to some of that stuff. Because it wasn't coming from nothing. There were people who were building institutions and it was having an effect on the community. So even in the bookstore you would see junkies coming in, guys you had seen the night before totally strung out, and they would come in the bookstore and they would talk to people. And they started buying books. So you would have a lot of people coming into the store who normally would never have gone into a bookstore before because we were in the heart of the inner city. So, for me, not to give mention to that, was unfortunate. And I felt the same way when Blackside did the Black Arts series, I tried to get some mention of the institutions that are helping to promote and continue these arts, but that didn't happen there either. So, you know, sometimes you win, sometimes. . . .

You have to decide which battles you're gonna fight. I really did battle a lot with Henry to the point that we were, by the end, barely speaking. 'Cause he really did have different politics than I do. But what I found was that I was arguing a lot and someone who wasn't involved with *Eyes* told me, "You have too much fire." Now I thought—it was a guy. It was a black guy, and I thought he was saying the usual kind of sexist thing. You know, "You need to tone it down." But then I said it to a friend of mine, Juadine, and she said, "Well you might want to" [*laughter*] "think about that." So I lowered the volume, and it really did help.

During this period when I was getting very heated, there was an older *New York Times* reporter, Tom Johnson, who said, "Fight no small wars." I said, that's a wonderful phrase. "Fight no small wars." And towards the end, I started really picking my battles. Because what had happened, I flared up so much, it was such a constant state that it was like, "Oh, that's just Judy." I started really remembering that. You really got to choose. Otherwise, it's almost like crying wolf. They just know that you're always gonna be fired up and they won't pay any attention to you. So, I got to the point where I really did pick my battles. Yeah.

But I did get screaming mad one time. Toward the end of the production on *Eyes* II, I'm sitting in my office and Michael Green, who was the marketing person, came in. Toyota had decided that they wanted to do a two-hour version of *Eyes* I, and they were going to market it to some of the black groups, NAA [NAACP], United Negro College Fund, groups like that. So they were looking for kinda famous people who could intro these pieces. Michael Green's a black guy and he says, "We're trying to find so-and-so to be one of the hosts." And he was asking me if I knew how to locate a few of them. And I said, "Well, who else is on the list to intro these pieces?" And he names these names and they're all male. And I went off, and I said "Michael!" And he realized—it was immediate. He realized, "Ooooh, I should never have done this." [*laughter*] I said, "I'm going down to Henry." And I went down and I asked the secretary, "Is Henry in?" and she said, "He's with

Dale." And I opened the door. I said, and I really, I raised my voice. I said, "How could you do this?! You know women were the bulwark of the movement! How could you do this!?" And he said something about, "Well, that's what Toyota wants." I said, "So, in other words, if they had said, 'we don't want any black people as hosts,' you would have gone for that too?!" I was so livid. And then I let out a scream. I said "ahhhhh!" [*screams*] And I went to the little neighborhood garden. There's a garden right down the street from the office. And I walked around the thing for awhile. It was one of those urban gardens, which is what I would do sometimes on a lunch hour. And I went back up, and I got my stuff, and I made a note, because by that time the "lock session" has started for one of the shows. It's Henry, Steve, and the two producers. And I'm supposed to be in the meeting, but I gave one of the producers a note, saying, "I will not be here because I would do more harm than good for you." And I went back out and came home. By the time I got home, two or three people had called me, one of them being Louis Massiah, another *Eyes* II producer. Because when I started screaming he came down because he thought I was hurt or somebody was hurt, and I told him what had happened in a way that I'm sure was barely coherent. But by the time I got home he had drawn up a list. He said, "I've submitted some names to Henry." One of them was Johnetta Cole, who was then president of Spelman, and half of the hosts ended up being women.

EC: So this is what? Late '80s, early '90s? And Toyota is explicitly asking for all men?

JR: Mmmm-hmm. Yep—'89. But it changed. Again, because of the producers. Now, after the fit that I threw, I suspect that Henry would have changed anyway, even without producers' input. But by that time Henry and I were so on the outs about the politics, I'm not sure whether he would've or not.

EC: You mentioned the importance of looking through *Stride Towards Freedom*, and seeing Jo Ann Robinson's name and finding her and interviewing her. And you said there were all these people that you knew were important to the movement that are missing. At that time, were you conscious that women explicitly were missing? Or were you just conscious that—

JR: No, I was aware that women were missing. Because when I'm looking at *Stride Towards Freedom*, what's amazing to me is that I find the name of a woman. That's what's amazing. It's not just that it's not King. It *is* that it's a woman. And that is absolutely, that's absolutely what's missing from much of what I was finding during the pre-*Eyes* I research stage. Except for Myrlie Evers—you would find her. And, of course, Rosa Parks.

EC: What do you see as the strengths and weaknesses of *Eyes*?

JR: Okay. The strengths for *Eyes* are that it reframes the history, so that it was not top-down. When I first started doing *Eyes* in 1978, I was the first full-time employee and for the first six months, I'm sitting there by myself, before there's a real producer/director who comes on board. And I'm looking through everything. Luckily, I had *Simple Justice*. But everything else was King-centered. I mean, *everything*: documentaries, literature, everything. Scholarship. Everything. So there was nothing in terms of local movement scholarship at that point. It was not there, period. I was not seeing then anything in the scholarship that reflected the movement that I knew, that I'd lived.

EC: What was that like?

JR: Oh, it pisses me off. It pissed me off, not having Fannie Lou Hamer and Unita Blackwell or Amzie Moore or Hartman Turnbow, not to mention, Mama Dollie in southwest Georgia. None of these people were in any of these histories. But, no, it was infuriating. Because it was like, this is not the way the movement was. So, first of all, we changed the scholarship. We helped. Because there were people who were talking about this. But we helped to validate this change in the scholarship. Also, in *Eyes*, you get real people talking. You don't have any scholars. There are no academics talking in *Eyes*. It's all the participants. Another strength, which I really didn't see the importance of—Henry did and I did not see until I saw it on the screen— was the importance of including government people and white racists. That was important. I didn't know it at the beginning. So I think those are the strengths. Another thing we do in *Eyes* is really give prominence to the black activists. You get white activist Virginia Durr, but you get her in the context of the black-led Montgomery Bus Boycott. So, one of the things that I'm actually happy about is that it gives the primary agency to the black activists.

The failings in *Eyes* I were the omissions. I'm not sure how I would define that. Not having self-defense in there. And I think that relates to Henry being a black filmmaker and Blackside being a black filmmaking company, a black company and not having any track record. And so, he might have felt he had to be careful. I think it was partly that. I think it was partly Henry. Self-defense just was not Henry.

EC: You've talked about some of the other things that were debated.

JR: True.

EC: Do you remember if self-defense was ever on the table for *Eyes* I?

JR: Not that I knew. So that means also that I did not bring it up. I don't remember ever bringing it up and it being shot down. Now, what I did bring up was—there was this sense, in *Eyes* I, that it was just about the white violence. But I said, "No, it's not just about the violence. It is the economic intimidation. It is people not being able to have loans." And that part is in, but I still don't think as much as it probably should have been. The self-defense—or at least resistance—comes in only two times that I remember. And that's Leo Lillard in the Nashville story where they talk about the students trying to hassle people, black folks who were buying during the Easter boycott. And then in Little Rock, you get the chili story, which is very much a resistance story. And the black staff clapping after Minnie Jean Brown accidentally-on-purpose throws this bowl of chili on this white student who has been hassling her.

EC: Now, with Lillard's story, that's not really self-defense, though, is it?

JR: No. No, you're right, it is not. You're right. I mixed the two up. This is, in fact, just enforcement. No, that's true. That's absolutely true.

EC: But did you bring it up—

JR: Because at least it was a sense of resistance and that's how I think about it.

EC: Or, it doesn't fit that—I mean, it's—

JR: Oh, it's not the neat definition of self-defense, you mean?

EC: Well, no, I guess I was just thinking it's enforcement, but it's also not a pretty part of the story.

JR: No.

EC: Black people enforcing—

JR: Yes. Against other black people. That's right. But, you are right, that's not self-defense. But—

EC: It's conflict.

JR: It's conflict, that's right.

EC: And it's not nonviolent. It's not a moral kind of plea, moral suasion.

JR: I think that's it. That's right. They are not just picketing, they are enforcing it. That's right. But we certainly never got anything about Hartman Turnbow. We just didn't get to include any examples of self-defense.

The other thing that I am sorry about is that you don't really get a sense of the history of black resistance that the movement comes from. Now, scholars had pointed that out to us, so Vecchione added this kind of whirlwind historical context at the beginning of that first segment of *Eyes* I. But that's all, because events were supposed to be very much kept in time, in the time of the story. The other thing we didn't acknowledge was *anything* that related to the CP, to the Communist Party. And that's specific to Henry, he just would not allow it. The other thing I would say, by the way, that was good about it was that there were no re-creations. Now, it is easier to maintain that when you have archival footage. So we had the luxury in *Eyes* of not doing them. The way we chose stories, there had to be archival footage. It was clear that you had to choose stories that had archival with them. We did Lowndes County and it was awhile before we found any footage of that. And that was a thing where we almost lost any portion of that story.

EC: So that means that, at some level, all these stories are still very much dependent on media coverage.

JR: Yes, for us, for the way we told the story at Blackside: media coverage and material from personal collections.

EC: How does the need to choose stories with archival footage shape the story that you tell?

JR: Well, it shaped which stories we selected, we chose to tell, not so much how we told the story, but which ones got chosen to be told.

EC: I guess what I meant was then, collectively, that is the story of the movement, right? So, people look at *Eyes*—

JR: Right, and that's the problem.

EC: And they see that as *the* movement. So, in some senses, then, those stories you've chosen become the movement.

JR: That's right. And the stories we haven't chosen are not seen as part of the movement. That's correct. And in fact, when I would go out on the road, I would oftentimes be asked by somebody who would be from, say, New Orleans or from some place else, and they would say, "How come you didn't do so-and-so because we were really struggling and we had a wonderful organization." And my stock answer was, "Well, we only had six hours, there's only so much you can do." But, the bottom line is, if there was not a lot of footage there, that story's not gonna get told.

And then, you also make other choices. For *Eyes* II, it became, okay, which rebellion do you do? Do you do Detroit or Newark? And there are still people who feel we should have done Newark, particularly because then you could see Kawaida and you could see the New Ark and Amiri Baraka and the organization, as opposed to just Detroit where it just seemed like it's aimless and that nothing came out of it. I remember sitting up onstage with Sam Pollard and Sheila Bernard, the two coproducers of the Detroit segment, after screening an early cut with scholars. I was the AP and after we finished showing that rough cut, it was like a silence. And then we got pummeled. And one of the things that I most remember is Michael Thelwell, who is a former SNCC person and has been forever a professor up at U. Mass, Amherst, and he said, "You're going to have to be very careful how you use the footage of the Detroit rebellion because," he said, "the lens was sympathetic when the media is covering the southern movement, but now you're on their home turf. You're on the northern media's home turf and they don't like it." And so, for example, you would get a lot of man-on-the-street interviews with black drunks, okay, who would be just talking and talking, and they would be seen as "the voice of the black community." And you really wouldn't get so much just regular people who were thinking about why this was happening.

EC: It's interesting because when you talk about the parts of the story that Hampton likes most, it seems like his preferences are fairly close to the kind of narrative that a lot of people get through textbooks and in general through pop culture. It seems, sort of, King, nonviolent-centric and integrationist and sort of a triumphant story of living up to American values. And certainly you get some of that with *Eyes*, but it seems like even *Eyes* I goes well beyond that in terms of bringing in more local people, local activists. And, you also see some of the failures of the federal government.

JR: And Henry was clear about that, about the failings, that that should be portrayed. But see, the other thing is that I can't stress enough: There were a lot of producers who were pushing for a lot of what you see in those shows, against what Henry might not have wanted.

EC: And I guess that's interesting to me because it sounds like he can be pushed, that he conceptualizes this or brings it forward. I don't know where the original idea comes from, whether it's his or he carries it forward.

JR: It's more his. I think when he first proposes this two hours, during the pre-*Eyes* version, in '78, it's totally his idea, although the stories in that were up to a lot of us to develop, or even to choose. But yeah.

EC: So, it's really a collaborative process.

JR: Absolutely. No, and that's one of the things. When I say he left me room to oppose him, he left room for the producers to oppose him too. And they did. He expected you to have a good argument. Now sometimes if he didn't want to hear it, he would just not meet with you. And that drove some people really crazy.

EC: I'm thinking about what scholarship was available to you all. And you've talked about this, right? But I guess I'm just kind of thinking, you've got Henry Hampton with this idea and you've got you, who were in the movement, but you don't know the day-to-day in Albany. You don't know the day-to-day in Birmingham. All of these things. You have a particular perspective that's shaped by the movement and the experiences you have, but there's still a lot of movement you don't know, even in SNCC. And then you've got these producers who don't have background in it and yet end up identifying these stories or identifying these—

JR: Because of the pre-interviews. Because one of the things that you don't have now, that you had back then, was enough time to do really strong, long pre-interviews on the phone with people. That's what's not allowed now because of decreased funding.

EC: So, at some level, *Eyes on the Prize* is shaped by primary research, oral histories.

JR: You got it. Oh, absolutely! People who are doing research, they're looking for footage, but they're also doing a lot of oral history. Yes.

EC: And so, that's probably one of the strengths of *Eyes on the Prize*: you're not relying on the existing scholarship, which doesn't deal with local movements. So that to some extent, *Eyes* I is a combination of the existing King-centric and white-centric scholarship and media coverage and the primary research that you all are doing on these communities through primarily oral histories.

JR: Correct, that is right.

EC: You said at one point you weren't sure whether the second series was going to have the perspective it needed to by the time it got through all the filters. In the end, what do you think?

JR: I don't know, it was a struggle. As I saw our producers winning some of the battles it became easier, but at the beginning I just wasn't sure. But it's producer pressure, always, that is moving things away from an overly traditional interpretation. And in the end I was happy with it. I think it *really is* a good series.

EC: So most of these producers don't come knowing much about the movement, don't have any experience with it, and they're fighting these battles over what they're learning from the research?

JR: You got it.

EC: So to some extent, you have film producers who are also functioning as historians, doing research on events they are just learning about and from that base they are able to fight to tell a more radical story?

JR: Yes, that's it. And, of course, the producers are also reading and talking to scholars who are specialists in certain aspects of this movement history. So it's all those influences.

EC: In the end, do you think the series is more a reflection of you or Henry or is it a merger?

JR: A merger, including—very strongly—the perspective of the show's producers.

EC: Can you give me some examples?

JR: Mmmm. Well in the Boston Busing segment for example. I think I would have preferred to see what had been in the first cut on Boston Busing, which was a sense of what black schools, like the Paige Academy here in Boston, were doing. And they were doing some really good stuff. It wasn't just black history and African continent and maps and stuff. It was the three Rs as well. And there was a rigor about that. And you saw that. Now you saw teachers in gelées and African traditional dress. And they appeared to be solid teachers, at least in the footage. And that got really cut. And what I heard from one of the members of the production staff, was that some people—and I don't know if it was Henry or not—felt that if the independent black schools were shown as so good, viewers would ask, "Why are the NAA and the folks trying to integrate the schools in South Boston? Why are they doing that? Why don't they just try and get more funding, get more support for the independent black schools?" Now, there's a way you could do that in narration. You could say, "As good as these schools were, they could only accommodate a certain number and it wasn't supported by tax dollars and that is not the solution. It's among the solutions that you can try, but it's not the main solution, 'cause our tax dollars should be going to public education for everyone." But you could have still seen the fullness of how interesting what they were doing at some of these black schools was. But that's not what happened. And I never called Henry on that, so I'm not sure. All I know is what I was told.

EC: Am I right that it was your work with *Eyes* that led to your involvement in teacher workshops and lectures on the movement?

JR: Yes, I was doing teacher training with *Eyes*, going to classrooms with *Eyes*. And there were things that I wanted the young people to know. Most especially young activists, but young people generally. And then to reach the larger community, meaning everybody. Because it wasn't so much that I wanted to correct the history. Certainly it was that. I wanted them to know what the movement really was, and how amazing it was and stuff. But, more than that, I wanted them to know what helped us function. And to know that we were not exceptional. It's what Dottie Zellner puts in the intro to

*Hands on the Freedom Plow* now, that we were just normal people.[13] That's one of the things that I always try and talk about, that if you don't know that it was regular folks who did the movement, then people don't know that they can do it again. It's a trick bag. So, if people keep saying to you that you need to be like Dr. King to effect change then you don't know that it was folks like you who did it.

Note: For more on *Hands on the Freedom Plow* and for Richardson's approach to teaching workshops and lectures, see "That Movement Responsibility: An Interview with Judy Richardson on Movement Values and Movement History," chapter 12, this volume.

## NOTES

1. See http://blacksidemedia.com (accessed June 10, 2010).

2. Charles M. Payne, "The Rough Draft of History," in *I've Got the Light of Freedom: The Organizing Tradition and the Mississippi Freedom Struggle* (Berkeley: University of California Press, 1995), 391–405.

3. Henry Hampton, *Eyes on the Prize. America's Civil Rights Movement, Mississippi: Is this America? (1962–1964)* (Alexandria, Va.: PBS Video, 1986).

4. Charles Payne surveys some of the media coverage of the MFDP's decision to reject the compromise orchestrated by Lyndon Johnson and writes that the reporters covering the Atlantic City convention "still found it hard to take seriously the idea that uneducated southern Blacks could be important political thinkers and actors. They could more easily be sympathetic than respectful." Payne, *I've Got the Light of Freedom*, 400. Hampton, *Mississippi: Is this America? (1962–1964)*.

5. Payne, *I've Got the Light of Freedom*, 418; Charles W. Eagles, "Toward New Histories of the Civil Rights Movement," *Journal of Southern History* 66 (Nov. 2000): 815–48.

6. For example, though *Eyes* introduces Black Power through Malcolm X, the production team set up SNCC's move toward Black Power with a brief segment on the Lowndes County Freedom Party (something Richardson pushed for). Here, they anticipate the argument made so compellingly by Hasan Kwame Jeffries—that SNCC's shift to Black Power was very explicitly grounded in their successful organizing in Lowndes County, work that immediately preceded Stokely Carmichael's election as chair and his public call for Black Power during the Meredith March. As Richardson points out in the interview, including Lowndes in the series was dependent on finding footage, clearly illustrating the challenges of incorporating local stories in a documentary series dependent on archival footage. See Hasan Kwame Jeffries, "SNCC, Black Power, and Independent Political Party Organizing in Alabama, 1964–1966," *Journal of African American History*

91 (Spring 2006): 171–93; and Hasan Kwame Jeffries, *Bloody Lowndes: Civil Rights and Black Power in the Alabama Black Belt* (New York: New York University Press, 2009).

*Eyes* also avoids setting up Carmichael and Martin Luther King Jr. as enemies representing opposite extremes. In addition to showing the two men walking side-by-side as they debated and discussed nonviolence, self-defense, and Black Power along a Mississippi highway during the Meredith March, the series uses an interview with Carmichael and footage of Carmichael listening to one of King's important anti-war speeches to convey a sense of the two men as friends and colleagues who, whatever their differences, shared a commitment to the struggle against racism, the Vietnam War, and economic inequality. Henry Hampton, *Eyes on the Prize. America's Civil Rights Movement. The Time Has Come (1964–1966)* (Alexandria, Va.: PBS Video, 1990); Henry Hampton, *Eyes on the Prize. America's Civil Rights Movement. The Promised Land (1967–1968)* (Alexandria, Va.: PBS Video, 1990).

7. Jacquelyn Dowd Hall has been particularly visible in pushing for an expanded time frame, though she argues most strongly for locating the origins of the movement in the 1930s. Jacquelyn Dowd Hall, "The Long Civil Rights Movement and the Political Uses of the Past," *Journal of American History* 91 (Aug. 2005): 1233–63. For a recent survey of the scholarship on Black Power, see Peniel Joseph, "The Black Power Movement: A State of the Field," *Journal of American History* 96 (Dec. 2009): 751–76. See also the introduction to this volume for a more detailed discussion of some of these historiographical debates and issues.

8. Charles Payne, "Sexism is a helluva thing," chapter 10, this volume. In the late 1970s, Bernice Johnson Reagon made a related point, explaining to an interviewer that some African Americans in Albany played a role in upholding the status quo, that the movement wasn't just black versus white. See Bernice Johnson Reagon and Dick Cluster, "The Borning Struggle: The Civil Rights Movement: An Interview with Bernice Johnson Reagon by Dick Cluster," *Radical History* 12, no. 6 (1978): 9–25, esp. 21.

9. Steven Lawson, in a recent essay taking issue with the long civil rights movement framework advocated by Jacqueline Dowd Hall, argues that *Eyes on the Prize* (presumably the first series) offers an effective narrative that does much to answer Hall's call for a counterpoint to the sanitized misuse of the civil rights movement. He writes, "In an unprecedented manner, this series weaves together the national and the local, ordinary men and women with more recognizable leaders, intragroup cooperation and competition, and mundane concerns with the aim of transforming America to make it 'a more perfect union.' It tears down myths that the accomplishments of this Civil Rights Movement were easy and that its participants were merely dreamers. It moves beyond Dr. King while understanding that the movement would have been very different without him. Hampton's *Eyes* has taken the Civil Rights Movement master narrative and reformulated it to include multiple perspectives of the people, black and white, who made the

movement and those who opposed it, those who had formal power and those who did not, all the while showing where this short Civil Rights Movement succeeded and where it failed." Steven Lawson, "Long Origins of the Short Civil Rights Movement, 1954–1968," unpublished essay in editor's possession. In another essay critiquing the long civil rights movement, Eric Arnesen observes that *Eyes* largely fails to connect post-1954 activism to the "strands of protest that preceded it." Despite that, he reflects, "I suppose I'd be satisfied if my students had, in fact, absorbed the chronologically misleading *Eyes* framework. At least it would be . . . something." [ellipses in original] Eric Arnesen, "Reconsidering the 'Long Civil Rights Movement,'" *Historically Speaking* 10 (April 2009): 31.

10. Judy Richardson to Emilye Crosby, e-mail, June 10, 2010.

11. For more on the different interpretations of the Albany Movement, see Bernice Johnson Reagon and Dick Cluster, "The Borning Struggle: The Civil Rights Movement: An Interview with Bernice Johnson Reagon by Dick Cluster," *Radical History*, 9–25, esp. 21. See also, J. Todd Moye, "Focusing Our Eyes on the Prize: How Community Studies Are Reframing and Rewriting the History of the Civil Rights Movement," chapter 5, this volume; and Emilye Crosby, introduction, this volume.

12. For further explanation of Richardson's reference to Carmichael's "prone" quote, see Emilye Crosby, "That Movement Responsibility: An Interview with Judy Richardson on Movement History and Legacies," chapter 12, this volume. See also, "SNCC Women and the Stirrings of Feminism," *A Circle of Trust: Remembering SNCC*, ed. Cheryl Lynn Greenberg (New Brunswick, N.J.: Rutgers University Press, 1998), 127–51.

13. Faith S. Holsaert, Martha Prescod Norman Noonan, Judy Richardson, Betty Garman Robinson, Jean Smith Young, and Dorothy M. Zellner, eds., *Hands on the Freedom Plow: Personal Accounts by Women in SNCC* (Urbana: University of Illinois Press, 2010), 1–6.

CHARLES M. PAYNE

# "Sexism is a helluva thing"

## Rethinking Our Questions and Assumptions

N ote: The following is a lightly edited transcript of a presentation by Charles Payne as part of the "Local Studies, a National Movement: Toward a Historiography of the Black Freedom Movement" Conversations in the Disciplines Conference at SUNY Geneseo, March 24–26, 2006.

Good morning. I want you to know that this time yesterday morning I was doing a talk in Atlanta and I stood up at the microphone and looked out at the audience, an audience of thirty or forty folks, three of whom were black, and I was thinking, "Why in the hell am I here?! What is the point?" So, this certainly feels more comfortable. I am glad that the story of the movement still has the power to draw in, on a gray Saturday morning, so many different kinds of people—men, women, different ages, you know. It's a comfortable-looking audience for me, and I know why I'm here. [*chuckle*]

I'm here in one sense just to say one thing: sexism is a helluva thing! Right? Sexism is a helluva thing. And you can think you know that, but you don't know that. [*chuckle*] That's sort of what I'm trying to say. Let me give you a couple cautionary tales.

Sandra Adickes, a member of SNCC (the Student Nonviolent Coordinating Committee), who worked in the Freedom Schools in Mississippi, has written what looks to be a very interesting book on that experience, her experience— *The Legacy of a Freedom School*.[1] There's a SNCC listserv and last month she was announcing her book to that listserv. Plus, she called me out! I believe I was eighteen years old the last time anybody called me out! To wit: this is an e-mail. I'm quoting, "In the *Legacy of a Freedom School*, I challenge Charles Payne's evaluation that teaching in Freedom School 'had relatively low status value'"— that's the phrase in quotes— "because women did most of the work; voter registration was the 'prestige assignment.'" And then, in her words, "I never found my work 'low-status.' The reports of women [freedom school] teachers in the SNCC archives reveal their commitment and pride in their work."[2]

So, that's her. Then, another woman, who also, I believe, worked in a Freedom School but who was in any case in Mississippi in the summer of 1964, wrote in response to that e-mail. "Yes, that's laughable. It's always easy to label whatever women do as 'low-status.' Typically puffed-up, self-importance of male academics." She's talking about me by the way, if you didn't associate that. "Typically puffed-up, self-importance of male academics, seeing men's work as *always* more important. I don't think the community felt that way at all." Note that point. "I don't think the community felt that way at all."[3] Right. Then there was another one from a third person, also in Mississippi that summer. "Nobody in the movement knew anything about low/high status. There would not have been a whole without all of the elements."[4]

And then what that led to was a series of sort of back-and-forth comments from other folk who were there.[5] Judy Richardson wrote this really wonderful defense of my work.[6] She was more positive than I would've been. [*chuckle*] And Charlie Cobb, who is, I think, usually and appropriately, credited with developing the idea of Freedom Schools, wrote back about the complexities in the word "status." And that there was a difference between people who were in the field and not in the field, and there were status associations which were attached to that. But anyway, he was writing just to complicate that.[7]

When I think about—I mean, lots of things are going on, right? Everyone is so offended when you say, "Well the work that you do is low-status." So, there's no surprise in that. But, the part that really caught me off guard: "Women in the community didn't feel what we did was low status." As soon as I read that it was like—snap! Yes, that's right! I don't even need to know the women. I think I know that culture well enough to know that adult black women in those cultures would *have revered* the work the schools were doing. I would not be at all surprised if, for a lot of the local women, the Freedom Schools were *more* important than the voter registration, in terms of how they would've prioritized it.

So, they're right. So, how did I get there? I hate making this kind of mistake. This is in a chapter where I am specifically trying to think about how women shape and change the movement in just absolutely, crucial ways. And even in the context of trying to do that, I wind up privileging some voices more than others without even thinking about it.

Part of the problem is that the question isn't a question. This is not a politicized question that activists and scholars are arguing over. If it had been raised to that level, I would've gone into the discussion more carefully. I would've looked at it from more angles. Nobody was arguing over this. It's been written dozens of times. It has never been challenged. It's sort of taken for granted. Right? I wouldn't have even called what I said an evaluation. I didn't think of it as that serious. I was simply repeating something which is repeated often in the record.

Hmmmm. Darn. That's the problem. Where does the record come from? Whose record, right? So, you know, if I thought back—and I'm actually, when I get some time, going to trace back through all my sources to see exactly how I got there. But, when I trace back, there are a number of oral histories in which people who are connected to the summer project talk about the hierarchy in terms of the way in which work was valued. And almost without exception, those who *say anything* about it, say that Freedom School work was devalued. What they don't say is, devalued by whom? No one says devalued by whom? And so it becomes this kind of general idea.

And when you think about it—the other source that we have, that I would've thought was unimpeachable, is the records kept by the offices which interviewed potential volunteers before they went South. One of the running themes in those records is this notion that they had to push people towards Freedom Schools because nobody wanted to do that. Everybody wanted to be in the Delta doing the voter registration. But if I think back on this, I need to go back and check—I'm pretty sure most of the folks putting those records together were, in fact, men. Okay? And so the degree to which those records reflect the priorities of the people keeping the records is problematic.

And all I am trying to say is that this whole discussion is far more complex than I realized when I was writing that, even though, in some sense, I was trying self-consciously to think carefully about these issues. Nonetheless, I still wind up privileging some viewpoints and disprivileging others on the basis of gender. And part of the reason I want to stress that I wound up doing that is because the records themselves have gender bias built into them. So, if I do what the scholar is trained to do—faithfully recreate and interpret the records—just doing that is going to often mean faithfully recreating certain kinds of gender bias. Sexism is a helluva thing! [*chuckle*]

Does anybody know the Haitian scholar, Michel-Rolph Trouillot, who writes about this problem? The problem isn't arguing with what scholars have said. The problem is arguing with what is not in the archives, what was not collected, the questions which were not asked or answered at the time. So, the progressive scholar has to retrain himself or herself to do that.[8]

Example two: I think that I will be talking this afternoon—I expect to be talking some about how literature on the civil rights/Black Power movement is changing. We've already had, with Robyn Spencer's talk this morning, just a wonderful example of how rich and exciting the new work is gonna be.[9] It's clear that the notion of a good 1960s/bad 1960s—it was all good before 1965 or 1966 and then all bad when Black Power came—that notion is going to be attacked and undermined. The idea that all the things that changed in America came out of the narrowly conceived southern civil rights movement proper is going to be destroyed. In fact, it already has been.

Nobody reads Herbert Haines's books about radical flank effect.[10] What he says is that the centrists wouldn't have gotten nearly as much as they did if they had not had the threat of radicals—had it not been for Malcolm X and the riots. You want to understand how the American higher education desegregated? It doesn't desegregate because of civil rights, it desegregates because of Black Power.

The first year that black students come onto these campuses in any numbers is 1968 in the fall. What happened in 1968 in the spring? American cities were burning and they were burning in the context of a rhetoric which said, "More of this to come, folk." And the institutional response to that was, "Let's open up the paths to the middle class." It doesn't come out of nonviolence. It doesn't come out of civil rights. It doesn't come out of folks in the South. It comes out of that national, urban eruption. That's the institutional response. So anyway, we're going to get this large literature, which celebrates and radicalizes what we have previously demonized—the radicalism, the militants of the movement. Hmmmm. That's good, isn't it? [*chuckle*] Yes, it sure is. [*chuckle*] Same question, right? What's imbedded in that language? What's imbedded in radicalism, militants? Where do our core conceptions, our gut conceptions, of those terms come from? What *exactly* is it we're validating?

For example, take the term "militants." So far as I know, almost all the time in these conversations when people refer to militants, they are saying something about how black people relate to white people. Question: give me a black-on-black situation. In that situation, what would "militant" constitute? What would it be if you thought of it? And this is a part of a long fixation, terrible among American social scientists (and pretty bad among American historians). Our literature on how blacks relate to other black folk is thin. It's thin over a 150-year period unless you're talking about pathological conceptions. The deviant black father, the dysfunctional black mother, and I don't even know if that's actually a relational literature, now that I think about it.

If you take that literature aside, all of our great literatures on African Americans tend to say a great deal about how they relate to white folk and very little about how they relate to one another—on a day-to-day, ordinary way. It is a question for everybody. I cannot get through a civil rights course without my students asking me, "How come whites and blacks couldn't get along in the movement? What happened?" They read enough to know that at some point there are strains among black people—North/South, folks that came into the movement early/ folks that came into the movement late, "this" ideology among blacks/ "that" ideology among blacks. They know that stuff is there, but they never sort of raise it up and say, "Professor Payne, can we talk about these issues among black folks?" Never, not once, is that raised up. I think that says something about how they have been trained.

Walter Rodney, speaking about blacks across the diaspora—if I remember the context—he said, "They do not understand that our historical experience has been speaking to white people, whether it be begging white people, justifying ourselves against white people, or even vilifying white people. Our whole context has been, 'That is the man to talk to.'" So that when we talk about radicals, when we talk about militants, to what degree is the way in which we conceive of those things shaped by this tradition that our whole context is talking about white folks? Let me push this article if folk don't know it. Vincent Harding's article, "History: White, Black, and Negro." For those of you who are or will be teaching, I think it's just one of the essential pieces.[11]

But, anyway, he makes the point that I am trying to make. He says, "There are three kinds of American history. First of all and most familiar is white history." What is white history? Well, that's what we all were raised on. The once and still dominant paradigm. It is a history in which people of color are relegated to the background of the basic story of American goodness and originality. But, it's basically a good story—a good story without black folks.

Then there's Negro history. And what is Negro history? This essay, by the way, taught me to hate all contributionist history. You'll see what I mean: "What contributions have you made?" Then there is Negro history, which he calls a kind of "me-too" history. Whatever white folks say they did, we say, "'Me too, me too!' Did Columbus discover America? 'Us too, us too, there were Negroes on the boat!' Did white men fight in a noble war against King

George? 'Us too, us too, Crispus Attucks died first. Don't forget our contributions!' Did white people have kings and queens? 'Us too, us too, remember
the empires of West Africa.' Did courageous white people open up the West?
'Well, there were black cowboys, there were black troopers, black trappers.
There were the brave Buffalo Soldiers, there were—'"

He turns that around on us. Now what did you just say? "There were the
'brave' Buffalo Soldiers." You said white Americans tried to exterminate a
people and black folk went along for the ride. That's what you said. That's
what's imbedded in that. Right? And that's what contributionist history is.
It is "Did you make a contribution?" The question you need to be asking is,
"What were you making the contribution to?"

And Negro history never does that. Negro history just says, "*Whatever
white folks did*, we did a little of that, too. We were there, too." And we're
happy to be included in that presence. So that the distinction that he wants to
make between Negro history and black history is that Negro history doesn't
take time to stop and interrogate the story. Right? By "black history" he
means a history that uses the story of African Americans as the basis for
questioning, for challenging the values and the assumptions which are imbedded in the other histories, imbedded in the master narrative.

Now that, at one level, could lead into a discussion about how we conceive of some of the categories in which we describe racial politics—militants, Afro-centric, black-to-the-bone. I mean, to what degree is there a kind
of "me-too-ism" imbedded in those? That's one set of questions.

There's another set of questions. It would be easy to translate his point
into gender terms. It's easy enough and we've all seen contributionist histories about women—"Women did it, too." Elaine Brown: "There was a woman
who was head of the Panthers"—without interrogating whether or not she
did anything different from what men had traditionally done. I mean, that's
sort of the perfect example. Just putting a face in a place, right, and saying
that that represents progress. It's easy to imagine that kind of history.

Among the young, black women scholars with whom I've worked the last
couple years, not all of them, but I've noticed enough—this group—all of
whom consider themselves feminist, all of whom consider themselves nationalist, and who are creating an intellectual and personal lifestyle well to
the left-of-center—is going to be a part of this valorizing or reevaluation of
the 1960s and they are attracted to certain kinds of questions, which sometimes seem to me to have imbedded in them certain kinds of problems.

In Professor Robyn Spencer's discussion, we got a description of Panther women who were involved in self-defense in the same way that men were. She *also* gave us a description of Panther women who were involved in the creation of community institutions in ways that very few men were. So you get this sort of complete picture.[12] What I am noticing among some of the young women that I work with is that they are much more drawn to the one side than to the other. So, Assata Shakur, the New York 21, gun battles with state troopers. Didn't that happen? Yes, it happened, it's important, it's not well enough known. But, at the same time, if I say, "You could argue that—all organizations have to deal with the problems of internal community. How do you keep working relationships, trust, mutuality among yourselves?" We have good anecdotal reason to believe that in this whole history women play a disproportionate role. I spent a significant part of my life, at one time, working with Chicago community organizations. And it was very much the women in those organizations who were the spirit, who handled the disagreements that developed, who made folk feel important, who prevented militant cultures from becoming cultures of put-downs, which was a problem going on around them at the time—"I'm blacker than you, I'm more radical than you," whatever the language is. So women sort of stopped that and made folks take a more complex and humane stance.

So, when I say to some of my students, "Yes, let's sort of study that. This notion of how movements maintain an internal sense of community is crucial. We have good reason to believe that women play a special role in it." "Well," they say, "but yeah, that's a traditional female role. That's what women always do. They always manage relationships. We don't want to do that. We want to see women who are doing nontraditional things."

And in a sense, that makes sense, you know. I can understand that. There's also a sense, obviously, in which that worries me. To some degree they're saying, "We're gonna valorize things that society valorizes." Right? And the kinds of things that society has valorized are very masculinist. So then we look at women to the degree that they fit our conception of militancy, of politics. That is what we are going to focus on and we are not necessarily going to look at other kinds of things. Right? All of which is to say, I just wonder if we can't come up with a nonmasculinist conception of militancy? What would that mean? What would that look like? And the fact that it is not a question we are considering is, I think, a problem.

The point I'm trying to make is that, not only is sexism a helluva thing be-

Figures 24 and 25  The Citizenship Schools, founded by Septima Clark, sNCC's
Freedom Schools, and Stokely Carmichael's canvassing in Lowndes County, Alabama,
to encourage voter registration and help build the Lowndes County Freedom Party
all suggest possibilities for developing a "non-masculinist conception of militancy."
Citizenship School on Johns Island (*above*), with Alice Wine (*second from left*),
Septima Clark (*center*), and Bernice Robinson (*standing*), 1959. Photograph by Ida
Berman, courtesy of Highlander Research and Education Center Archives. Stokely
Carmichael (*opposite*) canvassing in Lowndes County, Alabama, in July 1965, almost
a year before his use of the phrase "Black Power" on the June 1966 Meredith March
made him a national media figure and representative of a more traditional image of
black militancy. Courtesy of the Library of Congress, Prints and Photographs Division,
*Look* magazine, Photograph Collection, LC Look-Job 65-2434. For a partial transcript
of a Freedom School class led by Stokely Carmichael, see figure 33, chapter 14, p. 434.

cause it's imbedded in the records, it's a helluva a thing because it's imbedded
in the conceptual equipment that we have to think about the records. I mean,
the very concepts that we use to describe liberation are created by unfree-
dom. We are shaped by the society that we want to change, and we have its
contradictions within us. And so, knowing that, how do we begin to protect
ourselves, not simply from all that stuff out there, but from all that stuff that
is still there in the way in which we think about the problem even when we're
trying to think in a liberatory way. So, I'll pose the question. There are lots of
young people in the audience. So, you all just go and solve the question, that's
all. I've done my job. [*chuckle*]

For a transcript of Charles Payne's conference-closing keynote talk, "Why Study the Movement?," see chapter 14, this volume.

## NOTES

1. Sandra Adickes, *The Legacy of a Freedom School* (New York: Palgrave, 2005).

2. Sandra Adickes to SNCC-List, February 22, 2006 (copies of all of the cited SNCC listserv e-mails are in editor's possession); Payne writes, "Within the movement, Freedom School work always had relatively low status value. In part this was because women did much of the Freedom School work and because it wasn't as dangerous as other work. Voter registration was the prestige assignment. Looking back at the Freedom Schools from the hindsight of the last three decades is disturbing. Of all the models generated by the movement, it seems tragic that this one, an institution specifically attentive to the developmental needs of Black youngsters as a movement issue, was accorded little respect. At the time, though, for young people with a sense of urgency, Freedom Schools seemed a long slow road." Charles M. Payne, *I've Got the Light of Freedom: The Organizing Tradition and the Mississippi Freedom Struggle* (Berkeley: University of California Press, 2005), 305.

3. Sheila Michaels to SNCC-list, February 22, 2006.

4. Gloria Richardson Dandridge to SNCC-list, February 22, 2006.

5. For example, Wally Roberts writes, "Payne's sources for his assertion may be some of the men whom I observed even in Oxford before we went to Mississippi (as a [Freedom Summer] coordinator, I was there for both weeks) and that was that some of the men who were going to do voter registration work treated it as higher status work and even glamorized it because they thought it was more risky. That attitude, while not widespread, persisted throughout the summer." Wally Roberts to SNCC-list, February 22, 2006. See also, Charles Payne to SNCC-list, March 20, 2006; Gloria Clark to SNCC-list, March 20, 2006.

6. Judy Richardson wrote, "I'm sorry, folks, but I gotta say that, as important as the work of the Freedom Schools was absolutely seen to be (and let's not forget that Charlie Cobb was one of those instrumental in the writing of the curriculum), I don't believe it was as valued as the voter registration work. Voter registration work was considered front lines. Didn't mean that those who were doing that other work didn't feel absolutely integral and important to the struggle—just meant that it was seen as less than the voter registration work, just like a lot of other non-voter registration work. I can't remember any guy ever saying, 'Boy, I really wanna work in the Freedom Schools.' Matter of fact, when I kept saying to Jim Forman, 'I wanna go to the field.' I did NOT mean the Freedom Schools. I meant voter registration work. and there was a reason for this." Judy Richardson to SNCC-list, February 24, 2006.

7. After an off-list discussion with Richardson, Charlie Cobb wrote Payne with another perspective. "While the 1964 Freedom Schools now hold a semi-exalted place officially reflective of movement creativity, they really were an effort to come up with something the summer volunteers could do effectively, given their inexperience and given the reluctance of many of us to have them in the first place, without placing the full time staff (SNCC, CORE) in too great danger. The schools were an organizers' answer to that—they were coming; we had to use them meaningfully. We had long recognized the problem with schools and had made a couple of indirect stabs at dealing with it (e.g. nonviolent school in McComb, what Maria Varela was doing in Selma, Bob Moses' experiment with programmed learning) but had never thought of ourselves as organizing around education the way, say, Septima Clark did. Or even a program like SCLC's Citizenship Education Program (headed by Andy Young, I think). I do not think it was less valued in the way that Judy suggests—'I want to go into the field' (not work with freedom schools) but rather that being in the 'field' was distinctly different than being a freedom summer volunteer no matter what the work. This is partly racial in the sense that being in the 'field' also implied a different relationship with the black community than that of the volunteers. And finally in this regard, being in the 'field' partly meant shedding some of the remaining vestiges of being in Mississippi/the South as a missionary there to help the downtrodden. With the 1965 Voting Rights Act we could have moved seriously and aggressively into education/ freedom schools the way we had done with voter registration but our own internal chaos prohibited meaningful discussion about where we go from there. As I think Bob Moses said once, we were not even sure who 'we' were." Charles Cobb Jr. to Charles Payne and Judy Richardson, March 20, 2006 (in editor's possession).

8. Michel-Rolph Trouillot, *Silencing the Past: Power and the Production of History* (Boston: Beacon, 1995).

9. Payne is referencing the talk by Robyn Ceanne Spencer that preceded his on the panel, "Women, Gender, and Leadership." A version of Spencer's talk was subsequently published. See Robyn Ceanne Spencer, "Engendering the Black Freedom Struggle: Revolutionary Black Womanhood and the Black Panther Party in the Bay Area, California," *Journal of Women's History* 20, no. 1 (Spring 2008): 90–113.

10. Herbert H. Haines, *Black Radicals and the Civil Rights Mainstream, 1954–1970* (Knoxville: University of Tennessee Press, 1988).

11. Vincent Harding, "History: White, Negro, & Black," *Southern Exposure* 1, no. 3 (1974): 51–62. The quotes in the next few paragraphs are not direct quotes from Harding's essay, rather they are Payne's words, presented as quotes in a way that synthesized Harding's arguments.

12. Spencer's talk, which Payne is referencing, was subsequently published. Spencer, "Engendering the Black Freedom Struggle."

ROBYN C. SPENCER AND WESLEY HOGAN

# Telling Freedom Stories from the Inside Out

## Internal Politics and Movement Cultures in SNCC and the Black Panther Party

### THE HIDDEN STORY

The Student Nonviolent Coordinating Committee (SNCC) and the Black Panther Party (BPP) were organizations that defined an era. Founded by student activists in 1960, SNCC staffed the front lines against racist violence during the southern civil rights struggle and launched or took part in many influential grass-roots political campaigns during the 1960s. The BPP, founded in 1966 by community college students, challenged racism, poverty, and police brutality and grew to become one of the most visible organizations advocating Black Power. Although the scholarly literature on both of these organizations is rich, the internal life of the movements remains unexplored.[1] Though the ways people treat one another inside a movement serve as the essential building blocks of the movement, many activists and cultural commentators consider these relationships "private," "personal," or even "nonessential" matters.

Wesley Hogan would like to thank Robyn Spencer for her patience, dynamic writing, and analytical brilliance in this collaboration, as well as the SNCC and SDS people who agreed to be interviewed, and colleagues Emilye Crosby, Nishani Frazier, Sara Leland, and Dirk Philipsen, who kept her on task and brought their editorial power and prowess to the work. Of course no one above should be held responsible for any thickheadedness herein. Robyn Spencer would like to thank Wesley Hogan for her wonderful spirit of collaboration and brilliant theoretical insights. She would also like to thank Panther interviewees, Emilye Crosby for her persistent encouragement, editorial vision, and imagination, and Nishani Frazier for her excellent feedback.

This is especially true in the case of movement interiority, personal politics, and sexual dynamics. Although these areas usually fall under the rubric of "airing dirty laundry" or are considered irrelevant to public political activity and labeled "personal politics" by scholars and activists alike, they are essential to understanding the character and complexity of social movements and to recreating the historical moments in which those movements operated.[2] Much of formal political history and democratic theory has routinely overlooked the vitality and candor of people's internal social relations as a measurement of a movement's small-"d" democratic progress.

So why is it essential to know what happened inside these movements? Isn't it enough to know what they were able to accomplish in the world of external politics? In SNCC, the quality of interpersonal social interactions served as the fundamental glue holding the organization together. Black Panther Party members pointed to comradeship as a major component of their organizational experience and central to their political commitments. It is clear from interviewing former Panthers that they were not just committed to the organization, and "the people," they were deeply and profoundly committed to each other. To this day, hundreds of former members of the BPP and SNCC attend reunions not just to honor their previous (and usually ongoing) political commitments but to reconnect with comrades in a profoundly personal and political way.[3] In addition, the following case studies demonstrate that knowing something about the interior of these movements changes the questions we ask about how SNCC or the Panthers were able to get things done. In some cases, knowledge of interior dynamics overhauls our understanding of key initiatives or internal debates over strategy.

Thus as scholars work to reconceptualize the national civil rights movement, these interior movement dynamics must move to the center of the story. Still, in the years since the civil rights movement's peak, very few scholars have figured out either how to get at such material, or, once they have it, how to piece it together with other kinds of sources. In addition, historians — biographers largely excepted — have often thought the personal unimportant. (It may well be that we need to ask: why is the personal clearly justified in personal histories [biographies] but not as easily justified in collective biographies of groups? What is the basis for this double standard?) Even historians who believe that the personal is political have trouble including the personal in their historical analyses because movement veterans often withhold discussion of it.

Oral history has the potential to both help and hinder historians in gaining access to the interiors of social movements. Oftentimes the barrier to information and the key to information is one and the same: the interviewee. When historians embark on their research projects they quickly realize that sometimes the information they seek is exactly the information that movement activists are unwilling to share when the tape recorder is on. For one, many movement veterans don't necessarily see how internal relationships mattered to the larger story and they doubt its political significance. Second, given the dominant celebrity culture, discussion of such issues can easily be perceived as exploitative, gossipy, or a further encroachment on privacy. Third, many activists grew up in the movement, not just politically, but culturally and socially. It was a tumultuous time where they often felt, rightfully so, that their lives were on the line and acted accordingly. Given the struggles over defining the movement's legacy and impact, veterans sometimes associate discussions of interior life with criticism and seek to shift the discussion elsewhere—lamenting, for example, the fact that Stokely Carmichael's quip about "prone women" is better known than some of SNCC's organizing campaigns. Finally, and most important, movement veterans don't want to betray themselves or their friends over what seemed like personal matters and are worried that some of the personal truths will put the movement or individual members in a bad light.

It is true that we need much more evidence, and many more studies, to figure out how to determine whether a "personal" issue is historically relevant or not. How does the historian or movement activist suss out what is relevant and what is not? And what to do if there is disagreement? Nishani Frazier, historian of Congress of Racial Equality (CORE) and daughter of a movement veteran, reminds scholars to ask: "How much is too much when it comes to bringing the personal into history? What does having a more detailed inclusion of the personal in history mean for our broader understanding and exploration of the ultimate meaning of the past?" Frazier argues that "Maybe [we need] a more specific distinction of what kind of personal to put in" the past. She further suggests two key distinctions for deciding whether a personal issue is "historically relevant." If, for example, interior movement relationships impact the politics of the organization they should always be included, but scholars can be much more judicious—or leave out altogether—the way the politics of the organization impact personal life. Furthermore, if the weight of the personal lends itself to actionable presence in the unfolding of events, then the personal becomes relevant. If an activist gets tired and quits, it's actionable. If an activist gets tired and goes for a drive in the country—that's not historically relevant. Or, for example, if a male SNCC or BPP member has sex with several women and the women stew in anger with no clear transformation in the historical story line, it's not historically relevant. If the women send a memorandum to James Forman or Huey Newton, then it's actionable.[4]

Such complexities have made it difficult to render visible the historical origins of the glue that still binds these activists together. Shedding light on the interior of the movement has been challenging. While former Panthers are ready and willing to discuss election campaigns, community programs, and ideological shifts, questions about movement interiority have been met with reluctance and some have been disinclined to answer questions about how Panthers confronted the realities of class, color, and sexuality; how they negotiated housework and personal relationships; how they overcame conflicts; and how people who were, more often than not, teenagers forged bonds in the chaos of those revolutionary moments of the 1960s and 1970s. At that moment the historian runs up against the divide between the public political and the personal political. It is clear that public political work is perceived as the real story and the personal political is considered potential dirty laundry and in fact, too many of "those" types of questions can even throw the motivation of the interviewer into question.[5]

That these personal dynamics eventually began to take an (unreckoned) toll is a reality of history, which many prefer to avoid. A few examples connecting the personal to the political serve to illuminate this reality. One woman in SNCC had been a community organizer for several years by the mid-1960s. What kept her going was the feeling of being part of something larger than herself, that she and her compatriots were strong because they shared common goals and a common vision. But at some point she realized she was beginning to think private thoughts without speaking them. She feared some of her friends might ostracize her. She eventually realized she was risking her life for a strategy she was not sure she believed in any longer. She left the project, but as a result, two of her siblings (also in the group) did not speak to her for many years. In this case, the group's politics could no longer contain the personal and political growth this woman experienced. The lack of candor in her interior relationships in the group drove her to leave. A second example: in 1997, two former civil rights workers met for coffee. They

Figure 26  A look inside the movement in summer 1964: the Jackson, Mississippi, SNCC "freedom house." The man in the hat is Sandy Leigh, and the woman on the phone is Mary King. © 1978 George Ballis/Take Stock.

hadn't seen or spoken with each other in thirty-five years. They had once been political allies, lovers, and had faced down white supremacists' bullets multiple times. Now they had reconnected after a movement reunion. After exchanging some pleasantries, the woman asked: "Why did you really leave me for that white woman? Was it about me, or race, or what?" He replied: "I don't know, I still can't figure it out." The woman told him how painful it had been. The man acknowledged this. Their emotional wounds were sufficiently healed that finally, tentatively, they were able to reconnect. Even so, they had lived separate lives for three decades. This early private split resulted in her leaving a project to which she had been central.

Similar examples can be found in the history of the BPP. Leaving the organization was a tension-fraught endeavor for members at different points in its history. Panther Chief of Staff David Hilliard resigned from the BPP in 1974. A subsequent memo retroactively expulsed Hilliard for violating "a Party directive, namely continued contact (via phone visits) with an expelled

Party member, Brenda Presley." Hilliard had a close personal relationship with Presley and when her relationship with the organization ended, he was put in an untenable position.[6] After Hilliard left the organization, his brother June Hilliard, who had served as assistant chief of staff, resigned and was also retroactively expelled. This one incident demonstrates how personal relationships forged in the BPP or that predated the BPP sometimes outlasted it. In this case, internal politics was part of the answer to the question of some of the BPP's organizational shifts as these two key leadership positions were reconceptualized. Yet, such reasons for leaving remain invisible.[7] Another example can be found in the occasional retreats that some women in the BPP began to hold after the fortieth reunion in 1996 as way to heal past wounds. Intensely private affairs, these retreats provide a safe space for BPP women to talk frankly about their former relationships, not just with men but with other women.

These important personal relationships have remained outside of the historical record. The woman alienated from her siblings and the movement veterans having a coffee date had all been interviewed numerous times for civil rights histories, and they had many times told the stories of being shot, the tales of political campaigns, and had given interviewers numerous specifics to help recreate the feeling of what it was like to challenge Jim Crow. But they—and other movement veterans—rarely if ever talked about their personal lives in the movement: with whom they formed relationships, whether those lasted, their friendships that broke and reformed; pregnancies, marriages, and stories of who had come out of the closet; or the ways race had pulled them together or driven them apart. Not that they believed these issues to be apolitical. They just found it difficult to talk about them, because it was hard to see how such issues mattered to the larger freedom story. The BPP examples reflect another dynamic—the manipulation of silence. As a rank and file member, Presley has escaped the historical spotlight and her story resides in the silence of unasked questions. David and June Hilliard do not participate in scholarly interviews and have purposefully remained silent in order to exercise some control over their stories. The question of betrayal, privacy, friendship, and loyalty are all central to the decisions activists make about what story they tell.

The everyday details, textures, and tones of how people related to one another within the movement—for example, the Panthers' or SNCC's movement culture—are thus hard to uncover.[8] One has to piece it together, looking at thousands of documents and hundreds of interviews. Such work is not possible without the collective work of other scholars.[9] Feedback from movement veterans, friends, and colleagues keeps one from making many faulty assumptions or drawing erroneous conclusions.[10] That SNCC and Panther activists committed so many of their thoughts and reflections to paper also turned out to be invaluable. The constant FBI surveillance that both groups faced has provided yet another (problematic) window into movement interiors. Still, much of the work is tentative in this area. Most of the autobiographies we have are written by men and white women. We need a good deal more research, as well as primary sources (oral histories, letters, journals, etc.) from black women in particular, before we can be relatively confident that we understand how internal social dynamics unfolded in both SNCC and the Black Panther Party. Key questions or debates that no activists wanted to talk about, or wanted to talk about but could not find a way to bring forward, often provide the most important starting place. In SNCC, key submerged issues centered on (1) the utility of nonviolence, (2) what to do with the whites who wanted to work in the movement full time, and (3) sexuality. The BPP also ran up against internal and external barriers to putting issues such as sexuality and communal politics on the table and working through them productively.

This chapter argues that movement interiority matters and is key for the historical record. It examines the development of movement culture and interpersonal interactions in SNCC and the Black Panther Party and distinguishes between relevant and less significant interior issues, examines briefly how movement scholars can open up these conversations to get at interiority, and raises questions about how best to use it when constructing written or filmed history.

## SNCC AND ITS NONVIOLENT ETHIC

Nonviolence was never a universally embraced philosophy within the movement. Indeed, despite the group's name, some SNCC people challenged the utility of nonviolence from the beginning. Nonetheless, there did exist a commonly agreed-upon set of behaviors and values that may properly be described as a "nonviolent ethic" within the broader movement, and certainly within SNCC, between mid-1960 and the end of 1964. This approach derived from two major sources. The first sprung from a radical humanist approach developed by African Americans since the onset of the freedom struggle in the seventeenth century. As Charles Payne noted in 1995, young organizers in the 1960s "were bringing back to the rural Black South a refined, codified version of something that had begun there, an expression of the historical vision of ex-slaves, men and women who understood that, for them, maintaining a deep sense of community was itself an act of resistance."[11] The second source flowed from the practice of nonviolence as a way of life—the idea that one had to keep the social relationships inside the movement as fully "nonviolent" as those that the participants hoped to create in a new post-segregated America. But people who only used nonviolence as a *tactic* also largely embraced this ethic within the group. SNCC workers understood this ethic to be, in essence, the process of creating the new society itself. Furthermore, candor was essential—because it was practical. In the sit-ins, Freedom Rides, wade-ins, and pray-ins they organized throughout the South, movement workers had to believe that no one would ruin their nonviolent action by breaking the commitment to nonviolence. In the early days of 1960 to 1961, in the local sit-in and Freedom Rider communities, trust became a political necessity. Candor also became a prerequisite that was essential for SNCC in its work with local people on voter registration in the rural South between 1961 and 1965. Not to remain open and candid with one another could get one beaten or even killed. As one participant remembered, her boyfriend came on a sit-in even though he hadn't been truthful when asked by a movement leader if he was sure he could remain nonviolent. His evasion of the truth was devastating. Once on the action, he lashed back both verbally and physically at a white thug. Not only were all twenty-two people on the action arrested, but one of them was sexually assaulted in jail. Reminders of such truths haunted everyone, everywhere in SNCC.[12]

At "history's moving edge," as Charles Sherrod explained, SNCC had only their own past actions to serve as guides for future strategy.[13] They had to incorporate their experiential learning into their subsequent plans. For all its rhetorical simplicity, it is difficult to explain the effect of this habit of reflection. It encouraged innovation: mistakes were okay, as long as people learned from them. Making the same mistake twice was not all right—lives were at stake—so reflection became a political necessity.

It was due to these political realities that movement activists demanded mutual respect and reflection from themselves and one another. These were the essential ingredients of the movement's ability to recruit newcomers, sustain its internal cohesion and momentum, and secure the political victories that helped it to remain a vital political force in the nation. And yet such criteria were almost wholly invisible to political commentators outside of the movement, then and now.

Significantly, there were many difficulties to sustaining a movement based on the integrity of relationships and an open democratic process. What happened to the movement when individual relationships faltered, or dissolved altogether? The standards those within the movement now had for each other were quite high. More recent recruits did not necessarily fit into the group with ease. Whether potential activists stayed and adjusted, or whether they left in confusion, their interactions with others impacted the level of democratic social relations the group as a whole was able to achieve. So it was for each member who crossed the bridge from the majority culture into a movement culture centered largely in the nonviolent ethic of candor, respect, reflection, and mutual trust. Each person brought their personal history and personality. Despite the fact that they were "good people," more often than not both people's histories and personalities included many layers of authoritarian habits and behaviors.

This was the enormous challenge—rewarding though it could be—of a politics based on the integrity of interpersonal relationships. These were dangerous shoals; people often crashed up against different strategies to create change, or on the many ways race and white supremacy shaped people's actions and thoughts. Others found themselves smashing against a failed sexual encounter or love affair, or the differences between those who were formally credentialed (at Morehouse, Harvard, or Howard) and those who were educated by hard-won experience (the schools provided by Mississippi backroads and Georgia jails). Still others crashed against their need for individual recognition and mainstream success. These difficulties flashed to high visibility, in particular any time black SNCC workers and white volunteers tried to work together in a community without a base of prior relationships or successful attempts at genuine communication (Cambridge, Maryland, Greenwood, Mississippi, or Terrell County, Georgia, to name only a few). Both sides felt the great strain that the absence of productive, candid discussion often promotes. When conflicts proved intractable or permanent—such as when an activist couple's marriage fell apart—the community surrounding them experienced great stress. The problem of betrayal, and how to address it within the movement, then emerged as a major hurdle that movement activists could find no systemic way to clear.

Finally, it is now evident that when the movement at large no longer supported an environment promoting higher levels of candor, reflection, and trust than could be found in the traditional culture, it was, in fact, no longer a movement. The "radical manners" of candor and mutual respect were the lifeblood of the movement. Many in the movement discovered this core truth only after the fact.

## PANTHERS AND SEXUAL POLITICS

Even in an organization like the BPP where internal life was often under surveillance by the FBI and scholars have some access to internal documents generated within the organization such as memos and minutes from meetings, former Panthers are often the only source to really unpack the interior life of the organization. Sexual politics is an important subtheme in the Panthers' history that has remained underanalyzed by scholars. Although sexuality is just one aspect of interior life, it demonstrates well some of the issues at play and the challenges of trying to access a full, complex story that takes the personal seriously. On the one hand, there is the practical: the discomfort of the interviewer and the interviewee in broaching topics mainly understood as personal. This is further complicated by age and gender and cultural understandings about respect for elders and taboo topics. While this discomfort is real, when addressing other topics that are painful, such as fallen comrades and arrests, the interviewer and interviewee pair is often able to push through the discomfort due to the value they both place on adding the information to the historical record. In reality, internal politics is often perceived of low value to the historical record so the incentive to push past obvious roadblocks is also low. Yet these stories have the potential to challenge the unstated scholarly assumption that internal life in the BPP was a seedbed for dysfunction. They serve as signposts for scholars to begin tracking down the contentious personal bonds that both undergirded and undermined the political commitment of BPP members.

The Panthers were obviously influenced by and had an influence on the transformation of ideas of sexuality in the 1960s, especially in the Bay Area, where the counterculture, student movement, and women's liberation movement flourished. Yet activists have remained silent around issues of sexuality. One main reason is that scholars have not asked. Scholars have assumed that the "black sixties" involves a certain type of politics—policy oriented, protest rooted, goal oriented, self-perception altering, white supremacy challenging. And that the "white sixties" involved another type of politics—personal, experimental, transformative, and psychedelic—filled with counternarratives, counterhegemony, and "the counterculture," where the bold redefinition of self and community was par for the course. However, the history of Black Power intersected and overlapped with the narrative of the sixties in more complicated ways than scholars have previously acknowledged. Another key reason is what scholar Darlene Clark Hine has called dissemblance, reticence around issues of personal politics and sexuality attributable to the desire to avoid reinforcing racial stereotypes.[14] Discussions of race and sexuality immediately bump up against racist ideas of black sexual deviance, black female Jezebels, and black male studs that were alive and well in the 1960s and are still operational in the contemporary context where the researcher launches her or his inquiry. The light that Panthers shine on their sexual practice within and outside of the organization does have the potential to fuel stereotypes, feed rumor mills, and further discredit an organization that has suffered from its fair share of mainstream condemnation.

Gender further complicates this story. Tales of sexuality, which emerge as a thread in many (both black and white) male activists' 1960s memoirs, seem to be less acceptable for women. Male Panther leaders, such as Bobby Seale in *A Lonely Rage* and Eldridge Cleaver in *Soul on Ice*, have written explicitly about their sexual encounters yet Elaine Brown, in her autobiography *A Taste of Power*, was roundly criticized for her frank discussion of how intimate encounters (which crossed lines of both race and gender) sometimes shaped her political trajectory and other times were simply casual or exploratory. Although these memoirs were published decades apart it is clear that speaking out about sexuality is risky for black women, even when they speak in nonsensationalistic ways and contextualize their actions within the growing feminist movement.[15]

Thus these silences around sexuality and the BPP are not just due to historiographical gaps or white racism. They are also attributable to the politics of respectability rooted in everything from secular misogyny, religious notions of patriarchy, and social conservatism that still roundly condemns women's sexual freedom—while celebrating or tacitly accepting men's sexual freedom—in the black community. Speaking out about sex is especially costly for black women. When I asked one former Panther—who referred to himself as a "ladies man" during his time in the organization—about *A Taste of Power* he quipped (off the record), "I didn't know she fucked everybody." The standard couldn't be more doubled.[16]

Yet the silence effectively hides pathbreaking experimentation of all types around the idea of sexual pleasure and fascinating debates around monogamy, sexual freedom, birth control, children/childcare, and motherhood and fatherhood. It can also hide an ugliness that needs to be examined—rapes, manipulation and coercion around sexuality, undemocratic practices, and homophobia. Crucial parts of everyone's stories get lost when the internal experiences of social movements are not brought to life, but women's stories are uniquely invisible. Bettina Aptheker has written: "[I]f we were to put together an anthology of women activists from the sixties, with memoirs and ideas and thoughts and reflections and experiences, they would dwell in part on issues of power and control and politics, but they would also talk about the dailyness of struggle, of making connections, and of a long, slow process of meaningful change. They would also talk about other issues that are far more painful and far less pretty to look at, but that are absolutely essential for us."[17] Historians desperately need to see the stuff deemed "dirty laundry" that activists deem tangential to the real story and are uncomfortable discussing. How else will there be a full and true accounting? How else can those who want and need to learn from these social movements fully analyze them, and learn from their innovations as well as their mistakes?

In 1977, Panther leader Huey Newton initiated a discussion about dating within the organization. It is one of the few moments in Panther history where debates around gender and sexuality are openly discussed and there is a paper trail. Newton invited comment on the Party's unspoken norm of heterosexual female Panthers pursuing romantic and sexual relationships solely within the organization. This practice was rooted in the assumption that women were more likely to let personal emotions weaken their political commitment and allow men outside of the BPP to influence them to leave the organization. Although some women did what they pleased, others bought into the notion that BPP members could best understand and support each other's unorthodox lifestyles and strong political commitments. For them, politics had a role in the choice of a partner and they limited themselves to Panther men. In contrast, male Panthers dated community women on the assumption that men dating outside of the organization was a potential gain because they could attract their female partner to join. Male Panthers also dated Panther women.[18] This was a recipe for tension.

BPP members responded to Newton's request with an outpouring of emotions, opinions, and grievances that reflected a deep dissatisfaction with the organization's gender dynamics, internal structure, and relationship to the community. One woman wrote that women had played a major role in many revolutions but due to the sometimes insular lifestyles of some BPP members, "we barely see the masses much less have a chance to educate them." Consequently, she argued, myths of Panther women as "robots or some type of Black humanoid" abounded both inside and outside the BPP.[19] Her comments suggest that Panther women were not rejecting community men, but were rarely put in a position to interact with them due to the demands of their political work. This was not just a personal and social problem, but a political issue. This sentiment was echoed by another woman who argued that external relationships could root the Party more deeply in the community. She wrote: "If the sister has been around for a good while and her practice has proven her to be a responsible person, I think this can be a positive thing for the Party and for the particular man we may see. It may not even be with the intention of bringing him in as a member, but bringing us closer as friends and allies."[20] Another Panther woman argued that all Party members should be free to choose partners outside of the organization if they chose people "who have ideals and goals common to us." She pointed out that her "concern about male-female relationships extends beyond the sexual aspect. Ultimately it will take a new and humane society to alter the ways in which men and women in America treat each other."[21] Another woman wrote in stating that she agreed with the policy of women not dating outside the Party because she believed that men from the community would have a hard time understanding the rigors of a Panther woman's life and might express jealousy or influence the woman to leave.[22]

The outcome of this provocative dialogue, which largely took the form of memos to Newton, is uncertain. It created a space, however, for rank and file members to collectively discuss organizational policies, customs, and norms around a range of issues, including how courtship and sexuality related to politics and community organizing. And it also suggests that the interior politics of movements, especially related to sexuality, is critical to any understanding of the BPP's organizational history.

## SEXUALITY, RACE, AND THE EVOLUTION OF SNCC

What internal dynamics are critical, what is dirty laundry, and what is just irrelevant? To show how difficult this is to examine from multiple angles, a short case study may be helpful. To participants in SNCC, sexuality caused great conflict, sometimes determining who worked on what projects, how work got done (or didn't), and at key junctures, tilting the direction of the organization's political strategies. Sexuality is obviously interior, but why is the role of whites, and the "White Folks Project" in particular, a matter of interiority? In SNCC, "what to do with white people" became a submerged "internal" issue because of a central truth: this was a black movement in both leadership and grass-root support. Whites who wanted a role needed to learn a lot—quickly—about black cultures and institutions. They also had to be respectful and useful. For most whites in the early 1960s, this proved an overwhelming hurdle. At the same time, blacks needed the attention and resources that white participation drew into the movement. The resulting clashes over "what to do with whites in the movement" were sometimes discussed among blacks only, sometimes played out in individual relationships, and sometimes flashed to high visibility in explosive staff meetings. How then, can historians look at the ways movement participants handled these issues, in both their personal and professional activities?

Power, Frederick Douglass famously stated, concedes nothing without a demand. In the case of the civil rights movement, blacks made demands of whites in power. But was there a role for whites who wanted to be a part of the movement? And should whites ever be in leadership positions in a black-generated movement? Could whites overcome their own white supremacist acculturation and relate to blacks as full human beings, while at the same time maintaining respect for black culture and black traditions of struggle? How did understandings of sexuality and sexual relationships impact black-white and black-black relationships?

One way to get through the persistent and intensifying questions about the role of whites in the Mississippi movement in the early 1960s was to "get the white workers into the white community," recalled SNCC veteran Bob Moses. Moses, the architect of SNCC's Mississippi organizing drive, noted: "If we could somehow get white workers establishing some beachheads in the white communities, one, they would obtain some legitimacy; two, you'd get rid of the problem that [whites were] trying to pile up in the black community." It would also bring new allies to the Mississippi Freedom Democratic Party. "If you could turn up a meeting where you had real grass roots white people like you can turn up today at some meetings," Moses said in 1982, "and get the MFDP people to meet with them, they wouldn't have any problem meeting and resolving, talking to each other. So I felt that was the only way out."[23]

White movement veterans Sam Shirah and Ed Hamlett tried to set up one such project over the summer of 1964 in Biloxi: the "White Folks Project." Could white civil rights workers organize white people in the South to channel white anger away from blacks and toward their own freedom?[24] After training with the other Mississippi summer volunteers in Oxford, Ohio, this group spent an additional week at Highlander Folk School. In the previous three years' work in Mississippi, white workers had been beaten, shot at, and arrested as soon as they showed any solidarity with the black movement. This group chose to start work in Biloxi because it had always been a tourist town, had a military base, and people were used to outsiders; perhaps the townsfolk would not attack as violently as could be expected elsewhere in the state. However, SNCC people had no models for organizing among whites. Robert Pardun, who came with Judy Schiffer and Charlie Smith from Texas, explained that, even after the orientation in Oxford and the week at Highlander, "no one knew what we were going to do, who we were going to talk to." Pardun and Smith rented a house for the twenty staff members, but when they arrived the following day, all the locks had been changed. The landlord had found out who they were. They spent the summer in the Riviera Hotel.[25]

A young couple soon moved in down the hall from the Biloxi SNCC project, and began to spend time with them. Halfway into the summer, the man went to Shirah with a problem. He admitted that all his people were Klan and he therefore had been sent "to figure out how to get rid of [SNCC]," but after getting to know the SNCC workers, he'd reconsidered. He said, "[T]he South is not ever going to grow as long as there's this Klan violence trying to keep this one segment of the population down." His search for an alternative to the Klan had led him to the Nazi party, but after meeting the SNCC people, he "ended up becoming a delegate of the Freedom Democratic Party," one of the four whites in the state to do so. Shirah eventually had to arrange an escape for the white couple out of Mississippi because the Klan was trying to kill them.[26]

Aside from this one chance encounter, however, the group had very little idea of where to find open-minded whites. They went to the library daily to try and figure out who controlled what in Biloxi. They went to the military base and talked to the men there. They tried to convince the small business-men on the boardwalk to integrate. The latter nearly all said they would in-tegrate, but "just that they didn't want to be the first. They wanted to do it all together, so they didn't stand out." Trouble was bad for business.[27] At the end of the first month they traveled to Highlander for a second retreat. Myles Horton refocused them by "posing the right questions." Half returned to work with the white poor, the other ten sent out literature and met clandes-tinely with concerned white ministers and professionals.[28] "By and large we didn't have any idea of what solid role we could play," recalled Sue Thrasher, a southerner on the project. "We weren't in a community. We couldn't oper-ate a Freedom School. We couldn't work for the Mississippi Freedom Demo-cratic Party." After talking to the ministers, and to the small business own-ers, the SNCC workers found whites so afraid that the only role left to SNCC people was the role of "white liberals just trying to talk to people and get some support." "We spent a lot of time sitting around talking about what we should do," Thrasher noted.[29]

Shirah and the four staff who stayed on decided to focus solely on the poor. "The important work to be done is with poor folks and not with mod-erates and liberals," they felt. "The white poor have the political need of de-cent jobs, housing, education, and health. The movement must go to them and help them develop their own leadership rather than demand that the moderates and the liberals fight their political battles for them." Both the populist and labor movements had collapsed in part due to racial conflict; therefore, SNCC workers saw it as "the responsibility of the freedom move-ment, before the threat of the movement to the white poor further increases, to include them in our efforts." Neither blacks nor poor whites constituted a majority in any state or in the South as a whole. They would look to white or-ganizers in SNCC, CORE, SDS, and the Hazard Kentucky project for staff. Sit-ting down to set goals in the fall of 1964, they hoped that at the end of three years, fully one-third of movement work in Mississippi would be with the "one third of really poor folks in the state who are white."[30]

Though tens of thousands of white Mississippians were indeed poor, SNCC found no good way to reach them. "The workers came back burnt out from the white community," Moses observed. "They couldn't survive. It was a wasteland. There were no supports there." Thrasher went back to Nashville to form the Southern Students Organizing Committee office, Pardun went back to start several counterculture institutions in Texas, and Hamlett and the Shirahs continued to try to find ways to work with poor and middle-class whites, but within the labor movement. By the time larger numbers of whites began to organize as a result of the civil rights movement at the end of the 1970s, "they were out of phase with the [Mississippi] Freedom Democratic Party, which had faded." Thus, Bob Moses recognized, the question of whites' role in the movement in 1964 to 1966 "continued to fester because there was no clear way out at this point."[31]

sNCC had also been less than successful at trying to work with whites in other capacities. The Southern Conference Educational Fund had given sNCC $13,600 between 1961 and 1964 to work with white southern campuses. sNCC hired Bob Zellner—who did this work for two years—followed by Sam Shirah, then Ed Hamlett. When the leadership of the Texas Democratic Coalition requested two black sNCC organizers to work with them in black communities in Texas—all expenses paid—sNCC declined. The Appalachian Committee for Full Employment asked for two black women organizers in early 1964: sNCC did not respond. "We have not been willing to experiment even in cases where little if any risk is involved," Hamlett concluded at Waveland. "Our record of 'cooperation' with white-dominated groups—dedicated in some cases to radical change in the system, has been a pretty damn sorry one." Furthermore, the sCEF money was not allocated to the purpose for which it had been given, "organizing Southern white students."[32]

The disarray in white sNCC staffers' public work was compounded by the personal difficulties blacks and whites experienced relating to one another during this period. Race became an issue not because of race per se, but because whites, though well-meaning, almost always had a much lower level of experience with racism, less sophistication in addressing racism, and not very strong skills compared to their black sNCC peers in getting African Americans to overcome internalized submission in the face of white power.

Working with sNCC (and CORE) forced black women, white women, black men, and white men to confront the difficulties and complications of interracial and intraracial intimacy. Sexuality could make a positive difference, breaking through another interracial barrier. But it also proved enormously complicated and sometimes explosive to live, day-in, day-out, in the midst of political struggle. White male volunteers were seen by some black parents as predators in relation to their daughters in the movement. Black parents had faced the trauma of their daughters being threatened, assaulted, and raped by white men for generations. Why were white volunteers from the North any different from southern white men, they wondered? As one black man later summed up, there was also the issue of black men who were "Muslims during the day, and integrationists at night." Black women and white women found this issue almost impossible to talk through in their day-to-day lives, though it dramatically impacted their relationships. As Alice Walker's deft exploration of this issue in *Meridian* notes, black women often felt their beauty, self-worth, and belonging threatened when black partners broke off with them and took up with white women. White women could face a "sex test" on the projects: if a white woman didn't sleep with a black man, did that mean he saw her as racist? Sometimes different expectations rubbed uneasily against one another: a white movement woman described one of the black Freedom Singers visiting Swarthmore as "very fast and . . . looking for girls to make out with him." When he later approached white Swarthmore junior Mimi Feingold, who was not interested in a relationship, Feingold felt that she might be perceived as racist if she turned him down. Her friend Charlotte Phillips encouraged her to "tell him exactly how you feel. . . . I think the most important thing for everybody involved is to be as honest and open as possible. I think we have to stop seeing ourselves in these situations as Representatives of the White Girl, trying to Do the Right Thing with a Negro boy." The result of that poor solution, she noted, "is not helpful to anybody." However, Phillips noted that she understood how difficult it was to be honest in those situations, when "we have to prove ourselves continually, both to people with whom we come in contact and to ourselves."[33]

Feingold was perplexed. How should she respond to the casual advances of a young black man who barely knew her? Vernon Grizzard, another friend, suggested she "make eyes right back, in an equally insincere manner." Regardless of race, Grizzard noted, many people had superficial sexual relationships of the "I-wonder-how-far-I-can-get" sort. While race complicated this interaction, and "we can't help being conscious of being white with most Negroes," he noted, young black men also faced a "very perplexing situation." Some white women sought to have their physical attractiveness validated by black men, and explicitly sought out black boyfriends. A strong machismo standard in some parts of the movement put enormous pressure on black men. Everyone felt confused. Just as in the world outside the movement, bad decisions made out of confusion or impulse could happen to anyone. "In any relationship that continues," Grizzard advised, "that first re-buff will lose all significance for the boy—if he really gets to know you at all, he'll find out why you acted as you did, and he'll see that it has nothing to do with race."[34] Everyone remained confused throughout much of this period on the issue of interracial sex, but it continued to be at the center of the tensions over the role of whites in the movement throughout the decade. When blacks or whites tried to address it openly, it often sounded like blaming a group of people, and discussion was cut off. Rather than put the burden for this situation on black men, as did many in the white press and in the academy, it would be more historically accurate to emphasize that no one group was to blame, everyone was baffled, young, and confused, and facing daily white terror. And given the surreal level of hostility, racism, and violence of the culture surrounding the movement, it is essential to pay historical tribute to the many loving intraracial and interracial relationships that survived within the movement.[35]

Thus by the end of 1964 and into early 1965, whites in SNCC still struggled to find a place to work that made sense, and increasingly needed to find more honest ways to relate to one another, and with their black peers. Bob Moses saw his commitment to antiwar organizing going on in this period at least partly as "a way of helping the white students get out of the civil rights movement."[36] In this period, no one in SNCC could figure out how to talk frankly and openly about race in "mixed" company. Or how whites should do organizing work. Or how to make sense of the explosive impact of some sexual relationships. When SNCC workers, black and white, tried to bring these topics out into the open in the period between the summer of 1963 and the spring of 1964, such candid discussion almost always got shut down. By the beginning of 1965, this strangulation of both professional options (how do we organize whites?) and personal candor (how do we deal with interracial issues inside of SNCC?) pushed some blacks to start avoiding whites. In some cases, this was subtle. At other times, it meant that black workers simply did not talk with their white friends. By mid-decade, some blacks in SNCC explored separatist or nationalist stances that were gaining momentum both nationally and internationally.[37] One white activist noted that when blacks stopped talking to their white peers, that was it. There was no more interracial conversation until the whites left. And with the exception of Bob and Dottie Zellner, all whites had left SNCC by December 1966. While some black SNCC staff avoided whites because of the questions white involvement raised, other black staff stopped talking to their white peers because their political self was changing. This need to assert self and obtain more power meant there was simply no room for whites in the same way. In other words, the interpretive framework a historian uses for framing personal or interior issues must include the fluid nature of these issues compared to other historical documentary evidence.

None of the whites in SNCC were shocked by black workers' desire to create their own space and their own organizations. In fact, whites like Mary King and Jane Adams tried to explain—during the 1960s and later—both the ideas of black separatism and (distinct from separatism) the ideas behind "black power for black people" to whites outside of the movement. Mary King wrote to her father in 1967 that "the demonic-Stokely-of-the-news-media has been one of the most ardent people in trying to keep the last whites from being driven out of SNCC," and she urged those who didn't understand black power "to understand how deeply hurt and alienated is Black America. We have got to try to understand the feelings *behind* Black rejection of white help." Black Power "was liberating and made perfect sense," Jane Adams, a Mississippi SNCC volunteer, later reflected. "I knew it had to happen. It was the same thing a little later when women's consciousness began[,] . . . you have to have your own space. That's part of undoing oppression." She returned north after realizing she could not overcome the fact that older African American women with master's degrees whom she greatly respected from rural areas of the state "would say 'Yes, Miss Jane' and 'No, Miss Jane.'"[38] Still, it is hard for historians to address the multiple realities such black and white SNCC workers experienced. The whites felt almost mute with frustration by other whites' ignorance of the historical realities which led inevitably to Black Power. They understood the need of their black friends for separate space. What they didn't necessarily understand was how one recognized these realities while at the same time acknowledging the grieving and sense of loss whites felt when losing their movement friends who were black. It is worthwhile to ask if white women understand these issues more clearly after the women's movement gave them a set of parallel experiences to compare to black separatism. In many cases, it remained difficult to create a context for—much less a history of—these issues even thirty or forty years after the fact, as the documentation from movement reunions illuminates. Even if they could have found an open, trusting context to examine these realities, the power dynamics in which they operated were not going away just through conversation. How does anyone "talk through" the implications of slavery, Jim Crow, and their legacies? As this crushing historical burden sat atop their shoulders, those in the movement often turned to the coping mechanism of evasion.

Evasion—between blacks and whites, among whites talking to each other, and among blacks talking to each other—strangled the interior culture of the movement. The end of "movement culture" came at different times for different people. In the end, the small-"d" democrats in the movement—black and white—betrayed one another through silence. In what proved to be a grave denouement, people lost the ability to say things to one another that were truthful. Still, it is possible to judge the quality of SNCC's democratic achievements in the mid-1960s by the depth of despair evident in the questions that surfaced in this period: Charles Sherrod—one of the pioneers of the interracial beloved community—later asked of this period, "[There are times when] I hate white people. Can you deal with me if I say that?" Casey Hayden and Mary King said, "[W]omen don't have equal decision-making power. Why not?" Jimmy Bolton, a black staffer, asked of a now nearly all-black staff: "Why won't the SNCC-that-is-now accept me for who I am?"[39] They were attempts to unbetray everyone in the movement they had known by ending the disloyalty of silence. Even when people asked the question, and many people responded by talking about "the problem," few were open to accept others' perspectives. Perhaps honest and open-minded conversation might have helped sustain the internal culture and allowed the organization to address head-on both internal and external challenges. Without candor, those challenges limited the ways that individuals and the organization could move forward.

Despite the failure of the Biloxi White Folks Project, the confusion of the 1964 to 1965 period, and the eventual collapse of SNCC's movement culture, most SNCC people maintained a lifestyle over the subsequent five decades that reflected the values of the movement. As SNCC staffer Martha Prescod Norman Noonan recalled, "The movement was a very important thing for me, I was with people who were like me, who woke up in the morning, and worried about whether the world would change or not." It was an orientation she felt "permanent, that I don't ever see myself changing. So I never felt that I left the movement. I don't see the time I spent raising a family as separate from anything else I was doing. To me, that was just what came at that time in my life and I raise my children according to the same principles." As one member of the New Left said, "I always lived communally until I had kids.

Then I lived communally with my kids."[40] Movement veterans continued to operate "as if"—as if more truthfulness, more candor, more respect, and ultimately more equality could already be lived in the here and now. It is worthy of note that they did so in a world that maintained few institutions to support this orientation.

SNCC workers "put their bodies on the line whenever some issue of justice was at stake," Robert Pardun recalled. SNCC's insistence that "participatory democracy was more than just simple democracy; it *can* mean that you work for a candidate," and hold him or her accountable once elected. "But it can also mean that if you see that a restaurant is segregated, that you just go there and integrate it. And if they arrest you, you just do it again. You just keep doing it until you make the point that you're trying to make: Participating in that decision-making, being willing to take personal responsibility for what you do, was an important step forward."[41] SNCC people refused to participate in an unjust system. It put them in a position of power rather than a position of victim. To do this took an enormous level of motivation. No one in SNCC was a loner: they were sustained by one another. In the first half of the 1960s, they lived and worked with each other in a way that "made each other feel safe" even though every day they were risking their lives. If we are to figure out *how* this movement grew powerful enough to break apart Jim Crow, we must understand how those relationships were created and maintained, as well as the reasons why some of them eventually felt apart.

## PANTHERS: BUILDING COMMUNITY, BECOMING COMMUNITY

In the 1970s, the Black Panther Party turned its focus to community organizing in Oakland, California. Weakened by the impact of COINTELPRO (FBI counterintelligence program) on the organization and internecine struggles, many chapters nationwide closed or were dismantled and hundreds of Panthers moved to California, which became known as the BPP's "Base of Operations." To achieve "community control" the Panthers would try to entrench themselves in Oakland, hoping that the city would become a model for grass-roots organizing and community activism all over the country. The Panthers began to focus on building their organization into a lasting institution and strengthening the comradeship between members was part of this process. Things such as health care, child care, and education were not just social justice issues or private needs that the Panthers were fighting to support in poor Oakland communities, they were also organizational matters.

The strengthening of the Panthers' community programs in this period cannot be appreciated without understanding that they were bolstered not just to serve the local community but to serve the organization and its membership as part of the local community. As such interior politics were central to community politics because the organization was supposed to mirror the society they wanted to create. It was an attitude that falls in line with sociologist Winifred Breines's observation that the New Left engaged in prefigurative politics, the move to "create and sustain within the live practice of the movement, relationships and political forms that 'prefigured' and embodied the desired society."[42]

Politics infused all areas of Party members' lives and the borders between workplace and home space, public and private were blurred. The Party promoted a collective structure to facilitate the total commitment of its membership. They attempted to meet the needs of its cadre for food, clothing, and shelter. They created a Health Cadre whose job included keeping track of ill comrades and children, and tracking epidemics of the flu and other contagious illnesses that could spread quickly in a collective living situation. This Health Cadre was tied to the Health Clinic created in 1971 in Berkeley to provide free medical attention, medication, referrals, sickle cell testing, immunization, prenatal instruction, first aid kits, and community health surveys. Doctors and other health care professionals volunteered their services.[43] The Panthers also created a free ambulance service.[44] They believed that by showing the community that "it is possible to receive professional, competent and, above all, preventative, medical help without paying any money for it," they were teaching "the people . . . to understand that as taxpayers they do not have to stand for the lackadaisical treatment given to them by county hospitals and other public health facilities."[45]

In many ways, the Black Panther Party was like a family. Agenda items for Central Committee meetings included comrades' appearance and clothing needs, interpersonal conflict, and the maintenance of cleanliness in work areas. The collective distribution of Panther funds to buy shoes and clothing for comrades was discussed at one meeting. A memo to central body members dated August 16, 1972 brought up the need for a dialogue on Planned Parenthood within the Party, policies for expectant mothers, creation of an infirmary, and teaching remedial reading and math skills. The organization tried to create an alternative model of living for their membership based on democratic and nonindividualistic values.

For many of these members the attempts to shed individualism, confront ingrained ideas about gender and sexuality, build genuine bonds of mutual trust and respect with comrades, and provide social services to both comrades and communities in need was one of the most politicizing experiences of Black Power. Being a BPP member was not just a commitment to a political ideal, an organization, and a community—it was also a commitment to each other. Panther Bobby McCall recalled: "We ate together. We slept together. We lived together. We did everything together like a family, like an organization should. . . . We were a bunch of disciplined, organized young brothers and sisters who were determined to uplift the black community. It wasn't no joke being in the Party. It might have been called a party, but it was no party. We had a lot of fun with each other because we loved each other. We had a lot of family affairs. We always celebrated each other's birthdays . . . in a big way. We didn't celebrate holidays but we did celebrate life with each other."[46] This collective apparatus undergirded the Panthers' political endeavors in the 1970s. One could argue that without understanding these human relationships and how they helped sustain the organization and its political work that it is impossible to understand the Panthers' trajectory in the 1970s.

The Oakland Community School (OCS), which provided a model for community-based education, illustrates how these new ways of interacting within relationships embodied the BPP's collectivist philosophy. The school began as the Intercommunal Youth Institute in 1971, a school program catering to Party members' children who sometimes faced harassment at school due to their parents' politics.[47] Oakland parents appreciated the academic rigor and progressive educational philosophy that the Institute provided and soon the student base of the school expanded. The Panthers renamed the Institute the Oakland Community School and moved into a larger building that became known as the Oakland Community Learning Center (OCLC). The OCLC hosted community events, housed the Son of Man Temple, and provided a space for classes and programs on dance, drama, adult education, and music.[48]

The Panthers' took a holistic approach to the school. School director Ericka Huggins noted that: "We find out, for instance, that a mother needs certain things otherwise she won't be able to get her child to school. So, we have a welfare rights referral system. There's a senior citizens program functioning here. Quite often, the grandparents and older guardians of the children are involved in the SAFE program. . . . There's a teen program, for the older brothers and sisters of the children. That's how it started."[49]

The Panthers created a collective environment where students and teachers lived and learned together. Students were grouped according to ability rather than age. Panther literature stated: "Our students participate in determining the policies that govern them. They criticize each other (and their instructors) in order to correct mistakes and mistaken ideas. If they violate the rules that they themselves helped to make, then they are criticized before the collective. All of this is done with the understanding that we criticize with love, never with hatred. Never are children called stupid, dull, or dumb. No one child is forced to make a better grade than another. There are no grades. There is no negative competition. There is only the competition that will produce enthusiasm and prove, through action, that our capabilities are endless."[50] The OCS became the Panthers' most visible and successful community survival program, earning a nationwide reputation for excellence in community-based education. The staff of twenty-seven full-time accredited teachers taught students art, music, science, Spanish, environmental studies, and physical education.[51] In the summer students participated in a structured program of trips, classes, and recreational activities.[52] By May 12, 1976, approximately 125 children attended the OCS.[53] (See OCS photo, p. 397.)

According to Huggins: "People from all over the globe acknowledged the school as not only a great alternative to public education but an amazing experiment in community and a guiding force in the lives of students. It was more than a school. It was a community within itself. . . . We cared for the total child."[54] Students participated actively in school administration through the Youth Committee, which planned activities as well as administered discipline among students. Parents could join a Parents Advisory Board, created in 1976 as a medium through which parents could be involved in the school administration and activities, as well as contribute to OCS fund-raising efforts.[55] Although the OCLC allowed the Panthers to create a core group of community supporters anchored by the parents of the children who attended the OCS, the school would close its doors in 1982. Outsiders and journalists at the time described its closure as a result of declining financial support in the wake of financial misconduct charges against Newton. The reality is much more complex: it involved not just finances but the decline of membership's commitment to the collective communal structure. By the late 1970s, members' commitment to collective child care, to the sacrifices of subsuming their individual goals and desires for things like higher education, and their criticism of leadership often pushed them out of the organization despite their commitment to community programs like the ocs.

The Panthers' struggle to actualize community inside and outside of their organization therefore must warrant closer attention. Their debates over the relationship between the organization and the community, and the relationship between personal and societal transformation, can reveal much about the challenges of making social change. Historian Robin Kelley has argued that there is both scholarly and *activist* value in recovering the "alternative visions and dreams" of historical movements "who proposed a different way out of our constrictions" because they challenge us to "tap the well of our own collective imaginations." He argues that "without new visions we don't know what to build, only what to knock down."[56]

America's democratic cultural heritage may be thin, but the experiences of those inside sncc and the Black Panthers made it thicker. For this reason, young people are hungry to know and understand more about all that happened inside these freedom movements—the complexities and ambiguities as well as the triumphs we celebrate every January (Martin Luther King Day) and February (Black History Month). And there is a huge range of issues that speak to young people. Some of the conflicts that emerged in sncc and the bpp are the same as those percolating in the global justice movement today. There were conflicts between those who felt it essential to create a democratic process within the movement and those who wearied of discussion, defined democracy as a product not a process, and were eager to act. There were those who spoke in the language of democracy but derived power through centralization and hierarchy. The question of how to define and actualize internal democracy in organizations lies at the heart of many of the internal struggles that contemporary movements face.

In the 1960s, movement people faced the perils of righteousness, where some people tried to be "more radical than thou." Always, sex and sexuality, drug use, and lack of tact or interpersonal skills could also easily derail movement activity. People argued the merits of armed self-defense versus armed revolution and compared both to the strategy of nonviolent direct action. On race, there were spoken and unspoken conflicts: some issues were possible to put into words but one didn't always have a shared context. Other issues were felt, and present, but people could not find ways to put them into words.

Movement "quality control" remained a major hurdle: organizers knew that they needed large numbers of recruits to create fundamental societal change, but what should they do when people joined who disregarded the movement culture of either SNCC or the BPP and consequently drove others away? How did one hold people accountable in a voluntary movement? COINTELPRO and other (local and state) law enforcement oppression shaped the internal dynamics of the movement, forcing people to choose between a security culture and an open movement culture. Finally, few if any young people in the movement separated their "professional" lives from their personal lives. The quality of one's daily life was thus entirely tied to the quality of movement culture one experienced on any given day. These factors combined to intensify the actions and reactions of many inside the movement.

## INSIDE OUT: WHY THESE STORIES ARE INVISIBLE

There appear to be a series of factors at work that keep many of the most knowledgeable and thoughtful activists from the 1960s quiet about the insides of the movement. One, people who do know the stories haven't yet found a context in which to share them. Two, historians rarely know what kinds of questions to ask. Three, even when the historians ask, activists within the movement don't want to tell tales out of school—it's too much like dictating which dirty laundry gets aired.

The very ways historians are trained to gather and assess evidence create difficulty with getting the interior movement culture into the public historical record. Very little of the evidence for how these conflicts played out can be corroborated, and even less is quantifiable, and that makes some professional journalists, historians, and other cultural commentators uncertain of how to tell the story—or even how to get the story. At times, to open this kind of dialogue can end the interview. The interviewer should be, after all, trying to get on tape who matters to this person and why. What people and experiences have shaped him or her the most? The following excerpt exhibits some of these risks. It is taken about two-thirds of the way through an interview Hogan conducted with a SNCC veteran in the late 1990s:

WH: But there is one part I want to get to before I completely wear you out, and
    if you have time and opportunity later, I'd like to follow up on areas where we
    haven't been able to get to cover. But the one piece that [another SNCC veteran]

told me to talk to you about, that is one of the strands of my work that I mentioned earlier. I'm going to set it up, a little bit here, so you can kind of take a break, and lean back. I'm going to try and create a new context. I've had some good response to these kinds of questions so far, but you have to kind of change the tone a little bit.

SNCC VETERAN: OK.

WH: What I've noticed, it comes from some work that I did before I became an academic. In the movement itself, in trying to figure out how social movements work or don't work, one of the things that is crucial is the quality of the relationships inside between people, and the three qualities that seem to stick out time and again are the degree to which they're able to one, trust one another, two, be candid, and three, maybe even be kind. The quality of those relationships on the inside [of the movement] is a kind of glue.

SNCC VETERAN: Yes.

WH: And that's what, to some degree, allows people to stay in these movements and continue in these areas, rather than just have a movement come together and then dissipate, not really gel or come together at all.

SNCC VETERAN: Yes. I'm glad you picked up on this. That's right.

WH: But the problem is that the relationships are filled with pain and difficulty as well as self-discovery, joy, and sharing. That kind of stuff really rarely gets into the history, for these reasons. Yet it seems to me that it has a huge effect on the movement itself, and how it moves forward or doesn't. So, if that brings forward anything from you, where you think, "Yes, I relate to that," I'd like to ask you to talk about whether you think that that thesis is useful or not. Again, what I'm driving for is to figure out what makes movements work, what contributes to their coming apart. This interior quality needs a lot more exploration, so my questions aren't very good, because—

SNCC VETERAN: No, they're perfect. Yes, it was absolutely crucial. The reason that my closest friends now, are the ones that I got in SNCC all these years later is because there was a way that we dealt with each other that made it safe. We felt safe with each other. For instance—I could not speak, I was shy, I was in awe of everybody. Even if I couldn't do it in the larger meetings, I felt safe enough in, say, the Freedom Houses, to have far ranging discussions, to say stuff. I felt that people had my back. I always felt that I could depend on people. It wasn't just the depending on—it makes it sound like that [exercise] where somebody stands up, you fall over, and everyone has to catch you. It was more—I thought they had my interests at heart. That's what it was. From the smallest little thing. . . . Nobody made me feel stupid. Part of that has to do with the kind of folks who get attracted to SNCC, I think, has to do with the culture of SNCC that Miss [Ella] Baker helped to form, because I never remember her saying to anybody—Now she could be very hard. She is not all sunshine and light. And I remember being scared to death of Miss Baker. . . .

In this case, the historian was lucky. Other times, a very similar approach meant that Hogan was quickly shown the door.[57] Here, the SNCC veteran continued to share valuable experiences that laid bare the disappointments, broken hopes, rituals, and triumphs that made the movement "simply the most important thing I had, or have, ever done." Of course, historians then have to decide how to contextualize this material, have to acquire permission to use it, and must find other sources to corroborate or further complicate the story line. The interviewer's personal history must be taken into consideration.[58] It is often uncomfortable, unfamiliar, time-consuming, and requires a command of detail that can bewilder. However, the resulting narratives may well be the marrow of democratic activity.

More historians can view themselves as midwives to interior freedom stories—conduits that allow stories to be told with little investment in how they turn out—rather than imagine themselves as parents deeply invested in molding and shaping stories as a reflection of historians' vision. In other words, scholars can help make interior movement politics visible by empowering activists to speak on their own terms and willfully stepping into the background. This is one way to level the power relationships between academics—who often have access to publishers, travel money, and are vested with authority to speak for themselves and for others—and movement activists who sometimes can't even speak for themselves. For some activists dropping out of school and being in SNCC or the BPP also meant alienation from family support systems and often an arrest record. When the movement was over, they had limited options and many still live in the wake of their experiences in terms of lack of financial resources, lack of formal education, and lack of pensions or good health care. This is especially true at the rank and file level.

It has been hard for rank and file members to exert "ownership" over the BPP's history in the face of leaders who command big bucks and have been given the authority to not only tell their story but to tell "the story." It is no surprise that in this context scholars, even well-meaning ones, are seen as yet another group trying to tell "the story" and profit from it. Exciting things happen when former activists are empowered to tell their own story. For example, former Panther Elbert Howard has self-published his memoirs. Many other Panthers have followed suit.[59] These books have popular appeal and sell quickly at Panther community events, reunions, and conferences but scholars usually don't access them due to widely disparate analytical quality and methodology. However, these books tell stories that often don't appear elsewhere. Although *Mother's Son*, Dallas Panther Skip Shockely's self-published memoir, freely blends fact and fiction, it raises interesting questions about the Panthers' health advocacy that scholars can pursue in other mediums and with more traditional sources. Scholars can support these attempts to democratize the process and welcome the insights that movement veterans feel comfortable sharing on their own volition and in their private spaces. They can help create the intellectual space for SNCC and Panther women to feel comfortable adding their stories to the historical record on their own terms. Yes, these efforts will be a lot less neat than the tightly packaged, peer-reviewed monographs that we professional historians produce where every ambiguity has been squashed, all of the blood has been neatly sopped up, and anything unquantifiable has been omitted. However, reading those stories can help us refine our questions and point us to different answers. We daresay that it will bring us closer to how things really were.

SNCC veteran Judy Richardson is an example of an activist who has taken the lead in telling her story and helping others find a voice as well. At an Organization of American Historians symposium in 2003 she noted that movement history is often wrong in its evidence (or lack of it). For more than thirty years she has brought documentary films to the public that tell the story of the movement from an insider perspective. Another SNCC veteran has created an eighty-page "slander panders" summary listing historians' inaccuracies on SNCC alone. Also, how history is conceptualized by many historians contributes to the silence: we have not clearly explained why the quality of relationships inside the movement matters. Finally, while Black Power activists have suffered from mainstream exclusion, the civil rights movement has become a kind of sacred ground among historians and the broader public alike. Some people fear that criticizing anyone in the civil rights movement is unpatriotic, akin to burning the flag or sitting during the Pledge of Allegiance, while others fear that Black Power was too nihilistic and racially chauvinistic to contain broader lessons about human rights. Yet sanctifying or condemning the movement veterans dehumanizes them. We must find ways to be critical *and* supportive, demanding *and* open-hearted. We have to acknowledge the sobering realities people faced inside the movement as well as their magnificent aspirations that reshaped the country and, indeed, the world.

The way people treat one another inside civic movements is at least as important to politics as the larger tactics or strategies adopted by the group as a whole. Indeed, interiority often significantly impacts the tactics and strategies adopted by the group as a whole. In SNCC, this can be seen in the way movement organizers recruited whites, the jobs they were given, and how interracial debates unfolded within this "seed of the new society." In the BPP, interiority illuminates the importance of communal child care and family formation as key institutions within the organization's structure. It reveals how the Panthers engaged the cultural and sexual politics of the time and understood sexuality in ways that challenged and reinforced patriarchy. The importance of interiority is a major theoretical point, and one largely missing from discussions about democratic politics. As oral historians, we must sometimes work outside the bounds of our training and our comfort level to push activists to reveal not just outcomes but processes. Analyzing organizational building blocks and the lived experiences of membership can help reveal how SNCC and the BPP become vehicles for societal and personal transformation. As students of social movements, we must begin to ask a series of questions about the interior social relations of movements that up until now have remained largely off the historical radar. Then, individually and in collaboration with our sources and other movement historians, we need to scrutinize what interior movement information is worthy of inclusion, and how to frame the information itself. Above all, we need to note the fluid nature of individuals' thinking and contextual shifts. There are certainly more than two ways to view any given interaction, event, or process. If we pay attention to such interior questions, however, young people interested in political activism and social transformation in their own era will have a much firmer democratic heritage on which to draw for inspiration and grounding.

## NOTES

1. The extant literature on the interior relationships within movements is fairly thin. Debbie Louis, *And We Are Not Saved: A History of the Movement as People* (Garden City, N.Y.: Doubleday, 1970) is an early example from a movement veteran that scholars have largely ignored. Others who focus on this issue include Bernice Johnson Reagon, "Women and Culture Carriers in the Civil Rights Movement: Fannie Lou Hamer," in *Women in the Civil Rights Movement: Trailblazers and Torchbearers, 1941–1965*, ed. Vicki L. Crawford et al. (Atlanta: Georgia State University Press, 1990), 203–17; Charles M. Payne, *I've Got the Light of Freedom: The Organizing Tradition and the Mississippi Freedom Struggle* (Berkeley: University of California Press, 1995); Jo Freeman, *The Politics of Women's Liberation: A Case Study of an Emerging Social Movement and Its Relation to the Policy Process* (I Universe, 2000); David S. Meyer, Nancy Whittier, and Belinda Robnett, eds., *Social Movements: Identity, Culture and the State* (New York: Oxford University Press, 2002); the entire ouevre of Wini Breines; and Francesca Poletta, *Freedom is an Endless Meeting: Democracy in American Social Movements* (Chicago: University Chicago Press, 2004). Curtis Austin's important work examines the role of violence and its use in the internal life in the Panther Party—particularly retention of power and control—in maintaining the organization. Curtis Austin, *Up Against the Wall: Violence in the Making and Unmaking of the Black Panther Party* (Fayetteville: University of Arkansas Press, 2008). However, scholars and activists largely disagree with how important this interior culture is, and how important it is for historians to record it. Though we recognize that we are far from any definitive conclusions here, we are hoping to open up a fresh discussion on the issue.

2. For an excellent sociological analysis of internal movement culture see Verta Taylor and Nancy Whittier, "Analytical Approaches to Social Movement Culture: The Culture of the Women's Movement," in *Social Movements and Culture*, ed. Hank Johnston and Bert Klandermans (Minnesota: Routledge, 1995), 163–87.

3. SNCC has held well-attended anniversary conferences between 1979–2010 and the BPP continues to commemorate its founding with annual events such as October 2009's Black Panther Party History month and nationwide reunions every decade. See: http://www.sncc50thanniversary.org/program.html and http://www.itsabouttimebpp.com/Reunions/reunions_index.html. Of course, reunions can also serve as a continuous space for divisions and cliques as well, which perhaps should have long been dead. The fact that divisions can carry over for so long speaks to the depth of some of these conflicts.

4. Conversation between Hogan and Nishani Frazier, June 11, 2010.

5. In Spencer's interviews with Panther women, for example, she found that showing too much interest in the paternity of children (which she was interested in from the standpoint of how the organization viewed motherhood and fatherhood differently

and how views on the institution of marriage changed) pushed up against the women's sense of their own personal space and potentially positioned Spencer as someone digging for dirt.

6. David Hilliard details his long romantic involvement with Presley in David Hilliard and Lewis Cole, *This Side of Glory: The Autobiography of David Hilliard and the Story of the Black Panther Party* (New York: Lawrence Hill Books, 2001).

7. Expulsions were noted in memos dated January 24, 1974, January 26, 1974 (David Hilliard's resignation), February 28, 1974, March 11, 1974 (June Hilliard), March 21, 1974, and May 15, 1974. See "Innerparty Memorandum," Box 14, Huey P. Newton Foundation Records, Green Library, Stanford University, California (hereafter cited as HPN Papers).

8. The idea of "movement culture" is one most vividly introduced to the literature on social movements in Lawrence C. Goodwyn, *The Populist Moment: A Short History of the Agrarian Revolt in America* (New York: Oxford University Press, 1978).

9. For her work on SNCC, Hogan is indebted to the scholarship of Clay Carson, Cynthia Griggs Fleming, Wini Breines, Ron Grele, Bret Eynon, Charles Payne, and John Dittmer, as well as their generosity in sharing source material.

10. Hogan would like to especially thank coauthor Robyn Spencer, as well as Emilye Crosby, Nishani Frazier, Todd Moye, Hasan Jeffries, Tim Tyson, Paul Alkebulan, Renée Afanana Hill, and above all, Dirk Philipsen. As Crosby pointed out, just because colleagues help hold us in check, that doesn't mean this is always collaborative, though that is a key aspect. It also means we need to recognize, publicly and in writing, that it is a collaborative, challenging, and contested terrain—and therefore we and our readers need to hold multiple perspectives in our heads at one time.

11. Payne, *I've Got the Light of Freedom*, 405–6.

12. Anonymous interview, not for attribution. The person's desire for anonymity reflects the challenges of researching internal movement culture. For other examples of the importance of candor and trust within the movement, see Wesley C. Hogan, *Many Minds, One Heart: SNCC and the Dream for a New America* (Chapel Hill: University of North Carolina Press, 2007), 13–55, 118, 127, 157–59, 229, 242.

13. Charles Sherrod, interview by Bret Eynon, May 12, 1985. Columbia Oral History Project, Butler Library, Columbia University, New York.

14. Darlene Clark Hine, "Rape and the Inner Lives of Black Women in the Middle West: Preliminary Thoughts on the Culture of Dissemblance," *Signs* 14 (Summer 1989): 912–20.

15. See Elaine Brown, *A Taste of Power: A Black Woman's Story* (New York: Anchor: 1993). For a feminist analysis of Brown's sexual politics see Farah Jasmine Griffin's review in *Boston Review*, March/April 1993. Available at http://www.bostonreview.net/BR18.2/griffin.html. Accessed on June 20, 2010.

16. Much has been written on the necessity and practicality of the "politics of re-

spectability" within the black freedom struggle. Some important work includes Evelyn Brooks Higginbotham, *Righteous Discontent: The Women's Movement in the Black Baptist Church, 1880–1920* (Cambridge, Mass.: Harvard University Press, 1994); Kevin Gaines, *Uplifting the Race: Black Leadership, Politics, and Culture during the Twentieth Century* (Chapel Hill: University of North Carolina Press, 1996); E. Frances White, *Dark Continent of Our Bodies: Black Feminism and the Politics of Respectability* (Philadelphia: Temple University Press, 2001); Corey D. B. Walker, *A Noble Fight: African American Freemasonry and the Struggle for Democracy* (Urbana: University of Illinois Press, 2008).

17. Bettina Aptheker, "Women and the FSM," from the panel, "The Story of the Free Speech Movement," 1984 Free Speech Movement Reunion. Accessed January 18, 2010 at www.fsm-a.org/stacks/b_aptheker84.html.

18. Steve McCutchen, interview by Spencer, October 11, 1997, tape recording, Oakland, California.

19. "Memo to: Huey From: Dale re: Women in the Perty [sic]," October 4, 1977, Folder: "Reports on Comrades," Box 14, HPN Papers.

20. Memo from Roni Hagopian, August 21, 1977, Folder: "Reports on Comrades," Box 14, HPN Papers.

21. "Memo To: The Servant From: Comrade JoNina Abron," Folder: "Reports on Comrades," Box 14, HPN Papers.

22. "Memo To: The Servant From: Arlene Clark," August 9, 1977, Folder "Reports on Comrades," Box 14, HPN Papers.

23. Robert Moses, interview by Clayborne Carson, March 29–30, 1982.

24. Robert Pardun, interview by Wesley Hogan, June 22, 1998, Los Gatos, California.

25. Robert Pardun interview.

26. Ibid.

27. Ibid.

28. Len Holt, *The Summer That Didn't End* (New York: William Morrow & Co., 1965), 138.

29. Sue Thrasher, interview by Ronald Grele, Columbia University Oral History Project. See also Sue Thrasher, "Circle of Trust," in *Deep in Our Hearts: Nine White Women in the Freedom Movement* (Athens: University of Georgia Press, 2000), 233–36. Locales outside the Deep South often provided more opportunities for white antiracist organizing. For example, see Tracy K'Meyer's recent book on Louisville, *Civil Rights in the Gateway to the South* (Louisville: University Press of Kentucky, 2009); Thomas J. Sugrue, *Sweet Land of Liberty: The Forgotten Struggle for Civil Rights in the North* (New York: Random House, 2008); and Patrick D. Jones, *The Selma of the North: Civil Rights Insurgency in Milwaukee* (Boston: Harvard University Press, 2009).

30. Holt, *The Summer That Didn't End*, 140.

31. Robert Moses, interview by Carson.

32. Ed Hamlett, "sncc's Relationship to White-Dominated Organizations (Exclusive of the NAACP), n.d. [November 1964?], Mary King Papers, State Historical Society of Wisconsin, Madison, WI (hereafter cited as SHSW).

33. Alice Walker, *Meridian* (New York: Harvest Books, 2003); Charlotte Phillips to Mimi Feingold, June 26, 1963. Miriam Feingold Papers, SHSW.

34. Vernon Grizzard to Mimi Feingold, June 29, 1963, Frame 259, Reel 1, Miriam Feingold Papers, SHSW.

35. On interracial relationships in SNCC, see, for example, Kwame Ture's beautifully crafted memoir, Stokely Carmichael, with Ekwueme Michael Thelwell, *Ready for Revolution: The Life and Struggles of Stokely Carmichael (Kwame Ture)* (New York: Scribner, 2003) and Penny Patch's poignant essay, "Sweet Tea at Shoney's," in *Deep in Our Hearts*, 131–70. Such important memoirs allow corroboration of oral testimony, although they also illustrate some of the difficulties of relying on one person's vision alone. Bringing multiple accounts together allows historians to see activists' varying lenses, but also the ways memoirs may gently gloss over examples that in other accounts are very raw and personal.

36. Robert Moses, interview by Clayborne Carson.

37. Ibid.

38. Mary King to Poppa, June 21, 1967, and Mary King to Bishop Lloyd C. Wicke, August 1, 1967, Mary King Papers, SHSW. Adams, interview by Ron Chepesiuk, *Sixties Radicals, Then and Now: Candid Conversations with Those Who Shaped the Era* (Jefferson, N.C.: McFarland, 2007), 64.

39. Charles Sherrod, transcript, "A Fifteen Year Perspective on Progress in Race Relations, 1964–1979," Jackson, Miss., October 30, 1979. Folder 2, Mississippi's "Freedom Summer" Reviewed Papers, SHSW; Casey Hayden, speech for panel on "Feminists and Women: Their Roles, Rights, and Opportunities During the Movement," Jackson State University, Jackson, Mississippi, 1995, paper in the author's possession; Jimmy Bolton to Personnel Committee, March 9, 1965, Frame 689, Reel 1, SNCC Papers.

40. Martha P. Norman, interview by Eynon and Fishman; Jeff Jones, interview with Ron Grele, October 24, 1984, New York. Both available at the Columbia Oral History Project.

41. Robert Pardun interview.

42. Wini Breines, *Community and Organization in the New Left, 1962–1968: The Great Refusal* (New Brunswick, N.J.: Rutgers University Press, 1989), 6.

43. "Budget, 1971," Folder: "Black Panther Party No-Profit Corporations Including Black United Front," Box 34, HPN Papers.

44. Black Panther Party, ed., *The CoEvolution Quarterly* 3 (Fall 1974): 1.

45. Ibid., 22.

46. Bobby McCall, interview by Spencer, October 14, 1997, tape recording, San Francisco, California.

47. Michele Russell, "Conversation with Ericka Huggins. Oakland, California, 4/20/77," p. 17, 20, Box 1, HPN Papers.

48. Black Panther Party, ed, *The CoEvolution Quarterly*, Issue No. 3, Fall 1974.

49. Michele Russell, "Conversation with Ericka Huggins. Oakland, California, 4/20/77," p. 17, Box 1, HPN Papers.

50. "General Articles. Re: Youth Institute," Box 48, HPN Papers.

51. February 1976 article, Folder: "OCS Brochure," Box 4, HPN Papers.

52. "July 1977 Corporate Overview EOC," Folder: EOC, Box 4, HPN Papers.

53. Folder: "Montclair Article," Box 5, HPN Papers.

54. Folder: "OCS Brochure, Ericka Huggins as a member of the county education board, Trustee Area 6," Box 4, HPN Papers.

55. "July 1977 Corporate Overview EOC," Folder: EOC, Box 4, HPN Papers.

56. Robin Kelley, *Freedom Dreams: The Black Radical Imagination* (New York: Beacon Press, 2003), preface, ix.

57. Negative responses include: people responding in a self-aggrandizing way unsupported by peers or the written record, people who lie, people who follow the conventional narratives even though their own experience belies it, and people who simply will not answer.

58. On written corroboration and the validity of memories, see Trevor Lummis, "Structure and Validity in Oral Evidence," *International Journal of Oral History* 2, no. 2 (1983): 109–20. For some excellent, brief pieces that examine the complex issues raised by what oral historians call "reflexivity," see Valerie Yow, "'Do I Like Them Too Much?' Effects of the Oral History Interview on the Interviewer and Vice-Versa," *Oral History Review* 24, no. 1 (1997): 55–79; Belinda Bozzoli, "Interviewing the Women of Phokeng," in *The Oral History Reader*, ed. Robert Perks and Alistair Thomson (New York: Routledge, 2006), 155–65. For a more extended examination of these issues, see Valerie Yow, *Recording Oral History, Second Edition: A Guide for the Humanities and Social Sciences* (Lanham, Md.: Altamira Press, 2005).

59. Some examples of self-published books by Panthers: Elbert "Big Man" Howard, *Panther on the Prowl* (Self-published); Steve D. McCutchen aka Lil' Masia, *We Were Free for a While: Back to Back in the Black Panther Party* (Baltimore: Publish America, 2008); Skip Shockley, *Mother's Son* (Xlibris Corporation, 2009).

EDITED BY EMILYE CROSBY

# That Movement Responsibility

## An Interview with Judy Richardson on Movement Values and Movement History

**N**ote: This interview text is drawn from several in-depth interviews with Richardson, conducted by Emilye Crosby, between July 2005 and July 2007. The interviews have been consolidated, organized, and edited for clarity and readability. A brief introduction precedes the interview.

### INTRODUCTION

I first met Judy Richardson in spring 1999 in what might be considered typical SNCC fashion. I went to the George Eastman House in Rochester to hear four former SNCC staffers, including Richardson, talk about their photographic work with the organization. I was with a long-time SNCC friend, Worth Long, who was scheduled to speak the next day at Geneseo. After the presentation, Worth invited his SNCC friends to join him and all four immediately agreed. In exchange for lunch, they generously spent most of the afternoon with my students—talking about their work as movement activists, cultural documentarians, artists, and organizers. Richardson returned to Geneseo in spring 2005 for a more formal lecture and it was during this visit that we began the conversations that led to the interviews in this book.

It isn't really surprising that Judy agreed so quickly when I asked if I could interview her. Over the years, she has been extremely generous with her time, granting interviews and discussing projects with a seemingly endless succession of students and scholars. When we began our interviews, I didn't have any "product" in mind. I was primarily focused on recording her stories and increasingly absorbed by our in-depth and wide-ranging conversations. After several multi-day interview sessions, however, I began to think more about "doing something" with this material. I found Judy's experiences and perspective compelling and thought they could be valuable to others. When I raised the possibility, Judy didn't say no, but she also wasn't entirely sure. Although she never said it this way, I think she sees giving interviews as being about the history, while she was concerned that publishing an interview would put too much emphasis on her, possibly implying a sense of self-importance that she didn't feel and that she considered at odds with the movement values she absorbed and embraced with SNCC.

This same attitude is reflected in Judy's approach to her lectures and workshops on the movement. She never set out to do public speaking and was initially terrified to speak in front of, as she says, any group larger than three people. And yet, just as Judy's movement work brought her into *Eyes on the Prize*, her work on *Eyes* brought her into other ways of documenting and teaching movement history. When a lecture bureau called Blackside looking for someone who could talk about *Eyes*, the call was eventually referred to Judy, and shortly thereafter, Henry Hampton (Blackside's head and founder) asked her to take on the newly created position of education director. Richardson reflects that, among other things, this was a way for Hampton to keep her on payroll at a point when neither she nor Hampton saw her as a filmmaker and there wasn't any other obvious role for her in the company. Over the next few years, as Blackside became one of the premier documentary production companies in the nation, she moved back and forth between education work and production. (For example, she served as coproducer on Blackside's 1994 PBS documentary *Malcolm X: Make It Plain* for "The American Experience.")[1]

By the time Richardson left Blackside and began working with Northern Light Productions, she was a filmmaker. Although she has worked on a wide range of projects, movement history remains her passion, and in recent years she produced a one-hour PBS documentary, *Scarred Justice*, on the 1968 Orangeburg Massacre (S.C.), and all the videos for the National Park Service's Little Rock Crisis Visitor Center. In addition to her lectures, workshops, and filmmaking, Richardson continues to find many ways to document and share movement history. One of the most significant undertakings is the book *Hands on the Freedom Plow: Personal Accounts by Women in SNCC*. Richardson and five coeditors (all women who were on SNCC staff) have devoted considerable time over the past decade to this collection, which brings together contributions by fifty-two SNCC women.[2]

When Richardson makes presentations about the movement, she tends to talk very little about herself. Instead, she emphasizes the activism and potential of ordinary people—during the movement and today. She highlights her colleagues in SNCC and the local women and men who worked with and supported them. She draws extensively on her own study of the movement, sharing quotes and stories from a wide range of people. Holding up magazine covers and newspaper clippings, she tells stories about the work SNCC folk have continued to do since the movement, in part because she is so proud of their accomplishments, but also to make the point that so many of them have continued to struggle, and struggle effectively, for racial justice (as organizers, teachers, medical personnel, writers, artists, and more). She also makes it a point to address contemporary issues, even when they are uncomfortable. As she notes, it would undoubtedly be more fun and probably less stressful to focus only on the movement, telling glorious uplifting stories. And yet she feels a responsibility, one she attributes to the values of the movement, to use her talks to make connections between past and present, to draw attention to current injustices. Because of this, she often tackles challenging and contested topics like affirmative action, economic inequality, and unjust wars.

Watching Judy present you would never know that she struggled with public speaking or was terrified to stand in front of an audience. She exudes warmth and energy. Moreover, it is obvious that she is completely engaged, not only in what she's sharing, but in the comments and discussions that emerge from her presentations. This passionate interest in movement history and teaching was the basis for our conversations and collaboration. It is also evident when Judy attends conferences; she joins in fully—listening, discussing, considering. I first saw this at the March 2006 Local Studies Conference I organized at Geneseo. Richardson was among the keynote speakers, but her participation went well beyond that and students were especially captivated by the way she moved back and forth between the roles of teacher and learner, historical actor and documentarian.

For example, when Charles Payne addressed a debate that had recently flared on a SNCC listserv about perceptions of Freedom School teachers in the 1964 Summer Project, Richardson responded with her own memories and opinions about the scholarship. She has commented since that hearing Payne's analysis—of the ways some perceptions have been privileged over others—expanded her view, allowing her to see the issue from another angle. (See chapter 10 in this volume for a transcript of Payne's talk.) Students were also intrigued to learn that Richardson was among the SNCC organizers involved in the Lowndes County, Alabama, movement, the subject of Hasan Kwame Jeffries's research and conference talk. One student observed that in realizing this, he was "struck by how alive" movement history is. (He also reflected on the fact that the conference was organized, in part, around the actions taken more than forty years before by people who were then his age.)³ During the discussion following one of the first panels, Richardson mentioned "movement values." Payne referred back to that moment in his closing talk, first asking the audience to define what "movement values" meant to them and then asking Richardson to respond. (See chapter 14 in this volume for a transcript of Payne's conversation with conference participants.) Student Joseph Zurro later wrote, "[M]y heart raced a little because the way that she spoke seemed, in some ways, to be how I felt. Now, it's very easy for me to want to align my thoughts with those of a movement legend, but it's true! Judy Richardson said that for her the Movement was something that was 'very personal.' . . . What I thought I heard was that it was more about human-to-human interactions . . . and about applying all of your own good virtues each day and at all times."⁴

Another student commented that Richardson's keynote, which she used to read accounts by a number of SNCC women from an early version of *Hands on the Freedom Plow*, "infused all that we have been reading, and talking about in class, with such a vibrant, human voice that was truly a privilege to experience." After summarizing some of what she learned from the individual stories (including the importance of personal ties and the ways these women defined success in terms of their experiences and their communities), she concludes: "[B]y humanizing these true leaders of the movement, Richardson helped to further develop my understanding of just how critical local studies are."⁵ One student saw a connection between the way Richardson approached her keynote and what she had been learning in class about Ella Baker and the organizing tradition. "It was a great idea on her part to include and intertwine the many stories told by various SNCC members and other people in the movement. I think in this way, she understood that her story alone isn't the only valuable thing. . . . If you look at it in a symbolic way, you could say that she, like the movement, is not just a 'one person show,' but [it was] a group effort and the work of many people, not just one."⁶

In the interview that follows, Judy offers her view of what's important about the movement (including why interpretations matter) and reflects on what she tries to convey in her talks and workshops (including some of the themes that caught students' attention at the Local Studies Conference). We get a sense, too, of how her years in the movement (and those "movement values") remain central to her life. As she talks about how she approaches all of these efforts to document and share movement history—filmmaking, teaching, editing *Hands on the Freedom Plow*—we get important snapshots of the movement. We also get a sense of Judy, her passion and commitment, her perspective and insights. Like my students, I greatly enjoy hearing Judy speak. Even more, though, I value her openness and her willingness to question, to consider, to search for ways to explain and communicate. She wants people to know about the movement, not simply to relive or celebrate these experiences that were so central to her life, but because she believes knowing about the movement is crucial for today and tomorrow. For her, this is true of the high ideals *and* the nitty gritty of organizing; it includes everything from the messiness and the losses (whether personal or political) to the joy of community and the power of struggle. And while there is much we can learn from studying the movement, Judy emphasizes that, at its most basic, it teaches us that we must each take responsibility. And whether alone or with others, we must each find a way to act on what we believe.

## INTERVIEW

EMILYE CROSBY (EC): I know that you do teacher development workshops and speak to college audiences and other groups, especially for King Day. What are some of the things that you try to convey to your audiences?

JUDY RICHARDSON (JR): What I'm trying to get across are some essential things. One, that it wasn't just Dr. King. And that's usually how I close it. That the movement is folks just like those of us in this room. It's our cousins, our uncles, our church people, our fellow students. And if we don't know that it's people just like us, *just like us*, who did the movement, we won't know that we can do it again, and then the other side wins. So, it's primarily that. And secondly, if we do nothing, nothing changes. Now, I mentioned that to you earlier and you rightly said, "In fact, it can change and get worse," which is true. So, if you do nothing, it either stays the same or gets worse, particularly if you are a person of color, or unempowered, or poor, or in any way disadvantaged. And I don't mean you got to just struggle, struggle, struggle all your life. But you got to be aware that somewhere in this, you got to keep doing *something*. It can be a tutorial. 'Cause I keep saying to students, "Look, it may not be movement stuff. It may be you're doing a tutorial, and in that tutorial you do what we used to do in the Freedom Schools. You're not just doing reading and writing, you're talking about, 'Well, this is the Constitution, how would you change it to make it more equitable? How would you change it so that it works more for unempowered people?'" It's always thinking, I'm not going to use "outside-the-box," but thinking in a different way from the way people generally structure stuff.

Now, and the other thing I try to do is show them that it's not this quick thing. So, even in *Eyes*, you get this sense that you're having these protests in Selma and then in a few days you've got twenty thousand people marching across the Pettus Bridge in Selma. And it never happened that way. So particularly young people who are trying to organize, I will get them coming up after a speech on a campus, and they'll say, "You know it's only I and my two friends who come to meetings." And, I said, "Honey, first of all, if everybody who says they were in the movement, were in the movement, we'd be free now. But the other part of that is you need to understand, we shortened the length of time it took to get things moving in *Eyes*. We speeded stuff up. It doesn't take place in real time."

When I was in organizing in Cordele, southwest Georgia, I'd have weekly "mass" meetings. There were maybe four people in that mass meeting for a good two, three months. It was I, my coworker from the community, and her mother. And I think her uncle might have come once or twice, but I can't remember. The only reason I knew it was having an effect was because somewhere in there, within those, I guess two months, there was a police brutality case that had gone up, which had always been pro forma. Well, my coworker and her mother asked me to do up leaflets because I had a mimeograph machine in the office. And so I did up leaflets and they distributed them. They said you should not come to the session, to the courthouse. They distributed them, they went, they obviously organized the community, and they packed the courtroom. It had never happened before.

So, part of what I say to people, to young people, particularly, who are wondering how come it's only the same four people in their meetings, that's the way it was in the movement, too. But, you never know how that word is spreading and you never know when it's going to ignite something. You never know when it's gonna come to fruition. But again, if you do nothing, there's nothing to come to fruition, so you got to do something. So, yeah. They have this, this imagined kind of time span where things happen quickly. *Eyes* helps feed into that, but it is not true. So, you always have to say, "Look, the reality that you're dealing with—in that sense, anyway—is no different from what we were dealing with." But I also acknowledge that it *was* a very different time. I let them know that I don't think that what we're in now is the same as it was in 1960 or 1964. But, what I'm hoping they get is that there are certain movement principles and certain ways of working and organizing—certain tools that can facilitate the work that they're doing or that they might want to do—to help get them started and might sustain them and the communities they are organizing.

Movement people will sometimes say, "You young people just aren't doing diddly squat and da da da." Young folks don't need to hear that. What they need to hear is, this is how we did stuff. This is how we got started. These were the difficulties that we had. And not try to romanticize that. Now when I say romanticize, I don't mean that you don't talk about the glory of the movement, 'cause it was absolutely glorious to me. And it was a time that I felt extremely alive and, so, in some ways maybe I romanticize it too. But not to the point where you gloss over the difficulties or the failings of the movement. You want to acknowledge that as well.

Also, I always talk about the fact that we're not getting beat over the head just to sit down next to white people. That's real crucial. That we all— meaning the movement and local people even before the movement comes into a community—see it as, just, we have the same rights as every other American. So if we want to go into this lunch counter and sit wherever we want to, we should be able to do that. And voting is a factor of citizenship. So, it's mainly about being able to exercise rights as *Americans* that every- body else is exercising. And also economic equity, so I always put that in.

EC: Is there a certain point in the movement at which you begin to envision something that's actually different than the rights that people already have?

JR: Oh, interesting. Not, truthfully, not usually in the presentations I do.

EC: So, that's not something you address in the presentations. Is that some- thing you experienced as part of the movement?

JR: Yes, certainly. Good point. As far as the movement, I think my assumption was that you were gonna have the world that we talked about in the movement. Which was that people really wouldn't . . . want. It starts to sound like I'm about to do, go into Marx or something, which I really have never understood be-

Figure 27　Judy Richardson speaking to students at suny Geneseo, March 2005. Photograph by Ron Pretzer, courtesy of suny Geneseo.

cause I don't read political tracts. But there was a sense that if you're gonna do a day's work, you're supposed to get more than a dollar a day or two dollars a day. That's the reason I talk about the economic inequity and talk about: what does it mean to have ceos getting three hundred and four hundred times the wage of an average worker in their company? What does that mean?

ec: Some people talk about the Beloved Community. Did that mean anything to you in sncc?

jr: There was certainly a sense that we took care of one another, that we respected one another's opinion, that you never called somebody stupid. People did argue. They argued vociferously. But there really was a fundamental respect for other people and their opinions and that was important. That's something I carried with me.

ec: One of the things you said is that when you talk to students, you want to convey something of how wonderful the movement was and important, but also, not gloss over the difficulties. Do you have examples of the difficulties?

jr: Mmmm. Yeah. One of the things is that I don't think we realized how long it was gonna take. I think that I really did believe that once we got voting rights and got more black folks in power and got public accommodations, that it would just not be as difficult. Not that all the problems would be solved, just that it would not be as difficult. And I think it never occurred to me, for example, how getting black faces in positions of power—as somebody said, "black faces in high places," that *really was not gonna get it*. I mean, humph, there's Clarence Thomas, who's probably one of the worst. Well . . . among the worst.

EC: Are there some common assumptions that you confront, from college students or teachers?

JR: There's this idea that it's not a whole lot of black resistance before the Montgomery Bus Boycott. The civil rights movement just starts. That's a real big thing. It starts. With Rosa Parks. Nothing happens before then.

And there is always this assumption that it's just about integrating facilities, that the movement is just about that one thing. And it usually comes out in—"I had no idea that you all were working for economic equity." Because I usually read from the SNCC speech at the March on Washington which talks about the difference between a maid making a dollar a day in the home of a family making $70,000 a year. And I talk about SCLC organizing the Poor People's Campaign. And usually there's an anger that comes, particularly from black kids. This one black student said it publicly. Sometimes they'll come up to me, but this one, she said it in the audience. She said, "How come I didn't know all of this?" And they get mad, really mad. And she said, "I went to the best"—and that's the thing. She said, "I went to the best schools. Nobody told me about this."

Another misconception is they think it was all men. Even now. They really do think it was not only just Dr. King, but . . . just men. That's one of the reasons I became involved in *Hands on the Freedom Plow*, which is an anthology of SNCC women's writings and oral histories, which we solicited, collected, and edited over a period of, God, over twelve years.[7] Now when we first started it, Jean Wheeler Smith talked to me about bringing a team together, an editorial group. I will say that I think Jean was more concerned with whether there were white people on it than I was. But, I'm glad we did it that way. [*laughter*] So we had this group of six women as coeditors. In some ways *Hands* was an answer to *Deep in Our Hearts*, an anthology of white women's movement stories. Because our sense was that there needed to be something that represented SNCC women and that incorporated black

women and local women, particularly southern local women. So when we
first started—way back in '95, I think, is when we sent that first solicitation out—we sent it to a list of about 100 people. And in that solicitation,
we said we wanted stories that you've been telling your children, max thirty
pages. But we only want to include those who were based in the South for a
prolonged period of time. And we did that because we didn't want to have
mainly a lot of the 1964 Mississippi Summer volunteers. We wanted people
who were really integral to the work that SNCC was doing, and could represent it. So we asked for these stories and then when we started getting stuff
in, we realized that some folks were not gonna take the time to do this. So
Faith Holsaert went down and did oral histories in southwest Georgia. Dottie did an oral history with Annie Pearl Avery. I did an interview with Gloria
Richardson. And Jean Smith did the oral history with Mrs. Victoria Gray.

So one of the reasons for doing this was 'cause I kept getting this thing
with Stokely. And I got this from a scholar when I spoke at Rutgers in 2007.
He was a scholar, black scholar, and he said something in introducing our
panel that reflected the Stokely quote. You know, Stokely saying at Waveland, laughingly saying, "Ha, ha, ha, the best position for a woman is prone."
Now, the context for this quote is really important. This was at a point when
everybody in SNCC is doing position papers. He's being Stokely. Mary King
has already said in her book, "It was a joke!" Everybody took it as a joke.
And so to hear *this* from a black male scholar *in 2007* was—So then Courtland Cox, who was on the panel, too, got up to present and he starts talking
and then he said, "And then about that Stokely comment," and he turns to
me and pauses. And I said, "Don't worry, I got it covered." And everybody
laughed. And I did when it was my turn to present.

But part of it with *Hands* was to say, we were not this little submissive
group of women, which is how we often get framed now as SNCC women, because of Sara Evans and the so-called Stokely quote and how the white wom-
en's movement had sometimes portrayed this.[8] And we never felt unempowered. We never felt powerless. What comes through in these narratives is that
these women—and there are fifty-two of us coming from everywhere, so it's
not like we're just selecting and cherry-picking certain people. We *all* felt empowered, and for many of us, felt the most powerful that we have ever felt.
Now, I will say, how we saw that, sometimes, was affected by whether we were
white or black. Because whether we were white or black determined, sometimes, whether you went into the field, whether you were gonna endanger the

life of some black man by being there. There were a lot of reasons why white women didn't go into the field, were not sent into the field. And that's what's so wonderful about Casey Hayden's contribution to the book. She's very clear about the fact that she feels powerful throughout. And she understands why she's not supposed to go into the field, because it's gonna get some black man killed. And that she never feels that her project, her ideas, and her concepts are in any way devalued. And in fact they are very valued, so you have white women who really do see their time in SNCC as just amazing. And others who may have some problems with it. Yeah. So I guess part of it was, we wanted to hopefully end, forever, that conception of submissive little SNCC woman. No, I'm sorry. Not just submissive, oppressed. Oppressed SNCC women. Yes.

EC: Do you have a sense that women in SNCC did have less visibility—

JR: Oh gosh yes. Absolutely. Yeah. They were like, not there in the popular culture or the history. You didn't hear about Ruby Doris. I think about, in *Eyes on the Prize.* I often point out, in the Freedom Riders section, that Ruby Doris is in the paddy wagon footage. And I say to audiences, "That's Ruby Doris Smith Robinson, she was SNCC's Executive Secretary." And then afterward I explain who she is and that she did thirty days jail-no-bail in Rock Hill, S.C., and what she comes out of. So women were not seen as a presence within the SNCC history, and, yeah, we wanted the reality of that leadership to come through.

EC: What do you think are some of the most significant themes coming out of the book?

JR: Mmmm. Well, one thing is the sense of power that they had in the organization. The sense of power they felt they had, not as, necessarily, "leaders," but as activists, who were women, but who were activists within the organization. So this sense of power. I think you get also the sense of being preyed upon by white men in the communities where they grew up. And that comes out in southern black women's pieces. Certainly Bernice Johnson Reagon and Joann Christian. The role that family and community has in making them who they were and giving them the grounding to want to be part of this movement. The sense of things that had happened in their own community, like lynching. You get a history, you get a real sense of resistance in these black communities from these stories—even before the movement comes. But then what happens to some of those who resist and how the community has to get them out of harm's way, and send them to Chicago or wherever. Within the white women, you also get a sense that they also feel that have found a community. Which is why, for some of them, it is so hurtful when they can no longer be part of that.

Certainly self-defense is strong. That's everywhere. That's in Annie Pearl Avery's. That's in Joann Christian's. That's throughout. To the point, I remember that when Taylor Branch was nice enough to read the initial manuscript of *Hands*. And this was several years ago, when we had done a first edit, and it was unwieldy and probably 800 pages. He read it all and was so helpful! So he called me and we had like an hour-long conversation, probably over an hour. And he was going through the pieces that he thought were better than others and said if we wanted an entrée into Simon and Schuster, his publisher, he would certainly give that entrée. But then he said to me, and he said it a couple of times, that this self-defense thing was troubling. And then, when it came to the third time, I said, "Well, you know Taylor, though, that was the reality of the movement." And he said, a little wistfully, "Well, yeah, I know, but where does that lead?" But self-defense is definitely another through line, a theme that comes out of *Hands on the Freedom Plow*.

EC: So he thought that you should downplay that in the book? Edit it out?

JR: He never said that. See, that's what's interesting. He just said it was unfortunate. "It's unfortunate."

EC: And can you say a little bit more about your understanding of why he thought it was unfortunate?

JR: Because he's very much philosophically nonviolent, that's where his heart is. He loves the Nashville movement. He loves Beloved Community. He loves philosophical nonviolence. He's a nice guy and he's just personally uncomfortable with this whole idea of self-defense, and the only problem with that is that therefore, he does not include that very important piece of the movement in his narrative. And so people really do get a sense from his books that everybody is, during the "good movement" before '66, that they are philosophically nonviolent. And so it really misinterprets the movement in that way.

Prathia Hall has a wonderful piece about nonviolence in *Hands*, as a matter-of-fact. Prathia was very religious. Her mother and father had a church in Philadelphia. Prathia, before she died, had taken the Martin

Luther King Chair in the School of Religion at Boston University. And Prathia, in her piece in *Hands*, talks about being in this meeting during the Selma March that had a lot of SCLC people in it. And she said the whole issue of nonviolence came up, because folks were talking—after the horror of "Bloody Sunday"—about, "We want to go get some guns." And she said, she got so mad, because the SCLC people, she said, really did a kind of, not hijacking. It was manipulation. What SCLC folks said was, "If you can't be nonviolent, you can't be part of the movement." And she found that so horrible, even though she was philosophically nonviolent. But she said, "How can you say to somebody, after what has just happened, that you are not worthy of the movement if you can't espouse philosophical nonviolence?" And she just found that so abhorrent. And so she put that in her piece in *Hands*.⁹

EC: What are some of the other things you think are important about the movement that you emphasize—

JR: Sometimes in my talks I mention the time, in Winona, Mississippi, in 1963, where Fannie Lou Hamer, Annelle Ponder, and several other civil rights workers are arrested and beaten in jail. I talk about how Annelle is beaten bloody and how the jailor wants to be called "sir" and she won't say "sir." When Annelle comes out, the people who've come to get her out of jail look at her bloated face from the beating and somebody says, "Annelle, are you okay?" And when I first get to the Atlanta office, at some point, I see this photo of her face all beaten up. So, the folks getting her out of jail say, "Are you okay?" And she says, "Freedom!" When Nelson Mandela gets out of prison I think about these four people. There's no comparison—Mandela twenty-four years on Robbin Island and these four—plus Larry Guyot who gets arrested the next day when he goes to try to get them out—in a Winona jail. But what has happened is that if you continue to resist oppression, you sometimes become stronger than those who seek to oppress you. And that is what was similar in both of those cases.

So, I usually will talk about that and then I end usually with a quote from Melba Patilla, one of the Little Rock Nine. She mentions, in the first series of *Eyes on the Prize*: "There are times when I wondered if I was human." She talks about how they turned the water to scalding in the girls' locker room and stuff like that. And she says, "Sometimes I wondered, am I, am I less than human? And what's wrong with me?" 'Cause she's calling it back onto herself as a child. And then she just decides she's got to mellow out and she's got to find the strength in herself. And that survival is day-to-day and she finds the endurance and the strength to survive even the horrendous trials that they put her through in Little Rock. That is always, no matter where I am, no matter how short the speech has to be, that is always my last quote. Because it is how you survive oppression, both individually and as a community.

In the teacher workshops—the professional development sessions—I used to show teachers a lot of *Eyes* I. I now go into *Eyes* II, as well, which is much more relevant in terms of what we're dealing with today. I like to show "The Promised Land," which has Dr. King and the movement opposing the Vietnam War. Unfortunately, it doesn't have the part of his famous Riverside Church speech that I most like where he says that those who question why he's come out against the war not only really don't know him or his calling, they don't know the world in which *they* live. But at least the episode includes footage from that speech and how he's dealing with the Vietnam protest and the fact that other black leaders are coming out against him, like the NAACP and Roy Wilkins and Jackie Robinson and Senator Edward Brookes. I mean really acting as if he had no right to talk about what is then seen as international affairs and it's good 'cause Andy Young comes in and says, "It was almost like, 'Nigger stay in your place.'" And so I now show that segment, almost that full hour, because it also gets into the economic inequity part and what SCLC is doing in terms of Poor People's Campaign.[10] Now, I was surprised to find myself focusing on King because I had always been against this King-centered thing, but I find that it's helpful to show somebody like King in some ways becoming fairly radicalized; certainly he's moving even farther left in terms of his politics. And for the first time he is willing to oppose the Johnson administration where he wouldn't before. And coming out very, very strongly against the Vietnam War and that it meant something when he came out. And I combine that with the *Eyes* II segment on the assassination of Chicago Panthers Fred Hampton and Mark Clark, which relates to contemporary police brutality and the use of state power to silence dissent.

I always talk in my speeches, not just about the movement and its history and its values and the many people who made up the movement that I knew, but, I used to also talk about affirmative action: why that was important, what affirmative action for white people had always been like. And I always talk about growing economic inequity. And comparing it with other countries. And I always use statistical information, as I had learned to do in

SNCC, particularly from Jack Minnis, who was our director of research: you don't just spout off at the mouth. You ground your argument in facts and stats. So, I knew all of that and I had always used those other two things, affirmative action and economic inequality, which could be difficult to talk about to an audience. And they might get riled up and stuff, but, the bottom line of my speech, the core of it, was always the movement stuff, which made people feel good. But after 9/11, with these idiots in the White House, then it became, I've got to say something about the war, the soon-to-be war. And how do you let people know this is ridiculous, right? And unnecessary. Okay. So, I'm trying to figure out how you frame, to these kind of audiences, what they don't want to hear.

For example, I got a call to speak at the 2005 King breakfast for the NSA, the National Security Administration, as in the folks who are illegally wiretapping us. The first thing I thought was: do they not know what I talk about? And then I started thinking about how I would have to change the speech, because this was the NSA. And I knew I was going into what we used to call "the Belly of the Beast." And it was like—I really like people to like me when I'm speaking. And that's the thing. I like them to like me so they'll be able to hear what I'm saying. It may be difficult for them to hear some stuff, but at least they'll be open to most of it.

So after 9/11, I'm trying to figure out how you frame opposition to the Bush war—even before they dropped the bombs—but again, because of the movement, my assumption is *I've got to say it.* When the war is imminent and after it begins, I don't enjoy the speaking anymore and that's the problem. There was a whole period of about three years that I was on the road and not looking forward to the speeches. Before it had been primarily about the movement and I love talking about the movement because it reminds me about the wonderfulness of it. And so I love talking about it. And now, with Bush and the idiots, I no longer enjoy it. It's now more, "You really got to do this—you got to give folks proof that this war makes no sense." And I have to think about how I'm gonna steel myself and what documents I need to help me. So I'm clipping more of the *New York Times* and other mainstream press.

So I have to go into the NSA and I'm not sure how they're gonna receive me. Whereas they would have been more-or-less okay with affirmative action and talking about growing economic inequity, I'm now talking about war. And I'm opposing the Bush administration's unnecessary war, because that's how I frame it. So I remember talking to the woman who called me.

John Lewis had spoken there two days before me. And I say to the young woman, "So did John say anything about the war?" And she said, "No, but we loved him. He was so wonderful and he talked about the Selma March and—" Okay. So, I said, "But he didn't say anything about the war?" And she said, "Nooo, but—"

So, we're talking and I say, "Well, you know, I talk about Montgomery and who really was the foundation of the Montgomery movement," and I go through some stuff on the speech and then I said, "Now, I also talk about economic inequity." And, she said, "Oh, fine, okay." And I said, "And, I also, though, talk about the war." And there was this beat and she said, "Oh, you're gettin' sticky, now." Then she said, "Well, as long as you reference Dr. King because this *is* the annual King Day breakfast." And what her comment does is it turns me around in terms of how I can frame this for them. Now, I had always talked about King and SCLC and the Poor People's Campaign, and that would get me to economic injustice. But, what I now realize is that I can just say, "Well, he's also talking about opposition to the war." And then, because of her, I think, let me look at the Riverside speech that he gives in April of 1967, the year before he's killed. And it's a wonderful speech.

Now, it was wonderful, actually, that she said this because I reframed the way that I entered the documents—I usually use documents because my sense is nobody's going to believe me, Judy Richardson. It shouldn't just be your opinion, which is what I learned from the movement. And in terms of talking about the Iraq War, I started using the stuff that I thought they would hear. So I was using the Army War College Report. I use four-star Marine Corps Major Anthony Zinni, former head of Central Command. So, it was all that stuff that I figured, they can hear this. But because of this woman at NSA, I entered it through Dr. King's "Riverside speech."

Now, when I got to the event, I'm coming into *the* NSA, so I go through many check points, to the point that I can't even bring my cell phone inside. The deputy director meets me. He shows me a map on the wall that's an aerial map of this NSA compound. And then he shows me where things were before they tore them down after 9/11. What he's telling me is: This is how we had to secure the perimeter. And, more and more, I'm beginning to delete sections in the speech in my mind. I'm beginning to think, "Okay, this is not the place to say some of this, Richardson, 'cause . . ." and I rationalize it. Because, I say, "If you say this about the war, then they won't hear this about economic injustice. Or, they won't hear this about affirmative action." You rationalize in a way that will make you feel better about not doing what you know you should.

So, then I get into the breakfast and I'm sitting with the deputy director and the minister who's doing the invocation for the breakfast. In his prayer, he asks us to pray for "the brave men and women who are over there," but he doesn't stop there. He says, "Who are fighting for our liberty and our freedom in Iraq." And I start deleting more parts of the speech, like, unh uh. And then I don't know what happened. I'm not sure at what point I decide I'm just going to go ahead and say it. That I, that I have to say it. *That there is a responsibility to talk about this in this place. And that sense of responsibility comes from* SNCC. *It comes from nowhere else. It's like you cannot, you cannot be here and not do this.* So I get up there and I see these people and it's like, "Go for it." I did it. I did the speech that I had planned to do. What surprises me is that they give me a standing ovation. I am so surprised because I truly believed that some of these people were gonna walk out on the speech and that always breaks you. It breaks your rhythm and I'm just not confident enough that I'm going to be able to ignore that kind of thing totally. And, again, you really do want people to hear what you're saying. So they didn't walk out. They give me a standing ovation. And as I come off the stage, the minister shakes my hand. There is a line of, I would say, about fifteen people, to say something to me.

The first woman is this older white woman who says to me, "I am so glad you said what so many of us are thinking, but are afraid to say." And I actually hugged her and told her, "I was so worried about saying this." And I said—and this was true—"I have been worried about this for the last two months, since I knew I was gonna do this." Then there's a black woman behind her. And they all speak very softly, by the way. And she says, "You know, I used to want my daughter to work here, but I have not wanted that in some years." And then another woman, who comes up to me, who is also black, and she says, "I'm a senior staff person here." And she says, "We all know that this war should not have happened." She said, and she's real clear. She says, "And I'm not just saying, it's being done badly, I'm saying it should never have been waged." And it's like, why would I not have assumed that these people, who are sitting in the middle of this, would not know this. But also, I was amazed that they would acknowledge that.

And then there were a couple of guys, too, who came up, but they didn't say that kind of thing. They just thanked me for my speech and glad you came. Okay. But that there were so many people—oh, and one woman who was clearly not senior staff, black woman, tall black woman, who said, "I'm not going to speak too loudly," because she said, "I don't want any problems with my job." But she said, "I'm very happy that you were here." And then, matter-of-fact, she was the one who then said, "Now, don't expect to be invited back again." [*laughter*] It was so cute. That's right. I had forgotten that.

So at the end it was a relief. It was like, *okay.* First of all, I'm through this thing that has so worried me for the last two months. But, it was also that I didn't knuckle under. I didn't let myself get intimidated and I didn't self-censor. For me, that was that moment where it was like: Okay, are you gonna, are you gonna do this thing which you know you're supposed to do, even though it's gonna be hard, or are you gonna do the nice speech? 'Cause my speech is in segments, so I can really kind of cut to just the movement stuff—the past—if I want to. And I was really glad that I hadn't. I did what I thought the movement would expect of me. That was really what it was. This was the expectation. But that is part of what the movement does, I think, for all of us. Which is: there are things you are supposed to do.

It's why Dottie Zellner, I think, is in Jews Say No and continues to fight for human rights for Palestinians in the West Bank and Gaza. And she talks at synagogues and helps organize demonstrations where she is somewhat threatened. Not somewhat, she is threatened physically. And she continues to talk about it, because for her, this is what SNCC said to do. "Go into your community and try to right the wrongs there." Now, this is not an easy thing. But she carries that very seriously within her. It's also why Jean Smith, who is a psychiatrist, has focused on working with at-risk youth, particularly young people of color.

It's what Betty Garman does in her continuing to organize, do community organizing, which she loves. I, myself, could not handle it at this point. Because I can't stand all the internecine stuff. I don't have the stomach for it; I don't have the patience for it, either one. She has the patience and she's willing to struggle to get people empowered, both individually and as a community. And so she's willing . . . and loves it, loves working with community groups to get them moving even at a slow pace. She just has incredible patience and real insight in terms of what can work in order to move people from point A to point B. And to connect them with other communities.

For most of us who came out of the movement, there was a sense that we were responsible for leading our lives a certain way, didn't mean we couldn't have fun, didn't mean we couldn't dance and laugh and sing and do all that stuff. And rest sometimes. But it did mean that, overall, you had a responsibility to change stuff. Maybe little ways, maybe bigger ways. But you couldn't just sit by and let stuff happen without doing something. So I felt with that speech, I had, I had not shirked my responsibility. Yeah. That's more the way I would say it.

Note: For a discussion of Richardson's involvement in the making of *Eyes on the Prize*, see "Making *Eyes on the Prize*: An Interview with Filmmaker and SNCC Staffer Judy Richardson," chapter 9, this volume.

## NOTES

1. Judy Richardson to Emilye Crosby, June 10, 2010, e-mail. Judy Richardson interview by Emilye Crosby, May 28, 2010. David G. McCullough, Orlando Bagwell, Alfre Woodard, Steve Fayer, Judy Richardson, and Henry Hampton, *Malcolm X: Make It Plain* (Alexandria, Va.: PBS Video, 1994).

2. Faith S. Holsaert, Martha Prescod Norman Noonan, Judy Richardson, Betty Garman Robinson, Jean Smith Young, and Dorothy M. Zellner, eds., *Hands on the Freedom Plow: Personal Accounts by Women in SNCC* (Urbana: University of Illinois Press, 2010).

3. Greg Fair, Ella Baker Reading Group, Spring 2006 (hereafter EBRG).

4. Charles Payne, "Why Study the Movement?," chapter 14, this volume; Joseph Zurro, EBRG.

5. Ashley McKay, Hist266, Spring 2006.

6. Katie Snyder, Hist220, Spring 2006.

7. Holsaert, et al., eds., *Hands on the Freedom Plow*.

8. Sara Evans, *Personal Politics: The Roots of Women's Liberation in the Civil Rights Movement and the New Left* (New York: Vintage, 1980). See also, Mary King, *Freedom Song: A Personal Story of the 1960s Civil Rights Movement* (New York: William Morrow and Company, 1987); "SNCC Women and the Stirrings of Feminism," in *A Circle of Trust: Remembering SNCC*, ed. Cheryl Lynn Greenberg (New Brunswick, N.J.: Rutgers University Press, 1998), 127–51; Holsaert, et al., eds., *Hands on the Freedom Plow*.

9. Prathia Hall, "Bloody Sunday," in *Hands on the Freedom Plow*, 471–72.

10. Henry Hampton, *Eyes on the Prize. America's Civil Rights Movement*, vol. 5: *Power! (1966–68). The Promised Land (1967–1968)* (Alexandria, Va.: PBS Video, DVD edition, 2006).

JEANNE THEOHARIS

# Accidental Matriarchs and Beautiful Helpmates

*Rosa Parks, Coretta Scott King, and the Memorialization of the Civil Rights Movement*

On October 24, 2005, after nearly seventy years of activism, Rosa Parks died in her home in Detroit. Deserving a memorial to honor her lifetime of courageous service, what largely unfolded was a spectacle of national redemption to commemorate her death. Within days of her death, Rep. John Conyers Jr., who had employed Parks for twenty years in his Detroit office, introduced a resolution to honor Parks by having her body lie in state. After years of partisan rancor over the social justice issues most pressing to Parks and the shame of the federal government's negligence two months earlier during Hurricane Katrina, Congressional leaders on both sides of the aisle rushed to hold a national funeral for the "mother of the civil rights movement."

The first woman to lie in state at the nation's capitol (and the thirty-first person overall since 1852), Parks, who died in Detroit, was first flown to Montgomery for a public viewing and memorial service.[1] Secretary of State

I am grateful to Gaston Alonso, who shared my interest in the unfolding Parks memorial, and to Marwa Amer, Emilye Crosby, Prudence Cumberbatch, Johanna Fernandez, Arnold Franklin, Dayo Gore, Alejandra Marchevsky, Karen Miller, and Komozi Woodard, who offered insights and thoughtful conversation. Earlier versions of this article appeared in *First of the Month*, July 2006; and *Want to Start a Revolution*. "There Are No Accidents: On the Funerals of Rosa Parks and Coretta Scott King," *First of the Month*; *Want to Start a Revolution? Radical Women in the Black Freedom Struggle*, ed. Jeanne Theoharis, Komozi Woodard, and Dayo Gore (New York: New York University Press, 2009).

Condoleezza Rice attended that memorial, affirming that "without Mrs. Parks, I probably would not be standing here today as Secretary of State."[2] Parks's body was then flown to Washington, D.C. Longtime friend Federal Sixth Circuit Judge Damon Keith, who helped coordinate the memorial events, described the moving flight from Montgomery to Washington, D.C. The plane's captain, who was the first African American chief pilot of a domestic airline, announced on the loudspeaker that the plane would circle Montgomery twice in honor of Parks; then he proceeded to sing "We Shall Overcome." "There wasn't a dry eye in the plane," Keith recalled.[3] The body was met in D.C. by the National Guard and escorted to its place of honor at the Capitol.

At the Capitol, 40,000 Americans came to bear witness to her life and passing. President and Mrs. Bush laid a wreath on her cherry-wood coffin (which was kept simple and unadorned with other flowers, flags, or carvings). Supreme Court nominee Samuel Alito and Senate Majority Leader Bill Frist paid their public respects, with Frist proclaiming to the press: "Rosa Parks's bold and principled refusal to give up her seat was not an intentional attempt to change a nation, but a singular act aimed at restoring the dignity of the individual."[4] After lying in state, Parks's body was moved to the Metropolitan African Methodist Episcopal Church for a public memorial before an overflowing crowd.

Parks's coffin was then brought back to Detroit for two days of public viewing at the Museum of African American History. Thousands more waited in the rain to pay their respects to one of Detroit's finest citizens. With flags flown at half-mast on November 2, a massive seven-hour funeral celebration at the Greater Grace Temple brought 4,000 mourners and a parade of speakers and singers from Bill Clinton to Aretha Franklin to John Conyers.[5] Democratic presidential hopefuls Senators Barack Obama and Hilary Clinton focused on the quietness of her stand.[6] Thousands of people took the day off from work to wait outside to see a horse-drawn carriage bring Mrs. Parks's coffin to the cemetery. Six weeks later, President Bush signed a bill ordering a statue of Parks to be placed in the U.S. Capitol, the first ever of an African American, explaining, "By refusing to give in, Rosa Parks showed that one candle can light the darkness. . . . Like so many institutionalized evils, once the ugliness of these laws was held up to the light, they could not stand. Like so many institutionalized evils, these laws proved no match for the power of an awakened conscience—and as a result, the cruelty and humiliation of the Jim Crow laws are now a thing of the past."[7]

Like an elementary school pageant, buses became crucial to the symbolism of the event. Parks's protest was to be defined by the bus—not in the "total freedom" that she had sought—and thus the bus trailed her coffin around the country.[8] Sixty Parks family members and dignitaries traveled from Montgomery to Washington aboard three Metro buses draped in black bunting. The procession to and from the Capitol also included an empty vintage 1957 bus, dressed in black bunting, which followed the hearse, along with a procession of other city buses. On October 27, the cities of Montgomery and Detroit blocked off the front seats of their buses with black ribbons in her honor until her funeral November 2. The Henry Ford Museum in Dearborn, Michigan, offered free admission the day of her funeral so visitors could see the actual bus "where it all began."

Parks's body also became a crucial necessity for these public rites—brought from Detroit to Montgomery to Washington, D.C., and then back to Detroit for everyone to see. This personal moment with Parks's body served not simply as a private moment of grieving but also a public act of celebrating a nation who would honor her. It would not be enough to have memorial services; her body performed a sort of public communion where Americans would be able to visit her body and be sanctified. The hypervisibility of Parks's body worked to take attention away from the present injustices facing the nation. Less than two months after the federal government's gross inaction during Hurricane Katrina, and in the midst of a war where the Pentagon had forbidden the photographing of coffins returning from Iraq, Parks's coffin was to be the one seen and venerated. The decision to have her body lie in state at the Capitol honored Rosa Parks as a national dignitary but simultaneously reminded mourners that their experience was being sponsored by the federal government.

Three months later, on January 30, 2006, the nation was treated to a reprise when seventy-eight-year-old Coretta Scott King, with a similar legacy of more than fifty years of human rights activism, passed away. Having died in Mexico where she was receiving medical treatment, Coretta Scott King's body returned to Atlanta where it was carried through the streets on a horse-drawn carriage to the Georgia State Capitol. A bagpiper played "Amazing Grace."

King became the first woman and first black person to lie in state at the Georgia State Capitol. Her six-hour funeral was attended by Presidents Bush I and II, Clinton, and Carter—along with three planeloads of Congresspeople, three governors, and a slew of civil rights legends—and more than 10,000 people. A far more lavish affair than her husband's in 1968, her funeral service was held not at the King family church, Ebenezer Baptist, but in Bishop Eddie Long's New Birth Missionary Baptist Church. (In 2004, Coretta Scott King had opposed a march Bishop Long held to Martin Luther King's grave where Long denounced same-sex marriage and a woman's right to choose.)[9]

Because of the high-profile attendees, many civil rights comrades like Rep. John Lewis, Rev. Jesse Jackson, and Rev. C. T. Vivian, along with Georgia Congresswoman Cynthia McKinney, were not allowed to speak. And when President Bush decided to attend the funeral, longtime friend of the Kings Harry Belafonte—who had been asked to give a eulogy—was disinvited. Belafonte was such a close family friend that at Martin Luther King's graveside, Coretta had chosen to sit between him and her own father.[10] Yet Belafonte, who had been sharply critical of the Bush administration (as had Coretta Scott King herself), was no longer welcome at her funeral, perhaps because he would serve as a reminder of King's enduring critique of racial injustice and American foreign policy.[11]

On the day of the funeral, flags were flown at half-mast, according to President George W. Bush, to honor the "grace and beauty in all the seasons of her life." Bush told mourners, "In all her years, Coretta Scott King showed that a person of conviction and strength could also be a beautiful soul. . . . This kind and gentle woman became one of the most admired Americans of our time."[12] But despite the attempts to cordon off politics from the affair, they snuck in. Both Rev. Joseph Lowery and former President Jimmy Carter's remarks drew thunderous applause from the crowd and criticism from many political figures for the ways they sought to link King to the present day issues of injustice she had fought against. Rev. Lowery exclaimed, "But Coretta knew, and we know there are weapons of misdirection right down here. Millions without health insurance, poverty abound. For war, billions more, but no more for the poor."[13] President Carter went one step further, highlighting the ways the federal government had treated the Kings like criminals "with the civil liberties of husband and wife violated as they became the targets of secret government wiretapping, and other surveillance . . . [and] harassment from the FBI." He also underscored the need not simply "to acknowledge the great contributions of Coretta and Martin, but to remind us that the struggle for equal rights is not over. We only have to recall the color of the faces of those in Louisiana, Alabama, and Mississippi[,] [t]hose who are most devastated by Katrina[,] to know that there are not yet equal opportunities for all Americans."[14]

Understanding the historical significance of these women's deaths, many Americans took off work and journeyed long distances to pay tribute to these women's lives. And many friends and colleagues hoped to bear witness to the lifetime of political work these women had engaged in. They saw a public commemoration as a fitting honor to the greatness of these two civil rights legends, both of whom had continued to challenge the nation around issues of racial justice and human rights. Moreover, the passing of both women presented an opportunity to honor the lifetime of courageous service of two legends of the civil rights movement and to foreground the pivotal work of movement women not always fully recognized.

But the women who emerged in these public tributes bore only a fuzzy resemblance to Rosa Louise Parks and Coretta Scott King. Described by the *New York Times* as the "accidental matriarch of the civil rights movement," the Rosa Parks who surfaced in the deluge of political and media commentary was, first and foremost, "quiet." "Humble," "dignified," and "soft-spoken," she was "not angry" and "never raised her voice." Her contribution as the "mother of the movement" was defined over and over by that one act on the bus in December 1955.[15] A similar image of a "kind and gentle" Coretta Scott King dominated the public media; "obedient" and "beautiful," King's contribution was defined principally as her husband's "helpmate."[16] Held up as national heroines but stripped of their long histories of activism and continuing critique of American injustice, the memorialized Parks and King stood as gendered caricatures. In death, both became self-sacrificing mother figures for a nation who would use their bodies for a ritual of national rebirth. This public redemption entailed rewriting the movements these women had been a part of—disregarding their long political histories as well as the activism of many others who joined with them in the struggle.

The funerals of Parks and King demonstrate the public investment in particular histories of the civil rights movement. Scholars such as David Blight and Eric Foner have examined the political investments in the distorted popular histories of slavery and Reconstruction that emerged in the late nineteenth and early twentieth centuries. By portraying slavery as a relatively benign institution and Reconstruction as a decisive failure, these mythic histories served an important political function, helping to justify and entrench segregation and economic inequity at the turn of the last century.[17] Recasting history thus has long been an arena for legitimizing certain political interests. Looking at Parks's and King's funerals reveal the "memory wars," to use Blight's terminology, now at play around the civil rights movement.[18]

As with the history of Reconstruction, a mythic history of the civil rights movement solidified at the turn of the twenty-first century to serve contemporary political and economic needs. According to this popular story—and essential to the framing of both memorials—was the belief that the civil rights movement demonstrated the resiliency and redemptive power of American democracy. This movement proved the greatness of American values and the power of American dissent and self-improvement. A nonviolent struggle built by ordinary people, spurred by the act of a Montgomery seamstress, had corrected a crucial flaw in the American nation without overthrowing the government or engaging in a bloody revolution.[19] In this popular narrative, racism was cast as a flaw rather than a constitutive element of American democracy—which, once seen, was eliminated. This history of the civil rights movement provided a new cast of American heroes, courageous yet unthreatening, with their critique of American inequality located firmly in the past. With fallout from Hurricane Katrina threatening to expose this national myth-making, Parks's and King's funerals became the final coda on this narrative of progress: a woman who had been denied a seat on the bus was now a dignitary lying in state at the nation's Capitol.

The misinterpretations inherent in this mythic history have been challenged by a wealth of historical scholarship over the past two decades.[20] Taken together, this scholarship has demonstrated the depth and strength of racism throughout the United States and documented a national black freedom movement populated, shaped, and led by local people in communities across the country that began in the 1940s and extended through the 1970s. As historians have shown, these movements were not the inevitable outcome of American democracy or proof of the resiliency of American political institutions but the product of slow, tedious work, and tremendous physical, economic, and psychic sacrifice by many Americans over years and decades. Challenging the sanitized, Sunday-school version of the black freedom struggle, this new scholarship shows how these movements married self-defense with nonviolent direct action, radical economic critiques with desegregation, and voting rights with international solidarity.

Yet, the popular story that emerged around the funerals discounted this scholarship in favor of a history that served contemporary political needs. By honoring these individual women apart from the organizing they were a part of, by celebrating the movement but consigning it to the past of the old South, by reducing it to buses, soft voices, and accidental acts, the public memorials of Rosa Parks and Coretta Scott King reveal the saliency of this mythic history in our public life today. The construction of these women as accidental, supporting actors and quintessential American heroes was historically inaccurate but politically expedient. The variety of struggles in which Parks and King took part, the ongoing nature of the campaign against racial injustice, the connections between northern and southern racism, and the red-baiting and government harassment of movement activists (such as Parks and King) were given short shrift in their memorialization. Looking at the full picture of these women's lives and political work thus uncovers the series of myths around which this popular history of the civil rights movement has been constructed. And it gives a much broader and more complicated view of the breadth of these women's political lives and the black freedom struggle more generally—and of the persistence of structures of inequality and the enduring need for change in American society today.

## THE MYTH THAT SINGULAR ACTS MAKE A MOVEMENT

The public spectacle around Rosa Parks's death celebrated her courageous act but largely treated as background the decades of political activism that preceded and followed her bus stand and which gave the act its wider import. It overlooked the Parks who helped organize around the Scottsboro case in the 1930s and voting rights in the 1940s, who was the secretary of the NAACP and attended Highlander Folk School, who worried when she was in jail about the women in the cell with her who were too poor to afford bail, who worked with Robert Williams and Malcolm X as well as Martin Luther King. Indeed, there was nothing accidental about Rosa Parks's political stance on December 1, 1955 but, as she explained, it was "part of a life history of being rebellious against being mistreated because of my color."[21]

Born on February 4, 1913 in Tuskegee, Alabama, Rosa Louise McCauley was active in civil rights issues long before that fateful December day. Marrying the politically active Raymond Parks in December 1932, Rosa Parks joined with him in organizing on behalf of the nine young men who had wrongfully been convicted and sentenced to death in Scottsboro, Alabama. In 1943, she became the secretary of Montgomery's NAACP and worked closely with E.D. Nixon, the president of the chapter. For the next decade, alongside Nixon and a small group of other committed Montgomery activists, Parks sought to document, publicize, organize, and seek legal justice around cases of white-on-black brutality and contest segregation in Alabama. From 1943 to 1945 she also tried numerous times to register to vote, finally succeeding in 1945.*

Thus, Rosa Parks had been politically active for more than two decades before the bus incident. Besides her role as secretary, she founded and led the NAACP Youth Council. She attracted controversy when she took a group of young people to the Freedom Train exhibit and encouraged them to protest segregation in the downtown public library and on the city's buses. In the summer of 1955 Parks attended the Highlander Folk School, an interracial organizer training school started by Myles Horton in Tennessee. "I was 42 years old," she recalled, "and it was one of the few times in my life up to that point when I did not feel any hostility from white people. I experienced people of different races and backgrounds meeting together in workshops and living together in peace and harmony. I felt that I could express myself honestly without any repercussions or antagonistic attitudes from other people. . . . [I]t was hard to leave, knowing what I was going back to, but of course I knew I had to leave."[22]

By 1955, the Montgomery NAACP was looking for a test case against bus segregation. Two young women that year—Claudette Colvin and Mary Louise Smith—were arrested for refusing to give up their seats, though ultimately neither was deemed the kind of plaintiff that the NAACP wanted to back in a legal case. Parks grew frustrated with the runaround city officials were giving

---

* The following discussion of Parks's life and the Montgomery Bus Boycott is drawn from the following sources: Rosa Parks, *Rosa Parks: My Story* (New York: Dial Books, 1992); Douglas Brinkley, *Rosa Parks: A Life* (New York: Penguin, 2000); Jo Ann Robinson, *The Montgomery Bus Boycott and the Women Who Started It* (Knoxville: University of Tennessee Press, 1987); Stewart Burns, ed., *Daybreak of Freedom: The Montgomery Bus Boycott* (Chapel Hill: University of North Carolina Press, 1997); David Garrow, ed., *The Walking City: The Montgomery Bus Boycott, 1955–1956* (Brooklyn: Carlson Publishing, 1989); and Donnie Williams with Wayne Greenhaw, *The Thunder of Angels: The Montgomery Bus Boycott and the People Who Broke the Back of Jim Crow* (Chicago: Lawrence Hill Books, 2006).

them. "[A]ll of our meetings, trying to negotiate, bring about petitions before the authorities . . . really hadn't done any good at all."[23]

On December 1, 1955, Rosa Parks boarded a bus on her way home from work. She and three other black passengers were seated in a row toward the middle of the bus when a white man boarded the bus. There were no seats in the white section. By the terms of Montgomery's segregation, all four passengers would have to get up so one white man could sit down. When the driver, James Blake, with whom Parks had encountered trouble before, ordered them to give up their seats, the others got up but Parks refused. "I felt that, if I did stand up, it meant that I approved of the way I was being treated, and I did not approve."[24] Like other bus drivers in Montgomery, Blake carried a gun. He ordered her to move and when she refused again, had her arrested.

With more than a decade of political experience in trying to document legal malfeasance and white brutality, Parks was well aware of the risks of being arrested. Yet her bus stance is treated as the unwitting action of an old and tired seamstress, unconnected to a broader quest for justice. Parks herself critiqued the ways her action had come to be characterized: "I didn't tell anyone my feet were hurting. It was just popular, I suppose because they wanted to give some excuse other than the fact that I didn't want to be pushed around. . . . And I had been working for a long time—a number of years in fact—to be treated as a human being with dignity not only for myself, but all those who were being mistreated."[25]

Parks was taken to jail where she was allowed one phone call to her family and fined $14. Hearing that Parks had been arrested, community leaders— including E. D. Nixon, lawyers Fred Gray and Clifford Durr, and Women's Political Council president Jo Ann Robinson—sprang into action. Nixon saw in Parks the kind of plaintiff they had been looking for—middle-aged, religious, well-respected in the community, and known for her work on behalf of the NAACP. Perhaps most importantly, Nixon knew Parks was grounded and courageous enough to withstand the public harassment that would follow.

While the stance she took on the bus was a brave and independent choice, what made it the catalyst for a movement was certainly not a singular act. Instead, years of organizing by Parks and others in Montgomery had made people ripe for collective action. The boycott was actually called by the Women's Political Council (WPC), a local group of middle-class black women formed in 1946 to address racial inequities in the city. Indeed, the year before Parks's arrest, after the Supreme Court's ruling in *Brown v. Board of Educa-*

*tion*, WPC president Jo Ann Robinson, an English professor at Alabama State College, sent a letter to the mayor demanding action on the buses or people would organize a boycott. After hearing from lawyer Fred Gray that Parks had been arrested, Jo Ann Robinson decided to take action. With the help of two students, she stayed up all night making leaflets that called for a boycott of the buses the following Monday. The leaflet read: "Another Negro woman has been arrested and thrown into jail because she refused to get up out of her seat on the bus and give it to a white person. If we do not do something to stop these arrests, they will continue. . . . We are therefore asking every Negro to stay off the buses Monday in protest of the arrest and trial."[26]

The Women's Political Council distributed more than 50,000 leaflets across town to let people know of the boycott. Meanwhile, early the next morning, E. D. Nixon began calling Montgomery's black ministers—including Ralph Abernathy and a new young minister in town by the name of Martin Luther King Jr.—to convince them that they must support the boycott. While King initially hesitated, worried about being new in town and having a young family, he agreed to hold the meeting with other ministers at his church, preached about the action on Sunday, and would provide a galvanizing leadership in the months to come. Thus, Parks's action sparked a movement because there were a number of people and organizations in place to run with it.

That Monday, nearly every black person in Montgomery stayed off the buses—and at a packed mass meeting that evening, the community voted to continue the boycott (originally intended just as a one-day boycott) and formed a new organization, the Montgomery Improvement Association. People walked for miles throughout the winter, and an elaborate ride system was created with the use of private cars and black taxis.

But the city stood firm in its commitment to bus segregation. On February 21, 1956, Rosa Parks was indicted along with eighty-eight others, including Reverends King and Abernathy, E. D. Nixon, and Jo Ann Robinson, for their role in organizing a car pool to help maintain the boycott. Meanwhile, fearing that Parks's case would remain tied up in state court, African American lawyer Fred Gray had begun looking for plaintiffs in a case to challenge bus segregation through the federal courts.[27] Aurelia Browder, Susie McDonald, Claudette Colvin, and Mary Louise Smith, all women who had encountered discrimination on Montgomery buses, agreed to become plaintiffs in a civil action lawsuit. On February 1, 1956, Gray filed the case in U.S. District Court. The boycott lasted 381 days before black Montgomerians took their seats on the bus where they chose, after the Supreme Court's ruling in *Browder v. Gayle* outlawed segregation on buses. The black community stood together—and Montgomery's bus segregation was ruled illegal by the highest court in the land. As Parks herself later noted, "Four decades later I am still uncomfortable with the credit given to me for starting the bus boycott. Many people do not know the whole truth. . . . I was just one of many who fought for freedom."[28]

## THE MYTH THAT STATE-SPONSORED
## RACISM WAS A SOUTHERN PROBLEM

The blinding focus on Montgomery also misses the fact that Parks's activism did not end with the Montgomery Bus Boycott. It continued for four decades, after the Parkses moved to Detroit. Parks's many decades of social activism after that December day highlight the connections between northern and southern racism and the struggles for racial justice across the country. Receiving constant death threats and with few economic prospects in the city, the Parkses decided to leave Montgomery in the summer of 1957 for Detroit, where Rosa's brother had lived since 1946.[29] A year earlier, Parks had been to Detroit on the invitation of the militant United Auto Workers Local 600, where she spoke to the membership of the union on the boycott, linking northern and southern struggles for racial justice.[30]

The Parkses moved to a neighborhood "almost 100% Negro with the exception of about two families in the block where I live. In fact I suppose you'd call it just about the heart of the ghetto."[31] In Detroit, Rosa Parks was still considered "dangerous" and an outside agitator by many local citizens. And the Parks family struggled economically with both her and Raymond having difficulty finding stable work. Along with her employment (which was low-paying), she maintained her civil rights commitments with the NAACP, Highlander Folk School, and the SCLC. In 1963, she joined Martin Luther King at the front of Detroit's Great March to Freedom. That March, held weeks before the March on Washington, drew nearly two hundred thousand Detroiters. There, Parks recalled, King "reminded everybody that segregation and discrimination were rampant in Michigan as well as Alabama." Parks also made connections in her speeches between racial injustice and police brutality in Alabama and Michigan, referring to Detroit as "the northern promised land that wasn't."[32]

Parks took an interest in John Conyers's long-shot campaign for Michigan's First Congressional District in 1964. "To our great delight," according to Conyers, she became an active volunteer in his campaign for "Jobs, Justice, Peace."[33] Parks convinced Martin Luther King, despite his policy of not getting involved in any political races, to come to Detroit on behalf of the campaign. King spoke Easter weekend at Central Methodist Church and then endorsed Conyers's bid for Congress. According to Conyers, King's visit "quadrupled my visibility in the black community. . . . Therefore, if it wasn't for Rosa Parks, I never would have gotten elected."[34] On March 1, 1965, she was hired as part of the office staff for the newly elected Congressman's Detroit office. After nearly three decades of political work, this was Parks's first paid political job. "People called her a troublemaker," Conyers recalled, and the office and Parks herself received hate mail but she served on Conyers's staff for more than two decades.[35]

Doing much of the daily constituent services, Parks's work for Conyers focused on economic issues including welfare, education, and affordable housing, that disproportionately affected black Detroiters.[36] By the mid-1960s, housing for blacks in the city was decrepit, tremendously overcrowded, unsanitary, and unequal. The density in black neighborhoods was often more than twice that in white neighborhoods.[37] White vigilante violence had plagued those blacks who dared move into "white neighborhoods." Having lived in public housing herself (in the Cleveland Courts apartments in Montgomery), housing—and particularly public housing—was the social issue closest to her heart. Particularly as President Johnson's Great Society programs opened up funding for city needs, Parks lobbied to get a piece of that money for housing in Detroit.

Parks worked for Conyers till she retired in 1988. Simultaneously continuing a busy activist schedule, she made public appearances and speeches on scores of church programs, women's day events, rallies, and schools. She served as an honorary member of SCLC and joined numerous local organizations like the Women's Public Affairs Committee and the Detroit NAACP, local political campaigns, as well as numerous organizing efforts against the War in Vietnam.[38]

Not the meek and passive lady she is often presented to be, Parks believed in self-defense and admired Malcolm X and Robert Williams. Indeed, while seeing the tactical advantages of nonviolence, she shared their belief in self-defense. "[A]s far back as I remember, I could never think in terms

Figure 28 Rosa Parks greets children at the Black Panther Party Oakland Community School with director Ericka Huggins. Photograph courtesy of Ericka Huggins; Oakland Community School Yearbook/BPP Photographer.

of accepting physical abuse without some form of retaliation if possible."[39] A voracious reader, Parks read multiple newspapers a day and kept an extensive clippings file, interested in stories related to African Americans and in other pressing national issues such as the war in Vietnam and free speech at home.

But Parks's militancy has often been overlooked, due in part, according to Conyers, to the "discongruity" of Parks's radicalism "uncharacteristic for a neat, religious, demure, churchgoing lady."[40] Parks began making appearances at rallies sponsored by the Freedom Now Party, an all black political party started in Detroit in 1963. In February 1965, Parks received an award from the Afro-American Broadcasting Company, started by Milton and Richard Henry, Detroit activists who helped found the Freedom Now Party and, later, the Republic of New Africa. On February 14, 1965 they honored Parks at their First Annual Dignity Awards. Malcolm X gave the keynote speech (often referred to as his "Last Message" because it occurred a week before his assassination). Afterwards, Parks, who had long admired Malcolm X, spoke with him privately and got him to sign her program.[41]

Civil rights struggles in northern cities like Detroit had garnered few successes by the mid-1960s. This frustration, combined with persistent social and economic inequality and police brutality, triggered riots in nearly every major American city between 1964 and 1968. On July 23, 1967, police raided an illegal after-hours bar near the Parkses' home. The crowd refused to disperse and grew larger and more angry, leading to four days of rioting. The police grew more forceful and violent as well. According to Parks, "What triggered the riot in my opinion, to a considerable extent, was that between urban renewal and expressways, poor black people were bulldozed out of their homes."[42] Parks saw the 1967 riot as an outgrowth of the frustration people felt at the continuing inequities in a putatively liberal city such as Detroit. While never condoning random violence or theft, Parks could understand the uprising as "the result of resistance to change that was needed long beforehand."[43]

At the end of five days, forty-three people were dead—thirty at the hands of the police—and hundreds were injured, including eighty-five police officers. "What really went on," according to Conyers, "was a police riot."[44] Perhaps the most egregious incident took place on the fourth day when police killed three young men at the Algiers Motel. While the officers claimed a gun battle, no weapons were found and witnesses said the young men were deliberately murdered by the police. The Citizens Citywide Action Committee, popularly known as CCAC and chaired by Rev. Albert Cleage, stepped into the fray. Angered by the police cover-up, they decided to hold a mock trial to publicly call attention to the three deaths. Two thousand people packed Central Church on August 30, 1967 for the "People's Tribunal."[45] Milton Henry served as one of the two prosecutors; among the jurors were African American novelist John O. Killens and Rosa Parks. Parks's participation in the People's Tribunal shows the ways she was located in the midst of an emerging militancy in the city.

Parks continued her activism in the 1970s and the 1980s. She joined the Poor People's Movement in Washington, D.C., campaigned for George McGovern, opposed the war in Vietnam, helped to organize legal defense campaigns for Joan Little and Gary Tyler, attended the Gary Convention, and visited the Black Panther Party's Oakland Community School. She spearheaded the NAACP's protest of racially exclusive parks in Dearborn. By the 1980s, she had become active in the campaign to pressure the U.S. government and U.S. corporations to divest their holdings in South Africa. Alongside other activists in the Free South Africa Movement, she walked the picket lines in Washington, D.C., and spoke about divestment in numerous talks.[46] While popular notions end the civil rights movement with the passage of the Voting Rights Act or the assassination of Martin Luther King, Mrs. Parks's activism continued well beyond.

## BEYOND VOTING AND DESEGREGATION

Similarly, the memorialization of Coretta Scott King as Martin Luther King's wife and helpmate misses the wider critique of social injustice that underlaid her life's work. Coretta Scott was active in racial politics and the peace movement *before* marrying Martin Luther King Jr., and spoke up earlier and more forcefully against American involvement in Vietnam than her husband. An examination of her political commitments foregrounds the international dimensions of the civil rights struggle and the long-standing commitment to nonviolence, anticolonialism, and human rights around the world held by many civil rights activists. It also returns a much fuller and more militant picture of Martin Luther King's activism to public view, particularly his antipoverty work and opposition to the war in Vietnam, and the ways that Coretta Scott King helped shape this focus.

Coretta Scott, born on April 27, 1927 in Marion, Alabama, received her BA from Antioch College in music and elementary education. There Scott became politically active in the campus NAACP, the Race Relations and Civil Liberties Committees, and various peace activities.[47] Coretta Scott encountered discrimination at Antioch, when she was not allowed to student teach in the local public schools and the college sided with the school system's decision. "At that time, all of the teachers in the local public schools were white, even though the student body was integrated. . . . This . . . made me determined to become more involved in addressing issues of social and political injustice."[48]

Coretta Scott attended the Progressive Party convention and was a strong supporter of racial progressive Henry Wallace's 1948 independent bid for the U.S. presidency. An accomplished singer, she earned a scholarship to New England Conservatory of Music where she received her Bachelor of Music degree. In Boston she met Martin Luther King Jr., who was working on his doctorate at Boston University. According to King biographer Clayborne Carson, "[S]he was more politically active at the time they met than Martin was."[49] Independent and "ferociously informal," according to James Baldwin, she worried about how "circumscribed" her life might become if she married a pastor.[50]

Part of the attraction between her and Martin was political, as letters between the two of them reveal. While they were courting, Coretta sent Martin a copy of Edward Bellamy's socialist utopian novel *Looking Backward*. She later told Baldwin that her emerging relationship with Martin came to feel "somehow, preordained." They married in June 1953 and then moved to Montgomery in September 1954 where Martin had received his first pastorship.

Coretta Scott King's peace activism continued after her marriage, and in many ways her commitments to global peacemaking helped inspire his. (He had not been active around these issues before meeting her.) In 1958, Coretta spoke on her husband's behalf at the Youth March for Integrated Schools. Drawing inspiration from India's march to the sea and the underground railroad, Coretta King praised the young people for "proving that the so-called 'silent generation' is not so silent."[51] In 1957, she helped found the Committee for a Sane Nuclear Policy. In 1959, she and her husband traveled to India for five weeks to learn from the work of Mahatma Gandhi, meeting with India's prime minister Jawaharlal Nehru along with dozens of other local leaders and activists. And in 1962, she was a delegate for the Women's Strike for Peace to the Eighteen-Nation Disarmament Conference in Geneva, Switzerland.[52]

Coretta Scott King joined the Women's International League for Peace and Freedom and became even more vocal around peace issues as U.S. involvement in Vietnam escalated. After her husband received the Nobel Prize in 1964, she stressed to him "the role you must play in achieving world peace, and I will be so glad when the time comes when you can assume that role."[53] After that, Coretta pressed Martin even more forcefully to make this international dimension to nonviolence more prominent; their commitments to nonviolence meant they needed to oppose the use of violence to resolve conflict internationally as well as domestically.

While her husband wavered in his public opposition to the Vietnam War, after being attacked severely for his early criticisms of U.S. military involvement, Coretta Scott King remained steadfast in her public opposition to the war. In 1965, two years before her husband's famous sermon against the war at Riverside Church, Coretta Scott King addressed an antiwar rally at Madison Square Garden in New York City. Late in 1965, when her husband backed out of an address to a peace rally in Washington, she kept her commitment to speak.[54] Following her appearance, when a reporter asked Martin Luther King if he had educated Coretta on these issues, King replied, "She educated me."[55]

Coretta Scott King continued to push her husband to take a stronger stand against the war.[56] In April 1967, Martin Luther King made his famous declaration against the war at Riverside Church, decrying the resources being diverted from the War on Poverty to wage war in Vietnam and the use of black soldiers in a conflict thousands of miles away when their rights were not guaranteed at home. Then, while Martin spoke at the Spring Mobilization for Peace in New York, Coretta flew to San Francisco to speak at a peace demonstration of 60,000. In January 1968, missing celebrations of her husband's birthday in Atlanta, she joined 5,000 women in the Jeanette Rankin Brigade in Washington, D.C., to protest against the war. At the end of March, she presided over a conference in Washington, D.C., organized by the Women's International League for Peace and Freedom where she called for a ceasefire in Vietnam.[57]

Along with peace activism, issues of poverty and economic justice motivated both Coretta and Martin. After her husband's assassination in Memphis where he had gone to take part in a sanitation worker's strike, Coretta Scott King stepped in to fill the political void. Historian Michael Honey writes their partnership "came not only from personal love but also from a joint political commitment. . . . True to the patriarchal society in which they had been raised, Martin felt she should devote herself primarily to making a home and raising the children. She did that, but she did it in the context of two lives absolutely committed to changing the world. . . . Now, as the King family reeled from tragedy, Coretta began to demonstrate her own quiet and steely commitment to nonviolence."[58]

Understanding the tremendous work to be done in the wake of Martin's death, she committed to carrying on the fight for racial and economic justice: "The day that Negro people and others in bondage are truly free, on the day want is abolished, on the day wars are no more, on that day I know my husband will rest in a long-deserved peace."[59]

Four days after her husband's assassination, she traveled to Memphis to continue the planned march on behalf of the striking sanitation workers. "[W]e must have economic power," she proclaimed. "Every man deserves a right to a job or an income so that he can pursue liberty, life, and happiness."[60] Indeed, Coretta was resolute that an appropriate memorial for her husband's death was to continue the task of pursuing racial and economic justice.

## THE MYTH THAT THE MOVEMENT ENDED IN THE 1960S

At the heart of both Parks's and King's public memorializations was the distortion that the civil rights movement was long since over. An examination of Coretta Scott King's activities in the three decades following her husband's death counters the idea that the black freedom struggle ended with Martin Luther King's assassination. Coretta Scott King helped launch the Poor People's Campaign the month after her husband's death. At the end of his life, Martin Luther King was building a Poor People's Movement to descend on Washington and engage in massive civil disobedience. By making poverty visible and unignorable, they hoped to dramatize the widespread injustice of poverty in a nation as wealthy as the United States and force Congress and the president to action. But it was Coretta Scott King, Ralph Abernathy, and a host of other local leaders who took up the task of actually enacting the campaign.

On April 27, 1968, Coretta Scott King also delivered a speech at an antiwar demonstration in Central Park that Martin Luther King was supposed to have given. She linked her opposition to the war to antipoverty activism at home, drawing out what would be a persistent theme of hers on the multiple manifestations of violence in American politics. She saw the war abroad and economic injustice at home as "two sides of the same coin."

> [O]ur policy at home is to try to solve social problems through military means, just as we have done abroad. The bombs we drop on the people of Vietnam continue to explode at home with all of their devastating potential. There is no reason why a nation as rich as ours should be blighted by poverty, disease and illiteracy. It is plain that we don't care about our poor people, except to exploit them as cheap labor and victimize them through excessive rents and consumer prices.

She ended her speech with a call to the power of women to "heal the broken community now so shattered by war and poverty and racism."[61]

Even though welfare was a taboo among many civil rights leaders (who feared being associated with this stigmatized issue) and even though her husband had kept a distance from welfare rights, Coretta then linked the struggle for economic justice to the need for a real safety net for poor families. She decried the current proposal before Congress to cut welfare benefits as misguided and un-American. "It forces mothers to leave their children and accept work or training, leaving their children to grow up in the streets as tomorrow's social problems." King called for a guaranteed annual income for all Americans as a moral imperative—and encouraged people to join welfare mothers at the nation's capital on Mother's Day to "call upon congress to establish a guaranteed annual income instead of these racist and archaic measures, these measures which dehumanize God's children and create more social problems than they solve."[62]

On May 1, King kicked off the southern caravan of the Poor People's Campaign in Memphis with the song "Sweet Little Jesus Boy." She declared her own dream "where not some but all of God's children have food, where not some but all of God's children have decent housing, where not some but all of God's children have a guaranteed annual income in keeping with the principles of liberty and grace."[63] Coretta Scott King's vision was not ephemeral but one rooted in economic justice. Her Christianity was not an otherworldly religion but a living theology that saw Jesus as an advocate for the poor and oppressed. On May 12, she joined 7,000 welfare recipients and their allies from twenty cities at Cardozo High School in Washington, D.C., to decry the violence of poverty, call for the fulfillment of the spirit of the original 1935 Social Security Act, and kick off the D.C. events. The next month, on Solidarity Day, June 19, 1968, in the midst of the Poor People's encampment on the Mall in Washington, D.C., she gave a powerful speech to 50,000 people at the Lincoln Memorial. There she called on American women to "unite and form a solid block of women power" to fight racism, poverty, and war.[64]

The stand-by-your-man image of Coretta Scott King thus misses the extended critique of injustice that underlined her political work long after her husband's assassination. At both the Mother's Day March and then again on Solidarity Day, she decried the hypocrisy of a society "where violence against poor people and minority groups is routine." At a point when Black Power advocates were being criticized for their abandonment of nonviolent ideology, she reminded the nation of its own acts of violence: "Neglecting school children is violence. Punishing a mother and her family is violence.... Ignoring medical needs is violence. Contempt for poverty is violence. Even the lack of will power to help humanity is a sick and sinister form of violence."[65] (For more on the Mule Train and the Poor People's Campaign, see Amy Nathan Wright, "The 1968 Poor People's Campaign, Marks, Mississippi, and the Mule Train," chapter 4, this volume.)

Coretta reframed the political language of the time, foregrounding issues

Figure 29 Coretta Scott King kicks off the Poor People's Campaign in Memphis.
Photograph © 2010 Roland L. Freeman..

of economic violence prevalent throughout American society. As King biographer Thomas Jackson explained, "More forcefully than her husband had articulated, Coretta King connected poverty and policy neglect to systemic social violence."[66] She critiqued the stereotypes of poor black women, often cast as lazy, loud, and castrating figures, seeing it as a way to further disfigure women who advocated for themselves and to take attention away from the structural causes of black poverty and structural racism. Indeed, Coretta Scott King's analysis of poverty highlighted the intersections of race and gender that often kept black women poor and disregarded.

After her husband's assassination, she would spend the next three decades speaking out against poverty, working for peace and social justice around the world, and calling attention to AIDS and the need for gay rights. She did not simply seek to uphold her husband's legacy. Rather, she expanded it to address a variety of justice issues. Although she used the legacy of Martin Luther King to support her own independent activism, she was simultaneously always caught in his shadow. She spoke out on behalf of welfare rights, full employment, school desegregation, and against the Vietnam War. Yet there has been a tendency to treat her as an historical footnote; books allude to the fact that Coretta Scott spoke at a rally against Nixon's Family Assistance Plan in 1972, attended the black nationalist Gary Convention in 1972, joined marchers in Boston in 1975 to support school desegregation, and so on. Indeed, in the histories of these events, King's attendance is mentioned but not elaborated on, as it would be for other activists keeping the kind of full political schedule that she did.

In the 1980s, she took an active role in the anti-apartheid movement, attending demonstrations and, in 1984, being arrested outside the South African embassy. She traveled to South Africa, and subsequently met with President Ronald Reagan to urge divestment. And to the end of her life, she continued her international peace work. In the months leading up to the second Gulf War, King came out against the invasion: "A war with Iraq will increase anti-American sentiment, create more terrorists, and drain as much as 200 billion taxpayer dollars, which should be invested in human development here in America."[67]

She also became a vocal advocate of gay rights and the legalization of same-sex marriage. In the late 1990s, despite criticisms from civil rights leaders and her own children, Coretta Scott King chastened the nation "that Martin Luther King, Jr., said, 'Injustice anywhere is a threat to justice everywhere?' I appeal to everyone who believes in Martin Luther King, Jr.'s dream to make room at the table of brotherhood and sisterhood for lesbian and gay people."[68] King saw the struggle for gay rights as intimately connected to that of racial justice and stood firm against those Americans, even those in the black community, who would cast the battle for gay rights as dishonoring the spirit of the civil rights movement. In 2001, at the SCLC convention, she highlighted the threat of AIDS to the black community as "one of the most deadly killers of African-Americans. And I think anyone who sincerely cares about the future of black America had better be speaking out."[69] Decrying the dangers of legalized injustice, she opposed a Constitutional amendment banning same-sex marriage and reminded Americans that "gay and lesbian people have families, and their families should have legal protection, whether by marriage or civil unions."[70]

Coretta Scott King's politics extended past her husband's and far beyond the 1960s. Yet many of the memorials around her death dated the movement to the 1960s and placed her in Martin Luther King's shadow, missing her long-standing commitment to international peace, economic justice, and human rights.

## THE MYTH THAT THE NATION ALWAYS EMBRACED CIVIL RIGHTS ACTIVISTS

The funerals that celebrated these women as true American heroines also papered over the ways the government, along with many citizens, had for decades treated these women like subversives. With the exception of President Carter's speech, there was little public accounting for the ways that the FBI and the federal government just stood by when the Parks family and the King family—these celebrated "American heroes"—were receiving regular death threats. The memorials for Parks and the Kings largely whitewashed the decades of opposition to civil rights that brought economic hardship, violence, and government surveillance into the lives of these women and their families.

Parks's bus stand took a significant toll on her family's economic stability and safety. On January 7, 1956, Montgomery Fair discharged Parks. A week later, her husband resigned his job because his employer had prohibited any discussion of the boycott or even of Rosa Parks in the barbershop where he worked. Along with this economic hardship, the Parks family was receiving regular hate mail and death threats. Both Rosa and Raymond's health suffered.

Facing persistent death threats, red-baited as Communist sympathizers (particularly for Rosa's ties to Highlander), and unable to find work in the city, the Parkses decided to move to Detroit. But still they had trouble finding regular work and Rosa grew sicker, hospitalized in 1960 for ulcers. Not until 1965—a full decade after her bus stand—did the family gain a measure of economic stability (when John Conyers hired her). The harassment and hate mail also continued in Detroit, and Parks was often called a traitor. One 1972 letter to her read: "[W]hy didn't you stay down south? The North sure doesn't want you up here. You are the biggest woman trouble-maker ever, and should be put in jail for life imprisonment, but fortunately for you, the white citizens are very easygoing nice lawabiding, non-violent highly respectable citizens. You aren't."[71] Moreover, it is telling that in an America willing to spend millions of dollars on a three-state funeral celebration, Rosa Parks was forced to rely on a local church and the advocacy of friends to pay her rent in her last years.

The Kings also faced the persistent threat of violence and continual charges of being potential "Communists." The Kings's house was bombed in 1956, and they received near-incessant death threats and hate mail for more than a decade, along with persistent federal surveillance. Indeed, the King family was treated to near-constant FBI monitoring and harassment, instigated by FBI Director J. Edgar Hoover but okayed in 1963 by Attorney General Robert Kennedy for "national security" reasons. The FBI sent an anonymous tape of King's indiscretions to Coretta Scott King (along with a letter to Martin urging him to kill himself) on the eve of her husband's receipt of the Nobel Peace Prize. The FBI distributed this material to various Congressmen and journalists. While none of these journalists printed the files, they never exposed the FBI's considerable surveillance of King either. This monitoring continued even after Martin Luther King's assassination. Fearing that Coretta Scott King would "tie the anti-Vietnam movement to the civil rights movement," the Bureau maintained active surveillance of her for the next four years, dutifully reporting their findings to the Nixon administration.[72]

This public hatred and harassment went largely unmentioned in the context of the memorials. The history of the civil rights movement, as *Nation* columnist Gary Younge has observed, is mainly told without specific mention of those who opposed it. Somehow Parks and King can be honored without a corresponding public accounting by the people and public institutions that discredited these civil rights activists and attempted to preserve racial inequality. Younge writes, "That's because so much of Black History Month takes place in the passive voice. Leaders 'get assassinated', patrons 'are refused', women 'are ejected' from public transport. So the objects of racism are many but the subjects few. In removing the instigators, the historians remove the agency and, in the final reckoning, the historical responsibility."[73]

Businesses, local governments, and federal agencies all rushed to name buildings, streets, and even Michigan's Department of Homeland Security after Rosa Parks. Yet celebrating her became another tactic to avoid any public reckoning or responsibility for the racial injustice that these same institutions helped to perpetuate.

## THE MYTH THAT THESE WOMEN CHOSE THEIR GENDERED ROLES

The nation's memorialization of Parks and King rested on gendered caricature—both women were framed as having fought for justice sweetly and demurely. Both Parks and King were celebrated for their modesty and respectability, Parks for being quiet and never raising her voice, and King for being gentle and beautiful. Implicit in these celebrations was the desire to hold up a worthy type of protest in contrast to more militant, unseemly mobilizations. Lurking behind these characterizations was an unspoken castigation and stereotyping of other black women, for being outspoken and outraged, for being poor or overweight or loud or angry—and therefore not appropriate for national recognition.

Missed in the celebration of these women's "quietness" was the recognition of the forces and people who sought to keep Rosa Parks and Coretta Scott King quiet. From the first mass meeting in Montgomery in December 1955 to the March on Washington to the celebration of Parks's quietness in many civil rights leaders' eulogies, what must be recognized is that part of Rosa Parks's iconic status rested on this determined woman having to *be quiet*. On the evening of Parks's trial and the successful one-day boycott, 15,000 people gathered for a mass meeting at the Holt Street Baptist Church. Parks was recognized and introduced but not asked to speak, despite a standing ovation and calls from the crowd for her to do so. "I do recall asking someone if I should say anything," Parks remembered, "and someone saying, 'Why, you've said enough.'"[74] As historians Marisa Chappell, Jenny Hutchinson, and Brian Ward explain, "In order to reinforce Parks's image of unassailable respectability, movement leaders and the black press consistently downplayed—in fact, rarely mentioned—her involvement with the NAACP or Highlander."[75]

In part to allay Cold War suspicions of black militancy, Parks's role as the "mother of the movement" was constructed apart from her own political and employment history and seemed to preclude her from having a public leadership role, despite the scores of public appearances she was making. This image of her as a simple seamstress—and not also a longtime political activist—would come to take on a life of its own. And when the Parkses decided to leave Montgomery because she and her husband could no longer find work, no civil rights group—including the newly founded Southern Christian Leadership Conference or the Montgomery Improvement Association—offered her a job.

This lack of recognition and remuneration for women's roles was widespread among the national civil rights leadership. At the 1963 March on Washington, no women were asked to speak, and Coretta Scott King and the wives of other civil right leaders were not allowed to march with their husbands. Civil rights activist Pauli Murray protested to A. Philip Randolph, the March's organizer, "over the blatant disparity between the major role which Negro women have played and are playing at the crucial grass-roots levels of our struggle and the minor role of leadership they have been assigned in the national policy-making decision."[76] As a result of this pressure, Randolph included "A Tribute to Women" but still no woman spoke. Parks—along with a number of other women activists such as Gloria Richardson, Diane Nash, Myrlie Evers, and Daisy Bates—were asked to stand up and be recognized during the tribute. Parks herself criticized this sexism, telling Daisy Bates at the March on Washington that she hoped for a better day coming. And in her autobiography, Parks writes that the March "was a great occasion, but women were not allowed to play much of a role."[77] Indeed, the backgrounding of women in the movement was not lost on "the mother of the civil rights movement."

Despite numerous attempts to increase her role in the movement and expand her position beyond wife and mother, Coretta Scott King similarly encountered numerous roadblocks from her husband and his colleagues who saw women largely as helpmates. The Kings' marriage—and Martin Luther King's attitude toward the role of women—reflected many of the gendered assumptions prevalent in the 1950s and 1960s. As Coretta explained, "Martin had, all through his life, an ambivalent attitude toward the role of women. On the one hand, he believed that women are just as intelligent and capable as men and that they should hold positions of authority and influence. . . . But when it came to his own situation, he thought in terms of his wife being a homemaker and a mother for his children. He was very definite that he would expect whoever he married to be home waiting for him."[78]

This paradox sat at the heart of their marriage. Part of what attracted Martin to Coretta, and Coretta to Martin, was her politics and independence, and yet he also sought to limit her public role. Martin Luther King recalled that the "first discussion we had was about the question of racial and economic injustice and the question of peace. She had been actively engaged in movements dealing with these problems."[79] King wanted a wife who was "as dedicated as I was" and recognized Coretta's deep political convictions. But he also limited her role while they were married. Defying the images of her as a lovestruck appendage, Coretta Scott King also underscored the political convictions that underlined their relationship from its outset.

> I married Martin Luther King Jr., who I'd learned to love. It wasn't love . . . at first sight. But he was such an extraordinary human being, and our values were so similar, and our outlooks were so much alike, we made a good couple. . . . [A]s we were thrust into the forefront of the cause, it was my cause, too, from the very beginning. Because I had been an activist in college, and involved in the peace movement. . . . I could not have continued after he was no longer here if I hadn't had that kind of commitment. I always knew that I was called to do something. . . . I finally rationalized, after I met Martin, and it took a lot of praying to discover this, that this was probably what God had called me to do, to marry him.[80]

Coretta Scott King criticized the sexism of the movement and the ways women's roles were often overlooked in *New Lady* magazine in January 1966. "Not enough attention has been focused on the roles played by women in the struggle. By and large, men have formed the leadership in the civil rights struggle but . . . [w]omen have been the backbone of the whole civil rights movement."[81] Coretta sought a more public role throughout their marriage but to a certain extent, Martin attempted to keep her home and treated her, at times, as a supporting player in the movement. In the decades after her husband's death, Coretta was actually able to assume the public role that she had desired even throughout their marriage. As Michael Dyson argues, "After being made marginal in the movement by her husband—its greatest, most enduring symbol—Coretta King has come into her own."[82]

Tellingly, neither Rosa Parks nor Coretta Scott King was ever commissioned to write a full autobiography of their lives. Rosa Parks published a young adult autobiography *Rosa Parks: My Story*, an elementary school version (*I Am Rosa Parks*), and a book of quotes (*Quiet Strength*), while Coretta Scott King wrote and then reissued *My Life with Martin Luther King, Jr.* Even in the 1993 reissue, *My Life* ends with her husband's death and Coretta's self-effacing declaration, "In the same way that I had given him all the support I could during his lifetime, I was even more determined to do so now that he was no longer with us. Because his task was not finished, I felt that I must rededicate myself to the completion of his work."[83] The decades of her work after his assassination go unchronicled. *Rosa Parks: My Story*, while replete with interesting information about her politics and early life, also largely ignores Parks's political work after Montgomery and is written to appeal to younger readers. Their extant autobiographies thus contribute to their gendered public images as storybook characters and inspiring icons. Both women saw in the roles they were cast—mother of the civil rights movement and wife of its greatest leader—the potential to aid the civil rights struggle. Yet they also remained trapped by the limitations of these positions.

## TOWARD A MORE SUBSTANTIVE MEMORIALIZATION

The funeral celebrations of Rosa Parks and Coretta Scott King promoted an inspirational children's story of social change with a cast of gentle heroines, backward southern rednecks, and courageous public leaders. That both Parks and King were being honored as midwives of the movement, rather than its leaders or thinkers, was not coincidental. Long viewed as quiet and respectful, they could be cast as nonthreatening supporters of a movement that had run its course.

The funerals promoted a misleading but politically expedient history of these women's lives and the civil rights movement more broadly: Back in the day, racial injustice was rampant in the South, but not the rest of the nation. Rosa Parks's singular act and Martin Luther King's individual leadership caused the civil rights movement, which led the country to band together to address Jim Crow segregation. The nation now can unite to honor these

"American heroes" of the civil rights struggle confident in its own righteousness. Erasing the long history of opposition to the black freedom movement, which for decades rendered Parks's and King's extensive political activities "un-American," this fable presumed an unwavering national march toward a color blind American democracy. Such a mythology was all the more useful in a post-Katrina world, where honoring an old woman on a bus could divert attention from the national abandonment of people stranded in the Superdome.

A shell game of veneration, these national funerals marked not just the deaths of these women but the passing of American racism. Counter to what these women stood for, their memorials became a way for the nation to distance and distract itself from injustice in the present. They hid an organized, sustained freedom struggle behind a celebration of singular acts and remarkable individuals who had overcome the racism of the past. Ultimately, they consigned Parks's and King's critique of American society to distant history, even though both women had continued to speak out on racial justice and human rights in our own time.

## NOTES

1. Parks was the second African American to lie in state in the Capitol. The first black person honored was Jacob J. Chestnut, a Capitol police officer fatally shot in 1998.

2. Michael Janofsky, "Thousands Gather at the Capitol to Remember a Hero," *New York Times*, October 31, 2005.

3. Interview with Sixth Circuit Judge Damon Keith in his chambers, Detroit, Michigan, June 14, 2007.

4. *Associated Press*, October 25, 2005. Frist (R-TN) cosponsored a resolution with Senator Harry Reid (D-NV) that passed unanimously in the Senate for Parks to lie in state at the Capitol. Frist explained, "The Capitol Rotunda is one of America's most powerful illustrations of the values of freedom and equality upon which our republic was founded, and allowing Mrs. Parks to lie in honor here is a testament to the impact of her life on both our nation's history and future." "US Capitol Honours Civil Rights Leader Parks," *ABCNews Online*, October 30, 2005.

5. Judge Keith talked of the tremendous pressure he was under in balancing the dignitaries, politicians, entertainers, and other public figures: "Everybody wanted to speak." Keith interview.

6. Peter Slevin, "A Quiet Woman's Resonant Farewell," *Washington Post*, November 2, 2005.

7. Transcript of President Bush's remarks can be found at http://www.whitehouse
.gov/news/releases/2005/12/20051201-1.html.

8. Douglas Brinkley, *Rosa Parks: A Life* (New York: Penguin, 2000), 118.

9. Civil rights activist Julian Bond decided not to go to the funeral because Coretta
Scott King had been active on gay and lesbian rights and would not have approved of
the homophobia of the church and its pastor Bishop Long, who were hosting the service. Keith Boykin, "Why Julian Bond Skipped King's Funeral," www.KeithBoykin.com,
February 10, 2006. Dyana Berger, "Coretta Scott King dies at 78," and "Anti-gay church
to picket King's funeral," *Washington Blade*, February 3, 2006.

10. Coretta Scott King, *My Life With Martin Luther King, Jr.* (New York: Henry Holt
and Company, 1993), 307. The King children and, in particular, King's daughter, the Rev.
Bernice King, who gave the eulogy, along with Republican Party officials were in part
responsible for the decision to disinvite Belafonte.

11. Maya Angelou did make a point of noting the absence of Belafonte in her remarks.
A partial transcript of Angelou's speech can be found at http://www.democracynow
.org/2006/2/8/last_tributes_to_coretta_scott_king.

12. Shaila Dewan and Elisabeth Bumiller, "At Mrs. King's Funeral, a Mix of Elegy and
Politics," *New York Times*, February 8, 2006.

13. Partial transcripts of Rev. Joseph Lowery's speech can be found at http://www
.democracynow.org/article.pl?sid=06/02/08/1516213.

14. Partial transcripts of President Jimmy Carter's speech can be found at http://www
.democracynow.org/article.pl?sid=06/02/08/1516213.

15. Described as "unassuming seamstress" and "small act of defiance" in Maria New-
man, "Thousands Pay Final Respects to Rosa Parks in Detroit," *New York Times*, November 2, 2005; "accidental matriarch" in Michael Janofsky, "Thousands Gather at the Capitol to Remember a Hero," *New York Times*, October 31, 2005; as "quiet" and "humble"
in "US Civil Rights Icon Dies," *BBC*, October 25, 2005; and "Parks remembered for her
courage, humility," www.CNN.com, October 20, 2005; as "humble" in "Thousands Attend Rosa Parks funeral in Detroit," *USA Today*, November 2, 2005; as "quiet" in Peter
Slevin, "A Quiet Woman's Resonant Farewell," *Washington Post*, November 2, 2005; and
as "mild-mannered" and "gentle giant" in Cassandra Spratling, "Goodbye Mrs. Parks,"
*Detroit Free Press*, October 25, 2005. Even E. R. Shipp, who challenges the myths surrounding Parks's bus stand, eulogizes Parks in a way that contributes to the idea of her
as a nonpolitical actor: "That moment on the Cleveland Avenue bus also turned a very
private woman into a reluctant symbol and torchbearer in the quest for racial equality."
E. R. Shipp, "Rosa Parks, 92, Founding Symbol of Civil Rights Movement, Dies," *New
York Times*, October 25, 2005.

16. Described as the "matriarch of the movement" in "Coretta Scott King Dies,"
www.CNN.com, January 31, 2006. Shaila Dewan and Elisabeth Bumiller, "At Mrs. King's

Funeral, a Mix of Elegy and Politics," *New York Times*, February 8, 2006; as having "grace and serenity" in "Coretta Scott King dead at 78," www.MSNBC.com, January 31, 2006; as an "avid proselytizer for his vision" in Peter Applebome, "Coretta Scott King, 78, Widow of Dr. Martin Luther King Jr., Dies," *New York Times*, January 31, 2006; as having "poise, grace and enduring dignity " in Larry Copeland, "'Queen of black America' Coretta Scott King dies at 78," *USA Today*, January 31, 2006; as the "closest thing possible to African-American royalty" in Ernie Suggs, "Coretta Scott King 1927–2006," *Atlanta Journal Constitution*, January 31, 2006.

17. David Blight, *Race and Reunion: The Civil War in American Memory* (Cambridge, Mass.: Harvard University Press, 2001); Eric Foner, *Reconstruction* (New York: Harper, 1988); and Eric Foner, *Who Owns History* (New York: Hill and Wang, 2003).

18. Blight, *Race and Reunion*, 3–4.

19. See Renee Romano and Leigh Raiford, eds., *The Civil Rights Movement in American Memory* (Athens: University of Georgia Press, 2006); and Jacquelyn Dowd Hall, "The Long Civil Rights Movement and the Political Uses of the Past," *Journal of American History* 91 (March 2005): 1233–63.

20. I am dating this new scholarship with the publication of two crucial studies on the movement in Mississippi: John Dittmer, *Local People: The Struggle for Civil Rights in Mississippi* (Urbana: University of Illinois Press, 1994); and Charles M. Payne, *I've Got the Light of Freedom: The Organizing Tradition and the Mississippi Freedom Struggle* (Berkeley: University of California Press, 1995). On the southern movement, see, for instance, Chana Kai Lee, *For Freedom's Sake: The Life of Fannie Lou Hamer* (Chicago: University of Illinois Press, 2000); Bettye Collier Thomas and V. P. Franklin, eds., *Sisters in the Struggle: African-American Women in the Civil Rights-Black Power Movement* (New York: New York University Press, 2001); Belinda Robnett, *How Long? How Long? African American Women and the Struggle for Freedom and Justice* (New York: Oxford University Press, 1997); Barbara Ransby, *Ella Baker and the Black Freedom Movement: A Radical Democratic Vision* (Chapel Hill: University of North Carolina Press, 2003); Timothy B. Tyson, *Radio Free Dixie: Robert F. Williams & the Roots of Black Power* (Chapel Hill: University of North Carolina Press, 1999); Peter Levy, *Civil War on Race Street: The Civil Rights Movement in Cambridge, Maryland* (Gainesville: University Press of Florida, 2003); Emilye Crosby, *A Little Taste of Freedom: The Black Freedom Struggle in Claiborne County, Mississippi* (Chapel Hill: University of North Carolina Press, 2005); Wesley C. Hogan, *Many Minds, One Heart: SNCC's Dream for a New America* (Chapel Hill: University of North Carolina Press, 2007). On rethinking the southern focus of the movement, see Jeanne Theoharis and Komozi Woodard, eds., *Freedom North: The Black Freedom Struggle Outside of the South, 1940–1980* (New York: Palgrave Macmillan, 2002); and Jeanne Theoharis and Komozi Woodard, eds., *Groundwork: Local Black Freedom Movements in America* (New York: New York University Press, 2003); Clarence

Taylor, *Knocking at Our Own Door: Milton A. Galamison and the Struggle to Integrate New York City Schools* (New York: Columbia University Press, 1997); Martha Biondi, *To Stand and Fight* (Cambridge, Mass.: Harvard University Press, 2003); Matthew Countryman, *Up South* (Philadelphia: University of Pennsylvania Press, 2005); Josh Sides, *L.A. City Limits: African American Los Angeles from the Great Depression to the Present* (Berkeley: University of California Press, 2003); Quintard Taylor, *In Search of the Racial Frontier* (New York: W.W. Norton, 1998); and Robert Self, *American Babylon: Race and the Struggle for Postwar Oakland* (Princeton, N.J.: Princeton University Press, 2003).

21. Stewart Burns, *To the Mountaintop: Martin Luther King's Sacred Mission to Save America 1955–1968* (New York: Harper Collins, 2003), 18.

22. Rosa Parks, *Rosa Parks: My Story* (New York: Dial Books, 1992), 124.

23. Rosa Parks, *The Black Women Oral History Project Volume 8,* (Westport: Meckler, 1991), 253 (hereafter cited as BWOHP*).*

24. Parks, BWOHP, 254.

25. Interview of Rosa Parks by John H. Britton for The Civil Rights Documentation Project, September 28, 1967, 6 (hereafter cited as CRDP).

26. Jo Ann Gibson Robinson, *The Montgomery Bus Boycott and the Women Who Started It: The Memoir of Jo Ann Gibson Robinson* (Knoxville: University of Tennessee Press, 1987), 45–46.

27. Taylor Branch, *Parting the Waters* (New York: Simon & Schuster, 1988), 159.

28. Rosa Parks with Gregory Reed, *Quiet Strength* (Grand Rapids: Zondervan, 1994), 27.

29. Violence continued in Montgomery even after the desegregation of the buses, with snipers firing into the buses and the bombing of four black churches. Brinkley, *Rosa Parks*, 171.

30. Beth Bates, "'Double V for Victory' Mobilizes Black Detroit, 1941–1946," in Theoharis and Woodard, *Freedom North*, 23.

31. Parks, CRDP, 28.

32. Notes on her speech to the Alabama club, Rosa L. Parks Papers, 1955–1976, on file at the Walter Reuther Library, Wayne State University (hereafter cited as Rosa Parks Papers); Brinkley, *Rosa Parks*, 67.

33. John Conyers, "On Rosa Parks: She Earned the Title as Mother of the Civil Rights Movement," Interview with Amy Goodman, *Democracy Now*, October 25, 2005. Transcript can be found at www.democracynow.org/article.pl?sid=05/10/25/1421234.

34. Brinkley, *Rosa Parks*, 187.

35. Ibid., 189.

36. "America Salutes Rosa Parks," video on file at the Schomburg Library.

37. Sidney Fine, *Violence in the Model City* (Ann Arbor: University of Michigan Press, 1989), 4.

38. Parks's papers (housed at the Reuther Library) are full of programs, invitations, and political literature, demonstrating the robust political life Parks maintained during the 1960s and her considerable attention to the Black Power Movement.

39. Parks, CRDP, 19.

40. Ibid., 189.

41. I am grateful to Stephen Ward for helping me put these events together. Box 2, Rosa Parks Papers; Brinkley, *Rosa Parks*, 191–3.

42. Brinkley, *Rosa Parks*, 202–3.

43. "Whatever happened to Mrs. Rosa Parks," *Ebony*, August 1971.

44. Henry Hampton and Steve Fayer, *Voices of Freedom: An Oral History of the Civil Rights Movement from the 1950s through the 1980s* (New York: Bantam, 1990), 391.

45. Suzanne Smith, *Dancing in the Street: Motown and the Cultural Politics of Detroit* (Cambridge, Mass.: Harvard University Press, 1999), 200–2. Fine, *Violence in the Model City*, 286.

46. Roxanne Brown, "Mother of the Movement," *Ebony*, February 1988.

47. Coretta Scott King, "Address to Antioch Reunion," 2004. For transcript, see www .antioch-college.edu/Antiochian/archive/Antiochian_2004fall/reunion/king/.

48. Ibid.

49. "History Professor Clay Carson to publish King autobiography," Stanford News Service, October 27, 1998. Available at http://news.stanford.edu/pr/98/981027carsonfina .html.

50. James Baldwin, "The Dangerous Road before Martin Luther King," *Collected Essays* (New York: Library of America, 1998), 649–50.

51. Coretta Scott King, "Address at Youth March for Integrated Schools in Washington, D. C.," October 25, 1958, Martin Luther King Papers Project downloaded at mlk-kpp01.stanford.edu/ . . . /Vol4/25-Oct-1958_AddressAtYouthMarch.pdf.

52. According to *Boston Globe* columnist Derrick Jackson, the delegation was received by the U.S. representative to the talks as if they were "hysterical females." Derrick Jackson, "The King who led on world peace," *Boston Globe*, February 1, 2006.

53. King, *My Life with Martin*, 272–3.

54. Taylor Branch, *At Canaan's Edge: America in the King Years, 1965–68* (New York: Simon & Schuster, 2006).

55. Thomas F. Jackson, *From Civil Rights to Human Rights: Martin Luther King, Jr. and the Struggle for Economic Rights* (Philadelphia: University of Pennsylvania Press, 2007), 313.

56. Burns, *To the Mountaintop*, 321.

57. Michael Honey, *Going Down Jericho Road: The Memphis Strike, Martin Luther King's Last Campaign* (New York: W. W. Norton, 2007), 454.

58. Ibid., 453–54.

59. Ibid., 454.

60. "How Many Men Must Die?," *Life*, April 19, 1968, 34; "Coretta King: In Her Husband's Footsteps," *Ebony*, September 1968, 162.

61. A full transcript of her speech can be found at: http://grym.gnn.tv/blogs/20194/Transcript_of_Coretta_Scott_King_Central_Park_April_27_198.

62. Ibid.

63. Roland L. Freeman, *The Mule Train: A Journey of Hope Remembered* (Nashville: Rutledge Hill Press, 1998), 23.

64. Ibid., 109.

65. Jackson, *From Civil Rights to Human Rights*, 358.

66. Ibid., 358.

67. Coretta Scott King spoke out against war in a speech at the Metropolitan Community Foundation on January 16, 2003, declaring: "True homeland security should be about protection of liberties." A partial transcript can be found at www.blink.org.uk/pdescription.asp?key=1549&grp=27.

68. Mubarik Dahir, "Mrs. King's Legacy of Love," *AlterNet*, February 2, 2006. In 1998, she explained, "Homophobia is like racism and anti-Semitism and other forms of bigotry in that it seeks to dehumanize a large group of people, to deny their humanity, their dignity and personhood. . . . This sets the stage for further repression and violence that spread all too easily to victimize the next minority group." *Chicago Defender*, April 1, 1998, 1. King spoke at the 2003 Creating Change conference and, in 2004, linked the struggle for gay marriage to the civil rights struggle. "Coretta Scott King Gives Support to Gay Marriage," *USA Today*, March 24, 2004.

69. Dyana Berger, "Coretta Scott King Dies at 78," *Washington Blade*, February 3, 2006.

70. Ibid., and "Anti-gay church to picket King's funeral," *Washington Blade*, February 3, 2006.

71. Folder 1–7, Box 1, Rosa Parks Papers.

72. "FBI Spied on Coretta Scott King, Memos Show," August 30, 2007. Available at www.MSNBC.com.

73. Gary Younge, "White History 101," *The Nation*, March 5, 2007, 10.

74. Rosa Parks, Stephen Millner interview in David Garrow, *The Walking City: The Montgomery Bus Boycott, 1955–1956* (New York: Carlson, 1989), 563.

75. Marisa Chappell, Jenny Hutchinson, and Brian Ward, "'Dress modestly, neatly . . . as if you were going to church': Respectability, Class and Gender in the Montgomery Bus Boycott and the Early Civil Rights Movement" in *Gender and the Civil Rights Movement*, ed. Peter Lin and Sharon Monteith (New Brunswick: Rutgers University Press, 2004), 88.

76. Lynne Olson, *Freedom's Daughters: The Unsung Heroines of the Civil Rights Movement from 1830 to 1970* (New York: Simon and Schuster, 2001), 288.

77. Parks, *My Story*, 186.

78. Michael Eric Dyson, *I May Not Get There With You: The True Martin Luther King, Jr.* (New York: The Free Press, 2001), 212–13.

79. Ibid., 212. See also Clayborne Carson, *The Autobiography of Martin Luther King, Jr.* (New York: Grand Central, 2001). Coretta switched her program at the Conservatory from performing arts to musical education to fit with these expectations but then was largely thwarted in her desire to teach.

80. Interview with Coretta Scott King on *Tavis Smiley* (taped in January 2005 and aired February 2, 2006). The transcript can be found at www.pbs.org/kcet/tavissmiley/archive/200602/20060202.html.

81. Coretta Scott King, "The World of Coretta King: A Word with Trina Grillo," *New Lady*, January 1966, 34.

82. Dyson, *I May Not Get There With You*, 221.

83. King, *My Life with Martin*, 303–4.

CHARLES M. PAYNE

# Why Study the Movement?

## *A Conversation on Movement Values and Movement History*

**N**ote: The following is a lightly edited transcript of Charles Payne leading a discussion around the question of "Why study the movement?," which was the closing keynote at the "Local Studies, a National Movement: Toward a Historiography of the Black Freedom Movement" Conversations in the Disciplines Conference at SUNY Geneseo, March 24–26, 2006.[1]

CHARLES PAYNE: I don't think what's called for now is a "normal talk." And sixty percent of those talks is superfluous anyway. So we can cut most of what I was going to say. I was going to try to say something about where civil rights scholarship *seems* to be going and where I think it *should* be going. Alright? And the first part is just: a whole ton of stuff is coming out; some of it's good, some of it's bad. That's the first twenty minutes of my speech. What I would *like* to do—I'm going to hold off. I think I *may* talk about the latter part; I want to say something about where I think it *should* be going, so I may hold off and do a brief thing about it at the end.

Now I want to start getting some reaction from those of you who have been studying the Movement. I want to go back to this question which came up earlier in a different form. I actually want to ask you to comment on two questions: the first is simply, what is it that you are getting from studying the Movement? And I wonder if there's a racial difference in this. I'll explain why I'm asking this at some point. Do black students and white students get *exactly* the same thing from studying the Movement? So I want to get some of you who have been doing that to comment about it, what's coming across. Then, those of you who have been *teaching*, I wonder if what the students *say* they learn is what you think you're teaching. Is what you're sending out there what they're picking up on?

I need to think about how to articulate how important I think one of Judy Richardson's earlier comments was. It is one that I'm afraid will be missed and I don't want it to be, so I want to underscore it.[2] And it was to the effect that: wherever I've gone, whatever I've done, I have taken the *values* of my Movement experience with me. Now the question, then, is: when she said that, what did you understand her to mean? When she says "the values of her Movement experience," which have informed her subsequent life, how do you understand that phrase, "values from the Movement experience"? You will comment on that and then she will tell you whether you get it right or wrong. [*audience laughter*]

And let me say, or let *me* ask you if I rightly interpreted something earlier. When some of these issues came up in one conversation, I can't remember which, people were talking about Montgomery and Claudette Colvin was mentioned a couple of times.[3] I *thought* that was an example of people saying that "I realize from studying the Movement that more people can be historical actors." That's the way I was taking that. That's what I thought the message was. If that's *not* the case, let me know.

But any of you who are studying the Movement in any way, what are you getting out of it? What does it change about how you think and see these issues?

TARIK KITSON: For me, the reason why I study the civil rights movement is it explains why I'm treated the way I'm treated. And it explains things about my ancestors, my Mom, my Grandma, especially since I'm from the South.

PAYNE: You are from Greensboro?

KITSON: Right. I'm from North Carolina.

PAYNE: A particularly important site.

KITSON: Right. Also, you know, I wasn't really taught anything when I was a little kid in public school or anything like that. I'm from Greensboro, but knew nothing about it, as far as black history. When I got to Geneseo I learned *so much* about it and I teach a lot of people about stuff I've learned. I go back to Greensboro and I teach about where they're living at. And a lot of people who are like me, you know, a lot of black kids my age, they don't know anything about their history. And I like teaching them about it because it's very interesting. So, that's what I get out of the civil rights movement.

PAYNE: Can you say something about—in any kind of conversations, what kind of reactions you get from the people you are teaching?

KITSON: They just really surprised; they're surprised about a lot of things I talk to them about. Like why things are the way they are.

PAYNE: Good. Anyone else?

CORTEZ JONES: For me, learning about the Movement, it's kind of an inspiration now. And the reason I say that is because there's so many problems going on in modern day society and it's totally different from what the Movement was about back in the '50s and the '60s. Now, it's not us being oppressed by the white men or the white people, it's us being oppressed by *each other*. And learning about the Movement, I kind of get ideas and I kind of get an itch in my back: "What can I do in my own community, how they did it?" And learning about the Movement kind of helps me, guides me in that way.

And I had the pleasure of listening to Dorothy Cotton speak and she gave me this idea. I asked the question: If [Martin Luther] King was alive, what would he say to us and what would he do? And she said, "I can't tell you." She said, "What I could tell you is that he *is* dead." [*audience laughter*] The change is on me—which is good, though. And learning about the youths of SNCC and the things they did is really inspirational to me because now I feel that *I* can make a difference. So, inspiration.

PAYNE: Inspiration-slash-empowerment, right? Cause those don't have to go together. But this sense that I *feel* that I can make a difference, is what I'm referring to. Anyone else?

PETER ANDERSON: I'm Pete Anderson. I'm a graduate student at Binghamton but as I said, I graduated from Geneseo. I really enjoy studying the Movement for, along the same lines that Tarik and Cortez talked about. I, obviously, am not an African American, so I'm coming at it from a little bit of a different place. But I just fell in love with learning about it because it really tells a story about what our country is. And what can make our country a bad place, is what can make it a great place at the same time. I like passing the story on to people because I want people to know about what was going on and what the Movement was fighting for, and kind of the key issues that are still around today. The issues were around before the Movement and they're kind of always going to be around until something happens, like

Figure 30  Geneseo students (*left to right*) Christopher Basso (*partially cut off*), Erin Rightmyer (*background*), Jared DePass, Peter Anderson, Amanda Abold (*background*), Tarik Kitson, and Cortez Jones (*background*), at "Local Studies, a National Movement" Conference, March 25, 2006. Photograph courtesy of SUNY Geneseo.

a Movement, to really bring them up. So that's why I've enjoyed learning about the Movement so much.

PAYNE: And when you "pass it on," when you talk about it to others, what kind of reactions do you get?

ANDERSON: Most people are—Obviously there's always sort of a certain level of: "I just had no idea about that." And most people are incredibly interested. I worked with Tarik and Cortez when I was a student here at Geneseo and I loved working with them and I loved seeing how people react to the type of information that they're getting. And what's most interesting to me was a lot of times when [white] people learn about it, they're incredibly defensive about it. I think a lot of it comes with where the people are coming from, their background, whether it be racial or economic or social, and how some people are just like, "No, that couldn't happen here. That's not what we do." And you kind of see—

PAYNE: Give me an example.

ANDERSON: Like, I work with students who come from a very sheltered environment, the suburban environment. They're tucked away from the "bad cities" and the "bad people" who live there and so on and so forth. And you teach them about racism and they're like, "This doesn't exist." And they hear about the riots that happened, in Watts and so on and so forth, and they're, "Oh, they were just bad people, they weren't—"

PAYNE: "Crazy people! Crazy Negroes!"*

ANDERSON: Yes. Exactly. What Professor Jeffries talked about earlier. That's their visual impression. But, if I work with them long enough, they can finally start to see the connections and they're like, "They aren't that crazy. They're saying the same things that these people are saying and they weren't viewed as crazy." I don't know if I'm answering your question, but—

PAYNE: I'm not that sure where I'm going with the question. But your answer qualifies. One of the things you made me think is that— What he said at the end there: "that I get an initial reaction—I get an initially bad reaction, or negative reaction, or defensive reaction. If I keep pushing, then some people will hear me in a different way." I think in the individual lives of organizers, learning *that* is just a major crossing point. Because we tend to divide the world up into those who agree with us and those who don't, and those who don't we don't have much patience with. And precisely what becoming an organizer *is*, I think at some level, experientially, is learning to work through this initial rejection.

KRISTY SIRIANNI: I'm Kristy Sirianni and I go to Geneseo. The first thing I remember, actually, after coming here is taking a general civil rights class and watching the first clip Emilye showed. And I think it was with the Freedom Rides and watching African Americans getting beaten, and just tears

* Payne is referencing Hasan Kwame Jeffries's earlier talk, "Crazy Negroes and Out-of-Control Crackers," on the panel, "Moving Beyond Dichotomies." For student responses to Jeffries's talk, see "Conclusion: 'Doesn't everybody want to grow up to be Ella Baker?': Teaching Movement History" (this volume). Jeffries refers briefly to this concept in chapter 8 of this volume: "Remaking History: Barack Obama, Political Cartoons, and the Civil Rights Movement."

coming down my face. And I think studying with her, and seeing local movements for the first time for me, being able to put faces to the Movement and seeing people like Fannie Lou Hamer and Ella Baker who—Ella Baker, to me, is just a *complete* inspiration. I look at her as a woman who I would love to just live up to what she did.[4]

I have also had reactions like Pete's. I've had conversations with my roommates who are all white, twenty, nineteen-year-olds from prominent middle-class white families. And I've told them some of the stuff that I learned here and they are just, they don't believe me. They're adamant about not believing anything I have to say. And very defensive in some cases, about the same kind of stuff. It's just unbelievable that it's coming out of my mouth, but they don't want to hear it.

PAYNE: I'm in the process of writing an essay, the theme of which will be: militant ignorance. [*audience laughter*] "This couldn't have happened. It wasn't that way."

SARAH BUZANOWSKI: I'm Sarah Buzanowski and I'm a graduate student at Temple University in Philly and a Geneseo graduate. I study the Movement and what I get from it is, I think it mirrored my sense of where I'm going in life in terms of social justice issues, in terms of how I am in the fight for feminism, and how I work, how I do *my* history work, how I confront the questions, the ideologies, the issues of power that we're looking at, that a lot of people in this room are looking at. And it informs all that. I don't think we can really understand where any of this stuff is going without taking from those lessons. And I think, of all the history I've studied, from humanities with Professor Cook and the whole Rome thing, I think that the subject that's most relevant *to me* was the lessons I took from the Movement.

ERIN RIGHTMYER: I'm Erin Rightmyer, a senior at Geneseo. I remember being nine years old and watching the *Eyes on the Prize* videos. My Dad would get them from the library for me, so I've always been interested. But it wasn't until I started looking into it more and until I started studying women's studies, women's history as well, that I kind of saw the connections between women's—like how the students of SNCC could work to change big issues, but they would work on the grass-roots level. It inspires me to try to work with politics and try to change the big things, but do it on a very basic

Figure 31 Geneseo students (*left to right*) Kristy Sirianni, Sarah Buzanowski, Christopher Basso, at "Local Studies, a National Movement" Conference, March 25, 2006. Photograph courtesy of SUNY Geneseo.

level. So it gives me hope. I guess that's why I kind of enjoy studying it. I find that there's a lot of things that can be done from it.

PAYNE: This empowerment subtheme amongst you is very clear. For those of you who are teaching it, anyone want to say what you think your students are getting or what you want your students to get from the other side?

PAM BROOKS: My name is Pam Brooks. I teach at Oberlin College; this is my sixth year. This is such an amazing set of stories that Judy has shared with us and demonstrated so well.[5] I am connected to the Movement because I am black and female, and that is inseparable. I am connected because I am the daughter of Movement people and I want to teach this work because it inspires me over, and over, and over again. It never fails to bring me to tears and to bring me to soaring heights of admiration and respect. And I will *never* apologize for writing that kind of history or for reading it. And I am *so* thankful that the scholars in this room are doing the work they're doing. So, my students who come to Oberlin—

PAYNE: To a place with a history of a certain kind.

BROOKS: Which is a place with an *amazing* history. I can tell you some of those stories but we know them because we live in America. And this institution prides itself on its history of inclusion and although this institution is, indeed, a good place to *be*, as an academic who thinks in a particular way, [it is] my students [who] are a reward to me, they are a treasure for me.

I just returned from Jackson [Miss.] where I went, with them in tow, to a conference of Movement vets. The students were *outstanding* and so were the veterans, and so was their interaction. So there's a cadre of young people that eat this stuff up, [*gesturing to students in room*] just like these students. And who value this work because they see within it ways that they, too, can be directed and inspired to do the work that they know they can't avoid.

And they are given maps, small maps, and they're given handbooks. Chana Kai Lee's biography of Mrs. Hamer is a handbook, and Angela Davis's autobiography is a handbook.[6] And any of the pieces that they read and digest, we sit around and we talk about how now they're going to move forward. So, I love to do this work. I don't ever intend leaving—I mean, take me out feet first, I'm going to die writing on the blackboard. I'm not gonna stop!

RENEE ROMANO: Hi I'm Renee Romano, I teach at Wesleyan. My teaching the Movement has really changed since I've been teaching. When I started, I don't know what I was doing but I had this moment my second year of teaching when a student, after this big thing on the Movement, a big unit, said, "You know, the Movement didn't change anything. It just made whites more likely to kill black people." I thought, "Ok, I'm *really* doing something wrong."

PAYNE: There was a time at which that kind of remark was common among black students. Vincent Harding has written about this attitude that "the Movement didn't do anything."[7]

ROMANO: Well, it's still very common among students at my institution! There's a real cynicism. And I found teaching my cynical students has actually made me less cynical and more about John Lewis, Vincent Harding, thinking "what are the ways in which the Movement teaches people how to be fully human or offers models of human empowerment?" And one of the things I've been trying to challenge my students about—they will often say, "Things are harder now because the enemy is more diffuse." Right? "In the sixties, it was clear who was racist; it was clear who the enemy was." And I spend a lot of time talking about: imagine being in Mississippi in 1960, a Closed Society, and think about how bleak things could have looked to you if you had no hope. And then imagine the kinds of tools you have today if you want to change your world, from the Internet to a media, that at least you could potentially use, to all kinds of things. And trying to give them some perspective by using this past, about how even in incredibly trying, difficult times people *can* take some action to take control of their own lives and try to change their world. And I don't know if that's been successful with my very cynical students but that's at least what I try to do whenever I now teach the Movement.

PAYNE: Since you have the microphone and since I know you have a book coming out soon, would you say a sentence or two about the book that's coming out that's pertinent to this discussion?

ROMANO: Thank you! Sure. I've got a book coming out called *The Civil Rights Movement in American Memory*, which is an anthology of essays, and one of the big issues it's looking at is the ways in which the dominant narrative of the Movement is in fact being put to political use, as in often doing problematic political work in our culture in terms of closing off discussion about the complexity of the past, in terms of pinning the blame on a few specific individual bad men, the out-of-control crackers, and looking at the ways in which there's been commodification of Movement history and depoliticization of a lot of the Movement symbols, from the X Caps to the five magazine spreads of iconic Black Panther photos in a fashion spread. So it's a book that tries to, in a lot of different essays, look at all these kinds of things.[8]

UMEME SABABU: How you doing? My name is Umeme Sababu and I was born in Greenville, Mississippi. I teach at Edinboro University in Pennsylvania. And one of the things I really try to do is to make the Movement filled with complexity. You ask a lot of students the first day of class, "Who are some of the important people of the civil rights movement?" And after Rosa Parks and Dr. King, it's blank. So what I think to do is try to explore the complexities, the different organizations, and different individuals in the movement. A perfect example, on the second day of class, I was lecturing and I'm very emotional when I lecture. And the guy in front of me, he kept leaning back and after class he said, "How many times do you pray a day?" And I said, "Well, sometimes I don't pray at all." And he says, "Well, you're not a true Muslim."

And I said, "Well, I'm not Muslim at all!" But his perception was, because my name is Umeme Sababu, that I was some kind of radical, jihad Muslim, et cetera. So I try to explore the complexity. . . . The reason I'm here today, really, is to explore in more important detail this kind of false dichotomy between the "civil rights movement" and the "Black Power" movement.

SCOTT CORLEY: Hi, I'm Scott [Corley] and I teach at a two-year college in Binghamton and quite directly my objective in teaching what I teach, which is basically 100-level survey American history courses, is to have students understand how much of this is directly interconnected with American history. My students usually think, coming into my classes, and I daresay most other ones, that there's American history and then there's African American history. And I try to *change* that and integrate the two so that it's not so separate. And many of my students initially have a *really* hard time understanding that, in addition to what was just said, understanding the intricacies of the American history. So, those are the main things that I try to address.

BILL COOK: I'm Bill Cook, a teacher here at Genesco, and I'm the medievalist so I perhaps have a somewhat different kind of thing to say. I'm a self-taught person with regard to the civil rights movement and on a sabbatical in 1993 I found myself traveling around the Mississippi Delta and trying to learn some things that I should have learned when I was twenty years old. And I went into a church and went to Sunday school with a group, and when the group all got together they got up and said, "We think Brother Bill ought to address the group." And so I got up, without any preparation at all, and I had just been doing some thinking and some reading and I had also just gotten back from Europe and had been to Auschwitz and I said, "Let me tell you why I'm here. I'm here because I believe that I need to hear your story and I need to incorporate it into my story. And I want you to hear my story because you should incorporate it into your story." We had a wonderful dialogue and an interesting conversation. I've never quite taught my own courses the same after that.

I teach a Western Humanities course that a couple of people here have taken. It's required of all of our students and it is sort of your Plato and Dante and Shakespeare, the Bible, and such things. But we teach the course—the goal of the course is to talk about social, political, and moral alternatives. That's what the catalog says. And to do that, one doesn't just talk about Plato, one also talks about the modern times. One tries to make

Figure 32  Participants at "Local Studies, a National Movement" Conference, March 24, 2006. Photograph courtesy of SUNY Geneseo.

some links, and what I've been able to do because of some experiences I've had, and reading John [Dittmer]'s book and other books I've looked at in the past, I've been able to find ways of incorporating some of that story, that became my story,[9] so that it becomes all my students' story.[9] It can be something very simple like an assignment. I have an assignment where we, for example, talk about Martin Luther King as a humanities student by reading "A Letter from Birmingham City Jail." It's a wonderful assignment that I've given to students several times, where they can find, obviously, things from the Bible, from Sophocles, from Plato and from Thomas Aquinas and other places. But more than that, when I talk about democracy in Athens and what it might mean and what we might learn about the modern world by looking at that first democracy, or when we talk about certain other kinds of topics that come up in the course, I'm able to bring in other examples and broader examples so that our students really are able to see as much as possible what this old stuff has to inform us about the world in which we live.

And the most important thing: I used to have two pictures in my office. They are Francis of Assisi and Dante. I now have three pictures in my office: Francis of Assisi, Dante, and Fannie Lou Hamer. [*audience chuckles*]

PAYNE: That's a good story! Alright, I need to stop. I know there are any number of folk I would actually call on if I had time and *make* them say something.

This time last year I was on this external review for the Black Studies department at the University of California, Santa Barbara. They bring out a bunch of faculty and ask, "How's our department doing?" and I'm one of the bunch of faculty they brought in. And so the first thing you do is meet with the administration and they tell you what they want to know. And so I'm sitting with all of the honchos, and they said, "Well, you know, this is southern California, we don't have much of a black student population here. Do you guys really think we need to have a Black Studies program? We have an increasing Latino Studies program and maybe these resources should go there." Which is hardly the first time I've heard that. The underlying assumption is: "For whom is Black Studies? For whom is it taught? It's for black students." And there's almost always, almost a kind of therapeutic model of what it is you're doing: You're making black students feel good about themselves.

My impression as a teacher—I've been doing this for . . . close to thirty years. It's been a while! White students in some senses get more out of it than black students. For one of the things that I see happening to white *and* black students is that—and this will hearken back to things which were said earlier today. I forgot who said it. I think it was Judy: "Well, if they lied to me about this, what else have they lied to me about?" So, I find students saying, "I am no longer comfortable with what I'm been taught in U.S. History—or Medieval History. If there's a master narrative of the civil rights movement, is there a master narrative in the way they present the English language to us? What are the hidden assumptions and paradigms?" It's one of the most valuable things that we *do* in black studies and women's studies, is teach this kind of critique of the dominant paradigms. And to have a sense of both what the dominant paradigm is and what the critiques of it might be. If all you get out of college is that, you're well ahead of most people. And I think we do that in a way that the traditional departments do not.

Black students—my sense and my experience, and anybody wants to comment on this, please—get something else out of it. And Tarik touched on it. You touched on it when you referred to your ancestors. If I understand what black students are saying to me after they read this material, one of the *dominant* messages from them over the years has been: "I respect my ancestors in a different way having become acquainted with this material." And what does that tell you? It tells you they *disrespected* their ancestors before. This is one of those embedded dialogues that's so deeply drilled into us that we're not aware of it. I think each generation of African American youths has been taught to disrespect the previous generation in certain ways. And while that's a normal phenomenon among any people, I think given the degree of *stigma* attached to race in this country, it has particular weight among African Americans. It's particularly hard for us to respect our forebears. And part of the reason for that is that we're taught to think that they took it. I mean, the model that the younger generation has—and this would have been true in 1960. Right? The kids go out to the sit-in, the kids go, "Darn, I'm going to do this because my daddy didn't." Right? So this notion that your parents didn't struggle, your grandparents didn't struggle, and were therefore in a sense not "manly," collectively. And "manly" means worthy. That's something which has to be struggled with. And I think exposure to this kind of history helps folks rethink those kinds of issues, about the imagined past.

Let me say this, too, because I'm really sorry in a sense that I did my schedule so I can't be here for tomorrow morning's work with schoolteachers. I think that work is just particularly vital, not only because it would be nice if some people learned this before they got to college, but also because schoolteachers are the "niggers" of our time in a sense. It is the most disrespected, disregarded of all professions. It really is useful for teachers to think of themselves as the heirs to the Movement. To think of themselves as a part of that flow of people who are trying to *teach* in ways that will change the distribution of opportunity structures.

From time to time, Bob Moses has spoken to my classes and they ask that question, "What are you doing now?" He says, "I'm running the Algebra Project. I'm teaching math."[10] And they say, "Oh, you've left the Movement, huh?" [*laughs*] That's so far from his thinking! I've never seen him respond. I don't know what he thinks. Who knows? But anyway, connecting teachers to this history is, I think, very important. And I also want to say: this whole notion of finding models for oneself in this history—I, too, want to be like Ella Baker when I'm fully formed. But finding living, concrete, breathing, touchable models, as it were, is something else that I hear.

And there's this Charles Eagles article which says—which I think John Dittmer must have referred to yesterday—part of the problem with this certain generation of scholarship is all these people are interested in trying to restart the Movement.[11] Well I don't know if that's a problem. [*laughs*] I don't think that's a problem. If that's the case, if you are trying to render Movement history in ways that will do what they are saying, help students think about contemporary issues and help them think about their personal relationship with social change, well don't you want to get the story right? Doesn't that give you an additional—beyond the expectations of scholarship—an additional imperative to be right in what you say? I don't accept the idea that because you have this passionate commitment to a certain kind of history you therefore are more likely to distort it than the "objective" historian.

We don't have time now, but it would be interesting to speculate on this other question: What's negative about learning this history? Just to keep the conversation halfway honest. I don't think I have a particularly strong answer to that. But one thing I do worry about is this setting the bar too high, that you study these dramatic victories, and that *devalues* everything that is around you. I remember there was a time at which I was visiting college campuses in the Northeast. This was around the time that the anti-apartheid movement was starting and we asked—every place you go, you asked black students, "What's going on?" And they said, "Nothing. We're not political at all on this campus." And of course they might have a tutoring program in the community, they might have a mentoring program, they may be actually involved in lots of things, but they say, "We're not doing anything political here. There's nothing going on here." And they've gotten a certain conception of "political," right? And it's a big event, dramatic event, "political." And I wonder if sometimes in our teaching if we reinforce this notion.

Let me just see if I can get some reactions quickly to the other question. What are the values of the Movement? When Judy was referring to that, what went off in your mind? What do you think she means when she talks about the values that she took from the Movement? [*silence*] Just what I was afraid of!

WESLEY HOGAN: I don't know, there are a couple adjectives that came to mind that I jotted down because I think the question is such an important one. Relational. Active, like a way to actually *do* something. Communitarian, everybody does all the work and people are accountable to their friends. In other words, they do what they say they're going to do.

PAYNE: Anyone else? What are the values that animated this Movement, as you understand it? We can separate it from Judy. How do you understand the values that animated the Movement?

TODD MOYE: The important thing for me is that they defined the values for themselves and they very consciously thought about how they were doing that. Consciously refusing to use the values that had come down to them from the larger culture, and created an alternative culture, an alternative value system. So, to me, it's less important how you define what the value of their system was than to acknowledge that they so consciously created something aside from what had been handed down to them.

PAYNE: That *process*, not content. What are the questions in the Freedom School curriculum? "What is it that the majority culture has that we want? What is it that the majority culture has that we *don't* want? What is it that we have that we want to keep?"[12] Now Du Bois said—I wouldn't even try to capture his language—but in a speech in 1960 he said: African Americans have got to begin thinking about what of what we are we want to keep, otherwise everything's going to become crazy. That was April, 1960.[13] Anyone else want to say anything about this issue of values?

GREG FAIR: My name's Greg Fair. I'm a student at Geneseo. One thing that I think is really important, I know for me personally, and I think is part of what everybody's been talking about today, is the value of process maybe over outcome. And I know Ella Baker talked a lot about that and a big part of the Movement was what you learn through the process of trying something. And for me personally, it wasn't necessarily where you end up in the end that made it a success, it's what you got out of the process, what you got out of the intent.

BEN HOUSTON: Ben Houston from the University of Florida. I think the value that I associate is exactly what you said, which is simply the

Waveland : Work-Study Institute, Feb.-March, 1965. Notes
by Jane Stembridge about a class held by Stokely Carmichael, and
other related notes.

The most important class was "Stokely's speech class."
He put eight sentences on the blackboard, with a line between, like this:

| | |
|---|---|
| I digs wine | I enjoy drinking cocktails |
| The peoples wants freedom | The people want freedom |
| Whereinsoever the policemens goes they causes troubles | Anywhere the officers of the law go, they cause trouble |
| I wants to reddish to vote | I want to register to vote |

---

Stokely: What do you think about these sentences? Such as --
The peoples want s freedom?

Zelma: It doesn't sound right.

Stokely: What do you mean?
Zelma: "Peoples" isn't right.
Stokely: Docs it mean anything?
Milton: People means everybody. Peoples means everybody in ther
world.
Alma: Both sentences are right as long as you understand
them.
Henry: They're both Okay, but in a speech class you have to
use correct English.

(Stokely writes "correct English" in corner of blackboard.)

Zelma: I was taught at least to use the sentences on the rights
side.
Stokely: Does anybody you know use the sentences on the left?
Class: Yes.
Stokely: Are they wrong?
Zelma: In terms of English, they are wrong.
Stokely: Who decides what is correct English and what is in-
correct English?
Milton: People made rules. People in England, I guess.
Stokely: You all say some people speak like on the left side of
the board. Could they go anywhere and that way?
Could they go to Harvard?
Class: Yes - No. Disagreement.
Stokely: Does Mr. Turnbow speak like on the left side?
Class: Yes.
Stokely: Could Mr. Turnbow go to Harvard and speak like that?
I wants to reddish to vote.
Class: Yes.
Stokely: Would he be embarrassed?

Figure 33 Partial transcript from a Freedom School class led by Stokely Carmichael at
the Waveland Work-Study Institute, in February–March 1965. The class addressed the
Freedom School questions: "What does the majority culture have that we want? What
does the majority culture have that we don't want? What do we have that we want
to keep?" February–March 1965, transcript by Jane Stembridge, SNCC papers. (SNCC
microfilm, Reel 12, frame 693, recreation.)

Movement where people can disagree and yet they still end up singing together because I see that sadly lacking in modern society.

PAYNE: For me, in my perception for what's special in that SNCC culture is that ability to disagree, to fight one another like cats and dogs, and to maintain this other kind of sense of unity. And what *is* dangerous, I think, is when—and again, I think Komozi [Woodard] referred to this earlier— when we look back we think, "Oh, they were all unified then. They were all on the same page." No. It is *precisely* their ability to disagree that is so impressive for me about that culture.[14]

SPEAKER: I just think it's very important always to struggle against perceived injustice.

PAYNE: That's true. That just about covers all of it! Judy, would you mind commenting on that question? What do you see, when you say that phrase, "the values of the Movement"?[15]

JUDY RICHARDSON: What do I see as the values? I was thinking about that as people talked. It's interesting because for me it's also very personal. It's not just going out and struggling against injustice, which is certainly part of it. One of the things—For example, where I work, when we come back from a shoot, say for example, what I always talk about is team: "Boy, the team was amazing on this." Well, I learned that from the Movement, that you always give credit to the team, because that's who does it. And in some ways going into film was very much—was easier for me, because there was always this sense that it was collaborative. When I sit in the edit room with Chuck, who's this incredible African American editor who was on *Eyes* I and *Eyes* II, I pulled him over to Northern Light now, it's not *just* that I absolutely value what he says about the edit. It's also that—Thursday night before I left, the student intern at the company comes in and said, "You know, Chuck just said something about the cover letter for this." Now, this is totally outside his edit. But there is a way in which I know that Chuck has good sense, I mean, basically. Right? And that I need to learn to listen to him. Again, I learned that from the Movement. I learned how people's opinions were valued in a way that—Now I never felt that I would be attacked in a staff meeting.

PAYNE: Disagreed with, but not attacked.

RICHARDSON: That's absolutely right. Now I might have been in awe, which was true. I was in awe of all the SNCC people. Never said a word in staff meetings. Part of it was that it was so highly politicized that I knew if I came out and said something, I might be messing up somebody's political position, and that would be a problem. So the reason I didn't talk was not because I thought that somebody was going to be slamming me, because that would never happen in a SNCC meeting.

I guess it's also the sense that—[*pauses*] It's funny because, I mean, I never think of myself as philosophically nonviolent. I'm not. But there is a way that that seemed "in," in terms of ways that we dealt with each other, that was very interesting to me. And I think about that now, looking back. I don't know that I knew that then, because I didn't know the role that had in the national Movement and so-and-so-and-so. Yeah, it's very personal to me. The way you deal with one another.

KOMOZI WOODARD: Can I add my observations? I've interviewed a lot of sisters from the Movement. And one thing you see—They go on up in leadership very quickly. They go up in leadership. So, one of the sisters was the head of the Urban League when she was running a youth program throughout the state of New Jersey. Another one became the highest ranking woman at Public Service Gas and Electric. What they said to me was that what they learned from the Movement is that you could do anything.

RICHARDSON: Absolutely!

WOODARD: So, what you did in service of the *cause*, it taught you to go study the situation, learn the skills you had to learn, transform yourself to do this job. They took that "can do" attitude. And also the fact that many of those women would never have been afforded leadership opportunities in the power structure, they were running institutions in the Movement.

PAYNE: In the Movement.

WOODARD: So they took that experience and they just zoomed up in all these things because they had—And even me in journalism. [*turning to Judy*] I would have never met you; I ran a newspaper. So certain things— part of the denial of equality in this country is not only for you to not get credentials, but for you to not get hands-on experience. For you had been excluded from power meetings. How is it done? And the Movement, in a way, was a parallel structure where you had to get those skills. You had to run successful campaigns. You had to publicize issues. Right?

RICHARDSON: But you know something? What you're talking about are the skills that we learned. I mean, part of it is that, yeah, there's times I think about what I learned in the Movement, it's like the book, *Everything I Needed to Know, I Learned in Kindergarten.*[16] But that's separate to me. Because for me it was also—And when I talked about the difference between the Movement and [black] nationalism, for example? Okay. One of the things was that in the Movement, you valued all of us. So when I hear from Freddie Green and somebody else—She and another woman go to meet Maulana Karenga, somewhere out in Utah, or wherever they were. And they go with Ralph Featherstone who was from D.C. and was in the Movement, in SNCC. And the three of them walk in—and I'm not sure who, but one of the other brothers was in there, too—and Karenga says, "We don't talk to women." Now, we understood—Freddie Green and the other woman, *they* understood (because I got this from them). They understood Karenga saying that. What they *didn't* understand was Featherstone staying at the meeting. Because for them, we were all colleagues. We were coworkers. That was the value. And so for them to, for the guys to turn their back and say, "Well, you all should leave." That retort—

PAYNE: Violates that value.

RICHARDSON: That was the value.

WOODARD: I was at a merger meeting in a more radical setting. It was a multiracial meeting and part of my delegation was a white guy. And the people of color in the other organization were having loving phrases to the two black delegates from our group, and they kept attacking the white guy in my group. And so we had to say, "Now, wait a minute. He's with us. If you attack him, you attack us." So it's the same thing. But yes, you're right. If I had abandoned him in the middle of that meeting, how could we say we were brothers in the struggle and stuff like that? So I think that it is the team spirit.

RICHARDSON: Yes.

WOODARD: And that you take care of each other.

RICHARDSON: Yes! That's it! That's it.

WOODARD: No matter what.

RICHARDSON: No matter what.

PAYNE: Now I'm only repeating something you said earlier, several times in fact, but there's a moment in the history of nationalism in too many places, in which chauvinism triumphs over that sense of teamwork. And the result is there's a moment in which all that leadership talent is suppressed. Organization cannot go on.

Your first remark—there's an article in Dick Cluster's *They Should Have Served that Cup of Coffee*, where Bernice Reagon has this thing where she says, "I don't recognize any of these histories of the Albany Movement. It wasn't about what King did or what SNCC did. What's important is, the Movement taught me I can cross any line anybody draws around me."[17]

RICHARDSON: *Hello!*

PAYNE: That's all it is. "I can cross any line anybody draws around me." And so, it creates this expanded sense of one's own potential but also— because I want to stress this before I end—but also an expanded sense of human potential generally. Right? This notion that you cannot go—can't be a journalist unless you go to journalism school. No! I'm going to take some sixteen-year-old boy, put him behind a typewriter, and we're going to work this thing out until we get a newspaper out of him! There's an interview with Bob Moses where he says, "One of the things that the Movement did was credentialize poor people."[18] If you're going to college, once you leave SUNY, you think you've got the right to speak on anything and everything, right? If you don't go through this, where do you get that expanded sense of yourself and your entitlement? Well, the Movement did that for people. It gave them the sense that they had the right to—they had the right to speak.

RICHARDSON: Can I say just one more thing? That was the other thing. I mean, I'm coming out of Tarrytown, New York. I'm coming from the under-the-hill area, which is where all the black folks live. My mother has an eighth-grade education, but she's reading the *New York Post*, she's listening to Barry Gray.[19] My father was a union organizer at the plant. So it's all that other stuff. But, I come out of there with a sense that I'm privileged. I go on a full scholarship to Swarthmore. The thing that saved me was going into the Movement. Because otherwise—I listened to Miss Hamer in a way

I would never have listened to her coming out of Swarthmore. Right? I'm listening to Mrs. Blackwell in a whole different way, which is what helps me. Now, let me talk about the skills. So that when I'm doing interviews for *Eyes on the Prize*, it's a whole different thing. Because I understand these people got a lot of sense, they've got organizing, they've got brilliance. It's something I would *not* have understood except for the Movement.

PAYNE: And just let me say that, embedded in that, one of the critiques of elite education is that they keep telling you, you already know everything. You got the best education there is. And so when you're in contact with people who don't socially represent those types, you've been taught to not hear them. That's part of the socialization process that some of you are going through *right now*. And some of us are abetting that. [*chuckles*]

I got into this discussion as a way to get into this question of: where is the Movement now? And depending on how it's framed, I never know whether I should be encouraged or *dis*couraged by the way young people sort of raise that issue. One way to frame it is: "It is so much more difficult to start a movement now," for whatever reasons. . . . You can fill it in, some of that has been talked about. Well, it depends on what you mean by the "Movement." If you think of the Movement in terms of the values, if you think of the Movement as people who have consciously defined some set of values and are doing their best to live up to those values, while they're making some kind of change in society—if you think of it that way, it doesn't seem to me to be so impossible. But if you think of it as, "You've got to change the racial structure of the country," well, that's gonna take a little while! Good luck! But I am saying that thinking of the Movement in terms of tactics is fine, strategy is fine, but thinking of it in terms of culture, and a culture in which certain kinds of people could *develop*, could grow in certain kinds of ways, right? That, in some ways, seems to me to be more replicable than this notion of the Movement as attacking the barricades and doing all this other big stuff. Which is what people *mean*, I think, largely, when they say, "We can't do that right now." Well, that's maybe not the point. That's probably not the most useful way to think about it, about the Movement.

Last two things I will say. [*pause*] What Judy again made me start thinking about. Well, suppose all of the people whose stories she read, suppose she had said, "This is a book and everybody in it now is a stockbroker." Suppose she said, "All these folks are now selling stock, making lots of money, and *living good!*" [*audience laughter*] Suppose she had said that none of these people is doing anything remotely connected to social justice, human rights, right now. But then that's just the way it is. Now, would you feel differently about the book, had she said that? Because she emphasized the continuity between their lives then and their lives now.[20]

ROMANO: Yes.

PAYNE: Tell me why.

ROMANO: Otherwise they buy into the consumerist ethos of America which seems so problematic.

PAYNE: Well, that's the game that's here!

ROMANO: That's not a very good game, though.

PAYNE: Everybody else has bought into it; we're not criticizing everybody else. We're not criticizing the stockbrokers who have *always* been stockbrokers. We're criticizing the stockbrokers-who-used-to-be-activists. Right? There's an issue of equity here. And what is it about the stockbrokers-who-used-to-be-activists that bother us so? What's the nature of the underlying dialogue?

Let me give you a hypothesis. And Bob Moses actually comes to mind. Because I was about to say: a good example is a pain in the butt! [*chuckles*] [*audience laughter*] Bob Moses is a good example, and you know that guy's a pain in the butt. [*chuckles*] Why are they pains? Because they make you wonder what you should be doing. They make you wonder what you should be doing. Alright? And so, it seems to me that part of this "what-are-they-doing-now?" dialogue comes in some judgmental kind of sense. It's like the big brother or big sister that we really like, but in some ways they're an annoyance because they set these standards and now everybody expects us to live up to it. So it's a real ambivalence, I think, our relationship to the heroes and heroines of the sixties. In some ways their very presence, their very examples, the lives they've led raise the question: "Oh, what should I be doing in my life?" And so what am I doing when I say to them, "Well, you did six years in the Movement, but now you're into the credit card thing like all the rest of us. And therefore, your six years in the Movement are invalidated." I think *that's* the underlying, that's the underlying message that needs discussion. We take the people who have already contributed more than anybody else and we say, "If you don't continue contributing, it means you're not serious, you have sold out! Therefore we don't have to *think about* what the questions of your lives imply about our lives." I think that's the logic which is going on in that "What-is-it-they're-doing-now?" discussion. You can say the same thing about SDS, this whole notion of a way to protect ourselves, to take the sting out of the critical implications of the idea that *they* were more active, more involved than us. It's to say, "Yeah, but they've fallen off the pedestal now. They're down here with us. Thank God!" [*chuckles*] So I mean, I think there is something dishonest in that dialogue, for one.

And the last thing I want to say is something about this notion of human potential and what the Movement scholarship should be doing. We should be moving into the ghettos, is where I'm going to end up with this. One of the most fascinating parts of my Mississippi research project for me was trying to figure out why certain kinds of families stepped forward in the Delta, when it was dangerous, when there's no rational argument you can make that this thing is gonna work.[21] There's *no* rational reason to believe that! And when the oppression is so high, what's the reason that certain families—And the [Ladner sisters'] donut story that Judy read earlier summarizes virtually everything I know.[22] There's certain families which kept alive certain traditions and certain attitudes. Much of it seems to come down to this notion of: "Yeah, we may be at the bottom, but there are some things *we will not take.* We're not just going to take everything they give. We are going to *demand* respect." And if you show me the families which are conveying that message to kids in 1950, I think I can show you the families which are going to be the first to go to mass meetings in the 1960s. I think there is that. There is that.

So, if I mention to my students—The last few times that I was in Mississippi, I was sort of plausibly told by people who I believed, that I know would not lie, that children from the same families I described, as the leading Movement families of the 1960s, are now involved in selling drugs and gang-banging. For my students, that's a letdown. In fact, that's a letdown for some of you. They don't want *these* families to have *these* weaknesses. And so the class and I get into another thing because I don't see what the problem is. I don't understand why there's a problem. I don't understand why they think that families that produced activists can't also produce hoodlums. [*laughs*] And I think it's a fundamentally—And here I may be way off, but this is the way I think about it—

CROSBY: Can I ask you something about that?

PAYNE: Go ahead.

CROSBY: I'm thinking about, of course, your chapter where you talk about "They Kept the Story Before Me" and why these families are activist families—am I right? And you say, either there or somewhere else, it seems to me that part of your argument is about the way families teach the children. And so, for me, I might find what you're saying disappointing because it means that there's been a loss of transmitting this—the cultural values of why you say there are these Movement families in the first place. And so for me—I mean, I'm not sure because I've not thought about this; it's brand new. But for me, that would be the disappointment, that people who, the families who were able to do this were not able to continue it.

PAYNE: And that's a disappointment that *I* share. And a puzzlement that I share. And I think I would say that of the students I've been engaged with, that question of why those stories weren't passed on to the next generation, comes up time and time again. But I also get the impression that something else is going on.

SPEAKER: I think students tend to think there's something special or unique about certain individuals—

PAYNE: [*while nodding head in agreement*] Bam! Bam! See, my guess is that that's at least a part of it, a significant part of it. That there is fundamentally— the kinds of people who we revere as civil rights heroes and heroines are *one kind* of human. And the kind of people who are tearing up our cities right now, that's *another* kind of human. And never the twain shall meet! I mean, we have this deep sense of "they," whether "they" are Arabs or welfare mothers. "They" are motivationally and morally, fundamentally different from us, and therefore we cannot understand why they do what they do. We can't *understand* why these kids throw away their opportunities and destroy their own communities. We *can't* understand that! And when we say that, we're saying that they're fundamentally different from us. Because we can understand what we do, presumably. So all that "can't understand" rhetoric is putting folks—not in the category of being "different" but—in the category of being "other."

And so—What does this imply? Oh, and to me when I said I don't see a problem. See, it would seem to me that the parsimonious explanation, or expectation, would be listen: to venture out into a civil rights movement in a moment where that's chancy, and to venture out into criminal activities, in some ways that requires similar kinds of personality structures. You have to have some ability to organize, to connect. You have to have a certain kind of entrepreneurial attitude. You have to have this notion that I can envision something which is not here and get it or do it. It's going to be the nervy kids in either context who are going to push forward. And so it seems to me that we ought not be surprised that the same human potential that can produce civil rights, that can produce sNCC field secretaries, the same human potential, given a slightly different developmental set of opportunities, can become a damn fourteen-year-old murderer. Right? You twist one in one direction, but the potential is there. And the same families, therefore, which produce one thing at one time will produce another. Whether that's true in all cases or most cases, it seems to me to be a healthier paradigm for raising some of these questions. And so what that means to me, what I worry about—That question: what's the disadvantage of studying the civil rights movement? Well, I wonder if to some degree we study the Movement because we're more comfortable with studying the Movement than with studying the ghetto. The people in the ghetto are uncomfortable, messy, and embarrassing. Because the kinds of questions about racial inferiority and racial inequality and what keeps it going, that's raised by these folk in the ghetto, those are embarrassing and uncomfortable questions. So it seems to me, one of the things we have to think about is how could you do an analysis that doesn't separate those discussions. Because right now those are separate discussions, right? We don't discuss the history of the civil rights movement and issues of the contemporary ghetto in the same breath. So how do you create one discussion that will at least allow for the possibility of combining them? I'm not sure. But I'm not going to leave here without picking on Judy. [*chuckles*]

It seems to me that one part of the answer is that we begin to refocus much of what we do around this issue of human growth. Not the tactical victories, not the—If I could have done one thing more, if I could go back and redo that book—I don't know if any of you remember Mary Lane, but this woman who becomes just a wonderful woman local leader? I'd like to be able to do forty pages on how Mary Lane changes between 1962 and 1968. To see her going from being a woman who doesn't know she has a *right* to go into a meeting in her own community to somebody arguing with the governor, outfoxing Lyndon Johnson, who is leading a statewide campaign. She's the center of it: "You want something done, you go see Mary." I say something about what she is at the beginning and something about what she was like and how she was respected at the end, but there's no analysis. I don't even need analysis. What I need is a vivid picture of growth and change. Because when we have those kinds of pictures, when we have those kinds of pictures, when we see that people weren't always where they were, that they had to go through a process to get there, when we look at the developmental process, then I think it opens our minds up to the question: what would have happened if the process had been slightly different? What would have happened had she not had these models which she could identify with, come into her life? What would have happened to her? That question is sort of embedded. So this notion—and this is why the *Hands on the Freedom Plow* collection—That project is important to me for a whole bunch of reasons. One of them is that you see how people change. And if you think back to what you heard earlier today, I think you'll remember hearing this—Jean Wheeler Smith has this one essay, "I Found My Brave Self."[23]

RICHARDSON: That was in mine!

PAYNE: That was in yours. But that phrase: "I found a different part of me" in jail, she's saying. People found their brave selves, they found their smart selves, they found their organizational selves. And in the stories in this collection, you can see people changing. And that's one of the reasons why it's so important, and why you all [*motioning to Judy*] need to get done with it and get it out!

And I think that's probably everything I wanted to say. We have to begin to find ways to think about—and I think this is very much in the spirit of the Movement—to embrace the thing that makes you uncomfortable, to embrace what you fear. And the black underclass—I don't normally use that term but it's good rhetoric for what I'm saying. The black underclass makes us uncomfortable. We have to sort of find a way, in the same analysis of the black freedom struggle, to think through that set of questions and to hope that we can do that. To do what? Again, I think one of the most valuable things about the Movement is values, is that it opens us up constantly, it challenges constantly our ingrained notions about the limitations of human potential.

And I think that was everything that I intended to say except for: this has been a heck of a conference! And I only saw half of it! What the other half must have been! And to just thank *everybody*. Thank you.

## NOTES

1. The conference, "Local Studies, a National Movement: Toward a Historiography of the Black Freedom Movement," was funded in part by a SUNY Conversations in the Disciplines grant. The conference consisted of three panels. The first, "Local Studies: What Do They Tell Us? Why Do They Matter?," included presentations by J. Todd Moye, Jeanne Theoharis, Hasan Kwame Jeffries, and Robyn C. Spencer. The second, "Women, Gender, and Leadership," included presentations by Charles M. Payne, Jeanne Theoharis, and Robyn C. Spencer. The third, "Moving Beyond Dichotomies: Reframing Nonviolence vs. Violence, Integration vs. Nationalism, and Civil Rights vs. Black Power," included presentations by Wesley Hogan, Emilye Crosby, Hasan Kwame Jeffries, and Komozi Woodard. Payne's discussion, centered around "Why Study the Movement?," was the final keynote. The first two keynotes were: John Dittmer on "Southern Community Studies and Their Critics," and Judy Richardson, "Hands on the Freedom Plow: Personal Stories and Reflections from Women and SNCC." All sessions were recorded and are in editor's possession.

2. Payne is referencing Judy Richardson's earlier keynote, which was a reading of a selection of excerpts from what was then a draft of *Hands on the Freedom Plow*. Richardson, "Hands on the Freedom Plow" keynote; Faith Holsaert, Martha Prescod Norman Noonan, Judy Richardson, Betty Garman Robinson, Jean Wheeler Smith Young, and Dottie Zellner, eds., *Hands on the Freedom Plow: Personal Accounts by Women in SNCC* (Urbana: University of Illinois Press, 2010).

3. Claudette Colvin was a Montgomery, Alabama, teenager who was arrested for refusing to relinquish her seat on a bus several months before Rosa Parks's similar refusal sparked the Montgomery Bus Boycott. Colvin was also a plaintiff in the *Browder v. Gayle* lawsuit that led to a U.S. Supreme Court decision invalidating Montgomery's bus segregation laws. See Stewart Burns, ed., *Daybreak of Freedom: The Montgomery Bus Boycott* (Chapel Hill: University of North Carolina Press, 1997), 5–6, 19, 74–77.

4. For more about Ella Baker, her approach to social justice, and her role in the civil rights movement, see Charles M. Payne, *I've Got the Light of Freedom: The Organizing Tradition and the Mississippi Freedom Struggle* (Berkeley: University of California Press, 1995), esp. ch. 3; Charles M. Payne, "Ella Baker and Models of Social Change," *Signs: Journal of Women in Culture and Society* 14 (Summer 1989): 885–900; Barbara Ransby, "Behind-the-Scenes View of a Behind-the-Scenes Organizer: The Roots of Ella Baker's Political Passions," in *Sisters in the Struggle: African American Women in the Civil Rights-Black Power Movement*, ed. Bettye Collier-Thomas and V. P. Franklin (New York: New York University Press, 2001), 42–57; and Barbara Ransby, *Ella Baker and the Black Freedom Movement: A Radical Democratic Vision* (Chapel Hill: University of North Carolina Press, 2003).

5. Judy Richardson, "Hands on the Freedom Plow" keynote.

6. Chana Kai Lee, *For Freedom's Sake: The Life of Fannie Lou Hamer* (Urbana:

University of Illinois Press, 1999); Angela Y. Davis, *Angela Davis—an Autobiography* (New York: Random House, 1974).

7. For reflections by Vincent Harding on teaching movement history, see Vincent Harding, *Hope and History: Why We Must Share the Story of the Movement* (Maryknoll, N.Y.: Orbis Books, 1990).

8. Renee Christine Romano and Leigh Raiford, eds. *The Civil Rights Movement in American Memory* (Athens: University of Georgia Press, 2006). Romano is referencing Hasan Kwame Jeffries's earlier talk, "Crazy Negroes and Out-of-Control Crackers."

9. John Dittmer, *Local People: The Struggle for Civil Rights in Mississippi* (Urbana: University of Illinois Press, 1994).

10. For information about the Algebra Project and its connections to the civil rights movement, see www.algebra.org. See also, Robert Parris Moses and Charles E. Cobb Jr., *Radical Equations: Math Literacy and Civil Rights* (Boston: Beacon Press, 2001); Robert Moses, et al., "Organizing in the Spirit of Ella," *Harvard Educational Review* 59 (Nov. 1989): 423–43.

11. Charles Eagles writes, among other things, "[H]istorians have often lacked detachment because of their profound and justifiable moral commitment to the aims of the civil rights movement." Charles W. Eagles, "Toward New Histories of the Civil Rights Movement," *Journal of Southern History* 66, no. 4 (2000): 815–48, quote on p. 814, see esp. 816, 819, 839, 847–8.

12. For information about the Freedom Schools and their curriculum, see the Education & Democracy website, http://educationanddemocracy.org. See also, Charles M. Payne, *I've Got the Light of Freedom*, 301–6.

13. George Breathett, ed., "William Edward Burghardt Du Bois: An Address to the Black Academic Community," *Journal of Negro History* 60, no. 1 (Jan. 1975): 45–52.

14. Payne is referring Komozi Woodard's comments on the earlier panel, "Moving Beyond Dichotomies."

15. For an extended conversation with Judy Richardson on this and other questions, see "Making *Eyes on the Prize*: An Interview with Filmmaker and SNCC Staffer Judy Richardson," chapter 9, this volume; and "That Movement Responsibility: An Interview with Judy Richardson on Movement History and Legacies," chapter 12, this volume.

16. Robert Fulghum, *Everything I Ever Really Needed to Know I Learned in Kindergarten* (Evanston, Ill.: Press of War Schori, 1988).

17. Although Payne's references appear in quotations in the text, they are not direct quotes. The actual quote is:

> When I read about the Albany Movement, as people have written about it, I don't
> recognize it. They add up stuff that was not central to what happened. . . . I had
> grown up in a society where there were very clear lines. The older I got, the more
> I found what those lines were. The Civil Rights Movement gave me the power to

challenge *any* line that limits me. I got that power during the Albany Movement, and that is what it meant to me, just really to give me a real chance to fight and to struggle and not respect boundaries that put me down. Before then, I struggled within a certain context but recognized lines. Across those lines were powers that could do you in, so you just respect them and don't cross them. The Civil Rights Movement just destroyed that and said that if something puts you down, you have to fight against it. And that's what the Albany Movement did for Albany, Georgia.

Dick Cluster, ed., *They Should Have Served That Cup of Coffee: Seven Radicals Remember the 60s* (Boston: South End Press, 1979), 23. For a slightly different version of the interview, see Dick Cluster, ed., "The Borning Struggle: The Civil Rights Movement: An Interview with Bernice Reagon," *Radical History* 12, no. 6 (1978): 8–25.

18. For a portion of this interview, see "'This transformation of people': An interview with Bob Moses," in *Debating the Civil Rights Movement, 1945–1968*, Steven F. Lawson and Charles Payne, with introduction by James T. Patterson (Lanham, Md.: Rowman & Littlefield, 2006), 170–88.

19. Barry Gray is credited with initating talk radio and broadcast for many years from New York's WMCA station. For more, see "Barry Gray, Talk Radio Pioneer, Is Dead at 80," *New York Times*, December 22, 1996.

20. Judy Richardson, "Hands on the Freedom Plow" keynote. Holsaert, et al., eds., *Hands on the Freedom Plow.*

21. See especially, Payne, *I've Got the Light of Freedom*, chapter 7: "They Kept the Story Before Me: Families and Traditions," 207–35.

22. Payne is referencing an account by Joyce Ladner, read earlier in the day by Judy Richardson, about an incident that occurred when Ladner was a child. Judy Richardson, "Hands on the Freedom Plow" keynote. According to Joyce Ladner, when she and her sister Dorie Ladner were eleven and twelve years old, they went to a nearby store to buy donuts. As he was giving Dorie Ladner change, the white shopkeeper put his hand on her breast. "She took the bag of donuts and beat him across the head. . . . [W]e went home . . . and told my mother what happened. She said, 'You should have killed him.'" This account is in Cheryl Lynn Greenberg, ed., *Circle of Trust: Remembering* SNCC (New Brunswick, N.J.: Rutgers University Press, 1998), 140. See also, Joyce Ladner, "Standing Up for Our Beliefs," in *Hands on the Freedom Plow*, ed. Holsaert, et al., 217–22.

23. See Jean [Wheeler] Smith Young, "Do Whatever You Are Big Enough to Do," in *Hands on the Freedom Plow*, ed. Holsaert, et al., 240–49. The phrase, "I found my brave self" is not in this published account, but the account does illustrate the process of change that Payne is referencing.

EMILYE CROSBY

# Conclusion

## *"Doesn't everybody want to grow up to be Ella Baker?": Teaching Movement History*

**C**harles Payne closed the "Local Studies, a National Movement" Conference (which inspired this book) by leading a discussion framed by the question: "Why study the Movement?" (See chapter 14 for an edited transcript of this conversation.) After reflecting on that question, Chris Machanoff, a Geneseo student who had been studying the movement for three years, wrote,

> Many of the valuable things I take from studying the Movement I cannot explain well. A list of lessons could go on forever: The strengths of people under horrific conditions. The ability of people to bond and put aside differences after fundamental disagreements. The corrupting abilities of power, yet the simultaneous possibility to reject the corrupting abilities of power. The way people can blind themselves in order to justify injustice. How upset people can become when they feel their way of life/status quo is threatened. The power of experience in creating individuals; and the potential leadership in all individuals. The way we as a country narrowly define education, and what constitutes and passes as educated; the way one's lived experience is an important education, but is not considered relevant to those with power. The fact that "major-

The title quote is from Tiffany Izzo, Ella Baker Reading Group, Spring 2006.

For their interest, support, and insightful comments, I would like to thank Sarah Campbell, Patricia Crosby, Michelle Deardorff, Carol Faulkner, Wesley Hogan, Todd Moye, Judy Richardson, Renee Romano, and Kathleen Connelly. I was able to give earlier versions of this presentation at the Hamer Institute at Jackson State University and the SNCC 50th Anniversary Symposium at Brown University. I am grateful for the opportunity in both of these inspiring and intellectually stimulating gatherings.

ity rules," a supposedly democratic principle, can leave entire populations of people unaccounted for.[1]

As Machanoff's comments suggest, for many students, studying the movement—especially from a bottom-up, community-based perspective—is not just about learning a few new facts. Rather it offers an important opportunity to think seriously about issues fundamental to our society. Many also find that studying the movement brings to life historical interpretation and perspective, while teaching them to be more critical about information and to question much that they have been taught. It provides them with tools and insights for understanding contemporary society, introduces them to a meaningful model for citizenship, and offers an accessible approach to seeing themselves as historical actors.

In this vein, I have come to believe that in teaching movement history what *and* how we teach are *both* essential. I have found that students respond well to learning about the "organizing tradition" in an educational context that draws on its principles and lessons. As Payne explains, those who subscribed to the organizing tradition took a long view toward social change, one that emphasized developing leadership skills and efficacy. Most of all, they believed it was important for people "to see themselves as having the right and capacity to have some say-so in their own lives." Ella Baker, a key architect of the organizing tradition, "viewed education as a collective and creative enterprise requiring collaboration and exchange at every stage."[2] I try to apply this in a number of ways—through introducing students to the "ordinary people" who fueled the movement (people who were, as Judy Richardson says, just like them); through explicitly connecting content to skills; and through engaging students as active participants in their education.[3] There are many good pedagogical reasons for this approach, but one fundamental piece is that what students are learning is often at odds with (and even directly contradicts) so much of what they have been taught and believe (often unquestioningly). It is essential, then, that they approach their study (and reevaluate their beliefs) through their own analysis, not because someone tells them something different.

The Local Studies Conference at Geneseo offers a valuable opportunity to explore how students respond to learning movement history this way. Many of the students who attended the conference were taking their first class on the civil rights movement, while a smaller group was immersed in more in-

Figure 34 Ella Baker Reading Group (and friends), Spring 2006. (*left to right*): Cortez Jones, Scott Snowden, Christopher Machanoff, Erynne Mancini, Joseph Zurro, Erin Rightmyer, Tarik Kitson, Jared DePass, Claire Ruswick, Christopher Basso, Tiffany Izzo, Patrick O'Neill, Christina Pinnola, Christopher Bruce, Joseph Easton, Christopher Neels. Photograph courtesy of SUNY Geneseo. (See also images on p. 422, p. 425.)

tensive reading and discussion through the Ella Baker Reading Group. The latter was a group-directed study that (at the time of the conference) I had been leading (with an evolving mix of students) for five semesters. Although some of these students had done unusually in-depth study for undergraduates (and helped lay the foundation for a successful conference), they were also fairly typical of Geneseo students in their backgrounds and belief systems. And although they were self-selected in pursuing movement history, most developed their interest by chance.

This chapter explores student responses to the conference and, more generally, to studying movement history. It draws most heavily from the Ella Baker Reading Group student reflections, partly because these students were particularly absorbed in studying the movement, but also because they invested more in writing about the conference and what their movement study meant to them. Their reflections are supplemented by those from other students who attended the conference or who have written about studying the movement in other contexts. I am particularly interested in what students think about what they learn from studying movement history this way. What do they emphasize? What do they find most meaningful? What connections do they make to their own lives?

The Local Studies Conference reinforced the message of bottom-up movement history in a variety of ways. Many of the presenters drew on local struggles for their content. They also talked about process. The "scholars" shared stories about their motivations and challenges, acknowledged criticism of their work, discussed their mistakes, and raised questions. In doing this, they established an alternative to the more dominant expert-driven, top-down model many students are accustomed to. Even when the specific content and details were new to students, this approach drew them in and helped demystify the history, something that was reinforced as students discovered that they had actually read some of the primary sources and books that the scholars were referencing. For example, Chris Basso came to believe "I can do what they are doing. I can be a historian. I just have to be able to think, ask questions . . . and really analyze." Many students appreciated Todd Moye's personal explanation for why and how he came to study Sunflower County, Mississippi, as well as his story about returning to the community to present his work before the all-white, all-male, not very receptive Rotary Club. They could also identify with his description of being exposed to local movement history when he was a college student reading William Chafe's *Civilities and Civil Rights*.[4] (See chapter 5 for a version of Moye's presentation.)

Students were particularly responsive to the way Charles Payne opened his talk, "Sexism is a helluva thing," by discussing a recent, public critique of his work. (See chapter 10 for an edited transcript of Payne's talk.) Commenting that Payne wasn't at all defensive, Greg Fair observed, "Payne's attitude toward his error was one of the most important parts of his talk. He sent the message that it is okay to make mistakes as a historian/activist (mistakes are not something to be afraid of) but also that it is important not to ignore/deny them. They should be put to constructive use." Similarly, several students were impressed by John Dittmer's willingness to openly acknowledge that not all scholars embrace local studies, particularly commenting on the way Dittmer handled his discussion of Charles Eagles's critique that he, Payne, and others of their generation were "too sympathetic" to the movement.[5]

Perhaps most importantly, students met the scholars and activists, the *important people* they had read about and knew as authors, as "real people," ones who were friendly and interested in their opinions. In this vein, students especially appreciated the spirit of collective inquiry, the shared respect and mutuality, and the way the conversation was framed to include everyone—movement scholars and activists, but also nonspecialists, K–12 teachers, community members, and students. Sophomore Tarik Kitson wrote later that he had expected the conference to be "scholars arguing," and was pleasantly surprised to experience, instead, what Todd Moye referred to as "the Beloved Community of Black Freedom Struggle scholars." For Greg Fair, it was "energizing to spend time with people who take the movement seriously," while another student wrote, "I felt as though the students had just as much to give as the scholars. This was not only encouraging but humbling to know that we are all after the same goal, to share knowledge and expand our horizons."⁶

Many students made explicit connections between the ways presenters approached the conversation and what they were learning about Ella Baker and the organizing tradition. They saw this at work in the ways presenters asked questions and involved the audience. One observed, "In a lot of cases I think they were pulling an Ella Baker in that they often responded to a question with a question and forced you to think harder and reach the conclusion on your own." In particular, students commented on Payne's conference-closing keynote. Sophomore Joe Zurro noted that "by mid-afternoon I faintly remember hearing a collective, 'ow, my brain' from the student section. . . . But, I think that after Charles Payne found his way to the podium, everyone seemed to know that we were in for something good. . . . Right from the beginning the address turned into a discussion." Another observed, "In a style very reminiscent of Ella Baker and the Organizing Tradition, Payne listened to what each person had to say, and then asked a question which prompted the person to find the deeper meaning in what they were saying." Zurro recalls that when Payne asked students why they studied the movement, he scrambled to jot down some notes and organize his thoughts. Several weeks later, as he continued to struggle with articulating his own reasons for studying the movement, he commented, "I am sure that [Professor Payne] would have known just what question to ask, just what way to jiggle that key to unlock what's up there in my head that I can't even get at sometimes. He asked questions that I didn't know the answer to, but then he made me feel as if I knew the solutions all along." Students had a similar response to Judy Richardson's keynote, which she used to read stories from many SNCC women. One commented, "It was a great idea on her part to include and intertwine the many stories told by various SNCC members and other people in the movement. . . . If you look at it in a symbolic way, you could say that she, like the movement, is not just a 'one person show.'" She represented the way it was "the work of many people, not just one."[7]

At the conference, students appreciated seeing behind the neat historical accounts they read in their books—getting a sense of historians at work, developing confidence that they had something worthwhile to contribute, and, in some cases, seeing themselves as scholars (or activists). For many, learning the content of bottom-up history works in a similar way. Because it is so at odds with so much of what they've been taught, it provides powerful lessons about perspective, while reinforcing their analytical skills. After listening to the conference's opening panel, featuring four scholars talking about four different local struggles, a first year student concluded that "one cannot always believe what is commonly thought of as the truth" and that "the big picture isn't always the right picture." Another commented, "[I]t scares me to think that there is so much history that I have a false impression of." The conference strengthened her appreciation for "how thick the fog is surrounding the interpretation of history. Even when we think we are making progress in obtaining a more precise view of what happened, we still are blocked by biases." For Chris Basso, being able to analyze primary sources from the Montgomery Bus Boycott himself "had a huge impact on me. I began to question everything I've ever learned." Referencing Jeanne Theoharis's conference talk on the national response to Rosa Parks's death, he added, "It is unsettling to think that for most people in the country, this is all they think of Rosa Parks," that she was "'graceful, soft-spoken, graceful, kind, graceful, beautiful.' . . . It demonstrates the continuance of racist stereotypes through our popular history."[8] (See chapter 13 for Jeanne Theoharis's essay on the memorialization of Parks and Coretta Scott King.)

Through the study of bottom-up movement history, many students begin to more fully understand the importance of process, not just outcome, and develop an appreciation for what Ella Baker called "spadework."[9] Activists and leaders become more real and accessible, more like them, not so distant. When students learn that "dirt farmers," high school students, and domestic workers organized and mounted a sustained challenge to racism, they can begin to imagine themselves acting in historically important ways. Tiffany Izzo explains, "For a long time I had always put the leaders I had known on this pedestal of being inspired by some act of God, it never occurred to me that it was not that they had some special and rare power, but that everyone had that power and it was their choice to use that power that made them the people they were." She appreciated seeing the "inner workings" of change, observing that before she studied the movement, "I felt that change came from someone who decided to stand up and make an inspiring speech and 'lead the people.' These leaders were great minds who spent time thinking about things that the everyday person couldn't comprehend unless it was explained to them, which was their extraordinary role—to explain and lead. That sentence makes me chuckle in an odd way now."[10]

Students also become more comfortable with complexity and nuance as they grapple with the diversity and range of beliefs, tactics, and contexts that characterized the movement. (The movement was "nonviolent," right? But what does that mean? How does it relate to self-defense? Do all tactics fit these frameworks? What about voter registration and organizing? How do these tactics overlap? How do they work—or not work—in different contexts?) In fact, students' initial picture of the movement is almost invariably dominated by a static caricature of nonviolence that portrays blacks as loving, long-suffering Christians passively turning the other cheek. Katie Snyder explains, "As far as I knew, the civil rights movement was led by Martin Luther King Jr., and was nonviolent, which meant that African Americans sat at 'whites only' counters and were sprayed with water from fire hoses by the police. . . . I had an idea that people's homes were bombed, but I was told that they were 'nonviolent' and never carried weapons."[11] When Judy Richardson meets teachers through her workshops on the movement, she finds they "generally teach their students only the philosophy (as opposed to the *tactic*) of nonviolence as if it were the norm throughout the movement. And they teach it as a way of dealing with the issue of violence in their schools." In her view, one of the problems with this approach is that "young people, especially young African Americans, get turned off of the Movement because the only images they see are of folks getting beat over the head and singing 'We Shall Overcome.'"[12]

Teaching a more nuanced and complex explanation of nonviolence, along with the reality of armed self-defense in the movement, can help students more clearly see activists' agency, their tactical flexibility, the nature and extent of white resistance, and the life and death challenges of organizing without any meaningful legal protection.[13] Snyder explained, "After learning about self-defense, I find it *so* important to the movement, and how activists took on self-defense because the justice system wasn't there to protect them so they had to protect themselves." Students who have been taught to celebrate a nonviolent movement that deteriorated with the violence of Black Power can struggle to understand or accept the role self-defense actually played in the movement. After hearing my conference paper on self-defense, another student wrote, "[I]t is rather easy to confuse self-defense with violence, when in fact . . . self-defense was used by people who pledged to nonviolence, but who were not necessarily committed to it as a way of life. . . . I admit, that until you said that you object to pitting nonviolence against self-defense, I never really saw the possibility for the two to go hand-in-hand."[14] (See chapter 7 for my essay on the historiography of self-defense.)

It is just as crucial for students to learn two points about nonviolence: first, that it was not a given or the only tactic activists used *and* second, that it was *active*, not passive. It is also important for students to work through some of their often-unspoken assumptions and the double standards they've absorbed, ones that suggest African Americans had to remain nonviolent in order to somehow "earn" their citizenship rights. Students typically respond well to learning about nonviolence and self-defense in concrete, context-specific ways.

At the conference, what really grabbed their attention, however, were Wesley Hogan's comments that nonviolence is unnatural and counterintuitive for most people in our country and how, despite this, movement activists were sometimes able to use it to generate effective public protest and confrontation. (See chapter 6 for Hogan's essay on nonviolence.) A few students immediately connected Hogan's discussion to the U.S. response to the 9/11 attacks and their own antiwar organizing. Many of the self-identified activists were struggling to figure out what nonviolence meant to them. They assumed that they were nonviolent, but didn't really know what that meant or how to *act* on it. Hogan's talk didn't offer any simple answers, but it did provide them with a clearer context and sharper framework for considering their options.[15] Another student went in a different direction, noting that Hogan's presentation "made me reflect on whether or not our society has the potential to be nonviolent." She continued, "I have gone back and forth trying to decide if our fight against terrorism was legitimate. . . . I am certain now that what we are doing in the Middle East isn't going to cure terrorism."[16]

Hasan Kwame Jeffries's talk, "Crazy Negroes and Out-of-Control Crackers," touched on two topics that appear to be particularly important for students to grapple with—Black Power and the institutional nature of white supremacy. For students, the stereotypes around both of these subjects are every bit as strong as the mythology featuring King and Parks and, in fact, the pieces often reinforce each other. Most students have absorbed the lesson—almost without exception—that Black Power was "violent and racist," that it was "where the civil rights movement went wrong." At the same time, they tend to have a very limited and narrow understanding of white supremacy. They are generally taught that "racism is embodied by the N-word and burning crosses." Movement era violence is typically set up as *the* primary form of white resistance, but sometimes even that violence is downplayed. A student recently explained that he had the "impression that the absolute worst thing about being black in the South was having to use a different water fountain." For him, one of the most important things about studying the movement was coming to understand much more clearly "what was at stake."[17]

Chris Basso effectively captures the stereotypical good sixties, bad sixties framing of Black Power that reinforces the notion that white supremacy was embodied in the actions of a few extremists.

> The civil rights movement is seen as being good, the Black Power movement as being bad. The civil rights movement turns into this distorted picture of Martin Luther King, Rosa Parks, white liberals, and the federal government going to battle against crazy southern racists and their segregationist society. Once that was over, due to the passage of the Civil Rights Act of 1964 and the Voting Rights Act, the civil rights movement was over, and black people and other minorities should have had nothing else to complain about. But reckless and irresponsible blacks in the ghettoes started pointless riots and started screaming Black Power for no good reason. This is pretty much what most people see the civil rights and Black Power movement as.[18]

Claire Ruswick thought of Black Power as a "dangerous and radical movement, maybe even like a cult," a picture that came primarily from the movie *Forrest Gump*. After studying Black Power, she concluded "that I had been misled, like most of America, to believe that Black Power was a shallow movement that was only based on hatred and anger."[19]

After a Spring 2008 class, one white student reflected, "I always believed the racist stereotypes that Black Power was an angry, violent, mob-type movement that used guns and violence to get their way. . . . I only saw it as a way for blacks to get things they wanted, things that *they* didn't deserve to have (affirmative action-type things), because whites had them." Chris Bruce, who went to a New York City public high school that was almost 100 percent minority, learned about Black Power during "black history month." He recalls, "I always walked away with the notion that Black Power was the equivalent of white supremacists and the Ku Klux Klan." In a group discussion with students who had similar experiences, regardless of the racial make-up of their high schools, he considered the reasons for this pervasive miseducation. "I began to wonder if this was the result of the high school curriculum's Cliffs Notes version of the movement or was it something more than that? Was it a way to discredit members of the movement by calling them irrational and crazy like Hasan Jeffries said in his speech?"[20]

Jeffries's talk was eye-opening for students as he broke down some of the strategies used to trivialize Black Power and obscure nationwide institutional white supremacy. Claire Ruswick explains,

> According to Jeffries, throughout the history of black-white relations in America, people have used the excuse of "crazy Negroes" to ignore the real issues at stake. Just as southern whites used the term "outside agitators" to convince themselves that "their" blacks were happy, and it was just outsiders that were stirring up problems, Americans have used the idea of the "crazy Negroes" to convince themselves that blacks bringing their issues to the public, and speaking openly about social change, are just crazy. Americans hide behind the term "crazy" so they don't have to deal with the fact that these blacks might be speaking the truth about a deep-seated and real problem in America.[21]

Joe Zurro recalls not being sure he agreed with Jeffries when he first heard the presentation. After talking with his classmates and watching it again, however, he reflected, "I think one of the reasons Jeffries's speech resonated so much with me was because I had been guilty of what he warned against. What I think he was trying to get across to us was that we cannot make judgments, at least fair judgments, about an individual based on that individual's personality. By 'explaining away' Carmichael as a prophet of rage, and Malcolm X as a hateful person, we miss so much about what it is they are trying to get across. We get lost in the way they speak it, and refuse to examine critically the meaning."[22]

For Zurro and others, this idea was brought home most forcefully by Jeffries's example of Martin Luther King Jr. and the ways that, during his lifetime, he, too, was often portrayed as a "Crazy Negro." Reflecting on Jeffries's talk, Chris Basso writes, "In the dominant narrative of the civil rights movement, Martin Luther King is a saint. He was passive-resistant, he protested in a peaceful way and other people should try to emulate him. This completely ignores the fact that at times in his career, King was demonized by almost everybody. . . . He was that 'crazy Negro.' It makes me wonder whom today we think is just crazy and out of control?" A week later, Basso was still considering this question. "For many people in this country, Martin Luther King had a dream that white people and black people could live together. Problem solved, King is a hero. Like Judy Richardson said at the conference, 'Where is the King that called for a radical redistribution of wealth?' It's simply not taught, because that's Black Power rhetoric (if people even get to hear that part after all the 'hate whitey' nonsense) and because Martin Luther King solved all the nation's problems of race." He asks, "Why aren't we taught about the Martin Luther King that the government hated? He was a 'crazy Negro' in most people's eyes. Why is that so easily forgotten?"[23]

Students were just as struck by Jeffries's analysis of "out-of-control-crackers." Chris Bruce explains, "By calling Bull Connor an 'out-of-control cracker' you reduce white supremacy and the obstacles blacks had to face at the time." Basso reiterates that "[w]hat people fail to acknowledge is the deep systemic racism involved. The system of segregation was much more than the authority [of] restaurant owners, mayors, and crazy governors. Not to mention, this interpretation lets the northern racism, and the national racism in general, off the hook." He argues that "[d]emonizing certain characters in history as crazy racist white people allows for people to completely ignore the racism in their own lives, schools, communities, families, state, country. Racism only amounts to using the N-word and lighting crosses on fire." Arguing that "[p]eople still see racism as being individualistic rather than systemic," he followed Jeffries's lead and addressed Hurricane Katrina, which had hit New Orleans just seven months before, asking, "Why is a huge portion of our population (which conspicuously is also black) living at levels of poverty that are only attributed to Third World countries when so many in our country live in a disgusting amount of wealth and opportunity?" Then he offered a partial answer, "I feel like people think, 'Well, we're not racist. I mean yeah, there's a huge population of black people in New Orleans who are poor, but Condoleezza Rice is in the Cabinet.'"[24] As this suggests, when students develop a complex understanding of how white supremacy worked during the movement, they are often less likely to see it as something limited to either the past or the South. They begin to explore the ways it operates today and in the places they call home.

As part of their conference preparation, the students in the Ella Baker Reading Group read Jeffries's dissertation on the Lowndes County, Alabama, civil rights movement. As a result, they already had access to an unusually detailed and nuanced picture of both Black Power and white supremacy as it looked through the lens of a rural southern community. Even before hearing Jeffries's talk, they had rejected most of their stereotypical views of Black Power. However, as important as Jeffries's work can be in helping students approach Black Power with more complexity and insight, students appear to be particularly engaged by his portrait of the Lowndes County movement (and the formation of the Lowndes County Freedom Party [LCFP], symbolized by the snarling Black Panther) as a significant moment in American democracy. In Lowndes, SNCC's egalitarian approach to organizing combined with the "freedom rights" vision of local African Americans to form the basis for what Jeffries calls "freedom politics."[25] Students seem hungry for this alternative to "politics as usual" and they appear to have little trouble seeing this history of African Americans in rural Alabama as relevant to them and their lives. After reading Jeffries's dissertation, Claire Ruswick commented on "how close" the LCFP "came to reaching the values that the American political system is supposed to stand for." She saw it as a model demonstrating that "it is possible to have the kind of political participation and organization necessary to form a government that actually represents the people" and suggested that the LCFP offered a far more helpful story of democratic possibility than the George Washington story typically presented to schoolchildren.[26]

Two other groups of Geneseo students have read Jeffries's work—a manuscript draft and the recently published *Bloody Lowndes*—and had an opportunity to discuss it with him. In each case, they have responded to many of the same themes and details, quickly abandoning the pervasive and superficial characterization of Lowndes—as epitomizing all the stereotypical negatives of Black Power—to focus instead on what it illustrates about the potential of "freedom politics." As one student explained, "In 1965, the African American locals held the majority of the vote in Lowndes County, yet voter registration or black candidates' election into office wasn't the ultimate goal of the movement." Instead, they wanted the "local black community to remain politically engaged. Creating political education, voter awareness, and

Figure 35 Hasan Kwame Jeffries with Geneseo students, September 2007. Photograph by Ben Gajewski, courtesy of SUNY Geneseo.

holding people accountable, is the basis of Freedom Politics." Another student commented on "the importance of personal responsibility in obtaining freedom rights—a responsibility that cannot be delegated to 'leaders.'" He was particularly struck by the fact that the "Lowndes County Freedom Party had a platform before it had any candidates" and what that said about the importance of people as "an integral part of a democratic process."[27]

In fact, many students are drawn to the idea of "freedom politics," both historically and in terms of contemporary society. One described it as "incredibly compelling" and an important alternative, while another wrote "freedom politics are exactly what the American government needs." During Jeffries's spring 2010 visit to Geneseo, students appreciated both his scholarship and his willingness to use a historical lens to tackle contemporary political issues. Responding to audience questions, Jeffries made a clear distinction between having an African American president and "freedom politics." Quite a few students reacted positively to this point and to Jeffries's willingness to evaluate President Barack Obama's actions. One wrote, "[P]erhaps my favorite moment ... was his critique of Obama's failure to speak out on issues of race and injustice." Another highlighted the distinction Jeffries made between "black visibility" and "black power" or, as another student wrote, "why it is important to not simply get blacks elected but to get people elected who speak to the needs of the black community, for instance." One student summed up the response of many, writing, "[A]lthough the heyday of freedom politics seems behind us, Prof. Jeffries was able to convey an element of optimism for the future and at the same time challenge us to remember that what's past is prologue."[28]

Although the mythology that passes for the civil rights movement history in much of our society is a triumphant story that can work to help protect white privilege and the idea of American triumphalism, many students, regardless of race, embrace the opportunity to learn a more accurate, realistic history. At the end of a Fall 2008 class, one white student reflected that he began the semester knowing only the predictable "Disney-style historical narrative that . . . was a story of redemption and good swiftly defeating evil, with a few big heroes like Martin Luther King and Rosa Parks." He found that "[t]he truth, as always, is much more complicated, much less pretty and rosy, and much more grass roots." He preferred this, noting, "It felt much more honest and much more humane to be taught that the struggle for black rights was not just a linear one—that things did not just continually get better and better after 1954, that it wasn't just that whites woke up one day and saw the error and immorality of their ways." Another white student commented that a class on Black Power was both her most difficult and her favorite because it "forces me to think in new ways and to get past personal feelings when I'm researching, reading, or discussing an issue." After a class on movement historiography, a student wrote, "[I]n a way I feel liberated." He speculated that many people avoid a serious discussion of "civil rights because they are afraid that when race comes up the whole world will erupt. However, in this class . . . we embraced it, took it, and analyzed it. What we came out with was very enlightening and I have a whole new look on civil rights and the struggle for equality in every sense."[29]

For many students, learning complex, bottom-up movement history extends well beyond historical literacy. It gives them knowledge and skills that they can use to better understand contemporary issues and reconsider previously unexamined assumptions. While many become angry and dismayed about the distortions that masquerade as history, at the same time, they often feel empowered as they develop a stronger knowledge base and new skills. They look to the movement for inspiration and as a model. At the end of a

Spring 2009 class, one student observed, "I think what I've learned the most this semester was actually how much my education has failed me." She went on to ask, "Why can't our education system teach us a little bit more than just 'Rosa Parks didn't move from her seat because her feet were tired' or 'Martin Luther King Jr. was the only leader in the movement'?" For her, this is essential "because if we don't look at the civil rights movement as a whole, how can we really understand what is going on today?"[30] A student who attended the conference expressed similar concerns. Observing that even the movement "symbols" that she and others learn about have lost "their true historical significance," she asks, "How can we learn to face our present injustices with this type of information?" She continues, "On the other hand, the organizing tradition that Todd Moye spoke about," along with Jeanne Theoharis's description of the institutionalization of school segregation in many northern cities, "are tools that we can use, not simply facts."[31]

As her comment suggests, when students replace their myths with history, they become more engaged, not less. The story is still peopled with heroes, but they tend to be ones the students can more easily identify with, including young people, women, and others often discounted or seen as powerless by the broader society. One observed that it was "especially inspiring to see how students were able to fight for something they believed in. I think more young people need to do this today."[32] Tiffany Izzo, who identified as an activist before coming to college, was inspired and could easily relate when she saw photographs showing that students who had "organized campaigns for voter registration, demonstrations, and protests were hanging around and talking about their thoughts late at night. . . . It was like—I can do that, in fact—I *do* do that." Hearing personal stories from SNCC staffer Judy Richardson reinforced this connection and Izzo reflected that "[t]hese people became very real to me, they became role models."[33]

Another student explains that "[l]earning about ordinary people coming together and completely changing society helps me to believe that all of the negative things happening now can be changed too. I think studying the organizing tradition and local communities puts emphasis on the power of the individual, and helps people to see that they themselves can facilitate change." This, she notes, gave her a sense of "hope in the future," a sentiment others share. For Chris Machanoff, who works as a labor organizer, studying the movement provides "a valuable tool for analysis" and "a sense of needed hope in the current dire times." He continues, "When things look absolutely hopeless, studying a group of people who created a power base to challenge wrongs has kept me from becoming nihilistic." Another student echoed the themes of hope and empowerment, explaining that learning about SNCC inspires her to try to "change the political system today" and to "fight for women's health or against domestic violence on the grass-roots level."[34]

Tarik Kitson insists that learning an accurate history would go a long way in the fight against contemporary racism. For Greg Fair, the movement provides "a way to understand inequalities that exist today," along with a "sense of my own power and ability to fight for equality (racial, economic, educational)." He continues, "I must be a politically conscious person. I must seek out good information and base my life around it. I have learned to take the rest of the world more seriously and be familiar with America's relationships with other countries. I have also learned of the interconnectedness of freedom struggles around the world (and through time)." As Fair's comments suggest, even those who do not see themselves as activists can take quite a bit from studying the movement. Like Fair, it can motivate them to be better citizens, more engaged in the world. Claire Ruswick explains, "Studying the civil rights movement has helped me not grow into a ignorant bystander. Even if I might not become a devoted activist, I might be able to take a small role in making the situation better, because I am aware that it exists."[35]

For Joe Zurro (who began teaching in the Mississippi Delta after graduation), part of the significance comes from recognizing that "[t]hose who participated in the movement did not accept the values that were given them by the previous generations. The process, the conscious struggle, the defining of their own systems of thought became central to those involved in the movement." This has become an important model for him. "As I struggle toward living right, . . . I feel like I need the same sort of conviction to walk the road alone when I have to." He elaborated that the conference helped him see that he has "a responsibility as a potential historian, and as a citizen of the world (!) to allow for diversity of thought and action, and to make myself familiar with it before I make a judgment—and even then, to be conscious of redemption and forgiveness."[36] Like Zurro, many emphasize that the impact of studying the movement goes beyond an abstract concept of activism or justice, but influences the way they try to live on a daily basis. Claire Ruswick explains, "Studying the movement might inspire people to fight for the betterment of humanity, or a group of people, but I also think it is a deeply personal thing. It is about fighting for the betterment of yourself." Joe Zurro adds, "I try and live in such a way that the Movement could continue through me. I don't think I can form some organization that is going to sweep across this country and guarantee that gays and lesbians will have equal rights under the law. But, I can start by treating them as though they are equals (my god! they are!). And I can work and teach so that my friends will feel the same. The fight does continue!"[37]

For another student this is even more personal. When he began college, he believed "gay marriage was pushing the envelope too far" and did not think he should "shove [his] sexual orientation in someone's face." His attitude changed after studying the movement. Although he does not want to be "irresponsible" or imply that the issues facing African Americans in the sixties and gays today are equivalent, he has come to believe that both "the civil rights movement and the gay rights movement are all about human rights." He asks, "Why does someone have the right to tell me that I cannot marry someone of the same sex when 20, 30, 40 years ago they were telling blacks and whites that they could not marry?" He continues, "There was a time (and in some places there probably still is) that there were *biblical* justifications for segregation, lynching, the banning of interracial marriage. So why should I accept any biblical injunction that forbids my sexual orientation? In this aspect, the study of the civil rights movement has really affected me. This is definitely something that you don't get from the dominant narrative."[38]

When Payne asked students to explain what they learn from studying the movement, he speculated that there was a difference for black and white students. (For more on this, see chapter 14, Payne, "Why Study the Movement?.") Though there is certainly overlap, there do seem to be some variations in what they emphasize (both in the comments students made during the conference and in their subsequent reflections). Many African American students reference family ties, a (new) appreciation for the achievements of earlier generations (within their family and by blacks generally), and sometimes a sense of responsibility for taking advantage of the opportunities that others sacrificed to make possible. Chris Bruce, for example, said that "[t]o me, learning about the movement means self-discovery." Reading Stokely Carmichael's *Ready for Revolution* helped him situate himself (along with his Panamanian relatives) more explicitly within the African diaspora. He felt "a part of something bigger, a larger community." He also observed that studying the movement "allows me to have a better understanding about the obstacles and victories that my people faced. It gives me confidence and strength when I read about the movement. It's a constant reminder of all the sacrifices that had to be taken in order for me to be where I am now, a soon-to-be college graduate." Jared DePass also made family connections, explaining that his mother was from Farmville, Virginia, located in Prince Edward County, home to one of the five *Brown* cases. When the state of Virginia closed public schools for five years rather than follow a court-ordered desegregation plan, some of his aunts and uncles were affected. "Learning about . . . the struggles [that] members of my family had in an effort to receive an education really sparked an interest in me."[39]

White students are more likely to be surprised to discover the persistence of racism and more likely to have their fundamental beliefs challenged or vision expanded (something that some resist and others more readily appreciate). Claire Ruswick reflects, "Growing up in a sheltered middle-class world, it is easy to believe that racism doesn't exist, and that the poverty or violence I see on the news is a small problem limited to only a few regions of the country." She says that until she joined the Ella Baker Reading Group, she "didn't know that racism was still a problem in the United States." She explains, for example, that she now sees parallels in the attitudes of white parents who opposed busing for school desegregation in Boston in the 1970s and the attitudes of white parents in Ithaca, New York, who opposed a 2005 school restructuring plan that would send their children to school with larger numbers of minority students.[40]

The potential and challenges for teaching movement history are intertwined with the many ways that persistent white supremacy influences our society (including the mostly white students I teach at Geneseo). Almost all students, regardless of race, are miseducated about our country's racial history. While African American and other minority students are more likely to be exposed to competing narratives, all students have been raised in a cultural context that emphasizes that racism is no longer an issue, something that has been reinforced with Barack Obama's election and the now pervasive presumption among many that we have achieved a "post-racial America." One white student explained, "I think young people today are raised with the impression that racism is not a widespread part of culture anymore, and that blacks who complain about its impact are 'using' their minority status to obtain special privileges or sympathies that would not be afforded to them *if they were white 'like everybody else'*" (emphasis added).[41]

When I teach a course on school desegregation, for example, most white students begin the semester sure that our nation's schools are integrated. Until we look carefully at these issues using an evidence-based, analytical lens, the mythology that *Brown* ended segregation and the civil rights movement ended racism wins out over their lived experience of virtually all-white schools (often in close proximity to schools attended almost exclusively by minority students, schools that most consider inferior). Many white students also believe that African Americans and other minorities have special privileges and advantages, particularly in college admissions and hiring. They express certainty about this, even though they are at a school that enrolls approximately thirty African American students a year out of an entering class of over 1,000.[42]

Student prejudices and assumptions about race are exacerbated by the persistent overrepresentation of white authority in our society. At Geneseo, for example, the vast majority of the faculty (and top administrative staff) are white and very few white students have ever had African American teachers or principals or any contact with African American authority figures. In this context, many (white) students have absorbed an expectation that whites should be in charge, that their (white) way of doing things is the only correct or appropriate way. Few of them are even aware of this and even fewer examine it or the related, and also unacknowledged, corollary that African Americans must be somehow inferior. As students grapple with new ideas and ways of understanding race historically—through, among other things, considering how labels like "Crazy Negro," are used; developing an awareness of the double standard around nonviolence and black self-defense during the movement; and coming to understand the extent and persistence of institutional white supremacy (how it intersects with and goes beyond the Klan and burning buses)—they sometimes revisit these internalized stereotypes and biases. At the end of a class on Black Power, one student wrote, "I also liked the Black Power class because I am so used to the idea that whites should be in charge, that this allowed me to see a situation in which blacks were able to take command of the situation. I have never had a black administrator, teacher, manager, or anyone in authority over me."[43]

Another student commented on how hearing SNCC activist and Mississippi native Hollis Watkins speak changed her image of African Americans. She had a picture of "huge mental inequalities within the African American culture of the mid-1900s." Explaining that she was prepared to see African Americans of this era as "heros because of their courage," she adds that at

Figure 36  Hollis Watkins leading Geneseo students in a workshop on student activism, March 2, 2010. Photograph by Dan Barbato, courtesy of SUNY Geneseo.

the same time, "you can't help but see them in an inferior light. Their ways of speaking and dressing often gives the impression of inferiority which leads to feelings of pity." After hearing about rural Mississippi poverty, education, and family life firsthand from Watkins, she reflected, "[L]istening to his voice and wisdom, you get a sense of the intelligence that permeated his household. A man who speaks with such wisdom and reverence is hard to imagine as anything other than equal or even superior to yourself." She then concluded, "This expression of intelligence helps to show that while African Americans may have been oppressed, they were in no way less intellectual or incapable of rationality. The rights they fought to procure were as deserving to them as they are to any man, regardless of race."[44] Teaching accurate, nuanced history can help counter some of these problematic biases, as students become more aware of their assumptions, more aware of the structural bases for persistent inequality, more aware of the skills and insight of particular African Americans, and more aware of the validity of multiple worldviews and the legitimacy of a range of cultural frames of reference. As students gain insight about multiple viewpoints and ways of seeing the world, they almost invariably sharpen their analytical skills and develop a keener appreciation for perspective. They can then draw on these new skills and this new awareness throughout their study and their lives.

While I strongly believe teaching movement history can have a positive, even transformative, impact on students, there is little value in simply substituting a new celebratory bottom-up account for the existing top-down narrative. Toward the end of the Local Studies Conference, Payne suggested that in order to keep the discussion "halfway honest" we should ask if there are any negatives to studying the movement. He speculated that one could be setting the bar too high and seeing movement activists as somehow different or special. Along those lines, he challenged the audience to make connections between movement history and contemporary problems in urban ghettos. He argued that it was important not to ignore challenging or unpleasant problems, suggesting that if we see the movement in terms of the development of human potential, we can avoid the trap of putting activists on a pedestal, while simultaneously dismissing other people as less than or unworthy. One student was struck by this and she saw a parallel between "the idea that human beings have 'different potentials,'" and the idea "that only some people are extraordinary enough to be leaders."[45]

For her part, Claire Ruswick wondered if "studying the civil rights movement inspires people to work in their own communities to fight for justice" or "does it quench the yearning to make a difference in the world, even if you personally aren't doing anything?" For Chris Machanoff, Hasan Jeffries's talk was most important for his insistence that we not "valorize the movement, as much as we may want to, but instead critically analyze it in order to pull out the most important aspects." He observed that "one thing which came across from many historians is the difficulty, yet importance, of studying history which so recently occurred." He concluded that there was both a "special opportunity" and a real challenge in "responsibly using all the sources: oral histories, notes, records, and archives accurately," a challenge that, he observed, is heightened by the fact that "people involved in the Movement can critique one's work."[46]

Students believe that it is possible to identify with the best of the movement and still engage with the history in ways that are thoughtful and critical. Not everyone would agree. Charles Eagles, of course, is the most visible example, but many others share his concern that historians who rely on oral history, or as Komozi Woodard said of John Dittmer, "take the side of the people," cannot write rigorous, "objective" history. They would probably offer the same critique of teachers who emphasize the bottom-up lens, decentering King and the primacy of national institutions in favor of a more chaotic and complicated bottom-up lens that incorporates more people, more issues, more tactics, more conflict, more uncertainty, and fewer clear-cut victories. Payne responded to critics of bottom-up historians in his Geneseo talk and a year later in the preface to the 2007 edition of *I've Got the Light of Freedom*. In the latter he writes, "Giving young people a history they can use doesn't require any bending of the record. Quite the contrary. The more precisely and completely we can render the history, the longer it will be useful."[47]

Introducing students to bottom-up movement history—in content and approach—does not simply produce a different kind of kind of narrow, heroic story. At its most basic, students immediately confront the moral and Constitutional failures of their government. Students also learn about tactical and philosophical conflicts within the movement, along with the demoralizing impact of petty, personal squabbles. The heroes turn out to be "real" people, flaws and all. There aren't always victories and some of the ones that do occur are limited and short-lived. When Hasan Jeffries discussed his book, *Bloody Lowndes*, with students in my civil rights movement historiography course in February 2010, one of their burning questions was why he included a chapter about the 1970s and 1980s betrayal of "freedom politics." Why, they wanted to know, didn't he end his book earlier, on a more upbeat note? He acknowledged that the last chapter was "the hardest to write." But added that, as much as he would have "loved to end the book on a high note" with the triumphant election of long-time activist John Hulett as sheriff, that would have contributed to a distortion of sorts. More importantly, it would have meant "overlooking valuable lessons about the perils of power, lessons that everyone committed to democracy should learn."[48]

After the conference, a number of students struggled with the challenge of how to bring the movement history they were learning to a larger audience, especially k–12 classrooms. Chris Machanoff observed that one of the conference participants asked a "particularly difficult, yet important question: Given the complexity of the movement, how do we change what is taught with the constricted time and material allotted to teachers?" In trying to answer this, he observed that it would be impossible to cover the entire movement in all of its complexity, but suggested that replacing the "hierarchical narrative" with something "showing the Movement was truly a *mass* movement of ordinary people would be important. In the short term, this seems more feasible than expecting students to attain an understanding of all the Movement's specific intricacies." Claire Ruswick reflected on her newfound appreciation for the political nature of education and how people are confronted with sometimes difficult choices in what to teach. Although she argued that "we really need to do a massive restructuring of the way we teach" history, she had no clear sense of how to accomplish that.[49]

Tiffany Izzo didn't address how teachers should tackle bottom-up history, but made it clear that she thinks it is important. Explaining that studying the movement was one of the things that helped her "feel capable of fighting for anything I believe in," she suggests that movement history "ties a lot of the other things together. People have lives, they have experiences. There's no formula for a leader (which I also got from studying the movement), but teaching the movement, telling people they are capable of things they might have never considered and allowing them to build on their own experiences certainly can't hurt." Chris Basso, then a sophomore and one of two students who attended a Sunday morning workshop on teaching movement history, reflected on all of the challenges that the teachers described—from the limits of their own education to the implications of their students' marginalized economic status to the restrictions enforced by school boards and regulatory agencies. Despite this, he was "inspired and motivated" by the teachers' passion and commitment and by Payne's suggestion that teachers could be "the new civil rights activists." He left the conference committed to becoming a teacher and has just begun teaching in a New York City public high school.[50]

At the Local Studies Conference, students clearly responded well to meeting historians and activists, to being included in the conversation, and to the serious way others considered and reflected on issues that the students found relevant to their own lives. I have seen this repeatedly over the years as movement activists and historians have spent time at Geneseo giving lectures, but also, invariably, spending time talking with students, telling stories, listening to their concerns, and discussing contemporary issues. I have found that when students have an opportunity to meet activists or historians in connection with a class, it always increases their interest and helps them see the "academic" work as more meaningful. As important as this is, it isn't always possible and, even in optimum circumstances, such as for the students whose coursework included the conference, these interactions can only supplement other work. For the most part, teachers have to introduce students to movement activists, to historians and their work, in other ways. While it isn't the

Figure 37  Rochester teacher Chojy Schroeder (*left*) and Geneseo student Christopher
Basso during Judy Richardson's presentation at a teaching workshop, Local Studies,
a National Movement Conference, March 26, 2006. Photograph courtesy of SUNY
Geneseo.

same as talking to someone in person, firsthand accounts—including memoirs, oral histories, field reports, documentaries, and recordings—and good
scholarship can all bring the movement to life, with accuracy, complexity,
and in ways that students can relate to.

Movement history also invites an emphasis on skills and active engagement. Though students can learn skepticism and appreciation for depth in
many classes, the impact seems particularly striking and profound in the
context of movement history—probably because the content does directly
challenge pervasive normative myths. Although it can be a struggle at first,
many students respond well to complex or "messy" history and to being
asked to figure things out and draw their own conclusions. And they seem
particularly eager for history that can help them make sense of the world in
which they live. Many express a desire to be part of an educated, informed
society that embraces a realistic, usable history, one that can help, not undermine, efforts to fight for justice.

During the Local Studies Conference, one student said that she hoped to live up to Ella Baker's legacy. Payne later observed that "I, too, want to be like Ella Baker when I'm fully formed."[51] Recounting this afterward, Tiffany Izzo wrote, "This made me laugh. Doesn't everybody want to grow up to be Ella Baker?" before acknowledging, "In truth, many people might have not even heard her name before. It was nice to be in a community of people who do know, though, and would laugh and understand." She concluded, "The next step is figuring out how to get that across to people who haven't learned about those aspects of the movement—people who wouldn't get why someone would want to grow up to be Ella Baker."[52]

And this is our challenge. We must continue to question and learn. We must do a better job of communicating what we know, of ensuring that the insights from local struggles are central to the historiographical discussions and are incorporated into the curriculum, from elementary school through college and beyond. We must reclaim our symbols. It is crucial that our society understand that Rosa Parks was a lifelong activist and that when Martin Luther King Jr. was killed, he was considered, in the words of Hasan Kwame Jeffries, "a Crazy Negro." He was considered crazy because he was leading an interracial movement of the poor, critiquing the violence of war and poverty, and fighting for economic justice. In reclaiming the subjects of these distorted myths, we see how their activism fits more comfortably with what we learn from local movement studies and bottom-up history—including the importance of human, as well as civil rights, what Jeffries has described collectively as the "freedom rights" identified by African Americans at the point of emancipation.[53] Among other things, we must take seriously and be precise about the activism and struggle that preceded and followed the more visible mass movement of the 1950s and 1960s, while exploring the ways organizing and mobilizing intersected and diverged in the making of that mass movement. We must address, not just women's "contributions," but the ways women's participation shaped the movement. As a number of the pieces in this book illustrate, the entire picture shifts when women are brought into focus. In general, centering the ordinary people who did extraordinary things forces us to reconsider what this movement was about, how it worked, what it accomplished, and what remains to be done.[54] If we do all this, Ella Baker and her approach to life and social justice work will be as well-known as Martin Luther King's "I Have a Dream" speech and we will, at the very least, extend the community of people who can relate to and appreciate what it might mean to "grow up to be [like] Ella Baker." We may also extend the community of people who will take her approach to heart and join with their friends and neighbors to continue the struggle for justice.

## NOTES

1. Christopher Machanoff, Ella Baker Reading Group, Spring 2006. (Hereafter, EBRG.) Some of the student reflections quoted throughout have been edited very slightly to standardize punctuation, capitalization, and spelling. Copies of all student reflections are in author's possession.

2. Charles M. Payne, *I've Got the Light of Freedom: The Organizing Tradition and the Mississippi Freedom Struggle* (Berkeley: University of California Press, 1995), 68; Barbara Ransby, *Ella Baker and the Black Freedom Movement: A Radical Democratic Vision* (Chapel Hill, University of North Carolina Press, 2003), 362.

3. Emilye Crosby, "Making *Eyes on the Prize*: An Interview with Filmmaker and SNCC Staffer Judy Richardson," chapter 9, this volume.

4. Christopher Basso, EBRG; Amanda Abold, Hist266, Spring 2006; Katie Snyder, Hist266, Spring 2006; Mark Schuber, Hist266, Spring 2006; Angela Cassidy, Hist266, Spring 2006.

5. Greg Fair, EBRG; Liz Hoagland, Hist266, Spring 2006; Kim Kiniry, Hist266, Spring 2006; Angela Cassidy, Hist266, Spring 2006; Amanda Abold, Hist266, Spring 2006; John Dittmer, "Southern Community Studies and Their Critics," March 24, 2006, "Local Studies, a National Movement," Conference DVD (in author's possession). See also, Charles W. Eagles, "Toward New Histories of the Civil Rights Movement," *Journal of Southern History* 66, no. 4 (2000): 815–48.

6. Kristy Sirianni, EBRG; Tarik Kitson, EBRG; Gregory Fair, EBRG; Christopher Machanoff, EBRG. Tarik Kitson, EBRG; Todd Moye, "Local Studies: What Do They Tell Us? Why Do They Matter?" panel, March 24, 2006, "Local Studies, a National Movement," Conference DVD (in author's possession); Christopher Machanoff, EBRG. Greg Fair, EBRG; Liz Hoagland, Hist266, Spring 2006. Similarly, Machanoff described the conference as "refreshing," while Mark Schuber wrote, "[I]t was amazing to have so many different people give their opinions." Chris Machanoff, EBRG; Mark Schuber, Hist266, Spring 2006.

7. Christina Pinnola, EBRG; Joseph Zurro, EBRG. Ruswick was among the many students who commented on Payne's ability to ask helpful questions and, as she observed, "pick out all the problems and issues present, and articulate them in a manner that makes sense." Claire Ruswick, EBRG. Katie Snyder, Hist220, Spring 2006. The stories that Judy Richardson read from have subsequently been published. See Faith S. Holsaert, Martha Prescod Norman Noonan, Judy Richardson, Betty Garman Robinson,

Jean Smith Young, and Dorothy M. Zellner, *Hands on the Freedom Plow: Personal Accounts by Women in* SNCC (Urbana: University of Illinois Press, 2010).

8. Mark Schuber, Hist266, Spring 2006; Claire Ruswick, EBRG; Christopher Basso, EBRG; Jeanne Theoharis, "Women, Gender, and Leadership" panel, March 25, 2006, "Local Studies, a National Movement," Conference DVD (in author's possession). Theoharis's commentary on the popular response to the deaths of Rosa Parks and Coretta Scott King offered an important analytical model for many students who were learning to critique the movement mythologies they had been taught. Kristy Sirianni, EBRG; Justin Becker, Hist266, Spring 2006; Claire Ruswick, EBRG. See also Jeanne Theoharis, "Accidental Matriarchs and Beautiful Helpmates: Rosa Parks, Coretta Scott King, and the Memorialization of the Civil Rights Movement," chapter 13, this volume.

9. Payne, *I've Got the Light of Freedom*, 85.

10. Tiffany Izzo, EBRG.

11. Katie Snyder, Hist220, Spring 2006.

12. Judy Richardson to Afro-Am listserv, H-Net, February 20, 2006, http://h-net .msu.edu/cgi-bin/logbrowse.pl?trx=lm&list=H-Afro-Am (accessed July 7, 2010). An African American student who returned to college as an adult certainly had that reaction. He reflected, "The history I was told never made sense to me. I used to think Blacks were scared back then, timid, meek, and weak. I remember saying, 'Man I wouldn't put up with that crap!' 'If I was alive back then I would have drank in any water fountain I felt like!' I thought Martin Luther King was well intentioned but conservative and when I finally learned about Malcolm X, my interest in the Civil Rights Movement was somewhat renewed, yet I remained largely uninformed." Keven Adams, Hist220 final reflection, Spring 2010.

13. For more on teaching self-defense in the movement, see Emilye Crosby, "'This nonviolent stuff ain't no good. It'll get ya killed.': Teaching about Self-Defense in the African-American Freedom Struggle," in *Teaching the Civil Rights Movement*, ed. Julie Buckner, Houston Roberson, Rhonda Y. Williams, and Susan Holt (New York: Routledge, 2002), 159–73.

14. Katie Snyder, Hist220, Spring 2006; Liz Hoagland, Hist266, Spring 2006.

15. Christopher Neels, Hist266, Spring 2006; Jerry Emanuel, Hist266, Spring 2006.

16. Christopher Neels, Hist266, Spring 2006; Mark Schuber, Hist266, Spring 2006; Quote by Liz Hoagland, Hist266, Spring 2006.

17. Laura Warren Hill, comments on Local Studies Conference, in author's possession; David O'Donnell, Fall 2009 Hist220 final reflection. Kevin Muller, November 25, 2008 journal, Honr206; Daniel Bailey, Hist220 final reflection, Fall 2009.

18. Christopher Basso, EBRG.

19. Claire Ruswick, EBRG; Steve Tisch, et al., *Forrest Gump* (Hollywood, Calif.: Paramount Pictures, 1994).

20. Lisa Kress, Hist388 (Black Power and Structural Inequality), Spring 2008; Christopher Bruce, EBRG.

21. Claire Ruswick, EBRG.

22. Joseph Zurro, EBRG.

23. Ibid.; Christopher Basso, EBRG.

24. Christopher Bruce, EBRG; Christopher Basso, EBRG.

25. Hasan Kwame Jeffries, "Freedom Politics: Transcending Civil Rights in Lowndes County, Alabama, 1965–2000 (PhD diss., Ohio State University, 2002). Quotes from Hasan Kwame Jeffries, *Bloody Lowndes: Civil Rights and Black Power in the Alabama Black Belt* (New York: New York University Press, 2001), 4–6.

26. Claire Ruswick, Reflection on Jeffries, "Freedom Politics," EBRG, Spring 2006.

27. David Russell, Hist220, Jeffries reflection, March 2, 2010 (hereafter, Hist220, Jeffries); Jake Griffin, Hist220, Jeffries; Keven Adams, Hist220, Jeffries.

28. Alex Timmis, Hist220, Jeffries; Samantha Maurer, Hist220, Jeffries; Jade Johnson, Hist220, Jeffries; Keven Adams, Hist220 final reflection, Spring 2010; Keven Adams, Hist220, Jeffries.

29. Joel Dodge, Honr203, Fall 2008; Lisa Kress, Hist388 (Black Power and Structural Inequality), Spring 2008; Jake Griffin, Hist220 final reflection, Spring 2010.

30. Emily Keim, Hist266, Spring 2009. Judy Richardson observes that when she speaks to college audiences, students often express anger over what they have not been taught. Emilye Crosby, "That Movement Responsibility: An Interview with Judy Richardson on Movement History and Legacies," chapter 12, this volume.

31. Ashley McKay, Hist266, Spring 2006.

32. Tracy Webster, Hist266, Spring 2006. Similarly, Claire Ruswick noted that everyone likes stories about people "fighting for a just cause." Claire Ruswick, EBRG.

33. Tiffany Izzo, EBRG.

34. Hannah Prescott-Eberle, Hist266, Spring 2006; Christopher Machanoff, EBRG; Erin Rightmyer, EBRG.

35. Tarik Kitson, EBRG; Gregory Fair, EBRG; Claire Ruswick, EBRG.

36. Joseph Zurro, EBRG.

37. Claire Ruswick, EBRG; Joseph Zurro, EBRG.

38. Name withheld by request, EBRG.

39. Christopher Bruce, EBRG; Stokely Carmichael, with Michael Thelwell, *Ready for Revolution: The Life and Struggles of Stokely Carmichael (Kwame Ture)* (New York: Scribner, 2003); Jared DePass, EBRG.

40. Claire Ruswick, EBRG; Claire Ruswick to Emilye Crosby, e-mail, July 7, 2009.

41. Kevin Muller, November 25, 2008 journal, Honr206.

42. From Fall 2004 through Fall 2009, Geneseo enrolled an average of just under thirty-three new black students per year out of an average of 1,032 incoming students.

During the same years, an average of 116 total black students were enrolled (suggesting some problems with retention). The average for all minority students was just under 166 incoming students and 600 overall out of a total student body of 5,280. Students classified as Asian are the largest minority group on campus and one that is growing at a faster rate than any other. The number and percentage of African American faculty is even lower. As of Fall 2009 there were a total of four black faculty, including two who are tenured, out of a total of 207 full-time faculty. Geneseo Fact Book, 2009–10. http://www.geneseo.edu/webfm_send/2666 (accessed July 3, 2010, and in author's possession).

43. Lisa Kress, Hist388 (Black Power and Structural Inequality), Spring 2008.

44. Victoria Trosterud, reflection on talk by Hollis Watkins, March 6, 2010.

45. Charles Payne, "Why Study the Movement?," chapter 14, this volume; Hannah Prescott-Eberle, Hist266, Spring 2006.

46. Claire Ruswick, EBRG; Christopher Machanoff, EBRG.

47. Eagles, "Toward New Histories," 815–48. Komozi Woodard, Introduction for John Dittmer, March 24, 2006, "Local Studies, a National Movement," Conference DVD (in author's possession); Payne, *I've Got the Light of Freedom* (2007 edition), xxi.

48. Hasan Kwame Jeffries with Hist220: Interpretations in History: Civil Rights Movement, February 25, 2010, SUNY Geneseo; Hasan Kwame Jeffries, e-mail to author, June 26, 2010.

49. Christopher Machanoff, EBRG; Claire Ruswick, EBRG.

50. Tiffany Izzo, EBRG; Christopher Basso, EBRG; Teaching Workshop, March 26, 2006, "Local Studies, a National Movement" Conference, SUNY Geneseo.

51. Kristy Sirianni made this comment during Payne's closing keynote, "Why Study the Movement?" Charles Payne, "Why Study the Movement?," March 25, 2006, "Local Studies, a National Movement," Conference DVD (in author's possession). See also, Charles Payne, "Why Study the Movement?," chapter 14, this volume.

52. Tiffany Izzo, EBRG.

53. Jeffries, *Bloody Lowndes*, 4.

54. "Ordinary people who did extraordinary things," is a paraphrase of Charles Payne's assertion that "[p]art of the legacy of people like Ella Baker and Septima Clark is a faith that ordinary people who learn to believe in themselves are capable of extraordinary acts, or better, of acts that seem extraordinary to us precisely because we have such an impoverished sense of the capabilities of ordinary people. If we are surprised at what these people accomplished, our surprise may be a commentary on the angle of vision from which we view them." Payne, *I've Got the Light of Freedom*, 5.

# CONTRIBUTORS

EMILYE CROSBY is Professor of History at SUNY Geneseo where she has been awarded the Chancellor's Award for Excellence in Teaching and the Spencer Roemer Supported Professorship. She is author of *A Little Taste of Freedom: The Black Freedom Struggle in Claiborne County, Mississippi* (2005), which was awarded the Mississippi Historical Society McLemore Prize and the Organization of American Historians Liberty Legacy Honorable Mention. Her published essays include: "'Looking the Devil in the Eye': Race Relations and the Civil Rights Movement in Claiborne County History and Memory," *The Civil Rights Movement in Mississippi*, ed. Ted Ownby (forthcoming), and "'This nonviolent stuff ain't no good. It'll get ya killed.': Teaching about Self-Defense in the African-American Freedom Struggle," in *Teaching the Civil Rights Movement*, ed. Julie Buckner, Houston Roberson, Rhonda Y. Williams, and Susan Holt (2002).

JOHN DITTMER is Professor Emeritus of History at DePauw University. He has also taught at Brown and at MIT, and from 1967–1979 was a member of the history faculty at Tougaloo College. He is the author of *Black Georgia in the Progressive Era, 1900–1910* (1977), and *Local People: The Struggle for Civil Rights in Mississippi* (1994), which received the Bancroft Prize and the Lillian Smith Book Award for Nonfiction. His latest book, *The Good Doctors: The Medical Committee for Human Rights and the Struggle for Social Justice in Health Care* (2009), is now available in paperback from Bloomsbury Press.

LAURIE B. GREEN teaches history at the University of Texas at Austin, specializing in courses on comparative civil rights, race, and women's and gender studies. She is the author of *Battling the Plantation Mentality: Memphis and the Black Freedom Struggle*, published in 2007 by the University of North Carolina Press. The book won the 2008 Philip A. Taft Labor History Award, and was a finalist for 2008 OAH Liberty Legacy Award. She is now researching the politics of race, gender, and hunger during the antipoverty struggles of the 1960s and 1970s.

WESLEY HOGAN teaches the history of social movements, African American history, women's history, and oral history at Virginia State University. Her book on SNCC, *Many Minds, One Heart: SNCC and the Dream for a New America* (2007), won the Lillian Smith Book Award, the Scott-Bills Memorial Prize for best work in peace history, and the Library of Virginia nonfiction literary award. From 2006–2009 she was the codirector of the Institute for the Study of Race Relations, whose mission is to bring together community organizers, researchers, and young leaders to promote healthy communities. Between 2004–2008, she was active in bringing together the Algebra Project, the Young People's Project, and the Petersburg City Public Schools, and has recently coordinated an oral history project of the civil rights movement in Petersburg. Her current project with the philosopher Renée Afanana Hill is an interdisciplinary comparative examination of methods of rebuilding civic bodies in the wake of genocide or collective abuse in South Africa, Rwanda, Germany, the United States, and Argentina.

HASAN KWAME JEFFRIES earned his PhD in American history with a specialization in twentieth-century African American history from Duke University in 2002. He is currently Associate Professor of History in the Department of History and the Kirwan Institute for the Study of Race and Ethnicity at The Ohio State University. He is the author of *Bloody Lowndes: Civil Rights and Black Power in Alabama's Black Belt* (New York University Press, 2009).

CHARLES W. MCKINNEY JR. is an Assistant Professor of History at Rhodes College in Memphis, Tennessee, where he teaches classes on twentieth century United States history, the civil rights movement, black activism, and the African American Intellectual Tradition. He is the author of *Greater Freedom: The Evolution of the Civil Rights Struggle in Wilson, North Carolina* (2010). He is a founding member and Senior Fellow of the Jamestown Project, a diverse action-oriented think tank of new leaders who reach across boundaries and generations to make democracy real. His current project is a multidisciplinary response to the question posed by Martin Luther King Jr. in 1968—"Where Do We Go From Here?." In 1990 McKinney won the First Year Teacher of the Year award in the Compton (CA) Unified School District in South Central Los Angeles. He subsequently spent five years as the partnership manager for Public Allies, an Americorps leadership development program, and three years as a curriculum coordinator for a juvenile justice diversion program in Durham, North Carolina.

J. TODD MOYE is Associate Professor of History and Director of the Oral History Program at the University of North Texas. He is the author of *Let the People Decide: Black Freedom and White Resistance Movements in Sunflower County, Mississippi, 1945–1986* (2004), and *Freedom Flyers: The Tuskegee Airmen of World War II* (2010).

CHARLES M. PAYNE is the Frank P. Hixon Professor in the School of Social Service Administration at the University of Chicago, where he is also an affiliate of the Center for Urban School Improvement. His interests include urban education and school reform, social inequality, social change, and modern African American history. He is the author of *Getting What We Ask for: The Ambiguity of Success and Failure in Urban Education* (1984), and *I've Got the Light of Freedom: The Organizing Tradition in the Mississippi Civil Rights Movement* (1995). The latter has won awards from the Southern Regional Council, *Choice Magazine*, the Simon Wisenthal Center, and the Gustavus Myers Center for the Study of Human Rights in North America. He is coauthor of *Debating the Civil Rights Movement* (1999), and coeditor of *Time Longer than Rope: A Century of African American Activism, 1850–1950* (2003). He recently published *So Much Reform, So Little Change* (Harvard Education Publishing Group), which is concerned with the persistence of failure in urban schools.

JUDY RICHARDSON was a staff member with the Student Nonviolent Coordinating Committee (SNCC) in the early 1960s, working in the national office in Atlanta, and in Mississippi, Lowndes County, Alabama, southwest Georgia, and on Julian Bond's first campaign for the Georgia House of Representatives. In 1968 Richardson and a number of former SNCC workers organized Drum and Spear Bookstore in Washington, D.C. In the early 1980s, Richardson worked with the United Church of Christ Commission for Racial Justice, as director of information. She began her film career in 1978, working with Blackside's Henry Hampton on what later became the fourteen-hour PBS series, *Eyes on the Prize*. Also for Blackside, Richardson coproduced *Malcolm X: Make It Plain* in 1994. She is currently a Consulting Senior Producer with Northern Light Productions, and recently completed a one-hour PBS documentary *Scarred Justice* (2009), on the 1968 Orangeburg Massacre (S.C.) and all the videos for the National Park Service's new Little Rock Crisis Visitor Center. She and five other female activists from SNCC edited *Hands on the Freedom Plow: Personal Accounts by Women in* SNCC (University of Illinois Press, 2010).

ROBYN C. SPENCER is currently an Assistant Professor in the Department of History at Lehman College, City University of New York. Her areas of interest include black social protest after World War II, urban and working-class radicalism, and gender. She has published several articles and chapters, including "Engendering the Black Freedom Struggle: Revolutionary Black Womanhood and the Black Panther Party in the Bay Area, California," in the *Journal of Women's History* (2008). She is currently completing a book on the Oakland Black Panthers, *Repression Breeds Resistance: The Rise and Fall of the Black Panther Party in Oakland, CA 1966–1982*, and starting a new project, tentatively titled *No Justice, No Peace: Black Liberation Politics and the Movement Against the Vietnam War, 1955–1973*.

JEANNE THEOHARIS is Professor of Political Science and Endowed Chair in Women's Studies at Brooklyn College of City University of New York. She coedited *Freedom North: Black Freedom Struggles Outside of the South, 1940–1980* (2003), and *Groundwork: Local Black Freedom Movements in America* (2005) with Komozi Woodard, and *Want to Start a Revolution: Radical Women in the Black Freedom Struggle* (2009) with Dayo Gore and Komozi Woodard.

AMY NATHAN WRIGHT is an Assistant Professor in University Programs at St. Edward's University in Austin, Texas, where she teaches the literature of the modern black freedom struggle, as well as interdisciplinary courses on the rhetoric of the sixties, the history of marginalized groups in the United States, and contemporary social problems and issues of identity. She is currently completing her manuscript, "The Dream Deferred: Poverty, Race, and the 1968 Poor People's Campaign."

# INDEX

Abercrombie, Caude, 128

Abernathy, Ralph, 110, 118, 394, 402

Abold, Amanda, 422 *illus.*

abolition, 263

abolitionist movement, 173

activists, and historical interpretation,
  1–2, 5, 18–24, 36–37n47, 38n51,
  39n55, 358–60; and internal
  movement politics, 330–60. *See also*
  historiography; partisanship

Adams, Jane, 349

Adams, Victoria Gray, 281, 287, 375

Adickes, Sandra, 319–20

affirmative action, 272, 368, 379–82, 457,
  466

African diaspora, 464

afro, 92, 270, 305

Afro-American Broadcasting Company,
  397

AFSCME, 74

AIDS, 405–6

Alabama, 233, 262

Alabama, University of, 266

Albany Movement (Ga.), 161–62 *illus.*, 177
  *illus.*, 287, 295, 313; and historiography,
  18–20, 37n49, 157–62, 164, 166, 292,
  438; and nonviolence, 176, 182–83, 185,
  211, 220–21, 222

Algebra Project, 431, 440

Ali, Muhammad, 303–4

Alito, Samuel, 386

"America, We Loved You Madly," 278, 288

American Federation of State, County,
  and Municipal Employees. *See*
  AFSCME

American Indian Movement, 136

Anderson, Peter, 421–24, 422 *illus.*

Antioch College, 399

antipoverty activism, and the civil rights
  movement, 57, 60, 71, 73, 74, 75, 77;
  and the Poor People's Campaign, 109–
  38. *See also* economic issues; human
  rights; welfare rights activism

antipoverty programs, 49, 91. *See also*
  federal programs; War on Poverty

Appalachian Committee for Full
  Employment, 346

Aptheker, Bettina, 341

Aquinas, Thomas, 429

armed resistance, as a movement tactic,
  69, 198, 200, 201, 212, 216, 220,
  222–30, 233, 238, 252n62. *See also*
  historiography; retaliation; rhetoric;
  self-defense; Umoja, Akinyele;
  violence

armed self-defense. *See* self-defense

Army War College Report, 381

Athens, Greece, 429–30

Atlanta, Ga., movement in, 57, 166, 176,
  215, 279, 378

Atlantic City 1964 Convention. *See under*
  Democratic Party

Attica (N.Y.) prison rebellion, 303

Attucks, Crispus, 324

Auschwitz, 428
Avery, Annie Pearl, 375
Axelrod, Janet, 299

Bagley, Pat, 272
Bagwell, Orlando, 293–94, 306
Bailey, Dwight, 97
Bailey, Wallace, 95
Baker, Doris Shaw, 119, 133
Baker, Ella, 48 *illus.*, 262, 287, 358; and
    approach to leadership, 56, 58, 59,
    181–82, 369, 433, 449, 452, 453, 476n54;
    as inspiration, 424, 432, 472–73; and
    nonviolence/self-defense, 181–82, 184
Baldwin, James, 46, 400
Bambara, Toni Cade, 302
Baraka, Amiri, 271, 312
Barnes, Audrey, 286
Barnett, Ross, 44
Bartley, Numan V., 153
Basso, Christopher, and studying
    movement history, 422 *illus.*, 425 *illus.*,
    450 *illus.*, 451, 453, 456, 458, 470, 471
    *illus.*
Bates, Daisy, 409
Batson, Ruth, 290
Battle, Clinton, 155–56
*Bearing the Cross*, 148, 287
Beckwith, Byron de la, 45
Belafonte, Harry, 388
Bellamy, Edward, 400
Bellamy, Fay, 187, 216
beloved community, 373, 350; and
    Local Studies, a National Movement
    Conference, xi, 452; and nonviolence,
    179–82, 187, 377, 436
Berclaw, Nancy, 61
Bernard, Sheila, 312
Bevel, James, 172, 173, 180

*Beyond Atlanta*, 160
Bible, 179, 428–29, 464
Biloxi, Miss., 344–46, 350
Binghamton University (SUNY), 421
Birmingham Campaign (Ala.), 45, 158,
    220, 295, 313
Birmingham speech (by John F.
    Kennedy), 50
black community, and internal relations/
    differences, 55, 76–77, 83–84, 88–
    89, 156, 227, 282, 304, 317n8, 322–
    23. *See also* boycott, enforcement;
    nonviolence, debates over
black freedom struggle, as a way of
    defining the movement, 6, 12, 13, 14,
    59, 73, 83, 101, 148, 153
Black Hats (Port Gibson, Miss.), 1, 2,
    226–29, 232
Black History Month, 83, 355, 408, 457
black institutions, 21, 86, 88, 282, 325;
    and Black Power, 300, 301, 306, 309–
    10, 397. *See also* Drum and Spear
    Bookstore; Lowndes County Freedom
    Organization; parallel institutions
black nationalism (nationalists), and the
    movement, 49, 270–71, 282, 290, 300,
    301, 303, 306, 324, 348–49, 397, 405,
    437–38. *See also* Black Power; black
    radicals
Black Panther Party (Chicago), 379
Black Panther Party (Des Moines, Iowa),
    163
Black Panther Party (Lowndes County,
    Ala.), 13, 233, 254n82
Black Panther Party (Oakland-based),
    69, 74, 427; and gender in scholarship
    on, 324–25, 339–42, 351–53, 359; and
    internal politics, 330–60; and self-
    defense scholarship, 201, 224–25;

mentioned, 69, 163. *See also* Oakland Community Learning Center; Oakland Community School

Black Power, 269–72, 330, 466; in *Eyes on the Prize*, 280–81, 300, 301, 316–17n6; and local studies, 6, 13–14, 26, 163, 166, 230, 235, 456–61; and the Meredith March, 14, 49–50, 199, 211; and normative history, 5, 14, 15, 15, 26, 34n27, 50, 57, 269–72, 323–25, 340, 360, 403, 428, 456–61; and Stokely Carmichael, 13, 49, 166, 233, 301, 316–17n6, 326 *illus.*; and women, 34n38, 73. *See also* black nationalism; black radicals; historiography; separatism

Black Power studies, 11

black radicals/radicalism, 269–72, 282, 302, 456; and humanism, 336; and movement leadership, 58, 379; and Rosa Parks, 397, 409; and scholarly framing, 322–26, 379, 390, 397

Black Studies, 282, 304, 430

blackface caricature, 16

Blackside, 278–318 *passim*, 367

Blackside archives, 297

Blackwell, Unita, 281, 309, 439

Blight, David, 389–90

Block, Sam, 185

*Blood Done Sign My Name*, 238

*Bloody Lowndes*, 459, 469

Bloody Sunday, 221, 378

Bogalusa movement (La.), and the Deacons for Defense, 196, 203–7, 213, 214–15, 223–24, 226, 229–30, 232, 236

Bogalusa Voters League, 206

Bolden, Willie, and the Mule Train, 117, 118, 119, 124, 125, 128, 130

Bolling, Elmore, 268

Bolton, Jimmy, 350

Bond, Julian, 83, 279, 287, 291, 413n9

Booth, Dwayne, 265

Boss Crump political machine. *See* Crump, E. H. (Boss)

Boston, Mass., 290; and busing, 315, 465

Boston University, 399

bottom-up history, and the civil rights movement, 7, 9, 12, 17, 19–20, 24, 370–84; and teaching the movement, 448–73. *See also* historiography; teaching (and learning) movement history

boycott, 1, 2; and enforcement by black activists, 3, 183, 219, 226–28, 238, 252n69, 310; as tactic, 172–73, 174, 183, 206, 207, 226, 227. *See also* Montgomery Bus Boycott; school boycotts

Boyette, Bruce, 99–100

Braden, Anne, 187

Branch, Taylor, 148, 157, 158, 377

Brandon, Marjorie, 3–4

Branford, Charles, 85

Breines, Winifred, 352

bridge leaders, 57, 102

Brookes, Edward, 379

Brooks, Pam, 425–26

Browder, Aurelia, 394

*Browder v. Gayle*, 395

*Brown* decision, 10, 69, 162, 280, 466; and Mississippi, 43–44, 153, 154, 156

Brown, Elaine, 324, 340

Brown, Elsa Barkley, 61

Brown, Minnie Jean, 310

Brown, Sterling, 304

Browning, Joan, 159–61

Bruce, Christopher, and studying movement history, 450 *illus.*, 457–58, 464–65

Bryant, C. C., 195

Bryant, Ora, 195

Bryant's Chapel (Indianola, Miss.), 177

Bush administration (George W.), 380.
See also Bush, George W.

Bush, George H., 387

Bush, George W., 380, 386, 387, 388

Bush, Laura, 386

Butterfield, G. K., Jr., 81–83, 85

Butterfield, G. K., Sr., 83, 84, 88

Butterfield Lane (Wilson, N.C.), 84

Buzanowski, Sarah, 424, 425 illus.

Cambridge, Md., 185, 219, 279, 338

Camilla, Ga., 186

Canton, Miss., and the Meredith March,
49–50, 237, 293

Cap Cities, 284–85, 288, 290

Cardozo High School (Washington,
D.C.), 403

Carmichael, Stokely, 38n51, 50, 304, 327
illus., 464; and Blackside interview,
296–97; and Freedom Schools illus.,
434; and Lowndes County/ Black
Power, 13, 49, 166, 233, 301, 316–
17n6; and media portrayals, 262, 267,
269, 349, 457; and misuse of "prone"
comment, 297, 332, 375, 376; and
nonviolence, 176, 211, 212, 216–17,
221

Carson, Clayborne, 291, 399–400; and
"black freedom struggle," 12, 13, 148

Carter, Jimmy, 387, 388–89

Carthage, Miss., 186

cartoons, and Barack Obama's election,
25, 259–75

Cashin, John, 126

Center for Black Education (Washington,
D.C.), 306

"centerwomen," 57

Central Methodist Church (Detroit), 396,
398

Cha-Jua, Sundiata, 11

Chafe, William, 56; and local studies
scholarship, 5, 8, 10, 13–14, 19, 147–51,
165, 451

Chaney, James, 187, 286

Chappell, Marisa, 408

Chavis, Ben, 184

Chicano movement, 136

child care, and the Black Panther Party,
351, 353–55

Christian, Joann, 376

Christianity, 163, 173, 178–79, 270, 403,
454

chronology. See under historiography

Churchill, Ward, 188

Citizens Citywide Action Committee
(Detroit), 398

Citizens' Council, 7, 43, 45, 153–56. See
also segregationists; white resistance;
white supremacy

citizenship, and the civil rights
movement, 54, 56, 58, 61, 64, 65, 95,
103, 123, 155, 163, 199, 372, 449, 455

Citizenship School classes, 194, 196, 326
illus.

civil liberties, and the civil rights
movement, 379–80, 388–89, 391, 397,
407–8

Civil Liberties Committee (Antioch
College), 399

civil rights unionism, 9, 10, 11, 12. See also
long civil rights movement

Civil Rights Act of 1964, 47, 63, 162, 282,
456; and organized self-defense, 223,
228, 230, 231

Civil Rights Commission, 46, 73

*The Civil Rights Movement in American Memory*, 427

Civil Rights Movement Veterans of Mississippi, 426

*Civilities and Civil Rights*, and impact on movement scholarship, 5, 8, 13–14, 147–50, 163, 451

Claiborne County movement (Miss.). *See* Port Gibson movement.

*Claiborne Hardware, et al. v. NAACP, et al.*, 2

Clark, Mark, 379

Clark, Septima, 56, 58, 59, 326 *illus.*, 476n54

Clark, Thomas, 70

Clay, Byron, 136

Cleage, Albert, 398

Cleaver, Eldridge, 340

Clinton, Hillary, 386

Clinton, William (Bill), 386, 387

Closed Society, 43, 46, 427

club women, 65

Cluster, Dick, 438

Cobb, Charles, Jr. (Charlie), and Freedom Schools, 320, 328n6, 329n7; and unviolence and self-defense, 21, 38n54, 191n25, 194, 243n18, 253n74

COFO, 46, 227, 286

COINTELPRO, 351, 356

Colburn, David, 149

Cold War, 9, 178–79, 409

Cole, Johnetta, 308

Collins, Dora Lee, 133

Collins, Irene, 114

color blindness, 261–62, 412. *See also* "post-racial" America

Columbia, Tenn., 68

Colvin, Claudette, 392, 394, 420

Commission for Racial Justice. *See* United Church of Christ, Commission for Racial Justice

Committee for a Sane Nuclear Policy, 400

Communist Party, 407; and *Eyes on the Prize*, 303, 311; and the long civil rights movement, 12, 14, 33

community bridge leader. *See* bridge leader

community organizing, as approach, 91–104, 112, 182, 183, 262, 383, 470, 472; and the Black Panther Party, 351–56; in SNCC, 153, 156–57, 166, 227, 232–33, 236, 266, 286, 369, 370–72, 421, 424–25, 452–53, 459–60; and students, 423, 449, 451–54. *See also* Baker, Ella; historiography; Payne, Charles; SNCC

community studies. *See* historiography

Concerned Citizens, 156

Concord Baptist Church (Brooklyn), 299

Confederacy, 267

Congress of Racial Equality. *See* CORE

Congressional Challenge (MFDP), 48

Constitution, and the movement, 45, 179, 197, 224, 231, 371, 469

Conyers, John, and Rosa Parks, 385–86, 396, 398, 407

Cook, William (Bill), 424, 428–29

Copeland, Myrna, 120, 123

Corbett, Fannie, 81 *illus.*; biography of, 86–87; portrayals of, 81–85; and WCIA, 89, 91, 92–104

Cordele, Ga., 371

CORE, 219; and nonviolence, 185, 198, 203–6, 220; and self-defense, 198, 203–7, 223; mentioned, 44, 49, 90, 148, 181, 286, 293, 295, 306, 332, 345, 346

Corley, Scott, 428

Cornell University, 282, 304

Corporation for Public Broadcasting, 290, 299

Cosby, Bill, 298–99

Cotton, Dorothy, 421

Cottonreader, R. B., 113

Council of Federated Organizations. See COFO

counterculture, 339, 340, 346

Cox, Courtland, 191, 375

Crawford, Vicki, 56

Credentials Committee (Democratic Party), 47

Crosby, Emilye, 58, 147, 183–84, 284 *illus.*, 423

Crossley, Callie, 292, 300–1

Crowe, J. D., 266, 272

Crump, E. H. (Boss), 70

Cuba, 155

"culture of poverty," 115, 120, 138

Dahmer, Vernon, 195

Dante, 428–29, 430

Darden High School (Wilson, N.C.), 85

Davis, Angela, 303, 426

de Jong, Greta, 10, 198, 204–5

Deacons for Defense, 212, 213, 238; and Black Hats (Port Gibson, Miss.) 1, 2, 226–29, 232; in Bogalusa, La., 196, 203–7, 213, 214–15, 223–24, 226, 229–30, 232, 236; and gender, 208–9, 213–15; and historiography, 196, 198, 201, 203–9, 213–15, 223–32, 235, 250–51n59–60, 251–52n66; in Jonesboro, La., 199, 205, 207–8, 212–15, 223, 226, 232; and the Meredith March, 236–37; and organized self-defense, 223, 236; and southwest Mississippi, 227–29; and women's auxiliary, 213, 214. *See also* historiography; self-defense

*Deep in Our Hearts*, 374

Democratic Coalition (Tex.), 346

Democratic Party, 48, 259; Atlantic City convention (1964), 46–47, 195, 281; National Committee, 48, 49

demonstrations, and fighting back, 215–17, 219, 222; marches, 84, 88, 92, 93, 96, 184, 195, 227, 262; and nonviolent action, 14, 76, 157, 194, 206, 211, 215, 225, 230, 231, 262, 455. *See also* Freedom Rides; nonviolence; self-defense; sit-ins; *specific events*

Dennis, David (Dave), 204, 219–20, 286

Denson, Augusta, 132–33

DePass, Jared, 422 *illus.*, 450 *illus.*, 465

desegregation, as a movement goal, 116, 157, 158, 163, 172, 213, 231; in movement historiography, 9, 25, 103, 390; protests for, 83, 88. *See also* historiography; integration; interracial; multiracial activism; normative narrative; popular culture; school desegregation; segregation

Detroit, Michigan, 11, 67; and Rosa Parks, 385, 386, 387, 395–98, 407

Detroit uprising, 186, 312

Devine, Annie, 293

DeVinney, Jim, 292, 303

Diamond, Dion, 227

dissemblance, 340

Dittmer, John, 114, 228, 291, 429, 432; on black retaliation/ violence, 218–20; on the federal role in the movement, 24–25; and local studies scholarship, 8, 10, 18, 19, 152, 451, 468; on self-defense, 5, 21, 118, 195–97, 203–4, 209–10, 212

Doar, John, 291

domestic workers, 61, 62, 72. *See also* household forms

Donaldson, Ivanhoe, 187

Dorsey, James, 3

Douglass, Frederick, 343

Draper, Alan, 17–18

drug dealing, 441–43

Drum and Spear Bookstore (Washington, D.C.), 279–80, 306

Dryden, Marymal, 56

Du Bois, Shirley, 306

Du Bois, W. E. B., 433

Dunbar, Leslie, 45

Duncan, Ruby, 72

Durham freedom movement (N.C.), 56, 76

Durr, Clifford, 393

Durr, Virginia, 309

Dyson, Michael, 410–11

Eagles, Charles, and movement historiography, 7–8, 17, 18, 164–65, 281, 432, 451, 468

East Wilson Ministerial Association (N.C.), 100

Eastland, James, 43, 44, 153

Eastman House (Rochester, N.Y.), 366

Easton, Joseph, 450 *illus.*

economic constraints, 86–87. *See also* economic issues; economic retaliation; structural inequality

economic issues, and movement activism, 2, 14, 52–53, 60, 71–74, 85–104, 109–38, 155–56, 158, 161, 172–73, 181, 262–63, 264, 330, 372, 374, 401–6, 472; and movement history, 2, 6, 9, 12, 14, 151, 163, 262–63, 264, 265, 282, 310, 374, 390, 458. *See also* antipoverty activism; historiography; human rights; Poor People's Campaign; poverty; welfare rights activism

economic justice, after the movement, 373, 379–81, 388, 390, 396, 406, 463

economic retaliation, 43, 119, 210, 212, 406–7

Edelman, Marian Wright, 110, 290

Edinboro University, 427

education, 448, 467, 470; and the Black Panther Party, 351, 353–55; and funding, 88, 263; and persistent inequality, 114, 151–52, 396, 463. *See also* school boycott; school desegregation; teaching (and learning) movement history

Eighteen-Nation Disarmament Conference, 400

Eisenhower administration. *See* Eisenhower, Dwight D.

Eisenhower, Dwight D., 43, 50

Elaine, Ark., 268

electoral success, 83, 84, 85, 104. *See also* voting rights

Ella Baker Reading Group (Geneseo), xii, xvi, 422 *illus.*, 425 *illus.*, 450 *illus.*, 459, 465, 471 *illus.*

emancipation, 12, 472

employment, and African Americans, 86–87, 88, 89, 134–35, 157, 172, 262–63

Employment Security Commission, 87

Eskew, Glen, 10

Estes, Steve, 165, 211

Eudora AME Church (Marks, Miss.), 118

Evans, Sara, 375

Evers, Charles, 195, 204; and southwest Mississippi, 219, 226–28, 238

Evers, Medgar, 45, 195, 213, 218, 239; assassination of, 280, 285–86; funeral of, 219–20, 249n44

Evers, Myrlie, 285–86, 309, 409

*Everything I Needed to Know, I Learned in Kindergarten*, 437

*Eyes on the Prize*, 376, 378–79, 424, 435; and Judy Richardson, 26, 278–318, 367, 439; and portrayal of the movement timeframe, 371–72

Fair Employment Practices Committee, 263

Fair, Gregory, 433, 451, 452, 463

Fairclough, Adam, 157; on the Deacons for Defense, 206, 223, 230; and local studies scholarship, 8, 10, 162; on self-defense, 5, 21, 195–97, 204–6

Farmer, Leslie, 98–99

Farmer, Velma, 95

Farmville, Va., 465

Fayer, Steve, 286, 288, 300, 301, 308

FBI, and harassment/ surveillance, 47, 128, 336, 339, 351, 388, 406–7

FCD. *See* Fund for Community Development

FDP. *See* MFDP

Featherstone, Ralph, 437

Federal Bureau of Investigation. *See* FBI

federal government, 6, 24–25, 456; and harassment of activists, 407–8; and housing, 89, 91, 98–99; and inaction, 43–44, 224, 230, 240, 265, 292, 313, 469; and intervention, 196, 206, 223, 230, 231, 232. *See also* FBI, *individual laws, presidents, programs*

federal programs, and the movement, 98, 114–16, 131–32, 184. *See also specific programs*

Federalism, 45

Feimster, Crystal, 65

Feingold, Miriam (Mimi), 204–5, 347

feminism, 409–11, 424, 463. *See also* gender; gender norms/ stereotypes; historiography; sexism; women

FEPC. *See* Fair Employment Practices Committee

Fifteenth Amendment, 61, 183, 265

Fifteenth Annual Conference on Marketing and Public Relations in the Negro Market, 125

Fitch Drive (Wilson, N.C.), 84

Fitch, Milton, Jr., 85

Fitzsimmons, David, 263

Fleming, Cynthia Griggs, 10

Florida A&M, 69

Foner, Eric, 389

Food Stamp Act of 1964, 114

food stamps, 63, 72, 114–16, 132

Ford Foundation, 290, 299

Forman, James, 216–17, 220, 333

Forman, Mildred, 216

*Forrest Gump*, 456

Francis of Assisi, 430

Franklin, Aretha, 386

Franklin (Mr., of Quitman County, Miss.), 113

Fraser, Gerald, 287

Frazier, Nishani, 332

Free South Africa Movement, 399

freed people, 264

freedom, meanings of, 10–11, 13, 61–63, 65

*Freedom North*, 11

Freedom Now Party, 397

freedom politics, 166, 459–60, 469

Freedom Rides, 164, 202, 423; and *Eyes on the Prize*, 287, 294–95; and the Kennedy administration, 44–45; and the 1980s, 280; and nonviolence, 175–76, 182–83, 208, 216, 337

"Freedom Riders," 175, 215, 217, 221, 376

freedom rights, 11, 14, 166, 264, 275, 459, 472

Freedom Schools, 38n51, 181, 186, 231, 371; and portrayals in movement history, 319–20, 328n2, 328–29n5-n7, 368; and societal values, 433–34

Freedom Singers, 347

*Freedom Song*, 23–24, 39n55

freedom songs, 288. *See also individual names*

Freedom Summer. *See* Mississippi Summer Project

Freedom Train Caravan, 129, 392

Freeman, Roland, 119–27 *passim*, 122 *illus.*, 127 *illus.*, 130, 137, 404 *illus.*

Frist, Bill, 386

Fuller, Howard, 95

Fuller, Minnie, 91–96

Fund for Community Development (North Carolina), 91–98, 101, 103–4

funding, for *Eyes on the Prize*, 284–85, 288, 290, 297–99; and nonviolence/self-defense, 183, 187–88, 191–92n34, 199, 220, 236

Gandhi, Mahatma, 172, 173, 400

Garman, Betty, 383

Garrow, David, 148, 157, 158, 287, 291

Garvey, Marcus, 269

Gary Convention, 398, 405

Gaston Motel, Birmingham, Ala., 220

Gathering of Hearts, 135

Gathwright, Ned, 118

Gault, Charlayne Hunter, 298

gay rights, 388, 405–6, 413n9, 417n68, 464

Gaza, 383

gender, and the civil rights narrative, 25, 26, 34n28, 52–57, 59, 67, 75, 81–85, 101–4, 105n4, 245–46n28, 246n30,

246n32, 246–47n34, 247n37, 248n41-n42, 248–49n44, 389. *See also* feminism; historiography; sexism; women

gender norms/stereotypes, 62; of black women, 340, 405, 408, 442; and movement activism, 56–59, 210, 389. *See also* feminism; gender; historiography; racist stereotypes; sexism; women

Geneseo College (State University of New York), 366; and Local Studies, a National Movement Conference, xi, xvi, 147–48, 368, 448–73; students and movement history, xi-xii, xv-xvi, 14–15, 16, 420–25, 428, 433, 448–73

Ghana, 296

Giddings, Paula, 304–5

global justice movement, 355

*God's Long Summer*, 7

Goldwater, Barry, 46–47

Good, Paul, 49, 50

Good Neighbor Council, 88, 100

Goodman, Andrew, 286

Goodwyn, Lawrence, 159

Grady-Willis, Winston, 10, 166

Gray, Barry, 438

Gray, Fred, 393–94

Gray, Victoria. *See* Adams, Victoria Gray

Great Depression, 62, 67

Great March to Freedom (Detroit), 395

Great Society programs, 396. *See also* federal programs; War on Poverty

Green, Freddie, 437

Green, Laurie B., 10, 25

Green, Michael, 307

Greene, Christina, 10, 56, 58, 70

Greensboro, N.C., 420; and the civil rights movement, 13–14, 56, 150, 151

Greenville, Miss., 427

Greenville, N.C., 150–51

Greenwood, Miss., 49, 338; movement in, 185, 214, 219–20, 279

Gregory, Robin, 305

Grizzard, Vernon, 347

Groppi, James, 163

*Groundwork: Local Black Freedom Movements*, 11, 59, 163

Guinea, 296

Gulf War, 405

Guster, Leesco, 3, 58

Guyot, Lawrence, 56, 378

Haines, Herbert, 322

Hall, Jacqueline Dowd, 65; and movement historiography, 7, 8–10, 11, 12, 14

Hall, Leon, 113, 116

Hall, Prathia, 178, 221, 377–78

Hamer, Fannie Lou, 47, 48 *illus.*, 424, 438–39; biographies of, 56, 149, 426; and *Eyes on the Prize*, 281, 287, 309; and police violence in Winona, 179, 378; and self-defense, 184, 248n42; and Sunflower County movement, 10–11, 153, 155–56; mentioned, 430

Hamer Institute (Jackson State University), xiii, xiv

Hamlett, Ed, 344, 346

Hampton, Fred, 379

Hampton, Henry, 278–318 *passim*, 367

*Hands on the Freedom Plow*, 316, 367, 369–70, 425, 441, 443, 444; and nonviolence/ self-defense, 215–16, 377–78; as response to portrayals of SNCC women, 374–75

Hannah, John, 46

Hansson, Riber, 267

Harding, Vincent, 158, 323–24, 426

Hargrove, Bill, 217

Harlem, 215

Harlem uprising, 186

Harmony, Miss., 223

Harrell, Antoinette, 135

Harris, Don, 185

Harvard University, 338

haven communities, 232. *See also* self-defense

Hawthorne School (Washington, D.C.), 129

Hayden, Casey, 178, 350, 376

Hazard Kentucky project, 345

Head Start, 49, 110

Health Cadre (in the Black Panther Party), 352

health care, 463; and the Black Panther Party, 351–52, 359; as a movement issue, 54–55, 60, 71–74, 136, 345, 388, 405. *See also* gender; historiography; human rights

Henderson, Juadine, 307

Henderson, Vivian, 172

Henry, Aaron, 195

Henry Ford Museum, 387

Henry, Milton, 397–98

Henry, Richard, 397

Hicks, Jackie, 214

Hicks, Robert, 215

Highlander Folk School, 56, 344–45; and Rosa Parks, 391–92, 395, 407, 409

Hill, Lance, on the Deacons for Defense, 223–27, 229, 233–37; on gender, 208–9, 212–14, 245–46n28, 246n30, 246n32, 246–47n34, 247n37, 248n41–n42, 248–49n44; and self-defense historiography, 198–200, 203–7, 229, 230, 232, 235, 238

Hilliard, David, 334–35

Hilliard, June, 335
Hills, Minnie Lee, 130
Hine, Darlene Clark, 340
historical memory, 135, 151, 427; and
    Barack Obama's campaign, 259–
    75; and gender, 55, 57, 62, 81–85,
    101–4; and memorializations of
    Parks and King, 385–412. *See also*
    historiography; master narrative;
    normative narrative; oral history;
    popular culture
historiography, and chronology, 6–14,
    *passim*, 31n18, 51, 85, 147, 148, 156–57,
    159, 162–63, 165, 222–40, 281, 311,
    374–78, 399, 406; class, and economic
    issues, 60, 71–74, 81–104, 105n4,
    136–38, 155–56, 158, 161, 167n2; and
    defining success and failure, 18–20,
    37n49, 112–13, 137–38, 157–62, 230,
    292, 438; and *Eyes on the Prize*, 278–
    316; and local studies, 5–14, 15, 17, 19–
    20, 21, 24–26, 28n11–36n44 *passim*,
    53, 58–61, 104, 111–13, 136–38, 147–67,
    183–85, 194–98, 199, 200, 202, 205,
    209–10, 218–20, 222–23, 235, 239, 280,
    283, 287, 309, 313, 316–17n6, 472; and
    northern/ national movement, 6, 11–
    12, 281, 390–91, 395; and self-defense,
    2–3, 6, 20–24, 25, 194–240, 377, 390,
    396–97; and women/ gender, 25, 26,
    34n28, 52–59, 67, 75, 81–104, 105n4,
    149, 166, 167n2, 207–15, 245–46n28,
    246n30, 246n32, 246–47n34, 247n37,
    248n41-n42, 248–49n44, 287, 308–9,
    319–26, 332, 333–36, 339–42, 343, 346–
    48, 351–53, 359, 374–78, 403, 408–
    11, 472. *See also* bottom-up history;
    gender; human rights; interracial
    emphasis; long civil rights movement;
    master narrative; normative narrative;
    popular culture; radicalism; self-
    defense; top-down history; women;
    *individual authors, books*
Hodgson, Godfrey, 47
Hogan, Wesley, 25, 26, 221, 433, 455
Holmes County, Miss., 195, 196, 210, 236
Holsaert, Faith, 375
Holt Street Baptist Church
    (Montgomery), 408
Honey, Michael, 401
Hoover, J. Edgar, 407
Horton, Myles, 392
household forms, labor, and authority,
    61–63, 72, 75, 76, 77
housing, 396; as a civil rights issue, 14,
    16, 25, 81, 84–85, 89–95, 97–100,
    103–4, 110, 116, 121, 263, 398, 403; and
    evictions, 119–20
Housing and Urban Development. *See*
    HUD
Houston, Ben, 433, 435
Howard Beach, N.Y., 300
Howard, Elbert, 359
Howard, T. R. M. (wife of), 218
Howard University, 338; and Lyndon
    Johnson speech, 49, 50; and student
    protest, 282, 304–5
HUD, 90, 98–99
Huggins, Ericka, 353–54
Huie, William Bradford, 291
Hulett, John, 233, 262, 469
human rights, 127 *illus.*; in contemporary
    society, 383, 387, 388, 389, 396,
    399–406, 412, 464; and movement
    activism, 54–55, 60, 72, 74, 85–104,
    148, 153, 155–56, 231, 262–63, 264,
    275, 398; and movement history, 6,
    9, 10–11, 14, 81–85, 101–4, 111–13,

human rights (*continued*)
136–38, 163, 166, 262–63, 264, 275, 472; and the Mule Train, 109–38. *See also* economic issues; freedom rights; historiography; housing; welfare rights activism
humanism, 133, 336
Humphrey, Hubert, 47
Hurricane Katrina, xvi, 458; and racial politics, 385, 387, 388–89, 390, 412
Hurst, E. H., 23
Hutchinson, Jenny, 408
Hyatt, Margie, 117, 124

"I AM A MAN," 52, 74, 76
*I am Rosa Parks*, 411
*I've Got the Light of Freedom*, 18, 20, 152, 469
*In Re Debs*, 45
India, 172, 173, 400
Indian Trail (Caravan, Poor People's Campaign), 129
Indianola, Miss., 153–56, 177
Industrial Education Center (Wilson, N.C.), 92
infant mortality, 73–74
Ingram, Judith Allen, 56
integration, 88; and *Eyes on the Prize*, 300, 301, 303, 312–13; as a movement goal, 13, 151, 166, 180, 300, 374; in scholarship, 13, 282, 312–13. *See also* desegregation; interracial; multiracial activism
Intercommunity Youth Institute, 353
international issues, 463; and the civil rights movement, 155, 173, 218, 280, 390, 399–402
interracial, 374, 437, 464, 472; and the long civil rights movement framing, 9, 10, 12, 15, 295; rape, 65, 347; and the role of whites in SNCC, 336, 343–51, 360; and scholarly emphasis, 88, 280–81. *See also* integration; multiracial activism; White Folks Project
Iraq War, 380, 387, 388, 405
Ithaca, N.Y., 465
Izzo, Tiffany, and studying movement history, 450 *illus.*, 453–54, 462, 470, 472

Jackson, Jesse, 272, 388
Jackson, Jimmie Lee, 187
Jackson movement (Miss.), 45, 176
Jackson State College, 219
jail-no-bail, 376
Jeanette Rankin Brigade, 401
Jeffries, Hasan Kwame, 10, 66; and "Crazy Negroes and Out-of-Control Crackers" talk, 423, 455–59, 469–70, 472; and Geneseo students, 455–61; on the history of Lowndes County, Ala., 13–14, 25–26, 166, 183–84, 198, 232–35
Jews Say No, 383
Jim Crow/Jim Crow laws, 43, 335, 350; and representations in popular culture, 265, 266, 267, 272, 386, 411. *See also* segregation
Johnson administration. *See* Johnson, Lyndon B.
Johnson, Bertha Burres, children of, 122 *illus.*; and Mule Train, 118, 121, 125, 126, 130
Johnson, Eddie, 177
Johnson, Henry, 285, 286
Johnson, Lyndon B., and the movement, 43, 46–50, 162, 292, 379, 443; and the War on Poverty, 49, 60, 110, 396
Johnson, Marilyn, 67
Johnson, Tom, 307

Johnson-Humphrey ticket, 48

Jones, Cortez, 421, 422 *illus.*, 450 *illus.*

Jones, John Wesley, 100

Jonesboro movement (La.), and the
    Deacons for Defense, 199, 205, 207–8,
    212–15, 223, 226, 232

Joseph, Peniel, 11

Justice Department, 183; and violence
    against the movement, 206, 218, 233, 236

K'Meyer, Tracy, 10

Karenga, Maulana, 437

Katrina. *See* Hurricane Katrina

Katzenbach, Nicholas, 50

Kawaida (Newark, N.J.), 312

"Keep your Eyes on the Prize," 278, 288

Keith, Damon, 386

Kelley, Robin, 355

Kendrick, S. C. Rose, 120

Kennedy administration. *See* Kennedy,
    John F.

Kennedy, John F., 43, 44–46, 50

Kennedy Library, 291

Kennedy, Randall, 147

Kennedy, Robert, 44, 46, 110, 407

Kenyan liberation movement, 218

Killens, John O., 398

King, Coretta Scott, 15, 26, 44, 404 *illus.*;
    as activist, 399–406; and anti-war
    work, 399–402, 406, 407; on gay
    rights, 388, 405–6, 413n9, 417n68; and
    gender in the movement, 409–11; as
    Martin Luther King's wife, 389, 399,
    401, 403, 409–10; memorial for, 387–
    91, 402, 407–8, 411–12, 453

King, Marion, 186, 222

King, Martin Luther, Jr., 47, 49, 58, 149,
    160 *illus.*, 396, 421; and the Albany
    Movement, 19–20, 37n49, 157–62,
    221–22, 438; assassination of, 51, 111,
    117, 128, 148, 162, 399, 401–7 *passim*,
    411; and Barack Obama cartoons, 261–
    62; biographers of, 148, 149, 157–62,
    287, 399–400; and color-blindness,
    262; and Coretta Scott King, 389,
    399–401, 403, 405–6, 409–10; and the
    federal government, 45, 50; and the
    Memphis Sanitation Strike, 60, 63, 74;
    and the Montgomery Bus Boycott,
    391, 394; and nonviolence, 68, 93,
    178, 194, 197–98, 201, 207, 208–9, 216,
    217–18, 220, 221–22, 237; and the Poor
    People's Campaign, 109–10, 111, 381;
    as radical, 379, 381, 399–401, 457–58,
    472; and representing the movement,
    4, 5, 8, 15, 152, 194, 201, 227, 228, 259,
    261–62, 274, 287, 288, 292, 309, 370,
    374, 411, 427, 454, 461, 462, 469, 472;
    and self-defense, 197–98, 237; and the
    Vietnam War, 379, 381, 399–402; and
    violence against, 217, 218, 220, 407

King, Martin Luther, Jr. Day, 83, 85, 355,
    370; and Judy Richardson at NSA,
    380–83

King, Mary, 349, 350, 370, 375

Kirk, John A., 159–62

KKK. *See* Ku Klux Klan

Koch, Ed, 300

Kitson, Tarik, and movement history,
    420–21, 422 *illus.*, 431, 450 *illus.*, 452,
    463

Klan. *See* Ku Klux Klan

Ku Klux Klan, 61, 66, 185, 457; in
    Mississippi, 3, 4, 22–23, 46, 154, 344;
    and movement self-defense, 69, 196,
    203, 206, 229, 232–33; and portrayals
    of the movement, 267–68, 466. *See
    also* racist violence; white resistance

labor movement. *See* civil rights unionism; union activism

Lackey, Hilliard, 113

Lacy, Dave, 298, 302

Ladner, Dorie, 441, 447n22

Ladner, Joyce, 441, 447n22

Lafayette, Bernard, 186

Lambert, Miss., 135

Lane, Mary, 443–44

Lang, Clarence, 11

Langford, Howard, C., 120

Las Vegas, Nev., 72–73

Latino Studies program, 430

law enforcement, failures of, 197, 206, 223, 224, 226, 230–32; parallel, 232. *See also* Deacons for Defense; federal government; self-defense

Lawson, James, and nonviolence, 172–74, 178, 180, 216

Lawson, Steven F., 13, 148–49, 162

LCFO. *See* Lowndes County Freedom Organization

leadership, 460; defining, 85, 448, 453–54, 468; and gender, 54–59, 101–2, 214, 281, 376, 393–94, 409–10, 436. *See also* Baker, Ella; community organizing; gender; historiography; racial diplomacy; women; *individual people*

Lee, Chana Kai, 10, 426

Lee, Don. *See* Madhubuti, Haki

Lee, Herbert, 23

Leflore County, Miss., 236

*Legacy of a Freedom School*, 319–20

Leonard, Freddie, 294–95

*Let the People Decide*, 10

Lévi-Strauss, Claude, 65

Levy, Peter, 10, 198, 219

Lewis, Anthony, 44

Lewis, David Levering, 148, 157, 158

Lewis, John, 262, 266, 381, 388; and nonviolence, 172, 173, 180, 301, 426

Lewis, Peter, 261–62

liberals (white), 123, 150, 162, 345, 398, 456; and differences within the movement, 47–49, 269, 281, 301–2; and self-defense, 183, 187–88, 225, 235, 236

*Liberation* magazine, 198

Lillard, Leo, 294, 310–11

Lincoln, Abraham, 263–64

Lincoln Memorial, 259, 263, 403

Lipsitz, George, 229

Little, Joan, 398

Little Rock, Ark., 310, 379

Little Rock Crisis Visitor Center, 367

Little Rock Nine, 378–79

*Local People*, 18, 152

local studies. *See under* historiography

Local Studies, a National Movement: Toward a Historiography of the Black Freedom Movement Conference, xi, xvi, 147–48, 368–69, 444; and student reflections, 448–96; and talks by Charles Payne, 148, 319–29, 419–47; and teaching movement history, 419–47, 448–73

*A Lonely Rage*, 340

long civil rights movement, 162–63, 317–18n9; and local studies scholarship, 8–12, 14, 28, 32n22, 34n28

Long, (Bishop) Eddie, 388, 413n9

Long, Worth, 366; and unviolence, 22, 38n34, 202, 212, 240

Looby, Z. Alexander, 174

*Looking Backward*, 400

Lorraine Motel (Memphis, Tenn.), 75

Lotus, 299

Louisiana movement, and CORE, 204,

205; and the Deacons for Defense, 196, 199, 223–24, 226; and self-defense, 195–99 *passim*

Lowery, Joseph, 388

Lowndes County, Ala., and *Eyes on the Prize*, 283, 305–6, 311; movement in, 11, 13–14, 163, 166, 184, 232–35, 236, 254n82, 262, 263, 264, 268, 305, 459–61

Lowndes County Freedom Organization, 163, 233, 235, 262, 305, 459–60

Lowndesboro, Ala., 268

Luckie, Clarke, 268

lynching, 69, 197, 267, 376, 464; of Emmett Till, 64–66, 69. *See also* racist violence

Lynd, Staughton, 185–86

Machanoff, Christopher, and studying movement history, 448–49, 450 *illus.*, 462–63, 468, 469

Maddox, Lester, 128, 216

Madhubuti, Haki, 306

Malcolm X, 15, 48, 49, 188, 457; and *Eyes on the Prize*, 302–3; "Message to the Grassroots," 192n36; and Rosa Parks, 391, 396, 397; and self-defense, 201, 212, 224–25

*Malcolm X: Make It Plain*, 367

Mallisham, Joseph, 184

Mallory, Mae, 215

Mancini, Erynne, 450 *illus.*

Mandela, Nelson, 378

manhood, ideas of and the civil rights movement, 52–77, 325, 431; and self-defense historiography, 207–15. *See also* black radicals; gender; historiography; "politics of protection"; womanhood

Manzi, Jim, 299

March on Washington (1963), 129, 374, 395, 408, 409; and Obama Campaign cartoons, 259, 261, 262

marches. *See under* demonstrations

Marion, Ind., 267

Marisette, Andrew, 117, 128

Marks, Miss., and the Mule Train, 109–38 *passim*

Marsh, Charles, 7

Marshall, Burke, 44–45, 218, 291, 292

Martin Luther King Jr. Boulevard (Greenville, N.C.), 151

Martin Luther King Jr. Parkway (Wilson, N.C.), 84

Marx, Karl, 372–73

Maryland eastern shore protests, 176

masculinist, 325. *See also* black nationalism; gender; manhood; militancy

Massiah, Louis, 303, 308

master narrative, of the civil rights movement, 9, 10, 12, 163, 280, 324, 430; and the Wilson, N.C. movement, 83, 84, 101. *See also* historiography; normative narrative; popular culture; teaching (and learning) movement history; top-down history

maternal rights, 65. *See also* mothers

Matson, R. J., 259, 270

MCC. *See* Men's Civic Club (Wilson, N.C.) and Mississippi Cultural Crossroads (Port Gibson, Miss.)

McCain, James (Jim), 204

McCain, John, 266

McCall, Bobby, 353

McComb, Miss., 176, 183, 119, 220

McCoy, Eddie, 184

McCray, Samuel, 118, 134–35

McDew, Charles (Chuck), 39n55, 176

McDonald, Susie, 394

McGhee, Hazel, 58–59, 62, 76

McGhee, Laura, 185, 195, 214, 219

McGhee, Silas, 219–20

McGovern, George, 398

McGuire, Danielle, 69, 70

McKinney, Charles W., Jr. 10, 25

McKinney, Cynthia, 388

McKinnon, Lydia, 117

McKissick, Floyd, 90, 92

McKnight, Gerald D., 141

McLaurin, Charles, 176, 177, 178, 212

McMillen, Neil, 147, 153

media, and the Albany Movement, 157–58; and Barack Obama's campaign, 259, 260; and coverage of the movement, 149, 164, 194, 217, 220, 222, 235, 293, 311–12; and coverage of the Mule Train, 113, 118–20, 126–31 passim; and Eyes on the Prize, 295–96; and self-defense, 197, 249n49, 250n55. See also cartoons; popular culture; normative narrative

Meier, August, 148

memorializations. See Black History Month; cartoons; historical memory; King, Martin Luther, Jr., Day; King, Coretta Scott; popular culture; Parks, Rosa

memory. See historical memory

Memphis, Tenn., 60; and gender in the movement, 25, 52–55, 58, 68–70, 71–73, 76

Men's Civic Club (Wilson, N.C.), 88, 98, 100

Meredith, James, 45, 49, 136

Meredith March against Fear, 49–50, 199; and self-defense, 4, 223, 236–37; mentioned, 43, 110, 211. See also Black Power; Carmichael, Stokely; Deacons for Defense; self-defense

Meridian, 347

Metropolitan African Methodist Episcopal Church (Washington, D.C.), 386

MFDP, 50, 155, 227, 231; at the Atlantic City convention, 46–48, 195–96, 281; and White Folks Project, 344–45

Midwestern Caravan (Poor People's Campaign), 129

migration, 57, 61–62, 66–67, 86

Mileston, Miss., 223

militancy, 282; and gender, 207–15; and self-defense, 207–15, 222–40. See also black radicals/ radicalism; Black Power

Mills, Kay, 10

Milwaukee, Wisc., 263

Minnis, Jack, 380

Mississippi Burning, 22–23, 39n55

Mississippi Cultural Crossroads (Port Gibson, Miss.), xiv-xv

Mississippi Freedom Democratic Party. See MFDP

Mississippi movement, 22–24, 183, 262; and black retaliation/ violence, 219–20; and the federal government, 43–51; and self-defense, 195, 198–99, 201–5, 209, 212–13, 223–24, 226–28, 233, 236

Mississippi Summer Project, 46, 231, 236, 286; and Freedom School work, 319–21, 368; and normative portrayals, 8, 39n55, 280, 295, 375; and the role of whites, 336, 343–51; and self-defense, 198, 201, 218; mentioned, 202, 279. See also COFO; Freedom Schools; MFDP

Mondale, Walter, 47

Monroe, N.C., Robert Williams, and self-defense, 69, 76, 196, 197, 210, 215, 221, 230–31, 237

Montgomery, Ala., mentioned, 385–87, 392–95, 400, 406, 408, 409, 411. *See also* Montgomery Bus Boycott

Montgomery Bus Boycott, 261, 309, 381, 385–87 *passim*, 420, 453; and chronology, 162, 374; and *Eyes on the Prize*, 287, 374; and movement myths, 15, 261; and portrayals of nonviolence, 200, 217–18; and Rosa Parks, 392–95

Montgomery Improvement Association, 394, 409

Moore, Alice, 14

Moore, Amzie, 195, 309

Moore, Herman, 154, 155

Morehouse College, 338

Moses, Robert (Bob), 22, 46, 51, 438; and the Algebra Project, 431, 440; and unviolence, 203, 204, 239; and whites in SNCC, 343–46, 348

*Mother's Son*, 359

mothers, as activists, 58, 60, 70, 71, 72, 73–74, 103, 350–51, 402–3; and the Black Panther Party, 341, 352–53; and images of Rosa Parks and Coretta Scott King, 389; and the Mule Train, 121–23; and protecting children, 55, 69, 71, 87, 402–3. *See also* antipoverty activism; gender; health; historiography; racist stereotypes; welfare rights activism

movement, culture, 26, 330–60; as developing human potential, 439–44; goals of, 147, 151, 159, 260, 262, 263, 274, 275; mythologies in popular culture, 15–16, 25–26, 150, 260–61, 274–75, 342, 390–91, 395, 402, 406, 408, 412, 456, 461, 462, 466, 471–72;

values, 26, 366–84, 432–39, 463–64. *See also* activists; bottom-up history; historiography; partisanship; popular culture; master narrative; normative narrative; teaching (and learning) movement history; top-down history; *specific events, people, organizations, and issues*

Moye, Todd, 451, 462; on the Sunflower County movement, 10–11, 19, 25, 150, 152–53, 155–57, 184, 198, 202, 451

Moyers, Bill, 47

Mule Train, and the Poor People's Campaign, 25, 74–75, 112–13, 118–31, 133–38

multiracial activism, 110–11, 131, 133, 138, 437. *See also* interracial

Murray, Pauli, 409

Museum of African American History (Detroit), 386

Muslim, 270, 427–28

*My Life with Martin Luther King, Jr.*, 411

NAACP, 7, 8, 162, 307, 379, 399; and Rosa Parks, 391–93, 395–98, 409; and school desegregation, 43, 290, 315; and self-defense, 195–97, 203–4, 219, 226, 227; in southern communities, 2, 4, 23, 68, 69, 83, 92, 154, 155, 157, 174, 268

Nash, Diane, 409; and nonviolence, 172, 174, 175, 178, 179, 186

Nashville, Tenn., movement in, 172–75, 178, 216–17, 294, 310, 346, 377

Nasstrom, Kathryn, 57, 165

Natchez model, 226, 238

Natchez movement (Miss.), and self-defense, 198, 219, 226, 238

*Nation*, 407–8

Nation of Islam, 201

National Association for the Advancement of Colored People. *See* NAACP

National Security Administration, 380–83

nationalism. *See* black nationalism

Nazis, 344; resistance to, 173

Neels, Christopher, 450 *illus.*

*Negroes with Guns*, 188, 200

Nehru, Jawaharlal, 400

New Ark (Newark, N.J.), 312

New Communities, Inc. (southwest Ga.), 161

New Deal, 11

New England Conservatory of Music, 399

New Left, 352

New Birth Missionary Baptist Church (Atlanta, Ga.), 388

New York 21 (Twenty-One), 325

New York State Regents Curriculum, 22

Newark uprising, 186, 270, 312

Newton, Huey, 271, 333, 341–43, 354

9/11, 380, 381, 455

Nixon, E. D., 392–94

Nixon, Richard, 153, 405

Nobel Prize, 400

nonviolence, 93, 183–85; and breaking discipline, 215–22; and compassion, 173–74; critiques and rejection of, 188, 199, 201, 203, 206, 209; and historical interpretation, 5, 15, 21, 22, 25, 33–34n27, 163, 183–85, 188, 241n1, 241n10, 280, 322, 377, 390; and Laurie Pritchett's response, 157–58; and morality, 174–75, 178, 180, 182–83; and movement supporters, 187–88; philosophical, 68, 166, 174–75, 178–81, 183, 187, 194, 197, 199, 202, 204, 206, 211, 216, 220, 221, 222, 239, 247n38, 267, 337, 377–78; and protest, 88, 117, 118, 157–58, 174–75, 194, 205, 206, 211, 225, 232, 402, 454–55; and redemptive suffering, 178–79; and self-defense, 181–82, 184–86, 191n25, 192–93n37, 194–240, 244n19-n20, 245n25-n27, 454–55; and SNCC debates, 336–39; as a tactic, 173, 175, 176, 182–83, 187–88, 197, 203, 204, 211, 216, 222, 227, 231, 233, 239, 337, 351, 355, 376, 390, 396, 454–55; training in, 88, 172–74; as unmanly, 207–15; and war and poverty, 400–5. *See also* armed resistance; demonstrations; desegregation; historiography; "politics of protection"; retaliation; rhetoric; self-defense; sit-ins; unviolent; violence; *specific events, people, organizations, and tactics*

nonviolent workshops, 172–74

Noonan, Martha Prescod Norman, 350

Norman, Martha Prescod. *See* Noonan, Martha Prescod Norman

normative narrative, 16, 18; and Barack Obama's campaign, 259–75; and memorials of Rosa Parks and Coretta Scott King, 390–91, 407–12; and movement history, 1, 5, 9, 11, 15–18, 22, 24, 30, 33n27, 37n47, 39n55, 83–84, 85, 102, 163, 166, 188, 196–97, 241n1, 241n10, 280, 281, 282, 295–96, 312–13, 322–25, 374, 377, 427, 432; and teaching the movement, 448–73. *See also* historiography; popular culture; teaching (and learning) movement history; top-down history

Norrell, Robert, 10, 149, 151

Norris, Edgar, 89

North Carolina A & T, 150

Northeastern Caravan (Poor People's Campaign), 129
Northern Light Productions, 367, 435
NSA. *See* National Security Administration

O'Neill, Patrick, 450 *illus.*
Oakland, Cal., and the Black Panther Party, 351–56, 397 *illus.*, 398
Oakland Community Learning Center, 353–54
Oakland Community School, 353–54, 397, 398
Obama, Barack, 386, 460–61; the movement, and popular cartoons, 25–26, 259–74; and "post-racial" America, 15, 24, 465
Obama, Michelle, 270
Oberlin College, 425–26
OCLC. *See* Oakland Community Learning Center
OCS. *See* Oakland Community School
Office of Economic Opportunity, 50
Ole Miss, integration of, 45
open housing legislation, 263
Operation Life (Las Vegas, Nev.), 72
oral history, 321; and *Eyes on the Prize*, 283, 285, 287, 291, 292, 293, 313–14; and internal movement politics, 332–36, 356–60; and movement interpretations, 2, 17–18, 20–21, 22, 23, 24, 36n44, 38n51, 165–66, 468. *See also* activists; historiography; partisanship
Orangeburg Massacre (S.C.), 367
organizing tradition. *See* community organizing
Orleck, Annelise, 72
Oxford, N.C., 184, 238
Oxford, Ohio, 344

*Pacifism as Pathology*, 188
Paige Academy (Boston), 315
Palestinians, 383
Palmarin, Ines Soto, 135
pan-Africanist, 296
Panama, 464
parallel institutions, 231, 232, 437. *See also* black institutions
paramilitary, and self-defense, 224–29, 233, 235, 238. *See also* historiography; self-defense
Parchman Penitentiary (Miss.), 295
Pardun, Robert, 344, 346, 351
Parker, Jeff, 274
Parker, Mack Charles, 69
Parks, Raymond, 391, 395, 406–7
Parks, Rosa, 309, 374, 397 *illus.*, 472; after the bus boycott, 395–99; before the bus boycott, 391–92; and the bus boycott, 392–95; and costs of activism, 406–8; and gender in the movement, 408–9, 411; memorial for, 385–87, 389–91, 402, 407–8, 411–12, 453; and movement myths, 15, 26, 162, 427, 456, 461, 462, 472; and self-defense, 218, 396–97
*Parting the Waters*, 148
partisanship, and movement history, 7, 17–22, 36n44, 164–65, 306, 425, 432, 468–69. *See also* historiography; oral history
Patilla, Melba, 378–79
patriarchy, 210, 340, 360, 401. *See also* gender; sexism
Pauley, Frances Freeborn, 165
Payne, Charles M., 228, 281, 472; on black violence/ retaliation, 218; on community organizing, 84, 182, 337, 449, 476n54; and Local Studies, a

Payne, Charles M. (*continued*)
National Movement Conference, 319–
29, 419–47, 448, 451, 452, 462, 468–69,
472; and local studies scholarship,
8, 10, 19, 26, 152; other historians'
critique of, 17–18, 20, 469; on self-
defense, 5, 21, 195–97, 203–4, 209–10,
213–14; on tactical flexibility, 237, 239,
247n38; on women/ gender, 56, 58,
209–10, 319–29, 368
PBS, 282, 290, 295, 299, 367. *See also*
WGBH
Penn, William, 173
Pentagon, 188, 387
People's Tribunal (Detroit), 398
Perry, Albert, 210
Petersburg, Va., 176
Phillips, Charlotte, 347
Philpot, Sandra, 91–94
Phipps, Armstead, 110
Pinnola, Christina, 450 *illus.*
Pittman, E. B., 90–91
Planned Parenthood (in the Black
Panther Party), 352
Plato, 428–29
police brutality, 22, 50, 186, 330; as
inspiration, 117–20, 177, 203; and
movement activism, 63–64, 66–
68, 70, 74–75, 157, 371, 395; post-
movement, 280, 300, 379; and protests
against, 66–71, 398; in Winona jail,
179, 378. *See also* racist violence
political access, and movement activism,
46–48, 57, 75, 82, 155, 184, 233, 263–64;
and movement history, 2, 9, 50, 282,
459–60. *See also* electoral success;
voting rights
political cartoons. *See* cartoons
political education workshops, 233

"politics of protection," and the civil
rights narrative, 25, 55, 63–77
politics of respectability, 66–67, 88, 340,
408
Pollard, Sam, 305, 312
Ponder, Annell, 179, 184, 378
Poor People's Campaign, and economic
issues in the movement, 25, 60, 61, 72,
75, 109–38, 374, 379, 381, 402–4
"Poor People's Store," 125
popular culture, and Barack Obama's
campaign, 259–75; and memorials
for Rosa Parks and Coretta Scott
King, 385–91, 402, 406–8, 411–12;
and portrayal of the movement, 1, 12,
15–17, 22, 25, 37n47, 83, 101, 135, 188,
194, 200, 282, 283, 295–96, 311–13, 374,
427. *See also* cartoons; historiography;
master narrative; normative narrative
populist movement, 345
Porche, Faye, 124
Port Gibson movement (Miss.), 58, 183; and
learning about self-defense, 1–5; and
self-defense, 58, 226–29, 232, 236, 238
"post-racial" America, 15, 16, 17, 24, 272–
74, 412, 465. *See also* cartoons; color
blindness; teaching (and learning)
movement history
poverty, 25, 50, 467; and the Poor People's
Campaign, 109–12, 114–15, 118–21,
123, 125–27, 130, 133–37; and women's
movement activism, 55, 60, 71–74. *See
also* antipoverty activism; economic
issues; historiography; human rights;
Poor People's Campaign; welfare
rights activism
PPC. *See* Poor People's Campaign
Prague, 188
prejudice, 266, 267, 269, 272, 274. *See*

*also* structural inequality; white
supremacy
Presley, Brenda, 335
Prince Edward County, Va., 465
Pritchett, Laurie, 19, 157, 160 *illus.*
Progressive Party convention, 399
protection, politics of. *See* "politics of
protection"
psychological warfare, 4, 228. *See also*
rhetoric; self-defense
Public Broadcasting Service. *See* PBS
Public Service Gas and Electric, 436

*Quiet Strength*, 411
Quin, Aylene, 219
Quitman County Industrial High School
(Miss.), 117
Quitman County, Miss. *See* Marks, Miss.

Rabby, Glenda, 10
race riots. *See* rebellions; riots; *specific
cities*
*Race & Democracy*, 8
Race Relations Committee (Antioch
College), 399
racial diplomacy, 88, 98, 100. *See also*
leadership
racial privilege, 16–17. *See also* prejudice;
structural inequality; teaching (and
learning) movement history; white
supremacy
racist stereotypes, 443; and poverty, 72,
73, 74, 77, 114–15, 120, 138, 405, 442;
and sexuality, 340. *See also* gender
norms/ stereotypes
racist violence, 300, 396; against the
movement, 153, 174, 186–87, 196–97,
203, 204, 210, 212, 221, 226, 230, 231,
232–37, 240, 265–69, 348, 423–24;

before the movement, 265–68; and
gender, 61, 63–71, 337, 376–77; in
Marks, Miss., 118–20; and movement
narratives, 54–55, 267–69, 310, 454, 456;
and the sanitation strike, 63–64; and
self-defense, 4, 23, 25, 44, 196–97, 206,
214. *See also* police brutality; Ku Klux
Klan; lynching; rape; white resistance
radical. *See* black radicals
radicalism, in movement history, 9, 10, 11,
12, 13, 26, 379. *See also* black radicals
Raines, "Mama" Dollie, 309
Randolph, A. Philip, 409
Ransby, Barbara, 58
rape, 61, 64–65. *See also* racist violence
*Ready for Revolution*, 211, 317n8, 464
Reagan administration, 280, 405
Reagan, Ronald. *See* Reagan
administration
Reagon, Bernice Johnson, 211, 376; and
Albany Movement interpretations,
18–20, 37n49, 292, 438, 446–47n17
Reagon, Cordell, 157
rebellions, 163, 186, 201, 270. *See also*
riots; *specific cities*
Reconstruction, 61, 62, 66, 389–90
red-baiting, 391, 407
Republic of New Africa, 397
respectability, politics of. *See* politics of
respectability
Resurrection City (Poor People's
Campaign), 111, 119, 123, 129–30, 136
retaliation (and threats) by African
Americans, as part of the "nonviolent"
movement, 4, 183, 187, 199, 204, 210,
218–22, 228, 232, 237–39, 248–
49n44. *See also* armed resistance;
nonviolence; rhetoric; self-defense;
unviolent; violence

rhetoric (confrontational), by African Americans, as part of the "nonviolent" movement, 3, 217, 225–26, 228, 230, 235–36, 238. *See also* armed resistance; nonviolence; psychological warfare; retaliation; self-defense; unviolent; violence

Rice, Condoleezza, 386

Richardson, Gloria, 56, 375, 409

Richardson, Judy, 215, 220, 284 *illus.*, 320, 373 *illus.*; and *Hands on the Freedom Plow*, 425, 441, 443, 444; and interpreting movement history, 26, 38n51, 278–318, 359, 366–84, 449, 454, 458; and Local Studies Conference, 420, 430, 432–33, 435–40, 452–53, 462; and movement values, 420, 432–33, 435–40

Richmond, Va., 264

Rightmyer, Erin, 422 *illus.*, 424–25, 450 *illus.*

riots, 49, 128, 322, 398, 456. *See also* rebellions; *specific cities*

Riverside Church, N.Y., 400–1; and Martin Luther King's anti-Vietnam speech, 379, 381

Robbin Island (South Africa), 378–79

Roberts, John, 16, 18

Robinson, Amelia Boynton, 136

Robinson, Jackie, 379

Robinson, Jo Ann, 287, 308, 393–94

Robinson, Ruby Doris Smith, 149, 186, 376

Robinson, Virginia, 116

Robnett, Belinda, 57, 102

Rock Hill, S.C., 376

Rockefeller Foundation, 298

Rockefeller, Terry, 303

Rodney, Walter, 323

Rolling Fork, Miss., 187

Romano, Renee, 426–27, 440

*Rosa Parks: My Story*, 411

Rosen, Hannah, 61, 65

Rouse, Jacqueline, 56

Rudwick, Elliott, 148

Ruswick, Claire, and studying movement history, 450 *illus.*, 457–59, 463, 465, 469, 470

Sababu, Umeme, 427–28

Sacks, Karen, 57

San Francisco, Cal., 339

Sanford, Terry, 88

Sanitation Strike (Memphis), and Coretta Scott King, 401; and gender, 52, 54, 55, 63, 71, 72, 76; and Martin Luther King, 60, 63, 74, 111, 401

sanitation workers, 60, 62

*Scarred Justice*, 367

SCEF, 346

Schiffer, Judy, 344

Scholar Schools (*Eyes on the Prize*), 279, 283, 291, 302

school boycott, 118, 156, 184. *See also* education; school desegregation

school desegregation, 3, 104, 290, 315; after *Brown*, 43–44; and limitations today, 1, 15, 35n39, 465–66; as a movement goal, 151, 195, 263, 282, 405; as a response to riots, 322; and white resistance, 134–35, 465. *See also* education; school boycott; segregation; segregationist; teaching (and learning) movement history; white resistance

Schwerner, Michael, 286

SCLC, 58, 84, 149, 216, 262, 406; and the Albany Movement, 18–20, 157–62;

and philosophical nonviolence, 178, 181, 183, 185, 221–22, 378–79; and the Poor People's Campaign, 110–14, 116–32, 135–36, 137, 379, 381; and Rosa Parks, 395, 396; and self-defense, 203

Scottsboro case, 391 92

SDS, 345, 440

Seale, Bobby, 340

Seals, Rosie, 72

segregation, and contemporary schools, 15, 35n39, 462, 465–66; establishment of, 64, 389–90, 464; as a movement issue, 75, 83, 88–89, 91, 119, 157–58, 163, 173, 175–76, 180, 183, 211, 392–95, 458; and movement mythologies, 15, 265–66, 411, 466. See also desegregation; historiography; Jim Crow; racist violence; school desegregation; segregationists; white resistance; white supremacy

segregationists, 7, 149, 194–95, 456; and organized efforts, 44–46, 152–56. See also Citizens' Council; historiography; Jim Crow; Ku Klux Klan; racist violence; segregation; white resistance; white supremacy

self-defense, 68, 69, 70, 76, 118; and activist voices, 20–24; and Black Panther Party survival programs, 74; and chronology, 201, 222–40; on demonstrations, 215–22; and discourse about, 67–68, 76; and double standards, 22, 200, 223, 229–30, 240, 455, 466; and Eyes on the Prize, 281, 301, 309–11; and law enforcement, 4, 23, 25, 44, 196–97, 206, 214; and local studies, 194–98, 199, 200, 202, 205, 209–10, 218–20, 222–23, 235, 239; in movement historiography, 2–3, 6, 20–24, 25, 194–240, 377, 390, 396–97; and nonviolence, 4, 181–82, 184–86, 191n25, 192–93n37, 194–240, 244n19-n20, 245n25-n27, 454–55; organized, 197, 208, 222–40; in the Port Gibson movement (Miss.), 1–5, 226–29, 232; and public space, 197, 222–40; publicity, and visibility, 187–88, 191–92n34, 197, 199, 220–40; and women/ gender, 4, 58, 197, 201, 207 15, 239, 245 46n28, 246n30, 246n32, 246–47n34, 247n37, 248n41-n42, 248–49n44, 325, 396–97. See also armed resistance; historiography; nonviolence; "politics of protection"; psychological warfare; retaliation; rhetoric; self-defense; unviolent; violence; specific events, organizations, people, and tactics

Sellers, Cleveland, 304

Selma, Ala., 50, 186, 221, 222

Selma-to-Montgomery March, 50, 232–33, 378, 381

separatism, 348–49, 397. See also black nationalism

sexism, 340, 437, 438; Charles Payne on, 319–28, 438; and Eyes on the Prize, 307–9; critique by Coretta Scott King, 410; and perceptions of, 297, 332, 374–78; and scholarship, 65, 137, 307, 308–9, 319–26, 340, 375. See also gender; historiography; patriarchy; women

sexual assault. See racist violence; rape

sexuality, and movement history, 330–60. See also stereotypes; welfare rights activism

Shakespeare, William, 428

Shakur, Assata, 325

Sharecroppers' Union, 11

Sherrod, Charles, 337, 350; and the Albany
Movement, 157, 160–61, 292; and
nonviolence, 178, 179, 182, 183
Shields, Rudy, 3–4
Shipp, Thomas, 267
Shirah, Sam, 344–46
Shockely, Skip, 359
Shuttlesworth, Fred, 291
Simkins, Modjeska, 56
singing, in the civil rights movement, 118,
177, 221, 295, 435, 454
Sirianni, Kristy, 423–24, 425
sit-ins, 69, 88, 195, 287, 294, 337, 431;
in Greensboro, N.C., 150, 173–74;
in Nashville, Tenn., 173–75; and
nonviolence, 173–76, 182, 208
Sitkoff, Harvard, 149
Sitton, Claude, 291
slavery, 263, 350, 389
slavery era, 64
Smith, Abraham, 267
Smith, Charlie, 344
Smith, Hazel Brannon, 236
Smith, Jean Wheeler. See Young, Jean
Wheeler Smith
Smith, Jerome, 204
Smith, Mary Louise, 392, 394
Smith, Ruby Doris. See Robinson, Ruby
Doris Smith
SNCC, 46–47, 262, 437, 438, 443; and the
Albany Movement, 18–20, 157–62,
292; and Black Power, 13–14, 49, 166,
235, 301; and contemporary activism,
368, 379–84, 421; and internal
disagreements, 435–36; and Freedom
Schools, 319–21; and Judy Richardson,
279, 283, 286, 366–84; and Mississippi,
46, 153, 156, 266, 281, 295, 301; and

movement interpretations, 8, 18–19,
21–24, 39n55, 148; and nonviolence,
176, 178–88, 204, 215–17, 220, 221, 222,
267, 301; and organizing, 153, 156–57,
166, 227, 232–33, 236, 266, 286, 369,
370–72, 421, 424–25, 452–53, 459–60;
and the role of whites, 336, 343–51;
and self-defense, 203, 204, 223, 232–35;
and tactical flexibility, 199, 200, 202,
212–13, 236, 239, 240, 267. See also
activists; historiography; partisanship;
specific events, people, tactics
Snowden, Scott, 450 illus.
Snyder, Katie, 454–55
Social Security, 87, 115, 116, 132
Social Security Act, 403
Sojourners for Truth and Justice, 70
Solidarity Day (Poor People's Campaign),
129–30, 135, 403
Son of Man Temple (Oakland, Calif.), 353
Sophocles, 429
Sotomayor, Sonia, 16, 18
Soul on Ice, 340
South Africa, and the anti-apartheid
movement, 155, 173, 299, 398–99, 405,
432
Southern Caravan (Poor People's
Campaign), 129
Southern Christian Leadership
Conference. See SCLC
Southern Conference Education Fund.
See SCEF
Southern Regional Council (SRC), 45
Southern Students Organizing
Committee (SSOC), 346
southwest Georgia, 279, 375. See also
Southwest Georgia Project
Southwest Georgia Project, 158

Southwest Georgia Project for
  Community Education, 161
Spencer, Robyn C., 26, 322
Spring Mobilization for Peace, 401
SSOC. *See* Southern Students Organizing
  Committee
St. Augustine, Fla., 149, 176, 185
Stewart, Michael, 300
*Storming Caesars Palace*, 72
Strain, Christopher, on the Deacons for
  Defense, 223–24, 229–30; on self-
  defense, 193n37, 198–200, 208, 225, 238
*Stride Toward Freedom*, 157, 287, 308
Stringer, Emmett, 195
structural inequality, 439; and movement
  interpretations, 263, 265–69, 272,
  405, 458, 462, 466–67. *See also*
  historiography; master narrative;
  normative narrative; popular culture;
  prejudice; white supremacy
*The Struggle for Black Equality, 1954–80*,
  149
Student Nonviolent Coordinating
  Committee. *See* SNCC
Students for a Democratic Society. *See*
  SDS
suffrage campaigns, 65
Sunflower County (Miss.), and the civil
  rights movement, 10–11, 25, 150, 152–
  53, 155–57, 184, 202, 451
Sunflower County Freedom Democrats,
  155
Supreme Court, U.S., 15, 43–44, 45
Swarthmore College, 215, 279, 347, 438

Tallahassee, Fla., 69, 71
Tanzania, 280
Tarrytown, N.Y., 438

*A Taste of Power*, 340, 341
Taylor, Andrea, 298
teacher workshops, on movement history,
  284, 315–16, 367, 370, 379, 470
teachers, and the legacy of the movement,
  431–42, 470
teaching (and learning) movement
  history, from a bottom-up
  perspective, 17–18, 22–24, 26, 448–
  73; and contemporary issues, 421,
  424–25, 426–27, 432, 449, 455, 458,
  460, 461–65, 469, 470; and family,
  420, 431, 464–65; and inspiration/
  empowerment, 421, 424–27, 432,
  426, 449, 461–65; as a model for
  citizenship, 449, 459–61, 469, 471;
  and racial differences, 419, 430–31,
  464–65; and resistance to, 422–23,
  424, 465–66. *See also* historiography;
  master narrative; normative narrative;
  popular culture; textbooks
Temple University, 424
Terrell County, Ga., 338
textbooks, and movement history, 1, 8, 15,
  19, 22, 56, 283, 312–13
Thelwell, Michael, 304, 312
Theoharis, Jeanne, 26, 453, 463; and
  movement historiography, 11, 12, 15,
  59–60, 163
*They Should Have Served that Cup of
  Coffee*, 438
Thomas, Clarence, 374
Thomas, Earnest, 206, 229
Thornton, J. Mills, 10
Thrasher, Sue, 345
Tiananmen Square, 188
Till, Emmett, 64, 69, 291
Tobacco Worker's International Union, 87

top-down history, and the civil rights movement, 2, 5, 7–8, 12, 18, 19, 75, 188, 194, 200–1, 280, 283, 287, 288, 309, 313, 314, 432. *See also* bottom-up history; gender; historiography; master narrative; normative narrative; popular culture

Toyota, 307–8

Trouillot, Michel-Rolph, 321–22

Tuck, Stephen G. N., 10, 160–61, 162

Tucker, Nathaniel, 97

Ture, Kwame. *See* Carmichael, Stokely

Turnbow, Hartman, 309, 434; and self-defense, 195, 200, 213, 214, 236, 311

Turnbow, Mrs. "Sweets," 195

Turner, Nat, 269

Turnkey 3, 99

Tuscaloosa, Ala., 184, 199, 223

Tuskegee, Ala., 149

TWIU. *See* Tobacco Worker's International Union

Tyler, Gary, 398

Tyson, Timothy, 163, 215; on gender, 210–11; on retaliation/ violence in the movement, 238–39; on self-defense, 10, 21, 68, 163, 184, 185, 195–98, 210–11, 237, 238–39

UCCCRJ. *See* United Church of Christ, Commission for Racial Justice

Umoja, Akinyele, 212; on armed resistance, 224–27, 229, 238; on self-defense, 198–200, 204, 205, 223–24, 230, 232

un-violent. *See* unviolent

union activism, 438; and ties to the movement, 59, 74, 75, 87, 111, 156, 395. *See also* civil rights unionism; Sanitation Strike

Unitarian Church, 290

Unitarian Universalist Association, 290

United Auto Workers Local 600, 395

United Church of Christ, Commission for Racial Justice, 280, 290, 293, 300

United Negro College Fund, 307

University of Mississippi. *See* Ole Miss

unviolent, and framing movement activism, 21–22, 38n54, 202–7, 227, 239–40, 243–44n18. *See also* armed resistance; historiography; nonviolence; retaliation; rhetoric; self-defense; violence

uprisings. *See* rebellions; riots; *specific cities*

urban migration, and protest, 57, 61–62, 67

Urban League, 436

Varela, Maria, 329n7

Vecchione, Judith, 290, 311

veterans (military), and the civil rights movement, 64, 67–69, 196, 238

Vietnam War, 49, 50, 111; opposition to, 48, 186, 304, 348, 379, 396–97, 399–402, 406, 407

violence (and threats), by African Americans, 197, 214, 215–22, 229, 237–39. *See also* historiography; nonviolence; retaliation; rhetoric; self-defense; unviolent

Vivian, C. T., 174, 388

voter registration. *See* voting rights; political access

voting rights, 43; and the historical narrative, 25, 57, 75, 83, 148–49, 151, 319–21, 390; and other movement goals, 68, 75, 116; and movement activism, 1, 21, 22, 46, 88, 95, 154, 157,

177–84 *passim*, 191, 194, 195, 202–3, 206, 207, 227, 228, 231, 319–21, 372, 374, 391, 454, 459

Voting Rights Act of 1965, 183; and chronology, 9, 227, 228, 280, 282, 399; and political access, 14, 49, 50, 230, 233, 456

Walker, Alice, 347
Walker, Jenny, 217–18
Wallace, George, 266–67
Wallace, Henry, 399
Walls, Eddie, 4
War on Poverty, 49, 60, 110, 134, 396, 401
Ward, Brian, 408
Warner, Julius, 1–4
Warren, Earl, 43
Washington, D.C., and the Poor People's Campaign, 110–38 *passim*
Washington University (St. Louis), 297
Watkins, Hollis, 466–67
Watts uprising/ riot, 4, 186, 225, 270, 423
Waveland, Miss., 346
WCIA. *See* Wilson Community Improvement Association.
"We Shall Overcome," 386, 454
Weaver, Lillian, 93, 94, 99
Wedge, Bruce, 90–91
welfare rights activism, and the civil rights movement, 56–57, 71–74, 76, 92, 109, 111, 114, 115, 116, 121, 131–32, 402–3. *See also* antipoverty activism; economic issues, gender; historiography; household forms; human rights; mothers
Wells, Ida B., 64–65
Wells, Jimmie L., 117
Wendt, Simon, on self-defense, 198–200, 205, 223, 225, 229, 236, 238; on gender,

208–10, 213–14; on nonviolence, 220, 236, 237
Wesley, Mary, 72
Wesleyan University, 426
West Bank, 188, 383
West, Ben, 174–75
Western Caravans (Poor People's Campaign), 129
Western Humanities course (Geneseo), 428–29
WGBH, 285
Wheeler, Jean. *See* Young, Jean Wheeler Smith
white activists. *See* interracial; SNCC; White Folks Project
white resistance, 49; in historiography, 6, 7, 8–9, 25, 26, 30–31n17, 164–65, 260, 263, 266–67, 269, 281, 309; in Mississippi, 43–45, 134–35, 149, 152–56; to the Mule Train, 117–20; in popular accounts, 265–69, 275, 407–8, 412, 456, 458–59. *See also* Citizens' Council; economic retaliation; historiography; segregation; segregationists; structural inequality; white supremacy
white supremacy, 338; in contemporary society, 458, 462, 465–68; portrayals of, 12, 13, 15, 17, 19, 51, 87, 150, 162, 177, 195, 209, 224, 227, 236, 240, 263, 266–67, 269, 282, 338, 340, 456–59, 465, 466; psychological impact of, 173, 209, 346. *See also* Citizens' Council; historiography; Jim Crow; master narrative; normative narrative; popular culture; prejudice; racist violence; segregation; segregationists; structural inequality; white resistance
white violence. *See* racist violence

White Folks Project, 343–51

White, Theodore, 47

Whitten, Jamie, 114

Wilkins, Roy, 197, 204, 379

Williams, Ersalene, 70

Williams, Genevista, 121

Williams, Hosea, 113, 125

Williams, Juan, 300

Williams, Mabel, 210, 215

Williams, Robert, 198, 391, 396; and self-defense, 68–69, 195, 196–98, 199, 200, 203–4, 215, 221, 230–31, 237, 238, 239; and women/ gender, 71, 76, 208, 210, 224

Wilson Community Improvement Association (N.C.), 81, 84–85, 96–104

Wilson Housing Authority (N.C.), 98

Wilson, John, 97

Wilson movement (N.C.), 25, 81–108

Winona jail (Miss.), 179, 378

Withers, Ernest C., 52

Wolcott, Victoria, 67

Woman's College of the University of North Carolina, 150

womanhood, ideas of and the civil rights movement, 52–77. See also gender; historiography; manhood; "politics of protection"

women, 65, 308; and self-defense, 4, 58, 197, 201, 207–15, 239, 245–46n28, 246n30, 246n32, 246–47n34, 247n37, 248n41-n42, 248–49n44, 325, 396–97; and local studies scholarship, 53–54, 59–61; and the March on Washington, 408, 409; and the Montgomery Bus Boycott, 393–94; and the movement narrative, 6, 25, 34n28, 52–59, 67, 75, 81–104, 308–9, 369, 403, 408–11; and the Mule Train, 121–23, 124–25,

132–33; and theories about movement participation, 209–10, 212–13, 248n40, 325. See also antipoverty activism; gender; historiography; household forms; human rights; leadership; mothers; normative narrative; popular culture; sexism; welfare rights

"Women in the Civil Rights Movement. Trailblazers and Torchbearers: 1941–1965" Conference, 56

Women's International League for Peace and Freedom, 400, 401

women's liberation movement, 339, 349

Women's Political Council, 393–94

Women's Public Affairs Committee (Detroit), 396

women's studies, 424, 430

Woodard, Komozi, and local studies scholarship, 11, 12, 59–60, 152, 163, 468–69; on movement values, 435–38

Woods, Barbara, 56

Wright, Amy Nathan, 25, 75

Wright, Jeremiah, 269–70

Young, Andrew, 110, 129, 379

Young, Jean Wheeler Smith, 374, 375, 383, 444

Younge, Gary, 407–8

Youth March for Integrated Schools, 400

Zellner, Dorothy (Dottie), 315, 348, 375, 383

Zellner, Robert (Bob), 346, 348

Zinn, Howard, 158

Zinni, Anthony, 381

Zurro, Joseph, and studying movement history, 369, 450 illus., 452, 457–58, 463–64